John Parry.

Honda Civic
Owners Workshop Manual

R M Jex

Models covered

(4611 - 368)

Civic Hatchback, including special/limited editions
Petrol: 1.4 litre (1396cc) & 1.6 litre (1590cc)
Diesel: 1.7 litre (1686cc) CTDi

Does NOT cover Type R/Type S models with 2.0 litre petrol engine, 2-door Coupe or 1.3 litre electric hybrid Executive IMA Saloon
Does NOT cover 'new' Civic range introduced January 2006

© Haynes Publishing 2007

ABCDE
FGHIJ
KLMNO
PQRST

A book in the **Haynes Owners Workshop Manual Series**

ISBN **978 1 84425 611 2**

British Library Cataloguing in Publication Data
A catalogue record for this book is available from the British Library.

Printed in the USA

Haynes Publishing
Sparkford, Yeovil, Somerset BA22 7

Haynes North America, Inc
861 Lawrence Drive, Newbury Park, California 91320, USA

Haynes Publishing Nordiska AB
Box 1504, 751 45 UPPSALA, Sverige

D1437085

Contents

LIVING WITH YOUR HONDA CIVIC

Roadside repairs

Weekly checks

MAINTENANCE

Routine maintenance and servicing

Contents

REPAIRS AND OVERHAUL

Advanced driving

Many people see the words 'advanced driving' and believe that it won't interest them or that it is a style of driving beyond their own abilities. Nothing could be further from the truth. Advanced driving is straightforward safe, sensible driving - the sort of driving we should all do every time we get behind the wheel.

An average of 10 people are killed every day on UK roads and 870 more are injured, some seriously. Lives are ruined daily, usually because somebody did something stupid. Something like 95% of all accidents are due to human error, mostly driver failure. Sometimes we make genuine mistakes - everyone does. Sometimes we have lapses of concentration. Sometimes we deliberately take risks.

For many people, the process of 'learning to drive' doesn't go much further than learning how to pass the driving test because of a common belief that good drivers are made by 'experience'.

Learning to drive by 'experience' teaches three driving skills:

☐ Quick reactions. (Whoops, that was close!)
☐ Good handling skills. (Horn, swerve, brake, horn).
☐ Reliance on vehicle technology. (Great stuff this ABS, stop in no distance even in the wet...)

Drivers whose skills are 'experience based' generally have a lot of near misses and the odd accident. The results can be seen every day in our courts and our hospital casualty departments.

Advanced drivers have learnt to control the risks by controlling the position and speed of their vehicle. They avoid accidents and near misses, even if the drivers around them make mistakes.

The key skills of advanced driving are **concentration,** effective all-round **observation, anticipation** and **planning.** When **good vehicle handling** is added to these skills, all driving situations can be approached and negotiated in a safe, methodical way, leaving nothing to chance.

Concentration means applying your mind to safe driving, completely excluding anything that's not relevant. Driving is usually the most dangerous activity that most of us undertake in our daily routines. It deserves our full attention.

Observation means not just looking, but seeing and seeking out the information found in the driving environment.

Anticipation means asking yourself what is happening, what you can reasonably expect to happen and what could happen unexpectedly. (One of the commonest words used in compiling accident reports is 'suddenly'.)

Planning is the link between seeing something and taking the appropriate action. For many drivers, planning is the missing link.

If you want to become a safer and more skilful driver and you want to enjoy your driving more, contact the Institute of Advanced Motorists at www.iam.org.uk, phone 0208 996 9600, or write to IAM House, 510 Chiswick High Road, London W4 5RG for an information pack.

Working on your car can be dangerous. This page shows just some of the potential risks and hazards, with the aim of creating a safety-conscious attitude.

General hazards

Scalding

• Don't remove the radiator or expansion tank cap while the engine is hot.
• Engine oil, automatic transmission fluid or power steering fluid may also be dangerously hot if the engine has recently been running.

Burning

• Beware of burns from the exhaust system and from any part of the engine. Brake discs and drums can also be extremely hot immediately after use.

Crushing

• When working under or near a raised vehicle, always supplement the jack with axle stands, or use drive-on ramps. *Never venture under a car which is only supported by a jack.*
• Take care if loosening or tightening high-torque nuts when the vehicle is on stands. Initial loosening and final tightening should be done with the wheels on the ground.

Fire

• Fuel is highly flammable; fuel vapour is explosive.
• Don't let fuel spill onto a hot engine.
• Do not smoke or allow naked lights (including pilot lights) anywhere near a vehicle being worked on. Also beware of creating sparks (electrically or by use of tools).
• Fuel vapour is heavier than air, so don't work on the fuel system with the vehicle over an inspection pit.
• Another cause of fire is an electrical overload or short-circuit. Take care when repairing or modifying the vehicle wiring.
• Keep a fire extinguisher handy, of a type suitable for use on fuel and electrical fires.

Electric shock

• Ignition HT voltage can be dangerous, especially to people with heart problems or a pacemaker. Don't work on or near the ignition system with the engine running or the ignition switched on.

• Mains voltage is also dangerous. Make sure that any mains-operated equipment is correctly earthed. Mains power points should be protected by a residual current device (RCD) circuit breaker.

Fume or gas intoxication

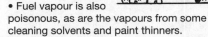

• Exhaust fumes are poisonous; they often contain carbon monoxide, which is rapidly fatal if inhaled. Never run the engine in a confined space such as a garage with the doors shut.
• Fuel vapour is also poisonous, as are the vapours from some cleaning solvents and paint thinners.

Poisonous or irritant substances

• Avoid skin contact with battery acid and with any fuel, fluid or lubricant, especially antifreeze, brake hydraulic fluid and Diesel fuel. Don't syphon them by mouth. If such a substance is swallowed or gets into the eyes, seek medical advice.
• Prolonged contact with used engine oil can cause skin cancer. Wear gloves or use a barrier cream if necessary. Change out of oil-soaked clothes and do not keep oily rags in your pocket.
• Air conditioning refrigerant forms a poisonous gas if exposed to a naked flame (including a cigarette). It can also cause skin burns on contact.

Asbestos

• Asbestos dust can cause cancer if inhaled or swallowed. Asbestos may be found in gaskets and in brake and clutch linings. When dealing with such components it is safest to assume that they contain asbestos.

Special hazards

Hydrofluoric acid

• This extremely corrosive acid is formed when certain types of synthetic rubber, found in some O-rings, oil seals, fuel hoses etc, are exposed to temperatures above 400°C. The rubber changes into a charred or sticky substance containing the acid. *Once formed, the acid remains dangerous for years. If it gets onto the skin, it may be necessary to amputate the limb concerned.*
• When dealing with a vehicle which has suffered a fire, or with components salvaged from such a vehicle, wear protective gloves and discard them after use.

The battery

• Batteries contain sulphuric acid, which attacks clothing, eyes and skin. Take care when topping-up or carrying the battery.
• The hydrogen gas given off by the battery is highly explosive. Never cause a spark or allow a naked light nearby. Be careful when connecting and disconnecting battery chargers or jump leads.

Air bags

• Air bags can cause injury if they go off accidentally. Take care when removing the steering wheel and/or facia. Special storage instructions may apply.

Diesel injection equipment

• Diesel injection pumps supply fuel at very high pressure. Take care when working on the fuel injectors and fuel pipes.

⚠️ *Warning: Never expose the hands, face or any other part of the body to injector spray; the fuel can penetrate the skin with potentially fatal results.*

Remember...

DO

• Do use eye protection when using power tools, and when working under the vehicle.

• Do wear gloves or use barrier cream to protect your hands when necessary.

• Do get someone to check periodically that all is well when working alone on the vehicle.

• Do keep loose clothing and long hair well out of the way of moving mechanical parts.

• Do remove rings, wristwatch etc, before working on the vehicle – especially the electrical system.

• Do ensure that any lifting or jacking equipment has a safe working load rating adequate for the job.

DON'T

• Don't attempt to lift a heavy component which may be beyond your capability – get assistance.

• Don't rush to finish a job, or take unverified short cuts.

• Don't use ill-fitting tools which may slip and cause injury.

• Don't leave tools or parts lying around where someone can trip over them. Mop up oil and fuel spills at once.

• Don't allow children or pets to play in or near a vehicle being worked on.

Honda Civic 5-door SE Executive (2005 model)

The latest UK-built Honda Civic (sometimes called the 'Swindon' Civic) went on sale in January 2001, replacing the previous successful Civic range. The Civic's bold long-wheelbase high-roof styling signals a change in thinking, and gives the car MPV-matching interior space and convenience, with features such as the facia-mounted gear lever freeing-up floor space – and in a car which is shorter than its predecessor.

The petrol engine range is essentially carried over from the previous Civic, but the engines are upgraded to boost engine power, while reducing fuel consumption and emissions. In the new car, both petrol engines are 16-valve SOHC designs, with the 1.6 litre unit having Honda's now-famous variable valve timing VTEC system. New to the range is a direct-injection common-rail diesel engine, which is a 1.7 litre 16-valve Isuzu-derived unit, featuring the latest in diesel engine technology.

As expected of a modern design, the new Civic offers high levels of passenger safety, scoring four stars in the Euro NCAP safety tests, with a particularly high score for pedestrian safety. To an impact-absorbing bodyshell with side impact beams are added front airbags and seat belt tensioners, with side airbags also fitted on most models. Disc brakes, ABS, EBD and Brake Assist are on many models; active as well as passive safety features strongly on the new car.

The model range is limited to 3- and 5-door Hatchbacks, but a wide variety of standard equipment and special-edition models have been available during the car's lifespan. The car has a high equipment level, even at the lower end of the model range. Besides the valuable safety equipment already mentioned, all feature electric power steering, rolling code engine immobiliser, central locking, electric mirrors and electric front windows. Air conditioning, an electric sunroof, CD player and satellite navigation are among the equipment fitted higher up the range.

The range received a minor facelift in November 2003, with detailed styling changes front and rear, projector-style headlights, and a space-saver spare wheel.

All models have front-wheel-drive, with a choice of five-speed manual transmission or an optional four-speed automatic on petrol models. The front suspension is of conventional MacPherson strut type, incorporating lower arms and an anti-roll bar; at the rear, a compact multi-link setup maximises the load area.

Your Honda Civic manual

The aim of this manual is to help you get the best value from your car. It can do so in several ways. It can help you decide what work must be done (even should you choose to get it done by a garage). It will also provide information on routine maintenance and servicing, and give a logical course of action and diagnosis when random faults occur. However, it is hoped that you will use the manual by tackling the work yourself. On simpler jobs it may even be quicker than booking the car into a garage and going there twice, to leave and collect it. Perhaps most important, a lot of money can be saved by avoiding the costs a garage must charge to cover its labour and overheads.

The manual has drawings and descriptions to show the function of the various components so that their layout can be understood. Tasks are described and photographed in a clear step-by-step sequence.

References to the 'left' and 'right' of the car are in the sense of a person in the driver's seat, facing forwards.

Acknowledgements

Thanks are due to Draper tools Limited, who provided some of the workshop tools, and to all those people at Sparkford who helped in the production of this manual.

We take great pride in the accuracy of information given in this manual, but car manufacturers make alterations and design changes during the production run of a particular car of which they do not inform us. No liability can be accepted by the authors or publishers for loss, damage or injury caused by any errors in, or omissions from, the information given.

Honda Civic 3-door Sport (2003 model)

The following pages are intended to help in dealing with common roadside emergencies and breakdowns. You will find more detailed fault finding information at the back of the manual, and repair information in the main chapters.

If your car won't start and the starter motor doesn't turn

☐ Open the bonnet and make sure that the battery terminals are clean and tight.
☐ Switch on the headlights and try to start the engine. If the headlights go very dim when you're trying to start, the battery is probably flat. Get out of trouble by jump starting (see next page) using a friend's car.
☐ If it's a model with automatic transmission, make sure the selector is in P or N.

If your car won't start even though the starter motor turns as normal

☐ Is there fuel in the tank?
☐ Has the engine immobiliser been deactivated? This should happen automatically when the key is inserted and turned to the first position.
☐ Is there moisture on electrical components under the bonnet? With the ignition off, wipe off any obvious dampness with a dry cloth. Spray a water-repellent aerosol product (WD-40 or equivalent) on ignition and fuel system electrical connectors like those shown in the photos. On petrol models, pay special attention to the ignition coil wiring connectors (which are under a plastic cover).

A Check the condition and security of the battery connections.

B Check that the ignition coils are securely connected (petrol models).

C With the ignition off, check the fuses and relays in the engine compartment fusebox. Fuse No 6 in particular controls the engine management system.

Check that electrical connections are secure (with the ignition switched off) and spray them with a water-dispersant spray like WD-40 if you suspect a problem due to damp

Jump starting

When jump-starting a car using a booster battery, observe the following precautions:

✔ Before connecting the booster battery, make sure that the ignition is switched off.

✔ Ensure that all electrical equipment (lights, heater, wipers, etc) is switched off.

✔ Take note of any special precautions printed on the battery case.

✔ Make sure that the booster battery is the same voltage as the discharged one in the vehicle.

✔ If the battery is being jump-started from the battery in another vehicle, the two vehicles MUST NOT TOUCH each other.

✔ Make sure that the transmission is in neutral (or PARK, in the case of automatic transmission).

 Jump starting will get you out of trouble, but you must correct whatever made the battery go flat in the first place. There are three possibilities:

1 The battery has been drained by repeated attempts to start, or by leaving the lights on.

2 The charging system is not working properly (alternator drivebelt slack or broken, alternator wiring fault or alternator itself faulty).

3 The battery itself is at fault (electrolyte low, or battery worn out).

1 Connect one end of the red jump lead to the positive (+) terminal of the flat battery

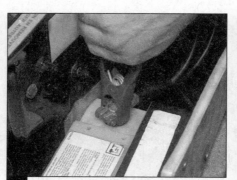

2 Connect the other end of the red lead to the positive (+) terminal of the booster battery.

3 Connect one end of the black jump lead to the negative (-) terminal of the booster battery

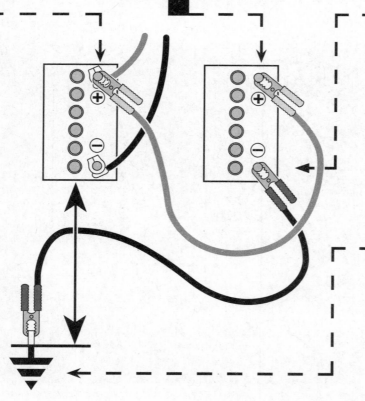

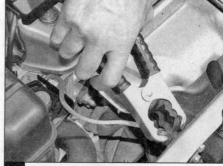

4 Connect the other end of the black jump lead to a bolt or bracket on the engine block, well away from the battery, on the vehicle to be started.

5 Make sure that the jump leads will not come into contact with the fan, drive-belts or other moving parts of the engine.

6 Start the engine using the booster battery and run it at idle speed. Switch on the lights, rear window demister and heater blower motor, then disconnect the jump leads in the reverse order of connection. Turn off the lights etc.

Wheel changing

Warning: Do not change a wheel in a situation where you risk being hit by other traffic. On busy roads, try to stop in a lay-by or a gateway. Be wary of passing traffic while changing the wheel – it is easy to become distracted by the job in hand.

Preparation

- When a puncture occurs, stop as soon as it is safe to do so.
- Park on firm level ground, if possible, and well out of the way of other traffic.
- Use hazard warning lights if necessary.
- If you have one, use a warning triangle to alert other drivers of your presence.
- Apply the handbrake and engage first or reverse gear (or Park on models with automatic transmission).
- Chock the wheel diagonally opposite the one being removed – a couple of large stones will do for this.
- If the ground is soft, use a flat piece of wood to spread the load under the jack.

Changing the wheel

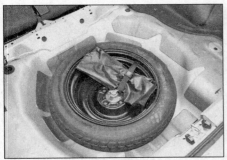

1 The spare wheel and tools are in the luggage compartment, under the boot floor panel. Lift up the panel's rear edge, take out the tool bag from the spare wheel, then unscrew the spare wheel retainer bolt anti-clockwise, and lift out the spare wheel.

2 Use the wheelbrace to loosen each wheel nut by half a turn. Remove the wheel trim if necessary to access the nuts, but note that some genuine Honda wheel trims are retained by the wheel nuts, and so cannot be removed with the nuts fitted.

3 Locate the jack head into the jacking point nearest the wheel to be changed. The jacking points are elongated tabs on the base of the door sills at the front and rear – the notched jack head should locate on the tab.

4 Turn the jack handle clockwise until the wheel is raised clear of the ground. Remove the nuts, take off the wheel trim where applicable, and lift the punctured wheel clear.

5 Fit the spare wheel, which may be of narrow 'space-saver' type (the wheel trim may not fit a space-saver wheel, so it should be stored in the boot). Refit the wheel nuts, and tighten moderately with the wheelbrace.

6 Lower the car to the ground, then finally tighten the wheel nuts in a diagonal sequence. Ideally, the wheel nuts should be slackened and retightened to the specified torque at the earliest opportunity.

Finally . . .

- Remove the wheel chocks.
- Stow the jack and tools in the correct locations in the car. On models with alloy wheels, the plastic centre cap must be pushed out before the retainer bolt can be used to hold the punctured wheel in place.
- Check the tyre pressure on the wheel just fitted. If it is low, or if you don't have a pressure gauge with you, drive slowly to the nearest garage and inflate the tyre to the correct pressure.
- On models with a space-saver spare wheel, this is for temporary use only. Drive with extra care, especially when cornering – limit yourself to a maximum of 50 mph, and to the shortest possible journeys, while it is fitted.
- Have the damaged tyre or wheel repaired as soon as possible.

Identifying leaks

Puddles on the garage floor or drive, or obvious wetness under the bonnet or underneath the car, suggest a leak that needs investigating. It can sometimes be difficult to decide where the leak is coming from, especially if the engine bay is very dirty already. Leaking oil or fluid can also be blown rearwards by the passage of air under the car, giving a false impression of where the problem lies.

 Warning: Most automotive oils and fluids are poisonous. Wash them off skin, and change out of contaminated clothing, without delay.

 HAYNES HiNT *The smell of a fluid leaking from the car may provide a clue to what's leaking. Some fluids are distinctively coloured. It may help to clean the car carefully and to park it over some clean paper overnight as an aid to locating the source of the leak.*
Remember that some leaks may only occur while the engine is running.

Sump oil

Engine oil may leak from the drain plug...

Oil from filter

...or from the base of the oil filter.

Gearbox oil

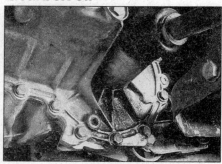

Gearbox oil can leak from the seals at the inboard ends of the driveshafts.

Antifreeze

Leaking antifreeze often leaves a crystalline deposit like this.

Brake fluid

A leak occurring at a wheel is almost certainly brake fluid.

Power steering fluid

Power steering fluid may leak from the pipe connectors on the steering rack.

Towing

When all else fails, you may find yourself having to get a tow home – or of course you may be helping somebody else. Long-distance recovery should only be done by a garage or breakdown service. For shorter distances, DIY towing using another car is easy enough, but observe the following points:

☐ Use a proper tow-rope – they are not expensive. The vehicle being towed must display an ON TOW sign in its rear window.
☐ Always turn the ignition key to the first position when the vehicle is being towed, so that the steering lock is released, and the direction indicator and brake lights work.
☐ Only attach the tow-rope to the towing eyes provided.

☐ Before being towed, release the handbrake and select neutral on the transmission.
☐ On models with automatic transmission, the car must be towed with its front wheels raised clear of the ground, or transmission damage may occur. Even on manual transmission models, if the front wheels cannot be suspended, the towing distance must not exceed 50 miles, at a maximum speed of 35 mph.
☐ Note that greater-than-usual pedal pressure will be required to operate the brakes, since the vacuum servo unit is only operational with the engine running.
☐ If the ignition is not switched on, or the battery is flat, the electric power steering may not work, resulting in very heavy steering.

☐ The driver of the car being towed must keep the tow-rope taut at all times to avoid snatching – this can be achieved by applying the brakes very gently, where this is appropriate.
☐ Make sure that both drivers know the route before setting off.
☐ Only drive at moderate speeds and keep the distance towed to a minimum. Drive smoothly and allow plenty of time for slowing down at junctions.

Introduction

There are some very simple checks which need only take a few minutes to carry out, but which could save you a lot of inconvenience and expense.

These *Weekly checks* require no great skill or special tools, and the small amount of time they take to perform could prove to be very well spent, for example:

☐ Keeping an eye on tyre condition and pressures, will not only help to stop them wearing out prematurely, but could also save your life.

☐ Many breakdowns are caused by electrical problems. Battery-related faults are particularly common, and a quick check on a regular basis will often prevent the majority of these.

☐ If your car develops a brake fluid leak, the first time you might know about it is when your brakes don't work properly. Checking the level regularly will give advance warning of this kind of problem.

☐ If the oil or coolant levels run low, the cost of repairing any engine damage will be far greater than fixing the leak, for example.

Underbonnet check points

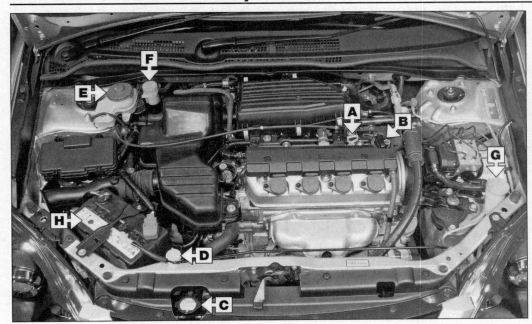

◄ 1.6 litre petrol engine (1.4 litre similar)

A *Engine oil level dipstick*

B *Engine oil filler cap*

C *Radiator cap*

D *Expansion tank filler cap*

E *Brake fluid reservoir*

F *Clutch fluid reservoir*

G *Washer fluid filler neck*

H *Battery*

Note: *All models have electric power steering. As this is not a hydraulically-operated system, no power steering fluid reservoir is present.*

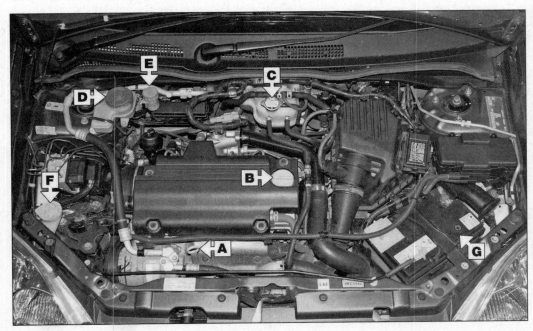

◄ 1.7 litre diesel engine

A *Engine oil level dipstick*

B *Engine oil filler cap*

C *Expansion tank filler cap*

D *Brake fluid reservoir*

E *Clutch fluid reservoir*

F *Washer fluid filler neck*

G *Battery*

Note: *All models have electric power steering. As this is not a hydraulically-operated system, no power steering fluid reservoir is present.*

Engine oil level

Before you start
✔ Make sure that the car is on level ground.
✔ Check the oil level before the car is driven, or at least 5 minutes after the engine has been switched off.

The correct oil
Modern engines place great demands on their oil. It is very important that the correct oil for your car is used (see *Lubricants and fluids*).

HAYNES HiNT *If the oil is checked immediately after driving the vehicle, some of the oil will remain in the upper engine components, resulting in an inaccurate reading on the dipstick.*

Car care
● If you have to add oil frequently, you should check whether you have any oil leaks. Place some clean paper under the car overnight, and check for stains in the morning. If there are no leaks, then the engine may be burning oil (see *Fault finding*.
● Always maintain the level between the upper and lower dipstick marks (see photo 2). If the level is too low, severe engine damage may occur. Oil seal failure may result if the engine is overfilled by adding too much oil.

1 On petrol engines, the dipstick is behind the engine, and has an orange handle; diesel models have a yellow-handled dipstick at the front (see *Underbonnet check points* for exact locations). Pull out the dipstick – on diesel engines, oil may drip onto the alternator below, so have a cloth ready.

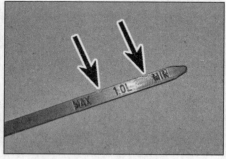

2 Using a clean rag or paper towel, wipe all the oil from the dipstick. Insert the clean dipstick into the tube as far as it will go, then withdraw it again. Note the oil level on the end of the dipstick, which should be between the lower (or MIN) and upper (or MAX) marks. Adding approximately 1.0 litre of oil will raise the level from the lower to the upper mark.

3 Oil is added through the filler cap on top of the engine. Unscrew the filler cap, then top-up the level – use a funnel to reduce spillage. Add the oil in small amounts, checking the level on the dipstick often – allow a minute or so for the oil added to reach the sump. Take care not to overfill.

Washer fluid level

● Screenwash additives not only keep the windscreen clean during bad weather, they also prevent the washer system freezing in cold weather – which is when you are likely to need it most. Don't top-up using plain water, as the screenwash will become diluted, and will freeze in cold weather.

 Warning: On no account use engine coolant antifreeze in the screen washer system – this may damage the paintwork.

1 The windscreen/tailgate washer fluid reservoir filler neck has a blue cap, and is located at the front of the engine compartment, behind either the left-hand headlight (petrol models) or the right-hand headlight (diesel models). Unclip and remove the cap.

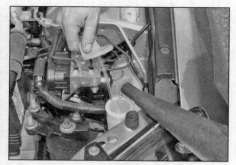

2 A 'tube dipstick' is attached to the cap – place a finger over the hole in the cap, and withdraw the tube; if sufficient fluid is present, a level will be seen in the tube. The bottle can safely be filled to the top. When topping-up the reservoir, a screenwash additive should be added in the quantities recommended on the bottle.

Coolant level

Warning: DO NOT attempt to remove the radiator cap nor the expansion tank cap when the engine is hot, as there is a very great risk of scalding. Only check the level when the system is cold, after the car has been standing for several hours (preferably, after being left overnight). Do not leave open containers of coolant about, as it is poisonous.

Car Care

● With a sealed-type cooling system, adding coolant should not be necessary on a regular basis. If frequent topping-up is required, it is likely there is a leak. Check the radiator, all hoses and joint faces for signs of staining or wetness, and rectify as necessary.

● It is important that antifreeze is used in the cooling system all year round, not just during the winter months. Don't top up with water alone, as the antifreeze will become diluted. **Note:** *Genuine Honda antifreeze comes pre-mixed, ready to use.*

1 On petrol models only, the level in the radiator itself should be checked first, and for this the engine must be **cold**. Turn the radiator cap anti-clockwise to the first stop, then press down and continue turning to remove it. The level should be up to the filler neck – top-up if necessary, using a suitable mixture of antifreeze and water. Refit the cap securely on completion.

3 Add a mixture of water and antifreeze to the expansion tank, until the coolant is up to the MAX mark. Use antifreeze of the same type (and colour) as that which is already in the system. Refit the cap securely.

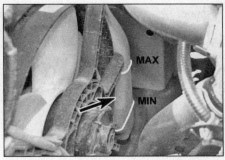

2 Next, the expansion tank level should be checked. On petrol models, the tank is at the front, next to the radiator. When the engine is cold, the level should be between the MIN and MAX marks. When the engine is hot, the level may rise slightly above the MAX mark. If topping-up is necessary, wait until the engine is **cold**, then remove the cap on the expansion tank.

4 On diesel models, only the expansion tank level needs to be checked. The tank is at the rear of the engine bay, mounted centrally, and has MIN and MAX marks on the side. If topping-up is necessary, with the engine **cold**, remove the tank's pressure cap. Add water and antifreeze until the coolant is up to the MAX mark, then refit the cap securely

Wiper blades

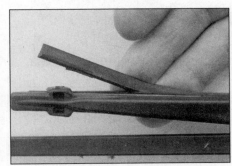

1 Check the condition of the wiper blades; if they are cracked or show any signs of deterioration, or if the glass swept area is smeared, renew them. For maximum clarity of vision, wiper blades should be renewed annually, as a matter of course.

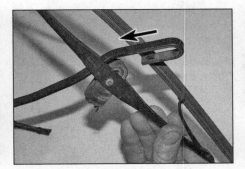

2 To remove a windscreen wiper blade, pull the arm fully away from the screen until it locks. Swivel the blade through 90°, then depress the locking clip at the base of the mounting block, and slide the blade out of the hooked end of the arm.

3 Don't forget to check the tailgate wiper blade as well, which unclips directly from the arm.

Tyre condition and pressure

It is very important that tyres are in good condition, and at the correct pressure - having a tyre failure at any speed is highly dangerous. Tyre wear is influenced by driving style - harsh braking and acceleration, or fast cornering, will all produce more rapid tyre wear. As a general rule, the front tyres wear out faster than the rears. Interchanging the tyres from front to rear ("rotating" the tyres) may result in more even wear. However, if this is completely effective, you may have the expense of replacing all four tyres at once! Remove any nails or stones embedded in the tread before they penetrate the tyre to cause deflation. If removal of a nail does reveal that the tyre has been punctured, refit the nail so that its point of penetration is marked. Then immediately change the wheel, and have the tyre repaired by a tyre dealer.

Regularly check the tyres for damage in the form of cuts or bulges, especially in the sidewalls. Periodically remove the wheels, and clean any dirt or mud from the inside and outside surfaces. Examine the wheel rims for signs of rusting, corrosion or other damage. Light alloy wheels are easily damaged by "kerbing" whilst parking; steel wheels may also become dented or buckled. A new wheel is very often the only way to overcome severe damage.

New tyres should be balanced when they are fitted, but it may become necessary to re-balance them as they wear, or if the balance weights fitted to the wheel rim should fall off. Unbalanced tyres will wear more quickly, as will the steering and suspension components. Wheel imbalance is normally signified by vibration, particularly at a certain speed (typically around 50 mph). If this vibration is felt only through the steering, then it is likely that just the front wheels need balancing. If, however, the vibration is felt through the whole car, the rear wheels could be out of balance. Wheel balancing should be carried out by a tyre dealer or garage.

1 *Tread Depth - visual check*
The original tyres have tread wear safety bands (B), which will appear when the tread depth reaches approximately 1.6 mm. The band positions are indicated by a triangular mark on the tyre sidewall (A).

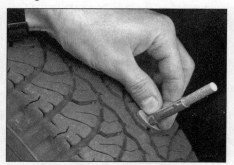

2 *Tread Depth - manual check*
Alternatively, tread wear can be monitored with a simple, inexpensive device known as a tread depth indicator gauge.

3 *Tyre Pressure Check*
Check the tyre pressures regularly with the tyres cold. Do not adjust the tyre pressures immediately after the vehicle has been used, or an inaccurate setting will result.

Tyre tread wear patterns

Shoulder Wear

Underinflation (wear on both sides)
Under-inflation will cause overheating of the tyre, because the tyre will flex too much, and the tread will not sit correctly on the road surface. This will cause a loss of grip and excessive wear, not to mention the danger of sudden tyre failure due to heat build-up.
Check and adjust pressures
Incorrect wheel camber (wear on one side)
Repair or renew suspension parts
Hard cornering
Reduce speed!

Centre Wear

Overinflation
Over-inflation will cause rapid wear of the centre part of the tyre tread, coupled with reduced grip, harsher ride, and the danger of shock damage occurring in the tyre casing.
Check and adjust pressures

If you sometimes have to inflate your car's tyres to the higher pressures specified for maximum load or sustained high speed, don't forget to reduce the pressures to normal afterwards.

Uneven Wear

Front tyres may wear unevenly as a result of wheel misalignment. Most tyre dealers and garages can check and adjust the wheel alignment (or "tracking") for a modest charge.
Incorrect camber or castor
Repair or renew suspension parts
Malfunctioning suspension
Repair or renew suspension parts
Unbalanced wheel
Balance tyres
Incorrect toe setting
Adjust front wheel alignment
Note: *The feathered edge of the tread which typifies toe wear is best checked by feel.*

Brake and clutch fluid levels

Warning:
Brake fluid can harm your eyes and damage painted surfaces, so use extreme caution when handling and pouring it.
Do not use fluid that has been standing open for some time, as it absorbs moisture from the air, which can cause a dangerous loss of braking effectiveness.

Safety first!

● If the reservoir requires repeated topping-up, this is an indication of a fluid leak somewhere in the system, which should be investigated immediately.

● The fluid level in the brake fluid reservoir will drop slightly as the brake pads wear down, but the fluid level must never be allowed to drop below the MIN mark.

● If a leak is suspected, the car should not be driven until the braking system has been checked. Never take any risks where brakes are concerned.

1 The two reservoirs are located next to each other, at the rear of the engine bay on the driver's side.

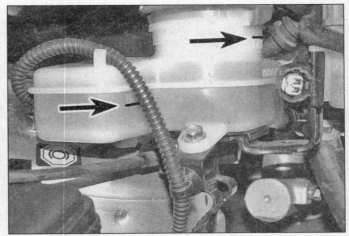

2 The brake fluid reservoir has a MAX mark at the top, near the neck, with the MIN mark lower down, at the side. The fluid level must be kept between these two marks – if the level drops below the MIN mark, air will enter the system, causing loss of braking ability.

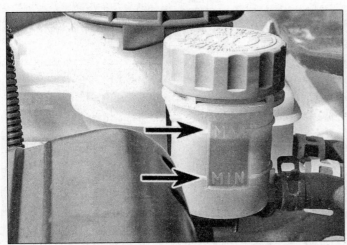

3 The smaller clutch fluid reservoir has MAX and MIN marks on the side.

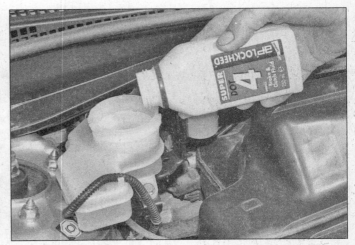

4 If topping-up is necessary, first wipe the area around the filler cap with a clean rag, then unscrew the cap. If the fluid in the reservoir is dark or dirty, it should be changed. Carefully add fluid, avoiding spilling it on surrounding paintwork. Use only the specified hydraulic fluid. After filling to the correct level, refit the cap securely, and wipe off any spilt fluid.

Battery

Caution: Before carrying out any work on the vehicle battery, read the precautions given in 'Safety first!' at the start of this manual.

✔ Make sure that the battery tray is in good condition, and that the clamp is tight. Corrosion on the tray, retaining clamp and the battery itself can be removed with a solution of water and baking soda. Thoroughly rinse all cleaned areas with water. Any metal parts damaged by corrosion should be covered with a zinc-based primer, then painted.

✔ Periodically (approximately every three months), check the charge condition of the battery as described in Chapter 5A.

✔ If the battery is flat, and you need to jump start your vehicle, see *Roadside Repairs*.

✔ The original-equipment battery is described as 'maintenance-free', but has removable cell covers, and the electrolyte level can be seen through the battery casing. If the level in any cell is obviously low, there is no harm in topping-up with a little distilled water.

HAYNES HINT *Battery corrosion can be kept to a minimum by applying a layer of petroleum jelly to the clamps and terminals after they are reconnected.*

1 The battery is located at the front of the engine compartment, behind either the right-hand headlight (petrol models) or the left-hand headlight (diesel models). The battery should be inspected periodically for damage such as a cracked case. Honda batteries have a condition indicator window, which should show either blue or green if all is well.

3 If corrosion (white, fluffy deposits) is evident, remove the cables from the battery terminals, clean them with a small wire brush, then refit them. Automotive stores sell a tool for cleaning the battery post . . .

2 Check the tightness of the battery cable clamps to ensure good electrical connections. You should not be able to move them. Also check each cable for cracks and frayed conductors.

4 . . . as well as the battery cable clamps.

Electrical systems

✔ Check all external lights and the horn. Refer to the appropriate Sections of Chapter 12 for details if any of the circuits are found to be inoperative.

✔ Visually check all accessible wiring connectors, harnesses and retaining clips for security, and for signs of chafing or damage.

HAYNES HINT *If you need to check your brake lights and indicators unaided, back up to a wall or garage door and operate the lights. The reflected light should show if they are working properly.*

1 If a single indicator light, brake light or headlight has failed, it is likely that a bulb has blown and will need to be renewed. Refer to Chapter 12 for details. If both brake lights have failed, it is possible that the brake pedal position switch, operated by the brake pedal, is to blame. Refer to Chapter 9 for details.

2 If more than one indicator light or headlight has failed, it is likely that either a fuse has blown, or that there is a fault in the circuit (see Chapter 12). The interior fuses are mounted underneath the steering column – turn the catch clockwise, and lower the fusebox lid. The fuse list is shown inside the lid.

3 To renew a blown fuse, first ensure the ignition is switched off (take out the key). Remove the fuse using the plastic tweezer tool provided (where applicable). Fit a new fuse of the same rating, available from car accessory shops. It is important that you find the reason that the fuse blew (see *Electrical fault finding* in Chapter 12).

Lubricants and fluids

Engine:

  Petrol . . . .   Engine oil, SAE 10W-30 or 10W-40, to specification API SJ or SL

  Diesel . . . .   Engine oil, SAE 5W-40, to specification ACEA B3

Cooling system . . . .   Ethylene glycol-based antifreeze suitable for use in mixed-metal engines – Honda All Season Type 2

Manual transmission . . . .   Honda Manual Transmission Fluid (MTF) – fully synthetic gear oil

Automatic transmission . . . .   Honda ATF-Z1

Brake and clutch systems . . . .   Hydraulic fluid to DOT 3 or DOT 4

Tyre pressures

Note: *The tyre pressures given here are a guide only. A sticker attached to the driver's door pillar shows the correct pressures for each particular car and its original-equipment tyres (**see illustration**). If new tyres are fitted, check with the tyre supplier or a Honda dealer for the latest tyre pressure information.*

	Front	Rear
Normal use (driver and one passenger)	30 psi (2.1 bar)	30 psi (2.1 bar)
All seats in use, and/or motorway driving	32 psi (2.2 bar)	32 psi (2.2 bar)
Towing	32 psi (2.2 bar)	38 psi (2.6 bar)
Emergency (space-saver) spare tyre		
All usage, front or rear	61 psi (4.2 bar)	

The tyre pressures are given on a sticker on the driver's door pillar

Chapter 1 Part A:
Routine maintenance and servicing – petrol engine models

Contents

Degrees of difficulty

Easy, suitable for novice with little experience	**Fairly easy,** suitable for beginner with some experience	**Fairly difficult,** suitable for competent DIY mechanic	**Difficult,** suitable for experienced DIY mechanic	**Very difficult,** suitable for expert DIY or professional

Lubricants and fluids

Refer to *Weekly checks* on page 0•17

Capacities*

Engine oil (including oil filter):	
1.4 litre engine (steel sump)	3.2 litres
1.6 litre engine (aluminium sump)	3.5 litres
Cooling system:	
Change	4.0 litres
Total	5.1 litres
Manual transmission	1.5 litres
Automatic transmission (fluid change)	2.7 litres
Washer fluid reservoir:	
Without headlight washers	2.5 litres
With headlight washers	5.0 litres
Fuel tank	50 litres

*All capacities are approximate.

Engine

Engine codes	See Chapter 2A
Valve clearances (engine cold):	
Intake	0.18 to 0.22 mm (0.007 to 0.009 in)
Exhaust	0.23 to 0.27 mm (0.009 to 0.011 in)
Idle speed (not adjustable)	700 ± 50 rpm
Auxiliary drivebelt deflection (midway between pulleys):	
New belt	5.6 to 6.5 mm
Used belt	8.5 to 11.0 mm

Ignition system

Spark plugs:	
Type	NGK ZFR5J-11 or Denso KJ16CR-L11
Electrode gap	1.0 to 1.1 mm (0.039 to 0.043 in)

Brakes

Friction material minimum thickness:	
Front brake pads	1.6 mm
Rear brake pads	1.6 mm
Disc minimum thickness:	
Front disc	19.0 mm
Rear disc	8.0 mm
Handbrake adjustment	6 to 10 clicks

Torque wrench settings

	Nm	lb ft
Alternator adjuster lockbolt	24	18
Alternator adjuster plate front bolt	44	32
Alternator upper mounting bolt	44	32
Automatic transmission drain plug	49	36
Engine block coolant drain bolt	78	58
Manual transmission drain plug	39	29
Manual transmission filler/level plug	44	32
Roadwheel nuts	108	80
Spark plugs	18	13
Sump drain plug:		
1.4 litre engine (steel sump)	44	32
1.6 litre engine (aluminium sump)	39	29

The maintenance intervals in this manual are provided with the assumption that you, not the dealer, will be carrying out the work. These are the minimum maintenance intervals recommended by us for cars driven daily. If you wish to keep your car in peak condition at all times, you may wish to perform some of these procedures more often. We encourage frequent maintenance, because it enhances the efficiency, performance and resale value of your car.

If the car is driven in dusty areas, used to tow a trailer, or driven frequently at slow speeds (idling in traffic) or on short journeys, more frequent maintenance intervals are recommended.

When the car is new, it should be serviced by a dealer service department (or other workshop recognised by the car manufacturer as providing the same standard of service) in order to preserve the warranty. The car manufacturer may reject warranty claims if you are unable to prove that servicing has been carried out as and when specified, using only original-equipment parts, or parts certified to be of equivalent quality.

Every 6000 miles or 6 months, whichever comes first

☐ Renew the engine oil and filter (Section 3)

Note: *Frequent oil and filter changes are good for the engine, so we recommend halving Honda's current interval, which is 12 000 miles or 12 months.*

Every 12 000 miles or 12 months, whichever comes first

☐ Check the braking system (Section 4)
☐ Check the steering and suspension components for condition and security (Section 5)
☐ Check the condition of the driveshaft gaiters (Section 6)
☐ Engine management and exhaust emission test (Section 7)
☐ Check the engine idle speed (Section 8)
☐ Check the operation of all electrical systems (Section 9)
☐ Check the exhaust system (Section 10)
☐ Check all components, pipes and hoses for fluid leaks (Section 11)
☐ Renew the pollen filter (Section 12)
☐ Check the automatic transmission fluid level (Section 13)
☐ Check the manual transmission oil level (Section 14)
☐ Lubricate all door locks and hinges, door stops, bonnet lock and release, and tailgate lock and hinges (Section 15)
☐ Carry out a road test (Section 16)

Every 24 000 miles or 2 years, whichever comes first

☐ Check and if necessary adjust the valve clearances (Section 17)
☐ Renew the air filter element (Section 18)
☐ Check the auxiliary drivebelt, and adjust or renew if necessary (Section 19)
☐ Renew the spark plugs (Section 20)

Every 60 000 miles or 5 years, whichever comes first

☐ Renew the timing belt, check the belt tensioner and the water pump (Section 21)

Note: *Honda recommend that the interval for timing belt renewal is 60 000 miles or 5 years. However, if the car is used mainly for short journeys or a lot of stop-start driving, it is recommended that the renewal interval is shortened. The actual belt renewal interval is very much up to the individual owner but, bearing in mind that severe engine damage will result if the belt breaks in use, we recommend you err on the side of caution.*

Every 72 000 miles or 6 years, whichever comes first

☐ Renew the automatic transmission fluid (Section 22)
☐ Renew the manual transmission fluid (Section 23)

Note: *On a car used mainly for short journeys, or for a lot of towing, this interval should be halved to 36 000 miles or 3 years. As with engine oil changes, changing the fluid will help to prolong the transmission's life.*

Every 3 years, regardless of mileage

☐ Renew the brake fluid (Section 24)

Every 5 years, regardless of mileage

☐ Renew the coolant (Section 25)

Note: *Some models may have been filled with Honda coolant which is claimed to have a 10-year life (typically, this type of coolant is orange or red in colour). If this is known to be the case, and only this coolant is used in the system, the 10-year renewal interval can be observed. The DIY owner may prefer to use the suggested shorter interval, especially if the coolant in the system is of unknown type.*

Underbonnet view of a 1.6 litre model (1.4 litre similar)

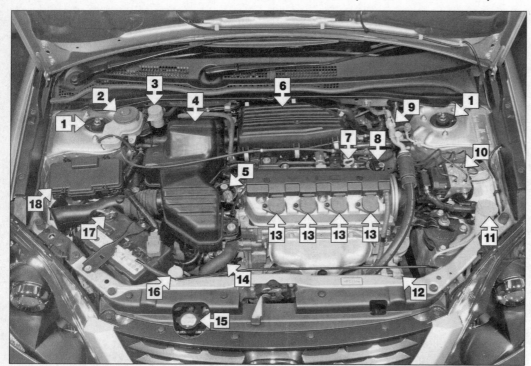

1 Front suspension strut upper mounting
2 Brake fluid reservoir
3 Clutch fluid reservoir
4 Inlet air resonator
5 EGR valve
6 Air cleaner
7 Engine oil dipstick
8 Engine oil filler cap
9 Air conditioning refrigerant pipe
10 ABS unit
11 Washer fluid filler neck
12 Alternator
13 Ignition coils
14 Radiator top hose
15 Radiator filler cap
16 Coolant expansion tank cap
17 Battery negative lead
18 Engine compartment fusebox

Front underbody view of a 1.6 litre model

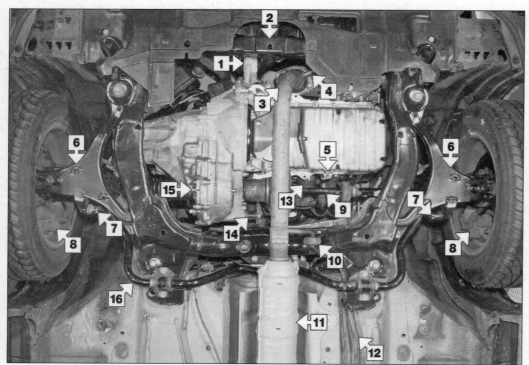

1 Engine front mounting
2 Subframe front support point
3 Exhaust front pipe
4 Primary oxygen sensor
5 Engine oil drain plug
6 Front suspension lower arm
7 Anti-roll bar drop link
8 Front brake caliper
9 Driveshaft
10 Exhaust mounting
11 Catalytic converter
12 Fuel and brake lines
13 Oil filter
14 Engine rear mounting
15 Manual transmission drain plug
16 Anti-roll bar

Rear underbody view

1 Centre rear support point
2 Exhaust rear mounting
3 Exhaust rear silencer
4 Fuel vapour separator
5 Charcoal canister
6 Two-way valve
7 Fuel tank
8 Rear anti-roll bar
9 Rear suspension strut
10 Rear suspension lower arm
11 Handbrake cable
12 Exhaust centre silencer

Maintenance procedures

1 General information

1 This Chapter is designed to help the home mechanic maintain his/her car for safety, economy, long life and peak performance.

2 The Chapter contains a master maintenance schedule, followed by Sections dealing specifically with each task in the schedule. Visual checks, adjustments, component renewal and other helpful items are included. Refer to the accompanying illustrations of the engine compartment and the underside of the car for the locations of the various components.

3 Servicing your car in accordance with the mileage/time maintenance schedule and the following Sections will provide a planned maintenance programme, which should result in a long and reliable service life. This is a comprehensive plan, so maintaining some items but not others at the specified service intervals, will not produce the same results.

4 As you service your car, you will discover that many of the procedures can – and should – be grouped together, because of the particular procedure being performed, or because of the proximity of two otherwise-unrelated components to one another. For example, if the car is raised for any reason, the exhaust can be inspected at the same time as the suspension and steering components.

5 The first step in this maintenance programme is to prepare yourself before the actual work begins. Read through all the Sections relevant to the work to be carried out, then make a list and gather all the parts and tools required. If a problem is encountered, seek advice from a parts specialist, or a dealer service department.

2 Regular maintenance

1 If, from the time the car is new, the routine maintenance schedule is followed closely, and frequent checks are made of fluid levels and high-wear items, as suggested throughout this manual, the engine will be kept in relatively good running condition, and the need for additional work will be minimised.

2 It is possible that there will be times when the engine is running poorly due to the lack of regular maintenance. This is even more likely if a used car, which has not received regular and frequent maintenance checks, is purchased. In such cases, additional work may need to be carried out, outside of the regular maintenance intervals.

3 If engine wear is suspected, a compression test (refer to Chapter 2A) will provide valuable information regarding the overall performance of the main internal components. Such a test can be used as a basis to decide on the extent of the work to be carried out. If, for example, a compression test indicates serious internal engine wear, conventional maintenance as described in this Chapter will not greatly improve the performance of the engine, and may prove a waste of time and money, unless extensive overhaul work is carried out first.

4 The following series of operations are those most often required to improve the performance of a generally poor-running engine:

Primary operations

a) Clean, inspect and test the battery (refer to Weekly checks).
b) Check all the engine-related fluids (refer to Weekly checks).
c) Check the condition and tension of the auxiliary drivebelt (Section 19).
d) Renew the spark plugs (Section 20).
e) Check the condition of the air filter, and renew if necessary (Section 18).
f) Check the condition of all hoses, and check for fluid leaks (Section 11).
g) Check the valve clearances (Section 17).

5 If the above operations do not prove fully effective, carry out the following secondary operations:

Secondary operations

All items listed under Primary operations, plus the following:

a) Check the charging system (refer to Chapter 5A).
b) Check the ignition system (refer to Chapter 5B).
c) Check the fuel system (refer to Chapter 4A).

3.4 Unscrewing the oil filler cap may help the oil to drain

3.5a The sump drain plug is at the rear – take care if the exhaust is hot

3.5b Move the drain plug clear quickly, and try not to drop it

Every 6000 miles or 6 months

3 Engine oil and filter renewal

1 Frequent oil and filter changes are the most important preventative maintenance procedures which can be undertaken by the DIY owner. As engine oil ages, it becomes diluted and contaminated, which leads to premature engine wear.

2 Before starting this procedure, gather together all the necessary tools and materials. Also make sure that you have plenty of clean rags and newspapers handy, to mop-up any spills. Ideally, the engine oil should be warm, as it will drain more easily, and more built-up sludge will be removed with it. Take care not to touch the exhaust or any other hot parts of the engine when working under the car. To avoid any possibility of scalding, and to protect yourself from possible skin irritants and other harmful contaminants in used engine oils, it is advisable to wear gloves when carrying out this work.

3 Firmly apply the handbrake, then jack up the front of the car and support it on axle stands (see *Jacking and vehicle support*). Unbolt and remove the engine undertray, referring if necessary to Chapter 11, Section 23.

4 Remove the oil filler cap **(see illustration)**.

5 Using a spanner, or preferably a suitable socket and bar, slacken the drain plug about half a turn. Position the draining container under the drain plug, then remove the plug completely **(see illustrations)**.

6 Allow some time for the oil to drain, noting that it may be necessary to reposition the container as the oil flow slows to a trickle.

7 After all the oil has drained, wipe the drain plug and the sealing washer with a clean rag. Examine the condition of the sealing washer, and renew it if it shows signs of scoring or other damage which may prevent an oil-tight seal. Clean the area around the drain plug opening, and refit the plug complete with the washer and tighten it to the specified torque.

8 Move the container into position under the oil filter. On all engines, the filter is located on the rear face of the cylinder block, above the left-hand driveshaft **(see illustration)**.

9 Use an oil filter removal tool to slacken the filter initially, then unscrew it by hand the rest of the way **(see illustration)**. Empty the oil from the old filter into the oil drain container. Check the filter to make sure the filter sealing ring has come off with it – if not, it may still be stuck to the engine, and should be removed.

10 Use a clean rag to remove all oil, dirt and sludge from the filter sealing area on the engine.

11 Apply a light coating of clean engine oil to the sealing ring on the new filter, then screw the filter into position on the engine. Tighten the filter firmly by hand only – **do not** use any tools.

12 Refit the engine undertray. Remove the old oil and all tools from under the car, then lower the car to the ground.

13 Fill the engine through the filler hole, using the correct grade and type of oil (refer to *Weekly checks* for details of topping-up). Pour in half the specified quantity of oil first, then wait a few minutes for the oil to drain into the sump. Continue to add oil, a small quantity at a time, until the level is up to the lower mark on the dipstick **(see illustration)**.

14 Start the engine and run it for a few minutes, while checking for leaks around the oil filter seal and the sump drain plug. Note that there may be a delay of a few seconds before the low oil pressure warning light goes out when the engine is first started, as the oil circulates through the new oil filter and the engine oil galleries before the pressure builds-up.

15 Stop the engine, and wait a few minutes for the oil to settle in the sump once more. With the new oil circulated and the filter now completely full, recheck the level on the dipstick, and add more oil as necessary.

16 Dispose of the used engine oil safely with reference to *General repair procedures*. It should be noted that used oil filters should not be included with domestic waste. Most local authority used oil 'banks' also have used filter disposal points alongside.

3.8 The oil filter is also at the rear, above the driveshaft

3.9 Unscrew and remove the oil filter

3.13 Fill the engine slowly, checking the dipstick often

4.6 Place a ruler across the inspection hole to check the pad thickness

5.4 Check the balljoint rubber boots for damage

5.6 Check for wheel bearing wear by rocking the wheel

Every 12 000 miles or 12 months

4 Braking system check

> ⚠️ **Warning: The dust created by the brake system is harmful to your health. Never blow it out with compressed air and don't inhale any of it. An approved filtering mask should be worn when working on the brakes. Do not, under any circumstances, use petroleum-based solvents to clean brake parts. Use brake system cleaner only. Try to use non-asbestos parts whenever possible.**

1 In addition to the specified intervals, the brakes should be inspected every time the wheels are removed or whenever a defect is suspected.

2 Any of the following symptoms could indicate a potential brake system defect:

a) The car pulls to one side when the brake pedal is depressed.

b) The brakes make squealing or dragging noises when applied.

c) Brake pedal travel is excessive.

d) The brake pedal pulsates when applied (if this happens during emergency braking only, this could be due to ABS operation, which can be felt through the pedal, and is not a cause for concern).

e) Brake fluid leaks, usually onto the inside of the tyre or wheel.

3 Loosen the wheel nuts.

4 Raise the car and place it securely on axle stands (see Jacking and vehicle support).

5 Remove the wheels.

Disc brakes

6 There are two pads (an outer and an inner) in each caliper. The pads are visible through inspection holes in each caliper **(see illustration)**.

7 If the lining material is less than the thickness listed in this Chapter's Specifications, renew the pads. **Note:** Keep in mind that the lining material is bonded to a metal backing plate – the metal plate is not included in this measurement.

8 If it is difficult to determine the exact thickness of the remaining pad material by the above method, or if you are at all concerned about the condition of the pads, remove the caliper(s), then remove the pads from the calipers for further inspection (refer to Chapter 9).

9 Once the pads are removed from the calipers, clean them with brake cleaner and remeasure them with a ruler or a vernier caliper.

10 Measure the disc thickness with a micrometer to make sure that it still has service life remaining. If any disc is thinner than the specified minimum thickness, renew it (refer to Chapter 9). Even if the disc has service life remaining, check its condition. Look for scoring, gouging and burned spots. If these conditions exist, remove the disc and have it resurfaced (see Chapter 9).

11 Before installing the wheels, check all brake pipes and hoses for damage, wear, deformation, cracks, corrosion, leakage, bends and twists, particularly in the vicinity of the rubber hoses at the calipers. Check the clamps for tightness and the connections for leakage. Make sure that all hoses and pipes are clear of sharp edges, moving parts and the exhaust system. If any of the above conditions are noted, repair, reroute or renew the pipes and/or fittings as necessary (see Chapter 9).

Drum brakes

12 The only satisfactory way to check the rear drum brake linings is to remove the drums as described in Chapter 9. This will also allow an inspection to be made of the rear wheel cylinder, which should be checked for signs of fluid leakage.

Brake servo check

13 Sit in the driver's seat and perform the following sequence of tests.

14 With the brake fully depressed, start the engine – the pedal should move down a little when the engine starts.

15 With the engine running, depress the brake pedal several times – the travel distance should not change.

16 Depress the brake, stop the engine and hold the pedal in for about 30 seconds – the pedal should neither sink nor rise.

17 Restart the engine, run it for about a minute and turn it off. Then firmly depress the brake several times – the pedal travel should decrease with each application.

18 If the brakes do not operate as described, the brake servo or its vacuum hose may have failed. Refer to Chapter 9.

Handbrake

19 Slowly pull up on the handbrake and count the number of clicks you hear until the handle is up as far as it will go. The adjustment is correct if you hear approximately 8 clicks. If you hear more clicks, the handbrake needs adjusting (see Chapter 9); fewer clicks, and the cables may have seized, or the brakes are dragging (not releasing).

5 Suspension and steering check

Wheel nut tightness check

1 Work around each wheel in turn, and check the tightness of the wheel nuts using a torque wrench.

2 If you suspect that the nuts have been over-tightened (as sometimes happens in certain garages), loosen and then tighten each nut (one at a time) to the specified torque.

Front suspension and steering

3 Raise the front of the car, and securely support it on axle stands (see Jacking and vehicle support).

4 Visually inspect the balljoint dust covers and the steering rack-and-pinion gaiters for splits, chafing or deterioration **(see illustration)**. Any wear of these components will cause loss of lubricant, together with dirt and water entry, resulting in rapid deterioration of the balljoints or steering gear.

5 Check the suspension strut for signs of fluid leakage from the shock absorber – if evident, this indicates that the shock absorber has failed (the car would fail an MoT in this condition). **Note:** Shock absorbers should always be renewed in pairs on the same axle.

6 Grasp the roadwheel at the 12 o'clock and 6 o'clock positions, and try to rock it **(see illustration)**. Very slight free play may be felt,

6.1 Check the driveshaft outer CV boots for splits

6.4 Though less susceptible to damage, the inner joint boots should also be checked

but if the movement is appreciable, further investigation is necessary to determine the source. Continue rocking the wheel while an assistant depresses the footbrake. If the movement is now eliminated or significantly reduced, it is likely that the hub bearings are at fault. If the free play is still evident with the footbrake depressed, then there is wear in the suspension joints or mountings.

7 Now grasp the wheel at the 9 o'clock and 3 o'clock positions, and try to rock it as before. Any movement felt now may again be caused by wear in the hub bearings or the steering track rod balljoints. If the outer balljoint is worn, the visual movement will be obvious. If the inner joint is suspect, it can be felt by placing a hand over the rack-and-pinion rubber gaiter and gripping the track rod. If the wheel is now rocked, movement will be felt at the inner joint if wear has taken place.

8 Using a large screwdriver or flat bar, check for wear in the suspension mounting bushes by levering between the relevant suspension component and its attachment point. Some movement is to be expected, as the mountings are made of rubber, but excessive wear should be obvious. Also check the condition of any visible rubber bushes, looking for splits, cracks or contamination of the rubber.

9 With the car standing on its wheels, have an assistant turn the steering wheel back-and-forth, about an eighth of a turn each way. There should be very little, if any, lost movement between the steering wheel and roadwheels. If this is not the case, closely observe the joints and mountings previously described. In addition, check the steering column universal joints for wear, and also check the rack-and-pinion steering gear itself.

10 The Civic has an electric power steering system, so there are no fluid hoses to check. However, the system has an EPS warning light on the instrument panel which should come on with the ignition, then go out as the engine starts. If this warning light operates correctly (and the other checks described previously are carried out) it can be assumed that the steering system is fault-free.

11 The efficiency of the shock absorbers may be checked by bouncing the car at each corner. Generally speaking, the body will return to its normal position and stop after being depressed. If it rises and returns on a rebound, the shock absorber is probably suspect.

Rear suspension

12 Chock the front wheels, then jack up the rear of the car and support securely on axle stands (see *Jacking and vehicle support*).

13 Working as described previously for the front suspension, check the rear hub bearings, the suspension bushes and the struts/shock absorbers for wear.

6 Driveshaft (CV) gaiter check

1 With the car raised and securely supported on stands, turn the steering onto full lock, then slowly rotate the roadwheel. Inspect the condition of the outer constant velocity (CV) joint rubber gaiters while squeezing the gaiters to open out the folds **(see illustration)**.

2 Check for signs of cracking, splits or deterioration of the rubber, which may allow the grease to escape and lead to water and grit entry into the joint.

3 Check the security and condition of the retaining clips.

4 Repeat these checks on the inner CV joints **(see illustration)**.

5 If any damage or deterioration is found, the gaiters should be renewed as described in Chapter 8.

7 Engine management and exhaust emission check

1 This check involves checking the engine management system operation by plugging an electronic tester into the system diagnostic socket to check the electronic control module (ECM) memory for faults (see Chapter 4A).

2 In addition, the exhaust emissions should be checked using suitable equipment. In the UK, the exhaust emissions are checked

anyway at the annual MoT test for cars over 3 years old.

3 In reality, if the car is running correctly and the engine management warning light in the instrument panel is functioning normally (coming on with the ignition lights, then going out), then this check need not be carried out. However, if any unusual running problems have been noted, it may be worth having a Honda dealer (or other competent garage with the necessary diagnostic equipment) carry out the check – it may be that a fault has occurred, and the car is running in its 'limp-home' back-up mode.

8 Idle speed check

1 Engine idle speed is the speed at which the engine runs when no throttle is applied, when the car is completely stopped. Note that it is normal for the idle speed to be held up for a second or two, before dropping to base idle – most cars will also run above idle while rolling to a stop, or when coasting downhill. The speed is critical to the performance of the engine itself, as well as many sub-systems.

2 The idle speed is under the control of the engine management module (ECM) and is not adjustable manually. If the idle speed is significantly different from that specified (which is also for an engine at full operating temperature), in the first instance, check the accelerator cable and throttle body.

3 Poor idle quality could be due to poor maintenance – change the engine oil, and carry out the primary operations listed in Section 2.

4 As a rough guide, an idle speed which is too high may be due to an 'air leak' – the engine is sucking in excess air somewhere (perhaps from a loose or split air or vacuum hose), and the ECM is compensating for the extra air by adding fuel.

5 An engine prone to stalling could be suffering a problem with one of the engine-driven ancillaries, such as the alternator, or the problem could be low fuel pressure. Also check the brake pedal position switch and vehicle speed sensor (see Chapter 4A, Section 11).

6 Ultimately, a persistent idle speed problem will have to be referred to a Honda dealer for diagnosis.

9 Electrical systems check

1 Check the operation of all electrical equipment, ie, lights, direction indicators, horn, wash/wipe system, etc. Refer to the appropriate Sections of Chapter 12 for details if any of the circuits are found to be inoperative.

9.2 Check the engine wiring harness for chafing or heat damage

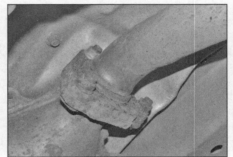

10.2 Check the exhaust joints for corrosion and leakage

10.4 Check the exhaust rubber mountings for perishing

2 Visually check all accessible wiring connectors, harnesses and retaining clips for security, and for signs of chafing or damage **(see illustration)**. Rectify any faults found.

10 Exhaust system inspection

1 With the engine cold (at least three hours after the car has been driven), check the complete exhaust system from the engine to the end of the tailpipe. Ideally, the inspection should be done with the car on a hoist to permit unrestricted access. If a hoist isn't available, raise the car and support it securely on axle stands (see *Jacking and vehicle support*).
2 Check the exhaust pipes and connections for evidence of leaks, severe corrosion and damage **(see illustration)**. Make sure that all brackets and hangers are in good condition and tight.
3 At the same time, inspect the underside of the body for holes, corrosion, open seams, etc, which may allow exhaust gases to enter the passenger compartment. Seal all body openings with silicone or body filler.
4 Rattles and other noises can often be traced to the exhaust system, especially the mounts and hangers. Try to move the pipes, silencer and catalytic converter. If the components can come in contact with the body or suspension parts, secure the exhaust system with new mounts **(see illustration)**.

11 Hose and fluid leak check

1 Visually inspect the engine joint faces, gaskets and seals for any signs of water or oil leaks. Pay particular attention to the areas around the cylinder head cover, cylinder head, oil filter and sump joint faces. Bear in mind that, over a period of time, some very slight seepage from these areas is to be expected – what you are really looking for is any indication of a serious leak. Should a leak be found, renew the offending gasket or oil seal by referring to the appropriate Chapters in this manual.
2 Also check the security and condition of all the engine-related pipes and hoses, all braking system pipes and hoses, and the fuel lines **(see illustrations)**. Ensure that all cable-

ties or securing clips are in place, and in good condition. Clips which are broken or missing can lead to chafing of the hoses, pipes or wiring, which could cause more serious problems in the future.
3 Carefully check the radiator hoses and heater hoses along their entire length **(see illustrations)**. Renew any hose which is cracked, swollen or deteriorated. Cracks will show up better if the hose is squeezed. Pay close attention to the hose clips that secure the hoses to the cooling system components. Hose clips can pinch and puncture hoses, resulting in cooling system leaks. If spring-type hose clips are used, it may be a good idea to substitute Jubilee clips.
4 Inspect all the cooling system components (hoses, joint faces, etc) for leaks.
5 Where any problems are found on cooling system components, renew the component or gasket with reference to Chapter 3.

11.2a Check the brake pipes . . .

11.2b . . . and hoses for corrosion and leaks . . .

11.2c . . . not forgetting the clutch pipe/ hose, where applicable

11.3a Check the radiator hoses . . .

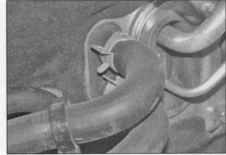

11.3b . . . and heater hoses, here at the bulkhead

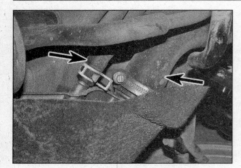

11.6 Check the fuel tank hoses for damage

6 With the car raised, inspect the fuel tank and filler neck for punctures, cracks and other damage. The connection between the filler neck and tank is especially critical **(see illustration)**. Sometimes a rubber filler neck

12.2 Lowering the glovebox

or connecting hose will leak due to loose retaining clamps or deteriorated rubber.

7 Carefully check all rubber hoses and metal fuel lines leading away from the fuel tank. Check for loose connections, deteriorated hoses, crimped lines, and other damage. Pay particular attention to the vent pipes and hoses, which often loop up around the filler neck and can become blocked or crimped. Follow the lines to the front of the car, carefully inspecting them all the way. Renew damaged sections as necessary. Similarly, whilst the car is raised, take the opportunity to inspect all underbody brake fluid pipes and hoses.

8 From within the engine compartment, check the security of all fuel, vacuum and brake hose attachments and pipe unions, and inspect all hoses for kinks, chafing and deterioration.

9 Where applicable, check the condition of the automatic transmission fluid pipes and hoses.

12 Pollen filter renewal

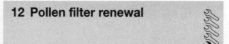

1 All models are equipped with a filter under the facia that cleans the air entering the car through the ventilation system. This filter is fine enough, apparently, to remove airborne pollen, so it doesn't take long for it to get blocked – when it does, the air output will be greatly reduced.

2 Open the glovebox. If the glovebox is full, it may be advisable to empty it now. Press the side panels of the glovebox inwards to release the stops, and swing the glovebox down further from the facia **(see illustration)**.

3 Unclip the pollen filter cover by levering the locktab upwards, then swing the cover up and remove it **(see illustration)**.

4 The pollen filter is actually in two sections, side by side behind the facia. Pull out the first one by gripping the small tab on the top. The other half of the filter's top tab can also be seen – grip it, and slide the filter sideways so that it too can be withdrawn from the filter housing **(see illustrations)**.

5 Remove each filter element from its frame, noting how it fits.

6 Observing the direction-of-fitting markings on the side of each element (the airflow arrows should point downwards), refit them to the frames **(see illustrations)**.

7 As far as possible, wipe the inside of the housing clean.

8 Establish which half of the new filter goes in first, and which way up it should be (the airflow arrows should point downwards, and the grip tabs should be side by side, facing into the car). Insert it into the slot, and slide it over. Check that the second half is also correctly aligned, then slot it home too.

9 Clip the filter cover back in place at the top, and secure with the locktab at the bottom.

10 Swing the glovebox back into place, and close it to complete.

12.3 Unclip the pollen filter cover at the bottom

12.4a Remove the first half of the filter . . .

12.4b . . . then slide the second half to the right . . .

12.4c . . . so that it too can be removed

12.6a Observing the airflow direction arrows . . .

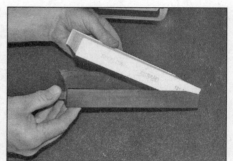

12.6b . . . fit the new filter elements to their frames

13 Automatic transmission fluid level check

1 The level of the automatic transmission fluid should be carefully maintained. Low fluid level can lead to slipping or loss of drive, while overfilling can cause foaming, loss of fluid and transmission damage.
2 The transmission fluid level should only be checked with the car parked on level ground.
3 Start the engine, warm it up to operating temperature (wait until the radiator fan comes on, and cuts out), then switch it off. The fluid level should be checked within one minute of switching off the engine.
4 Remove the dipstick – it's accessed between the fusebox and the inlet air resonator, and has a yellow loop on top (see illustration). Note that the dipstick has to be twisted slightly to remove it – it has a sealing cap built into the stick which must locate so that the arrow on the cap faces forwards.
5 Wipe the fluid from the dipstick with a clean rag, and re-insert it.
6 Pull the dipstick out again and note the fluid level, which should be between the upper and lower marks on the dipstick. If the level is low, add the specified automatic transmission fluid through the dipstick opening, using a funnel.
7 Add just enough of the specified fluid to fill the transmission to the proper level. It takes about 0.8 litre to raise the level from the lower mark to the upper mark, so add the fluid a little at a time and keep checking the level until it is correct.
8 The condition of the fluid should also be checked along with the level. If the fluid at the end of the dipstick is black or a dark reddish brown colour, or if it emits a burned smell, the fluid should be changed (see Section 22). If you are in doubt about the condition of the fluid, purchase some new fluid and compare the two for colour and smell.

14 Manual transmission fluid level check

1 The manual transmission does not have a dipstick. To check the fluid level, raise the car and support it securely on axle stands (see *Jacking and vehicle support*). The filler/level plug is in front of the right-hand driveshaft, on the transmission's extension housing. Remove the plug, noting that a square key will be needed (on our car, a 1/2-inch square socket extension fitted). If the lubricant level is correct, it should be up to the lower edge of the hole (see illustration).
2 If the transmission needs more lubricant (if the level is not up to the hole), add more through the filler/level hole. If there is sufficient access, a funnel can be used, but most transmission fluid bottles have a flexible tube

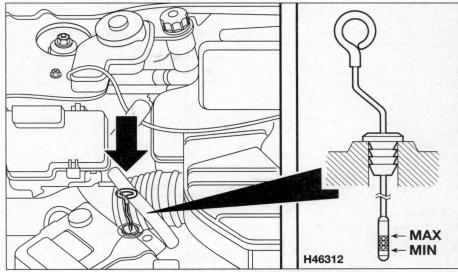

← MAX
← MIN

H46312

13.4 Automatic transmission fluid dipstick details

attached, which is better suited – by squeezing the bottle, fluid can be added from almost any angle. Stop filling the transmission when the lubricant begins to run out the hole.
3 Refit the plug and tighten it securely. Drive the car a short distance, then check for leaks.

15 Hinge and lock lubrication

1 Work around the car and lubricate the hinges of the bonnet, doors and tailgate with a light machine oil (see illustration).
2 Lightly lubricate the bonnet release mechanism and exposed section of inner cable with a smear of grease.
3 Check the security and operation of all hinges, latches and locks, adjusting them where required. Check the operation of the central locking system.
4 Check the condition and operation of the tailgate struts, renewing them both (as described in Chapter 11) if either is leaking or no longer able to support the tailgate securely when raised.

16 Road test

Instruments and electrical equipment

1 Check the operation of all instruments and electrical equipment.
2 Make sure that all instruments read correctly, and switch on all electrical equipment in turn, to check that it functions properly.

Steering and suspension

3 Check for any abnormalities in the steering, suspension, handling or road 'feel'.
4 Drive the car, and check that there are no unusual vibrations or noises.
5 Check that the steering feels positive, with no excessive 'sloppiness', or roughness, and check for any suspension noises when cornering and driving over bumps.

Drivetrain

6 Check the performance of the engine, clutch, transmission and driveshafts.

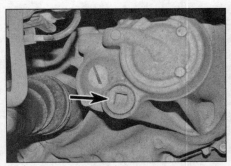

14.1 Manual transmission filler/level plug

15.1 Lightly oil all the hinges, door check straps, etc

7 Listen for any unusual noises from the engine, clutch and transmission.

8 Make sure that the engine runs smoothly when idling, and that there is no hesitation when accelerating.

9 Check that, where applicable, the clutch action is smooth and progressive, that the drive is taken up smoothly, and that the pedal travel is not excessive. Also listen for any noises when the clutch pedal is depressed.

10 Check that all gears can be engaged smoothly without noise, and that the gear

lever action is smooth and not abnormally vague or 'notchy'.

11 On automatic transmission models, make sure that all gearchanges occur smoothly, without snatching, and without an increase in engine speed between changes. Check that all of the gear positions can be selected with the car at rest. If any problems are found, they should be referred to a Honda dealer or specialist.

12 Listen for a metallic clicking sound from the front of the car, as the car is driven slowly in a circle with the steering on full-lock. Carry out this check in both directions. If a

clicking noise is heard, this indicates wear in a driveshaft joint (see Chapter 8).

Braking system

13 Make sure that the car does not pull to one side when braking, and that the wheels do not lock when braking hard.

14 Check that there is no vibration through the steering when braking.

15 Check that the handbrake operates correctly, without excessive movement of the lever, and that it holds the car stationary on a slope.

Every 24 000 miles or 2 years

17 Valve clearance check and adjustment

1 The valve clearances must be checked and adjusted with the engine cold.

2 Remove the cylinder head cover and the timing belt upper cover as described in Chapter 2A.

3 Remove the spark plugs as described in Section 20. The spark plugs are due to be renewed at this interval, so unless the valve clearances are being checked for any other reason, obtain a new set of plugs for refitting.

4 Set No 1 piston to TDC by turning the engine using a socket (19 mm) on the crankshaft pulley bolt. The camshaft sprocket has an UP mark on one of its spokes, and two line markings opposite each other on its inner rim. At No 1 TDC, the UP mark should be uppermost (at the twelve o'clock position), and the two line marks aligned with the cylinder head top surface **(see illustrations)**.

5 With the engine in this position, the four valves for No 1 cylinder can be checked and adjusted.

6 Start with the intake valve clearance. Insert a feeler gauge of the correct thickness (see this Chapter's Specifications) between the

valve stem and the rocker arm. Withdraw it, and you should feel a slight drag. If there's no drag or a heavy drag, loosen the locknut and undo the adjuster screw. Carefully tighten the adjuster screw until you can feel a slight drag on the feeler gauge as you withdraw it **(see illustrations)**.

7 Hold the adjuster screw with a screwdriver (to stop it turning) and tighten the locknut. Recheck the clearance to make sure it hasn't changed. Repeat the check-and-adjust procedure on the other No 1 cylinder intake valve, then on the two exhaust valves. Note that the inlet and exhaust valve clearances are different.

8 Rotate the crankshaft pulley 180° anti-clockwise (the camshaft pulley will turn 90°) until No 3 piston is at TDC. With No 3 at TDC, the UP mark on the camshaft sprocket will be at the nine o'clock position, in line with the front surface of the cylinder head. Check and adjust No 3 cylinder valves.

9 Rotate the crankshaft pulley 180° anti-clockwise until No 4 piston is at TDC. With No 4 piston at TDC, the UP mark on the camshaft sprocket will be pointed straight down, and the line markings should again align with the cylinder head top surface. Check and adjust No 4 cylinder valves.

10 Rotate the crankshaft pulley 180° anti-clockwise to bring No 2 piston to TDC. The UP mark on the camshaft sprocket should be

17.4a The camshaft sprocket UP mark should be uppermost . . .

17.4b . . . and the lines on the inner rim should align with the head

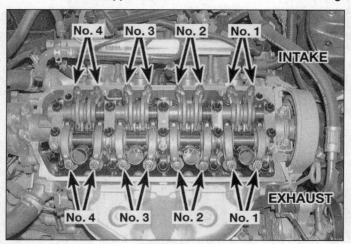

17.6a Valve layout

17.6b Hold the adjuster screw while the locknut is tightened

at the three o'clock position, in line with the rear surface of the cylinder head. Check and adjust No 2 cylinder valves.

11 Though there should be no real need, the engine can be turned again to bring No 1 back to TDC, and the clearances can be rechecked. If the engine is then turned further in sequence, the clearances for the remaining three cylinders can be rechecked.

12 On completion, refit the timing belt upper cover and cylinder head cover as described in Chapter 2A. Spark plug fitting details are in Section 20.

18.1a Remove the centre screw . . .

18.1b . . . then release the clips around the edge . . .

19 Air filter element renewal

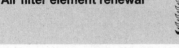

1 Remove the screw in the centre of the air filter cover, then release a total of six spring clips which secure the edges of the cover – use a flat-bladed screwdriver if the clips are stiff **(see illustrations)**.

2 Lift off the cover for access to the filter element **(see illustration)**.

3 Lift the air filter element out of the housing, and wipe out the inside of the air cleaner housing with a clean rag **(see illustration)**.

4 While the air cleaner cover is off and the element is removed, be careful not to drop anything down into the air cleaner assembly.

5 Fit the new element into the air cleaner housing, making sure it seats properly.

6 Install the air cleaner cover, and secure with the six clips, which can be snapped into place by pressing on the curved part of the clip. Tighten the central bolt securely.

19 Auxiliary drivebelt check, adjustment and renewal

Checking

1 Due to their function and material makeup, a drivebelt is prone to failure after a long period of time, and should therefore be inspected regularly.

2 With the engine stopped, inspect the full length of the drivebelt for cracks and separation of the belt plies. It will be necessary to turn the

18.2 . . . and lift off the air cleaner cover

engine (using a spanner or socket and bar on the crankshaft pulley bolt) in order to move the belt from the pulleys so that the belt can be inspected thoroughly. Twist the belt between the pulleys so that both sides can be viewed. Also check for fraying, and glazing which gives the belt a shiny appearance. Check the pulleys for nicks, cracks, distortion and corrosion.

3 The belt tension is checked by pushing the belt at a distance halfway between the pulleys. Push firmly with your thumb and see how much the belt moves (deflects).

4 Renew the belt if it shows any sign of wear or damage.

Adjustment

5 The drivebelt is adjusted by moving the alternator – a worm-drive adjuster is fitted below the unit. Where applicable, the air conditioning compressor is rigidly mounted.

6 Loosen the left-hand front wheel nuts, then

18.3 Removing the air cleaner element

jack up the front of the car, and support it on axle stands (see *Jacking and vehicle support*). Remove the left-hand front wheel.

7 Remove the engine undertray (see Chapter 11, Section 23).

8 Loosen the alternator upper and lower mounting bolts, and the bolt on the adjuster plate **(see illustrations)**.

9 Before adjusting, temporarily retighten the alternator upper mounting bolt to half the specified torque.

10 Turn the adjuster bolt (which has a wing-nut type head) to adjust the belt tension **(see illustration)**. Use the belt deflection figures specified as a guide – to some extent, setting belt tension is a matter of experience and 'feel'. Clearly the belt must not be too loose (though multi-ribbed belts are less likely to slip than the older vee-belt type), but don't over-adjust, as this will lead to expensive wear in the alternator and compressor bearings.

19.8a Loosen the alternator upper mounting bolt . . .

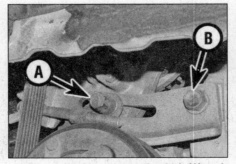

19.8b . . . the lower mounting bolt (A) and adjuster plate bolt (B)

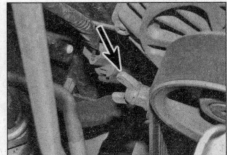

19.10 Turn the wing-nut fitting to adjust the belt tension

19.14 Removing the auxiliary drivebelt

11 When the belt tension is satisfactory, tighten the lower mounting bolt, adjuster plate bolt and the alternator upper mounting bolt to their specified torques. Recheck the belt tension when all the bolts have been

20.3a Release the cover fasteners with a screwdriver . . .

tightened, as tightening then can affect the tension.

12 If a new belt has been fitted, refit the wheel and lower the car to the ground. Run the engine for about 5 minutes, and recheck the belt tension. Honda recommend that, after this 5-minute period, the tension is reset to the deflection specified for a used belt.

13 On completion, refit the engine undertray and the wheel, then lower the car to the ground and tighten the wheel nuts to the specified torque.

Renewal

14 To renew a belt, follow the above procedure for drivebelt adjustment, but slip the belt off the pulleys and remove it **(see illustration)**.

15 Take the old belt with you when purchasing new ones, in order to make a direct comparison for length, width and design.

16 Fit the new belt around the pulleys, making sure the belt ribs sit properly in the pulley grooves – turn the engine by hand to ensure the belt has seated before adjusting it as described previously in this Section.

20 Spark plug renewal

1 The correct functioning of the spark plugs is vital for the correct running and efficiency of the engine. It is essential that the plugs fitted are appropriate for the engine; suitable types are specified at the beginning of this Chapter, or in the car's handbook. If the correct type is used and the engine is in good condition, the spark plugs should not need attention between scheduled renewal intervals. Spark plug cleaning is rarely necessary, and should not be attempted unless specialised equipment is available, as damage can easily be caused to the firing ends.

2 Ensure that the ignition is switched off (take out the key).

3 Remove the plastic cover which sits over the ignition coil connectors on top of the engine, by turning the two quick-release fasteners a quarter-turn anti-clockwise using a flat-bladed screwdriver. Lift the cover off **(see illustrations)**.

4 Wipe around the coils and the top of the engine as necessary – it is essential that dirt does not enter the engine when the spark plugs are removed.

5 Unscrew the nut securing each ignition coil to the top of the engine **(see illustration)**.

6 Lift the first coil slightly to detach it from the spark plug, but note that it is still plugged in at this point **(see illustration)**.

7 Press the locking tab on the first coil's wiring connector, and slide the connector back to disconnect it from the coil **(see illustration)**.

8 Lift the coil out of the engine **(see illustration)**.

9 Using a slim spark plug socket, unscrew and remove the first spark plug **(see illustration)**. The spark plugs on these models are recessed, so a long extension will also be necessary.

10 Examination of the spark plugs will give

20.3b . . . and lift the cover off the ignition coils

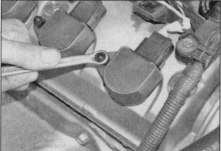

20.5 Unscrew the ignition coil mounting nut

20.6 Lift the coil off the spark plug . . .

20.7 . . . then disconnect the wiring plug at the rear . . .

20.8 . . . and lift it out completely

20.9 Unscrew and remove the spark plugs

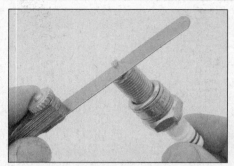

20.15a Measuring the spark plug gap with a feeler blade

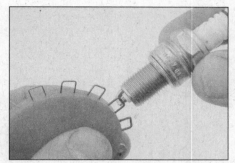

20.15b Measuring the spark plug gap with a wire gauge

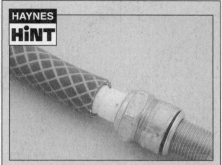

HAYNES HiNT

It's often difficult to insert spark plugs into their holes without cross-threading them. To avoid this possibility, fit a short length of rubber or plastic hose over the end of the spark plug. The flexible hose acts as a universal joint, to help align the plug with the plug hole. Should the plug begin to cross thread, the hose will slip on the spark plug, preventing thread damage to the aluminium cylinder head.

a good indication of the condition of the engine. As each plug is removed, examine it as follows.

11 If the insulator nose of the spark plug is clean and white, with no deposits, this is indicative of a weak mixture or too hot a plug (a hot plug transfers heat away from the electrode slowly, a cold plug transfers heat away quickly).

12 If the tip and insulator nose are covered with hard black-looking deposits, then this is indicative that the mixture is too rich. Should the plug be black and oily, then it is likely that the engine is fairly worn, as well as the mixture being too rich. If the insulator nose is covered with light tan to greyish-brown deposits, then the mixture is correct and it is likely that the engine is in good condition.

13 Where multi-electrode plugs are fitted, the electrode gaps are all preset, and **no** attempt should be made to bend the electrodes – fit the plugs straight out of the packet.

14 If standard single-electrode plugs are fitted, the spark plug electrode gap is of considerable importance. If the gap is too large or too small, the size of the spark and its efficiency will be seriously impaired and it will not perform correctly under all engine speed and load conditions. The gap quoted at the start of this Chapter is suitable for the plugs also specified, but may not be if other makes of plug are used.

15 To set the gap, measure it with a feeler blade or spark plug gap gauge and then carefully bend the outer plug electrode until the correct gap is achieved. The centre electrode should never be bent, as this may crack the insulator and cause plug failure, if nothing worse. If using feeler blades, the gap is correct when the appropriate-size blade is a firm sliding fit **(see illustrations)**.

16 Special spark plug electrode gap adjusting tools are available from most motor accessory shops, or from some spark plug manufacturers.

17 Before fitting the spark plugs, check that the threaded connector sleeves on top are tight, and that the plug exterior surfaces and threads are clean. Though not essential, a little copper grease applied to the plug threads may make the plugs easier to remove next time.

18 Fit the new plug into the spark plug socket, then offer it into the engine with the long extension. A proper spark plug socket has a rubber insert fitted, which is very useful for gripping the plug during this stage of fitting – use an ordinary deep socket, and the plug will fall out.

19 Tighten the plug initially by hand – this way, it is possible to feel whether the plug is going in correctly (there should be little or no effort needed), or whether it is misaligned and is cross-threading **(see Haynes Hint)**. After several turns, the plug will be felt to 'seat' (contact the cylinder head).

20 Using a torque wrench, tighten the plug to the specified torque. Alternatively, tighten the plug no more than about half a turn after it seats. Do not over-tighten the plugs, or the alloy threads in the cylinder head will be damaged.

21 Offer the ignition coil into the engine so that the hole in the coil mounting plate aligns with the stud on the engine, and fit it over the plug. Reconnect the coil wiring plug, ensuring that a good connection is made, then press the coil firmly down over the mounting stud and onto the plug. Fit the coil mounting nut, and tighten it securely.

22 Repeat the procedure for the remaining coils and spark plugs. It is advisable to work on one coil and plug at a time, to avoid mixing up the coils, though they appear to be identical.

23 On completion, refit the plastic cover over the coils, and secure by turning the fasteners a quarter-turn clockwise.

Every 60 000 miles or 5 years

21 Timing belt renewal

Refer to the information given in Chapter 2A. At the same time, check the condition of the timing belt tensioner, and renew this also if necessary – many dealers and parts suppliers now sell timing belt 'kits', which include a new tensioner, and any additional idler pulleys. As the timing belt on petrol engines also drives the water pump, the pump should be inspected for signs of leakage (any powdery deposits, typically white or anti-freeze-coloured, underneath the pump are suspicious). Since the timing belt would have to be removed again in the event of water pump failure (and a water pump which seizes might wear the timing belt), many owners renew the pump as a matter of course, particularly if it is known to have completed a high mileage.

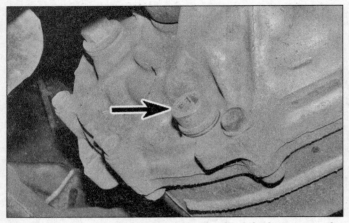

23.4a The manual transmission drain plug is at the bottom, on the right-hand side

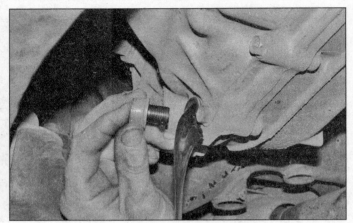

23.4b Unscrew the plug, and allow the fluid to drain

Every 72 000 miles or 6 years

22 Automatic transmission fluid renewal

1 The fluid should be drained when hot, preferably immediately after the car has been driven.

 Warning: Fluid temperature can exceed 120°C in a hot transmission. Wear protective gloves.

2 Raise the front of the car and place it on axle stands for access to the transmission drain plug (see *Jacking and vehicle support*).
3 Move the tools and drain pan under the car, being careful not to touch any of the hot exhaust components.
4 Place the drain pan under the transmission and remove the drain plug – it's located on the right-hand side of the transmission, near the bottom, and an Allen key or socket will be needed to undo it. Be sure the drain pan is in position, as fluid will come out with some force.
5 Once the fluid is drained, clean the drain plug and reinstall it securely, using a new sealing washer. Lower the car to the ground.

6 Pull out the dipstick, then add new fluid to the transmission through the dipstick tube. Use a funnel to prevent spills. It is best to add a little fluid at a time, continually checking the level with the dipstick (see Section 13). The engine should be left switched off at this stage.
7 When the fluid level reaches the upper mark on the dipstick, start the engine and slowly shift the selector into all positions, then shift into P and apply the handbrake. Let the engine warm up to operating temperature (wait until the radiator fan has come on, and gone off).
8 Turn off the engine and check the fluid level as described in Section 13.

23 Manual transmission fluid renewal

1 The fluid should be drained when hot, preferably immediately after the car has been driven. Park the car on level ground to begin with.
2 Raise the front of the car and place it on

axle stands for access to the transmission drain plug (see *Jacking and vehicle support*).
3 Move the tools and drain pan under the car, being careful not to touch any of the hot exhaust components.
4 Place the drain pan under the transmission and remove the drain plug – it's located on the right-hand side of the transmission, near the bottom, and a square key will be needed (on our car, a 3/8-inch socket extension fitted) **(see illustrations)**. Be sure the drain pan is in position, as fluid will come out with some force.
5 Once the fluid is drained, clean and refit the drain plug, using a new sealing washer and tightening it to the specified torque. Lower the car to the ground, and make sure that it is level.
6 Remove the filler/level plug, which is located higher up the transmission casing, behind the right-hand driveshaft. Again, a square plug is fitted – this time (on our car at least) a 1/2-inch socket extension can be used. Add new fluid until it begins to run out of the filler hole (see Section 14). On completion, refit the filler/level plug – use a new sealing washer and tighten it to the specified torque.

Every 3 years (regardless of mileage)

24 Brake fluid renewal

 Warning: Brake hydraulic fluid can harm your eyes and damage painted surfaces, so use extreme caution when handling and pouring it. Do not use fluid that has been standing open for some time, as it absorbs moisture from the air. Excess moisture can cause a dangerous loss of braking effectiveness.

1 The procedure is similar to that for the

bleeding of the hydraulic system as described in Chapter 9.
2 Working as described in Chapter 9, open the first bleed screw in the sequence, and pump the brake pedal gently until nearly all the old fluid has been emptied from the master cylinder reservoir. Top-up to the MAX level with new fluid, and continue pumping until only the new fluid remains in the reservoir, and new fluid can be seen emerging from the bleed screw. Tighten the screw, and top the reservoir level up to the MAX level line.
3 Work through all the remaining bleed screws in the sequence until new fluid can be seen at all of them. Be careful to keep the master

cylinder reservoir topped-up to above the MIN level at all times, or air may enter the system and greatly increase the length of the task.

 Old hydraulic fluid is invariably much darker in colour than the new, making it easy to distinguish the two.

4 When the operation is complete, check that all bleed screws are securely tightened, and that their dust caps are refitted. Wash off all traces of spilt fluid, and recheck the master cylinder reservoir fluid level.
5 Check the operation of the brakes before taking the car on the road.

Every 5 years (regardless of mileage)

25 Coolant renewall

Note: *Some models may have been filled with Honda coolant which is claimed to have a 10-year life (typically, this type of coolant is orange or red in colour). If this is known to be the case, and only this coolant is used in the system, the 10-year renewal interval can be observed. The DIY owner may prefer to use the suggested shorter interval, especially if the coolant in the system is of unknown type.*

⚠️ **Warning: Refer to Chapter 3 and observe the warnings given. In particular, never remove the radiator cap or expansion tank filler cap when the engine is running, or has just been switched off, as the cooling system will be pressurised and hot, and the consequent escaping steam and scalding coolant could cause serious injury. If the engine is hot, the electric cooling fan may start rotating even if the engine is not running, so be careful to keep hands, hair and loose clothing well clear when working in the engine compartment.**

⚠️ **Warning: Wait until the engine is cold before starting this procedure.**

Cooling system draining

1 Switch on the ignition, then turn the heater temperature control to the maximum heat position. Turn off the ignition.
2 To drain the system, first remove the radiator cap. Place a thick cloth over the radiator cap, then turn the cap anti-clockwise as far as the first stop and wait for any pressure to be released, then depress it and turn it further anti-clockwise to remove it. Similarly, remove the expansion tank cap **(see illustrations)**.
3 If additional working clearance is required, apply the handbrake, then jack up the front of the car and support it on axle stands (see *Jacking and vehicle support*).
4 Remove the engine undertray (see Chapter 11, Section 23), then place a large drain tray underneath, and loosen the radiator

drain tap. Allow the coolant to drain into the tray **(see illustrations)**. On completion, retighten the drain tap securely.
5 Move the drain tray to the rear of the engine, underneath the oil filter. Below and to the right of the oil filter is the engine block coolant drain bolt – unscrew the bolt and allow the rest of the system contents to drain into the tray **(see illustration)**.
6 When the block has been drained of coolant, refit the drain bolt using a new washer, and with a little liquid gasket applied to its threads. Tighten the block drain bolt to the specified torque, then refit the undertray. Where necessary, lower the car to the ground.
7 Honda also stipulate that the contents of the expansion tank should be drained when renewing the coolant. Realistically, unless suitable syphoning equipment is available (and remember, antifreeze is poisonous), this will mean removing the tank to pour out the contents. To remove the tank, refer to Chapter 3.

Cooling system flushing

8 If coolant renewal has been neglected, or if the antifreeze mixture has become diluted, then in time the cooling system may gradually lose efficiency, as the coolant passages become restricted due to rust, scale deposits, and other sediment. The cooling system efficiency can be restored by flushing the system clean.
9 The radiator should be flushed independently

of the engine, to avoid unnecessary contamination.

Radiator flushing

10 Disconnect the top and bottom hoses and any other relevant hoses from the radiator, with reference to Chapter 3.
11 Insert a garden hose into the radiator top inlet. Direct a flow of clean water through the radiator, and continue flushing until clean water emerges from the radiator bottom outlet.
12 If after a reasonable period, the water still does not run clear, the radiator can be flushed with a good proprietary cleaning agent. It is important that the manufacturer's instructions are followed carefully. If the contamination is particularly bad, remove the radiator, insert the hose in the radiator bottom outlet, and reverse-flush the radiator.

Engine flushing

13 Remove the thermostat as described in Chapter 3 then, if the radiator top hose has been disconnected from the engine, temporarily reconnect the hose.
14 With the top and bottom hoses disconnected from the radiator, insert a garden hose into the radiator top hose. Direct a clean flow of water through the engine, and continue flushing until clean water emerges from the radiator bottom hose.
15 On completion of flushing, refit the thermostat and reconnect the hoses with reference to Chapter 3.

25.2a Remove the radiator cap . . .

25.2b . . . and the expansion tank cap

25.4a Loosen the radiator drain tap . . .

25.4b . . . and let the coolant drain into a suitable container

25.5 The engine block coolant drain bolt is at the rear, next to the oil filter

25.24 Filling the expansion tank

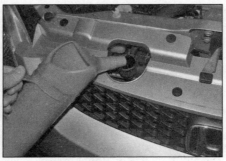

25.25 Fill the radiator slowly, to prevent airlocks

Antifreeze mixture

It is rare to ever drain the cooling system completely – a small quantity will remain. If the system has been extensively flushed with clean water, this remaining quantity will in fact be plain water. For this reason, some people will first fill the system with the required quantity of neat antifreeze (half the total system capacity, for a 50% mixture), and then complete the filling process with plain water. This ensures that the resulting coolant (once it has mixed inside the engine) is not 'diluted' by old coolant or water remaining in the system.

16 Honda state that, if the only antifreeze used is the type with which the system was first filled at the factory (see *Lubricants and fluids*) it will last 10 years. This is subject to it being used in the recommended concentration, unmixed with any other type of antifreeze or additive, and topped-up when necessary using only that antifreeze. No other type of antifreeze should be mixed with it – if this happens; to restore the 10-year life, the system must be drained and thoroughly reverse-flushed before fresh coolant is poured in.

17 If the car's history (and therefore the quality of the antifreeze in it) is unknown, owners who wish to follow Honda's recommendations are advised to drain and thoroughly reverse-flush the system, before refilling with fresh coolant.

18 If any antifreeze other than Honda's is to be used, the coolant must be renewed at regular intervals to provide an equivalent degree of protection; the conventional recommendation is to renew the coolant every three years.

19 Honda's own antifreeze is usually supplied pre-mixed, and is therefore ready to use. If you are using any other type of antifreeze, to give the recommended mixture ratio, 50% (by volume) of neat antifreeze must be mixed with 50% of clean, soft water; however, always note the antifreeze manufacturer's instructions (also see the Haynes Hint).

20 Before adding antifreeze, the cooling system should be completely drained, preferably flushed, and all hoses checked for condition and security. Fresh antifreeze will rapidly find any weaknesses in the system.

21 After filling with antifreeze, a label should be attached to the expansion tank, stating the type and concentration of antifreeze used, and the date installed. Any subsequent topping-up should be made with the same type and concentration of antifreeze.

Cooling system filling

22 Before attempting to fill the cooling system, make sure that all hoses and clips are in good condition, and that the clips are tight. If removed, refit the expansion tank (and battery).

23 Check that the heater temperature control has not been moved from the maximum heat position. If there is a chance it has been disturbed, temporarily switch on the ignition and set the control to maximum heat, then switch the ignition off once more.

24 Fill the expansion tank until the level reaches the MAX mark, then refit the expansion tank cap **(see illustration)**.

25 Slowly fill the system through the radiator filler cap until the coolant level reaches the top of the radiator filler neck **(see illustration)**. Wait a few minutes for the level in the radiator to stabilise, then **loosely** refit the radiator cap. The cap is fitted loosely at this stage to prevent a build-up of pressure in the system, and to allow the release of any trapped air.

26 Start the engine and let it run at idle until the engine reaches normal operating temperature, as indicated by the temperature gauge, or by the radiator cooling fan cutting in and out at least twice.

27 Switch off the engine, then check the level in the radiator and expansion tank, and top-up if necessary.

28 Refit the radiator cap tightly, then run the engine again briefly, and check for leaks.

29 Switch off the engine, and allow it to cool for at least an hour, and preferably, leave overnight.

30 With the engine completely cold, check and top-up the coolant level in the radiator and expansion tank as necessary.

Airlocks

31 If, after draining and refilling the system, symptoms of overheating are found which did not occur previously, then the fault is almost certainly due to trapped air at some point in the system, causing an airlock and restricting the flow of coolant; usually, the air is trapped because the system was refilled too quickly.

32 If an airlock is suspected, first try gently squeezing all visible coolant hoses. A coolant hose which is full of air feels quite different to one full of coolant when squeezed. After refilling the system, most airlocks will clear once the system has cooled, and been topped-up.

33 While the engine is running at operating temperature, switch on the heater and heater fan, and check for heat output. Provided there is sufficient coolant in the system, any lack of heat output could be due to an airlock in the system.

34 Airlocks can have more serious effects than simply reducing heater output – a severe airlock could reduce coolant flow around the engine. Check that the radiator top hose is hot when the engine is at operating temperature – a top hose which stays cold could be the result of an airlock (or a non-opening thermostat).

35 If the problem persists, stop the engine and allow it to cool down **completely**, before unscrewing the radiator and expansion tank caps or loosening the hose clips and squeezing the hoses to bleed out the trapped air. In the worst case, the system will have to be at least partially drained (this time, the coolant can be saved for re-use) and flushed to clear the problem.

Radiator cap check

36 Clean the radiator cap, and inspect the seal inside the cap for damage or deterioration. If there is any sign of damage or deterioration to the seal, fit a new pressure cap. If the cap is old, it is worth considering fitting a new one for peace of mind – they are not expensive. If the pressure cap fails, excess pressure will be allowed into the system, which may result in the failure of hoses, the radiator, or the heater matrix.

Chapter 1 Part B:
Routine maintenance and servicing – diesel engine models

Contents

Degrees of difficulty

Easy, suitable for novice with little experience	**Fairly easy,** suitable for beginner with some experience	**Fairly difficult,** suitable for competent DIY mechanic	**Difficult,** suitable for experienced DIY mechanic	**Very difficult,** suitable for expert DIY or professional

Lubricants and fluids
Refer to *Weekly checks* on page 0•17

Capacities*
Engine oil (including oil filter) .... 5.0 litres
Cooling system:
    Change.. 4.0 litres
    Total .... 5.3 litres
Manual transmission .... 2.0 litres
Washer fluid reservoir:
    Without headlight washers................................ 2.5 litres
    With headlight washers .... 5.0 litres
Fuel tank.. 50 litres
All capacities are approximate.

Idle speed (not adjustable)......................... 850 ± 50 rpm

Brakes
Friction material minimum thickness:
    Front brake pads .... 1.6 mm
    Rear brake pads.. 1.6 mm
Disc minimum thickness:
    Front disc .... 19.0 mm
    Rear disc .... 8.0 mm
Handbrake adjustment.................................... 6 to 10 clicks

Torque wrench settings

	Nm	lbf ft
Oil filter housing cover	25	18
Roadwheel nuts	108	80
Sump drain plug..	78	58

The maintenance intervals in this manual are provided with the assumption that you, not the dealer, will be carrying out the work. These are the minimum maintenance intervals recommended by us for cars driven daily. If you wish to keep your car in peak condition at all times, you may wish to perform some of these procedures more often. We encourage frequent maintenance, because it enhances the efficiency, performance and resale value of your car.

If the car is driven in dusty areas, used to tow a trailer, or driven frequently at slow speeds (idling in traffic) or on short journeys, more frequent maintenance intervals are recommended.

When the car is new, it should be serviced by a dealer service department (or other workshop recognised by the car manufacturer as providing the same standard of service) in order to preserve the warranty. The car manufacturer may reject warranty claims if you are unable to prove that servicing has been carried out as and when specified, using only original-equipment parts, or parts certified to be of equivalent quality.

Every 6000 miles or 6 months, whichever comes first

☐ Renew the engine oil and filter (Section 3)

Note: *Frequent oil and filter changes are good for the engine, so we recommend halving Honda's current interval, which is 12 000 miles or 12 months.*

Every 12 000 miles or 12 months, whichever comes first

☐ Check the braking system (Section 4)
☐ Check the steering and suspension components for condition and security (Section 5)
☐ Check the condition of the driveshaft gaiters (Section 6)
☐ Engine management and exhaust emission test (Section 7)
☐ Check the engine idle speed (Section 8)
☐ Check the operation of all electrical systems (Section 9)
☐ Drain any water from the fuel filter (Section 10)
☐ Check the exhaust system (Section 11)
☐ Check all components, pipes and hoses for fluid leaks (Section 12)
☐ Renew the pollen filter (Section 13)
☐ Check the manual transmission oil level (Section 14)
☐ Lubricate all door locks and hinges, door stops, bonnet lock and release, and tailgate lock and hinges (Section 15)
☐ Carry out a road test (Section 16)

Every 24 000 miles or 2 years, whichever comes first

☐ Renew the air filter element (Section 17)
☐ Check the auxiliary drivebelt, and renew if necessary (Section 18)
☐ Renew the fuel filter (Section 19)

Every 60 000 miles or 5 years, whichever comes first

☐ Renew the timing belt, and check the belt tensioner (Section 20)

Note: *Honda recommend that the interval for timing belt renewal is 60 000 miles or 5 years. However, if the car is used mainly for short journeys or a lot of stop-start driving, it is recommended that the renewal interval is shortened. The actual belt renewal interval is very much up to the individual owner but, bearing in mind that severe engine damage will result if the belt breaks in use, we recommend you err on the side of caution.*

Every 72 000 miles or 6 years, whichever comes first

☐ Check and if necessary adjust the valve clearances (Section 21)
☐ Renew the manual transmission fluid (Section 22)

Note: *On a car used mainly for short journeys, or for a lot of towing, this interval should be halved to 36 000 miles or 3 years. As with engine oil changes, changing the oil or fluid will help to prolong the transmission's life.*

Every 3 years, regardless of mileage

☐ Renew the brake fluid (Section 23)

Every 5 years, regardless of mileage

☐ Renew the coolant (Section 24)

Note: *Some models may have been filled with Honda coolant which is claimed to have a 10-year life (typically, this type of coolant is orange or red in colour). If this is known to be the case, and only this coolant is used in the system, the 10-year renewal interval can be observed. The DIY owner may prefer to use the suggested shorter interval, especially if the coolant in the system is of unknown type.*

Underbonnet view

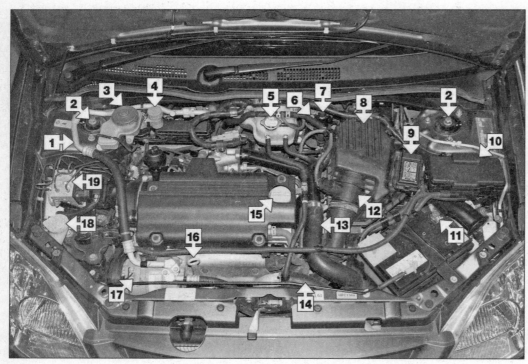

1 Air conditioning refrigerant pipe
2 Front suspension strut upper mounting
3 Brake fluid reservoir
4 Clutch fluid reservoir
5 Coolant expansion tank cap
6 Fuel filter
7 Hand-priming bulb
8 Air cleaner
9 Auxiliary fusebox
10 Engine compartment fusebox
11 Battery negative lead
12 Airflow sensor
13 Intercooler outlet hose
14 Intercooler inlet hose
15 Engine oil filler cap
16 Engine oil dipstick
17 Air conditioning compressor
18 Washer fluid filler neck
19 ABS unit

Front underbody view

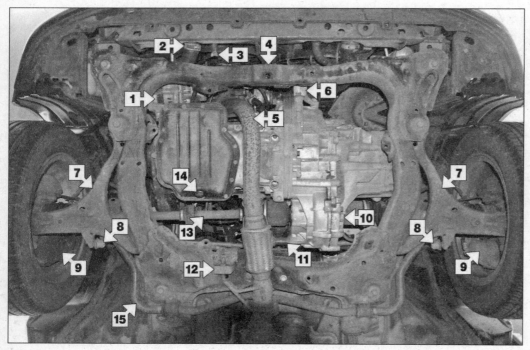

1 Alternator
2 Radiator bottom hose
3 Radiator drain tap
4 Subframe front support point
5 Exhaust front pipe
6 Engine front mounting
7 Front suspension lower arm
8 Anti-roll bar drop link
9 Front brake caliper
10 Transmission drain plug
11 Engine rear mounting
12 Exhaust mounting
13 Driveshaft
14 Engine oil drain plug
15 Anti-roll bar

Rear underbody view (petrol model shown)

1 Centre rear support point
2 Exhaust rear mounting
3 Exhaust rear silencer
4 Rear anti-roll bar
5 Fuel tank
6 Rear suspension strut
7 Rear suspension lower arm
8 Handbrake cable
9 Exhaust centre silencer

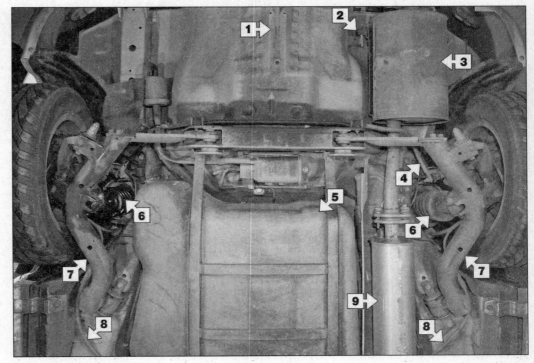

Maintenance procedures

1 General information

1 This Chapter is designed to help the home mechanic maintain his/her car for safety, economy, long life and peak performance.
2 The Chapter contains a master maintenance schedule, followed by Sections dealing specifically with each task in the schedule. Visual checks, adjustments, component renewal and other helpful items are included. Refer to the accompanying illustrations of the engine compartment and the underside of the car for the locations of the various components.
3 Servicing your car in accordance with the mileage/time maintenance schedule and the following Sections will provide a planned maintenance programme, which should result in a long and reliable service life. This is a comprehensive plan, so maintaining some items but not others at the specified service intervals, will not produce the same results.
4 As you service your car, you will discover that many of the procedures can – and should – be grouped together, because of the particular procedure being performed, or because of the proximity of two otherwise-unrelated components to one another. For example, if the car is raised for any reason, the exhaust can be inspected at the same time as the suspension and steering components.
5 The first step in this maintenance

programme is to prepare yourself before the actual work begins. Read through all the Sections relevant to the work to be carried out, then make a list and gather all the parts and tools required. If a problem is encountered, seek advice from a parts specialist, or a dealer service department.

2 Regular maintenance

1 If, from the time the car is new, the routine maintenance schedule is followed closely, and frequent checks are made of fluid levels and high-wear items, as suggested throughout this manual, the engine will be kept in relatively good running condition, and the need for additional work will be minimised.
2 It is possible that there will be times when the engine is running poorly due to the lack of regular maintenance. This is even more likely if a used car, which has not received regular and frequent maintenance checks, is purchased. In such cases, additional work may need to be carried out, outside of the regular maintenance intervals.
3 If engine wear is suspected, a compression test (refer to Chapter 2B) will provide valuable information regarding the overall performance of the main internal components. Such a test can be used as a basis to decide on the extent of the work to be carried out. If, for example,

a compression test indicates serious internal engine wear, conventional maintenance as described in this Chapter will not greatly improve the performance of the engine, and may prove a waste of time and money, unless extensive overhaul work is carried out first.
4 The following series of operations are those most often required to improve the performance of a generally poor-running engine:

Primary operations

a) Clean, inspect and test the battery (refer to Weekly checks).
b) Check all the engine-related fluids (refer to Weekly checks).
c) Check the condition and tension of the auxiliary drivebelt (Section 18).
d) Check the condition of the air filter, and renew if necessary (Section 17).
e) Renew the fuel filter (Section 19).
f) Check the condition of all hoses, and check for fluid leaks (Section 12).

5 If the above operations do not prove fully effective, carry out the following secondary operations:

Secondary operations

All items listed under Primary operations, plus the following:
a) Check the charging system (refer to Chapter 5A).
b) Check the preheating system (refer to Chapter 5A).
c) Check the fuel system (refer to Chapter 4B).

3.4 Remove the oil filler cap at the start

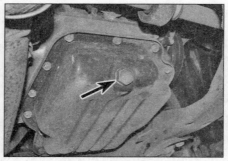

3.5a The drain plug is at the rear of the sump

3.5b Unscrew and remove the drain plug – try not to drop it

Every 6000 miles or 6 months

3 Engine oil and filter renewal

1 Frequent oil and filter changes are the most important preventative maintenance procedures which can be undertaken by the DIY owner. As engine oil ages, it becomes diluted and contaminated, which leads to premature engine wear.

2 Before starting this procedure, gather together all the necessary tools and materials. Also make sure that you have plenty of clean rags and newspapers handy, to mop-up any spills. Ideally, the engine oil should be warm, as it will drain more easily, and more built-up sludge will be removed with it. Take care not to touch the exhaust or any other hot parts of the engine when working under the car. To avoid any possibility of scalding, and to protect yourself from possible skin irritants and other harmful contaminants in used engine oils, it is advisable to wear gloves when carrying out this work.

3 Firmly apply the handbrake then jack up the front of the car and support it on axle stands (see *Jacking and vehicle support*). Unbolt and remove the engine undertray, referring if necessary to Chapter 11, Section 23.

4 Remove the oil filler cap **(see illustration)**.

5 Using a spanner, or preferably a suitable socket and bar, slacken the drain plug about half a turn. Position the draining container under the drain plug, then remove the plug completely **(see illustrations)**.

6 Allow some time for the oil to drain, noting that it may be necessary to reposition the container as the oil flow slows to a trickle.

7 After all the oil has drained from the sump, wipe the drain plug and the sealing washer with a clean rag. Examine the condition of the sealing washer, and renew it if it shows signs of scoring or other damage which may prevent an oil-tight seal. Clean the area around the drain plug opening, and refit the plug complete with the washer and tighten it to the specified torque.

8 Refit the engine undertray. Remove the old oil and all tools from under the car, then lower the car to the ground.

9 The oil filter housing is located on the rear of the cylinder block, and is accessed from above. To improve access, unclip the wiring harness from the bracket above the filter, then unbolt the bracket itself **(see illustrations)**.

10 Using a large socket, unscrew the top of the oil filter housing, and remove it with the old filter element **(see illustrations)**.

11 Slide off the old element, and dispose of it. Remove the two O-rings from the filter housing, and fit new ones – these should be provided with the new filter element **(see illustrations)**.

12 Slide on the new element, and make sure it is fully seated **(see illustration)**.

13 Offer the filter assembly into position, and screw it on. Tighten the housing cover to the specified torque.

3.9a Access to the oil filter housing is hampered by wiring harnesses . . .

3.9b . . . so unclip the harnesses from the bracket . . .

3.9c . . . then remove the two bolts . . .

3.9d . . . and take off the wiring harness bracket

3.10a Unscrew the oil filter housing . . .

3.10b . . . and remove it with the filter element

3.11a Slide off the old element

3.11b Take off the larger upper O-ring . . .

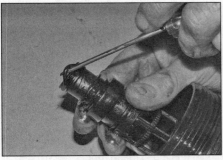

3.11c . . . and the smaller lower one, and fit new ones

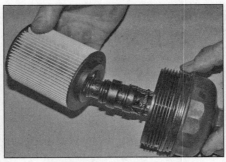

3.12 Fit the new element

3.15 Refill the engine slowly

14 Refit the wiring harness bracket, and clip the harnesses back into position.
15 Fill the engine through the filler hole, using the correct grade and type of oil (refer to *Weekly checks* for details of topping-up). Pour in half the specified quantity of oil first, then wait a few minutes for the oil to drain into the sump. Continue to add oil, a small quantity at a time, until the level is up to the lower mark on the dipstick **(see illustration)**. Adding approximately a further 1.0 litre will bring the level up to the upper mark on the dipstick.
16 Start the engine and run it for a few minutes, while checking for leaks around the oil filter housing and the sump drain plug. Note that there may be a delay of a few seconds before the low oil pressure warning light goes out when the engine is first started, as the oil circulates through the new oil filter and the engine oil galleries before the pressure builds-up.

17 Stop the engine, and wait a few minutes for the oil to settle in the sump once more. With the new oil circulated and the filter now completely full, recheck the level on the dipstick, and add more oil as necessary.
18 Dispose of the used engine oil safely with reference to *General repair procedures*. It should be noted that used oil filters should not be included with domestic waste. Most local authority used oil 'banks' also have used filter disposal points alongside.

Every 12 000 miles or 12 months

4   Braking system check

⚠ *Warning: The dust created by the brake system is harmful to your health. Never blow it out with compressed air and don't inhale any of it. An approved filtering mask should be worn when working on the brakes. Do not, under any circumstances, use petroleum-based solvents to clean brake parts. Use brake system cleaner only. Try to use non-asbestos parts whenever possible.*

1 In addition to the specified intervals, the brakes should be inspected every time the wheels are removed or whenever a defect is suspected.
2 Any of the following symptoms could indicate a potential brake system defect:

a) The car pulls to one side when the brake pedal is depressed.
b) The brakes make squealing or dragging noises when applied.
c) Brake pedal travel is excessive.
d) The brake pedal pulsates when applied (if this happens during emergency braking only, this could be due to ABS operation, which can be felt through the pedal, and is not a cause for concern).
e) Brake fluid leaks, usually onto the inside of the tyre or wheel.

3 Loosen the wheel nuts.
4 Raise the car and place it securely on axle stands (see *Jacking and vehicle support*).
5 Remove the wheels.

Disc brakes

6 There are two pads (an outer and an inner) in each caliper. The pads are visible through inspection holes in each caliper **(see illustration)**.

7 If the lining material is less than the thickness listed in this Chapter's Specifications, renew the pads. **Note:** *Keep in mind that the lining material is bonded to a metal backing plate and the metal plate is not included in this measurement.*

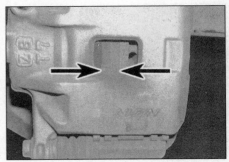

4.6 Place a ruler across the inspection hole to check the pad thickness

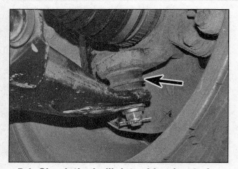

5.4 Check the balljoint rubber boots for damage

8 If it is difficult to determine the exact thickness of the remaining pad material by the above method, or if you are at all concerned about the condition of the pads, remove the caliper(s), then remove the pads from the calipers for further inspection (refer to Chapter 9).

9 Once the pads are removed from the calipers, clean them with brake cleaner and re-measure them with a ruler or a vernier caliper.

10 Measure the disc thickness with a micrometer to make sure that it still has service life remaining. If any disc is thinner than the specified minimum thickness, renew it (refer to Chapter 9). Even if the disc has service life remaining, check its condition. Look for scoring, gouging and burned spots. If these conditions exist, remove the disc and have it resurfaced (see Chapter 9).

11 Before installing the wheels, check all brake pipes and hoses for damage, wear, deformation, cracks, corrosion, leakage, bends and twists, particularly in the vicinity of the rubber hoses at the calipers. Check the clamps for tightness and the connections for leakage. Make sure that all hoses and pipes are clear of sharp edges, moving parts and the exhaust system. If any of the above conditions are noted, repair, reroute or renew the pipes and/or fittings as necessary (see Chapter 9).

Drum brakes

12 The only satisfactory way to check the rear drum brake linings is to remove the drums

5.6 Check for wheel bearing wear by rocking the wheel

as described in Chapter 9. This will also allow an inspection to be made of the rear wheel cylinder, which should be checked for signs of fluid leakage.

Brake servo check

13 Sit in the driver's seat and perform the following sequence of tests.

14 With the brake fully depressed, start the engine – the pedal should move down a little when the engine starts.

15 With the engine running, depress the brake pedal several times – the travel distance should not change.

16 Depress the brake, stop the engine and hold the pedal in for about 30 seconds – the pedal should neither sink nor rise.

17 Restart the engine, run it for about a minute and turn it off. Then firmly depress the brake several times – the pedal travel should decrease with each application.

18 If the brakes do not operate as described, the brake servo, its vacuum hoses, or the vacuum pump, may have failed. Refer to Chapter 9.

Handbrake

19 Slowly pull up on the handbrake and count the number of clicks you hear until the handle is up as far as it will go. The adjustment is correct if you hear approximately 8 clicks. If you hear more clicks, the handbrake needs adjusting (see Chapter 9); fewer clicks, and the cables may have seized, or the brakes are dragging (not releasing).

5 Suspension and steering check

Wheel nut tightness check

1 Work around each wheel in turn, and check the tightness of the wheel nuts using a torque wrench.

2 If you suspect that the nuts have been over-tightened (as sometimes happens in certain garages), loosen and then tighten each nut (one at a time) to the specified torque.

Front suspension and steering

3 Raise the front of the car, and securely support it on axle stands (see *Jacking and vehicle support*).

4 Visually inspect the balljoint dust covers and the steering rack-and-pinion gaiters for splits, chafing or deterioration **(see illustration)**. Any wear of these components will cause loss of lubricant, together with dirt and water entry, resulting in rapid deterioration of the balljoints or steering gear.

5 Check the suspension strut for signs of fluid leakage from the shock absorber – if evident, this indicates that the shock absorber has failed (the car would fail an MoT in this condition). **Note:** *Shock absorbers should always be renewed in pairs on the same axle.*

6 Grasp the roadwheel at the 12 o'clock and 6 o'clock positions, and try to rock it **(see illustration)**. Very slight free play may be felt, but if the movement is appreciable, further investigation is necessary to determine the source. Continue rocking the wheel while an assistant depresses the footbrake. If the movement is now eliminated or significantly reduced, it is likely that the hub bearings are at fault. If the free play is still evident with the footbrake depressed, then there is wear in the suspension joints or mountings.

7 Now grasp the wheel at the 9 o'clock and 3 o'clock positions, and try to rock it as before. Any movement felt now may again be caused by wear in the hub bearings or the steering track rod balljoints. If the outer balljoint is worn, the visual movement will be obvious. If the inner joint is suspect, it can be felt by placing a hand over the rack-and-pinion rubber gaiter and gripping the track rod. If the wheel is now rocked, movement will be felt at the inner joint if wear has taken place.

8 Using a large screwdriver or flat bar, check for wear in the suspension mounting bushes by levering between the relevant suspension component and its attachment point. Some movement is to be expected, as the mountings are made of rubber, but excessive wear should be obvious. Also check the condition of any visible rubber bushes, looking for splits, cracks or contamination of the rubber.

9 With the car standing on its wheels, have an assistant turn the steering wheel back-and-forth, about an eighth of a turn each way. There should be very little, if any, lost movement between the steering wheel and roadwheels. If this is not the case, closely observe the joints and mountings previously described. In addition, check the steering column universal joints for wear, and also check the rack-and-pinion steering gear itself.

10 The Civic has an electric power steering system, so there are no fluid hoses to check. However, the system has an EPS warning light on the instrument panel, which should come on with the ignition, then go out as the engine starts. If this warning light operates correctly (and the other checks described previously are carried out) it can be assumed that the steering system is fault-free.

11 The efficiency of the shock absorbers may be checked by bouncing the car at each corner. Generally speaking, the body will return to its normal position and stop after being depressed. If it rises and returns on a rebound, the shock absorber is probably suspect.

Rear suspension

12 Chock the front wheels, then jack up the rear of the car and support securely on axle stands (see *Jacking and vehicle support*).

13 Working as described previously for the front suspension, check the rear hub bearings, the suspension bushes and the struts/shock absorbers for wear.

6 Driveshaft (CV) gaiter check

1 With the car raised and securely supported on stands, turn the steering onto full lock then slowly rotate the roadwheel. Inspect the condition of the outer constant velocity (CV) joint rubber gaiters while squeezing the gaiters to open out the folds **(see illustration)**.
2 Check for signs of cracking, splits or deterioration of the rubber, which may allow the grease to escape and lead to water and grit entry into the joint.
3 Check the security and condition of the retaining clips.
4 Repeat these checks on the inner CV joints **(see illustration)**.
5 If any damage or deterioration is found, the gaiters should be renewed as described in Chapter 8.

6.1 Check the driveshaft outer CV boots for splits

6.4 Though less susceptible to damage, the inner joint boots should also be checked

7 Engine management and exhaust emission check

1 This check involves checking the engine management system operation by plugging an electronic tester into the system diagnostic socket to check the electronic control unit (ECU) memory for faults (see Chapter 4B).
2 In addition, the exhaust emissions should be checked using suitable equipment. In the UK, a smoke test is performed at the annual MoT test for cars over 3 years old.
3 In reality, if the car is running correctly and the engine management warning light in the instrument panel is functioning normally (coming on with the ignition lights, then going out), then this check need not be carried out. However, if any unusual running problems have been noted, it may be worth having a Honda dealer (or other competent garage with the necessary diagnostic equipment) carry out the check – it may be that a fault has occurred, and the car is running in its 'limp-home' back-up mode.

8 Idle speed check

1 Engine idle speed is the speed at which the engine runs when no throttle is applied, when the car is completely stopped. Note that it is normal for the idle speed to be held up for a second or two, before dropping to base idle – most cars will also run above idle while rolling to a stop, or when coasting downhill. The speed is critical to the performance of the engine itself, as well as many sub-systems.
2 The idle speed is under the control of the engine management module (ECM) and is not adjustable manually. If the idle speed is significantly different from that specified (which is also for an engine at full operating temperature), in the first instance, check the accelerator cable.
3 Poor idle quality could be due to poor maintenance – change the engine oil, and carry out the primary operations listed in Section 2.
4 An engine prone to stalling could be suffering a problem with one of the engine-driven ancillaries, such as the alternator, or the problem could be low fuel pressure. Also check the brake pedal position switch and vehicle speed sensor (see Chapter 4B, Section 10).
5 Ultimately, a persistent idle speed problem will have to be referred to a Honda dealer for diagnosis.

9 Electrical systems check

1 Check the operation of all electrical equipment, ie, lights, direction indicators, horn, wash/wipe system, etc. Refer to the appropriate Sections of Chapter 12 for details if any of the circuits are found to be inoperative.
2 Visually check all accessible wiring connectors, harnesses and retaining clips for security, and for signs of chafing or damage. Rectify any faults found.

10.2 Access under the filter is limited, so we used a cap as a drain container

10 Fuel filter water draining

1 The fuel filter is located at the rear of the engine compartment, next to the coolant expansion tank. To gain access, remove the air cleaner as described in Chapter 4B.
2 Obtain a suitable small container into which the filter can be drained (we used the cap from an aerosol can) **(see illustration)**. Place rags or paper towel under the filter assembly to catch any spillages. Do not allow diesel fuel to contaminate components such as the starter motor, the coolant hoses or any wiring.
3 Connect a tube to the drain screw on the base of the fuel filter **(see illustration)**. Place the other end of the tube into your container. Alternatively, if your container can be placed close enough, drain the filter directly into it.
4 Unscrew the drain screw and allow the filter to drain until clean fuel, free of dirt or water, emerges from the tube (approximately 100 to 150 ml is usually sufficient).
5 Securely close the drain screw and remove the container, tube, and rag, mopping-up any spilt fuel.
6 On completion, dispose safely of the drained fuel.
7 Squeeze the hand-priming bulb on the side of the filter a few times, to refill the filter with fuel – when the bulb becomes stiff, the filter should be full **(see illustration)**.
8 Refit the air cleaner as described in Chapter 4B.

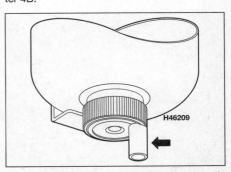

H46209

10.3 Attach a tube to the fitting (arrowed) on the fuel filter water drain screw

10.7 Squeeze the hand-priming bulb until it becomes stiff

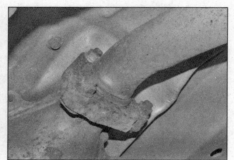

11.2 Check the exhaust joints for corrosion and leakage

12 Hose and fluid leak check

9 Start the engine, and let it run for a minute or two. If it starts, then stops, squeeze the hand-priming bulb a few more times, then try again. If necessary, refer to Chapter 4B and bleed the fuel system.

10 With the engine running, check all disturbed components carefully to ensure that there are no leaks.

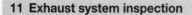

11 Exhaust system inspection

1 With the engine cold (at least three hours after the car has been driven), check the complete exhaust system from the engine to the end of the tailpipe. Ideally, the inspection should be done with the car on a hoist to permit unrestricted access. If a hoist isn't

available, raise the car and support it securely on axle stands (see *Jacking and vehicle support*).

2 Check the exhaust pipes and connections for evidence of leaks, severe corrosion and damage **(see illustration)**. Make sure that all brackets and hangers are in good condition and tight.

3 At the same time, inspect the underside of the body for holes, corrosion, open seams, etc, which may allow exhaust gases to enter the passenger compartment. Seal all body openings with silicone or body filler.

4 Rattles and other noises can often be traced to the exhaust system, especially the mounts and hangers. Try to move the pipes, silencer and catalytic converter. If the components can come in contact with the body or suspension parts, secure the exhaust system with new mounts.

1 Visually inspect the engine joint faces, gaskets and seals for any signs of water or oil leaks. Pay particular attention to the areas around the cylinder head cover, cylinder head, oil filter and sump joint faces. Bear in mind that, over a period of time, some very slight seepage from these areas is to be expected – what you are really looking for is any indication of a serious leak. Should a leak be found, renew the offending gasket or oil seal by referring to the appropriate Chapters in this manual.

2 Also check the security and condition of all the engine-related pipes and hoses, all braking system pipes and hoses, and the fuel lines **(see illustrations)**. Ensure that all cable-ties or securing clips are in place, and in good condition. Clips which are broken or missing can lead to chafing of the hoses, pipes or wiring, which could cause more serious problems in the future.

3 Carefully check the radiator hoses and heater hoses along their entire length **(see illustration)**. Renew any hose which is cracked, swollen or deteriorated. Cracks will show up better if the hose is squeezed. Pay close attention to the hose clips that secure the hoses to the cooling system components. Hose clips can pinch and puncture hoses, resulting in cooling system leaks. If the crimped-type hose clips are used, it may be a good idea to substitute Jubilee clips.

4 Inspect all the cooling system components (hoses, joint faces, etc) for leaks.

5 Where any problems are found on cooling system components, renew the component or gasket with reference to Chapter 3.

6 With the car raised, inspect the fuel tank and filler neck for punctures, cracks and other damage **(see illustration)**. The connection between the filler neck and tank is especially critical. Sometimes a rubber filler neck or connecting hose will leak due to loose retaining clamps or deteriorated rubber.

7 Carefully check all rubber hoses and metal fuel lines leading away from the fuel tank. Check for loose connections, deteriorated hoses, crimped lines, and other damage. Pay particular attention to the vent pipes and hoses, which often loop up around the filler neck and can become blocked or crimped. Follow the lines to the front of the car, carefully inspecting them all the way. Renew damaged sections as necessary. Similarly, whilst the car is raised, take the opportunity to inspect all underbody brake fluid pipes and hoses.

8 From within the engine compartment, check the security of all fuel, vacuum and brake hose attachments and pipe unions, and inspect all hoses for kinks, chafing and deterioration.

12.2a Check the engine-related hoses for splits

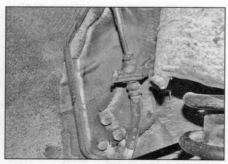

12.2b Check the brake pipes and hoses for corrosion and leaks

12.3 Check the coolant hoses

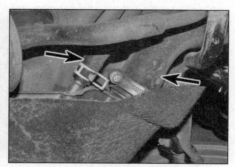

12.6 Check the fuel tank hoses for damage

13 Pollen filter renewal

1 All models are equipped with a filter under the facia that cleans the air entering the car through the ventilation system. This filter is fine enough, apparently, to remove airborne pollen, so it doesn't take long for it to get blocked – when it does, the air output will be greatly reduced.

2 Open the glovebox. If the glovebox is full, it may be advisable to empty it now. Press the side panels of the glovebox inwards to release the stops, and swing the glovebox down further from the facia **(see illustration)**.

3 Unclip the pollen filter cover by levering the locktab upwards, then swing the cover up and remove it **(see illustration)**.

4 The pollen filter is actually in two sections, side by side behind the facia. Pull out the first one by gripping the small tab on the top. The other half of the filter's top tab can also be seen – grip it, and slide the filter sideways so that it too can be withdrawn from the filter housing **(see illustrations)**.

5 Remove each filter element from its frame, noting how it fits.

6 Observing the direction-of-fitting markings on the side of each element (the airflow arrows should point downwards), refit them to the frames **(see illustrations)**.

7 As far as possible, wipe the inside of the housing clean.

8 Establish which half of the new filter goes in first, and which way up it should be (the airflow arrows should point downwards, and the grip tabs should be side by side, facing into the car). Insert it into the slot, and slide it over. Check that the second half is also correctly aligned, then slot it home too.

9 Clip the filter cover back in place at the top, and secure with the locktab at the bottom.

10 Swing the glovebox back into place, and close it to complete.

14 Manual transmission fluid level check

1 The manual transmission does not have a dipstick. To check the fluid level, raise the car and support it securely on axle stands (see *Jacking and vehicle support*). The filler/level plug is behind the left-hand driveshaft, and access is not easy **(see illustration)**. Remove the plug – if the lubricant level is correct, it should be up to the lower edge of the hole.

2 If the transmission needs more lubricant (if the level is not up to the hole), add more through the filler/level hole. If there is sufficient access, a funnel can be used, but most transmission fluid bottles have a flexible tube attached, which is better suited – by squeezing the bottle, fluid can be

added from almost any angle. Stop filling the transmission when the lubricant begins to run out the hole.

3 Refit the plug and tighten it securely. Drive the car a short distance, then check for leaks.

13.2 Lowering the glovebox

13.3 Unclip the pollen filter cover at the bottom

13.4a Remove the first half of the filter . . .

13.4b . . . then slide the second half to the right . . .

13.4c . . . so that it too can be removed

13.6a Observing the airflow direction arrows . . .

13.6b . . . fit the new filter elements to their frames

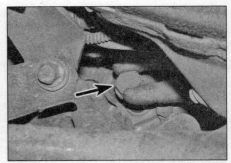

14.1 Removing the transmission filler/level plug

15.1 Lightly oil all the hinges, door check straps, etc

15 Hinge and lock lubrication

1 Work around the car and lubricate the hinges of the bonnet, doors and tailgate with a light machine oil **(see illustration)**.
2 Lightly lubricate the bonnet release mechanism and exposed section of inner cable with a smear of grease.
3 Check the security and operation of all hinges, latches and locks, adjusting them where required. Check the operation of the central locking system.
4 Check the condition and operation of

the tailgate struts, renewing them both (as described in Chapter 11) if either is leaking or no longer able to support the tailgate securely when raised.

16 Road test

Instruments and electrical equipment

1 Check the operation of all instruments and electrical equipment.
2 Make sure that all instruments read correctly, and switch on all electrical equipment in turn, to check that it functions properly.

Steering and suspension

3 Check for any abnormalities in the steering, suspension, handling or road 'feel'.
4 Drive the car, and check that there are no unusual vibrations or noises.
5 Check that the steering feels positive, with no excessive 'sloppiness', or roughness, and check for any suspension noises when cornering and driving over bumps.

Drivetrain

6 Check the performance of the engine, clutch, transmission and driveshafts.

7 Listen for any unusual noises from the engine, clutch and transmission.
8 Make sure that the engine runs smoothly when idling, and that there is no hesitation when accelerating.
9 Check that the clutch action is smooth and progressive, that the drive is taken up smoothly, and that the pedal travel is not excessive. Also listen for any noises when the clutch pedal is depressed.
10 Check that all gears can be engaged smoothly without noise, and that the gear lever action is smooth and not abnormally vague or 'notchy'.
11 Listen for a metallic clicking sound from the front of the car, as the car is driven slowly in a circle with the steering on full-lock. Carry out this check in both directions. If a clicking noise is heard, this indicates wear in a driveshaft joint (see Chapter 8).

Braking system

12 Make sure that the car does not pull to one side when braking, and that the wheels do not lock when braking hard.
13 Check that there is no vibration through the steering when braking.
14 Check that the handbrake operates correctly, without excessive movement of the lever, and that it holds the car stationary on a slope.

Every 24 000 miles or 2 years

17.2a Unclip the wiring harness from the back . . .

17.2b . . . and from the side of the air cleaner

17.3a Unclip the hose from the side . . .

17.3b . . . then pull off the vacuum hose

17 Air filter element renewal

1 The air cleaner is located at the rear of the engine compartment, between the coolant expansion tank and the battery.
2 The air cleaner housing has two sections of wiring harness clipped across the back and side – lift the harness out of the plastic clips, noting how it is routed **(see illustrations)**.
3 Similarly, unclip the hose lower down on the side of the housing, then pull off the small vacuum hose from its pipe stub on the housing **(see illustrations)**.
4 The engine compartment auxiliary fusebox is also clipped to the air cleaner cover – lift it upwards a little to release it **(see illustration)**.
5 Release the four spring clips securing the air cleaner cover. Access to these clips is limited, but a screwdriver may be used to prise the clips free **(see illustration)**.
6 Lift the cover off, noting that the air hose and wiring are still attached. Swing the cover forwards to access the filter element **(see illustration)**.
7 Lift the air filter element out of the housing, then wipe out the inside of the air cleaner housing with a clean rag **(see illustration)**.

8 While the air cleaner cover is off and the element is removed, be careful not to drop anything down into the air cleaner assembly – lay the cover loosely back into place.

9 Fit the new element into the air cleaner housing, making sure it seats properly.

10 Install the air cleaner cover, and secure with the four clips, which can be snapped into place by pressing on the curved part of the clip.

11 Reconnect the small vacuum hose to the stub on the side of the housing, then clip the other hose into place. Similarly, clip the two sections of wiring harness to the back and side. Finally, clip the fusebox back onto the side of the cover.

18 Auxiliary drivebelt check and renewal

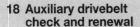

Checking

1 Drivebelts are prone to failure after a long period of time, and should therefore be inspected regularly.

2 For a proper check to be carried out, loosen the right-hand front wheel nuts, then jack up the front of the car and support it on axle stands (see *Jacking and vehicle support*). Remove the right-hand front wheel.

3 Unscrew the bolts and remove the engine undertray (see Section 3).

4 Inspect the full length of the drivebelt for cracks and separation of the belt plies. It will be necessary to turn the engine (using a spanner or socket and bar on the crankshaft pulley bolt) in order to move the belt from the pulleys so that the belt can be inspected thoroughly. Twist the belt between the pulleys so that both sides can be viewed. Also check for fraying, and glazing which gives the belt a shiny appearance. Check the pulleys for nicks, cracks, distortion and corrosion.

5 If the belt shows signs of wear or damage, it must be renewed.

6 Over time, the belt may stretch to the point where the automatic tensioner cannot tension it. The tensioner has a pointer fitted, which should not be beyond the mark on the tensioner bracket **(see illustration)** – if it is, a new belt is needed.

Renewal

7 If not already done, access the belt as described in paragraphs 2 and 3.

8 If the drivebelt is to be re-used, mark the direction of travel to ensure it is refitted the same way round. Note the run of the drivebelt around the pulleys **(see illustration)**.

9 Using a socket on the centre bolt, turn the drivebelt tensioner clockwise to release the tension, then slip the drivebelt from the pulleys **(see illustrations)**.

10 If required, a lock pin (such as a drill bit of suitable size) can be inserted through the hole

17.4 Unclip the fusebox

17.5 Release the air cleaner cover spring clips

17.6 Lift the air cleaner cover forwards to access the filter

17.7 Remove the filter element, noting how it is fitted

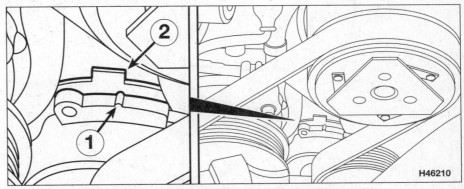

18.6 Tensioner pointer (1) must not be beyond mark (2)

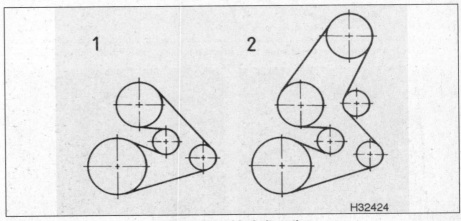

18.8 Auxiliary drivebelt routing

1 Without air conditioning   *2 With air conditioning*

18.9a Turn the drivebelt tensioner clockwise . . .

18.9b . . . then slip the belt from the pulleys

in the tensioner arm, to lock the tensioner in the retracted position – we found this rather difficult on our project car, and probably unnecessary **(see illustration)**.

11 Manoeuvre the new drivebelt into position and seat it on the pulley grooves. Release the tensioner and check again that the drivebelt is correctly seated.

12 Refit the undertray, then refit the front wheel. Lower the car to the ground, and tighten the wheel nuts to the specified torque.

19 Fuel filter renewal

1 To gain access to the filter, remove the air cleaner as described in Chapter 4B.

2 Remove the single bolt at the top securing the fuel filter guard plate, then unhook the plate and remove it **(see illustration)**.

3 Pull the hand-priming bulb forwards at the base, then the top, to release the hoses from their clips **(see illustration)**. Move the bulb clear for access to the filter.

4 Clean around the two hose connections on top of the filter – it is essential that no dirt enters the system. Squeeze the spring clips to release the hoses, and disconnect both of them from the filter – note the fitted position of each hose **(see illustration)**.

5 Unscrew the two bolts securing the filter mounting bracket, and lift out the filter and bracket **(see illustrations)**.

6 Loosen the filter bracket's clamp bolt, and withdraw the filter, noting the position of the pipes and bleed bolt on top, in relation to the bracket **(see illustrations)**.

7 Open the drain tap on the case of the old filter, and drain any fuel into a suitable container **(see illustration)**. Dispose of the drained fuel and empty filter safely and responsibly.

8 Fit the new filter into the bracket, positioning it the same way as the old filter (with the bleed bolt at the rear), and tighten the clamp bolt **(see illustration)**.

9 Offer the filter and bracket back into position, then fit and tighten the two bracket mounting bolts securely.

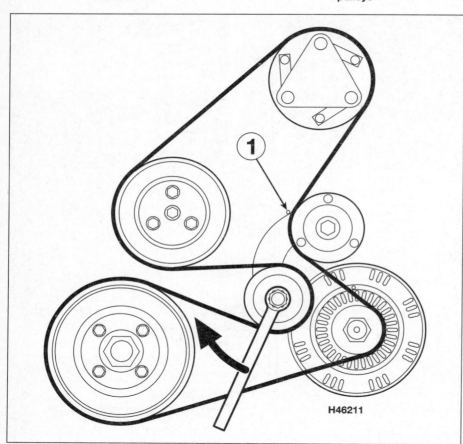

H46211

18.10 Turn the tensioner clockwise, then insert a locking pin (1) in the tensioner arm

19.2 Unbolt and remove the filter guard plate

19.3 Unclip the hand-priming bulb

19.4 Disconnect the two hoses from the top of the filter

19.5a Fuel filter bracket bolts (A) and clamp bolt (B)

19.5b Removing the filter and bracket

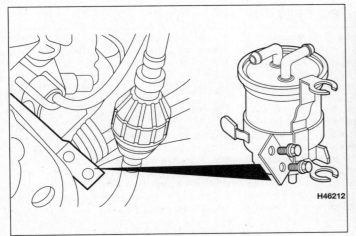

19.6a Fuel filter removal details

19.6b Loosen the clamp bolt and take out the filter

10 Reconnect the two hoses to their original locations on top of the filter, and secure with the spring clips. If preferred, the spring clips can be updated with Jubilee clips.

11 Squeeze the hand-priming bulb several times until it goes hard.

12 Refit the air cleaner as described in Chapter 4B.

13 Try to start the engine – preferably, have an assistant on hand to help bleed the fuel system as described in Chapter 4B.

19.7 Drain out the old filter before disposal

19.8 Fit the new filter into the bracket, bleed bolt to the rear

Every 60 000 miles or 5 years

20 Timing belt renewal

Refer to the information given in Chapter 2B. At the same time, check the condition of the timing belt tensioner, and renew this also if necessary – many dealers and parts suppliers now sell timing belt 'kits', which include a new tensioner, and any additional idler pulleys.

Every 72 000 miles or 6 years

21 Valve clearance check and adjustment

Refer to Chapter 2B.

22 Manual transmission fluid renewal

1 The fluid should be drained when hot, preferably immediately after the car has been driven. Park the car on level ground to begin with.

2 Raise the front of the car and place it on axle stands for access to the transmission drain plug (see *Jacking and vehicle support*).

3 Move the tools and drain pan under the car, being careful not to touch any of the hot exhaust components.

4 Place the drain pan under the transmission and remove the drain plug – it's located on the left-hand side of the transmission, near the bottom **(see illustration)**. Be sure the drain pan is in position, as fluid will come out with some force.

5 Once the fluid is drained, clean and refit the drain plug, using a new sealing washer and tightening it securely. Lower the car to the ground, and make sure that it is level.

6 Remove the filler/level plug, which is located higher up the transmission casing, behind the left-hand driveshaft. Add new fluid until it begins to run out of the filler hole (see Section 14). On completion, refit the filler/level plug – use a new sealing washer and tighten it securely.

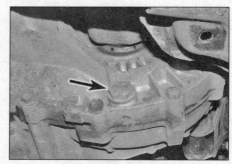

22.4 The transmission drain plug is located at the bottom

Every 3 years (regardless of mileage)

23 Brake fluid renewal

⚠️ *Warning: Brake hydraulic fluid can harm your eyes and damage painted surfaces, so use extreme caution when handling and pouring it. Do not use fluid that has been standing open for some time, as it absorbs moisture from the air. Excess moisture can cause a dangerous loss of braking effectiveness.*

1 The procedure is similar to that for the bleeding of the hydraulic system as described in Chapter 9.

2 Working as described in Chapter 9, open the first bleed screw in the sequence, and pump the brake pedal gently until nearly all the old fluid has been emptied from the master cylinder reservoir. Top-up to the MAX level with new fluid, and continue pumping until only the new fluid remains in the reservoir, and new fluid can be seen emerging from the bleed screw. Tighten the screw, and top the reservoir level up to the MAX level line.

3 Work through all the remaining bleed screws in the sequence until new fluid can be seen at all of them. Be careful to keep the master cylinder reservoir topped-up to above the MIN level at all times, or air may enter the system and greatly increase the length of the task.

> **HAYNES HiNT** *Old hydraulic fluid is invariably much darker in colour than the new, making it easy to distinguish the two.*

4 When the operation is complete, check that all bleed screws are securely tightened, and that their dust caps are refitted. Wash off all traces of spilt fluid, and recheck the master cylinder reservoir fluid level.

5 Check the operation of the brakes before taking the car on the road.

Every 5 years (regardless of mileage)

24 Coolant renewal

Note: *Some models may have been filled with Honda coolant which is claimed to have a 10-year life (typically, this type of coolant is orange or red in colour). If this is known to be the case, and only this coolant is used in the*

24.2 Remove the expansion tank cap

system, the 10-year renewal interval can be observed. The DIY owner may prefer to use the suggested shorter interval, especially if the coolant in the system is of unknown type.

⚠️ *Warning: Refer to Chapter 3 and observe the warnings given. In particular, never remove the expansion tank filler cap when the engine is running, or has just been switched off, as the cooling system will be pressurised and hot, and the consequent escaping steam and scalding coolant could cause serious injury. If the engine is hot, the electric cooling fan may start rotating even if the engine is not running, so be careful to keep hands, hair and loose clothing well clear when working in the engine compartment.*

⚠️ *Warning: Wait until the engine is cold before starting this procedure.*

Cooling system draining

1 Switch on the ignition, then turn the heater temperature control to the maximum heat position. Turn off the ignition.

2 To drain the system, first remove the expansion tank filler cap. Place a thick cloth over the cap, then turn the cap anti-clockwise as far as the first stop and wait for any pressure to be released, then depress it and turn it further anti-clockwise to remove it **(see illustration)**.

3 If additional working clearance is required, apply the handbrake, then jack up the front of the car and support it on axle stands (see *Jacking and vehicle support*).

4 Remove the bolts securing the undertray, then place a large drain tray underneath, and loosen the radiator drain tap. Allow the coolant to drain into the tray. On completion, retighten the drain tap and refit the undertray. Where necessary, lower the car to the ground.

5 Honda also stipulate that the contents of the expansion tank should be drained when renewing the coolant. Realistically, unless suitable syphoning equipment is available (and remember, antifreeze is poisonous), this will mean removing the tank to pour out the contents. To remove the tank, refer to Chapter 3.

24.22a Filling the expansion tank

24.22b MAX and MIN marks on the side of the expansion tank

Cooling system flushing

6 If coolant renewal has been neglected, or if the antifreeze mixture has become diluted, then in time, the cooling system may gradually lose efficiency, as the coolant passages become restricted due to rust, scale deposits, and other sediment. The cooling system efficiency can be restored by flushing the system clean.

7 The radiator should be flushed independently of the engine, to avoid unnecessary contamination.

Radiator flushing

8 Disconnect the top and bottom hoses and any other relevant hoses from the radiator, with reference to Chapter 3.

9 Insert a garden hose into the radiator top inlet. Direct a flow of clean water through the radiator, and continue flushing until clean water emerges from the radiator bottom outlet.

10 If after a reasonable period, the water still does not run clear, the radiator can be flushed with a good proprietary cleaning agent. It is important that the manufacturer's instructions are followed carefully. If the contamination is particularly bad, remove the radiator, insert the hose in the radiator bottom outlet, and reverse-flush the radiator.

Engine flushing

11 Remove the thermostat as described in Chapter 3 then, if the radiator top hose has been disconnected from the engine, temporarily reconnect the hose.

12 With the top and bottom hoses disconnected from the radiator, insert a garden hose into the radiator top hose. Direct a clean flow of water through the engine, and continue flushing until clean water emerges from the radiator bottom hose.

13 On completion of flushing, refit the thermostat and reconnect the hoses with reference to Chapter 3.

Antifreeze mixture

> **HAYNES HINT**
> *It is rare to ever drain the cooling system completely – a small quantity will remain. If the system has been extensively flushed with clean water, this remaining quantity will in fact be plain water. For this reason, some people will first fill the system with the required quantity of neat antifreeze (half the total system capacity, for a 50% mixture), and then complete the filling process with plain water. This ensures that the resulting coolant (once it has mixed inside the engine) is not 'diluted' by old coolant or water remaining in the system.*

14 Honda state that, if the only antifreeze used is the type with which the system was first filled at the factory (see *Lubricants and fluids*) it will last 10 years. This is subject to it being used in the recommended concentration, unmixed with any other type of antifreeze or additive, and topped-up when necessary using only that antifreeze. No other type of antifreeze should be mixed with it – if this happens; to restore the 10-year life, the system must be drained and thoroughly reverse-flushed before fresh coolant is poured in.

15 If the car's history (and therefore the quality of the antifreeze in it) is unknown, owners who wish to follow Honda's recommendations are advised to drain and thoroughly reverse-flush the system, before refilling with fresh coolant.

16 If any antifreeze other than Honda's is to be used, the coolant must be renewed at regular intervals to provide an equivalent degree of protection; the conventional recommendation is to renew the coolant every three years.

17 Honda's own antifreeze is usually supplied pre-mixed at 50/50 strength, and is therefore ready to use. If you are using any other type of

antifreeze, to give the recommended mixture ratio, 50% (by volume) of neat antifreeze must be mixed with 50% of clean, soft water; however, always note the antifreeze manufacturer's instructions (also see the Haynes Hint).

18 Before adding antifreeze, the cooling system should be completely drained, preferably flushed, and all hoses checked for condition and security. Fresh antifreeze will rapidly find any weaknesses in the system.

19 After filling with antifreeze, a label should be attached to the expansion tank, stating the type and concentration of antifreeze used, and the date installed. Any subsequent topping-up should be made with the same type and concentration of antifreeze.

Cooling system filling

20 Before attempting to fill the cooling system, make sure that all hoses and clips are in good condition, and that the clips are tight. If removed, refit the expansion tank.

21 Check that the heater temperature control has not been moved from the maximum heat position. If there is a chance it has been disturbed, temporarily switch on the ignition and set the control to maximum heat, then switch the ignition off once more.

22 Slowly fill the expansion tank until the level reaches the MAX mark **(see illustrations)**. Wait for the level to stabilise, then **loosely** refit the expansion tank cap. The cap is fitted loosely at this stage to prevent a build-up of pressure in the system, and to allow the release of any trapped air.

23 Start the engine and let it run at idle until the engine reaches normal operating temperature, as indicated by the temperature gauge, or by the radiator cooling fan cutting in and out at least twice.

24 Switch off the engine, then check the level in the expansion tank, and top-up if necessary.

25 Refit the expansion tank cap tightly, then

run the engine again briefly, and check for leaks.

26 Switch off the engine, and allow it to cool for at least an hour, and preferably, leave overnight.

27 Top-up the coolant level in the expansion tank as necessary.

Airlocks

28 If, after draining and refilling the system, symptoms of overheating are found which did not occur previously, then the fault is almost certainly due to trapped air at some point in the system, causing an airlock and restricting the flow of coolant; usually, the air is trapped because the system was refilled too quickly.

29 If an airlock is suspected, first try gently squeezing all visible coolant hoses. A coolant hose which is full of air feels quite different to one full of coolant, when squeezed. After refilling the system, most airlocks will clear once the system has cooled, and been topped-up.

30 While the engine is running at operating temperature, switch on the heater and heater fan, and check for heat output. Provided there is sufficient coolant in the system, any lack of heat output could be due to an airlock in the system.

31 Airlocks can have more serious effects than simply reducing heater output – a severe airlock could reduce coolant flow around the engine. Check that the radiator top hose is hot when the engine is at operating temperature – a top hose which stays cold could be the result of an airlock (or a non-opening thermostat).

32 If the problem persists, stop the engine and allow it to cool down **completely**, before unscrewing the expansion tank cap or loosening the hose clips and squeezing the hoses to bleed out the trapped air. In the worst case, the system will have to be at least partially drained (this time, the coolant can be saved for re-use) and flushed to clear the problem.

Expansion tank cap check

33 Remove the expansion tank cap when the system is cold. Clean the cap, and inspect the seal inside for damage or deterioration. If there is any sign of damage or deterioration to the seal, fit a new pressure cap. If the cap is old, it is worth considering fitting a new one for peace of mind – they are not expensive. If the pressure cap fails, excess pressure will be allowed into the system, which may result in the failure of hoses, the radiator, or the heater matrix.

Chapter 2 Part A:
Petrol engine in-car repair procedures

Contents

Degrees of difficulty

Easy, suitable for novice with little experience	**Fairly easy,** suitable for beginner with some experience	**Fairly difficult,** suitable for competent DIY mechanic	**Difficult,** suitable for experienced DIY mechanic	**Very difficult,** suitable for expert DIY or professional

Specifications

General

Engine type	Four-cylinder, in-line, water-cooled. Single overhead camshaft, 16-valve. VTEC system on 1.6 litre engine
Manufacturer's engine codes*:	
1.4 litre	D14Z5 or D14Z6
1.6 litre	D16V1 or D16W7
Bore	75.0 mm
Stroke:	
1.4 litre	79.0 mm
1.6 litre	90.0 mm
Capacity:	
1.4 litre	1396 cc
1.6 litre	1590 cc
Firing order	1-3-4-2 (No 1 cylinder at timing belt end)
Direction of crankshaft rotation	Anti-clockwise (viewed from timing belt end of engine)
Compression ratio:	
1.4 litre engine	10.4:1
1.6 litre engine	9.4:1

* See Vehicle identification in the Reference section

Compression pressures

Nominal	13.0 bar (189 psi)
Minimum	9.5 bar (138 psi)
Maximum difference between any two cylinders	2.0 bar (29 psi)

Camshaft

Endfloat:	
Nominal	0.05 to 0.15 mm
Wear limit	0.5 mm

Crankshaft oil seal

Fitted depth in housing	0.5 to 0.8 mm below front face

Flywheel

Runout on clutch surface	0.15 mm maximum

Lubrication system

Oil pump type. . . . . Rotor type, driven directly from crankshaft
Minimum oil pressure, engine hot:
    At idle speed. . . . . 0.7 bar (10 psi)
    At 3000 rpm . . . . 3.5 bar (51 psi)
Oil pump clearances:
    Inner-to-outer rotor radial clearance. . . . . 0.20 mm maximum
    Outer rotor-to-body radial clearance . . . . 0.20 mm maximum
    Rotor endfloat. . . . . 0.15 mm maximum

Torque wrench settings

	Nm	lbf ft
Accessory bracket bolts:		
8 mm bolts	24	18
10 mm bolts	44	32
Alternator upper mounting bolt	44	32
Big-end bearing cap bolts*	32	24
Camshaft bearing cap/rocker assembly bolts:		
8 mm bolts	20	15
6 mm bolts	12	9
Camshaft sprocket bolt (oiled)	37	27
Crankshaft position sensor bolt	12	9
Crankshaft oil seal housing bolts	10	7
Crankshaft pulley bolt:		
Stage 1	20	15
Stage 2	Angle-tighten a further 90°	
Cylinder head bolts:		
Stage 1	20	15
Stage 2	49	36
Stage 3	67	49
Cylinder head cover bolts	10	7
Driveplate bolts	74	55
Engine-to-transmission bolts	64	47
Engine/transmission mountings:		
Front mounting:		
Bracket-to-engine bolts:		
M10 bolt	54	40
M12 bolts	64	47
Through-bolt*	64	47
Left-hand mounting:		
Side bracket-to-engine bolts	44	32
Upper bracket mounting nuts	54	40
Rear mounting:		
Bracket-to-mounting through-bolt	64	47
Bracket-to-transmission bolts	64	47
Mounting-to-subframe bolts	59	44
Right-hand mounting:		
Mounting-to-transmission nuts, bolt and through-bolt	54	40
Exhaust front pipe-to-manifold bolts*	22	16
Flywheel bolts	118	87
Front subframe bolts:		
M10 bolts	59	44
M14 bolts*	103	76
Main bearing cap bolts:		
Stage 1 (all engines)	25	18
Stage 2:		
1.4 litre engine	44	32
1.6 litre engine	51	38
Oil pressure switch	18	13
Oil pump:		
Mounting bolts	10	7
Oil pressure relief valve plug	39	29
Pump inner cover screws	7	5
Oil pump pick-up tube/strainer nuts and bolts	11	8
Roadwheel nuts	108	80
Rocker assembly/camshaft bearing cap bolts:		
8 mm bolts	20	15
6 mm bolts	12	9

Torque wrench settings (continued)

	Nm	lbf ft
Sump drain plug:		
Steel sump (1.4 litre engine)	44	32
Aluminium sump (1.6 litre engine)	39	29
Sump nuts and bolts	12	9
Sump stiffener bracket bolts:		
M8 bolts	24	18
M10 bolts	44	32
Timing belt cover bolts	10	7
Timing belt tensioner bolt	44	32
VTEC oil pressure switch	22	16
VTEC solenoid mounting bolts	10	7

* Use new bolts

---

1 General information

How to use this Chapter

This Part of Chapter 2 is devoted to in-car repair procedures for the petrol engines. All procedures concerning engine removal and refitting, and engine block/cylinder head overhaul can be found in Chapter 2C.

Most of the operations included in this Part are based on the assumption that the engine is still fitted in the car. Therefore, if this information is being used during a complete engine overhaul, with the engine already removed, many of the steps included here will not apply.

The Specifications included in this Part of Chapter 2 apply only to the procedures contained in this Chapter. Chapter 2C contains the Specifications necessary for cylinder head and engine block rebuilding.

Engine description

This engine goes against the modern trend for 16-valve engines, in that it only has a single overhead camshaft (SOHC). The result is a more complicated set of rocker arms, and a multi-lobe camshaft, to operate all the valves. In addition, the 1.6 litre version of the engine incorporates the VTEC (Variable Valve Timing and lift Electronic Control) system, which electronically alters valve timing to enhance engine performance. For more information on the VTEC system, see Section 9 of this Chapter.

The engines are lightweight in design with an aluminium alloy block (with steel cylinder liners) and an aluminium alloy cylinder head. The crankshaft rides in a single carriage unit that houses the renewable insert-type main bearings, with separate thrust bearings at the number four position assigned the task of controlling crankshaft endfloat.

The pistons have two compression rings and one oil control ring. The semi-floating piston pins are press-fitted into the small end of the connecting rod. The connecting rod big-ends are also equipped with renewable insert-type plain bearings.

The engine has a centrifugal impeller-type water pump, driven by the timing belt, to circulate coolant around the cylinders and combustion chambers and through the inlet manifold.

Lubrication is handled by a rotor-type oil pump mounted on the front of the engine under the timing belt cover, driven directly by the crankshaft. The oil is filtered continuously by a cartridge-type filter mounted on the rear of the engine.

Operations with engine in car

The following operations can be carried out without having to remove the engine from the car:

a) *Removal and refitting of the cylinder head.*
b) *Removal and refitting of the timing belt and sprockets.*
c) *Renewal of the camshaft oil seal.*
d) *Removal and refitting of the rocker shaft and camshaft.*
e) *Removal and refitting of the sump.*
f) *Removal and refitting of the connecting rods and pistons*.*
g) *Removal and refitting of the oil pump.*
h) *Renewal of the crankshaft oil seals.*
i) *Renewal of the engine mountings.*
j) *Removal and refitting of the flywheel/ driveplate.*

* Although the operation marked with an asterisk can be carried out with the engine in the car after removal of the sump, it is better for the engine to be removed, in the interests of cleanliness and improved access. For this reason, the procedure is described in Chapter 2C.

2 Compression test – description and interpretation

1 When engine performance is down, or if misfiring occurs which cannot be attributed to the ignition or fuel systems, a compression test can provide diagnostic clues as to the engine's condition. If the test is performed regularly, it can give warning of trouble before any other symptoms become apparent.

2 The engine must be fully warmed-up to normal operating temperature, the battery must be fully-charged, and the spark plugs must be removed (see Chapter 1A). The aid of an assistant will also be required.

3 The ignition system must be disabled

for this test – this should be achieved by disconnecting the ignition coils when the spark plugs are removed.

4 The fuel pump must also be disabled, by removing fuse No 17 from the interior fusebox. **Note:** *This may cause a temporary fault code to be stored in the ECM, so the engine management warning light may be lit on completion. After a number of successful starts, the codes should clear themselves – if not, refer to Chapter 4A, Section 10.*

5 Fit a compression tester to No 1 cylinder spark plug hole (No 1 is at the timing belt end, which on this engine, is nearest the passenger-side inner wing). The type of tester which screws into the plug thread is to be preferred.

6 Have the assistant hold the throttle wide open and crank the engine on the starter motor; after one or two revolutions, the compression pressure should build-up to a maximum figure, and then stabilise. Record the highest reading obtained.

7 Repeat the test on the remaining cylinders, recording the pressure in each.

8 All cylinders should produce very similar pressures; any difference greater than that specified indicates the existence of a fault. Note that the compression should build-up quickly in a healthy engine. Low compression on the first stroke, followed by gradually-increasing pressure on successive strokes, indicates worn piston rings. A low compression reading on the first stroke, which does not build-up during successive strokes, indicates leaking valves or a blown head gasket (a cracked head could also be the cause). Deposits on the undersides of the valve heads can also cause low compression.

9 If the pressure in any cylinder is reduced to the specified minimum or less, carry out the following test to isolate the cause. Introduce a teaspoonful of clean oil into that cylinder through its spark plug hole, and repeat the test.

10 If the addition of oil temporarily improves the compression pressure, this indicates that bore or piston wear is responsible for the pressure loss. No improvement suggests that leaking or burnt valves, or a blown head gasket, may be to blame.

11 A low reading from two adjacent cylinders is almost certainly due to the head gasket having blown between them; the presence of coolant in the engine oil will confirm this.

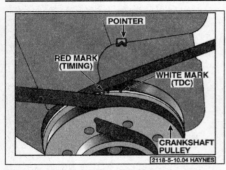

3.5 Align the white (TDC) mark on the pulley with the belt cover marks

3.7a Camshaft sprocket has an UP mark on one of its spokes . . .

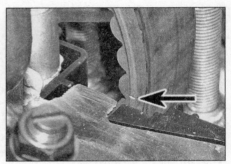

3.7b . . . and two small line marks on the inner rim

12 If one cylinder is about 20 per cent lower than the others, and the engine has a slightly rough idle, a worn camshaft lobe could be the cause.

13 If the compression reading is unusually high, the combustion chambers are probably coated with carbon deposits. If this is the case, the cylinder head should be removed and decarbonised.

14 On completion of the test, refit the spark plugs (see Chapter 1A), refit the main fuel injection relay fuse and reconnect the wiring connector to the distributor.

3 Top Dead Centre (TDC) for No 1 piston – locating

1 Top Dead Centre (TDC) is the highest point in the cylinder that each piston reaches as

it travels up and down when the crankshaft turns. Each piston reaches TDC on the compression stroke and again on the exhaust stroke, but TDC generally refers to piston position on the compression stroke.

2 Positioning No 1 piston at TDC is an essential part of many procedures, such as timing belt or camshaft removal.

3 Before beginning this procedure, be sure to place the (manual) transmission in neutral and apply the handbrake or chock the rear wheels. Also remove the spark plugs (see Chapter 1A).

4 In order to bring any piston to TDC, the crankshaft must be turned using the method outlined below. When looking at the auxiliary drivebelt end of the engine, normal crankshaft rotation is anti-clockwise (towards the front of the car). Always rotate the engine anti-clockwise; clockwise rotation may cause incorrect adjustment of the timing belt. The preferred method is to turn the crankshaft

with a socket (19 mm) and ratchet attached to the crankshaft pulley bolt.

5 Turn the crankshaft until the white (TDC) notch in the crankshaft pulley is aligned with the twin pointers on the timing belt cover. Note that the crankshaft pulley will also have a number of red marks – these are ignition timing marks, and are before top dead centre (BTDC) **(see illustration)**.

6 Remove the timing belt upper cover as described in Section 6.

7 The camshaft sprocket has an UP mark on one of its spokes, and two line markings opposite each other on the **inside** rim. At No 1 TDC, the UP mark should be uppermost (in the twelve o'clock position), and the two line marks aligned with the cylinder head top surface **(see illustrations)**.

8 After No 1 piston has been positioned at TDC on the compression stroke, TDC for any of the remaining cylinders can be located by turning the crankshaft in 180° increments and following the firing order (refer to the Specifications). Rotating the engine 180° past TDC for cylinder No 1 will put the engine at TDC compression for cylinder No 3.

4 Cylinder head cover – removal and refitting

Removal

1 Remove the ignition coils as described in Chapter 5B.

2 Unscrew the dome nut from each of the two accelerator cable support brackets, then move the cable to one side **(see illustrations)**. If more involved work is planned (such as removing the cylinder head), refer to Chapter 4A and disconnect the cable from the throttle body.

3 Remove the bolt from each end of the coil wiring plug busbar, then release the clip at the rear and unclip the harness at the front. Lift the busbar off the engine, and move to one side **(see illustrations)**.

4 Release the spring clip and disconnect the breather hose from the back of the cylinder head cover **(see illustration)**.

5 Pull out the engine oil dipstick and remove it **(see illustration)**.

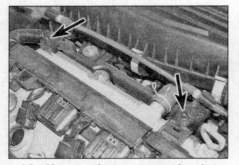

4.2a Unscrew the two support bracket dome nuts . . .

4.2b . . . and move the accelerator cable clear

4.3a Remove the bolt from each end of the wiring plug busbar . . .

4.3b . . . release the clip at the rear . . .

4.3c . . . and unclip the harness at the front . . .

4.3d . . . then lift off the busbar and move it clear

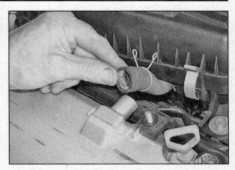

4.4 Disconnect the breather hose from the back of the cover

6 At the rear of the cover, lift the wiring harness off the studs, and move it clear **(see illustration)**.

7 Unscrew and remove the five cover bolts, noting their fitted positions, as they are of different lengths (the two longer bolts are at the rear) **(see illustrations)**. Recover the bolt washers from the cylinder head cover – new ones should be obtained if any are damaged.

8 Lift off the cover, and recover the gaskets – there is one main seal around the edge of the cover, and four circular ones around the coil/spark plug holes **(see illustrations)**. These can be re-used if in good condition, but if the main gasket especially has seen long service, a new one is recommended.

Refitting

9 Clean the mating surfaces of the cylinder head and the valve cover. Clean the surfaces

4.5 Remove the engine oil dipstick

with a rag soaked in gasket remover or cellulose thinners.

10 Fit the rubber gasket into the groove around the valve cover perimeter. Apply beads of liquid sealant (available from Honda dealers) to the 'corners' where the cylinder

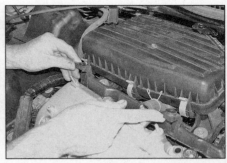

4.6 Lift the rear wiring harness off the rear studs

head mates with the rocker arm assembly **(see illustration)**. **Note:** *The cover must be fitted within five minutes of applying the sealant. If more time has elapsed, remove the old residue and re-apply the sealant.*

11 The four circular seals should be fitted so

4.7a Unscrew the five cover bolts . . .

4.7b . . . noting that the two rear bolts are longer than the others

4.8a Lift off the cylinder head cover . . .

4.8b . . . then recover the main gasket . . .

4.8c . . . and the four circular seals

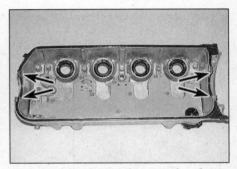

4.10 Apply sealant to the curved surfaces of the main gasket

5.2 Use a screwdriver through one of the starter bolt holes to lock the engine

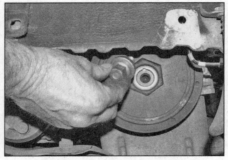

5.4a Unscrew and remove the bolt . . .

5.4b . . . then remove the crankshaft pulley . . .

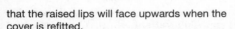

5.4c . . . and recover the Woodruff key

5.7 Use an angle-gauge for the second stage of tightening

that the raised lips will face upwards when the cover is refitted.

12 Offer the cover into position, holding the main gasket in place by holding it up in the rocker cover recesses either end. Make sure the coil/spark plug seals locate properly on the 'tubes' in the cylinder head (help them on using a small screwdriver), and shuffle the cover slightly to locate the main gasket.

13 Refit the cover bolts into their original positions, using new washers if necessary. Tighten them progressively to the specified torque.

14 The remainder of refitting is the reverse of removal, noting the following points:

a) *If difficulty is experienced refitting the ignition coils, this is probably due to one of the cover's circular seals having been displaced during fitting.*

b) *On completion, run the engine and check for signs of oil leaks.*

5 Crankshaft pulley – removal and refitting

Removal

1 Remove the auxiliary drivebelt as described in Chapter 1A.

2 The crankshaft pulley must now be held stationary while the bolt is loosened. Remove the starter motor as described in Chapter 5A and have an assistant engage a wide-bladed screwdriver through one of the starter motor bolt holes, and into the teeth of the starter ring gear **(see illustration)**. The alternative method (for manual transmission models only) of having an assistant engage a gear and apply the foot-brake, is unlikely to work – the bolt is very tight.

3 The crankshaft pulley bolt will be extremely tight. First, ensure that the car is securely

supported. Only use good-quality, close-fitting tools for this job – if something slips, it may result in injury. For extra leverage, use a long-handled breaker (or 'cracker') bar, or slip a piece of substantial tubing over the socket handle, to make it longer. If an extension bar is used on the socket, rest the outer end of the extension bar (the end nearest the handle) on another axle stand, to keep it horizontal – this improves leverage, and reduces the chance of the socket slipping off under load.

4 Unscrew and remove the bolt (which has an integral washer), and slip off the pulley. Note which way up the pulley fits – it engages on a keyway at the top. The Woodruff key which sits in the crankshaft may be loose – it's best to recover it, and store it with the pulley **(see illustrations)**.

Refitting

5 Wipe clean the pulley and the mating surfaces of the crankshaft and its sprocket. Also clean the pulley bolt and washer. Though not specifically required by Honda, consider using a new bolt when refitting – this should be done in any case if the bolt appears damaged.

6 Lightly oil the bolt threads and the underside of the bolt head, then offer in the pulley, the same way up as was noted on removal, and engage the notch in the slot on the crankshaft. Tighten the bolt by hand, and check that the pulley is properly seated.

7 Using the same method as for removal, prevent the crankshaft pulley from turning as the bolt is tightened. Tighten the bolt to the specified torque, then through the specified angle (which is equivalent to a quarter-turn) **(see illustration)**.

8 Refit and tension the auxiliary drivebelt as described in Chapter 1A.

6 Timing belt covers – removal and refitting

Upper cover

1 Support the engine under the sump, using a jack and a block of wood to spread the load.

2 Unscrew and remove the three nuts securing the engine left-hand mounting upper bracket, and lift the bracket off **(see illustrations)**.

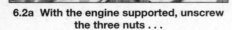

6.2a With the engine supported, unscrew the three nuts . . .

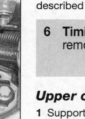

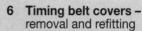

6.2b . . . and lift off the left-hand mounting upper bracket

3 On models with air conditioning, one of the refrigerant pipes is routed right over the top of the cover, making access difficult. Remove the single bolt from the pipe support bracket above the timing belt cover, and the pipe can then be moved a little (though still not much) **(see illustration)**.

4 Carefully release the grommet around the TDC sensor wiring plug from the upper cover, then disconnect the plug and move the wiring clear **(see illustration)**.

5 Unscrew the three upper cover retaining bolts, and remove the cover **(see illustrations)**. Note that the lower bolt is longer than the other two.

6 Refitting is a reversal of removal, noting the following points:

a) *Ensure that the TDC sensor is securely reconnected, and the grommet is fully refitted.*

b) *Tighten the engine left-hand mounting upper bracket nuts to the specified torque.*

Lower cover

7 Remove the crankshaft pulley as described in Section 5.

8 Remove the upper cover, as described previously in this Section.

9 Unscrew the four lower cover retaining bolts, unclip the wiring harness attached to the rear, and withdraw the cover **(see illustrations)**.

10 Check the condition of the cover's rubber seal, and ensure that it is seated in the cover groove before refitting **(see illustration)**.

11 Refitting is a reversal of removal, noting the following points:

a) *Refit the crankshaft pulley as described in Section 5.*

b) *Refit the timing belt upper cover as described previously in this Section.*

Inner (rear) cover

12 Remove the camshaft sprocket as described in Section 8.

13 Unscrew the inner cover retaining bolt, and remove the cover.

14 Refitting is a reversal of removal. Refit the camshaft sprocket as described in Section 8.

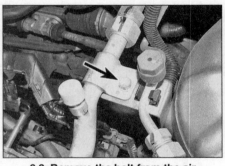

6.3 Remove the bolt from the air conditioning pipe support bracket

6.5a Remove the cover bolts . . .

7 Timing belt – removal, inspection and refitting

Removal

1 Disconnect the battery negative lead, and position the lead away from the battery (also see *Disconnecting the battery*).

2 Chock the rear wheels and apply the handbrake.

3 Loosen the wheel nuts on the left front wheel and raise the front of the car. Support the front of the car securely on axle stands (see *Jacking and vehicle support*). Remove the left front wheel.

4 Unbolt and remove the engine undertray.

5 Remove the spark plugs and the auxiliary drivebelt (see Chapter 1A).

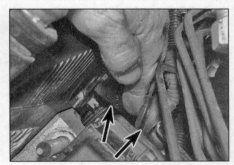

6.4 Release the grommet from the TDC sensor wiring plug

6.5b . . . and take off the upper cover – note TDC sensor wiring plug location

6 Remove the cylinder head cover as described in Section 4.

7 Set the engine to TDC on No 1 piston (see Section 3).

8 Remove the crankshaft pulley as described in Section 5. Given the amount of effort required to loosen the crankshaft pulley bolt, the engine may have moved from the TDC position – temporarily refit the pulley, and recheck that the engine is at TDC.

9 Remove any tools used to jam the starter ring gear.

10 Remove the timing belt upper and lower covers as described in Section 6.

11 Remove the alternator as described in Chapter 5A – the alternator upper mounting bolt passes through the engine left-hand mounting side bracket, but note that the bolt cannot be withdrawn with the alternator fitted, as it hits the inner wing.

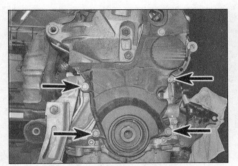

6.9a Remove the four bolts . . .

6.9b . . . and withdraw the lower cover

6.10 Check that the cover seal is located in its groove

7.12 Unbolt and remove the left-hand mounting side bracket

7.13a Unscrew the single mounting bolt . . .

7.13b . . . and move the crankshaft sensor clear

12 The side mounting bracket is secured with five bolts – two from the side, and three from the front. Remove these bolts, and withdraw the side mounting bracket **(see illustration)**. Recover the alternator upper mounting bolt – note that this bolt will have to be refitted with the bracket.

13 Remove the bolt securing the crankshaft position sensor (just behind the crankshaft sprocket), and remove the sensor without disconnecting it **(see illustrations)**.

14 Note that the crankshaft sprocket has a timing mark on its front face, which should be aligned with a pointer on the oil pump. This mark can only just be seen 'through' the timing belt, and it is advisable to make your own paint marks on the crankshaft sprocket and oil pump **(see illustrations)**. Recheck the alignment of the camshaft sprocket also, before removing the belt.

15 If you intend to re-use the timing belt

(which is not recommended), use white paint or chalk to mark the belt with an arrow to indicate the direction of rotation.

16 Loosen the timing belt tensioner bolt, then turn the tensioner anti-clockwise by fitting a 6 mm Allen key into the hole provided on the tensioner flange **(see illustrations)**. Hold the tensioner to relieve the belt tension.

17 Noting how it is routed around the sprockets and tensioner, slip the belt off the sprockets and remove it **(see illustrations)**. It is possible that the camshaft sprocket will turn slightly when the belt is removed – this is nothing to worry about, but note which way the sprocket has moved, and how far, as it will have to be turned back when the new belt is being fitted.

Caution: Once the belt has been removed, do not turn the camshaft (or the crankshaft) by more than a few degrees, otherwise the valves will hit the pistons.

Inspection

18 Check the timing belt for wear (especially on the thrust side of the teeth), cracks, splits, fraying and oil contamination. Renew the belt if any of these conditions are noted. **Note:** *Unless the engine has very low mileage, it's common practice to renew the timing belt every time it's removed. Don't refit the original belt unless it's in like-new condition. Never refit a belt in questionable condition.*

19 Rotate the belt tensioner pulley by hand and move it from side-to-side, checking for play and rough rotation. Renew it if roughness or play is detected. Some parts suppliers sell timing belt 'kits', which include the belt and a new tensioner – for maximum safety, a new tensioner should always be fitted with a new belt.

20 As the timing belt also drives the water pump, the pump should be inspected for signs of leakage (any powdery deposits, typically

7.14a The crankshaft sprocket timing marks are hard to see with the belt in place . . .

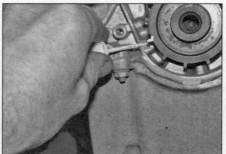

7.14b . . . so make your own marks on the sprocket and engine

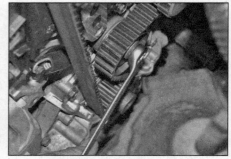

7.16a Loosen the tensioner bolt . . .

7.16b . . . then use an Allen key (or bit) to turn the tensioner anti-clockwise

7.17a Unhook the timing belt from the crankshaft sprocket . . .

7.17b . . . then remove it from the top

7.25a Fit the timing belt around the sprockets . . .

7.25b . . . then over the tensioner – note the Allen key . . .

7.25c . . . being used in the hex fitting in the tensioner flange

white or antifreeze-coloured, underneath the pump are suspicious). Since the timing belt would have to be removed again in the event of water pump failure (and a water pump which seizes might wear the timing belt), many owners renew the pump as further peace-of-mind, particularly if it is known to have completed a high mileage.

21 If there are signs of oil contamination on the belt, the belt end of the engine should be washed down and the source of the leak traced. The most likely sources are the camshaft or crankshaft oil seals. Some mechanics even renew these seals routinely when a new timing belt is being fitted on a high-mileage engine. Refer to Sections 12 and 18.

Refitting

22 Check that the timing mark on the crankshaft sprocket is still aligned with the pointer on the oil pump (or that your own marks are in alignment).

23 The camshaft sprocket should still be positioned so that the UP mark is uppermost, with the two line markings on the inner rim aligned with the cylinder head surface. It is possible that the sprocket has moved, under pressure from the valve springs. When the new belt is being fitted, the sprocket must be turned back into alignment – turn the sprocket as little as possible to achieve this, as more than a few degrees of rotation will cause piston-to-valve contact.

24 If a new belt tensioner is being fitted, fit this now as described in Section 8.

25 Fit the timing belt tightly around the crankshaft sprocket. If necessary, have an assistant turn the camshaft sprocket the few degrees required to achieve alignment, and hold it there with a spanner on the sprocket bolt while the timing belt is fitted around the sprocket teeth. Feed the belt under the water pump pulley, then over the tensioner pulley – if the old tensioner is being re-used, turn the tensioner with an Allen key **(see illustrations)**.

26 Check that the belt tensioner bolt is still only hand-tight, allowing the tensioner maximum freedom of movement to tension the belt.

27 Check that the camshaft and crankshaft timing marks are in the correct alignment. If not, and the belt is 'out' by a tooth, the belt will

have to removed again and refitted correctly before proceeding.

28 Make sure the car is out of gear (manual transmission) and that any locking tools have been removed from the starter ring gear.

29 Carefully turn the crankshaft anti-clockwise six revolutions, and check that the timing marks come back into alignment. If the crankshaft binds or seems to hit something, do not force it, as the valves may be hitting the pistons. If this happens, the belt is incorrectly fitted. If necessary, reset the engine to TDC, then remove the belt and repeat the refitting procedure.

30 If all is well, tighten the belt tensioner bolt to the specified torque. Note that the tensioner bolt is **not** intended to lock the tensioner in position – even with the bolt tight, the tensioner will move, to maintain belt tension during its service life.

31 Refit the crankshaft position sensor, and tighten its bolt to the specified torque.

32 Refit the engine side mounting bracket, together with the alternator upper mounting bolt. The mounting bolts should be hand-tight only to begin with. Tighten the front three bolts, then the two side bolts, to the specified torque.

33 Refit the alternator as described in Chapter 5A.

34 Refit the timing belt covers as described in Section 6, then refit the crankshaft pulley as described in Section 5. If the engine was set back to TDC, note that the crankshaft pulley's white timing mark should align with the pointers on the timing belt lower cover.

35 Further refitting is a reversal of removal.

8.2 Unbolt the tensioner, and unhook the spring

8 Timing belt tensioner and sprockets – removal and refitting

Timing belt tensioner

Removal

1 Remove the timing belt as described in Section 7.

2 Unscrew the tensioner mounting bolt completely, then unhook the spring from its locating stud on the engine, and remove the tensioner **(see illustration)**.

Refitting

Note: *This is the refitting procedure given by Honda if a new tensioner is being fitted. In practice, it seemed to make very little difference whether the tensioner was 'pinned' before fitting, or at what point the tensioner spring was hooked onto the engine stud.*

3 A new tensioner will be supplied with a looped pin fitted through the small holes on the tensioner and its baseplate (the other end of the pin locates in the tensioner's hex fitting) **(see illustration)**. This pin must remain fitted until the timing belt has been installed. If no pin is supplied, fit a 3 mm drill bit (or other locking pin) through the two small holes.

4 Fit the spring to the tensioner, then offer the tensioner up to the engine, and fit the mounting bolt, tightened only loosely at this stage – the tensioner must be free to move **(see illustrations)**. Do not hook the tensioner spring onto the engine yet.

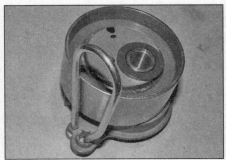

8.3 A new tensioner is fitted with a looped pin, which stays fitted until the belt is on

8.4a Fit the spring into the hole in the tensioner . . .

8.4b . . . then loosely bolt the tensioner onto the engine

8.5a Start fitting the belt around the crankshaft sprocket . . .

8.5b . . . then under the water pump and over the tensioner

8.6a Using a suitable hooked tool . . .

8.6b . . . pull the tensioner spring end over the stud on the engine

5 Fit the timing belt tightly around the crankshaft sprocket. If necessary, have an assistant turn the camshaft sprocket the few degrees required to achieve alignment, and hold it there with a spanner on the sprocket bolt while the timing belt is fitted around the sprocket teeth. Feed the belt under the water pump pulley, then over the tensioner pulley **(see illustrations)**.

6 Making sure that the belt does not slip off the tensioner pulley, hook the tensioner spring around the stud on the engine – use a suitable hooked tool, or a stiff piece of wire. Ensure that the spring end is located in the groove on the stud, and cannot slip off **(see illustrations)**.

7 Check that the camshaft and crankshaft timing marks are in the correct alignment. If not, and the belt is 'out' by a tooth, the belt will have to removed again and refitted correctly before proceeding.

8 Make sure the car is out of gear (manual transmission) and that any locking tools have been removed from the starter ring gear.

9 Carefully turn the crankshaft anti-clockwise six revolutions, and check that the timing marks come back into alignment. If the crankshaft binds or seems to hit something, do not force it, as the valves may be hitting the pistons. If this happens, the belt is incorrectly fitted. If necessary, remove the belt and repeat the refitting procedure.

10 Tighten the tensioner mounting bolt to the specified torque, then remove the locking pin or drill bit from the tensioner **(see illustrations)**.

11 Continue refitting the removed components as described in Section 7, paragraph 29 onwards.

Camshaft sprocket

12 Remove the timing belt upper cover as described in Section 6.

13 Slacken the camshaft sprocket retaining bolt, but leave it fitted hand-tight. To stop the camshaft turning, use a locking tool which fits between the sprocket spokes, which can be fabricated from two lengths of steel strip (one long, the other short) and three nuts and bolts. One nuts and bolt should form the pivot of the forked tool, with the remaining two nuts and bolts at the tips of the forks to engage with the sprocket spokes **(see illustration)**.

14 Remove the timing belt as described in Section 7.

Caution: If a sprocket holding tool is not used, and the sprocket turns significantly while its bolt is being loosened, there is a danger of valves hitting pistons.

15 Unscrew and remove the sprocket bolt, and remove the sprocket, noting that it has a locating key which sits in a notch on the camshaft.

16 If the sprocket is being removed to fit a new camshaft oil seal, unscrew the bolt and

8.10a Tighten the tensioner mounting bolt to the specified torque . . .

8.10b . . . then remove the tensioner locking pin

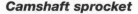

8.13 Use a home-made holding tool when loosening the sprocket bolt

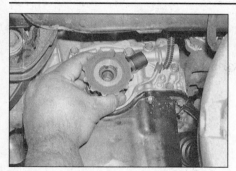

8.20a Slide off the crankshaft sprocket . . .

take off the timing belt's plastic inner cover from the cylinder head.

17 Refitting is a reversal of removal, noting the following points:

 a) *Fit the sprocket onto the camshaft, ensuring that its locating key enters the slot on the shaft.*

 b) *Fit the sprocket bolt, with oiled threads, and tighten to the specified torque. Use the sprocket-holding tool used for removal to prevent the sprocket turning.*

 c) *Refit the timing belt as described in Section 7.*

Crankshaft sprocket

18 Remove the timing belt as described in Section 7.

19 Note the alignment mark on the sprocket front face and the pointer on the oil pump – this will make aligning and refitting the sprocket easier.

20 The sprocket locates in a keyway on the

9.10a Unclip the wiring plug from its bracket . . .

9.11a Unscrew the three mounting bolts . . .

crankshaft itself, and should just slide off. Some models may have a timing belt guide plate fitted behind the sprocket, which should also be removed if access to the crankshaft oil seal is required **(see illustrations)**.

21 Refitting is a reversal of removal, noting the following points:

 a) *Where applicable, refit the belt guide plate before fitting the sprocket – note that its concave side should face inwards.*

 b) *Align the sprocket and oil pump marks, and slide the sprocket onto the keyway.*

 c) *Refit the timing belt as described in Section 7.*

9 VTEC system – description and component renewal

Description

1 The VTEC system (Variable Valve Timing and lift Electronic Control) is used on several models throughout the Honda range. In the Civic covered by this manual, only the 1.6 litre engine has a VTEC system, known as VTEC-II.

2 The differences between the non-VTEC (1.4 litre) engine and the VTEC counterparts are strictly in the components and operation of the valvetrain. All other engine components are identical.

3 The engine management computer has the ability to alter valve lift and timing through the use of different camshaft inlet valve lobes. The computer turns the system on or off, depending on sensor input.

9.10b . . . and separate the plug halves

9.11b . . . and lift off the solenoid

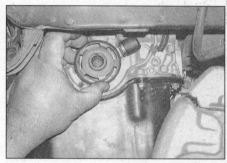

8.20b . . . and where applicable, the timing belt guide

4 The following parameters are used on both systems to determine VTEC operation:

 Engine speed (rpm).
 Vehicle speed (mph).
 Throttle position sensor output.
 Engine load measured by the manifold absolute pressure sensor.
 Coolant temperature.

5 The camshaft used in the VTEC system has different primary and secondary inlet valve lobe profiles (lift and duration specifications).

6 At low speeds, the secondary valve operates on its own camshaft lobe, which has very low lift and duration (compared to the primary valve). This limited valve operation provides good low-end torque and responsiveness.

7 When performance is needed, the secondary rocker arm is locked together (through the use of an electrically-controlled, hydraulic system) with the primary rocker arm. **Note:** *The secondary rocker arm no longer contacts its own camshaft lobe, until the system is disengaged.* When activated, both valves open to the full lift and duration of the primary camshaft lobe, increasing performance at higher engine speeds.

VTEC solenoid valve

8 Remove the air cleaner and inlet air resonator as described in Chapter 4A.

9 The solenoid valve is mounted on the back of the cylinder head, at the transmission end.

10 Unclip the solenoid valve wiring plug from its mounting bracket, then separate the plug halves **(see illustrations)**.

11 To remove the solenoid separately, unscrew the three mounting bolts and separate it from

9.11c Recover the double O-ring seal

9.12a If required, the solenoid plunger . . .

9.12b . . . and spring can be removed

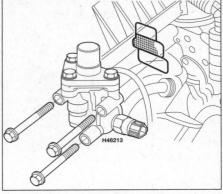

9.13a Valve housing removal details

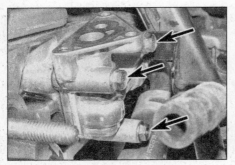

9.13b Remove the three bolts . . .

9.13c . . . and take off the valve housing

remove it with the wiring harness bracket from the engine. Anticipate a small amount of oil spillage as the valve is removed. Recover the seal/filter – a new one should be used when refitting (see illustrations).

14 Refitting is a reversal of removal, noting the following points:

a) Wipe the mating faces clean, then fit a new seal/filter.

b) Tighten the valve mounting bolts to the specified torque.

c) Check the engine oil level, and top-up if necessary (see Weekly checks).

VTEC oil pressure switch

15 Remove the air cleaner and inlet air resonator as described in Chapter 4A.

16 The pressure switch is mounted on the back of the cylinder head, at the transmission end.

17 Disconnect the switch wiring plug (see illustration). Note that access to the switch itself is hampered by a wiring support bracket, attached by two bolts to the VTEC valve housing.

18 Unclip the EVAP hose from the top of the wiring support bracket (see illustration).

19 Remove the VTEC valve housing bolt which secures the wiring support bracket, then loosen the lower bolt, and tilt the bracket to the side for access to the pressure switch (see illustrations).

20 Unscrew and remove the switch – anticipate a little oil spillage as this is done.

the valve housing. Recover the double O-ring – a new one should be used when refitting (see illustrations).

12 If required, the valve's operating plunger and spring can be extracted from the housing

for inspection and renewal (see illustrations).

13 To remove the valve housing, unscrew the three mounting bolts (note that two of these bolts also secure a wiring bracket) and

9.13d Recover the seal/filter

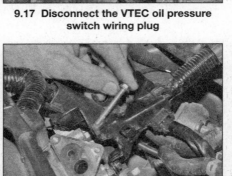

9.17 Disconnect the VTEC oil pressure switch wiring plug

9.18 Unclip the EVAP hose from the wiring support bracket

9.19a Remove the upper bolt from the wiring support bracket . . .

9.19b . . . then loosen the lower bolt, and pivot the bracket clear

Recover the O-ring seal – a new one should be used when refitting **(see illustrations)**.
21 Refitting is a reversal of removal, noting the following points:

  a) *Wipe clean the mating faces, and fit a new O-ring seal to the switch.*
  b) *Tighten the switch and solenoid valve mounting bolts to the specified torque.*
  c) *Check the engine oil level, and top-up if necessary (see Weekly checks).*

10 Rocker shaft assembly – removal, inspection and refitting

Note: *The camshaft bearing caps are removed together with the rocker arm assembly. To prevent the transmission end of the camshaft from popping up due to timing belt tension after the assembly is removed, have an assistant hold the camshaft down, then refit the bearing cap on that end to hold it in place until reassembly (assuming the timing belt remains fitted).*

Removal

1 Remove the cylinder head cover (see Section 4).
2 Completely loosen (but do not remove) all the valve adjuster screws, to remove all valve spring pressure from the rocker shaft components.
3 Set the engine to No 1 piston on TDC as described in Section 3.
4 Loosen the camshaft bearing cap bolts a quarter-turn at a time, in the **reverse** order of the tightening sequence shown later in this Section. Though the bolts must be loosened fully, it is a good idea to leave the bolts fitted, as this will help to keep the bearing caps, springs and rocker arms together.
5 If the camshaft bearing caps are removed from the assembly and they don't have numbers on them, number them before removal **(see illustration)**. Be sure to put the marks on the same ends of all the caps to prevent incorrect orientation of the caps during refitting.

9.20a Unscrew the pressure switch . . .

9.20b . . . and recover the O-ring

10.5 The camshaft bearing caps are numbered – the arrows point to the timing belt end

10.6 Remove the camshaft bearing caps, bolts and rocker arm assembly

6 Lift the rocker arm and shaft assembly from the cylinder head **(see illustration)**.
7 Extract the oil control jet from the head, using a suitable screw **(see illustration)**. Check that the jet is clear by blowing through it. A new O-ring should be used when the jet is refitted.

Inspection

8 If you wish to dismantle and inspect the rocker arm assembly, remove the retaining bolts and slip the rocker arms, springs, collars and bearing caps off the shafts. Mark the relationship of the shafts to the bearing caps and keep the components in order. They must

be reassembled in the same positions they were removed from.
Caution: On VTEC engines, it is a good idea to bundle the inlet rocker arms together with rubber bands.
9 Thoroughly clean the components and inspect them for wear and damage. Check the rocker arm faces that contact the camshaft and the rocker arm tips. Check the surfaces of the shafts that the rocker arms ride on, as well as the bearing surfaces inside the rocker arms, for scoring and excessive wear **(see illustration)**. Renew any parts that are damaged or excessively worn. Also, make sure the oil holes in the shafts are not blocked.

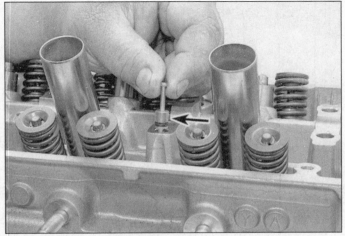

10.7 Removing the oil control jet (arrowed), using a screw

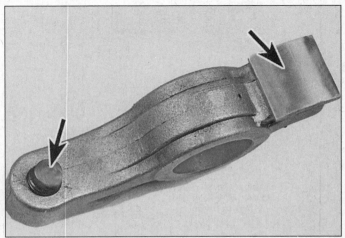

10.9 Check the contact face and adjuster tip for damage or wear

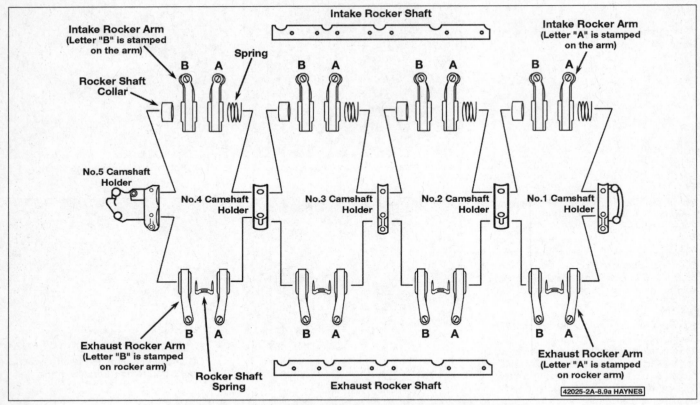

10.10a Exploded view of the rocker arms and shafts (1.4 litre engine)

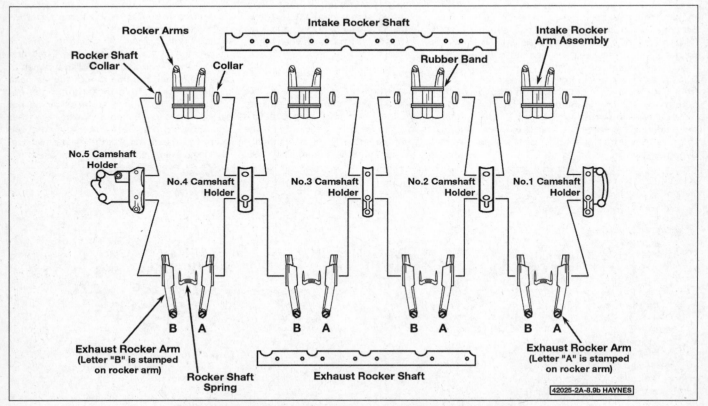

10.10b Exploded view of the rocker arms and shafts (1.6 litre engine)

Refitting

10 Lubricate all components with clean engine oil, and reassemble rocker arms onto the shafts. When refitting the rocker arms, shafts and springs, note the markings and the difference between the left- and right-hand side components **(see illustrations)**.

11 Refit the oil control jet to the head, using a new O-ring – ensure that it seats fully.

12 Coat the camshaft lobes and journals with clean engine oil. Apply suitable sealant (liquid gasket, available from Honda dealers) to the cylinder head contact surfaces of bearing caps 1 and 5, and refit the rocker arm assembly.

13 Tighten the camshaft bearing cap bolts a little at a time, in the proper sequence **(see illustration)** to the torque listed in this Chapter's Specifications.

14 The remainder of refitting is the reverse of removal. Adjust the valve clearances as described in Chapter 1A.

15 Run the engine and check for oil leaks and proper operation.

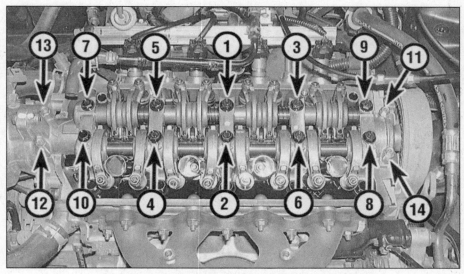

10.13 Rocker arm assembly bolt tightening sequence

---

11 Camshaft –
removal, inspection and refitting

Removal

1 If the camshaft sprocket is to be separated from the camshaft, remove it first as described in Section 8.

2 Remove the timing belt as described in Section 7.

3 Remove the rocker arm assembly (see Section 10). If the camshaft bearing caps are removed from the assembly and they don't have numbers on them, number them before removal. Be sure to put the marks on the same ends of all the caps to prevent incorrect orientation of the caps during refitting.

4 Lift out the camshaft, wipe it off with a clean rag, remove the camshaft seal and set the camshaft aside.

Inspection

5 To check camshaft endfloat:
a) *Refit the camshaft and secure it with the caps.*
b) *Mount a dial indicator on the cylinder head with the pointer resting on the camshaft nose.*
c) *Using a large screwdriver as a lever at the opposite end, move the camshaft forward-and-backward and note the dial indicator reading.*
d) *Compare the reading with the endfloat listed in this Chapter's Specifications.*
e) *If the indicated reading is excessive, either the camshaft or the cylinder head is worn. Renew parts as necessary.*

6 Check the camshaft bearing journals and caps for scoring and signs of wear. If they are worn, exchange the cylinder head with a new or rebuilt assembly.

7 Check the cam lobes for wear:
a) *Check the toe and ramp areas of each cam lobe for score marks and uneven wear. Also check for flaking and pitting.*
b) *If there's wear on the toe or the ramp, renew the camshaft, but first try to find the cause of the wear. Look for abrasive substances in the oil and inspect the oil pump and oil passages for blockage. Lobe wear is usually caused by inadequate lubrication or dirty oil.*

8 Inspect the rocker arms for wear, scoring and pitting of the contact surfaces (see Section 10).

9 If any of the conditions described above are noted, the cylinder head is probably getting insufficient lubrication or dirty oil. Make sure you track down the cause of this problem (low oil level, low oil pump capacity, clogged oil passage, etc) before refitting a new cylinder head, camshaft or rocker arm assembly.

Refitting

10 Thoroughly clean the camshaft, the bearing surfaces in the head and caps and the rocker arms. Remove all sludge and dirt. Wipe off all components with a clean, lint-free cloth.

11 Lubricate the camshaft bearing surfaces in the head and the bearing journals and lobes on the camshaft with clean engine oil.

Caution: Failure to adequately lubricate the camshaft and related components can cause serious damage to bearing and friction surfaces during the first few seconds after engine start-up, when the oil pressure is low or nonexistent.

12 Carefully lower the camshaft into position, with the keyway in the 12 o'clock position. Using an appropriate-sized driver, deep socket or section of pipe, fit a new camshaft seal with the open (spring) side facing in.

13 Refit the rocker arm assembly (see Section 10).

14 Rotate the camshaft as necessary and refit the camshaft sprocket with the UP mark stamped on the camshaft sprocket at the twelve o'clock position.

15 Where removed, refit the camshaft sprocket as described in Section 8.

16 Refit the timing belt and related components as described in Section 7.

17 The remainder of refitting is the reverse of removal.

---

12 Camshaft oil seal –
renewal

1 Remove the camshaft sprocket as described in Section 8.

2 Punch or drill two small holes opposite each other in the oil seal. Screw a self-tapping screw into each hole, and pull on the screws with pliers to extract the seal.

3 Alternatively, seals can sometimes be removed by pushing them in at the bottom – this will often have the effect of forcing the top of the seal outwards, making it easier to lever the seal out.

4 Clean the seal housing, and polish off any burrs or raised edges which may have caused the seal to fail.

5 Lightly lubricate the new seal with engine oil, then offer it into position with the seal lips facing inwards. Note that some seals have line markings across them, which are intended to align with the cylinder head top surface. Drive the seal into position, using a suitable tubular drift, such as a socket, which bears only on the hard outer edge of the seal. Take care not to damage the seal lips during fitting.

6 Refit the camshaft sprocket as described in Section 8.

13.6 Disconnect the coolant hoses from the housing

13.7 Unbolt the earth straps from the coolant housing

13 Cylinder head –
removal and refitting

Note: *Allow the engine to cool completely before beginning this procedure.*

Removal

1 Disconnect the battery negative lead, and position the lead away from the battery (also see *Disconnecting the battery*).

2 Drain the cooling system and remove the spark plugs (see Chapter 1A).

3 Remove the air cleaner and inlet air resonator as described in Chapter 4A.

4 Disconnect the accelerator cable from the throttle body as described in Chapter 4A, and remove the cable from its support brackets, noting how it is routed.

5 Also referring to Chapter 4A if necessary,

disconnect the brake servo vacuum hose, crankcase breather hose and charcoal canister (EVAP) hose from the throttle body, noting their fitted positions (label the hoses if required).

6 Release the hose clips and disconnect three of the four coolant hoses from the coolant housing at the end of the cylinder head (one of the small coolant hoses to the idle air valve need not be removed). The fitted position of each hose should be apparent when reassembling, but label the hoses if necessary **(see illustration)**.

7 Disconnect the earth straps which are fitted to the coolant housing **(see illustration)**.

8 Behind the coolant housing, unclip the hose and wiring harness from the metal coolant pipe. Remove the two mounting bolts along its length, then release the large spring-type hose clip and pull off the rubber hose at the rear. Pull the metal pipe rearwards to release it from the coolant housing – there

will be some resistance from the O-rings **(see illustrations)**.

9 Where applicable, trace the air conditioning pipe across the top of the engine, and remove the bolt from its front support bracket so that the pipe can be moved clear of the head without disconnecting it **(see illustration)**.

10 Noting their fitted positions, disconnect the wiring plugs from the following components, as applicable:
   a) *Idle air control valve (throttle body).*
   b) *Throttle position sensor (throttle body).*
   c) *Canister purge valve (rear of engine compartment).*
   d) *Engine coolant temperature sensor (coolant housing).*
   e) *Radiator fan switch (thermostat housing).*
   f) *Crankshaft position sensor (crankshaft sprocket).*
   g) *TDC sensor (timing belt upper cover).*
   h) *EGR solenoid valve (1.4 litre engine).*
   i) *VTEC solenoid valve and oil pressure switch (1.6 litre engine).*
   j) *Oil pressure switch (just above the oil filter).*

11 Noting how it is routed, release the wiring harness from the inlet manifold.

12 Remove the exhaust and inlet manifolds as described in Chapter 4A.

13 Remove the camshaft sprocket and timing belt inner cover as described in Section 8.

14 Working in the **reverse** order of the tightening sequence shown later in this Section, progressively loosen the cylinder head bolts by a quarter-turn at a time until all ten are fully loosened.

15 Lift the cylinder head off the engine, noting that two dowels are used at the front. If resistance is felt, don't prise between the head and block gasket mating surfaces – damage to the mating surfaces will result. Instead, try to rock the head free, by inserting a suitable blunt lever (such as a hammer handle) into the inlet or exhaust ports.

16 Remove the head from the engine, and set it down on a clean, flat surface – remember at all times to avoid damage to the gasket sealing surfaces.

17 Cylinder head dismantling and inspection procedures are covered in detail in Chapter 2C. Check the cylinder head for warpage, especially if the engine has been overheated following head gasket failure.

13.8a Unclip the wiring harness from the metal coolant pipe . . .

13.8b . . . then remove the mounting bolts . . .

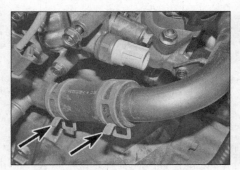

13.8c . . . release the hose clips and pull off the rubber hose at the rear . . .

13.8d . . . and pull the pipe out of the housing

13.9 Remove the air conditioning support pipe bracket bolt

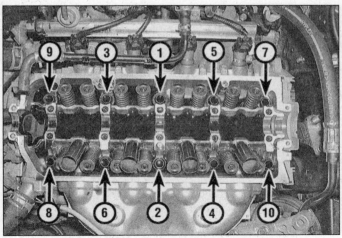

13.27 Cylinder head bolt tightening sequence

14.3a Unscrew the bolts . . .

Preparation

18 The mating surfaces of the cylinder head and block must be perfectly clean when the head is refitted.

19 Use a gasket scraper to remove all traces of carbon and old gasket material, then clean the mating surfaces with gasket remover or cellulose thinners. If there's oil on the mating surfaces when the cylinder head is fitted, the gasket may not seal correctly and leaks may develop.

20 When cleaning the engine block, fill the cylinders with clean rags to keep out debris. Use a damp rag to remove material that falls into the cylinders. Since the cylinder head and engine block are made of aluminium, aggressive scraping can cause damage. Be careful not to scratch or gouge the mating surfaces with the scraper.

21 Check the block and cylinder head mating surfaces for nicks, deep scratches and other damage. If damage is slight, it can be removed with a fine file; if it's excessive, machining may be the only alternative.

22 Use a tap of the correct size to clean the threads in the cylinder head bolt holes. Dirt, corrosion, sealant and damaged threads will affect torque readings. As far as possible, ensure that there is no water or oil in the head bolt holes in the block – if this is not either soaked out or blown out, the resulting hydraulic pressure when the bolts are fitted may crack the block.

23 Although not specifically required by Honda, it is advisable to buy a new set of cylinder head bolts for refitting. These bolts are subject to significant pressure, and if one should fail during retightening, considerable extra expense and inconvenience will be incurred. It is certainly not recommended to re-use a set of bolts more than once.

24 If new bolts are not being fitted, wire-brush the threads of the old ones thoroughly, and if available, use a die of the correct size (failing this, a nut of the right size will do) to chase the threads clean.

Refitting

25 Place a new gasket on the engine block, and locate it over the two dowels at the front. Check to see if there are any markings (such as TOP) on the gasket to indicate how it is to be fitted. Those identification marks must face up.

26 Place the cylinder head carefully onto the engine, and locate it on the two dowels. Try to disturb the gasket as little as possible.

27 Lightly oil the threads and the underside of the heads of the cylinder head bolts, then refit them. Tighten the bolts in the recommended sequence, in stages, to the torque listed in this Chapter's Specifications **(see illustration)**. Because of the critical function of cylinder head bolts, the manufacturer specifies the following conditions for tightening them:

a) *A beam-type or dial-type torque wrench is preferable to a preset (click-stop) torque wrench. If you use a preset torque wrench, tighten slowly and be careful not to overtighten the bolts.*

b) *If a bolt makes any sound while you're tightening it (creaking, clicking, etc), loosen it completely and tighten it again in the specified stages.*

28 Refit the timing belt inner cover, then refit the camshaft sprocket as described in Section 8.

29 Refit the timing belt as described in Section 7.

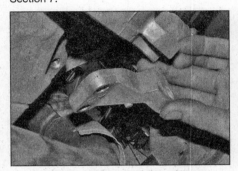

14.3b . . . and remove the stiffener brackets from the engine

30 Adjust the valve clearances as described in Chapter 1A, then refit the cylinder head cover as described in Section 4.

31 Refit the remaining parts in the reverse order of removal.

32 Be sure to refill the cooling system and check all fluid levels.

33 Run the engine until normal operating temperature is reached. Check for leaks and proper operation.

14 Sump – removal and refitting

Removal

1 Warm-up the engine, then drain the oil as described in Chapter 1A. Though not strictly necessary, it makes sense to fit a new oil filter at the same time.

2 Raise the car and support it securely on axle stands (see *Jacking and vehicle support*). Remove the bolts and take off the engine undertray.

3 Unscrew the bolts and remove the engine stiffener bracket(s) from the engine and sump **(see illustrations)**.

4 Progressively loosen and remove the nuts and bolts securing the sump to the engine block **(see illustrations)**.

14.4a The sump is secured by a combination of nuts and bolts

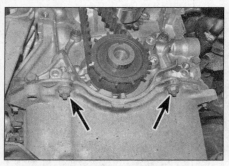

14.4b At the crankshaft pulley end, two nuts are used

14.7 Removing the sump on a 1.6 litre engine

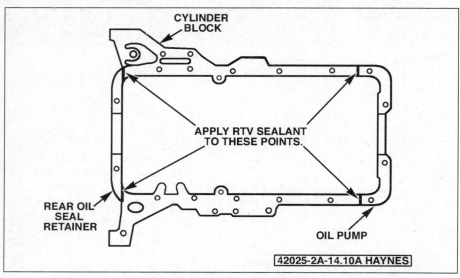

14.12 Apply sealant on the sump mating flange as shown (1.4 litre engine)

5 To make room for the sump to be removed, the exhaust front section must be lowered. Unscrew the three manifold-to-downpipe nuts and separate the joint. Trace the wiring from both of the oxygen sensors back to their wiring plugs, and disconnect – unclip the wiring from its support clips too. Unhook the exhaust front mounting rubber, and lower the exhaust onto an axle stand or similar, to prevent strain.

6 On 1.4 litre engines, tap on the sump with a soft-faced hammer to break the gasket seal, then detach the sump from the engine. Don't prise between the block and sump mating surfaces.

7 On 1.6 litre engines, break the sealant joint by striking the casting with the palm of the hand, or using a wide plastic spatula carefully inserted in the joint between the sump and cylinder block. On no account lever between the mating faces with metal tools, as this will almost certainly damage them, resulting in leaks when finished. Providing care is taken, a large screwdriver could be used in the drain hole, to prise down the sump **(see illustration)**.

Preparation

8 Using a gasket scraper, remove all traces of old gasket and/or sealant from the engine

block and the sump. Also make sure the threaded bolt holes in the block are clean.

9 Thoroughly clean the sump. On 1.4 litre engines with a steel sump, check the gasket flanges for distortion, particularly around the bolt holes. If necessary, place the pan on a wood block and use a hammer to flatten and restore the gasket surface.

10 Clean the mating surfaces on the engine block, and remove any oil residue which will prevent the new gasket from sealing properly – on 1.6 litre engines, this is essential for the sealant to bond.

14.13 On 1.6 litre engines, apply the sealant in a continuous bead

Refitting

1.4 litre engines

11 Apply a 2 mm wide bead of suitable sealant (liquid gasket, available from Honda dealers) to the top of the gasket where it curves upwards where the oil pump and the oil seal retainer mate, then fit the gasket onto the sump

12 Apply additional 2 mm wide beads of liquid sealant (4 places) to the engine block where the oil seal retainer and the oil pump meet the cylinder block **(see illustration)**. Once the sealant is applied, the sump must be fitted within five minutes, or the residue removed and fresh sealant applied.

1.6 litre engines

13 Apply a continuous 4 mm wide bead of sealant to the sump mating surface of the engine, keeping the bead to the inside of the bolt holes, and making sure the bead overlaps at the end (to give a complete seal all round) **(see illustration)**. Do not apply excess sealant, as this may end up inside the engine.

14 Once the sealant is applied, the sump must be fitted within five minutes, or the residue removed and fresh sealant applied.

All engines

15 Carefully place the sump in position, and refit the nuts and bolts finger-tight.

16 Starting with the nuts and bolts closest to the centre of the sump and working outward in a criss-cross pattern, tighten the nuts and bolts in three equal steps to the torque listed in this Chapter's Specifications. Don't overtighten them, or leakage may occur.

17 Refit the engine stiffener bracket(s) to the engine and sump, and tighten the bolts to the specified torque.

18 Wipe off any excess sealant from the sump before it dries, or trim it off carefully with a sharp knife – pulling it off by hand may remove it completely from the joint, leading to leaks.

19 Refit the exhaust front section, using a new gasket (refer to Chapter 4A if necessary). Ensure that the oxygen sensor wiring is reconnected properly, and that the wiring is refitted to its clips – this is essential, to keep it away from the hot exhaust.

20 Wait at least 30 minutes (or the time stated on the sealant packaging) before refilling the engine with oil as described in Chapter 1A, then start the engine and check for oil leaks.

15 Oil pump – removal, inspection and refitting

Removal

1 Remove the timing belt as described in Section 7.

2 Remove the crankshaft sprocket as described in Section 8.

3 Remove the sump as described in Section 14.

15.4 Oil pick-up tube and strainer nuts and bolts

15.5 Oil pump mounting bolts

4 Unscrew two nuts and two bolts, and remove the oil pick-up tube and strainer from the pump housing and the main bearing cap bridge **(see illustration)**. Recover the pick-up tube flange gasket – a new one will be needed for refitting.

5 Remove the four mounting bolts from the oil pump housing, and separate the assembly from the engine **(see illustration)**. Note that the oil pump is located on two dowels, and sealant is used as a gasket. Do not prise between the pump mating faces to remove it, unless absolutely necessary – if the mating faces get damaged, they will not seal properly.

Inspection

6 Undo the screws and dismantle the oil pump. You may need to use an impact screwdriver to loosen the pump inner cover screws without stripping the heads.

7 Check the oil pump rotor-to-cover-clearance, tooth tip clearance and rotor-to-body clearance. Compare your measurements to the figures listed in the Specifications. Renew the pump if any of the measurements exceed the specified limits.

8 Remove the pressure relief valve bolt and extract the spring and pressure relief valve plunger from the pump housing. Check the spring for distortion and the relief valve plunger for scoring. Renew parts as necessary.

9 Refit the pump rotors. Pack the spaces between the rotors with petroleum jelly (this will prime the pump).

10 Apply thread-locking compound to the pump inner cover screws, refit the cover and tighten the screws to the torque listed in this Chapter's Specifications. Refit the oil pressure relief valve and spring assembly, then refit the plug, and tighten to the specified torque.

Refitting

11 Apply a thin coat of sealant (liquid gasket, available from Honda dealers) to the pump housing-to-block sealing surface, and fit a new O-ring in the pump housing.

12 Refit the pump housing to the engine block, locating it over the two dowels, and tighten the five mounting bolts to the torque listed in this Chapter's Specifications.

13 Refit the oil pick-up tube and strainer, using a new tube flange gasket. Tighten the two nuts and bolts to the torque listed in this Chapter's Specifications.

14 Refit the sump (see Section 14).

15 Fit a new crankshaft oil seal as described in Section 18.

16 The remainder of refitting is the reverse of removal. Add the specified type and quantity of oil as described in Chapter 1A, then start the engine and check for leaks.

16 Oil pressure switch –
removal and refitting

1 The oil pressure switch is a vital early warning of low oil pressure. The switch operates the oil warning light on the instrument panel – the light should come on with the ignition, and go out almost immediately when the engine starts.

2 If the light does not come on, there could be a fault on the instrument panel, the switch wiring, or the switch itself. If the light does not go out, low oil level, worn oil pump (or sump

pick-up blocked), blocked oil filter, or worn main bearings could be to blame – or again, the switch may be faulty.

3 If the light comes on while driving, the best advice is to turn the engine off immediately, and not to drive the car until the problem has been investigated – ignoring the light could mean expensive engine damage.

Removal

4 Firmly apply the handbrake, then jack up the front of the car and support it securely on axle stands (see *Jacking and vehicle support*).

5 The oil pressure switch is mounted directly above the oil filter **(see illustration)**. Place a container below the oil filter as a precaution against oil spillage, then unscrew and remove the filter for access to the switch. A new filter will not be needed when refitting unless the old one is damaged.

6 Trace the wiring from the switch across to the wiring plug, which is clipped onto a bracket to the right. Unclip the plug and disconnect it.

7 Pull back the rubber boot, then slowly unscrew the switch and remove it – if a ring spanner is used, this has to be passed over the switch plug, and along the wiring **(see illustration)**.

8 Clean the switch threads and the switch location. If the same switch is being refitted, clean the switch threads with a wire brush.

16.5 Oil pressure switch – seen from below, with oil filter removed

16.7 Pull back the boot, and unscrew the switch

16.9 When refitting the switch, apply RTV sealant to the threads

Refitting

9 Apply a little liquid gasket (RTV sealant) to the switch threads, then fit the switch and tighten it to the specified torque **(see illustration)**. Fit the oil filter.

10 Reconnect the wiring plug, then refit the undertray and lower the car to the ground.

11 Check the engine oil level, as described in *Weekly checks*.

17 Flywheel/driveplate – removal and refitting

Removal

1 Raise the car and support it securely on axle stands (see *Jacking and vehicle support*), then refer to the appropriate Part of Chapter 7 and remove the transmission.

2 On manual transmission models, remove the pressure plate and clutch disc (see Chapter 6) Now is a good time to check/renew the clutch components and pilot bearing.

3 Remove the bolts that secure the flywheel/driveplate to the crankshaft – note that they have bi-hex heads, but any normal splined socket should undo them **(see illustration)**. To stop the crankshaft turning, insert a flat-bladed screwdriver through one of the starter motor bolt holes, into the ring gear teeth (manual transmission models), or insert a long punch through one of the holes in the driveplate and allow it to rest against a projection on the engine block (automatic transmission models).

4 Remove the flywheel/driveplate from the crankshaft. Since the flywheel is heavy, be sure to support it while removing the last bolt.

5 Clean the flywheel to remove grease and oil. Inspect the surface for cracks, rivet grooves, burned areas and score marks. Light scoring can be removed with emery cloth. Check for cracked and broken ring gear teeth. Lay the flywheel on a flat surface and use a straight-edge to check for warpage.

6 Clean and inspect the mating surfaces of the flywheel/driveplate and the crankshaft. If the oil seal is leaking, renew it before refitting the flywheel/driveplate (see Section 18).

7 Wire-brush the bolt threads, and check their condition before re-using them. These bolts are subject to significant stress, and while not specifically required by Honda, it is advisable to renew flywheel/driveplate bolts whenever they are disturbed.

Refitting

8 Position the flywheel/driveplate against the crankshaft. Note that some engines have an alignment dowel or staggered bolt holes to ensure correct refitting. Before refitting the bolts, apply thread-locking compound to the threads.

9 Prevent the flywheel/driveplate from turning by using one of the methods described in paragraph 3. Using a diagonal pattern, tighten the bolts to the specified torque.

10 The remainder of refitting is the reverse of the removal procedure.

18 Crankshaft oil seals – renewal

Timing belt end

1 Remove the timing belt as described in Section 7.

2 Remove the crankshaft sprocket and the belt inner guide (where fitted) as described in Section 8.

3 Carefully prise the seal out of the oil pump housing with a seal removal tool or a screwdriver **(see illustration)**. Sometimes, pushing the top of the seal inwards will force the bottom out, making it easier to lever out. Don't scratch the seal bore or damage the

17.3 Unscrew the six flywheel bolts

crankshaft in the process (if the crankshaft is damaged, the new seal will end up leaking).

4 Clean the bore in the oil pump housing, and coat the outer edge of the new seal with engine oil or multi-purpose grease.

5 Using a socket with an outside diameter slightly smaller than the outside diameter of the seal, carefully drive the seal into place with a hammer, with the seal spring towards the engine **(see illustration)**. If a socket is not available, a short section of a large-diameter pipe will work.

6 Refit the belt inner guide (where applicable) with its concave side facing inwards, and the crankshaft sprocket.

7 Refit the timing belt as described in Section 7.

8 Start the engine and check for leaks.

Transmission end

Note: Renewal of the oil seal and retainer as a unit are covered in Chapter 2C.

9 Remove the flywheel/driveplate (see Section 17).

10 The seal can be renewed without removing the sump or seal retainer. Use a screwdriver and a rag to carefully pry the seal out of the housing **(see illustration)**. Use the rag to be sure no nicks are made in the crankshaft seal surface.

11 Apply a film of clean oil to the crankshaft seal journal and the lip of the new seal, and carefully tap the seal into place. The lip is stiff, so carefully work it onto the seal journal of the crankshaft with a smooth object like the end of a socket extension **(see illustration)**. Tap the seal into the retainer with a seal driver. If

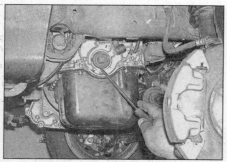

18.3 Carefully prise the oil seal out with a removal tool or screwdriver

18.5 Drive in a new seal with a socket the same diameter as the seal

18.10 Prise out the oil seal with a removal tool or screwdriver

a seal driver isn't available, a large socket or piece of pipe, with an outside diameter slightly smaller than that of the seal, can be used. Don't rush it, or you may damage the seal.

12 The seal's fitted depth in the housing is important – this is specified at the start of this Chapter. The new seal must not be driven in past this measurement – check using a straight-edge and feeler blades.

13 The remaining steps are the reverse of removal.

14 Start the engine and check for oil leaks.

19 Engine mountings
– inspection and renewal

Inspection

1 If improved access is required, raise the front of the car and support it securely on axle stands. Where necessary, undo the retaining bolts and remove the undertray from beneath the engine/transmission.

2 Check the mounting rubber to see if it is cracked, hardened or separated from the metal at any point; renew the mounting if any such damage or deterioration is evident.

3 Check that all the mountings' fasteners are securely tightened; use a torque wrench to check if possible.

4 Using a large screwdriver or a pry bar, check for wear in the mounting by carefully levering against it to check for freeplay; where this is not possible, enlist the aid of an assistant to move the engine/transmission

18.11 Working the seal over the journal with a socket extension bar

back-and-forth, or from side-to-side, while you watch the mounting. While some freeplay is to be expected even from new components, excessive wear should be obvious. If excessive freeplay is found, check first that the fasteners are correctly secured, then renew any worn components as described below.

Renewal

Note: *Before slackening any of the engine mounting bolts/nuts, the relative positions of the mountings to their various brackets should be marked to ensure correct alignment upon refitting.*

Left-hand upper bracket

5 First support the weight of the engine under the sump, using a trolley jack with a block of wood placed on its head.

6 Unscrew the three nuts securing the left-hand mounting upper bracket, and lift the bracket off the studs **(see illustrations)**.

7 Refitting is a reversal of removal. Tighten the nuts to the specified torque.

Left-hand lower mounting

8 Remove the upper mounting bracket as described previously in this Section.

9 The lower half of the mounting is secured to the inner wing by three bolts – remove these, and lift off the lower mounting **(see illustration)**. Check the rubber section for signs of perishing, cracks, or deterioration of the metal-to-rubber bonding.

10 Refitting is a reversal of removal. Tighten the bolts to the specified torque.

Left-hand side bracket

11 Remove the upper mounting bracket as described previously in this Section.

12 Remove the alternator as described in Chapter 5A – the alternator upper mounting bolt passes through the engine left-hand mounting side bracket, but note that the bolt cannot be withdrawn with the alternator fitted, as it hits the inner wing.

13 The side mounting bracket is secured with five bolts – two from the side, and three from the front. Remove these bolts, and withdraw the side mounting bracket **(see illustrations)**. Recover the alternator upper mounting bolt – note that this bolt will have to be refitted with the bracket.

14 Refitting is a reversal of removal. Refit the engine side mounting bracket (and alternator upper bolt), with all bolts fitted hand-tight only to begin with. Tighten the front three bolts, then the two side bolts, to the specified torque.

19.6a With the engine supported, unscrew the three nuts . . .

19.6b . . . and lift off the left-hand mounting upper bracket

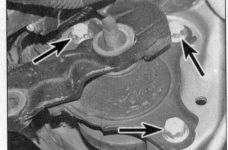

19.9 Left-hand lower mounting-to-wing bolts

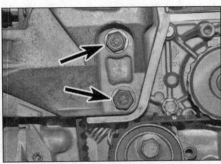

19.13a The side bracket has two bolts on the side . . .

19.13b . . . and these three in front

19.13c Removing the side mounting bracket

19.18 Removing the through-bolt and 'captive' nut from the engine front mounting

19.19a Unscrew the three bolts . . .

19.19b . . . and take off the front mounting

19.23 Removing the rear mounting through-bolt, with damper weight

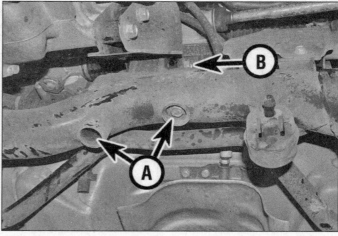

19.24a Two of the rear mounting-to-subframe bolts (A) – also note through-bolt (B)

15 Refit the alternator as described in Chapter 5A, and the upper bracket as described previously in this Section.

Front mounting

16 Firmly apply the handbrake, then jack up the front of the car and support it on axle stands.

17 Support the weight of the engine/transmission under the sump using a trolley jack with a block of wood placed on its head – this is just to relieve the pressure on the through-bolt. Removing the front mounting will only allow the engine to move on its remaining mountings, so providing they are in sound

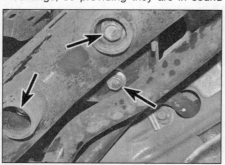

19.24b Showing the three rear mounting-to-subframe bolts

condition, removing the front mounting will not leave the engine dangerously unsupported.

18 Unscrew the through-bolt from the front mounting – note that the nut is effectively 'captive', as it has a locating lug on its base (see illustration).

19 Separate the mounting from the bracket on the subframe. If necessary, remove the three bolts and take off the mounting from the front of the engine (see illustrations).

20 Refitting is a reversal of removal. Tighten all nuts and bolts to their specified torques.

Rear mounting

21 Firmly apply the handbrake, then jack

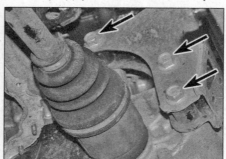

19.25 Rear mounting bracket-to-transmission bolts

up the front of the car and support it on axle stands.

22 Support the weight of the engine/transmission under the sump using a trolley jack with a block of wood placed on its head. Removing the front mounting will only allow the engine to move on its remaining mountings, so providing they are in sound condition, removing the front mounting will not leave the engine dangerously unsupported.

23 Working from below, unscrew and remove the mounting through-bolt, noting that it has a damper weight attached (see illustration).

24 If required, the lower part of the mounting can be unbolted from the subframe – there are three bolts in all, and they are of different lengths (see illustrations).

25 Similarly, there are three bolts securing the mounting bracket to the transmission (see illustration).

26 Refitting is a reversal of removal. Tighten all nuts and bolts to their specified torques.

Right-hand mounting

27 Remove the inlet air resonator and air inlet duct as described in Chapter 4A.

28 Remove the battery and its tray as described in Chapter 5A.

29 Support the weight of the transmission using a trolley jack with a block of wood placed on its head.

19.30a Right-hand mounting upper nuts and bolt, and through-bolt

19.30b Removing the right-hand mounting through-bolt

30 Unscrew and remove the mounting through-bolt, then lower the transmission slightly on the jack, to separate the mounting **(see illustrations)**.

31 To remove the transmission bracket, unscrew the two mounting nuts and single bolt on top of the transmission **(see illustration)**.

32 If required, the other part of the mounting can be unbolted from the inner wing/chassis leg **(see illustration)**.

33 Refitting is a reversal of removal. Tighten all nuts and bolts to their specified torques.

19.31 Removing the right-hand mounting upper bracket

19.32 Right-hand mounting-to-inner wing bolts

Notes

Chapter 2 Part B:
Diesel engine in-car repair procedures

Contents

Degrees of difficulty

Easy, suitable for novice with little experience 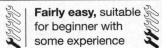	**Fairly easy,** suitable for beginner with some experience	**Fairly difficult,** suitable for competent DIY mechanic	**Difficult,** suitable for experienced DIY mechanic	**Very difficult,** suitable for expert DIY or professional

Specifications

General

Engine type	Four-cylinder, in-line, water-cooled. Belt-driven double overhead camshaft, 16 valves
Manufacturer's engine code	4EE2
Bore	79.0 mm
Stroke	86.0 mm
Capacity	1686 cc
Firing order	1-3-4-2 (No 1 cylinder at timing belt end)
Direction of crankshaft rotation	Clockwise (viewed from timing belt end of engine)
Compression ratio	18.4:1

Compression pressures

Nominal	28.6 bar (415 psi)
Minimum	25.5 bar (370 psi)
Maximum difference between any two cylinders	1.5 bar (22 psi)

Valve clearances

Engine cold (inlet and exhaust)	0.40 ± 0.05 mm

Camshaft

Endfloat	N/A
Maximum permissible radial run-out	0.05 mm

Lubrication system

Oil pump type	Rotor-type, driven by timing belt	
Minimum oil pressure at idle speed, engine hot	1.27 bar (18 psi)	
Oil pump clearances:	**Standard**	**Service limit**
Outer rotor-to-body clearance	0.24 to 0.36 mm	0.40 mm
Inner-to-outer rotor clearance	0.13 to 0.15 mm	0.20 mm
Rotor endfloat	0.035 to 0.100 mm	0.150 mm

Torque wrench settings

	Nm	lbf ft
Alternator mounting bracket-to-engine bolts:		
M10 bolts	48	35
M14 bolts	68	50
Baffle plate bolts	19	14
Big-end bearing cap nuts*:		
Stage 1	25	18
Stage 2	Angle-tighten a further 100°	
Camshaft bearing cap nuts/bolts:		
M8 size	22	16
M10 size	43	32
Camshaft housing bolts	22	16
Camshaft sprocket	64	47
Crankshaft oil seal housing bolts	10	7
Crankshaft pulley bolts	17	13
Crankshaft sensor plate bolts	12	9
Crankshaft sprocket bolt*	196	145
Cylinder head bolts*:		
Stage 1	40	30
Stage 2	Angle-tighten a further 60°	
Stage 3	Angle-tighten a further 60°	
Cylinder head cover bolts	10	7
Dipstick tube upper bolt to engine	50	37
EGR valve to manifold	25	18
Engine-to-transmission bolts:		
M10 bolts	40	30
M12 bolts	60	44
Engine/transmission mountings:		
Front mounting:		
Bracket-to-engine bolts	91	67
Through-bolt	64	47
Left-hand mounting:		
Mounting-to-transmission nuts, bolt and through-bolt	54	40
Rear mounting:		
Bracket-to-transmission bolts	69	51
Mounting-to-subframe bolts	59	44
Right-hand mounting:		
Bracket-to-engine bolts	17	13
Upper bracket mounting nuts	54	40
Flywheel bolts*:		
Stage 1	29	21
Stage 2	Angle-tighten a further 60°	
Front subframe bolts:		
M10 bolts	59	44
M14 bolts*	103	76
Fuel pump sprocket nut	69	51
Main bearing cap bolts*	88	65
Oil filter housing centre bolt	110	81
Oil filter housing cover	25	18
Oil pressure relief valve bolt	30	22
Oil pressure switch	20	15
Oil pump cover retaining bolts	10	7
Oil pump pick-up/strainer bolts	19	14
Oil pump sprocket nut	44	32
Roadwheel nuts	108	80
Sump bolts:		
Main casting-to-block/transmission bolts	10	7
Sump pan-to-main casting bolts	10	7
Drain plug	78	58
Thermostat housing to cylinder head	24	18
Thermostat housing cover	24	18
Timing belt idler pulley bolt	80	59
Timing belt tensioner bolt	49	36
Water pump pulley bolts	10	7

* Use a new nut/bolt

1 General information

This Part of Chapter 2 describes those repair procedures that can reasonably be carried out on the diesel engine while it remains in the car. If the engine has been removed from the car and is being dismantled as described in Part C, any preliminary dismantling procedures can be ignored.

Note that, while it may be possible physically to overhaul items such as the piston/connecting rod assemblies while the engine is in the car, such tasks are not normally carried out as separate operations. Usually, several additional procedures (not to mention the cleaning of components and of oilways) have to be carried out. For this reason, all such tasks are classed as major overhaul procedures, and are described in Part C of this Chapter.

Part C describes the removal of the engine/transmission unit from the car, and the full overhaul procedures that can then be carried out.

Engine description

The diesel engine is of the sixteen-valve, in-line four-cylinder, double overhead camshaft (DOHC) type, mounted transversely at the front of the car with the transmission attached to its left-hand end. The engine is actually of Isuzu origin, and is also used in several Vauxhall models.

The crankshaft runs in five main bearings. Thrustwashers are fitted to No 2 main bearing shell (upper half) to control crankshaft endfloat.

The connecting rods rotate on horizontally-split bearing shells at their big-ends. The pistons are attached to the connecting rods by gudgeon pins, which are a sliding fit in the connecting rod small-end eyes and retained by circlips. The aluminium-alloy pistons are fitted with three piston rings – two compression rings and an oil control ring.

The cylinder block is made of cast iron and the cylinder bores are an integral part of the block. On this type of engine, the cylinder bores are sometimes referred to as having 'dry liners'.

The inlet and exhaust valves are each closed by coil springs, and operate in guides pressed into the cylinder head.

The inlet camshaft is driven by the crankshaft via a timing belt, and rotates directly in the camshaft housing. The exhaust camshaft is driven by the inlet camshaft, via a spur gear. The camshafts operate the valves via followers, which are situated directly below the camshafts. Valve clearances are adjusted using shims which are fitted between the camshafts and followers.

Lubrication is by means of an oil pump, which is also driven by the timing belt. It draws oil through a strainer located in the sump, and then forces it through an externally-mounted filter into galleries in the cylinder block/crankcase. From there, the oil is distributed to the crankshaft (main bearings) and camshaft. The big-end bearings are supplied with oil via internal drillings in the crankshaft, while the camshaft bearings also receive a pressurised supply. The camshaft lobes and valves are lubricated by splash, as are all other engine components. An oil cooler is fitted to keep the oil temperature stable under arduous operating conditions.

Operations with engine in car

The following work can be carried out with the engine in the car:
a) *Compression pressure testing.*
b) *Cylinder head cover – removal and refitting.*
c) *Timing belt cover – removal and refitting.*
d) *Timing belt – removal and refitting.*
e) *Timing belt tensioner and sprockets – removal and refitting.*
f) *Valve clearances – checking and adjustment.*
g) *Camshaft and followers – removal, inspection and refitting.*
h) *Cylinder head – removal and refitting.*
i) *Connecting rods and pistons – removal and refitting.**
j) *Sump – removal and refitting.*
k) *Oil pump – removal, overhaul and refitting.*
l) *Oil cooler – removal and refitting.*
m) *Crankshaft oil seals – renewal.*
n) *Engine/transmission mountings – inspection and renewal.*
o) *Flywheel – removal, inspection and refitting.*
p) *Camshaft housing – removal and refitting.*
* *Although the operation marked with an asterisk can be carried out with the engine in the car after removal of the sump, it is better for the engine to be removed, in the interests of cleanliness and improved access. For this reason, the procedure is described in Chapter 2C.*

2 Compression test – description and interpretation

Compression test

Note: *A compression tester specifically designed for diesel engines must be used for this test.*

1 When engine performance is down, or if misfiring occurs which cannot be attributed to the fuel system, a compression test can provide diagnostic clues as to the engine's condition. If the test is performed regularly, it can give warning of trouble before any other symptoms become apparent.

2 A compression tester specifically intended for diesel engines must be used, because of the higher pressures involved. The tester is connected to an adapter which screws into the glow plug or injector hole. On these models, an adapter suitable for use in the glow plug holes will be required, due to the design of the injectors. It is unlikely to be worthwhile buying such a tester for occasional use, but it may be possible to borrow or hire one – if not, have the test performed by a garage.

3 Unless specific instructions to the contrary are supplied with the tester, observe the following points:
a) *The battery must be in a good state of charge, the air filter must be clean, and the engine should be at normal operating temperature.*
b) *All the glow plugs should be removed before starting the test (see Chapter 5A).*
c) *Disconnect the four injector wiring plugs to prevent the engine from running or fuel from being discharged.*

4 There is no need to hold the accelerator pedal down during the test, because the diesel engine air inlet is not throttled.

5 Crank the engine on the starter motor; after one or two revolutions, the compression pressure should build-up to a maximum figure, and then stabilise. Record the highest reading obtained.

6 Repeat the test on the remaining cylinders, recording the pressure in each.

7 All cylinders should produce very similar pressures; any difference greater than that specified indicates the existence of a fault. Note that the compression should build-up quickly in a healthy engine; low compression on the first stroke, followed by gradually-increasing pressure on successive strokes, indicates worn piston rings. A low compression reading on the first stroke, which does not build-up during successive strokes, indicates leaking valves or a blown head gasket (a cracked head could also be the cause). Deposits on the undersides of the valve heads can also cause low compression.
Note: *The cause of poor compression is less easy to establish on a diesel engine than on a petrol one. The effect of introducing oil into the cylinders ('wet' testing) is not conclusive, because there is a risk that the oil will sit in the recess on the piston crown instead of passing to the rings.*

8 On completion of the test, reconnect the fuel pump wiring connector, then refit the glow plugs as described in Chapter 5A.

Leakdown test

9 A leakdown test measures the rate at which compressed air fed into the cylinder is lost. It is an alternative to a compression test, and in many ways it is better, since the escaping air provides easy identification of where pressure loss is occurring (piston rings, valves or head gasket).

10 The equipment needed for leakdown testing is unlikely to be available to the home mechanic. If poor compression is suspected, have the test performed by a suitably-equipped garage.

3.5 Align the crankshaft pulley timing mark with the pointer on the oil pump cover

3.7a The camshaft sprocket can be locked using a 6 mm bolt . . .

3.7b . . . and the fuel pump sprocket by an 8 mm bolt

3 Top dead centre (TDC) for No 1 piston – locating

Note: *If the engine is to be locked in position with No 1 piston at TDC on its compression stroke, then a M6 and M8 bolt will be required.*

1 In its travel up and down its cylinder bore, Top Dead Centre (TDC) is the highest point that each piston reaches as the crankshaft rotates. While each piston reaches TDC both at the top of the compression stroke and again at the top of the exhaust stroke, for the purpose of timing the engine, TDC refers to the piston position (usually number 1) at the top of its compression stroke.

2 Number 1 piston (and cylinder) is at the right-hand (timing belt) end of the engine, and its TDC position is located as follows. Note

that the crankshaft rotates clockwise when viewed from the right-hand side of the car.

3 Disconnect the battery negative terminal. **Note:** *Before disconnecting the battery, refer to Disconnecting the battery in the reference section at the rear of this manual.* To improve access to the crankshaft pulley, apply the handbrake, then loosen the right-hand front wheel nuts, jack up the front of the car and support it on axle stands (see *Jacking and vehicle support*). Remove the right-hand front wheel and where necessary, undo the retaining bolts and remove the undertray from beneath the engine/transmission.

4 Remove the timing belt upper cover as described in Section 6.

5 Using a socket and extension bar on the crankshaft sprocket bolt, rotate the crankshaft until the notch on the crankshaft pulley rim is aligned with the pointer on the base of the oil pump cover **(see illustration)**. In this position,

the alignment notch on the crankshaft sprocket will be in the vertical position. Once the mark is correctly aligned, No 1 and 4 pistons are at TDC.

6 To determine which piston is at TDC on its compression stroke, check the position of the timing holes in the camshaft and fuel pump sprockets. When No 1 piston is at TDC on its compression stroke, both sprocket holes will be aligned with the threaded holes in the cylinder head/block, and both exhaust camshaft lobes for cylinder No 1 are pointing upwards if viewed through the oil filler hole. If the timing holes are 180° out of alignment then No 4 cylinder is at TDC on its compression stroke; rotate the crankshaft through a further complete turn (360°) to bring No 1 cylinder to TDC on its compression stroke.

7 With No 1 piston at TDC on its compression stroke, if necessary the camshaft and fuel pump sprockets can be locked in position. Secure the camshaft sprocket in position by screwing a M6 bolt into the hole in the cylinder head and lock the fuel pump sprocket in position by screwing a M8 bolt into the cylinder block **(see illustrations)**.

4 Cylinder head cover – removal and refitting

Removal

1 Remove the engine top cover, which is secured by four bolts **(see illustration)**.

2 Unscrew the three bolts securing the injector wiring harness, then disconnect the injector wiring plugs, labelling the plugs if necessary to ensure correct refitting **(see illustration)**.

3 Remove the three bolts securing the injector fuel return pipe to the engine.

4 Pull out the securing clips from the four return pipe connections to the injectors, then lift off the return 'rail' from the injectors by pulling squarely upwards **(see illustration)**. Recover the O-ring seal from each injector – new seals should be used when refitting.

5 Remove the injector pipes as described in Chapter 4B.

6 Noting which way round they are fitted, unscrew the two bolts securing each of the four injector pipe seal plates, and remove

4.1 Removing the engine top cover

4.2 Remove the three injector harness bracket bolts

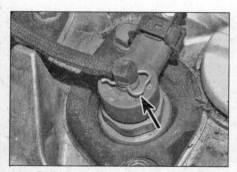

4.4 Pull out the fuel return pipe securing clips

4.6 Injector pipe seal plate bolts

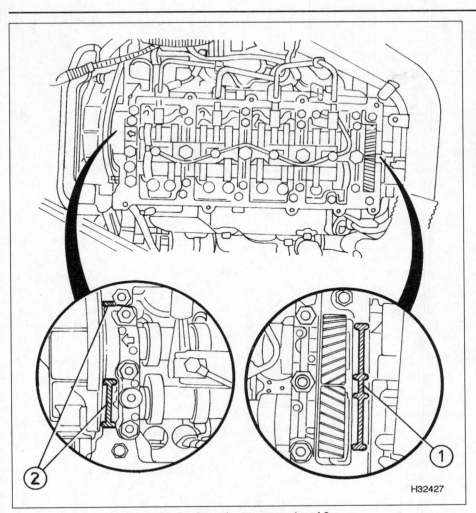

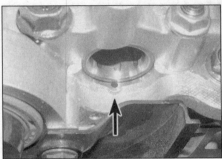

4.9b Ensure the borehole is not covered in sealant

4.11 The injector rear seals are marked 'upper' and 'outside'

4.9a Apply sealant to areas 1 and 2

them from the rear of the cylinder head cover **(see illustration)**. Similarly, remove the four injector seal plates from the top of the cover.

7 Release the hose clip, and disconnect the breather hose at the front of the cover. Unscrew the ten cover bolts and lift off the cover, noting that sealant is used at each end, which may cause it to stick initially.

Refitting

8 Ensure the cover and cylinder head surfaces are clean and dry, then fit the seal to the cover groove. Check the condition of the O-ring seal on the underside of the cover and renew if necessary.

9 Apply sealant (liquid gasket) to the mating surfaces as shown. Ensure that the oil borehole at the right-hand end of the exhaust camshaft is not covered in sealant **(see illustrations)**.

10 Carefully lower the cover into position, ensuring the seal remains correctly seated. Refit the cylinder head cover retaining bolts and tighten them in a diagonal sequence to the specified torque, starting in the centre and working outwards.

11 The remainder of the reassembly procedure is a reversal of removal, noting the following points:

a) *Ensure the injector wiring plugs and return pipes are refitted correctly and securely.*

b) *The injector rear seals are marked 'upper' and 'outside'. Fit the seals and make sure that the centre of the seal is pushed over the injector taper **(see illustration)**. The injector top seals are similarly marked.*

c) *Refit the injector pipes and bleed the fuel system as described in Chapter 4B.*

d) *On completion, start the engine and check for oil and fuel leaks.*

5 Crankshaft pulley – removal and refitting

Removal

1 Remove the auxiliary drivebelt as described in Chapter 1B.

2 Slacken and remove the four small retaining bolts securing the pulley to the crankshaft sprocket and remove the pulley from the engine **(see illustration)**. Prevent crankshaft rotation by engaging a gear – with the handbrake applied, this should be enough to hold the pulley.

Refitting

3 Refit the pulley to the crankshaft sprocket, aligning the pulley hole with the sprocket locating pin. Refit the pulley retaining bolts, tightening them to the specified torque.

4 Refit the auxiliary drivebelt as described in Chapter 1B.

5 Refit the engine undertray and roadwheel, then lower the car to the ground and tighten the wheel nuts to the specified torque.

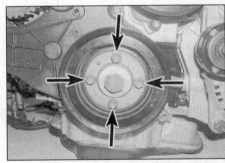

5.2 Remove the four small bolts securing the crankshaft pulley

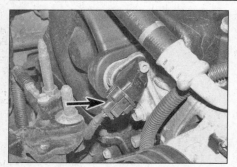

6.6 Disconnect the camshaft position sensor at the front of the cover

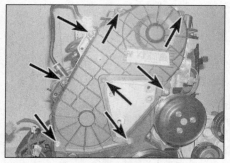

6.9 Remove the eight bolts from the timing belt upper cover

6.13 Timing belt lower cover bolts

6.14a Withdraw the adapter plate from the engine

6.14b Temporarily refit the timing belt tensioner lower bolt

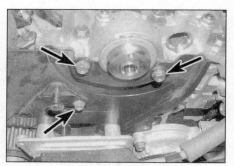

6.18 Timing belt rear cover bolts

6 Timing belt covers – removal and refitting

Removal

Upper cover

1 Honda recommend removing the water pump pulley and auxiliary drivebelt as part of the upper cover removal process, but we found this to be unnecessary. However, the drivebelt would have to be removed anyway for access to the timing belt. If the water pump pulley is to be removed, loosen the three pulley bolts before the drivebelt is removed as described in Chapter 1B.

2 The engine right-hand mounting must be removed. First support the weight of the engine under the sump, using a trolley jack with a block of wood placed on its head.

3 Unscrew the small bolt securing the earth strap to the engine right-hand mounting, and move the strap clear.

4 Unscrew the three nuts securing the right-hand mounting upper bracket, and lift the bracket off the studs.

5 Unscrew the three bolts securing the right-hand mounting lower (side) bracket to the 'triangular' adapter plate on the engine – note that the lowest of the three bolts is shorter than the other two. Withdraw the bracket from the engine.

6 Disconnect the wiring plug from the camshaft position sensor, located at the front of the upper cover **(see illustration)**.

7 Unclip the wiring harness from the front of the cover, noting how it locates over the front stud/bolt for the camshaft position sensor wiring harness.

8 Remove the front stud/bolt and the rear bolt securing the camshaft position sensor wiring harness, and move it clear of the upper cover.

9 Remove the eight upper cover retaining bolts and withdraw the cover, noting how it fits around the camshaft position sensor. The cover bolts are of different lengths, with the four shorter bolts uppermost and to the rear **(see illustration)**.

Lower cover

10 With reference to Chapter 1B, remove the auxiliary drivebelt.

11 Remove the upper cover as described previously in this Section.

12 With reference to Section 5, remove the crankshaft pulley.

13 Undo the three retaining bolts, and remove the lower cover from the oil pump housing **(see illustration)**.

14 Manoeuvre the 'triangular' adapter plate from the engine, noting how it fits. Temporarily refit the bolt retaining the timing belt tensioner pulley bracket **(see illustrations)**.

Rear (inner) cover

15 Remove timing belt as described in Section 7.

16 With reference to Section 8, remove the timing belt tension and guide rollers, camshaft sprocket and fuel pump sprocket.

17 Detach the tensioner spring retainer.

18 Undo the three retaining bolts, and remove the timing belt rear cover **(see illustration)**.

Refitting

19 Refitting is the reverse of removal, ensuring all retaining bolts/nuts are tightened securely.

7 Timing belt – removal, inspection and refitting

Removal

1 Position No 1 cylinder at TDC on its compression stroke as described in Section 3. Lock the camshaft and fuel pump sprockets in position by screwing the bolts into the threaded holes in the cylinder head/block.

2 Remove the crankshaft pulley as described in Section 5.

3 Unbolt and remove the timing belt upper and lower covers with reference to Section 6.

4 Slacken the timing belt tensioner retaining bolt, then turn the tensioner anti-clockwise to release the belt tension, and retighten the bolt.

5 Slide the timing belt off its sprockets and remove it from the engine. Though it should not be necessary, if wished, the belt retainer ring screwed to the camshaft sprocket can be removed first. If the belt is to be re-used (which is not recommended), use white paint or similar to mark the direction of rotation on the belt. **Do not** rotate the camshafts or crankshaft until the timing belt has been refitted.

Inspection

6 Check the timing belt carefully for any signs

7.9 Align the crankshaft sprocket notch with the oil pump cover pointer

7.10 Timing belt routing

of uneven wear, splitting or oil contamination, and renew it if there is the slightest doubt about its condition. If the engine is undergoing an overhaul and is approaching the specified interval for belt renewal (see Chapter 1B) renew the belt as a matter of course, regardless of its apparent condition.

7 When fitting a new belt, it is recommended that a new tensioner and idler pulley are also fitted – these are often sold as a kit with a new belt, when purchased from a Honda dealer. Therefore, most people renew these as a matter of course, but they should definitely be renewed if there is any sign of roughness when the tensioner and idler pulleys are spun by hand.

8 If signs of oil contamination are found, trace the source of the oil leak and rectify it, then wash down the engine timing belt area and all related components to remove all traces of oil.

Refitting

9 On reassembly, thoroughly clean the timing belt sprockets and ensure the camshaft and fuel pump sprockets are locked correctly in position. Temporarily refit the crankshaft pulley to the sprocket and check that the pulley cut-out is still aligned with the pointer on the oil pump cover; the mark on the crankshaft sprocket should also be aligned with the mark on the oil pump cover **(see illustration)**.

10 Remove the pulley and fit the timing belt over the crankshaft, oil pump, fuel pump and camshaft sprockets, ensuring that the belt rear run is taut (ie, all slack is on the tensioner pulley side of the belt). Do not twist the belt sharply while refitting it. Ensure that the belt teeth are correctly seated centrally in the sprockets, and that the timing marks remain in alignment. If a used belt is being refitted, ensure that the arrow mark made on removal points in the normal direction of rotation, as before **(see illustration)**.

11 Tension the belt initially by slowly loosening the tensioner pulley bolt, and allowing the pulley to contact the belt.

12 Check that the crankshaft sprocket timing mark is still correctly positioned, then remove the locking bolts from the fuel pump and camshaft sprockets.

13 Ensure the tensioner bolt is still loose, then rotate the crankshaft pulley approximately 60° **backwards** (anti-clockwise) to automatically adjust the timing belt tension. Hold the crankshaft pulley and tensioner pulley stationary, and securely tighten the tensioner bolt.

14 Rotate the crankshaft smoothly through two complete turns in the normal direction of rotation to settle the timing belt in position. Realign the crankshaft sprocket timing mark, and check that the camshaft and fuel pump sprocket locking bolts can be refitted.

15 Slacken the tensioner bolt, then rotate the crankshaft pulley approximately 60° **backwards** (anti-clockwise) to automatically adjust the timing belt tension. Hold the crankshaft pulley and tensioner pulley stationary, and tighten the tensioner bolt to the specified torque.

16 Return the crankshaft to TDC and make a final check that the sprocket timing mark/holes are correctly positioned.

17 As a final (rough) check that the belt tension is satisfactory, grip the belt between the thumb and finger in the middle of its longest run, and try to twist it. It should only be possible to twist the belt between 45 and 90°,

8.3 Removing the camshaft sprocket – note locating pin and hole

using moderate pressure – excessive twisting may damage the belt. If necessary, reset the belt tensioner, turn the engine through two complete turns, then recheck.

18 If removed, refit the belt retainer ring to the camshaft sprocket, and tighten the screws securely. Refit the timing belt covers and the crankshaft pulley as described in Sections 5 and 6.

8 Timing belt tensioner and sprockets – removal and refitting

Camshaft sprocket

Removal

1 Remove the timing belt as described in Section 7. Prior to attempting to unscrew the sprocket retaining bolt, turn the crankshaft 60° **backwards** (anti-clockwise) to prevent any accidental piston-to-valve contact.

2 Screw the sprocket locking bolt fully into position, then slacken and remove the sprocket retaining bolt, using the locking bolt to prevent rotation.

3 Unscrew the locking bolt and remove the sprocket from the end of the camshaft, noting which way round it is fitted **(see illustration)**. If the sprocket locating pin is a loose fit, remove it from the camshaft end and store it with the sprocket for safe-keeping.

Refitting

4 Ensure the locating pin is in position, then refit the sprocket to the camshaft end, aligning its locating hole with the pin.

5 Refit the sprocket retaining bolt, then align the timing hole with the cylinder head hole and screw in the locking bolt. Use the locking bolt to retain the sprocket, and tighten the sprocket bolt to the specified torque. Rotate the crankshaft 60° **forwards** (clockwise) until the groove in the crankshaft timing belt sprocket is at '12 o'clock' and aligns with the cast-in mark on the oil pump cover.

8.8 Using a sprocket holding tool when loosening the fuel pump sprocket nut

8.10 Using a puller to remove the fuel pump sprocket

8.11 Align the keyway in the sprocket with the Woodruff key in the shaft

6 Refit the timing belt as described in Section 7.

Fuel pump sprocket

Removal

7 Remove the timing belt as described in Section 7.

8 Screw the sprocket locking bolt fully into position to prevent rotation. Alternatively, a suitable tool can be made using two lengths of steel strip (one long, the other short), and three nuts and bolts; one nut and bolt forms the pivot of a forked tool, with the remaining two nuts and bolts at the tips of the 'forks' to engage with the sprocket spokes **(see illustration)**.

9 Slacken and remove the sprocket retaining nut.

10 Remove the sprocket from the fuel pump shaft, noting which way around it is fitted. If the Woodruff key is a loose fit in the pump shaft, remove it and store it with the sprocket for safe-keeping. **Note:** *The sprocket is a*

tapered-fit on the fuel pump shaft, and in some cases a suitable puller may be needed to free it from the shaft **(see illustration)**.

Refitting

11 Ensure the Woodruff key is correctly fitted to the pump shaft then refit the sprocket, aligning the sprocket groove with the key **(see illustration)**.

12 Refit the retaining nut and tighten it to the specified torque, using the holding tool or the locking bolt to prevent rotation.

13 If not already done, align the sprocket timing hole with the threaded hole in the cylinder block, and screw in the locking bolt.

14 Refit the timing belt as described in Section 7.

Crankshaft sprocket

Removal

15 Remove the timing belt as described in Section 7.

16 Slacken the crankshaft sprocket retaining bolt. To prevent crankshaft rotation, have an assistant select top gear and apply the brakes firmly. If the engine is removed from the car, it will be necessary to lock the flywheel (see Section 19). Honda dealers use a special holding tool which engages in two of the holes on the sprocket face.

17 Unscrew the retaining bolt and washer, and remove the crankshaft sprocket from the end of the crankshaft. If the sprocket is a tight fit, draw it off the crankshaft using a suitable puller **(see illustration)**. If the Woodruff key is a loose fit in the crankshaft, remove it and store it with the sprocket for safe-keeping.

18 Slide the flanged spacer off the crankshaft, noting which way around it is fitted.

Refitting

19 Refit the flanged spacer to the crankshaft with its convex surface facing away from the oil pump housing **(see illustration)**.

20 Ensure the Woodruff key is correctly fitted then slide on the crankshaft sprocket aligning its groove with the key.

21 Refit the retaining bolt and washer then lock the crankshaft by the method used on removal, and tighten the sprocket bolt to the specified torque setting **(see illustration)**.

22 Refit the timing belt as described in Section 7.

Oil pump sprocket

Removal

23 Remove the timing belt as described in Section 7.

24 Slacken and remove the sprocket retaining nut. Prevent the oil pump sprocket from rotating by passing a socket and extension bar through the sprocket, and onto one of the oil pump cover bolts.

25 Remove the sprocket from the oil pump shaft, noting which way around it is fitted.

Refitting

26 Refit the sprocket, aligning it with the flat on the pump shaft, and fit the retaining nut. Tighten the sprocket retaining nut to the specified torque, using the socket and extension bar to prevent rotation **(see illustration)**.

27 Refit the timing belt as described in Section 7.

8.17 Slide the crankshaft sprocket from the shaft

8.19 Fit the flanged spacer with the convex side away from the oil pump cover

8.21 Refit the crankshaft sprocket bolt and washer

8.26 Use a socket and extension bar on an oil pump cover bolt to lock the sprocket

Tensioner assembly

Removal

28 Remove the timing belt as described in Section 7.

29 Carefully unhook the tensioner spring plate, unscrew the retaining bolts and remove the tensioner assembly from the engine **(see illustration)**.

Refitting

30 Fit the tensioner assembly to the engine, tightening its retaining bolts by hand only. Refit the tensioner spring.

31 Refit the timing belt as described in Section 7.

Idler pulley

Removal

32 Remove the timing belt as described in Section 7.

33 Slacken and remove the retaining bolt, and remove the idler pulley from the engine **(see illustration)**.

Refitting

34 Refit the idler pulley and tighten the retaining bolt to the specified torque.

35 Refit the timing belt as described in Section 7.

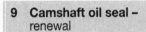

9 Camshaft oil seal – renewal

1 Remove the camshaft sprocket as described in Section 8.

2 Carefully punch or drill a small hole in the oil seal. Screw in a self-tapping screw, and pull on the screw with pliers to extract the seal **(see illustration)**.

3 Clean the seal housing, and polish off any burrs or raised edges which may have caused the seal to fail in the first place.

4 Lubricate the lips of the new seal with clean engine oil, and press it into position using a suitable tubular drift (such as a socket) which bears only on the hard outer edge of the seal. Take care not to damage the seal lips during fitting; note that the seal lips should face inwards **(see illustration)**.

5 Refit the camshaft sprocket as described in Section 8.

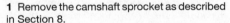

10 Valve clearances – checking and adjustment

Checking

1 The importance of having the valve clearances correctly adjusted cannot be overstressed, as they vitally affect the performance of the engine. The engine must be cold for the check to be accurate. The clearances are checked as follows.

2 Apply the handbrake, then loosen the

8.29 Unhook the timing belt tensioner spring plate

9.2 Pull the screw to extract the seal

right-hand front wheel nuts, jack up the front of the car and support it on axle stands (see *Jacking and vehicle support*). Remove the right-hand front roadwheel to gain access to the crankshaft pulley. Remove the engine undertray, which is secured by a number of bolts.

3 Remove the cylinder head cover as described in Section 4, and with reference to Chapter 4B, remove the fuel injectors.

4 Using a socket and extension on the crankshaft sprocket bolt, rotate the crankshaft in the normal direction of rotation (clockwise when viewed from the right-hand end of the engine) until the notch on the crankshaft pulley is correctly aligned with the pointer on the base of the oil pump cover.

5 Now rotate the crankshaft in the normal direction (clockwise) until the inlet camshaft lobes for No 1 cylinder (nearest the timing belt end of the engine) and the exhaust camshaft lobes for No 3 cylinder are pointing away from the followers. This indicates that these valves are completely closed, and the clearances can be checked.

6 On a piece of paper, draw the outline of the engine with the cylinders numbered from the timing belt end. Show the position of each valve, together with the specified valve clearance. Note that the clearance for both the inlet and exhaust valves is the same.

7 With the cam lobes positioned as described in paragraph 5, using feeler blades, measure the clearance between the base of both No 1 cylinder inlet cam lobes and No 3 cylinder exhaust cam lobes and their followers. Record the clearances on the paper **(see illustration)**.

8.33 Removing the timing belt idler pulley

9.4 Pressing the oil seal into position using a socket

8 Rotate the crankshaft pulley through a half a turn (180°) to position No 3 cylinder inlet camshaft lobes and No 4 cylinder exhaust camshaft lobes pointing away from their followers. Measure the clearance between the base of the camshaft lobes and their followers and record the clearances on the paper.

9 Rotate the crankshaft pulley through a half a turn (180°) to position No 2 cylinder exhaust camshaft lobes and No 4 cylinder inlet camshaft lobes pointing away from their followers. Measure the clearance between the base of the camshaft lobes and their followers and record the clearances on the paper.

10 Rotate the crankshaft pulley through a half a turn (180°) to position No 1 cylinder exhaust camshaft lobes and No 2 cylinder inlet camshaft lobes pointing away from their followers. Measure the clearance between the base of the camshaft lobes and their followers and record the clearances on the paper.

10.7 With the cam lobe pointing away from the follower, measure the clearance

10.14 Carefully depress the follower and slide the shim out

10.15 The thickness of each shim should be stamped on one of its surfaces

11 If all the clearances are correct, refit the cylinder head cover (see Section 4), and injectors (see Chapter 4B), then refit the roadwheel and lower the car to the ground and tighten the wheel nuts to the specified torque. If any clearance measured is not correct, adjustment must be carried out as described in the following paragraphs.

Adjustment

12 Rotate the crankshaft pulley until the lobe of the valve to be adjusted is pointing directly away from the follower. **Note:** *Ensure that the crankshaft is **not** positioned at TDC, as when a valve follower is depressed to remove the shim, the valve will strike the piston.*

13 Rotate the follower until the groove on its upper edge is facing towards the front of the engine (exhaust followers), or rear of engine (inlet followers).

14 In the absence of the special Honda tools, position a large flat-bladed screwdriver between the edge of the follower and the base of the camshaft. Use the screwdriver to carefully depress the follower until there is enough clearance to allow the shim to be slid out from between the follower and camshaft (a magnetic tool is particularly useful for this task) **(see illustration)**.

15 Clean the shim, and measure its thickness with a micrometer. The shims carry thickness markings, but wear may have reduced the original thickness, so be sure to check **(see illustration)**.

16 Add the measured clearance of the valve to the thickness of the original shim then

subtract the specified valve clearance from this figure. This will give you the thickness of the shim required. For example:

Clearance measured of valve	0.35 mm
Plus thickness of original shim	2.70 mm
Equals	3.05 mm
Minus clearance required	0.40 mm
Thickness of shim required	2.65 mm

17 Obtain the correct thickness of shim required and lubricate it with clean engine oil. Carefully depress the follower and slide the shim into position, with the thickness number downwards, ensuring it is correctly located.

HAYNES HINT *It may be possible to correct the clearances by moving the shims around between the valves, but do not rotate the engine with any shims missing. Keep a note of all the shim thicknesses to assist valve clearance adjustment when they need to be done again.*

18 Repeat the procedure given in paragraphs 12 to 17 on the remaining valves which require adjustment.

19 Rotate the crankshaft a few times to settle all shims in position the recheck the valve clearances before refitting the cylinder head cover (see Section 4), and fuel injectors (Chapter 4B)

20 Refit the roadwheel, then lower the car to the ground and tighten the wheel nuts to the specified torque.

Removal

1 Remove the cylinder head cover as described in Section 4.

2 Remove the fuel injectors as described in Chapter 4B.

3 Remove the camshaft sprocket as described in Section 8.

4 Undo the nuts and remove the No 5 bearing cap from the left-hand (transmission) end of the camshafts.

5 The exhaust camshaft gear incorporates a backlash compensating gear. This must now be locked to the fixed exhaust camshaft gear by inserting a suitably-sized bolt/rod into the hole on the inboard face of the fixed gear, and through into the backlash compensating gear. This prevents the spring preload of the compensating gear being lost when either camshaft is removed **(see illustration)**.

6 Working in a spiral pattern from the outside in, slacken the remaining camshaft bearing cap retaining nuts/bolts by one turn at a time, to relieve the pressure of the valve springs on the bearing caps gradually and evenly. Once the valve spring pressure has been relieved, the nuts/bolts can be fully unscrewed and removed. Note the fitted position of the two central bolts which have a stud extension for the camshaft cover.

Caution: If the bearing caps are carelessly slackened, the bearing caps might break. If any bearing cap breaks then the complete cylinder head assembly must be renewed; the bearing caps are matched to the head and are not available separately.

7 Remove the bearing caps, noting each cap's correct fitted location. The bearing caps are numbered 1 to 5 (No 5 cap having already been removed) and the arrow on each cap points towards the timing belt end of the engine.

8 Lift the camshafts out of the cylinder head.

9 Obtain sixteen small, clean plastic containers, and label them for identification. Alternatively, divide a larger container into compartments. Lift the followers and shims out from the top of the cylinder head and store each one in its respective fitted position. Make sure the followers and shims are not mixed to ensure the valve clearances remain correctly adjusted on refitting **(see illustration)**.

Inspection

10 Examine the camshaft bearing surfaces and camshaft lobes for signs of wear ridges and scoring. Renew the camshaft if any of these conditions are apparent. Examine the condition of the bearing surfaces both on the camshaft journals and in the cylinder head. If the head bearing surfaces are worn excessively, the cylinder head will need to be renewed.

11.5 Insert a bolt through the fixed gear into the backlash compensating gear

11.9 Lift out the cam followers and shims

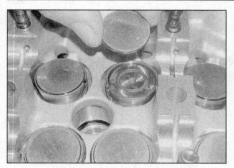

11.13 Ensure each shim is correctly located

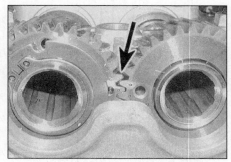

11.14 Align the camshaft gear marks (arrowed)

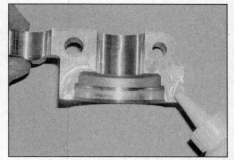

11.16 Apply a smear of sealant to the No 1 camshaft-bearing cap

11 Support the camshaft end journals on V-blocks, and measure the run-out at the centre journal using a dial gauge. If the run-out exceeds the specified limit, the camshaft should be renewed.

12 Examine the followers and their bores in the cylinder head for signs of wear or damage. If any follower is visibly worn, it should be renewed.

Refitting

13 Where removed, lubricate the followers with clean engine oil, and carefully insert each one into its original location in the cylinder head. Ensure each shim is correctly located in the top of the its relevant follower **(see illustration)**.

14 Rotate the crankshaft approximately 60° **backwards** (anti-clockwise) as a precaution against accidental piston-to-valve contact. Lubricate the camshaft followers with clean engine oil, then lay the camshafts in position. Check that the exhaust camshaft backlash compensating gear is still locked to the fixed gear. Ensure that the mark on the outer face exhaust camshaft gear lies between the two marks on the outer face of the inlet camshaft gear, and that the marks are approximately level with the upper edge of the camshaft housing **(see illustration)**. Note: *If the exhaust*

camshaft is being renewed, it will be necessary to obtain the Honda tool (5-8840-9051-0) to pretension the backlash compensating gear prior to installation.

15 Ensure the mating surfaces of the bearing caps and camshaft housing are clean and dry, and lubricate the camshaft journals and lobes with clean engine oil.

16 Apply a smear of suitable sealant (liquid gasket, available from Honda dealers) to the areas of the camshaft housing No 1 bearing cap mating surface **(see illustration)**.

17 Refit the No 1 to 4 camshaft bearing caps in their original locations on the cylinder head. The caps are numbered 1 to 5 (No 1 cap being at the timing belt end of the engine) and the arrow cast onto the top of each cap should point towards the timing belt end of the engine **(see illustration)**.

18 Refit the No 1 to 4 bearing cap nuts/bolts, tightening them by hand only.

19 Remove the bolt/rod locking the backlash compensating gear to the exhaust camshaft fixed gear, and refit the No 5 camshaft bearing cap.

20 Working in the specified sequence, tighten the nuts/bolts by one turn at a time to gradually impose the pressure of the valve springs evenly on the bearing caps **(see illustration)**. Repeat this sequence until all bearing caps

are in contact with the cylinder head, then go around in the specified sequence and tighten them to the specified torque.

Caution: If the bearing caps are carelessly tightened, the bearing caps might break. If any bearing cap breaks then the complete cylinder head assembly must be renewed; the bearing caps are matched to the head and are not available separately.

21 Fit a new camshaft oil seal as described in Section 9.

22 Refit the camshaft sprocket and timing belt as described in Sections 7 and 8.

23 Check the valve clearances as described in Section 10, then refit the cylinder head cover as described in Section 4, and the fuel injectors as described in Chapter 4B.

12 Camshaft housing – removal and refitting

Removal

1 Remove the camshaft sprocket as described in Section 8, and the cylinder head cover as described in Section 4. Remove the two bolts securing the timing belt rear cover to the camshaft housing **(see illustration)**.

11.17 The camshaft bearing cap arrows should point towards the timing belt end

11.20 Camshaft bearing cap tightening sequence

12.1 Remove the two timing belt rear cover bolts from the camshaft housing

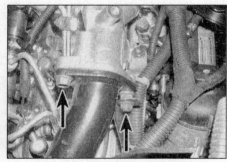

12.3 Undo the intercooler air pipe bolts (one has a stud with a nut attached)

12.4a Recover the EGR pipe gasket

12.4b Undo the large EGR union nut

12.6 Remove the compressor mounting bracket

12.8 Remove the camshaft housing gasket

2 With reference to Chapter 4B, remove the fuel injectors.

3 Remove the bolts securing the intercooler air pipe and bracket to the left-hand end of the camshaft housing and inlet manifold.

Undo the retaining clips and release the pipe from the inlet trunking **(see illustration)**.

4 Undo the bolts securing the EGR (exhaust gas recirculation) pipe to the exhaust manifold and the left-hand end of the camshaft housing.

Undo the large union at the EGR valve, and remove the pipe **(see illustrations)**. It should now be possible to remove the left-hand rear transport eye from the camshaft housing.

5 Unbolt the fuel return pipe, and disconnect the heater plug wiring connectors.

6 Release the refrigerant hoses from the retaining clip on the right-hand side inner wing. Without undoing the refrigerant pipes, disconnect the wiring plug, unbolt the air conditioning compressor from its support bracket (three bolts), and position it clear of the engine. Use a cable-tie or similar to tie the compressor to the front crossmember out of the way. Undo the three bolts and remove the compressor support bracket **(see illustration)**.

7 Slacken the camshaft housing retaining bolts 1/2 turn at a time in the **reverse** of the sequence shown in illustration 12.11.

8 Undo the bolts completely and remove the camshaft housing. Remove and discard the gasket **(see illustration)**.

Refitting

9 Ensure all mating surfaces are clean and free from any gasket or sealant residue.

10 Prior to refitting the housing, check that the camshaft gears are correctly aligned, with the mark on the outer face of the exhaust gear between the marks on the outer face of the inlet gear (see Section 11, paragraph 14)

11 With a new gasket in place, position the camshaft housing on to the cylinder head, and tighten the housing bolts evenly and gradually to the specified torque, in the sequence shown **(see illustration)**.

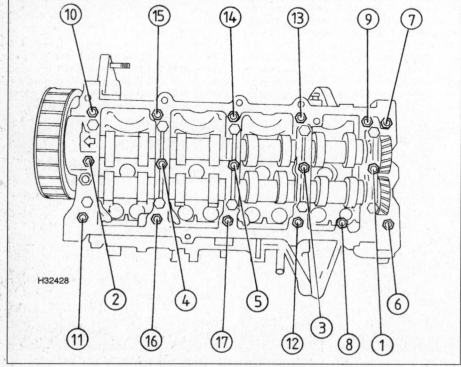

H32428

12.11 Camshaft housing bolts tightening sequence

13.4 Store the followers the correct way up

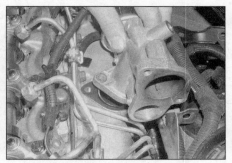

13.7 Removing the EGR valve

13.8 Detach the EVRV vacuum hose and wiring plug

12 Refitting is a reversal of removal. noting the following points:

a) *Check the valve clearances and adjust if necessary (Section 10).*

b) *Tension the timing belt as described in Section 7.*

c) *Check the fuel leak-back pipe and hose for leaks.*

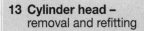

13 Cylinder head –
removal and refitting

Caution: Be careful not to allow dirt into the fuel pump or injector pipes during this procedure.
Note: New cylinder head bolts will be required on refitting.

Removal

1 Drain the cooling system as described in Chapter 1B.

2 Remove the camshaft sprocket as described in Section 8.

3 Slacken and remove the bolts securing the timing belt rear cover to the end of the cylinder head/camshaft housing.

4 With reference to Section 12, remove the camshaft housing. As a precaution, obtain sixteen small, clean plastic containers, and label them for identification. Alternatively, divide a larger container into compartments. Lift the followers out from the top of the cylinder head and store each one in its respective fitted position **(see illustration)**.

5 Undo the four retaining bolts and manoeuvre

the exhaust manifold heat shield out of the engine compartment. If the bolts are in poor condition, obtain new ones for reassembly.

6 Remove the nuts and bolts securing the exhaust manifold to the cylinder head, and recover the washers. Using a Torx socket, slacken and remove the two manifold retaining studs, and gently pull the manifold away from the engine. Alternatively, remove the exhaust manifold as described in Chapter 4B.

7 Unscrew the retaining bolts, disconnect the vacuum pipe, and remove the EGR valve **(see illustration)**.

8 Detach the vacuum hose and wiring plug from the EVRV **(see illustration)**.

9 Unbolt the fuel return pipe from the back of the head.

10 Disconnect the wiring harness from the glow plugs (see Chapter 5A).

11 Release the retaining clip and disconnect the coolant hose from the left-hand rear of the cylinder head **(see illustration)**.

12 Disconnect the coolant temperature sensor, unscrew the retaining bolts and pull the thermostat housing and wastegate vacuum pipe bracket away from the left-hand end of the cylinder head **(see illustration)**.

13 Working in the **reverse** of the sequence shown in illustration 13.33, progressively slacken the cylinder head bolts by half a turn at a time, until all bolts can be unscrewed by hand.

14 Lift out the cylinder head bolts and recover the washers.

15 Lift the cylinder head away; seek assistance if possible, as it is a heavy assembly **(see illustration)**. Remove the gasket, noting

the two locating dowels fitted to the top of the cylinder block. If they are a loose fit, remove the locating dowels and store them with the head for safe-keeping. Keep the head gasket for identification purposes (see paragraph 24).

16 If the cylinder head is to be dismantled for overhaul, then refer to Part C of this Chapter.

Preparation for refitting

17 The mating faces of the cylinder head and cylinder block/crankcase must be perfectly clean before refitting the head. Use a hard plastic or wood scraper to remove all traces of gasket and carbon; also clean the piston crowns. Take particular care, as the surfaces are damaged easily.

18 Also, make sure that the carbon is not allowed to enter the oil and water passages – this is particularly important for the lubrication system, as carbon could block the oil supply to any of the engine's components. Using adhesive tape and paper, seal the water, oil and bolt holes in the cylinder block/ crankcase.

19 To prevent carbon entering the gap between the pistons and bores, smear a little grease in the gap. After cleaning each piston, use a small brush to remove all traces of grease and carbon from the gap, then wipe away the remainder with a clean rag. Clean all the pistons in the same way.

20 Check the mating surfaces of the cylinder block/crankcase and the cylinder head for nicks, deep scratches and other damage. If slight, they may be removed carefully with a file, but if excessive, machining may be the only alternative to renewal.

13.11 Disconnect the coolant pipe from the cylinder head

13.12 Unbolt the wastegate vacuum pipe bracket

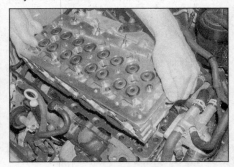

13.15 Lift the cylinder head away

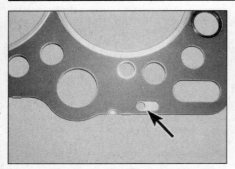

13.24 Cylinder head gasket identification hole (arrowed)

13.25 Measure the piston projection at the highest points between the valve cut-outs

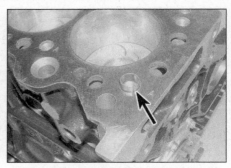

13.29 Check the locating dowels are in place

21 Ensure that the cylinder head bolt holes in the crankcase are clean and free of oil. Syringe or soak up any oil left in the bolt holes. This is most important in order that the correct bolt tightening torque can be applied and to prevent the possibility of the block being cracked by hydraulic pressure when the bolts are tightened.

22 The cylinder head bolts must be discarded and renewed, regardless of their apparent condition. They are 'stretch' bolts, and if they are re-used, the head will not be tightened down fully and evenly – either that, or the bolts will snap. A set of new bolts is not expensive.

23 If warpage of the cylinder head gasket surface is suspected, use a straight-edge to check it for distortion. Refer to Part C of this Chapter if necessary.

24 On this engine, the cylinder head-to-piston clearance is controlled by fitting different thickness head gaskets. The gasket thickness can be determined by looking at the left-hand front corner of gasket and checking on the number of holes **(see illustration)**.

Holes in gasket	Gasket thickness
No holes	1.45 mm
One hole	1.50 mm
Two hole	1.55 mm

The correct thickness of gasket required is selected by measuring the piston protrusions as follows.

25 Ensure that the crankshaft is still correctly positioned in the TDC position. Mount a dial test indicator securely on the block so that its pointer can be easily pivoted between the piston crown and block mating surface. Zero the dial test indicator on the gasket surface

of the cylinder block then carefully move the indicator over No 1 piston and measure the its protrusion at its highest point between the valve cut-outs, and then again at its highest point between the valve cut-outs at 90° to the first measurement **(see illustration)**.

26 Rotate the crankshaft half a turn (180°) to bring No 2 and 3 pistons to TDC. Ensure the crankshaft is accurately positioned then measure the protrusions of No 2 and 3 pistons at the specified points. Once both pistons have been measured, rotate the crankshaft through a further one and a half turns (540°) to bring No 1 and 4 pistons back to TDC.

27 Select the correct thickness of head gasket required by determining the largest amount of piston protrusion, and using the following table.

Piston protrusion measurement	Gasket thickness required
0.630 to 0.696 mm	1.45 mm (no holes)
0.697 to 0.763 mm	1.50 mm (one hole)
0.764 to 0.830 mm	1.55 mm (two holes)

Refitting

28 Wipe clean the mating surfaces of the cylinder head and cylinder block/crankcase.

29 Check that the two locating dowels are in position then fit a new gasket to the cylinder block **(see illustration)**.

30 If not already positioned at TDC, rotate the crankshaft so that No 1 piston is at its highest point in the cylinder. Now turn the crankshaft 60° **backwards** (anti-clockwise). This is to ensure that whist the cylinder head and camshafts are being refitted, there is little

chance of accidental piston-to-valve contact.

31 With the aid of an assistant, carefully refit the cylinder head assembly to the block, aligning it with the locating dowels.

32 Carefully enter each new cylinder head bolt into its relevant hole (do not drop them in). Screw all bolts in, by hand only, until finger-tight.

33 Working progressively and in the sequence shown starting from the centre, tighten the cylinder head bolts to their Stage 1 torque setting, using a torque wrench and suitable socket **(see illustration)**.

34 Once all bolts have been tightened to the Stage 1 torque, working again in the specified sequence, go around and tighten all bolts through the specified Stage 2 and 3 angles. It is recommended that an angle-measuring gauge is used to ensure accuracy **(see illustration)**. If a gauge is not available, use white paint to make alignment marks prior to tightening; the marks can then be used to check that the bolt has been rotated through the correct angle.

35 Refitting is a reversal of removal, bearing in mind the following points:

a) Prior to refitting the timing belt, turn the crankshaft 60° in the normal direction of rotation (clockwise) to TDC on No 1 cylinder until the groove in the crankshaft sprocket aligns with the cast-in mark on the oil pump housing (see illustration 7.9).

b) After refitting the injectors and pipes, check all unions for leaks (see Chapter 4B).

c) Ensure all wiring is correctly routed secured

d) Check the valve clearances as described in Section 10.

e) On completion, top-up the coolant system as described in Chapter 3.

13.33 Tighten the bolts to the Stage 1 setting . . .

13.34 . . . then to the Stage 2 setting

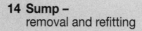

14 Sump –
removal and refitting

Removal

1 Disconnect the battery negative terminal (see *Disconnecting the battery*).

2 Firmly apply the handbrake, then jack up the front of the car and support it on axle stands (see *Jacking and vehicle support*).

Undo the retaining bolts and remove the engine undertray.

3 Drain the engine oil as described in Chapter 1B, then fit a new sealing washer and refit the drain plug, tightening it to the specified torque. It makes sense to fit a new oil filter at the same time, but this is not essential.

4 Slacken and remove the bolts securing the sump lower pan to the main casting, then remove the sump pan from underneath the car **(see illustrations)**.

5 To remove the main casting from the engine, remove the exhaust system front pipe as described in Chapter 4B.

6 Undo the two bolts securing the oil dipstick guide tube to the main sump casting.

7 Progressively slacken and remove the nuts and bolts securing the main casting to the base of the cylinder block/oil pump cover and transmission. Break the joint by striking the casting with the palm of the hand, or using a wide plastic spatula carefully inserted in the joint between the sump and cylinder block. On no account lever between the mating faces with metal tools, as this will almost certainly damage them, resulting in leaks when finished. Providing care is taken, a large screwdriver could be used in the drain hole, to prise down the sump. Lower the casting away from the engine and withdraw it from underneath the car.

8 While the sump main casting is removed, take the opportunity to check the oil pump pick-up/strainer for signs of clogging or splitting. If necessary, unbolt the pick-up/strainer and remove it from the engine along with its sealing ring **(see illustration)**. The strainer can then be cleaned easily in solvent or renewed.

Refitting

9 Remove all traces of dirt, oil and sealant from the mating surfaces of the sump main casting and pan, the cylinder block and (where removed) the pick-up/strainer.

10 Where necessary, fit a new sealing ring to the oil pump pick-up/strainer and fit the strainer to the base of the cylinder block **(see illustration)**. Refit the strainer retaining bolt and tighten it to the specified torque.

11 Ensure the main casting and cylinder

14.4a Remove the sump lower pan bolts

14.4b If the lower pan is stuck, ease it away using a wide-bladed scraper

14.8 Remove the oil pick-up pipe and strainer

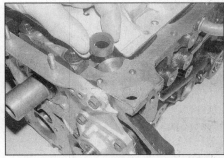

14.10 Fit a new oil pick-up pipe sealing ring

block mating surfaces are clean and dry, and apply a coat of suitable sealant (liquid gasket, available from Honda dealers) to the upper mating surface of the casting.

12 Position a new dipstick guide tube rubber seal on the main casting **(see illustration)**.

13 Offer up the main casting and loosely refit all the retaining nuts and bolts **(see illustration)**. Note that the four long bolts correspond with the bolts holes at the rear of the casting. If the sump is being fitted with the engine removed from the car and separated from the transmission, use a straight-edge to ensure that the rear face of the casting is flush with the transmission mounting face of the cylinder block. Working out from the centre in a diagonal sequence, progressively tighten the main casting retaining bolts to the specified torque setting.

14 Refit the bolts securing the main casting to the transmission housing and tighten them to the specified torque.

15 Ensure that the oil dipstick guide tube is correctly positioned, refit the retaining bolts, and tighten to the specified torque.

16 Refit the exhaust front pipe as described in Chapter 4B.

17 Ensure the main casting and sump pan mating surfaces are clean and dry and apply a coat of suitable sealant (liquid gasket, available from Honda dealers) to the upper mating surface of the pan. Refit the pan to the base of the main casting and tighten its retaining bolts to the specified torque **(see illustration)**.

18 Refit the engine undertray, lower the car to the ground then fill the engine with fresh oil, with reference to Chapter 1B.

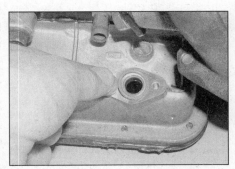

14.12 Position a new oil dipstick guide tube sealing ring

14.13 Refit the sump main casting

14.17 Apply a bead of sealant and refit the pan to the sump main casting

15.6a Remove the oil pump inner rotor . . .

15.6b . . . and outer rotor

15.9 Measure the inner rotor tip-to-outer rotor clearance

15 Oil pump – removal, inspection and refitting

Note: *The oil pressure relief valve is screwed into the cylinder block and cannot be removed without disturbing the fuel pump (see paragraph 7).*

Removal

1 Remove the timing belt as described in Section 7.

2 Remove the oil pump and crankshaft timing belt sprockets as described in Section 8.

3 Remove the sump main casting as described in Section 14.

4 Slacken and remove the retaining bolts then slide the oil pump cover off the end of the crankshaft, taking great care not to lose the locating dowels. Remove the sealing ring, which is fitted around the oil pump housing section of the cover, and discard it.

5 Using a suitable marker pen, mark the surface of the pump outer rotor; the mark can then be used to ensure the rotor is refitted the correct way around.

6 Remove the oil pump inner and outer rotors from the cylinder block **(see illustrations)**.

7 If necessary, remove the fuel pump as described in Chapter 4B, and unscrew the oil pressure relief valve assembly from the rear of the cylinder block, where it is located on the right-hand side of the fuel pump lower mounting bracket. Remove the sealing ring.

Inspection

8 Clean the components, and carefully examine the rotors, pump housing and cover for any signs of scoring or wear. Renew any component which shows signs of wear or damage. If the pump housing in the cylinder block is marked then seek the advice of a Honda dealer on the best course of action.

9 If the components appear serviceable, fit the rotors into the housing and measure the clearance between the outer rotor and pump housing, and the inner rotor tip-to-outer rotor clearance using feeler blades **(see illustration)**. Also measure the rotor endfloat, and check the flatness of the end cover. If the clearances exceed the specified tolerances, renew the worn components.

10 If the relief valve has been removed, check that the valve piston is free to move easily and return smoothly under spring pressure. If not renew the valve assembly.

Refitting

11 Where removed, fit a new sealing ring to the oil pressure relief valve, then refit the valve assembly to the cylinder block and tighten it to the specified torque setting.

12 Lubricate the pump rotors with clean engine oil and refit them to the pump housing, using the mark made prior to removal to ensure the outer rotor is fitted the correct way around.

13 Prior to refitting, carefully lever out the crankshaft and oil pump oil seals using a flat-bladed screwdriver. Lubricate the new oil seals

with a little silicone grease, then ensuring that each seal's sealing lip is facing inwards, press them squarely into the housing using a tubular drift which bears only on the hard outer edge of the seal. Press each seal into position so that it is flush with the housing, then lubricate the oil seal lips with clean engine oil **(see illustration)**.

14 Ensure the mating surfaces of the oil pump and cylinder block are clean and dry, and the locating dowels are in position. Remove all traces of sealant from the threads of the pump cover bolts.

15 Fit a new seal into the groove around the oil pump housing section of the cover, and apply a bead of suitable sealant (liquid gasket, available from Honda dealers) to the pump cover mating surface **(see illustration)**.

16 Carefully manoeuvre the oil pump cover into position, taking great care not to damage the oil seal lips on the crankshaft and inner rotor shaft. Locate the cover on the dowels making sure the pump sealing ring remains correctly positioned.

17 Apply a smear of sealant to the threads of each cover retaining bolt, then refit all bolts and tighten them to the specified torque. Note that the longer bolt corresponds to the lower left-hand bolt hole in the cover.

18 Refit the timing belt sprockets and belt as described in Sections 7 and 8, then refit the sump as described in Section 14.

19 On completion refill the engine with clean oil as described in Chapter 1B.

16 Oil pump seal – renewal

1 Remove the oil pump sprocket as described in Section 8.

2 Carefully punch or drill a small hole in the oil seal. Screw a self-tapping screw into the seal, and pull on the screw with pliers to extract the seal **(see illustration)**.

Caution: Great care must be taken to avoid damage to the oil pump.

3 Clean the seal housing, and polish off any burrs or raised edges which may have caused the seal to fail in the first place.

15.13 The seal fits flush with the housing

15.15 Fit a new seal to the oil pump cover

16.2 Pull the screw to extract the seal

17.6 Fit a new sealing ring to the recess in the cooler

17.7 Refit the oil filter housing centre bolt

4 Lubricate the lips of the new seal with clean engine oil, and press it into position using a suitable tubular drift (such as a socket) which bears only on the hard outer edge of the seal. Take care not to damage the seal lips during fitting; note that the seal lips should face inwards.

5 Refit the oil pump sprocket as described in Section 8.

17 Oil cooler – removal and refitting

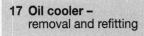

Removal

1 Firmly apply the handbrake, then jack up the front of the car and support it on axle stands (see *Jacking and vehicle support*). Undo the bolts and remove the undertray to gain access to the oil cooler, which is situated on the left-hand rear of the cylinder block.

2 Drain the cooling system as described in Chapter 1B. Alternatively, clamp the oil cooler coolant hoses directly above the cooler, and be prepared for some coolant loss as the hoses are disconnected. To improve access to the coolant hoses, remove the charge air pipe/hose (see Chapter 4B).

3 Position a suitable container beneath the oil filter. Release the retaining clip and disconnect the return hose.

4 Release the clips and disconnect the coolant hoses from the oil cooler, and release the wiring loom retaining clip.

5 Remove the single bolt securing the oil filter housing to the cylinder block. Discard the sealing ring; a new one must be used on refitting.

Refitting

6 Fit a new sealing ring to the recess in the rear of the cooler, then offer the cooler to the cylinder block **(see illustration)**.

7 Ensure that the oil cooler return hose is correctly positioned, and that the lug of the oil filter housing engages correctly, then refit the centre bolt and tighten it to the specified torque **(see illustration)**.

8 Reconnect the coolant hoses to the cooler, and secure them in position with the retaining clips.

9 Lower the car to the ground. Top-up the engine oil level as described in Chapter 1B.

10 If removed, refit the air inlet duct.

11 Refill or top-up the cooling system as described in Chapter 1B or *Weekly checks* (as applicable). Start the engine, and check the oil cooler for signs of leakage.

18 Oil pressure switch – removal and refitting

1 The oil pressure switch is a vital early warning of low oil pressure. The switch operates the oil warning light on the instrument panel – the light should come on with the ignition, and go out almost immediately when the engine starts.

2 If the light does not come on, there could be a fault on the instrument panel, the switch wiring, or the switch itself. If the light does not go out, low oil level, worn oil pump (or sump pick-up blocked), blocked oil filter, or worn main bearings could be to blame – or again, the switch may be faulty.

3 If the light comes on while driving, the best advice is to turn the engine off immediately, and not to drive the car until the problem has been investigated – ignoring the light could mean expensive engine damage.

Removal

4 The oil pressure switch is mounted on the rear of the engine, next to the oil cooler.

5 Remove the air cleaner as described in Chapter 4B.

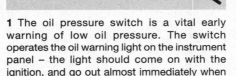

19.2 Fabricate a locking tool to retain the flywheel

6 Disconnect the switch wiring plug.

7 Place a drain container under the switch – the amount of oil lost should be quite small.

8 Anticipating oil spillage, slowly unscrew the switch and remove it.

9 Clean the switch threads and the switch location. If the same switch is being refitted, clean the switch threads with a wire brush.

Refitting

10 Apply a little liquid gasket to the switch threads, then fit the switch and tighten it to the specified torque.

11 Reconnect the wiring plug, then refit the air cleaner as described in Chapter 4B.

12 Check the engine oil level, as described in *Weekly checks*.

19 Flywheel – removal, inspection and refitting

Removal

1 Remove the transmission as described in Chapter 7A, then remove the clutch assembly as described in Chapter 6.

2 Prevent the flywheel from turning by locking the ring gear teeth **(see illustration)**. Alternatively, bolt a strap between the flywheel and the cylinder block/crankcase. Make alignment marks between the flywheel and crankshaft using paint or a suitable marker pen.

3 Slacken and remove the retaining bolts and plate, then remove the flywheel **(see illustration)**. Do not drop it, as it is very heavy.

19.3 Remove the flywheel bolts and recover the plate

20.7 The seal fits flush with the housing

Discard the flywheel bolts – these are subject to significant stress, and should always be renewed after removal.

Inspection

4 Examine the flywheel for wear or chipping of the ring gear teeth. Renewal of the ring gear is possible but is not a task for the home mechanic; renewal requires the new ring gear to be heated (up to 180° to 230°C) to allow it to be fitted.
5 Examine the flywheel for scoring of the clutch face. If the clutch face is scored, the flywheel may be surface-ground, but renewal is preferable.
6 If there is any doubt about the condition of the flywheel, seek the advice of a Honda dealer or engine reconditioning specialist. They will be able to advise if it is possible to recondition it or whether renewal is necessary.

Refitting

7 Clean the mating surfaces of the flywheel and crankshaft.
8 Apply a drop of locking compound to the threads of each of the new flywheel retaining bolts, then refit the flywheel and retaining plate and install the new bolts. If the original is being refitted align the marks made prior to removal.
9 Lock the flywheel using the method employed on dismantling then, working in a diagonal sequence, evenly and progressively tighten the retaining bolts to the specified Stage 1 torque setting.
10 Once all bolts have been tightened to the Stage 1 torque, go around and tighten all

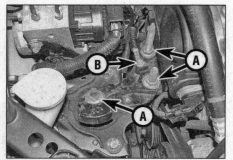

21.7 Right-hand mounting upper bracket nuts (A) – note earth strap bolt (B)

bolts through the specified Stage 2 angle. It is recommended that an angle-measuring gauge is used during the final stages of the tightening, to ensure accuracy. If a gauge is not available, use white paint to make alignment marks prior to tightening; the marks can then be used to check that the bolt has been rotated through the correct angle.
11 Refit the clutch as described in Chapter 6, then remove the locking tool and refit the transmission as described in Chapter 7A.

20 Crankshaft oil seals – renewal

Timing belt end

1 Remove the crankshaft sprocket as described in Section 8.
2 Carefully punch or drill two small holes opposite each other in the oil seal. Screw a self-tapping screw into each and pull on the screws with pliers to extract the seal.
3 Clean the seal housing and polish off any burrs or raised edges which may have caused the seal to fail in the first place.
4 Lubricate the lips of the new seal with clean engine oil and ease it into position on the end of the shaft. Press the seal squarely into position until it is flush with the housing. If necessary, a suitable tubular drift which bears only on the hard outer edge of the seal can be used to tap the seal into position. Take great care not to damage the seal lips during fitting and ensure that the seal lips face inwards.
5 Wash off any traces of oil, then refit the crankshaft sprocket as described in Section 8.

Flywheel end

6 Remove the flywheel as described in Section 19.
7 Renew the seal as described in paragraphs 2 to 4 **(see illustration)**.
8 Refit the flywheel as described in Section 19.

21 Engine/transmission mountings – inspection and renewal

Inspection

1 If improved access is required, raise the front of the car and support it securely on axle stands. Where necessary, undo the retaining bolts and remove the undertray from beneath the engine/transmission unit.
2 Check the mounting rubber to see if it is cracked, hardened or separated from the metal at any point; renew the mounting if any such damage or deterioration is evident.
3 Check that all the mountings' fasteners are securely tightened; use a torque wrench to check if possible.
4 Using a large screwdriver or a pry bar, check for wear in the mounting by carefully levering against it to check for free play;

where this is not possible, enlist the aid of an assistant to move the engine/transmission back-and-forth, or from side-to-side, while you watch the mounting. While some free play is to be expected even from new components, excessive wear should be obvious. If excessive free play is found, check first that the fasteners are correctly secured, then renew any worn components as described below.

Renewal

Note: *Before slackening any of the engine mounting bolts/nuts, the relative positions of the mountings to their various brackets should be marked to ensure correct alignment upon refitting.*

Right-hand mounting

5 First support the weight of the engine under the sump, using a trolley jack with a block of wood placed on its head.
6 Unscrew the small bolt securing the earth strap to the engine right-hand mounting, and move the strap clear.
7 Unscrew the three nuts securing the right-hand mounting upper bracket, and lift the bracket off the studs **(see illustration)**.
8 Unscrew the three bolts securing the right-hand mounting lower (side) bracket to the 'triangular' adapter plate on the engine – note that the lowest of the three bolts is shorter than the other two. Withdraw the bracket from the engine.
9 Refitting is a reversal of removal. Tighten all nuts and bolts to their specified torques.

Front mounting

10 Firmly apply the handbrake, then jack up the front of the car and support it on axle stands.
11 Support the weight of the engine/transmission under the sump using a trolley jack with a block of wood placed on its head. Removing the front mounting will only allow the engine to move on its remaining mountings, so providing they are in sound condition, removing the front mounting will not leave the engine dangerously unsupported.
12 Unscrew the nut and withdraw (or tap out) the through-bolt from the front mounting.
13 Separate the mounting from the bracket on the front subframe. If necessary, the mounting can be unbolted and removed from the front of the engine.
14 Refitting is a reversal of removal. Tighten all nuts and bolts to their specified torques.

Rear mounting

15 Firmly apply the handbrake, then jack up the front of the car and support it on axle stands.
16 Support the weight of the engine/transmission under the sump using a trolley jack with a block of wood placed on its head. Removing the front mounting will only allow the engine to move on its remaining mountings, so providing they are in sound condition, removing the front mounting will not leave the engine dangerously unsupported.

17 Working from below, unscrew the three mounting bolts, noting their positions as they are of different lengths.

18 Slacken and remove the two bolts securing the rear mounting to the subframe, and the nut securing the mounting to the transmission bracket, then manoeuvre the assembly out from underneath the car.

19 Refitting is a reversal of removal. Tighten all nuts and bolts to their specified torques.

Left-hand mounting

20 Remove the air cleaner assembly as described in Chapter 4B.

21 Remove the battery and its tray as described in Chapter 5A.

22 Support the weight of the transmission using a trolley jack with a block of wood placed on its head.

23 Unscrew the two mounting nuts and single bolt on top of the transmission. Lower the transmission slightly on the jack, to separate the mounting.

24 If required, the mounting can either be unbolted from the inner wing/chassis leg, or the through–bolt can be unscrewed and removed to separate the mounting and its bracket.

25 Refitting is a reversal of removal. Tighten all nuts and bolts to their specified torques.

Notes

Chapter 2 Part C:
Engine removal and overhaul procedures

Contents

Degrees of difficulty

Easy, suitable for novice with little experience	**Fairly easy,** suitable for beginner with some experience 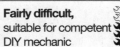	**Fairly difficult,** suitable for competent DIY mechanic 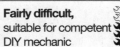	**Difficult,** suitable for experienced DIY mechanic	**Very difficult,** suitable for expert DIY or professional

Specifications

General

Manufacturer's engine codes*:
  1.4 litre petrol (D14Z5 and D14Z6) . . . . 66 kW SOHC 16V, non-VTEC
  1.6 litre petrol (D16V1 and D16W7) . . . . 81 kW SOHC 16V, VTEC
  1.7 litre diesel (4EE2) . . . . 74 kW DOHC 16V common-rail diesel
* See Vehicle identification in the Reference section

Engine block

Bore:
  Petrol engines. . . . . 75.0 mm (nominal), 75.07 mm (max)
  Diesel engines:
    Nominal. . . . . 79.0 mm
    Size group A. . . . . 79.001 to 79.010 mm
    Size group B. . . . . 79.011 to 79.020 mm
    Size group C. . . . . 79.021 to 79.030 mm
  Maximum cylinder bore ovality. . . . . 0.015 mm
  Maximum cylinder bore taper. . . . . 0.015 mm

Pistons and rings

Piston diameter:
   Petrol engines . . . . 74.98 to 74.99 mm (nominal), 74.97 mm (min)
   Diesel engines:
      Size group A . . . . 78.930 to 78.939 mm
      Size group B . . . . 78.940 to 78.949 mm
      Size group C . . . . 78.950 to 78.959 mm
Piston-to-bore clearance:
   Petrol engines . . . . 0.010 to 0.040 mm (nominal), 0.050 mm (max)
   Diesel engines . . . . 0.061 to 0.079 mm
Piston ring end gaps (fitted in bore):
   Petrol engines:
      Top compression ring . . . . 0.15 to 0.30 mm (nominal), 0.60 mm (max)
      Second compression ring . . . . 0.30 to 0.45 mm (nominal), 0.60 mm (max)
      Oil control ring . . . . 0.20 to 0.70 mm (nominal), 0.80 mm (max)
   Diesel engines:
      Top compression ring . . . . 0.25 to 0.35 mm
      Second compression ring . . . . 0.20 to 0.30 mm
      Oil control ring . . . . 0.20 to 0.40 mm
Piston ring-to-groove clearance:
   Petrol engines:
      Top compression ring . . . . 0.035 to 0.060 mm (nominal), 0.130 mm (max)
      Second compression ring . . . . 0.030 to 0.055 mm (nominal), 0.130 mm (max)
   Diesel engines:
      Top compression ring . . . . 0.09 to 0.15 mm
      Second compression ring . . . . 0.07 to 0.15 mm
      Oil control ring . . . . 0.02 to 0.15 mm

Crankshaft

Endfloat (maximum):
   Petrol . . . . 0.45 mm
   Diesel . . . . 0.20 mm

Cylinder head

Head warpage limit:
   Petrol engines . . . . 0.05 mm
   Diesel engines . . . . 0.1 mm
Cylinder head height:
   Petrol engines . . . . 92.95 to 93.05 mm
   Diesel engines . . . . 94.95 to 95.05 mm

Valves

Valve stem-to-guide clearance (maximum):	**Inlet**	**Exhaust**
Petrol engines . . .	0.16 mm	0.22 mm
Diesel engines . . .	0.08 mm	0.10 mm
Valve spring free length:		
1.4 litre engine . . .	58.70 mm	58.70 mm
1.6 litre engine . . .	56.49 mm	58.70 mm
Diesel engine . . .	44.63 mm	44.63 mm

Torque wrench settings

Refer to Chapter 2A and 2B Specifications

---

1 General information

Included in this portion of Chapter 2 are the general overhaul procedures for the cylinder head and internal engine components.

The information ranges from advice concerning preparation for an overhaul and the purchase of new parts to detailed, step-by-step procedures covering removal and refitting of internal engine components and the inspection of parts.

After Section 5, the information has been written based on the assumption that the engine has been removed from the car. For information concerning in-car engine repair, as well as removal and refitting of the external components necessary for the overhaul, see Chapter 2A or 2B.

The Specifications included in this Part are only those necessary for the inspection and overhaul procedures which follow. Refer to Chapter 2A or 2B for additional Specifications, and all torque wrench settings.

It's not always easy to determine when, or if, an engine should be completely overhauled, as a number of factors must be considered.

High mileage is not necessarily an indication that an overhaul is needed, while low mileage doesn't preclude the need for an overhaul. Frequency of servicing is probably the most important consideration. An engine that's had regular and frequent oil and filter changes, as well as other required maintenance, will most likely give many thousands of miles of reliable service. Conversely, a neglected engine may require an overhaul very early in its life.

Excessive oil consumption is an indication that piston rings, valve seals and/or valve guides are in need of attention. Make sure that oil leaks aren't responsible before deciding that the rings and/or guides are defective. Perform a cylinder compression check to determine the extent of the work required (see Chapter 2A or 2B as applicable).

Loss of power, rough running, knocking or metallic engine noises, excessive valvetrain noise and high fuel consumption rates may also point to the need for an overhaul, especially if they're all present at the same time. If a complete service doesn't remedy the situation, major mechanical work is the only solution.

An engine overhaul involves restoring the internal parts to the specifications of a new engine. During an overhaul, the piston rings are renewed and the cylinder walls are reconditioned (rebored and/or honed). If a rebore is done by an automotive engineering workshop, new oversize pistons (where available) will also be fitted. The main bearings and connecting rod bearings are generally renewed and, if necessary, the crankshaft may be reground to restore the journals. Generally, the valves are serviced as well, since they're usually in less-than-perfect condition at this point. While the engine is being overhauled, other components, such as the distributor, starter and alternator, can be rebuilt as well. The end result should be a like new engine that will give many trouble-free miles. **Note:** *Critical cooling system components such as the hoses, auxiliary drivebelts, thermostat and water pump should be renewed when an engine is overhauled. The radiator should be checked carefully to ensure that it isn't blocked or leaking (see Chapter 3). If you purchase a rebuilt engine or short block, some reconditioners will not warranty their engines unless the radiator has been professionally flushed. Also, be sure to check the oil pump carefully, as described in Chapter 2A or 2B.*

Before beginning the engine overhaul, read through the entire procedure to familiarise yourself with the scope and requirements of the job. Overhauling an engine isn't difficult, but it is time-consuming. Plan on the car being tied up for a minimum of two weeks, especially if parts must be taken to an automotive engineering workshop for repair or reconditioning. Check on availability of parts and make sure that any necessary special tools and equipment are obtained in advance. Most work can be done with typical hand tools, although a number of precision measuring tools are required for inspecting parts to determine if they must be renewed. Often an automotive engineering workshop will carry out the inspection of parts and offer advice concerning reconditioning and renewal. **Note:** *Always wait until the engine has been completely dismantled and all components, especially the engine block, have been inspected before deciding what service and repair operations must be performed by an automotive engineering workshop. Since the block's condition will be the major factor to consider when determining whether to overhaul the original engine or buy a rebuilt one, never purchase parts or have machine work done on other components until the*

block has been thoroughly inspected. As a general rule, time is the primary cost of an overhaul, so it doesn't pay to refit worn or substandard parts.

As a final note, to ensure maximum life and minimum trouble from a rebuilt engine, everything must be assembled with care in a spotlessly-clean environment.

Engine overhaul

The home mechanic is faced with a number of options when performing an engine overhaul. The decision to renew the engine block, piston/connecting rod assemblies and crankshaft depends on a number of factors, with the number one consideration being the condition of the block. Other considerations are cost, access to engineering workshop facilities, parts availability, time required to complete the project and the extent of prior mechanical experience.

Give careful thought to which alternative is best for you and discuss the situation with local automotive engineering workshops, automotive parts dealers and experienced reconditioners before ordering or purchasing renewal parts.

Some of the rebuilding alternatives include:

Individual parts

If the inspection procedures reveal the engine block and most engine components are in re-usable condition, purchasing individual parts may be the most economical alternative. The block, crankshaft and piston/connecting rod assemblies should all be inspected carefully. Even if the block shows little wear, the cylinder bores should be surface honed.

Short block

A short block consists of an engine block with a crankshaft and piston/connecting rod assemblies already refitted. All new bearings are incorporated and all clearances will be correct. The existing camshaft, valvetrain components, cylinder head(s) and external parts can be bolted to the short block with little or no engineering work necessary.

Long block

A long block consists of a short block plus an oil pump, sump, cylinder head, cylinder head cover, camshaft and valve train components, timing sprockets and belt. All components are installed with new bearings, seals and gaskets incorporated throughout. The refitting of manifolds and external parts is all that's necessary.

2 Engine removal – methods and precautions

If you've decided the engine must be removed for overhaul or major repair work, several preliminary steps should be taken.

Locating a suitable place to work is extremely important. Adequate work space,

along with storage space for the car, will be needed. If a workshop or garage isn't available, at the very least a flat, level, clean work surface made of concrete or tarmac is required.

Cleaning the engine compartment and engine before beginning the removal procedure will help keep tools clean and organised.

The engine is normally removed as a unit with the transmission – the transmission can be removed on its own first, but this hardly offers any benefits if the engine must also be removed. The car's body should be raised and supported securely, sufficiently high that the subframe can be removed, then the engine/transmission is unbolted as a single unit and lowered to the ground; the engine/transmission can then be withdrawn from under the car and separated. An engine hoist, crane or A-frame is ideal for supporting the engine and lowering it out, but the job can also be accomplished using an engine support bar, mounted across the engine bay on the inner wing channels. Supporting the engine/transmission from below should be considered a last resort. Make sure the equipment is rated in excess of the combined weight of the engine and transmission. Safety is of primary importance, considering the potential hazards involved in removing the engine/transmission from the car.

If the engine is being removed by a novice, a helper should be available. Advice and aid from someone more experienced would also be helpful. There are many instances when one person cannot simultaneously perform all of the operations required when lifting the engine out of the car.

Plan the operation ahead of time. Arrange for or obtain all of the tools and equipment you'll need prior to beginning the job. Some of the equipment necessary to perform engine removal and refitting safely and with relative ease are (in addition to an engine hoist) a heavy duty trolley jack, complete sets of spanners and sockets as described in the rear of this manual, wooden blocks and plenty of rags and cleaning material for mopping-up spilled oil, coolant and petrol. If the hoist must be hired, be sure to arrange for it in advance and perform all of the operations possible without it beforehand. This will save you money and time.

Plan for the car to be out of use for quite a while. A engineering workshop will be required to perform some of the work the DIY-er can't accomplish without special equipment. These workshops often have a busy schedule, so it would be a good idea to consult them before removing the engine in order to accurately estimate the amount of time required to rebuild or repair components that may need work.

Always be extremely careful when removing and refitting the engine. Serious injury can result from careless actions. Plan ahead, take your time and a job of this nature, although major, can be accomplished successfully.

3.5 Unbolt the earth strap from the transmission

3.8 Unbolt the two earth straps from the coolant housing

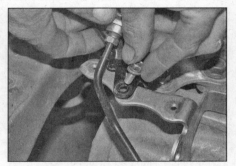

3.9a Unbolt the pipe/union bracket from the transmission . . .

3.9b . . . then unbolt and remove the slave cylinder

3.10a Disconnect the two gearchange cables . . .

3.10b . . . then unbolt the bracket from the transmission

3 Engine (petrol) – removal and refitting

Note: *The engine and transmission must be removed together, as a single unit. Read through the following steps carefully and familiarise yourself with the procedure before beginning work. Also at this point it may be helpful to use a penetrating fluid or spray on nuts and bolts that may be difficult to remove, such as exhaust manifolds, engine mountings, etc. An engine hoist or crane will be required.*

Removal

1 Open the bonnet, and support it in its widest-open position.
2 Depressurise the fuel system as described in Chapter 4A.

3 Disconnect the battery negative lead, and position the lead away from the battery (also see *Disconnecting the battery*).
4 Referring to Chapter 4A if necessary, unbolt and remove the inlet air resonator, inlet air duct and air cleaner.
5 Unbolt the earth strap next to the left-hand engine/transmission mounting **(see illustration)**.
6 Remove the battery and its tray as described in Chapter 5A.
7 Trace the battery positive leads to the engine compartment fusebox. Noting the fitted position of the two leads, unscrew their mounting bolts and disconnect them. Release the battery cables from their retaining clips.
8 Unbolt the two earth straps from the coolant housing **(see illustration)**.
9 On manual transmission models, trace the fluid pipe back from the slave cylinder to the fluid hose union, unbolt the pipe/union

support bracket, then unbolt and remove the cylinder **(see illustrations)**.
Caution: Be careful not to bend or kink the clutch hydraulic pipe, and don't depress the clutch pedal while the slave cylinder is removed.
10 Also on manual transmission models, disconnect the shift and selector cables from their levers on the transmission – each is secured by a split pin, and there are two washers. Unhook the cables, then unscrew the three bolts securing the cable support bracket to the transmission, and lift it clear, taking care not to bend the cables **(see illustrations)**.
11 On automatic transmission models, refer to Chapter 7B and disconnect the selector cable at the transmission end. The fluid cooler hoses must also be disconnected from the pipes at the front of the transmission – anticipate some fluid spillage, and either plug or tape over the open connections.
12 Locate the charcoal canister (EVAP) hose on the back of the throttle body, and either disconnect it there, or at the connection on the engine compartment bulkhead **(see illustration)**.
13 Release the hose clip and disconnect the vacuum hose from the front of the brake servo.
14 Disconnect the accelerator cable from the throttle body by loosening the adjuster locknut and unhooking the inner cable end fitting **(see illustration)**.
15 Separate the quick-release fittings (squeeze together the upper and lower tabs) and disconnect the fuel supply and EVAP hoses from the fuel rail **(see illustration)**. Either plug or tape over the open connections.

3.12 Disconnect the charcoal canister hose from the throttle body

3.14 Loosen the adjuster nuts and lift off the accelerator cable

3.15 Disconnect the supply hose from the fuel rail

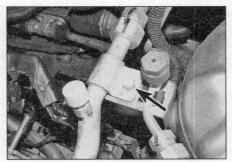

3.16 Remove the bolt from the air conditioning pipe support bracket

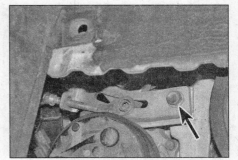

3.18 Remove the bolt securing the alternator adjuster bracket

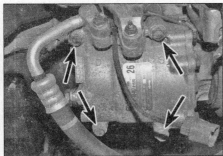

3.19a Remove the four compressor mounting bolts . . .

3.19b . . . then move it aside, and tie it up

3.24 Disconnect the hoses from the coolant housing

16 Where applicable, remove the bolt from the air conditioning support bracket so that the pipe can be moved clear without disconnecting it **(see illustration)**.

17 Loosen the front wheel nuts, and if possible, also loosen both driveshaft nuts while the car is still on the ground. Jack up the front of the car, and support it on axle stands (see *Jacking and vehicle support*). Note that the car must be raised sufficiently high for the engine and transmission to be lowered out and withdrawn from underneath. Remove the front wheels and the engine undertray.

18 Remove the alternator as described in Chapter 5A. Also unbolt the alternator adjuster front bolt, and take off the adjuster bracket **(see illustration)**.

19 Remove the four bolts securing the air conditioning compressor, then remove it from the engine and tie it to one side without

disconnecting or straining the hoses **(see illustrations)**.

20 Drain the cooling system and transmission as described in Chapter 1A. The engine oil does not have to be drained to remove the engine, but if the engine is to be dismantled after removal, it makes sense to drain the oil now.

21 Though not essential, it is advisable to remove the radiator (and, where applicable, the air conditioning condenser) as described in Chapter 3. This is primarily to reduce the chance of them being damaged as the engine is removed – if preferred, protect the rear of the radiator by placing some thick card, or a piece of old carpet, behind it.

22 Remove the exhaust front pipe as described in Chapter 4A.

23 Remove the driveshafts as described in Chapter 8.

24 Release the hose clips and disconnect a

total of four coolant hoses from the coolant elbow at the side of the cylinder head **(see illustration)**. The fitted position of each hose should be apparent when reassembling, but label the hoses if necessary.

25 Release the hose clips and disconnect the heater hoses at the bulkhead **(see illustration)**.

26 Attach an engine hoist to the engine lifting eyes, and raise it so that the engine's weight is supported. The engine can be supported from below, but note that enough room must be left for the subframe to be lowered out.

27 Unscrew the engine front mounting through-bolt (note that the nut is 'captive', and won't turn), then separate the mounting **(see illustration)**.

28 Unscrew the through-bolt from the engine rear mounting, noting that there is a damper weight fitted to it **(see illustration)**.

29 Unscrew the through-bolt from the right-

3.25 Disconnect the heater hoses from the bulkhead

3.27 Unscrew the front mounting through-bolt

3.28 Remove the rear mounting through-bolt and damper weight

3.29a Unscrew the right-hand mounting through-bolt . . .

3.29b . . . then unbolt the upper bracket

3.30a Unscrew the three nuts . . .

3.30b . . . and lift off the left-hand mounting upper bracket

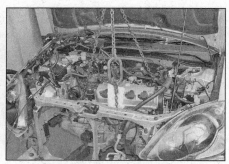

3.34 Lowering out the engine

hand (transmission) mounting, then unbolt and remove the upper mounting bracket **(see illustrations)**.

30 Unscrew the three nuts on the engine left-hand upper mounting, and lift off the upper bracket **(see illustrations)**.

31 Remove the front subframe as described in Chapter 10.

32 Check around the engine and transmission from above and below, to make sure there is nothing still attached or in the way which will prevent it from being lowered out. Also make sure there is enough room under the front of the car for the engine/transmission to be lowered out and withdrawn.

 HAYNES HiNT *Lowering the engine/ transmission onto a large board, some strong card, or even an old piece of carpet, will not only protect it from damage, but will make it easier to drag out from under the car.*

33 With the help of an assistant, begin by lowering the engine a little so that it clears its left- and right-hand mountings. Stop at this point, and check once more that nothing remains connected, and that nothing is in danger of getting caught up as the engine is lowered.

34 Carefully lower the engine out, while your assistant guides the engine past any obstructions **(see illustration)**. When clear of the car, lower it to the ground. Be prepared to steady the engine when it touches down, to

stop it toppling over. Withdraw the assembly from under the car, and remove it to wherever it will be worked on.

Separation

35 To separate the transmission from the engine, first remove the starter motor with reference to Chapter 5A.

36 Unscrew the bolts and remove the engine stiffener bracket(s) from the engine and sump. Also unbolt and remove the clutch cover plate.

37 Progressively unscrew and remove the transmission-to-engine bolts.

38 With the help of an assistant, withdraw the transmission directly from the engine, making sure that its weight is not allowed to bear on the transmission input shaft. On automatic transmission models, push the torque converter back into the transmission – take care that it does not fall out as the transmission is removed.

Refitting

39 Refitting is a reversal of removal, noting the following additional points:

a) Make sure that all mating faces are clean, and use new gaskets where necessary.

b) Tighten all nuts and bolts to the specified torque setting, where given.

c) On manual transmissions, apply a smear of high-melting-point grease to the splines of the transmission input shaft. Do not apply too much, otherwise there is the possibility of the grease contaminating the clutch friction disc.

d) On automatic transmissions, if the torque

converter was removed, refit it using a new O-ring seal. Have an assistant ready to keep the converter pressed into the housing as the transmission is refitted.

e) Fit new circlips to the grooves in the inner end of each driveshaft CV joint, and ensure that they fully engage as they are fitted into the transmission.

f) Replenish the transmission oil, and check the level with reference to Chapter 1A.

g) Refill the cooling system (and where applicable, the engine oil), as described in Chapter 1A.

h) As the front subframe was removed, have the front wheel alignment checked at the earliest opportunity.

4 Engine (diesel) – removal and refitting

Note: *The engine and transmission must be removed together, as a single unit. Read through the following steps carefully and familiarise yourself with the procedure before beginning work. Also at this point it may be helpful to use a penetrating fluid or spray on nuts and bolts that may be difficult to remove, such as exhaust manifolds, engine mountings, etc. An engine hoist or crane will be required.*

Removal

1 Open the bonnet, and support it in its widest-open position.

2 Remove the battery and its tray as described in Chapter 5A.

3 Trace the battery positive lead to the engine compartment fusebox. Noting the fitted position of the lead, unscrew the two mounting bolts, and disconnect it. Also unscrew the nut and disconnect the second lead from the battery negative terminal. Unclip the small fusebox from the main relay plate.

4 Referring to Chapter 4B if necessary, unbolt and remove the air cleaner and inlet air duct.

5 Refer to Chapter 6 if necessary and unbolt the clutch slave cylinder. Trace the fluid pipe back from the cylinder to the fluid hose union, and unbolt the pipe/union support bracket. *Caution: Be careful not to bend or kink the*

clutch hydraulic pipe, and don't depress the clutch pedal while the slave cylinder is removed.

6 Disconnect the shift and selector cables from their levers on the transmission – each is secured by a split pin, and there are two washers. Unhook the cables, then pull up the metal 'horse-shoe' clips securing the cables to the mounting bracket, and place the cables to one side, taking care not to bend them **(see illustration)**.

7 Disconnect the two small coolant hoses from the front of the expansion tank **(see illustration)**.

8 Release the hose clip and disconnect the brake servo vacuum hose from the vacuum pump (on the back of the alternator).

9 Release the clips and disconnect the intercooler hoses from the front of the engine **(see illustrations)**.

10 Trace the wiring harness from the bulkhead by the expansion tank to the wiring plug on the back of the engine, and disconnect it. Release the harness from its clips.

11 Unbolt and remove the engine top cover **(see illustration)**. Release the hose clips and disconnect the fuel supply and return hoses from the fuel high-pressure pump, noting their fitted locations.

12 In the engine compartment, disconnect the accelerator position sensor wiring plug – this is located close to the bulkhead on the passenger's side, under a plastic cover **(see illustration)**. Release the wiring harness securing clips.

13 Loosen the front wheel nuts, and if possible, also loosen both driveshaft nuts while the car is still on the ground. Jack up the front of the car, and support it on axle stands (see *Jacking and vehicle support*). Note that the car must be raised sufficiently high for the engine and transmission to be lowered out and withdrawn from underneath. Remove the front wheels and the engine undertray.

14 Drain the cooling system and transmission as described in Chapter 1B. The engine oil does not have to be drained to remove the engine, but if the engine is to be dismantled after removal, it makes sense to drain the oil now.

15 Remove the auxiliary drivebelt as described in Chapter 1B.

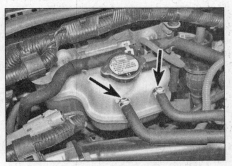

4.6 Slide up the horse-shoe clips to release the gearchange cables

4.7 Disconnect the two front hoses from the expansion tank

4.9a Loosen the hose clip and disconnect the intercooler air inlet hose at the front . . .

4.9b . . . the outlet hose can be disconnected at the side of the engine

16 Remove the exhaust front pipe as described in Chapter 4B.

17 Remove the driveshafts as described in Chapter 8.

18 Under the car, disconnect the air conditioning compressor wiring plug, then remove the bolt securing the compressor wiring harness. Support the compressor, then remove the three mounting bolts and move the compressor clear of the engine, **without** disconnecting or straining any of the pipework. Tie the compressor up to a convenient point (such as the front crossmember) – do not leave it hanging.

19 Remove the three bolts securing the compressor mounting bracket, and remove the bracket from the engine.

20 Release the hose clips and disconnect the coolant hoses from the thermostat housing at the side of the cylinder head **(see illustration)**. The fitted position of each hose should be

apparent when reassembling, but label the hoses if necessary. Also disconnect the hoses from either end of the coolant pipe which runs across the transmission.

21 Disconnect the radiator top and bottom hoses. Though not essential, it is advisable to remove the radiator (and, where applicable, the air conditioning condenser) as described in Chapter 3. This is primarily to reduce the chance of them being damaged as the engine is removed – if preferred, protect the rear of the radiator by placing some thick card, or a piece of old carpet, behind it.

22 Attach an engine hoist to the engine lifting eyes, and raise it so that the engine's weight is supported. The engine can be supported from below, but note that enough room must be left for the subframe to be lowered out.

23 Unscrew the engine front mounting through-bolt (note that the nut is 'captive', and won't turn), then separate the mounting.

4.11 The engine top cover is secured by four bolts

4.12 Unclip the plastic cover from the throttle quadrant to access the sensor

4.20 Disconnect the coolant hoses from the thermostat housing

4.26 Remove the three nuts from the right-hand mounting, and lift off the bracket

24 Unscrew the through-bolt from the engine rear mounting, noting that there is a damper weight fitted to it.

25 Unscrew the through-bolt from the left-hand (transmission) mounting, then unbolt and remove the upper mounting bracket.

26 Unscrew the three nuts on the engine right-hand upper mounting, and lift off the upper bracket **(see illustration)**.

27 Remove the front subframe as described in Chapter 10.

28 Check around the engine and transmission from above and below, to make sure there is nothing still attached or in the way which will prevent it from being lowered out. Also make sure there is enough room under the front of the car for the engine/transmission to be lowered out and withdrawn.

> **HAYNES HINT** *Lowering the engine/transmission onto a large board, some strong card, or even an old piece of carpet, will not only protect it from damage, but will make it easier to drag out from under the car.*

29 With the help of an assistant, begin by lowering the engine a little so that it clears its left- and right-hand mountings. Stop at this point, and check once more that nothing remains connected, and that nothing is in danger of getting caught up as the engine is lowered.

30 Carefully lower the engine out, while your assistant guides the engine past any obstructions. When clear of the car, lower it to

6.2 A labelled plastic bag can be used to store the valve components

the ground. Be prepared to steady the engine when it touches down, to stop it toppling over. Withdraw the assembly from under the car, and remove it to wherever it will be worked on.

Separation

31 Progressively unscrew and remove the transmission-to-engine bolts.

32 With the help of an assistant, withdraw the transmission directly from the engine, making sure that its weight is not allowed to bear on the transmission input shaft.

33 Recover the transmission adapter plate (spacer ring) and the two location dowels.

Refitting

34 Refitting is a reversal of removal, noting the following additional points:
- a) Make sure that all mating faces are clean, and use new gaskets where necessary.
- b) Tighten all nuts and bolts to the specified torque setting, where given.
- c) Apply a smear of high-melting-point grease to the splines of the transmission input shaft. Do not apply too much, otherwise there is the possibility of the grease contaminating the clutch friction disc.
- d) Fit new circlips to the grooves in the inner end of each driveshaft CV joint, and ensure that they fully engage as they are fitted into the transmission.
- e) Replenish the transmission fluid, and check the level with reference to Chapter 1B.
- f) Refill the cooling system (and where applicable, the engine oil), as described in Chapter 1B.
- g) As the front subframe was removed, have the front wheel alignment checked at the earliest opportunity.

5 Engine overhaul – dismantling sequence

1 It's much easier to dismantle and work on the engine if it's mounted on a portable engine stand. A stand can often be hired quite cheaply from an equipment hire workshop. Before it's mounted on a stand, the flywheel/driveplate should be removed from the engine.

2 If a stand isn't available, it's possible to dismantle the engine with it blocked up on the floor. Be extra careful not to tip or drop the engine when working without a stand.

3 If you're going to obtain a rebuilt engine, all external components must first be removed, to be transferred to the new engine, just as they will if you're doing a complete engine overhaul yourself. These include:

  Alternator, air conditioning compressor, etc, and mounting brackets.
  Emissions control components.
  Ignition coils and spark plugs (petrol models).
  Thermostat and housing cover.
  Water pump.
  Fuel injection components.

  Inlet/exhaust manifolds.
  Oil filter.
  Engine mountings.
  Clutch and flywheel, or driveplate.

Note: *When removing the external components from the engine, pay close attention to details that may be helpful or important during refitting. Note the fitted position of gaskets, seals, spacers, pins, brackets, washers, bolts, wiring and other small items.*

4 If you're obtaining a short block, which consists of the engine block, crankshaft, pistons and connecting rods all assembled, then the cylinder head, sump and oil pump will have to be removed as well. See *Engine overhaul* in Section 1 for additional information regarding the different possibilities to be considered.

5 If you're planning a complete overhaul, the engine must be dismantled in the following general order (as applicable):

  Inlet and exhaust manifolds.
  Cylinder head cover.
  Timing belt covers.
  Timing belt and sprockets.
  Rocker arm assembly/camshaft housing and camshaft(s).
  Cylinder head.
  Water pump.
  Sump.
  Oil spray nozzles (diesel engines).
  Oil pump and pick-up tube.
  Rear main oil seal retainer.
  Main bearing caps (or bearing cap bridge) and lower main bearings.
  Piston/connecting rod assemblies.
  Crankshaft and upper main bearings.

6 Cylinder head – dismantling

Note: *New and rebuilt cylinder heads are commonly available for most engines at dealer parts departments and some automotive reconditioning specialists. Due to the fact that some specialised tools are necessary for the dismantling and inspection procedures, and new parts aren't always readily available, it may be more practical and economical for the home mechanic to purchase an exchange head rather than taking the time to dismantle, inspect and recondition the original.*

1 Cylinder head dismantling involves removal of the inlet and exhaust valves and related components. The rocker arm assembly (or camshaft housing) and camshaft(s) must be removed before beginning the cylinder head dismantling procedure (see Part A or B of this Chapter). Label the parts or store them separately so they can be refitted in their original locations.

2 Before the valves are removed, arrange to label and store them, along with their related components, so they can be kept separate and refitted in their original locations **(see illustration)**.

6.3a Using a valve spring compressor . . .

6.3b . . . compress the valve spring until the collets can be removed from the valve

6.3c Remove the compressor then lift off the spring retainer . . .

6.3d . . . and remove the valve spring

6.3e Pull the seal off the top of the valve guide . . .

6.3f . . . then remove the spring seat

3 Compress the springs on the first valve with a spring compressor and remove the collets. Carefully release the valve spring compressor and remove the retainer, the spring and the spring seat (if used) **(see illustrations)**.

4 Pull the valve out of the head. If the valve binds in the guide (won't pull through), push it back into the head and deburr the area around the stem and the collet groove with a fine file or fine emery cloth **(see illustration)**.

5 Repeat the procedure for the remaining valves. Remember to keep all the parts for each valve together so they can be refitted in the same locations. **Note:** *On 1.6 litre petrol models, remember to remove the oil control jet and O-ring from the cylinder head (see Chapter 2A, Section 10).*

6 On diesel engines, use a suitable drift to drive out the four injector heat sleeves from the head, and recover the O-ring seal fitted at the top of each one – new seals should be

6.4 If the valve stem won't pull through, deburr the end with a file or fine emery cloth

used when reassembling. Mark the sleeves for position when removing – they should be refitted to their original locations.

7 Once the valves and related components have been removed and stored in an organised manner, the head should be thoroughly cleaned and inspected. If a complete engine overhaul is being done, finish the engine dismantling procedures before beginning the cylinder head cleaning and inspection process.

7 Cylinder head – cleaning and inspection

1 Thorough cleaning of the cylinder head and related valvetrain components, followed by a detailed inspection, will enable you to decide how much valve service work must be done during the engine overhaul. **Note:** *If the engine was severely overheated (after a head gasket failure), the cylinder head is probably warped, and will need to be skimmed at least – if badly warped, a new head may even be required.*

Cleaning

2 Scrape all traces of old gasket material and sealant off the head gasket, inlet manifold and exhaust manifold mating surfaces. Be very careful not to gouge the cylinder head. Special gasket removal solvents that soften gaskets and make removal much easier are available at automotive parts stores.

3 Remove all built-up scale from the coolant passages.

4 Push a stiff wire brush through the various

holes to remove deposits that may have formed in them.

5 Run an appropriate-size tap into each of the threaded holes to remove corrosion and thread sealant that may be present. If compressed air is available, use it to clear the holes of debris produced by this operation.

⚠ **Warning: Wear eye protection when using compressed air.**

6 Clean the camshaft housing or bearing cap bolt threads with a wire brush.

7 Clean the cylinder head with degreaser and dry it thoroughly. Compressed air will speed the drying process and ensure that all holes and recessed areas are clean. **Note:** *Decarbonising chemicals are available, and may prove very useful when cleaning cylinder heads and valvetrain components. They're very caustic and should be used with caution. Be sure to follow the instructions on the container.*

8 Clean the rocker arms and bearing caps and dry them thoroughly (don't mix them up during the cleaning process). Compressed air will speed the drying process and can be used to clean out the oil passages.

9 Clean all the valve springs, spring seats, collets and retainers with degreaser and dry them thoroughly. Do the components from one valve at a time to avoid mixing up the parts.

10 Scrape off any heavy deposits that may have formed on the valves, then use a motorised wire brush to remove deposits from the valve heads and stems. Again, make sure the valves don't get mixed up.

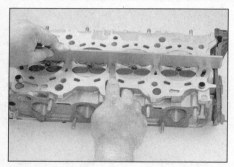

7.12 Check the head for warpage by trying to slip a feeler blade under the straight-edge

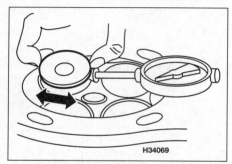

7.14 Check the valve stem-to-guide clearance (valve lateral movement) with a DTI

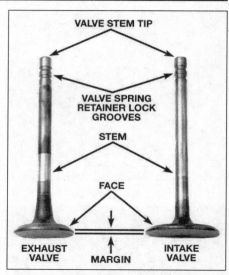

7.15 Check for valve wear at the points shown here

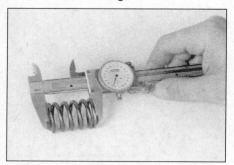

7.16 Measure the free length of each valve spring

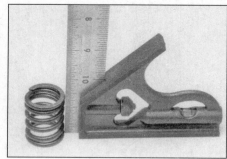

7.17 Check each valve spring for squareness

Inspection

Cylinder head

11 Inspect the head very carefully for cracks, evidence of coolant leakage and other damage. If cracks are found, check with an automotive engineering workshop concerning repair. If repair isn't possible, a new/reconditioned cylinder head should be obtained.

12 Using a straight-edge and feeler blade, check the head gasket mating surface for warpage **(see illustration)**. If the warpage exceeds the specified limit, it may be resurfaced at an automotive engineering workshop, provided it is not reduced below the specified minimum height.

13 Examine the valve seats in each of the combustion chambers. If they're pitted, cracked or burned, the head will require engineering work that's beyond the scope of the home mechanic.

14 Check the valve stem-to-guide clearance by measuring the lateral movement of the valve head with a dial indicator gauge (DTI) attached securely to the head **(see illustration)**. The valve must be in the guide and approximately 10 mm off the seat. After this is done, if there's still some doubt regarding the condition of the valve guides, they should be checked by an automotive engineering workshop (the cost should be minimal).

Valves

15 Carefully inspect each valve face for uneven wear, deformation, cracks, pits and burned areas. Check the valve stem for scuffing and the neck for cracks. Rotate the

valve and check for any obvious indication that it's bent. Look for pits and excessive wear on the end of the stem **(see illustration)**. The presence of any of these conditions indicates the need for valve reconditioning by an automotive engineering workshop.

Valve components

16 Check each valve spring for wear (on the ends) and pits. Measure the free length and compare it to this Chapter's Specifications **(see illustration)**. Any springs that are shorter than specified have sagged and shouldn't be re-used.

17 Stand each spring on a flat surface and check it for squareness with a carpenter's square **(see illustration)**. If any of the springs are distorted or sagged, renew all of them with new parts.

18 Check the spring retainers and collets for obvious wear and cracks. Any questionable

8.3 Grind-in the valve with a reciprocating rotary motion

parts should be renewed, as extensive damage will occur if they fail during engine operation.

8 Valves and seats – reconditioning

1 If the valves are in satisfactory condition, they should be ground (lapped) into their respective seats, to ensure a smooth gas-tight seal. If the seat is only lightly pitted, or if it has been recut, fine grinding compound **only** should be used to produce the required finish. Coarse valve-grinding compound should **not** be used unless a seat is badly burned or deeply pitted; if this is the case, the cylinder head and valves should be inspected by an expert to decide whether seat recutting, or even the renewal of the valve or seat insert, is required.

2 Valve grinding is carried out as follows. Place the cylinder head upside-down on a bench.

3 Smear a trace of the appropriate grade of valve-grinding compound on the seat face, and press a suction grinding tool onto the valve head. With a semi-rotary action, grind the valve head to its seat, lifting the valve occasionally to redistribute the grinding compound **(see illustration)**. A light spring placed under the valve head will greatly ease this operation.

4 If coarse grinding compound is being used, work only until a dull, matt even surface is produced on both the valve seat and the valve, then wipe off the used compound and repeat the process with fine compound. When a smooth unbroken ring of light grey matt finish is produced on both the valve and seat, the grinding operation is complete. **Do not** grind in the valves any further than absolutely necessary, or the seat will be prematurely sunk into the cylinder head.

9.2 Insert the valves into their original locations

9.3 Gently tap the valve seals into place with a deep socket

9.5a Fit the spring (closely-wound coils toward the head) and retainer over the valve stem

5 When all the valves have been ground-in, carefully wash off all traces of grinding compound using paraffin or a suitable degreaser before reassembly of the cylinder head.

9 Cylinder head – reassembly

1 Ensure that the cylinder head is completely clean before attempting reassembly.
2 Beginning at one end of the head, lubricate and refit the first valve **(see illustration)**.
3 Dip the new seal in clean engine oil, then fit over the valve and onto the guide. Using a hammer and a deep socket or seal refitting tool, gently tap each seal into place until it's completely seated on the guide **(see illustration)**. Don't twist the seals during refitting, or they won't seal properly. **Note:** *On petrol engines, the valve stem seals are colour-coded; white for the inlet valves and black for the exhaust valves.*
4 Refit the valve spring seat.
5 Position the valve springs and retainers over the valves. Place the end of the valve spring with the closely-wound coils toward the cylinder head. Compress the springs with a valve spring compressor and carefully refit the collets in the groove, then slowly release the compressor and make sure the collets seat properly. Apply a small dab of grease to each collet to hold it in place if necessary **(see illustrations)**.
6 Repeat the procedure for the remaining valves. Be sure to return the components to their original locations – don't mix them up.

9.5b Compress the spring and locate the split collets in the recess in the valve stem

7 On diesel engines, fit a new O-ring seal to the top of each injector heat sleeve, then refit the four sleeves to their original locations, making sure they are tapped fully home.
8 Apply clean engine oil to all the valvetrain components, then refit the camshaft(s) and rocker shaft assembly (or camshaft housing) as described in Chapter 2A or 2B.

10 Pistons and connecting rods – removal

Note: *Prior to removing the piston/connecting rod assemblies, remove the cylinder head, sump, oil pump pick-up tube, oil pump and baffle plate (see Chapter 2A or 2B).*
1 Use your fingernail to feel if a ridge has formed at the upper limit of ring travel (about 6 mm down from the top of each

9.5c Apply a dab of grease to each collet to hold them in place on the valve stem

cylinder). If carbon deposits or cylinder wear have produced ridges, they must be completely removed with a scraper or ridge reamer **(see illustration)**. Follow the reamer manufacturer's instructions. Failure to remove the ridges before attempting to remove the piston/connecting rod assemblies may result in piston breakage.
2 After the cylinder ridges (if any) have been removed, turn the engine upside-down so the crankshaft is facing up.
3 On diesel engines, the baffle plate must be removed first to access the connecting rods **(see illustration)**.
4 The existing numbers on the connecting rods indicate the rod bore size, not the position in the engine. Use a small centre punch to make the appropriate number of indentations on each rod and cap (1, 2, 3, etc, depending on the cylinder they're associated with) **(see illustrations)**.

10.1 A ridge reamer is required to remove the ridge from the top of each cylinder

10.3 Unbolt the baffle plate from the base of the cylinder block – diesel engines

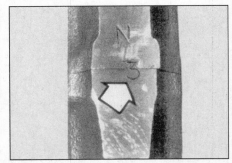

10.4a The stamped numbers indicate the big-end bore size

10.4b Mark the cylinder number on each connecting rod and cap with a centre punch

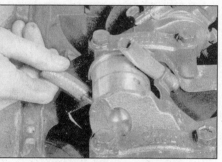

10.6 Fit sections of rubber or plastic hose over the rod bolts before removing the pistons

5 Loosen each of the connecting rod cap nuts half a turn at a time until they can be removed by hand. Remove the No 1 connecting rod cap and bearing shell. Don't drop the bearing shell out of the cap.

6 Slip a short length of plastic or rubber hose over each connecting rod cap bolt to protect the crankshaft journal and cylinder wall as the piston is removed **(see illustration)**.

7 Remove the bearing shell, and push the connecting rod/piston assembly out through the top of the engine. Use a wooden hammer handle to push on the upper bearing surface in the connecting rod. If resistance is felt, double-check to make sure that all of the ridge was removed from the cylinder.

8 Repeat the procedure for the remaining cylinders.

9 After removal, reassemble the connecting rod caps and bearing shells in their respective

connecting rods and fit the cap nuts finger tight. Leaving the old bearing shells in place until reassembly will help prevent the connecting rod bearing surfaces from being accidentally scratched or gouged.

10 Don't separate the pistons from the connecting rods at this stage.

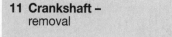

11 Crankshaft – removal

Note: *The crankshaft can be removed only after the engine has been removed from the car. It's assumed that the flywheel or driveplate, timing belt, sump, oil pick-up tube and oil pump, and baffle plate have already been removed. The oil seal retainer must be unbolted and separated from the block before proceeding with crankshaft removal.*

11.1 Place a DTI gauge against the end of the crankshaft to check endfloat

11.3 The endfloat can also be checked with a feeler blade at the thrustwasher journal

12.5a Use a hammer and punch to knock the core plugs sideways in their bores

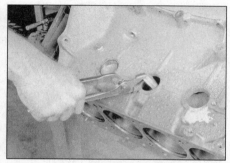

12.5b Pull the core plugs from the block using pliers

1 Before the crankshaft is removed, check the endfloat. Mount a dial indicator gauge (DTI) with the stem in line with the crankshaft and touching the end **(see illustration)**. **Note:** *The main caps and main-cap bridge should be in place and tightened to the specified torque.*

2 Push the crankshaft all the way to the right and zero the dial indicator gauge. Next, lever the crankshaft to the left as far as possible and check the reading on the dial indicator gauge. The distance that it moves is the endfloat. If it's greater than specified, check the crankshaft thrust surfaces for wear. If no wear is evident, new thrustwashers should correct the endfloat.

3 If a dial indicator gauge isn't available, feeler blades can be used. Gently lever or push the crankshaft all the way to the left of the engine. Slip feeler blades between the crankshaft and the back face of the front thrustwasher to determine the clearance **(see illustration)**.

4 Remove the main bearing caps and or bridge assembly. If necessary, use the bolts as levers to remove the caps. Try not to drop the bearing shells if they come out with the caps.

5 Carefully lift the crankshaft out of the engine. It may be a good idea to have an assistant available, since the crankshaft is quite heavy. With the bearing shells in place in the engine block, return the caps to their respective locations on the engine block, refit the main bearing caps/bridge and tighten the bolts finger-tight.

12 Engine block – cleaning

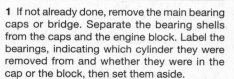

1 If not already done, remove the main bearing caps or bridge. Separate the bearing shells from the caps and the engine block. Label the bearings, indicating which cylinder they were removed from and whether they were in the cap or the block, then set them aside.

2 On diesel engines, carefully prise out the oil jets from the block.

3 Using a gasket scraper, remove all traces of gasket material from the engine block. Be very careful not to scratch or gouge the gasket sealing surfaces.

4 Remove all of the covers and threaded oil gallery plugs from the block. The plugs are usually very tight – they may have to be drilled out and the holes retapped. Use new plugs when the engine is reassembled.

5 Remove the core plugs from the engine block. To do this, knock one side of the plug into the block with a hammer and a punch, then grasp them with large pliers and pull them out **(see illustrations)**.

6 If any of the castings are extremely dirty, all should be steam-cleaned.

7 After the block is steam-cleaned, clean all oil holes and oil galleries one more time. Brushes specifically designed for this purpose are available at most automotive parts stores.

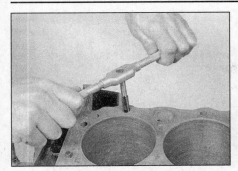

12.9 All bolt holes in the block should be cleaned and restored with a tap

12.11 A large socket on an extension can be used to drive in the new core plugs

12.13 Oil spray nozzles – diesel engines

Flush the passages with warm water until the water runs clear, dry the block thoroughly and wipe all machined surfaces with a light, rust preventive oil. If you have access to compressed air, use it to speed the drying process and blow out all the oil holes and galleries.

 Warning: Wear eye protection when using compressed air.

8 If the block isn't extremely dirty or sludged up, you can do an adequate cleaning job with hot soapy water and a stiff brush. Take plenty of time and do a thorough job. Regardless of the cleaning method used, be sure to clean all oil holes and galleries very thoroughly, dry the block completely and coat all machined surfaces with light oil.
9 The threaded holes in the block must be clean to ensure accurate torque readings during reassembly. Run the proper size tap into each of the holes to remove rust, corrosion, thread sealant or sludge and restore damaged threads **(see illustration)**. If possible, use compressed air to clear the holes of debris produced by this operation. Now is a good time to clean the threads on the head bolts and the main bearing cap bolts as well (though it is recommended that new bolts are used). **Note:** *New main bearing bolts **must** be used on diesel engines.*
10 Refit the main bearing caps/bridge, and tighten the bolts finger-tight.
11 After coating the sealing surfaces of the new core plugs with sealant, fit them in the engine block **(see illustration)**. Make sure they're driven in straight and seated properly, or leakage could result. Special tools are available for this purpose, but a large socket, with an outside diameter that will just slip into the core plug, a 1/2 inch drive extension and a hammer will work just as well.
12 Apply sealant to the new oil gallery plugs and thread them into the holes in the block. Make sure they're tightened securely.
13 On diesel engines, check that the piston oil spray nozzles are clear, then refit them to the cylinder block. Press the nozzles securely into position, ensuring that each one is positioned exactly at a right-angle to the crankshaft axis **(see illustration)**.
14 If the engine isn't going to be reassembled right away, cover it to keep it clean.

13 Engine block – inspection

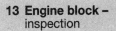

1 Before the block is inspected, it should be cleaned as described in Section 12.
2 Visually check the block for cracks, rust and corrosion. Look for stripped threads in the threaded holes. It's also a good idea to have the block checked for hidden cracks by an automotive engineering workshop that has the special equipment to do this type of work. If defects are found, have the block repaired, if possible, or renewed.
3 Check the cylinder bores for scuffing and scoring.
4 Measuring the cylinder bores for ovality, tapering and wear should be entrusted to an automotive engineering workshop or specialist. Not only are specialist tools required, but also the experience to operate them.
5 If the cylinder walls are badly scuffed or scored, or if they're oval or tapered beyond the limits (refer to a dealer or specialist), have the engine block rebored and honed at an automotive engineering workshop. If a rebore is done, oversize pistons and rings will be required.
6 Using a precision straight-edge and feeler blade, check the block gasket surface (the surface that mates with the cylinder head) for distortions **(see illustrations)**.
7 If the cylinders are in reasonably good condition and not worn to the outside of the

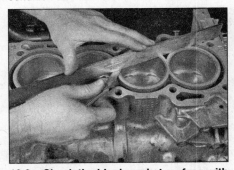

13.6a Check the block gasket surface with a precision straight-edge and feeler blades

limits, and if the piston-to-cylinder clearances can be maintained properly, then they don't have to be rebored. Honing is all that's necessary – ask at an automotive engineering workshop or specialist.

14 Pistons and connecting rods – inspection

1 Before the inspection process can be carried out, the piston/connecting rod assemblies must be cleaned and the original piston rings removed from the pistons. **Note:** *Always use new piston rings when the engine is reassembled.*
2 Using a piston ring expander tool, carefully remove the rings from the pistons. Be careful not to scratch or gouge the pistons in the process.
3 Scrape all traces of carbon from the top of the piston. A hand held wire brush or a piece of fine emery cloth can be used once the majority of the deposits have been scraped away. Do not, under any circumstances, use a wire brush mounted in a drill motor to remove deposits from the pistons. The piston material is soft and may be eroded away by the wire brush.
4 Use a piston ring groove cleaning tool to remove carbon deposits from the ring grooves. If a tool isn't available, a piece broken off the old ring will do the job. Be very careful to remove only the carbon deposits – don't remove any metal and do not scratch the sides of the ring grooves **(see illustrations)**.

13.6b Lay the straight-edge across the block, diagonally and from end-to-end

14.4a The piston ring grooves can be cleaned with a special tool, as shown here . . .

14.4b . . . or a section of a broken ring

14.10 Measure the piston diameter at a 90° angle to the gudgeon pin

5 Once the deposits have been removed, clean the piston/rod assemblies with degreaser and dry them with compressed air (if available). Make sure the oil return holes in the back sides of the ring grooves are clear.

 Warning: Wear eye protection when using compressed air.

6 If the pistons and cylinder walls aren't damaged or worn excessively, and if the engine block isn't rebored, new pistons won't be necessary. Normal piston wear appears as even vertical wear on the piston thrust surfaces and slight looseness of the top ring in its groove. New piston rings, however, should always be used when an engine is rebuilt.
7 Carefully inspect each piston for cracks around the skirt, at the pin bosses and at the ring lands.
8 Look for scoring and scuffing on the thrust faces of the skirt, holes in the piston crown and burned areas at the edge of the crown. If the skirt is scored or scuffed, the engine may have been suffering from overheating and/or abnormal combustion, which caused excessively high operating temperatures. The cooling and lubrication systems should be checked thoroughly. A hole in the piston crown is an indication that abnormal combustion (pre-ignition) was occurring. Burned areas at the edge of the piston crown are usually evidence of spark knock (detonation). If any of the above problems exist, the causes must be corrected or the damage will occur again. The causes may include inlet air leaks, incorrect

fuel/air mixture, low octane fuel, ignition timing and EGR system malfunctions.
9 Corrosion of the piston, in the form of small pits, indicates coolant is leaking into the combustion chamber and/or the crankcase. Again, the cause must be corrected or the problem may persist in the rebuilt engine.
10 Measure the piston across the skirt, at a 90° angle to the gudgeon pin, at the height from the bottom of the skirt listed in this Chapter's Specifications **(see illustration)**.
11 Check the piston-to-rod clearance by twisting the piston and rod in opposite directions. Any noticeable play indicates excessive wear, which must be corrected. The piston/connecting rod assemblies should be taken to an automotive engineering workshop or specialist to have the pistons and rods resized and new gudgeon pins installed. Renewing the gudgeon pins requires several special tools including an hydraulic press.
12 On petrol engines, if the pistons must be removed from the connecting rods for any reason, they should be taken to an automotive engineering workshop or specialist. While they are there have the connecting rods checked for bend and twist, since they have special equipment for this purpose. **Note:** *Unless new pistons and/or connecting rods must be installed, do not dismantle the pistons and connecting rods.*
13 On diesel engines, the gudgeon pins are of the floating type, secured in position by two circlips. The pistons and connecting rods can be separated as follows. Using a small flat-bladed screwdriver, prise out the circlips,

and push out the gudgeon pin. Hand pressure should be sufficient to remove the pin. Identify the piston and rod to ensure correct reassembly. Discard the circlips – new ones **must** be used on refitting. Reassemble the piston and connecting rod so that the mark (dot) on the piston crown is on the same side as the raised mark which is cast onto the side of the connecting rod **(see illustrations)**.
14 Check the connecting rods for cracks and other damage. Temporarily remove the rod caps, lift out the old bearing shells, wipe the rod and cap bearing surfaces clean and inspect them for gouges and scratches. After checking the rods, renew the old bearings, slip the caps into place and tighten the nuts finger tight. **Note:** *If the engine is being rebuilt because of a connecting rod knock, be sure to fit new rods.*

15 Crankshaft – inspection

1 Clean the crankshaft using paraffin or a suitable degreaser, and dry it, preferably with compressed air if available. Be sure to clean the oil holes with a pipe cleaner or similar probe, to ensure that they are not obstructed.

 Warning: Wear eye protection when using compressed air.

2 Check the main and big-end bearing journals for uneven wear, scoring, pitting and cracking.
3 Big-end bearing wear is accompanied by distinct metallic knocking when the engine is running (particularly noticeable when the engine is pulling from low speed) and some loss of oil pressure.
4 Main bearing wear is accompanied by severe engine vibration and rumble – getting progressively worse as engine speed increases – and again by loss of oil pressure.
5 Check the bearing journal for roughness by running a finger lightly over the bearing surface. Any roughness (which will be accompanied by obvious bearing wear) indicates that the crankshaft requires regrinding (where possible) or renewal.
6 Check for burrs around the crankshaft

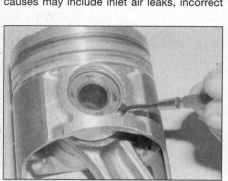

14.13a Prise out the piston circlip

14.13b The connecting rod and piston crown marks must be on the same side

oil holes (the holes are usually chamfered, so burrs should not be a problem unless regrinding has been carried out carelessly). Remove any burrs with a fine file or scraper, and thoroughly clean the oil holes as described previously.

7 Accurate measuring of the crankshaft bearing journals requires special tools and the experience to use them. Consequently, it is recommended that the task be entrusted to an automotive engineering workshop or specialist. If the crankshaft requires machining, they will be able to carry out the work and supply suitable undersize bearing shells.

8 Check the oil seal contact surfaces at each end of the crankshaft for wear and damage. If the seal has worn a deep groove in the surface of the crankshaft, consult an engine overhaul specialist; repair may be possible, but otherwise a new crankshaft will be required.

16 Main and big-end bearings – inspection

1 Even though the main and big-end bearings should be renewed during the engine overhaul, the old bearings should be retained for close examination, as they may reveal valuable information about the condition of the engine **(see illustration)**.

2 Bearing failure can occur due to lack of lubrication, the presence of dirt or other foreign particles, overloading the engine, or corrosion. Regardless of the cause of bearing failure, the cause must be corrected (where applicable) before the engine is reassembled, to prevent it from happening again.

3 When examining the bearing shells, remove them from the cylinder block, the main bearing caps, the connecting rods and the connecting rod big-end bearing caps. Lay them out on a clean surface in the same general position as their location in the engine. This will enable you to match any bearing problems with the corresponding crankshaft journal.

4 Dirt and other foreign matter gets into the engine in a variety of ways. It may be left in the engine during assembly, or it may pass through filters or the crankcase ventilation system. It may get into the oil, and from there into the bearings. Metal chips from machining operations and normal engine wear are often present. Abrasives are sometimes left in engine components after reconditioning, especially when parts are not thoroughly cleaned using the proper cleaning methods. Whatever the source, these foreign objects often end up embedded in the soft bearing material, and are easily recognised. Large particles will not embed in the bearing, and will score or gouge the bearing and journal. The best prevention for this cause of bearing failure is to clean all parts thoroughly, and keep everything spotlessly-clean during engine assembly. Frequent and regular engine oil and filter changes are also recommended.

5 Lack of lubrication (or lubrication breakdown) has a number of interrelated causes. Excessive heat (which thins the oil), overloading (which squeezes the oil from the bearing face) and oil leakage (from excessive bearing clearances, worn oil pump or high engine speeds) all contribute to lubrication breakdown. Blocked oil passages, which usually are the result of misaligned oil holes in a bearing shell, will also oil-starve a bearing, and destroy it. When lack of lubrication is the cause of bearing failure, the bearing material is wiped or extruded from the steel backing of the bearing. Temperatures may increase to the point where the steel backing turns blue from overheating.

6 Driving habits can have a definite effect on bearing life. Full-throttle, low-speed operation (labouring the engine) puts very high loads on bearings, tending to squeeze out the oil film. These loads cause the bearings to flex, which produces fine cracks in the bearing face (fatigue failure). Eventually, the bearing material will loosen in pieces, and tear away from the steel backing.

7 Short-distance driving leads to corrosion of bearings, because insufficient engine heat is produced to drive off the condensed water and corrosive gases. These products collect in the engine oil, forming acid and sludge. As the oil is carried to the engine bearings, the acid attacks and corrodes the bearing material.

8 Incorrect bearing refitting during engine assembly will lead to bearing failure as well. Tight-fitting bearings leave insufficient bearing running clearance, and will result in oil starvation. Dirt or foreign particles trapped behind a bearing shell result in high spots on the bearing, which lead to failure.

9 As mentioned at the beginning of this Section, the bearing shells should be renewed as a matter of course during engine overhaul; to do otherwise is false economy.

17 Engine overhaul – reassembly sequence

1 Before reassembly begins, ensure that all new parts have been obtained, and that all necessary tools are available. Read through the entire procedure to familiarise yourself with the work involved, and to ensure that all items necessary for reassembly of the engine are at hand. In addition to all normal tools and materials, thread-locking compound will be needed. A tube of liquid sealant will also be required for the joint faces that are fitted without gaskets.

2 To save time and avoid problems, engine reassembly must be done in the following general order:

Piston/connecting rod assemblies.
Crankshaft and main bearings.
Crankshaft transmission end oil seal and retainer.
Oil baffle plate (diesel).

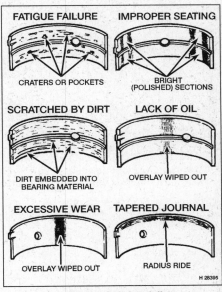

16.1 Typical bearing failures

Oil pump and oil pump pick-up.
Sump.
Cylinder head.
Camshaft(s) and rocker shaft assembly (or housing).
Water pump.
Timing belt and sprockets.
Inlet and exhaust manifolds.
Timing belt covers.
Cylinder head cover.
Flywheel/driveplate.

3 At this stage, all engine components should be absolutely clean and dry, with all faults repaired. The components should be laid out (or in individual containers) on a completely clean work surface.

18 Piston rings – refitting

1 Before fitting the new piston rings, the ring end gaps must be checked.

2 Lay out the piston/connecting rod assemblies and the new ring sets so the ring sets will be matched with the same piston and cylinder during the end gap measurement and engine assembly.

3 Insert the top (No 1) ring into the first cylinder and square it up with the cylinder walls by pushing it in with the top of the piston **(see illustration)**. The ring should be near the bottom of the cylinder, at the lower limit of ring travel.

4 To measure the end gap, slip feeler blades between the ends of the ring until a gauge equal to the gap width is found **(see illustration)**. The feeler blade should slide between the ring ends with a slight amount of drag. Compare the measurement to this Chapter's Specifications. If the gap is larger

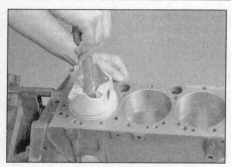

18.3 The ring must be square in the cylinder bore – push it down with a piston

18.4 With the ring square in the cylinder, measure the end gap with a feeler blade

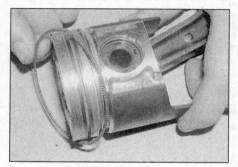

18.9a Fit the expander ring . . .

18.9b . . . followed by the oil control ring

18.12 Fit the compression rings with any identification marks uppermost (arrowed)

or smaller than specified, double-check to make sure you have the correct rings before proceeding.

5 If the gap is too small, it must be enlarged or the ring ends may come in contact with each other during engine operation, which can cause serious engine damage. The end gap can be increased by filing the ring ends very carefully with a fine file. Mount the file in a vice equipped with soft jaws, slip the ring over the file with the ends contacting the file teeth and slowly move the ring to remove material from the ends. When performing this operation, file only from the outside in.

6 Excess end gap isn't critical unless it's greater than the service limit listed in this Chapter's Specifications. Again, double-check to make sure you have the correct rings for the engine.

7 Repeat the procedure for each ring that will be fitted in the first cylinder and for each ring in the remaining cylinders. Remember to keep rings, pistons and cylinders matched up.

8 Once the ring end gaps have been checked/corrected, the rings can be fitted on the pistons.

9 The oil control ring (lowest one on the piston) is usually installed first. It's composed of three separate components. Slip the spacer/expander into the groove **(see illustration)**. If an anti-rotation tang is used, make sure it's inserted into the drilled hole in the ring groove. Next, fit the lower side rail. Don't use a piston ring refitting tool on the oil ring side rails, as they may be damaged. Instead, place one end of the side rail into the groove between the spacer/

expander and the ring land, hold it firmly in place and slide a finger around the piston while pushing the rail into the groove **(see illustration)**. Next, fit the upper side rail in the same manner.

10 After the three oil ring components have been fitted, check to make sure both the upper and lower side rails can be turned smoothly in the ring groove.

11 The No 2 (middle) compression ring is installed next. It's usually stamped with a mark, which must face up, toward the top of the piston. **Note:** *Always follow the instructions printed on the ring package or box – different manufacturers may require different approaches. Don't mix up the top and middle rings, as they have different cross-sections.*

12 Use a piston ring refitting tool and make sure the identification mark is facing the top of the piston, then slip the ring into the middle groove on the piston **(see illustration)**. Don't

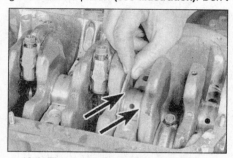

19.6 The thrustwashers (arrowed) are fitted to No 4 main bearing – grooves facing out

expand the ring any more than necessary to slide it over the piston.

13 Fit the No 1 (top) compression ring in the same manner. Make sure the mark is facing up. Be careful not to confuse the No 1 and No 2 rings.

14 Repeat the procedure for the remaining pistons and rings.

19 Crankshaft – refitting

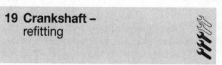

Note: *It is recommended that new main bearing shells are fitted regardless of the condition of the original ones.*

Note: *If you're working on an engine with a main bearing cap bridge, fit the piston/connecting rod assemblies first (see Section 21), placing all of the pistons at Top Dead Centre so the connecting rods don't interfere with crankshaft refitting.*

1 It's assumed at this point that the engine block and crankshaft have been cleaned, inspected and repaired or reconditioned.

2 Position the engine with the bottom facing up.

3 Remove the main bearing caps and/or bridge assembly.

4 Remove the original bearing shells from the block and the main bearing caps. Wipe the bearing surfaces of the block and caps with a clean, lint-free cloth. They must be kept spotlessly clean. **Note:** *Don't touch the faces of the new bearing shells with your fingers. Oil and acids from your skin can etch the bearings.*

5 Clean the back sides of the new main bearing shells and lay one in each main bearing saddle in the block. If one of the bearing shells from each set has a large groove in it, make sure the grooved insert is fitted in the block. Lay the other bearing from each set in the corresponding main bearing cap. Make sure the tab on the bearing shell fits into the recess in the block or cap.

6 On petrol engines, the flanged thrustwashers must be fitted in the No 4 cap and saddle (counting from the left of the engine) **(see illustration)**.

7 On diesel engines, using a little grease,

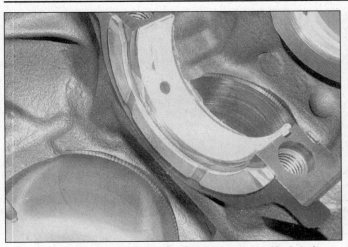

19.7 On diesel engines, fit the thrustwashers to No 2 main bearing – grooves facing out

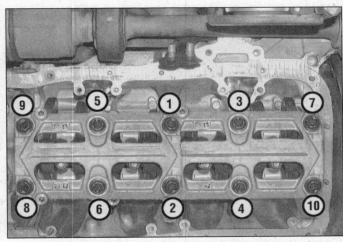

19.15 Main bearing cap bridge assembly tightening sequence – petrol engine

stick the thrustwashers to each side of the No 2 main bearing upper location; ensure that the oilway grooves on each thrustwasher face outwards **(see illustration)**.

8 Also on diesel engines, refit the sensor plate (if removed) to the flywheel end of the crankshaft, and tighten the three bolts to the specified torque.

9 Clean the faces of the bearings in the block and the crankshaft main bearing journals with a clean, lint-free cloth.

10 Check or clean the oil holes in the crankshaft, as any dirt here can go only one way – straight through the new bearings.

11 Clean the bearing faces in the block, then apply a thin, uniform layer of clean engine oil to each of the bearing surfaces. Be sure to coat the thrust faces as well as the journal face of the thrust bearing.

12 Make sure the crankshaft journals are clean, then lay the crankshaft back in place in the block.

13 Clean the faces of the bearings in the caps/bridge, then oil the bearings liberally.

14 Refit the main bearing caps and/or bridge assembly.

15 Fit the new main bearing bolts, with their threads and underside of the heads oiled. Following the recommended sequence, tighten all main bearing cap bolts to the torque

listed in Chapter 2A or 2B Specifications **(see illustration)**.

16 Rotate the crankshaft a number of times by hand to check for any obvious binding.

17 Check the crankshaft endfloat with feeler blades or a dial indicator gauge (DTI) as described in Section 11. The endfloat should be correct if the crankshaft thrust faces aren't worn or damaged and new bearings have been fitted.

18 Refer to Section 20 and fit the new oil seal.

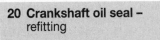

20 Crankshaft oil seal – refitting

Petrol engines

Note: *The crankshaft must be fitted and the main bearing caps bolted in place before the new seal and retainer assembly can be bolted to the block.*

1 Remove the old seal from the retainer with a hammer and punch by driving it out **(see illustration)**. Be sure to note how far it's recessed into the retainer bore before removing it; the new seal will have to be recessed an equal amount. Be very careful

not to scratch or otherwise damage the bore in the retainer or oil leaks could develop.

2 Make sure the retainer is clean. The seal must be pressed squarely into the retainer bore, so hammering it into place isn't recommended. If you don't have access to a press, sandwich the retainer and seal between two smooth pieces of wood and press the seal into place with the jaws of a large vice. If you don't have a vice big enough, lay the retainer on a workbench and drive the seal into place with a wood block and hammer **(see illustration)**. The piece of wood must be thick enough to distribute the force evenly around the entire circumference of the seal. Work slowly and make sure the seal enters the bore squarely.

3 Using a feeler blade, confirm that the clearance (or fitted depth) between the seal and the retainer is equal all the way around **(see illustration)**. The clearance is given in Chapter 2A Specifications.

4 Place a thin coat of liquid sealant (available from Honda dealers) to the entire edge of the retainer.

5 Lubricate the seal lips with multi-purpose grease or engine oil before you slip the seal/ retainer over the crankshaft and bolt it to the block. Be sure to use a new gasket. **Note:** *Apply a film of liquid sealant to both sides of the gasket before refitting.*

20.1 Support the retainer on wood blocks and drive out the oil seal with a punch

20.2 Drive the new seal squarely into the retainer with a wood block

20.3 Check the clearance between the seal and retainer using a feeler blade

20.8 Apply sealant to the oil seal housing mating surface

20.9 Fit the input shaft guide into the end of the crankshaft

6 Tighten the retainer bolts, a little at a time, to the torque listed in the Chapter 2A Specifications. Trim the gasket flush with the sump gasket surface, being careful not to scratch it.

Diesel engines

7 Ensure that the mating surfaces of the oil seal housing and cylinder block are clean and dry. Note the correct fitted depth of the oil seal, then tap/lever the seal out of the housing.
8 Apply a smear of sealant to the oil seal housing mating surface, and make sure that the locating dowels are in position **(see**

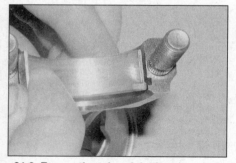

21.3 Ensure the tabs of the bearing shell engage with the notch

illustration). Slide the housing over the end of the crankshaft, and into position on the cylinder block. Put a drop of locking compound on the threads, then tighten the retaining bolts to the specified torque setting.
9 Fit the transmission input shaft guide into the end of the crankshaft **(see illustration)**.
10 Refit/reconnect the piston connecting rod assemblies to the crankshaft as described in Section 21. Referring to Part B of this Chapter, fit a new crankshaft oil seal, then refit the flywheel, oil pump cover, cylinder head, timing belt sprockets and a new timing belt.

21 Pistons and connecting rods – refitting

1 Before fitting the piston/connecting rod assemblies, the cylinder walls must be perfectly clean, the top edge of each cylinder must be chamfered, and the crankshaft must be in place.
2 Remove the cap from the end of the No 1 connecting rod (check the marks made during removal). Remove the original bearing shells and wipe the bearing surfaces of connecting rod and cap with a clean, lint-free cloth. They must be kept spotlessly clean.
Note: *Don't touch the faces of the new bearing shells with your fingers. Oil and acids from your skin can etch the bearings.*
3 Clean the back side of the new upper bearing shell, then lay it in place in the connecting rod. Make sure the tab on the bearing fits into the recess in the rod **(see illustration)**. Don't hammer the bearing shell into place and be very careful not to scratch or gouge the bearing face. Lubricate the bearing face with clean engine oil.
4 Clean the back side of the other bearing shell and fit it in the rod cap. Again, make sure the tab on the bearing fits into the recess in the cap, and lubricate the bearing face with clean engine oil.
5 Position the piston ring gaps at intervals around the piston **(see illustrations)**.
Caution: DON'T position any ring gap in line with the gudgeon pin hole or at the piston thrust surfaces (90° to gudgeon pin).
6 Tap out the old big-end bolts, and fit new ones **(see illustration)**. Slip a section of plastic or rubber hose over each bolt.
7 Lubricate the piston and rings with clean engine oil and attach a piston ring compressor to the piston. Leave the skirt protruding about 6 mm to guide the piston into the cylinder. The rings must be compressed until they're flush with the piston.
8 Rotate the crankshaft until the No 1 connecting rod journal is at BDC (bottom dead centre) and apply a coat of engine oil to the cylinder bores.
9 With the dot mark or arrow on top of the piston facing the timing belt end of the engine **(see illustration)**, gently insert the piston/connecting rod assembly into the No 1 cylinder bore and rest the bottom edge of the ring compressor on the engine block.
10 Tap the top edge of the ring compressor to make sure it's contacting the block around its entire circumference.
11 Gently tap on the top of the piston with

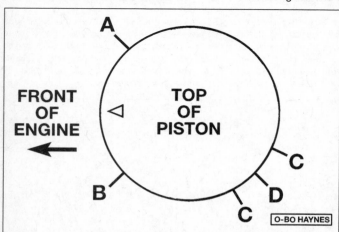

21.5a Petrol engine ring end gap positions – align oil control ring spacer gap at D, oil control ring side rails at C, second compression ring at A, and top compression ring at B

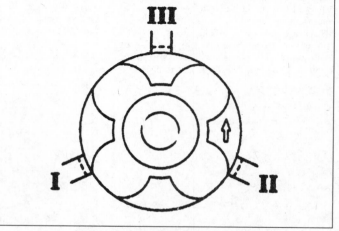

21.5b Piston ring end gap positions – diesel engines

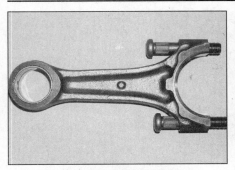

21.6 Renew the big-end bolts – diesel engines

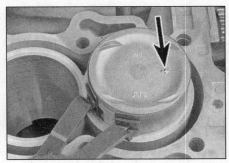

21.9 Fit the pistons with the mark (arrowed) towards the timing belt end of the engine

21.11 Tap the piston assembly into the cylinder using a hammer handle

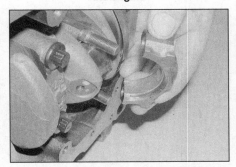

21.12a Lubricate the bearing surface and refit the bearing cap

21.12b Use an angle gauge to accurately tighten the bearing cap bolts – diesel engines

the end of a wooden or plastic hammer handle **(see illustration)** while guiding the end of the connecting rod into place on the crankshaft journal. The piston rings may try to pop out of the ring compressor just before entering the cylinder bore, so keep some pressure on the ring compressor. Work slowly, and if any resistance is felt as the piston enters the cylinder, stop immediately. Find out what's catching and fix it before proceeding. Do not, for any reason, force the piston into the cylinder – you might break a ring and/or the piston.

12 Slide the connecting rod into place on the journal, then remove the protective hoses from the rod cap bolts. Lubricate and fit the rod cap, tightening the nuts to the torque listed in Chapter 2A or 2B Specifications **(see illustrations)**.

13 Repeat the entire procedure for the remaining pistons/connecting rods.

14 The important points to remember are:

a) *Keep the back sides of the bearing shells and the insides of the connecting rods and caps perfectly clean when assembling them.*

b) *Make sure you have the correct piston/ rod assembly for each cylinder.*

c) *The arrow or dot mark on the piston must face the timing belt end of the engine.*

d) *Lubricate the cylinder bores with clean oil.*

e) *Lubricate the bearing faces when fitting the rod caps.*

f) *Where applicable, refit the main bearing cap bridge assembly before proceeding to the next paragraph.*

15 After all the piston/connecting rod assemblies and the main bearing cap bridge (if fitted) have been properly fitted, rotate the crankshaft a number of times by hand to check for any obvious binding.

22 Engine – initial start-up after overhaul

1 With the engine refitted in the car, double-check the engine oil and coolant levels. Make a final check that everything has been reconnected, and that there are no tools or rags left in the engine compartment.

Petrol models

2 Remove the spark plugs (see Chapter 1A).

3 Disable the fuel system by removing the fuse No 6 from the engine compartment fusebox (or see Chapter 12 – wiring diagrams).

Caution: To prevent damage to the catalytic converter from unburnt fuel, it is important to disable the fuel system.

4 Turn the engine on the starter until the oil pressure warning light goes out. If the light fails to extinguish after several seconds of cranking, check the engine oil level and that the oil filter is correctly fitted. Assuming these are correct, check the oil pressure switch wiring – do not progress any further until you are satisfied that oil is being pumped around the engine at sufficient pressure.

5 Refit the spark plugs (Chapter 1A), refit the fuel pump fuse, then switch on the ignition and listen for the fuel pump; it will run for a little longer than usual, due to the lack of pressure in the system.

Diesel models

6 Disable the engine management system by removing the fuse No 6 from the engine compartment fusebox (or see Chapter 12 – wiring diagrams).

7 Turn the engine on the starter until the oil pressure warning light goes out. If the light fails to extinguish after several seconds of cranking, check the engine oil level and the oil filter. Assuming these are correct, check the security of the oil pressure switch wiring – do not progress any further until you are satisfied that oil is being pumped around the engine at sufficient pressure.

8 Refit the engine management fuse.

9 Bleed the fuel system as described in Chapter 4B, Section 5.

All models

10 Start the engine, noting that this also may take a little longer than usual, due to the fuel system components being empty.

11 While the engine is idling, check for fuel, coolant and oil leaks. Don't be alarmed if there are some odd smells and smoke from parts getting hot and burning off oil deposits.

12 Keep the engine idling until hot water is felt circulating through the top hose, check that it idles reasonably smoothly and at the usual speed, then switch it off.

13 After a few hours, recheck the oil and coolant levels, and top-up as necessary (*Weekly checks*).

14 If new components such as pistons, rings or crankshaft bearings have been fitted, the engine must be run-in for the first 500 miles. Do not operate the engine at full-throttle, or allow it to labour in any gear during this time. It is recommended that the oil and filter be changed at the end of this period.

Notes

Chapter 3
Cooling, heating and air conditioning systems

Contents

Degrees of difficulty

Easy, suitable for novice with little experience	Fairly easy, suitable for beginner with some experience	Fairly difficult, suitable for competent DIY mechanic	Difficult, suitable for experienced DIY mechanic	Very difficult, suitable for expert DIY or professional

Specifications

General

Coolant capacity	See Chapter 1A or 1B
Cooling fan:	
Switch-on temperature:	
Petrol models	91 to 95°C
Diesel models:	
First speed	93 to 97°C
Second speed..	98 to 102°C
Switch-off temperature....................................	3 to 8°C below actual switch-on temperature
Pressure cap rating	0.95 to 1.25 bar
Thermostat:	
Petrol engines:	
Opens at..	76 to 80°C
Fully open at	90°C
Diesel engines:	
Opens at..	83 to 87°C
Fully open at	100°C
Valve lift at fully open	8.0 mm (minimum)
Air conditioning:	
Refrigerant type	R134a
Refrigerant quantity	500 to 550g

Torque wrench settings

	Nm	lbf ft
Air conditioning compressor mounting bolts:		
Petrol models	22	16
Diesel models...	25	18
Coolant temperature gauge sender	10	7
Coolant temperature switch..................................	24	18
Thermostat housing cover bolts:		
Petrol models	12	9
Diesel models...	24	18
Thermostat housing-to-block bolts	12	9
Water pump bolts:		
Petrol models	12	9
Diesel models...	24	18

1 General information and precautions

Engine cooling system

All models covered by this manual employ a pressurised engine cooling system with thermostatically-controlled coolant circulation. An impeller-type water pump mounted on the engine block pumps coolant through the engine. The coolant flows around each cylinder and toward the rear of the engine. Cast-in coolant passages direct coolant around the intake and exhaust ports, near the combustion chamber areas and in close proximity to the exhaust valve guides.

A wax pellet type thermostat controls engine coolant temperature. During warm-up, the closed thermostat prevents coolant from circulating through the radiator. As the engine nears normal operating temperature, the thermostat opens and allows hot coolant to travel through the radiator, where it is cooled before returning to the engine. Diesel models feature something which Honda call a 'water glow plug'; screwed into the thermostat housing next to the temperature gauge sender, this actually warms the water passing through the housing during engine warm-up, under the control of the engine management ECM.

The cooling system is sealed by a pressure cap, which raises the boiling point of the coolant and increases the cooling efficiency of the radiator.

Heating system

The heating system consists of a blower fan and heater matrix located in the heater housing, the hoses connecting the heater matrix to the engine cooling system and the heater/air conditioning controls on the facia. Hot engine coolant is supplied to the heater control valve located in the heater supply hose in the engine compartment. When the heater temperature control is turned to hot, a cable- or motor-operated air flap door opens to expose the heater matrix to the passenger compartment, and another cable opens the heater valve. When required, a fan switch on the control panel activates the blower motor,

2.3 Release the spring-type hose clips using pliers

which forces air through the matrix, increasing the supply of warm air.

Air conditioning system

See Section 10.

Precautions

Cooling system

Do not attempt to remove the radiator cap (petrol models) or expansion tank filler cap, nor to disturb any part of the cooling system with the engine hot, as there is a risk of scalding. If the cap must be removed before the engine and radiator have fully cooled down (even though this is not recommended) the pressure in the cooling system must first be released. Cover the cap with a thick layer of cloth, to avoid scalding, and slowly unscrew the filler cap until a hissing sound can be heard. When the hissing has stopped, showing that the pressure is released, slowly unscrew the filler cap until it can be removed. If more hissing sounds are heard, wait until they have stopped before unscrewing the cap completely. At all times keep well away from the filler opening.

Do not allow antifreeze to come in contact with your skin or painted surfaces of the car. Rinse off spills immediately with plenty of water. Never leave antifreeze lying around; as it can be fatal if ingested.

If the engine is hot, the electric cooling fan may start rotating even if the engine is not running, so be careful to keep hands, hair and loose clothing well clear when working in the engine compartment.

Air conditioning system

On models with an air conditioning system, it is necessary to observe special precautions whenever dealing with any part of the system, its associated components and any items which necessitate disconnection of the system. If for any reason the system must be disconnected, entrust this task to a refrigeration engineer.

Refrigerant must not be allowed to come in contact with a naked flame, otherwise a poisonous gas will be created. Do not allow the fluid to come in contact with the skin or eyes.

2 Cooling system hoses – disconnection and renewal

Note: *Refer to the precautions given in Section 1 of this Chapter before starting work.*

1 If the checks described in the appropriate part of Chapter 1 reveal a faulty hose, it must be renewed as follows.

2 First drain the cooling system (see the appropriate part of Chapter 1); if the antifreeze is not due for renewal, the drained coolant may be re-used, if it is collected in a clean container.

3 Release the hose clips from the hose concerned. Almost all the standard clips fitted at the factory are the spring type, released

by squeezing its tangs together with pliers, at the same time working the clip away from the hose stub **(see illustration)**. These clips can be awkward to use, can pinch old hoses, and may become less effective with age, so may have been replaced with Jubilee clips (released by turning the screw).

4 Unclip any wires, cables or other hoses which may be attached to the hose being removed. Make notes for reference when reassembling if necessary.

5 Note that the coolant unions are fragile (most are made of plastic); do not use excessive force when attempting to remove the hoses. If a hose proves to be difficult to remove, try to release it by rotating the hose ends before attempting to free it – if this fails, try gently prising up the end of the hose with a small screwdriver to 'break' the seal.

> **HAYNES HINT** *If the hose is stiff, use a little soapy water as a lubricant, or soften the hose by soaking it with hot water. If all else fails, cut the coolant hose with a sharp knife, then slit it so that it can be peeled off in two pieces. Although this may prove expensive if the hose is otherwise undamaged, it is preferable to buying a new radiator.*

6 Before fitting the new hose, smear the stubs with washing-up liquid or a suitable rubber lubricant to aid fitting. **Do not** use oil or grease, which may attack the rubber.

7 Fit the hose clips over the ends of the hose, then fit the hose over its stubs. When refitting hose clips, give some thought to how easy they will be to remove in the future – make sure the screw fitting or spring tangs will be accessible.

8 Work each hose end fully onto its outlet, check that the hose is settled correctly and is properly routed, then slide each clip along the hose until it is behind the outlet flared end before tightening it securely. Spring-type clips must have the ends squeezed together, and the clip positioned over the outlet flared end, then released. Do not over-tighten screw-type clips, as this may damage the hoses (and even the unions).

9 Refill the cooling system as described in Chapter 1A or 1B. Run the engine, and check that there are no leaks.

10 Recheck the tightness of the hose clips on any new hoses after a few hundred miles.

3 Thermostat – removal, testing and refitting

Note: *Refer to the precautions in Section 1 of this Chapter before starting work.*

1 As the thermostat ages, it will become slower to react to changes in water temperature ('lazy'). Ultimately, the unit may stick in the open or closed position, and this causes problems.

A thermostat which is stuck open will result in a very slow warm-up; a thermostat which is stuck shut will lead to rapid overheating.

2 Before assuming the thermostat is to blame for a cooling system problem, check the coolant level. If the system is draining due to a leak, or has not been properly filled, there may be an airlock in the system (refer to the coolant renewal procedure in Chapter 1A or 1B).

3 If the engine seems to be taking a long time to warm up (based on heater output), the thermostat could be stuck open. Don't necessarily believe the temperature gauge reading – some gauges never seem to register very high in normal driving.

4 A lengthy warm-up period might suggest that the thermostat is missing – it may have been removed or inadvertently omitted by a previous owner or mechanic. Don't drive the car without a thermostat – the engine management system's ECM will then stay in warm-up mode for longer than necessary, causing emissions and fuel economy to suffer.

5 If the engine runs hot, use your hand to check the temperature of the radiator top hose. If the hose isn't hot, but the engine clearly is, the thermostat is probably stuck closed, preventing the coolant inside the engine from escaping to the radiator – renew the thermostat. Again, this problem may also be due to an airlock (refer to the coolant renewal procedure in Chapter 1A or 1B).

6 If the radiator top hose is hot, it means that the coolant is flowing (at least as far as the radiator) and the thermostat is open. Consult the *Fault diagnosis* section at the end of this manual to assist in tracing possible cooling system faults, but a lack of heater output would now definitely suggest an airlock or a blockage.

7 To gain a rough idea of whether the thermostat is working properly when the engine is warming up, without dismantling the system, proceed as follows.

8 With the engine completely cold, start the engine and let it idle, while checking the temperature of the radiator top hose. Periodically check the temperature indicated on the coolant temperature gauge – if overheating is indicated, switch the engine off immediately.

9 The top hose should feel cold for some time as the engine warms up, and should then get warm quite quickly as the thermostat opens.

10 The above is not a precise or definitive test of thermostat operation, but if the system does not perform as described, remove and test the thermostat as described below.

Removal

11 Drain the cooling system (see Chapter 1A or 1B). If the coolant is relatively new or in good condition, save and re-use it.

Petrol models

12 Disconnect the electrical connector from the radiator fan switch. Note that access

3.12a On petrol models, disconnect the top hose . . .

3.13 Disconnect the radiator bottom hose from the thermostat cover

to the thermostat is greatly improved by disconnecting the top hose from the coolant housing **(see illustrations)**.

13 Release the hose clip, then detach the radiator hose from the cover **(see illustration)**.

14 Remove the two thermostat cover bolts and detach the housing cover **(see illustration)**. If the cover is stuck, tap it with a soft-faced hammer to jar it loose. Be prepared for some coolant to spill as the seal is broken.

15 Note how it's fitted, then remove the thermostat **(see illustration)**. Recover the rubber seal from the thermostat – a new one should be used when refitting.

Diesel models

16 Remove the air cleaner as described in Chapter 4B. Access to the top of the thermostat housing is also improved by removing the large intercooler air duct, after loosening the hose clips.

3.15 Withdraw the thermostat from the housing

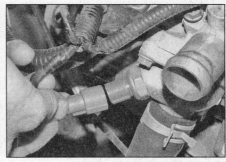

3.12b . . . and unplug the radiator fan switch

3.14 Unscrew the bolts, and remove the cover

17 Release the hose clips, and disconnect the radiator hose and heater hose from the thermostat cover **(see illustration)**.

18 Remove the two thermostat cover bolts and detach the housing cover. If the cover is stuck, tap it with a soft-faced hammer to jar it loose. Recover the cover gasket – a new one should be used when refitting.

19 Lift out the thermostat **(see illustration overleaf)**.

Testing

Note: *Frankly, if there is any question about the operation of the thermostat, it's best to renew it – they are not usually expensive items. Testing involves heating in, or over, an open pan of boiling water, which carries with it the risk of scalding. A thermostat which has seen more than five years' service may well be past its best already.*

20 If the thermostat remains in the open

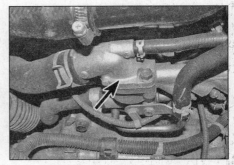

3.17 Thermostat housing location – diesel models

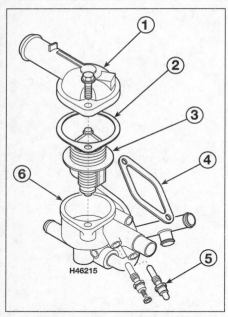

**3.19 Thermostat housing details –
diesel models**

1 Thermostat cover
2 Cover gasket
3 Thermostat
4 Thermostat housing gasket
5 Water glow plug
6 Thermostat housing

position at room temperature, it is faulty, and must be renewed as a matter of course.

21 Check to see if there's a open temperature marking stamped on the thermostat.

22 Using a thermometer and container of water, heat the water until the temperature corresponds with the temperature marking stamped on the thermostat. If no marking is found, start the test with the water hot, and heat slowly until it boils.

23 Suspend the (closed) thermostat on a length of string in the water, and check that maximum opening occurs within two minutes, or before the water boils.

24 Remove the thermostat and allow it to cool down; check that it closes fully.

25 If the thermostat does not open and close as described, or if it sticks in either position, it must be renewed.

**4.8 Remove the two upper mounting bolts
from each fan, and lift it off**

Refitting

26 Refitting is a reversal of removal, but note the following additional points:

  a) *Clean all mating surfaces thoroughly before reassembly.*

  b) *Fit a new cover gasket or rubber seal, as applicable.*

  c) *On petrol models, the thermostat should be fitted so that the bypass pin is at the top.*

  d) *Tighten all bolts to their specified torque wrench settings (where given).*

  e) *Ensure the coolant hose clips are positioned so that they do not foul any other components, and so they can easily be removed in future, then fit them securely. Consider updating the spring clips with Jubilee ones.*

  f) *Refill the cooling system (see Chapter 1A or 1B).*

---

4 Radiator and condenser fans
  – testing, removal and refitting

⚠️ *Warning: To avoid possible injury or damage, DO NOT operate the engine with a damaged fan. Do not attempt to repair fan blades – renew a damaged fan.*

Testing

Note: *Models equipped with air conditioning have two complete fan circuits – one for the condenser and one for the radiator. The following procedures apply to both.*

1 To test a fan motor, disconnect the two-pin electrical connector at the motor, and use bridging wires to connect the fan directly to the battery. If the fan still doesn't work, renew the motor. The radiator fan wiring plug is on the right-hand side of the front crossmember, with the condenser fan plug on the left (left and right as seen from the driver's seat) – do not confuse these plugs with those for the bonnet alarm switch or the air conditioning compressor clutch.

2 If the motor tests OK, check the fuse and relay (see Chapter 12), the fan switch, the condenser fan relay (also mounted in the engine compartment fusebox) if equipped, or the wiring which connects the components. **Note:** *On some models, the condenser fan relay is mounted directly in front of the condenser on the driver's side of the engine compartment.*

3 On petrol models, only one switch is fitted – the radiator fan switch is screwed into the thermostat cover. Diesel models have a two-speed fan, requiring two switches – both are screwed into the top of the radiator.

4 To test a radiator fan switch, remove the switch electrical connector and, using an ohmmeter, check for continuity across the terminals of the switch with the engine cold. The switch should not have continuity while the coolant is below the specified switch-on temperature. Start the engine and allow the engine to reach normal operating temperature.

Stop the engine and check for continuity again. The radiator fan switch should show continuity when the coolant temperature reaches or exceeds the switch-on temperature. If the switch fails to show continuity above this temperature, renew it.

5 The air conditioning condenser fan is controlled by the ECM. If the condenser fan fails to operate with the air conditioning on after all other checks have been completed, check for a low refrigerant charge or have the ECM diagnosed by a dealership service department or specialist.

Removal

6 Disconnect the battery negative lead, and position the lead away from the battery (also see *Disconnecting the battery*).

7 All the fans are bolted to the back of the radiator, and clearance to get on the bolts is limited, particularly at the bottom. Honda suggest that, in all cases, the radiator should first be removed as described in Section 5, and the fan/shroud assemblies unbolted afterwards. Having checked this on our project car, we have to agree.

8 With the radiator assembly removed, unbolt the fans as required **(see illustration)**. While the whole of the radiator is accessible, take the opportunity to thoroughly clean the fins, using a stiff paintbrush.

Refitting

9 Refitting is a reversal of removal, noting the following points:

  a) *Tighten the fan mounting bolts securely.*

  b) *Refit the radiator as described in Section 5.*

  c) *On completion, check the fan operation, either as described in Section 4, or by starting the engine and allowing it to reach operating temperature – if this method is chosen, do not allow the engine to overheat.*

---

5 Radiator –
  removal and refitting

Note 1: *Refer to the precautions in Section 1 of this Chapter before starting work.*

Note 2: *If the reason for removing the radiator is to cure a leak, note that minor leaks can sometimes be cured with the radiator in place, by using one of the proprietary radiator sealants.*

Removal

1 Jack up the front of the car, and support it on axle stands (see *Jacking and vehicle support*). Remove the bolts and take off the engine undertray.

2 Drain the cooling system as described in Chapter 1A or 1B.

Petrol models

3 Remove the front bumper and bumper crossmember as described in Chapter 11.

4 Release the clips and disconnect the

radiator top and bottom hoses. On models with automatic transmission, clamp the two small fluid cooler hoses at the base of the radiator before carefully disconnecting them, to reduce fluid loss to a minimum.

5 Work along the crossmember (or 'slam panel'), disconnecting the following wiring plugs (as applicable):
   a) Radiator cooling fan.
   b) Air conditioning compressor clutch.
   c) Air conditioning condenser fan.

6 On models with air conditioning, the condenser prevents the radiator from being removed. Working as described in Section 11, unbolt the condenser, but note that the pipes on the passenger side do not have to be disconnected – once the condenser is free, pull it out on the driver's side slightly, and support it on an axle stand or similar.

7 Unbolt the radiator upper support brackets at each end, and lift them off.

Diesel models

8 Work along the crossmember (or 'slam panel'), disconnecting the following wiring plugs (as applicable):
   a) Radiator cooling fan.
   b) Bonnet lock alarm switch.
   c) Air conditioning compressor clutch.
   d) Air conditioning condenser fan.

9 Carefully release or cut through the cable-ties securing the wiring harness to the crossmember.

10 Unscrew the bolts along the crossmember securing the upper support brackets for the radiator and air conditioning condenser (where fitted). As the bolts and brackets are removed, note their fitted positions for refitting.

11 Remove a further bolt at each end of the crossmember, and one at the base of the panel's central support. Carefully lift out the crossmember **(see illustration)**.

12 Trace the two air hoses from the top of the intercooler, and disconnect them from the engine.

13 Release the clips and disconnect the radiator top and bottom hoses, and the expansion tank hoses.

All models

14 Carefully lift out the radiator, noting that its lower pegs locate into rubber supports. Tilt the radiator to one side, to avoid spilling any remaining coolant on the paintwork.

15 Unbolt the fan assemblies from the back of the radiator as required.

16 Inspect the radiator for leaks and damage. If it needs repair, have a radiator repair specialist perform the work, as special techniques are required.

17 Debris and dirt can be removed from the radiator by spraying with a garden hose from the engine side.

18 Inspect the radiator mounts for deterioration, and renew if necessary.

Refitting

19 Refitting is a reversal of removal, noting the following points:

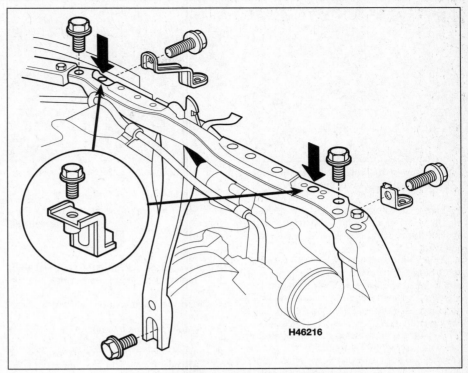

5.11 Front crossmember removal details

   a) Guide the radiator onto its lower mountings, taking care not to damage the fins on the surrounding components.
   b) On diesel models, note that the front crossmember fits over the radiator upper mounting pegs.
   c) Refit the radiator, expansion tank and intercooler hoses correctly and securely (as applicable). Consider updating any spring-type clips with Jubilee clips.
   d) Refill the cooling system as described in Chapter 1A or 1B.
   e) On automatic transmission models, check and if necessary top-up the transmission fluid level as described in Chapter 1A.

6 Expansion tank – removal and refitting

Note: Refer to the precautions in Section 1 of this Chapter before starting work.

Petrol models

1 The expansion tank is mounted adjacent to the radiator in the right-hand front corner of the engine compartment (right as seen from the driver's seat).

2 Remove the battery as described in Chapter 5A.

3 Trace the overflow hose from the radiator neck to the top of the tank. Remove the cap with the hose still attached. Lift the reservoir off its mountings and up out of the engine compartment.

4 Pour the coolant into a container – if it is clean, and the coolant is not due for renewal, it can be saved for re-use.

5 Wash out and inspect the reservoir for cracks. If it's damaged, renew it.

6 Refitting is the reverse of removal.

Diesel models

7 The expansion tank on diesel models is mounted centrally at the rear of the engine compartment.

8 Disconnect the two hoses at the front of the tank, noting their respective locations, and also pull off the overflow hose under the cap.

9 Have a container ready underneath the tank, then release the hose clip and disconnect the lower hose. Allow the coolant to drain – if it is clean, and the coolant is not due for renewal, it can be saved for re-use.

10 Undo the two mounting bolts, and lift the tank off the bulkhead.

11 Wash out and inspect the reservoir for cracks. If it's damaged, renew it.

12 Refitting is the reverse of removal.

7 Water pump – inspection, removal and refitting

Note: Refer to the precautions in Section 1 of this Chapter before starting work.

Inspection

1 A failure in the water pump can cause serious engine damage due to overheating.

7.8a Remove the water pump bolts – note that this one is shortest

7.8b Withdraw the pump from the engine

7.8c Remove the old O-ring from the pump's groove

2 There are two ways to check the operation of the water pump while it's fitted on the engine. If the pump is defective, it should be renewed.

3 Water pumps are equipped with weep (or vent) holes. If a failure occurs in the pump seal, coolant will leak from the hole – on petrol engines, the timing belt cover will have to be removed as described in Chapter 2A for a complete check.

4 Even if the pump's weep hole is not actually wet when inspected, an established coolant leak will show up as a powdery deposit (often white or antifreeze-coloured) under the hole.

5 If the water pump shaft bearings fail, there may be a howling or scraping sound at the pump while it's running. Shaft wear can be felt with the timing belt or drivebelt removed if the water pump pulley is rocked up-and-down (with the engine not running).

Petrol models

Removal

6 Drain the cooling system (see Chapter 1A). If the coolant is relatively new or in good condition, save and re-use it.

7 Remove the timing belt as described in Chapter 2A.

8 Remove the four water pump mounting bolts, noting that the bolt nearest the timing belt tensioner is shorter than the others, and detach the water pump from the engine. Prise the O-ring seal from the pump's groove – a new one must be used when refitting **(see illustrations)**.

9 Note that it is not possible to overhaul the pump. If it is faulty, the unit must be renewed complete.

Refitting

10 Clean the bolt threads, and if available, use a tap to clean the threaded holes in the engine.

11 Clean the engine and new water pump mating surfaces.

12 Carefully set a new O-ring in the groove of the pump.

13 Offer the pump up to the engine, then fit the bolts and tighten them progressively to the specified torque.

14 Refit the timing belt as described in Chapter 2A. It is recommended that a new belt is fitted, unless the existing one is known to have been changed recently.

15 Refill and bleed the cooling system as described in Chapter 1A.

Diesel models

Removal

16 Apply the handbrake, then jack up the front of the car and support it on axle stands (see *Jacking and vehicle support*). Remove the bolts and lower out the engine undertray.

17 Loosen the three water pump pulley bolts, but do not remove them at this stage – loosening the bolts is more easily done while the auxiliary drivebelt is still fitted.

18 Remove the auxiliary drivebelt as described in Chapter 1B.

19 Drain the cooling system as described in Chapter 1B.

20 Unscrew and remove the pulley bolts, and remove the pulley from the pump **(see illustration)**.

21 Unscrew and remove the five water pump mounting bolts **(see illustration)**.

22 Withdraw the water pump from the cylinder block, noting that it may be necessary to tap the pump lightly with a soft-faced mallet to free it from the cylinder block.

23 Recover the gasket and discard it; a new one must be used on refitting **(see illustration)**.

24 Note that it is not possible to overhaul the pump. If it is faulty, the unit must be renewed complete.

Refitting

25 Clean the bolt threads, and if available, use a tap to clean the threaded holes in the engine.

26 Ensure that the pump and cylinder block mating surfaces are clean and dry.

27 Refit the water pump to the cylinder block, together with a new gasket.

28 Insert the mounting bolts and tighten progressively to the specified torque.

29 Refit the pump pulley and tighten the bolts by hand at this stage.

30 Refit the auxiliary drivebelt as described in Chapter 1B, then tighten the pump pulley bolts fully.

31 Refit the undertray and lower the car to the ground.

32 Refill and bleed the cooling system as described in Chapter 1B.

7.20 Removing the water pump pulley – diesel models

7.21 Water pump mounting bolts – diesel models

7.23 Recover the water pump gasket – diesel models

8 Cooling system sensors and switches – removal and refitting

⚠ **Warning: Wait until the engine is completely cool before beginning this procedure.**

Coolant temperature sensor

1 Refer to Chapter 4A or 4B.

Radiator fan switch

2 To test the switch, refer to Section 4.

Petrol models

3 The radiator fan switch is screwed into the thermostat cover – do not confuse it with the coolant temperature sensor, which is located in the coolant housing on the end of the cylinder head **(see illustration)**.
4 Either drain the cooling system as described in Chapter 1A, or, if the new switch can be fitted immediately, anticipate some small loss of coolant when the old switch is removed.
5 Disconnect the switch wiring plug, then unscrew the switch and remove it. Recover the O-ring seal – a new one should be used when refitting **(see illustrations)**.
6 Fit the switch with a new O-ring, and tighten securely.
7 Reconnect the switch wiring plug securely.
8 On completion, either refill or top-up the cooling system (see Chapter 1A or *Weekly checks*).

Diesel models

9 The two radiator fan switches are screwed into the top of the radiator. The higher-temperature switch is the one nearer the end of the radiator.
10 Either drain the cooling system as described in Chapter 1B, or, if the new switch can be fitted immediately, anticipate some small loss of coolant when the old switch is removed.
11 Disconnect the switch wiring plug, then unscrew the switch and remove it. Recover the O-ring seal – a new one should be used when refitting.
12 Fit the switch with a new O-ring, and tighten securely.
13 Reconnect the switch wiring plug securely.
14 On completion, either refill or top-up the cooling system (see Chapter 1B or *Weekly checks*).

Condenser fan switch

15 Refer to Section 4.

Water glow plug (diesel models)

16 The water glow plug is screwed into the thermostat housing, behind the coolant temperature sensor. Our project car actually had three such plugs.
17 Either drain the cooling system as described in Chapter 1B, or, if the new plug can be fitted immediately, anticipate some

8.3 Radiator fan switch – petrol models

small loss of coolant when the old plug is removed.
18 Unscrew the nut and disconnect the wiring from the plug, then unscrew the plug and remove it. Recover the O-ring seal – a new one should be used when refitting.
19 Check that the old and new plugs are of the same power rating – this is denoted by a coloured band, which will be either silver or green.
20 Fit the plug with a new O-ring, and tighten securely.
21 Reconnect the wiring, and secure with the nut.
22 On completion, either refill or top-up the cooling system (see Chapter 1B or *Weekly checks*).

9 Heater/ventilation system components – removal and refitting

Note: *On models with climate control ('automatic' air conditioning), various other heating and ventilation control components are fitted in addition to the items listed in this Section – these are covered in Section 11.*

Air vents

1 The facia panel end vents are screwed directly into the end of the main facia panel, and so can only be removed once the facia panel itself has been removed, as described in Chapter 11. Each vent is secured by four screws.
2 The centre vents are an integral part of the

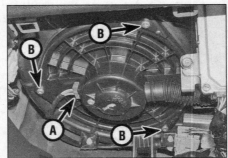

9.7a Blower motor wiring plug (A) and three mounting screws (B)

8.5a Disconnect the switch wiring plug . . .

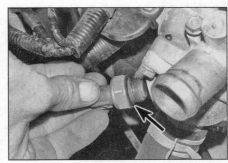

8.5b . . . then unscrew and remove it – note the O-ring seal

facia centre panel, which is removed as part of the heater control panel procedure described later in this Section.

Blower motor components

3 The blower motor is located behind the glovebox.
4 Remove the glovebox and the kick panel from the passenger footwell, as described in Chapter 11.
5 Though not essential for all tasks listed below, more working room will be created by removing the engine management ECM as described in Chapter 4A or 4B.

Motor and fan

6 Disconnect the motor wiring plug, which is directly below the motor, to the left.
7 Remove the three motor securing screws, and withdraw the motor and fan from the housing **(see illustrations)**.
8 Refitting is a reversal of removal.

9.7b Removing the blower motor

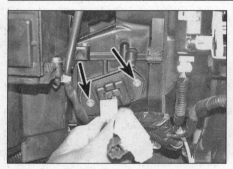

9.10 Disconnect the resistor pack wiring plug (mounting screws arrowed)

9.11 Removing the blower motor resistor pack

9.14 Disconnect the recirculation motor wiring plug

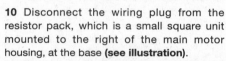
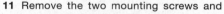

9.17 The plastic brace across the glovebox aperture must be cut at these points

Resistor pack

9 If the blower fan will only operate on its fastest speed, or not at all, the resistor pack may be faulty. Gain access to the blower motor as described in paragraphs 4 and 5.

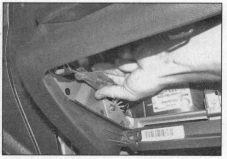

9.18a Remove the four screws inside . . .

10 Disconnect the wiring plug from the resistor pack, which is a small square unit mounted to the right of the main motor housing, at the base **(see illustration)**.

11 Remove the two mounting screws and

9.18b . . . and remove the glovebox frame

withdraw the pack from the housing **(see illustration)**.

12 Refitting is a reversal of removal.

Recirculation motor

13 When the recirculation switch is operated, a motor on the side of the blower motor housing operates the flap door to close off the supply of incoming air. Gain access to the blower motor as described in paragraphs 4 and 5.

14 Reach up by the right-hand side of the housing, and disconnect the recirculation motor wiring plug – do not confuse it with the resistor pack plug, which is lower down at the front **(see illustration)**.

15 The motor is secured by three screws to the side (a small bracket in front, secured by a single bolt, may also have to be removed). Remove the screws and withdraw the motor.

16 Refitting is a reversal of removal.

Complete housing

17 If the facia panel has not been removed, the housing will prove difficult to remove. At the base of the glovebox aperture is a plastic cross-brace, which Honda say must be cut through at each end, just inside the bolt holes, to allow the blower housing to be removed **(see illustration)**. As this is done, take care not to damage any other components.

18 At the top of the glovebox aperture is a frame running across, which is secured by two screws at either end. Remove the four screws and take out the glovebox frame **(see illustrations)**.

19 Disconnect the wiring plug from the blower motor itself (underneath), and the plug from the resistor pack (above and to the right) **(see illustrations)**.

20 Noting how it is routed, release the wiring from the support clips, tracing it back to the two further wiring plugs underneath to the right. Disconnect these two plugs, then undo two screws and remove the lower support bracket **(see illustrations)**.

21 Disconnect the recirculation control motor wiring plug on the right of the assembly, and free the wiring from its clips **(see illustration 9.14)**.

22 The housing is secured by two nuts and three bolts – unscrew these, noting their fitted positions, and withdraw the blower housing from under the facia **(see illustrations)**.

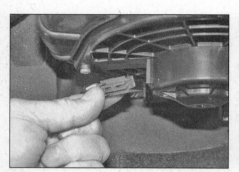

9.19a Disconnect the blower motor plug underneath . . .

9.19b . . . and the resistor pack plug in front

9.20a Undo the two screws from below . . .

9.20b . . . and take off the lower support bracket

9.22a Remove the blower housing bolt on the top left . . .

9.22b . . . and another underneath . . .

9.22c . . . with a further bolt at the top right

9.22d There is a mounting nut on the top right . . .

9.22e . . . and a further one at floor level, by the EPS control unit

23 Refitting is a reversal of removal.

Heater control panel

24 Remove the driver's side facia lower trim panels, the glovebox, and the gear lever surround panel, as described in Chapter 11, Section 27.

25 On models without air conditioning, or with 'non-climate' or 'manual' air conditioning (identifiable by not having AUTO on the controls), trace the air distribution and temperature cables down to the base of the heater unit, and disconnect them from their operating levers. One cable runs down on each side of the heater unit.

26 Remove the two screws at the base of the panel, visible from the front. Then, working through the openings on either side of the facia centre panel, remove the panel securing bolt on either side **(see illustrations)**.

27 The centre panel is now secured by

several clips all around its edges. If possible, start to free the panel by pushing it from behind. When the panel is free, disconnect the wiring plugs from the back – these will include (depending on model) the radio unit

9.22f Removing the blower motor housing

wiring, aerial lead, fan switch plug and climate control wiring connectors **(see illustrations)**. Withdraw the panel, noting the routing of the two control cables which will still be attached (where applicable).

9.26a Remove the two screws at the front . . .

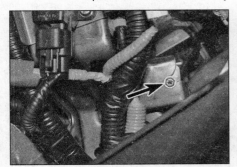

9.26b . . . then each side retaining screw must be removed . . .

9.26c . . . by working through the glovebox aperture . . .

9.26d . . . and from the driver's side footwell

9.27a Start to free the panel from behind . . .

9.27b . . . until it is free, and can be withdrawn

9.27c Disconnect the radio aerial lead . . .

9.27d . . . and the various wiring plugs from behind the panel

9.28 The vertical switch panel can be unscrewed and removed

9.29 The smaller switch panel has a screw at each end

28 The main control panel (with vertically-stacked control knobs) can be removed if required by first carefully pulling off the knobs, then removing the screws securing it to the facia centre panel **(see illustration)**.

29 The switch panel running across the

bottom of the centre panel is secured by a single screw at each end, and may also be removed if required **(see illustration)**. Note that the switches are only available as an assembly, not individually.

30 To renew a bulb, twist the relevant

bulbholder anti-clockwise and remove it from the rear of the panel. The ones on our car appear to be one-piece items (ie, bulb and holder are supplied together) **(see illustration)**.

31 Where applicable, the control cables can be disconnected from their knobs and renewed if required. Be sure to route the new cables as directly down to their connections on the heater unit as possible.

32 Refitting is a reversal of removal. As applicable, ensure that the wiring plugs and control cables are correctly and securely reconnected. Check the operation of the cables before clipping the facia centre panel into position.

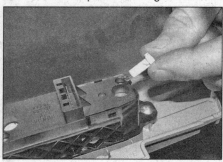

9.30 Twist and remove the bulbholder

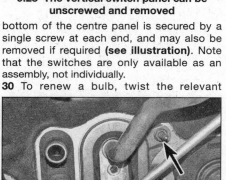

9.33a Unscrew the two air conditioning pipe flange nuts . . .

Heater unit

33 On models with air conditioning, have the system discharged by a Honda dealer, or other suitably-equipped specialist. At the same time, have the evaporator connections at the bulkhead disconnected, then do not use the system until it has been reconnected and recharged. The evaporator connections are next to the heater pipes, and the pipe flange is secured with two nuts **(see illustrations)**. Do not disconnect them without having the system discharged first – see Section 10.

34 Either drain the cooling system as described in Chapter 1A or 1B, or clamp the heater hoses at their bulkhead connections.

35 Working in the engine compartment, release the cable clamp, then disconnect the temperature control cable from the heater control valve **(see illustration 9.52)**.

36 Release the spring clips and disconnect

9.33b . . . and separate the flange from the bulkhead – note the rubber grommet

9.36 Release the spring clips and disconnect the heater hoses

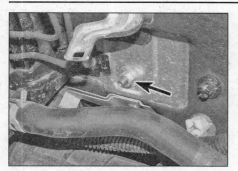

9.37 Unscrew the heater unit mounting nut from the bulkhead

9.40a Underneath the heater unit, the wiring harness is secured with foam tape . . .

9.40b . . . as well as the more usual clips and ties

the two heater hoses from their bulkhead connections **(see illustration)**. Anticipate some loss of coolant as this is done, even if the system has been drained – wipe this off any electrical parts or painted surfaces.

37 Unscrew and remove the heater unit mounting nut from the bulkhead **(see illustration)**.

38 Remove the facia panel and crossmember as described in Chapter 11.

39 Remove the complete blower motor housing as described previously in this Section.

40 Check around the heater unit and disconnect all the wiring plugs, noting their locations – models with automatic air conditioning will have more plugs than those without **(see illustrations)**.

41 The heater unit is secured by two bolts from the top, and a single bolt at the front, at floor level. Remove the bolts, and with the help of an assistant, lift the heater unit slightly, and pull it rearwards away from the bulkhead. Note that, as this is done, the unit will separate itself from the drain tube in the floor at the front, and possibly from the twin-vent duct at floor level. The heater pipes will be withdrawn through the bulkhead – be sure to recover the sealing grommet for refitting **(see illustrations)**.

42 Refitting is a reversal of removal, noting the following points:

a) When offering the unit into place, make sure the grommet is fitted to the heater pipes, and that they fit properly into their holes in the bulkhead. Also ensure

the heater unit engages with the floor drain tube and that the floor vent duct is correctly fitted.

b) Ensure that the heater hoses are correctly and securely reconnected, and remember to refit the heater mounting nut on the engine compartment side of the bulkhead.

c) Refit the blower motor housing as described in this Section, and the crossmember and facia as described in Chapter 11.

d) Where applicable, have the air conditioning evaporator pipes reconnected (using new O-rings if necessary) and the system recharged by a Honda dealer or air conditioning specialist.

e) Either refill or top-up the cooling system (Chapter 1A, 1B or Weekly checks).

f) Reconnect and if necessary adjust the

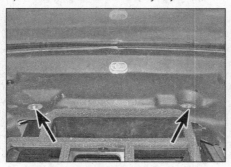

9.41a The heater unit has two upper mounting bolts . . .

heater control valve cable as described later in this Section.

Heater matrix

43 Remove the heater unit as described previously in this Section.

44 On models with air conditioning, remove the six screws securing the expansion valve cover, and take off the cover for access to the evaporator. Carefully withdraw the evaporator from the housing (refer to Section 11).

45 If not already done, remove the bulkhead grommet from the two heater pipes which supply the matrix. Remove the four screws and take off the heater pipe flange cover **(see illustrations)**.

46 Remove the four screws securing the pipe side cover to the heater housing, and take it off **(see illustrations)**.

47 Taking care not to bend the heater pipes, withdraw the matrix from the housing **(see**

9.41b . . . and one mounting bolt at floor level

9.41c When removing the heater unit . . .

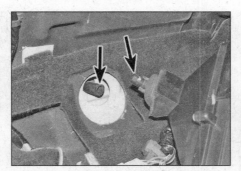

9.41d . . . note the evaporator drain pipe and tube at the front

9.45a Take off the bulkhead grommet from the heater pipes . . .

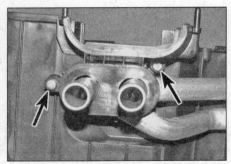

9.45b . . . then remove the screws (two of four shown) . . .

9.45c . . . and lift off the pipe flange cover

9.46a Remove the screws (three of four shown) . . .

9.46b . . . and take off the pipe side cover

illustration). Even if the system was drained of coolant, it is likely that some will remain in the matrix, so keep the pipes uppermost to prevent spillage.

48 If the matrix has been leaking, it may be possible for a radiator specialist to repair it, but ultimately, a new matrix might be the better solution.

49 Refitting is a reversal of removal.

Heater control valve

50 Either drain the cooling system as described in Chapter 1A or 1B, or clamp the heater hoses either side of the valve.

51 Release the cable clamp, then disconnect the temperature control cable from the heater control valve operating lever.

52 Release the spring clip from the hose at either end, then disconnect the heater hoses from the valve (see illustration).

53 Unbolt the support bracket from the bulkhead, and remove it from the engine compartment.

54 Refitting is a reversal of removal, noting the following points:

a) Reconnect the heater hoses securely, then either refill or top-up the cooling system (Chapter !A, 1B or Weekly checks).

b) Reconnect and if necessary adjust the heater control valve cable as described later in this Section.

Cable adjustment

55 If not already done, in the engine compartment, release the cable clamp on the valve operating lever, then disconnect the cable from the lever.

56 Remove the driver's lower facia trim panel as described in Chapter 11.

57 Working in the driver's footwell, release the cable clamp and disconnect the cable from the air flap door lever on the heater unit.

9.47 Withdraw the heater matrix from the housing

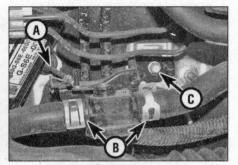

9.52 Heater control valve cable (A), hoses (B) and bracket bolt (C)

58 Turn the temperature control to the fully cold position, and switch on the ignition.

59 Reconnect the cable to the air flap door lever. Make sure the cable outer sleeve is touching the stop on the side of the heater unit, then clip the cable into the clamp.

60 Back in the engine compartment, turn the valve operating lever to the fully-closed position (anti-clockwise, viewed from above).

61 Reconnect the cable to the valve operating lever, then pull gently on the cable outer sleeve to take out any slack, and fit it into the cable clamp.

62 Check the operation of the heater temperature control on completion.

10 Air conditioning system
– general information,
checks and precautions

General information

An air conditioning system is available on some models. It enables the temperature of incoming air to be lowered; it also dehumidifies the air, which makes for rapid demisting and increased comfort. Two types of air conditioning are fitted – manual and automatic (climate control).

The cooling side of the system works in the same way as a domestic refrigerator. Refrigerant gas is drawn into a belt-driven compressor, and passes into a condenser in front of the radiator, where it loses heat and becomes liquid. The liquid passes through an expansion valve to an evaporator, where it changes from liquid under high pressure to gas under low pressure. This change is accompanied by a drop in temperature, which cools the evaporator. The refrigerant returns to the compressor and the cycle begins again.

Air blown through the evaporator passes to the blower housing, where it is mixed with hot air blown through the heater matrix, to achieve the desired temperature in the passenger compartment. On models with automatic air conditioning ('climate control'), the flap doors on the heater unit and blower housing are operated directly by electric motors, rather than by cables. Otherwise, the heating and ventilation system works in the same way as on other models.

Checks

The following maintenance checks should be performed on a regular basis to ensure that the air conditioning continues to operate at peak efficiency.

a) Inspect the condition of the compressor drivebelt. If it is worn or deteriorated, renew it (see Chapter 1A or 1B).

b) Check the drivebelt tension and, if necessary, adjust it – petrol models only (see Chapter 1A).

c) Inspect the system hoses. Look for cracks, bubbles, hardening and deterioration. Inspect the hoses and all fittings for oil bubbles or leakage. If there is any evidence of wear, damage or leakage, have the hose(s) renewed by a Honda dealer or air conditioning specialist.

d) Inspect the condenser cooling fins for leaves, insects and any other foreign material that may have embedded itself in the fins. Use a 'fin comb' or compressed air to remove debris from the condenser.

e) If you hear water sloshing around behind the facia, or have water dripping on the carpet, the drain tube at the front of the heater unit may be blocked. It should not be necessary to remove the heater unit to cure this – jack up the front of the car, then locate and clear the drain outlet.

It's a good idea to operate the system for about ten minutes at least once a month. This is particularly important during the winter months, because long term non-use can cause hardening, and subsequent failure, of the seals. Remember that a useful side-effect of using the air conditioning system is that it aids demisting.

The most common cause of poor cooling is simply a low system refrigerant charge. Many new cars are seemingly under-filled at the factory, and after a few years, the system becomes less effective. Front-end collision damage of any kind may also cause the system to lose gas. Take the car to a Honda dealer or air conditioning specialist, and have the system refilled – part of this process is to check for leaks before filling, and many garages will not make a charge for this if the system is discovered to have a leak **(see Tool tip)**.

If the air conditioning system is working properly, when the system is switched on with the engine running there should be an audible clunk as the compressor clutch engages. However, if the system is low on gas (low charge), the clutch will not engage.

Because of the complexity of the air conditioning system and the special equipment necessary to service it, in-depth troubleshooting and repairs are not included in this manual. For more complete information on the air conditioning system, refer to the *Haynes Air Conditioning Techbook*. However, renewal procedures for the major components are included.

Precautions

⚠️ *Warning: The refrigerant is potentially dangerous, and should only be handled by qualified persons. If it is splashed onto the skin, it can cause frostbite. It is not itself poisonous, but in the presence of a naked flame (including a cigarette) it forms a poisonous gas.*

Uncontrolled discharging of the refrigerant is dangerous, and damaging to the environment. It follows that any work on the air conditioning system which involves opening the refrigerant circuit must **only** be carried out by a Honda dealer or an air conditioning specialist.

Do not operate the air conditioning system

Many car accessory shops sell one-shot air conditioning recharge aerosols. These generally contain refrigerant, compressor oil, leak sealer and system conditioner. Some also have a dye to help pinpoint leaks.

⚠️ *Warning: These products must only be used as directed by the manufacturer, and do not remove the need for regular maintenance.*

if it is known to be short of refrigerant; the compressor may be damaged.

11 Air conditioning system components – removal and refitting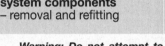

⚠️ *Warning: Do not attempt to open the refrigerant circuit. Refer to the precautions at the end of Section 10.*

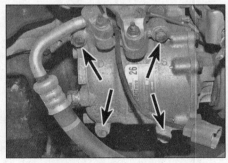

11.2a Remove the four compressor mounting bolts . . .

11.3 On diesel models, the flexible hose unions are on top

Compressor

1 If necessary, the compressor can be unbolted and moved aside, without disconnecting its flexible hoses, after removing the auxiliary drivebelt (see Chapter 1A or 1B) and disconnecting the wiring plug.

2 On petrol models, also remove the condenser fan as described in Section 4, and the alternator as described in Chapter 5A. The compressor is secured with four bolts – take care not to damage the radiator fins as the compressor is moved out of position **(see illustration)**.

3 On diesel models, the compressor is mounted high up on the engine, and has three mounting bolts. An added complication with this compressor is that the flexible hose unions are on top, which makes moving it aside for other tasks more difficult **(see illustration)**.

4 Refitting is a reversal of removal. Tighten the mounting bolts to the specified torque.

Evaporator

5 Remove the heater unit as described in Section 9.

6 Remove the six screws securing the expansion valve cover, and take off the cover for access to the evaporator. Carefully withdraw the evaporator from the housing **(see illustrations)**.

7 Refitting is a reversal of removal.

Condenser

8 If the condenser is being removed completely, the air conditioning refrigerant must be discharged by a Honda dealer or air conditioning specialist before starting.

11.2b . . . then move it aside, and tie it up

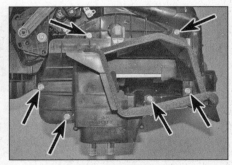

11.6a Remove the six screws . . .

11.6b . . . then lift off the expansion valve cover . . .

11.6c . . . and withdraw the evaporator core

11.10a Unbolt the receiver/dryer bottle mounting bracket from the inner wing . . .

11.10b . . . and unclip the rigid pipe

11.11a Unbolt the condenser upper mounting brackets . . .

11.11b . . . and lift the condenser out of its radiator support clips

Afterwards, the car can still be driven, but make sure the air conditioning system stays switched off.

9 The condenser is accessed by removing the front bumper and bumper crossmember as described in Chapter 11.

10 To create more movement in the refrigerant pipes, reach behind the condenser, unbolt the receiver/dryer bottle mounting bolt, and detach it from the inner wing. Also unclip the rigid pipe from the inner wing (see illustrations).

11 Unscrew the mounting bracket bolt from each top corner, then lift the condenser out of the support clips on the radiator (see illustrations).

12 If the condenser is only being removed for access to other components (such as the radiator), swing out the driver's side of the condenser, taking care not to place strain on the pipes on the passenger side. Rest the condenser on an axle stand.

13 To remove the condenser, with the system discharged, unscrew the pipe union bolts and separate the unions (see illustrations). Recover the O-ring from each union – new ones must be used when reassembling.

14 Refitting is a reversal of removal. Use new O-rings if the pipes were disturbed, and have the system recharged by a Honda dealer or air conditioning specialist.

Condenser fan

15 Refer to Section 4.

Heating/ventilation control motors

Note: *On models with automatic air*

conditioning (climate control), electric motors are used instead of the cables on lesser models. Control cables are still used on models with manual air conditioning, and a cable is still fitted to the heater valve in the engine compartment.

Air distribution control motor

16 Remove the glovebox as described in Chapter 11, and the engine management ECM as described in Chapter 4A or 4B.

17 From the front passenger's footwell, reach up on the left-hand side of the heater unit and disconnect the wiring plug from the base of the control motor (see illustration).

18 Remove the three mounting screws, and withdraw the motor from the heater unit, noting how the operating rod engages with the motor.

11.13a Remove the bolt from each condenser refrigerant union . . .

11.13b . . . and separate them – note the O-ring, which must be renewed

11.17 Disconnect the air distribution control motor wiring plug

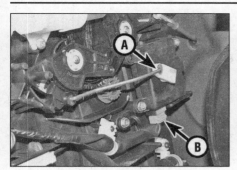

11.24 Temperature control motor operating rod (A) and wiring plug (B)

11.27 Prise out the sun sensor from the top of the facia . . .

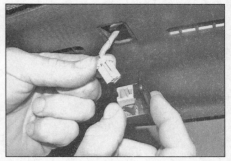

11.28 . . . and disconnect the wiring plug (seen with facia removed)

11.32a Disconnect the sensor wiring plug . . .

11.32b . . . and pull off the air hose

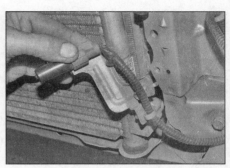

11.35 Unbolt the mounting bracket and remove the outside temperature sensor

19 Refitting is a reversal of removal, noting the following points:

a) *Ensure that the motor engages properly with the air flap operating lever.*

b) *Make sure the battery negative lead is still disconnected before reconnecting the ECM.*

c) *Check the operation of the motor on completion.*

Temperature (air mix) control motor

20 Remove the driver's side facia lower trim panel (the one nearest the centre of the car) as described in Chapter 11.

21 To gain access, the fusebox must be removed from under the facia. First disconnect the battery negative lead, and position the lead away from the battery (also see *Disconnecting the battery*) – this is **essential** before continuing.

22 The fusebox is secured by one main bolt at the top, but there are also a number of wiring plugs to disconnect – try to disturb the fusebox wiring as little as possible.

23 From the driver's footwell, reach up on the right-hand side of the heater unit and disconnect the wiring plug from the base of the control motor.

24 Remove the three mounting screws, and withdraw the motor from the heater unit, noting how the operating rod engages with the motor **(see illustration)**.

25 Refitting is a reversal of removal, noting the following points:

a) *Ensure that the motor engages properly with the air flap operating lever.*

b) *Make sure the battery negative lead is still disconnected before reconnecting the fusebox.*

c) *Check the operation of the motor on completion.*

Sun sensor

26 Fitted only to models with automatic air conditioning, the sun sensor allows the system to compensate for the additional cabin temperature generated in sunny conditions. The sensor is located in the centre of the facia panel, just behind the windscreen.

27 Taking care not to scratch the facia, and noting its fitted orientation, prise the sensor out using a small flat-bladed screwdriver **(see illustration)**. Note: *When we tried this on our project car, the top of the sensor broke off, and the sensor fell down inside the facia. As we were taking the facia out at the time, this wasn't a problem, but otherwise, the very limited access would make retrieving the sensor difficult.*

28 Disconnect the wiring plug from the sensor, and remove it completely **(see illustration)**. Make sure the plug doesn't fall back inside the facia.

29 Refitting is a reversal of removal. Ensure the sensor is fitted the right way round (with its wiring plug at the rear, facing into the car).

Cabin temperature sensor

30 Fitted only to models with automatic air conditioning, the sensor monitors cabin temperature so that the system can maintain the temperature selected. The sensor is located on the facia panel to the left of the steering wheel, behind a small grille.

31 Release the turn-buckle fastener, then unclip and remove the fusebox cover.

32 Reach in behind the grille, disconnect the wiring plug, then pull off the air hose from the rear of the sensor. Push the sensor grille out from behind, and remove it **(see illustrations)**.

33 Refitting is a reversal of removal. Ensure the sensor's air hose and wiring plug are securely refitted.

Outside temperature sensor

34 The outside air temperature sensor is mounted on the left-hand side of the front bumper's lower grille.

35 Reach inside the grille, and unclip the sensor by pulling it forwards off its side mounting bracket. Alternatively, the bracket itself can be unbolted and pulled clear **(see illustration)**.

36 Disconnect the sensor wiring plug, and remove it.

37 Refitting is a reversal of removal. Ensure the sensor is securely clipped back into place.

Chapter 4 Part A:
Fuel and exhaust systems – petrol models

Contents

Degrees of difficulty

Easy, suitable for novice with little experience	**Fairly easy,** suitable for beginner with some experience	**Fairly difficult,** suitable for competent DIY mechanic	**Difficult,** suitable for experienced DIY mechanic	**Very difficult,** suitable for expert DIY or professional

Specifications

General

Manufacturer's engine codes*:
1.4 litre petrol (D14Z5 and D14Z6)	66 kW SOHC 16V, non-VTEC
1.6 litre petrol (D16V1 and D16W7)	81 kW SOHC 16V, VTEC

See Vehicle identification in the Reference section

System type
All models .... Honda PGM-FI (Programmed Fuel Injection) multi-point sequential injection system

Fuel system data
Fuel pump type	Electric, immersed in tank
Fuel pressure	2.8 to 3.3 bar

Specified idle speed:
1.4 litre engines	700 ± 50 rpm
1.6 litre engines	750 ± 50 rpm
Idle mixture CO content	0.1 % maximum
Injector resistance	10 to 13 ohms

Recommended fuel
Minimum octane rating .... 95 RON unleaded (UK unleaded premium).
Leaded fuel must **not** be used

Torque wrench settings

	Nm	lbf ft
Crankshaft position sensor mounting bolt	12	9
Exhaust front pipe-to-centre section nuts*	33	24
Exhaust front pipe-to-manifold bolts*	22	16
Exhaust manifold heat shield upper bolts*	31	23
Exhaust manifold nuts*	31	23
Exhaust rear silencer bolts*	22	16
Floor guide channel bolts (3-door)	38	28
Fuel rail mounting nuts	12	9
Fuel tank support frame bolts	38	28
Inlet manifold mounting bolts/nuts	24	18
TDC sensor mounting bolt	10	7
Throttle body mounting bolts/nut	10	7

* *Use new bolts/nuts*

1 General information and precautions

The fuel system consists of a fuel tank, an electric fuel pump (located in the fuel tank), a fuel pump relay, the fuel rail and fuel injectors, an air cleaner assembly and a throttle body. All models are equipped with a multi-point sequential electronic fuel injection system, which essentially means it has four injectors (one per cylinder) which operate in firing order. Various sensors are used to supply information to the Engine Control Module (ECM), and from this information the module is able to determine the optimum settings for both fuelling and ignition timing. This Chapter deals with the fuel side of the system – refer to Chapter 5B for ignition-specific details. However, many of the sensors (described in Section 11) have a dual role, with their information being relevant to the correct operation of the fuel and ignition systems.

Fuel injection system

Sequential injection uses timed impulses to inject the fuel directly into the inlet port of each cylinder according to its firing order. The injectors are controlled by the ECM, which monitors various engine parameters and delivers the exact amount of fuel required into the inlet ports. The throttle body serves only to control the amount of air passing into the system. Because each cylinder is equipped with its own injector, much better control of the fuel/air mixture ratio is possible.

On models with automatic transmission, the system components and sensors are essentially the same, but because there are additional transmission control parameters, the control module is known by Honda as the Powertrain Control module, or PCM. For simplicity, however, we shall refer to the control module throughout as the ECM

An electric fuel pump, pressure regulator and fuel level sender unit are located inside the fuel tank. Fuel is pumped from the fuel tank to the fuel rail, which is equipped with a pressure damper to smooth out the flow of fuel. The system is 'returnless' – there is no return feed to the tank. Fuel vapours from the tank are stored in a canister at the rear of the tank, and supplied to the throttle body through a separate pipe.

Exhaust system

The exhaust system includes an exhaust manifold, primary and secondary oxygen sensors, a three-way catalytic converter, a centre section with silencer, and a rear silencer.

The catalytic converter is an emissions control device added to the exhaust system to reduce pollutants. Refer to Chapter 4C for more information regarding the catalytic converter and other emission control components.

Precautions

Extreme caution should be exercised when dealing with either the fuel or exhaust systems. Fuel is a potentially-explosive liquid, and extreme care should be taken when dealing with the fuel system. The exhaust system is an area for exercising caution, as it will remain hot for some time after the engine is switched off. Serious burns can result from even momentary contact with any part of the exhaust system, and the fire risk is ever-present. The catalytic converter in particular runs at very high temperatures.

When removing the engine control module (ECM), do not touch the terminals, as there is a chance that static electricity may damage the internal electronic components.

> ⚠️ **Warning: Many of the procedures in this Chapter require the removal of fuel lines and connections, which may result in some fuel spillage. Before carrying out any operation on the fuel system, refer to the precautions given in Safety first! at the beginning of this manual, and follow them implicitly. Petrol is a highly-dangerous and volatile liquid, and the precautions necessary when handling it cannot be overstressed.**

2 Fuel system – depressurisation

Note: *Refer to the warning in Section 1 before proceeding.*

> ⚠️ **Warning: The following procedures will merely relieve the pressure in the fuel system – remember that fuel will still be present in the system components, and take precautions accordingly before disconnecting any of them.**

1 The fuel system referred to in this Chapter is defined as the fuel tank and tank-mounted fuel pump/fuel gauge sender unit, the fuel rail, the fuel injectors, and the metal pipes and flexible hoses of the fuel lines between these components. All these contain fuel, which will be under pressure while the engine is running and/or while the ignition is switched on.

2 The pressure will remain for some time after the ignition has been switched off, and must be relieved before any of these components is disturbed for servicing work.

3 Whichever depressurisation method is used, bear in mind the following points:
a) *Plug the disconnected pipe ends, to minimise fuel loss and prevent the entry of dirt into the fuel system.*
a) *Note that, once the fuel system has been depressurised and drained (even partially), it will take significantly longer to restart the engine – perhaps several seconds of cranking – before the system is refilled and pressure restored.*

Method 1

4 The simplest depressurisation method is to disconnect the fuel pump electrical supply. With the ignition switched off, remove the fuel pump fuse (typically, No 17 in the interior fusebox). Try to start the engine – allow the engine to idle until it stops through lack of fuel. Turn the engine over once or twice on the starter to ensure that all pressure is released, then switch off the ignition – do not forget to refit the fuse when work is complete. **Note:** *This method may cause a temporary fault code to be stored in the ECM, so the engine management warning light may be lit on completion. After a number of successful starts, the codes should clear themselves – if not, refer to Section 10.*

Method 2

5 Place a suitable container beneath the connection or union to be disconnected, and have a large rag ready to soak up any escaping fuel not being caught by the container. Slowly open the connection or loosen the union nut to avoid a sudden release of pressure, and position the rag around the connection, to catch any fuel spray which may be expelled.

3 Accelerator pedal – removal and refitting

1 From inside the car, remove the driver's side facia closing panel to gain access to the accelerator pedal (see Chapter 11, Section 27).
2 Working in the driver's footwell, operate the accelerator pedal by hand, and unhook the cable end fitting from the top of the pedal, sliding it out to the right **(see illustration)**.

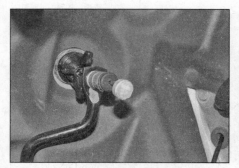

3.2 Unhook the cable from the top of the accelerator pedal

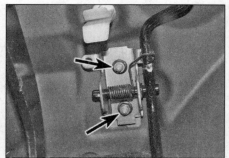

3.3 Unscrew the two mounting nuts, and remove the accelerator pedal

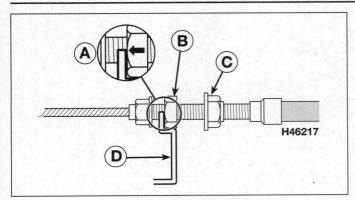

4.11 Accelerator cable initial adjustment

A Adjust until no clearance   C Locknut
   exists here   D Cable mounting bracket
B Adjuster nut

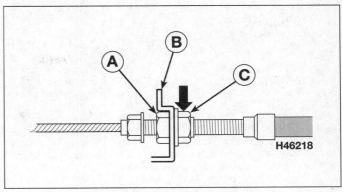

4.12 Accelerator cable final adjustment

A Adjuster nut   C Locknut
B Cable mounting bracket

3 Unscrew the retaining nuts and remove the pedal assembly from the bulkhead (**see illustration**).

4 If the pedal is defective, the complete assembly will have to be renewed.

5 Refit the pedal assembly and tighten its retaining nuts securely.

6 Refit the trim panel to the facia on completion.

7 Check the pedal operation before taking the car out on the road – if necessary, adjust the accelerator cable as described in Section 4.

4 Accelerator cable – removal, refitting and adjustment

Removal

1 Remove the air cleaner as described in Section 6.

2 Open the throttle body quadrant, and unhook the accelerator cable end fitting from it.

3 Trace the cable round to the bulkhead, then loosen the cable locknut, lift the cable from the bracket and move it to one side.

4 Trace the cable back round the engine compartment, freeing it from any clips, and noting how it is routed.

5 Remove the driver's side facia closing panel to gain access to the accelerator pedal (see Chapter 11, Section 27).

6 Working in the driver's footwell, operate the accelerator pedal by hand, and unhook the cable end fitting from the top of the pedal, sliding it out to the right. Feed the cable back into the engine compartment, releasing the bulkhead grommet.

7 Withdraw the cable from the engine side, and remove it.

Refitting

8 Refitting is a reversal of removal. On completion, adjust the cable as described later in this Section.

Adjustment

9 The adjustment should be carried out with the engine at operating temperature – if necessary, loosely refit the cable and start the engine, running it until the radiator cooling fan has come on and gone off.

10 If not already done, loosen the cable adjuster and locknuts, and remove the cable from the mounting bracket.

11 The first stage of adjustment is carried out with the cable end stop touching the top lip of the cable mounting bracket – note that this means the cable will be sitting up from its normal position. Rest the cable onto the top lip of the bracket, so that the cable end stop is on one side, and the adjuster nut on the other, and tighten the adjuster nut until the slack is just removed from the cable (**see illustration**).

12 Once the position of the adjuster nut has been set, lift the cable off the mounting bracket, and fit it properly back down in place, so that the bracket is now between the adjuster and locknuts (**see illustration**).

13 Tighten the locknut up to the mounting bracket, without disturbing the cable or the adjuster nut.

14 Without starting the engine, have an assistant depress the accelerator pedal fully, and check that the throttle quadrant opens fully. Similarly check that the quadrant returns to the idle position when the pedal is released.

5 Fuel lines and fittings – general information

Note: *Refer to the warning in Section 1 before proceeding.*

1 Quick-release couplings are employed at several unions in the fuel feed and return lines.

2 Before disconnecting any fuel system component, relieve the pressure in the system as described in Section 2, and equalise tank pressure by removing the fuel filler cap. Also note the routing of all hoses and pipes, and the orientation of all clamps and clips to ensure correct refitting.

3 Some of the quick-release connections have a plastic cover over them, which must be unclipped first for access.

4 Release the protruding locking lugs on each fuel line union, by squeezing them together and carefully pulling the coupling apart. Use rag to soak up any spilt fuel. Where the unions are colour-coded, the pipes cannot be confused. Where both unions are the same colour, note carefully which pipe is connected to which, and ensure that they are correctly reconnected on refitting.

5 To reconnect one of these couplings, press them together until they are locked. Switch the ignition on to pressurise the system, and check for any sign of fuel leakage around the disturbed coupling before attempting to start the engine.

6 Checking procedures for the fuel lines are included in Chapter 1A.

7 Always use genuine fuel lines and hoses when renewing sections of the fuel system. Do not fit substitutes constructed from inferior or inappropriate material, or you could cause a fuel leak or a fire.

6 Air cleaner and inlet air resonator – removal and refitting

Air cleaner

1 Remove the air cleaner element as described in Chapter 1A.

2 Though not essential, access is improved by releasing the accelerator cable from its two support brackets, and lifting the cable clear (**see illustration**).

3 On the passenger side of the air cleaner, disconnect the inlet air temperature sensor wiring plug (**see illustration**).

6.2 Unclip the accelerator cable from the two support brackets

6.3 Disconnect the inlet air temperature sensor

6.4 Air cleaner mounting bolts

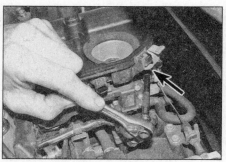

6.5a Loosen the Jubilee clip securing the air cleaner to the throttle body

6.5b Jubilee clip seen with air cleaner removed

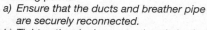

6.6 Removing the air cleaner

4 Unscrew the three mounting bolts (two at the front, one at the side) **(see illustration)**.
5 Insert a cross-head screwdriver (or better, an 8 mm socket on an extension) under the air cleaner on the passenger side, and

loosen the Jubilee clip which secures the air cleaner to the top of the throttle body **(see illustrations)**.
6 Lift the air cleaner off the throttle body, pull off the breather hose from the stub on the

back of the engine, then pull the air cleaner sideways off the duct from the resonator, and remove it from the engine **(see illustration)**.
7 Refitting is a reversal of removal, noting the following points:
  a) *Ensure that the ducts and breather pipe are securely reconnected.*
  b) *Tighten the air cleaner-to-throttle body Jubilee clip securely, to prevent air leaks which will upset the proper running of the engine.*
  c) *Reconnect the inlet air temperature sensor wiring plug securely.*

Inlet air resonator

8 To improve access, remove the air cleaner as described previously in this Section.
9 Unclip the fuel hoses and the wiring harness from the rear of the resonator **(see illustrations)**.
10 Unscrew the three mounting bolts (two on the engine side of the resonator, and one on the other side, behind the headlight) **(see illustrations)**.
11 Pull back the rubber boot on the inlet air duct to disconnect it from one side of the resonator, then pull the resonator duct out of the air cleaner and remove it **(see illustrations)**.
12 Refitting is a reversal of removal.

Inlet air duct

13 Remove the resonator as described previously in this Section. Although the duct can be unbolted and separated from the resonator while the resonator is still in place, if the resonator is not removed, the duct cannot be withdrawn.

6.9a Unclip the fuel hoses – note mounting bolt (arrowed) . . .

6.9b . . . and the wiring harness from the resonator

6.10a One of the resonator mounting bolts at the front of the engine . . .

6.10b . . . and another behind the headlight

6.11a Pull back the boot from the inlet air duct . . .

6.11b . . . and remove the resonator

6.14a Unscrew the inlet air duct bolt on the inner wing . . .

6.14b . . . and the other at the opposite end of the duct

6.15a Prise off the battery wiring harness . . .

6.15b . . . then remove the inlet air duct

14 Unscrew the two mounting bolts (one on the inner wing, the other behind the rubber boot where the duct joins the resonator) **(see illustrations).**
15 Unclip the battery wiring harness from the top of the duct, then withdraw it from the engine compartment **(see illustrations).**
16 Refitting is a reversal of removal.

7 Fuel pump/gauge sender unit – removal and refitting

Removal

1 Unscrew the fuel filler cap – this is done to equalise the pressure in the tank.
2 Depressurise the fuel system as described in Section 2.
3 Remove the rear seat cushion as described in Chapter 11.

4 Prise up the plastic clips at the front, and lift the carpet over the seat belt buckles **(see illustrations).**
5 Unscrew the four screws securing the tank access panel to the car floor, and carefully

7.4a Prise up the clips at the front . . .

lift it up – there's wiring attached to it **(see illustrations).**
6 Disconnect the pump/sender unit wiring plug inside, and move the access panel clear **(see illustration).**

7.4b . . . and lift out the carpet

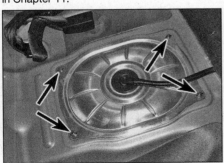

7.5a Remove the four screws . . .

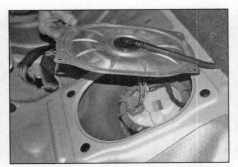

7.5b . . . and lift up the tank access panel

7.6 Disconnect the wiring plug inside

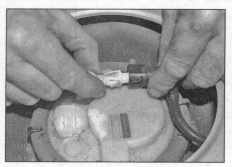

7.7 Squeeze and release the fuel hose

7.8a We marked the collar's fully-tightened position before unscrewing it . . .

7.8b . . . using an oil filter strap wrench

7.9a Remove the retaining collar . . .

7 Release the fitting on the fuel hose on top of the sender unit, and disconnect it, anticipating a small amount of fuel spillage. Either plug or tape over the hose ends. The quick-release fittings are typically released by squeezing

the upper and lower tabs on the plastic collar while sliding the hose off **(see illustration)**.

8 The sender unit is secured using a threaded plastic collar, which will be tight. As access to it is limited by the hole in the car floor, Honda

mechanics use a special three-legged gripping tool which engages the ribs on the collar's sides. An equivalent to this tool is available from several tool manufacturers. With care, it may be possible to unscrew the collar using slip-joint water pump pliers, an oil filter strap wrench, or even tap the collar round with a screwdriver, but care must be taken not to damage either the collar or the tank **(see illustrations)**.

9 Unscrew and remove the collar, then carefully lift the pump and sender unit out of the tank. Lift the unit straight up, then turn it to keep the fuel level float from catching on the tank opening. Recover the sealing ring – if this is in poor condition, a new one should be used when refitting **(see illustrations)**.

10 The unit may be dismantled if required – this should be fairly self-evident, but should only be attempted if spare parts are known to be available **(see illustrations)**. Typically, the unit will have to be renewed complete.

Refitting

11 If necessary, fit a new sealing ring to the sender unit, prior to fitting.

12 Refit the unit to the tank, taking care not to catch the sender unit's float. Align the rib mark on top of the unit between the two marks at the front of the tank **(see illustration)**.

13 Refit the collar to the fuel tank and tighten it securely.

14 Reconnect the fuel hoses to their original positions on the cover, ensuring each fitting clicks securely into position, and reconnect the wiring plug.

15 Start the engine and check for fuel leaks. If all is well, refit the access cover, carpet, and the rear seat cushion.

---

8 Fuel tank –
removal and refitting

Removal

1 Before removing the fuel tank, all fuel must be drained from the tank. Since a fuel tank drain plug is not provided, it is therefore preferable to carry out the removal operation when the tank is nearly empty. The remaining fuel can then be syphoned or hand-pumped from the tank.

2 Unscrew the fuel filler cap – this is done to equalise the pressure in the tank.

3 Remove the rear seat cushion as described in Chapter 11.

4 Unscrew the four screws securing the tank access panel to the car floor, and carefully lift it up (see Section 7).

5 Disconnect the sender unit wiring plug inside, and move the access panel clear.

6 Release the fitting on the fuel hose on top of the sender unit, and disconnect it, anticipating a small amount of fuel spillage. Either plug or tape over the open connections. The quick-release fittings are typically released by squeezing the upper and lower tabs on the plastic collar while sliding the hose off.

7.9b . . . and withdraw it from the tank

7.10a The external components can be released with a small screwdriver . . .

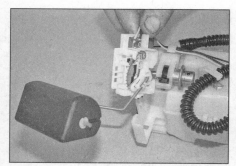

7.10b . . . then disconnected and removed

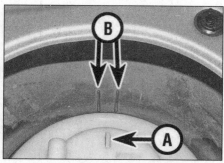

7.12 Align the rib on the sender (A) between the tank markings (B)

7 Jack up the rear of the car, and support it on axle stands (see *Jacking and vehicle support*).
8 Working in the left-hand rear wheel arch, remove the three nuts and take off the plastic cover panel from the fuel pipes which run from the filler to the tank.
9 Release the spring clip securing the fuel EVAP hose and the quick-release connections by squeezing the lugs together **(see illustration)**.
10 Loosen the large hose clip and disconnect the filler neck hose from the tank.
11 Position a jack (and a large flat piece of wood, to spread the load) under the tank, and just take its weight. Place the jack and wood centrally, so that the tank's support frame can be lowered.
12 Taking care that the tank does not move, loosen and remove the four support frame mounting bolts, and lower the frame **(see illustration)**.
13 With the aid of an assistant to steady the tank on the jack, lower the jack and remove the tank out from under the car. Note that the tank may 'stick' on the underseal. Try and keep the tank as level as possible, especially if it still contains fuel – if the tank tips, the fuel will run to one end, and the tank may slide off the jack.
14 As the tank is lowered, check for any hoses which may still be attached, and disconnect them as they become accessible.
15 If the tank is contaminated with sediment or water, remove the fuel gauge sender unit (Section 7), and swill the tank out with clean fuel. The tank is injection-moulded from a synthetic material – if seriously damaged, it should be renewed. However, in certain cases, it may be possible to have small leaks or minor damage repaired. Seek the advice of a specialist before attempting to repair the fuel tank.

Refitting

16 Refitting is the reverse of the removal procedure, noting the following points:
  a) *When lifting the tank back into position, take care to ensure that none of the hoses become trapped between the tank and body. Refit the support frame and tighten the bolts to the specified torque..*
  b) *Ensure all pipes and hoses are correctly routed and all hose unions are securely joined.*
  c) *On completion, refill the tank with a small*

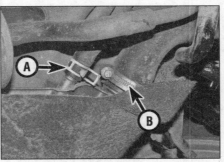

8.9 Disconnect the EVAP hose (A) and the filler neck hose (B)

amount of fuel, and check for signs of leakage prior to taking the car out on the road.

9 Fuel filler flap and cable – removal and refitting

Fuel filler flap

1 Open the filler door, then unscrew the nut inside and detach the opening spring **(see illustrations)**.
2 If possible, mark the position of the hinge relative to the body, to make refitting easier.
3 Unscrew and remove the two hinge bolts (note that the lower one has a stud for the opening spring), and withdraw the flap from the car **(see illustration)**.
4 Refitting is a reversal of removal. The position of the flap can be adjusted using the

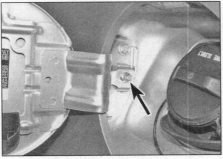

9.1a Unscrew the nut . . .

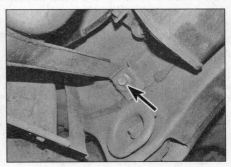

8.12 Unscrew the four tank support frame mounting bolts

hinge bolts if necessary. Use touch-up paint as required on the hinge bolts and around the hinge on completion.

Fuel flap cable

5 Working as described in Chapter 11, Section 27, remove the front sill trim panel on the driver's side, and the luggage area trim panel (or rear side trim panel) on the passenger's side. It is also useful to remove the rear seat cushion.
6 Loosen the bolt securing the cable operating lever – the bolt is at the back of the lever, and is accessed from the side (it's only visible at floor level). The bolt only has to be loosened, as the lever assembly is mounted on a slotted fitting – unhook the lever from the side of the car **(see illustration)**.
7 Release the cable end fitting by sliding it sideways out of the lever. Pull the cable down at the back of the lever to free it from its slot **(see illustration)**.

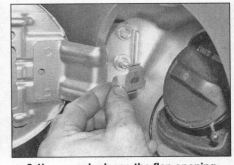

9.1b . . . and release the flap opening spring

9.3 Remove the two hinge bolts, and take off the flap

9.6 The operating lever mounting bolt is on a slotted fitting

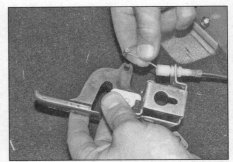

9.7 Unhook the end fitting, then unclip the cable outer

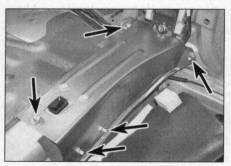

9.9 Unbolt and remove the metal plate on 3-door models

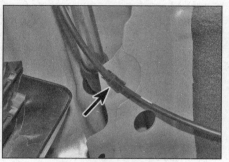

9.10 Unclip the cable at the rear . . .

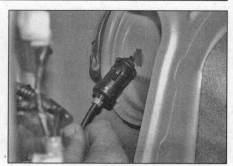

9.11 . . . then twist the lock through 90°, and release it from the body

8 Trace the cable back along the sill, then across the front of the rear seat – fold the carpet back as necessary for access. The cable is held in place by strips of tape, so new tape will probably be needed when refitting.

9 On 3-door models, the cable passes through a strengthening plate bolted to the floor, in front of the rear seat – remove the five mounting bolts, and take off the plate (see illustration).

10 At the rear, the cable is secured to the side of the boot by a plastic clip, which will have to be carefully prised out (see illustration).

11 Release the filler flap lock from the side of the boot by turning it 90° anti-clockwise, and the cable can be removed completely (see illustration).

12 Refitting is a reversal of removal, noting the following points:
 a) Ensure that the cable is routed as before, and secured by the tape.
 b) On 3-door models, tighten the guide channel bolts to the specified torque.
 c) Check the operation before refitting the removed trim.

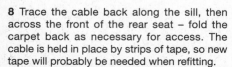

10 Fuel injection system
 – checking and
 fault code clearing

Note: Refer to the warning note in Section 1 before proceeding.

1 If a fault appears in the engine management system, first ensure that all the system wiring connectors are securely connected and free of corrosion. Then ensure that the

10.2 The diagnostic connector is under the steering column, on the left

fault is not due to poor maintenance; ie, check that the air cleaner filter element is clean, the valve clearances are correct, the cylinder compression pressures are correct and the engine breather hoses are clear and undamaged, referring to Chapter 1A or Chapter 2A.

2 If these checks fail to reveal the cause of the problem, the car should be taken to a suitably-equipped Honda dealer for testing. A diagnostic connector is incorporated in the engine management system wiring harness, into which dedicated electronic test equipment can be plugged – the connector is located under the steering column, on the left (see illustration). The test equipment is capable of 'interrogating' the engine control module (ECM) electronically and accessing its internal fault log (reading fault codes).

3 Fault codes can only be extracted from the ECM using a dedicated fault code reader. A Honda dealer will obviously have such a reader, but they are also available from other suppliers. It is unlikely to be cost-effective for the private owner to purchase a fault code reader, but a well-equipped local garage or auto-electrical specialist will have one.

4 Using this equipment, faults can be pinpointed quickly and simply, even if their occurrence is intermittent. Testing all the system components individually in an attempt to locate the fault by elimination is a time-consuming operation that is unlikely to be fruitful (particularly if the fault occurs dynamically), and carries a high risk of damage to the ECM's internal components.

5 Experienced home mechanics equipped with a suitable tachometer or other diagnostic equipment may be able to check the engine idle speed; if found to be out of specification, the car must be taken to a suitably-equipped Honda dealer for assessment. The engine idle speed is not manually adjustable; incorrect test results indicate the need for maintenance (check for leaking air/vacuum hoses, or use a proprietary injector cleaning treatment) or a fault within the injection system.

Clearing fault codes

6 Most of the components and sensors which make up the engine management system will log a fault code in the ECM memory in

the event of a fault. When this happens, the engine management warning light on the instrument panel will come on. In some cases, the ECM will substitute its own default value instead of the correct sensor reading, and although it can still be driven safely, the car will suffer driveability problems, often especially noticeable when cold.

7 Once the faulty component has been identified and the problem corrected (usually by fitting a new component), the fault code must be cleared. In some cases, this will happen automatically once the ignition has been switched on and off enough times – if the fault does not recur, it may clear itself.

8 To clear fault codes manually requires the use of a fault code reader tool as described at the start of this Section. However, codes may also be cleared by the DIY mechanic, as follows.

9 With the ignition off, remove fuse No 6 from the engine compartment fusebox for at least 10 seconds, then refit it. Switch the ignition on, and the fault should have cleared.

10 If the engine management light remains on (or comes back on later), either the same fault still exists, or there is another faulty component triggering a different fault code. Check that any new components have been correctly fitted, and especially that their wiring plugs are clean and secure.

11 Fuel injection system
 electronic components
 – removal and refitting

Throttle body

1 Remove the air cleaner as described in Section 6.

2 Turn the throttle body quadrant by hand, and unhook the accelerator cable end fitting from it. Trace the cable round to the bulkhead, then loosen the cable locknut, lift the cable from the bracket and move it to one side (see illustrations).

3 Disconnect the wiring plugs from the idle air control valve, throttle position sensor and canister purge solenoid valve (see illustrations). Label the plugs if necessary, to ensure correct refitting.

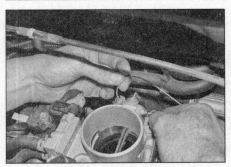

11.2a Open the throttle by hand, then unhook the cable end fitting

11.2b Loosen the locknut, and lift the cable out of the support bracket

11.3a Disconnect the wiring plug from the idle air control valve . . .

11.3b . . . throttle position sensor . . .

11.3c . . . and canister purge solenoid valve

11.4a Release the spring clips . . .

4 The idle air control valve has two coolant hoses attached, so either clamp the hoses or be prepared for a small amount of coolant loss (draining the cooling system is the only other option). Release the clips and disconnect the two coolant hoses each from the idle

air control valve – mark the hoses to ensure correct refitting **(see illustrations)**.
5 Similarly, disconnect the hoses from the canister purge solenoid valve – to improve access, disconnect the MAP sensor wiring plug **(see illustrations)**.

6 Unscrew the nut and three bolts securing the throttle body to the inlet manifold. Ensure that nothing remains attached to it, then lift it off the mounting stud. Recover the rubber seal from the base of the throttle body and discard it. It is essential that a new seal is

11.4b . . . then mark the hoses for position . . .

11.4c . . . before disconnecting them from the idle air control valve

11.5a Disconnect the hose at the front . . .

11.5b . . . then disconnect the MAP sensor wiring plug . . .

11.5c . . . and disconnect the hose at the rear of the purge valve

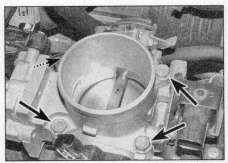

11.6a Throttle body mounting bolts (nut hidden)

11.6b Removing the throttle body

11.6c Recover the throttle body seal from the inlet manifold

11.10a Use a small screwdriver to release the plug catch . . .

11.10b . . . then pull off the injector wiring plugs

11.10c When all four plugs are free, lift the harness off the mounting studs

11.11 Release the clip on the EVAP hose connection to the fuel rail

used whenever the throttle body is disturbed – failure to do so will give rise to air leaks, which will upset the smooth running of the engine **(see illustrations).**

7 Refitting is a reversal of removal, noting the following points:

a) *Use a new seal, and tighten the throttle body bolts/nut to the specified torque.*
b) *Ensure that the wiring plugs and hoses are correctly refitted. If any of the hoses show signs of perishing or split ends, new hoses should be obtained.*

c) *Refit and adjust the accelerator cable as described in Section 4.*
d) *Check the coolant level, and top-up if necessary (Weekly checks).*

Fuel injectors

8 Depressurise the fuel system as described in Section 2.

9 Remove the air cleaner and inlet air resonator as described in Section 6.

10 Disconnect the wiring plugs from the following components (label the wiring if necessary, to ensure correct refitting):

a) *Throttle position sensor (in front of the throttle body).*
b) *Canister purge solenoid valve (to the left of the throttle body).*
c) *MAP sensor (also to the left of the throttle body, on the manifold).*
d) *All four fuel injectors (it is essential that the injector wiring plugs are not mixed up, though this is unlikely in practice). When the plugs have been disconnected, lift the moulded harness off the two studs at the back of the cylinder head cover, and move it clear (see illustrations).*

11 Release the hose clip and disconnect the EVAP system hose from the fuel rail **(see illustration).**

12 Lift and remove the curved plastic cover from the fuel supply hose connection. Squeeze the upper and lower lugs on the quick-release connection, and pull the hose from the fuel rail **(see illustration).**

13 Unscrew the two bolts securing the wiring harness support bar at the rear of the cylinder head, and lift it off **(see illustrations).**

11.12 Squeeze and release the fuel supply hose connection

11.13a Unscrew the two bolts . . .

11.13b . . . and lift off the wiring harness support bar

11.14 Unscrew the two fuel rail mounting nuts

14 Unscrew the two fuel rail mounting nuts **(see illustration)**.

15 Ease the fuel rail out by pulling carefully and equally on both ends of the rail – there will be some resistance from the injector lower O-ring seals. Recover the injector lower O-ring seals, and the small spacer from each mounting stud **(see illustrations)**. Remove the rail to a clean working area.

16 Slide out the metal locking clip which secures each injector to the rail, then pull the injector free, noting which way round they are fitted – again, there will be resistance from the upper O-ring. Remove and discard the upper O-ring – a new set should be obtained for refitting **(see illustrations)**.

17 Refitting is a reversal of removal, noting the following points:

a) Use new O-ring seals, and ensure the injectors are located in the rail the same way round as noted on removal – the wiring plug sockets should face the front of the car when the rail is installed.

b) Seat the rail and injectors fully home, and tighten the mounting nuts to the specified torque.

c) Refit all hoses and wiring plugs securely.

d) On completion, switch on the ignition to pressurise the system, and check for leaks.

Fuel pressure damper

18 The fuel pressure damper is located in the fuel rail, and its function is to smooth out any fuel pressure peaks from the fuel pump and regulator in the fuel tank. To access the damper, remove the fuel rail and injectors as described previously in this Section. The damper is secured in its fuel rail housing by a large circlip – remove the circlip and withdraw the damper, noting its O-ring seal **(see illustration)**.

19 Refitting is a reversal of removal. Use a new O-ring, and ensure the damper is fully seated and secured with the circlip. Refit the fuel rail and injectors using the information in this Section.

Fuel pressure regulator

20 Remove the fuel pump as described in Section 7. The fuel pressure regulator is clipped to the side of the pump/sender unit – disconnect the quick-release fittings and separate the regulator from the unit. Note the O-ring seal used on the upper connection, which must be renewed whenever it is disturbed.

21 Refitting is a reversal of removal.

Fuel filter unit

22 The filter unit is mounted inside the fuel tank, and forms part of the fuel pump/sender unit. Unlike an externally-mounted filter, this is not a routine maintenance item, and is intended to last the life of the car. However, if low fuel pressure is diagnosed, it could be that the filter is blocked, rather than the fuel pump being faulty.

23 Remove the fuel pump as described in Section 7. The filter is mounted on top of the pump, secured by two side clips. Carefully prise up the tabs to release the filter unit, then disconnect the two quick-release fuel hose connections and remove it.

24 Refitting is a reversal of removal.

Throttle position sensor

25 The throttle position sensor is fitted to the front of the throttle body, and signals the position of the throttle butterfly to the ECM. The sensor is mated to the throttle body in production, and is not intended to be removed. In the event that a throttle position sensor problem is suspected, consult a Honda dealer or Honda parts specialist for advice, as it appears (at the time of writing) that the only solution is a new throttle body.

Manifold absolute pressure (MAP) sensor

26 The sensor is mounted directly on top of the inlet manifold, and provides the ECM with information on the vacuum level in the manifold. The ECM uses this to calculate the engine load, and the appropriate fuelling – for example, if the vacuum measured is low, this suggests that the throttle is wide-open, and more fuel will be supplied.

27 Remove the air cleaner as described in Section 6.

28 The sensor is mounted on the manifold, to the left of the throttle body (left as seen from the driver's seat).

29 Disconnect the sensor wiring plug, then unscrew the mounting bolt and withdraw the sensor from the manifold – note that the sensor has an O-ring seal **(see illustrations)**.

30 Refitting is a reversal of removal. Use a new O-ring if necessary, and tighten the mounting bolt securely.

11.15a Ease out the fuel rail, and remove it

11.15b Recover the spacer from each fuel rail mounting stud

11.16a Removing an injector locking clip

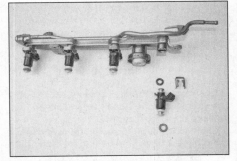

11.16b Fuel rail, with one injector assembly removed

11.16c Fuel injector, O-rings and metal locking clip

11.18 The fuel pressure damper is secured using a circlip

11.29a Disconnect the wiring plug from the MAP sensor . . .

11.29b . . . then unscrew the mounting bolt . . .

11.29c . . . and withdraw it from the inlet manifold – note the O-ring seal

11.33a Disconnect the wiring plug . . .

11.33b . . . then withdraw the inlet air temperature sensor . . .

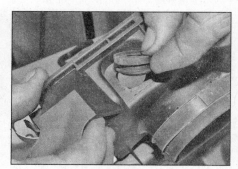

11.33c . . . and its sealing grommet

Inlet air temperature sensor

31 The inlet air temperature sensor is mounted in the air cleaner, and informs the ECM of the temperature of the incoming air.

32 Remove the air cleaner element as described in Chapter 1A.

33 The temperature sensor is mounted in the side of the air cleaner – disconnect the wiring plug, then pull the sensor out, noting its sealing grommet (see illustrations).

34 Refitting is a reversal of removal. Use a new grommet if necessary, and ensure that the sensor is fully seated.

Idle air control valve

35 The idle air control valve is mounted on the side of the throttle body, and is the primary means by which the ECM controls idle speed – as more air is allowed to 'bleed' into the manifold, more fuel is supplied, and the idle speed rises.

36 Remove the air cleaner as described in Section 6.

37 The valve is mounted on the right-hand side of the throttle body (right as seen from the driver's seat). The valve itself is fitted onto the rear of another small housing, which circulates coolant around the throttle body. However, the valve has two tamperproof screws fitted, meaning that this coolant housing is the one that must be removed to take off the valve.

38 Either clamp the two coolant hoses, or be prepared for a small amount of coolant loss (draining the cooling system is the only other option).

39 Disconnect the wiring plug from the back of the valve, then release the hose clips and disconnect the two coolant hoses from the side (mark the hoses to ensure correct refitting) (see illustrations).

40 Remove the three mounting screws and withdraw the valve from the throttle body (see illustrations).

41 Recover the valve's rubber seal – it is strongly recommended that a new one is

11.39a Disconnect the wiring plug at the rear . . .

11.39b . . . then disconnect the two coolant hoses at the front

11.40a Remove the three screws . . .

11.40b . . . and withdraw the control valve assembly from the throttle body

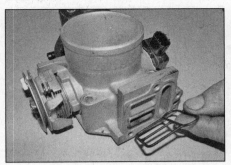

11.41 Always use a new seal when refitting

11.45 Coolant temperature sensor

11.46 Disconnect the sensor wiring plug . . .

11.47a . . . then using a deep socket . . .

11.47b . . . unscrew and remove the sensor

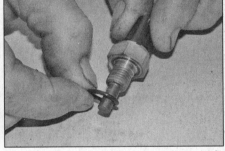

11.48 Use a new O-ring when refitting the sensor

used when refitting, as a worn seal may result in coolant leaking into the throttle body, and so into the engine **(see illustration)**. Also, air leaking past a worn seal will upset the running of the engine.

42 Refitting is a reversal of removal, noting the following points:

a) *Use a new seal, and tighten the mounting bolts securely.*

b) *Ensure that the hoses and wiring plug are securely reconnected.*

c) *Top-up the cooling system if necessary (see Weekly checks).*

Coolant temperature sensor

43 Either drain the cooling system as described in Chapter 1A or, if the new switch can be fitted immediately, anticipate some small loss of coolant when the old switch is removed.

44 Remove the inlet air resonator as described in Section 6.

45 The coolant temperature sensor is located at the transmission end of the head, screwed into the top of the coolant housing **(see illustration)**. Note that a faulty coolant temperature sensor is often the prime cause of poor running after a cold start, or poor fuel economy.

46 Disconnect the wiring plug from the sensor **(see illustration)**.

47 Unscrew the sensor (a 17 mm deep socket will be needed) and recover the O-ring – a new one should be used when refitting **(see illustrations)**. Mop-up any spilled coolant.

48 Refit the sensor to the housing, using a new O-ring, and tighten the sensor securely **(see illustration)**.

49 Reconnect the wiring plug to the sensor,

then refit the inlet air resonator as described in Section 6.

50 Refill or top-up the cooling system, as applicable (see Chapter 1A or *Weekly checks*).

Crankshaft position sensor

51 Remove the timing belt upper and lower covers as described in Chapter 2A.

52 The sensor is mounted behind the crankshaft sprocket, and informs the ECM of crankshaft speed and position.

53 Disconnect the wiring plug, then unscrew the mounting bolt and remove the sensor from the engine **(see illustrations)**.

54 Refitting is a reversal of removal. Tighten the sensor mounting bolt to the specified torque.

TDC sensor

55 Remove the timing belt upper cover as described in Chapter 2A.

11.53a Disconnect the wiring plug, then unscrew the mounting bolt . . .

56 The sensor is mounted below the camshaft sprocket, and informs the ECM of TDC position.

57 Unscrew the sensor mounting bolt and withdraw the sensor – note that it has a lug which locates in a recess on the cylinder head.

58 Refitting is a reversal of removal. Tighten the sensor mounting bolt to the specified torque.

Oxygen sensors

59 Refer to Chapter 4C.

Canister purge solenoid valve

60 Refer to Chapter 4C.

Exhaust gas recirculation valve

61 Refer to Chapter 4C.

Knock sensor

62 Refer to Chapter 5B.

11.53b . . . and remove the crankshaft sensor

11.65 Disconnect the wiring plug from the vehicle speed sensor – seen from below

11.66a Unscrew the sensor mounting bolt . . .

11.66b . . . and withdraw the vehicle speed sensor

Vehicle speed sensor

63 The vehicle speed sensor is mounted on top of the transmission, at the rear, in line with the right-hand driveshaft. The sensor is driven by a gear, in much the same way as the older speedometer drive, and provides an electronic signal of the vehicle speed. This information is used by the engine management ECM, electric power steering system (EPS) and anti-lock braking system (ABS), besides the speedometer itself.

64 Access to the sensor is easiest from below – jack up the front of the car, and support it on axle stands (see *Jacking and vehicle support*).

65 Reach up from behind the transmission, and disconnect the wiring plug from the speed sensor **(see illustration)**.

66 Unscrew the sensor mounting bolt, then withdraw the sensor from the transmission – there may be some resistance, both from the O-ring seal and from the sensor drive gear **(see illustrations)**.

67 Refitting is a reversal of removal, noting the following points:

a) Clean the mating faces of the sensor and transmission, and use a new O-ring if necessary. Expect the sensor to twist as it meshes with the transmission gear, then turn it to align the mounting bolt hole.

b) Tighten the sensor mounting bolt securely, and ensure that the wiring plug is securely reconnected.

Engine control module (ECM)

Note: *The ECM contains the immobiliser coding which was programmed into it when*

the car was new. If a new ECM is fitted, the immobiliser coding will have to be programmed into it by a Honda dealer before the car will start.

68 Disconnect the battery negative lead, and position the lead away from the battery (also see *Disconnecting the battery*). This is **essential** when working on the ECM – if the module's wiring connector is unplugged when the battery is still connected, this will almost certainly damage the module.

69 The module is located inside the car, behind the glovebox. Remove the glovebox as described in Chapter 11, Section 27.

70 Above the ECM, where applicable, remove the relay mounting nut and the nut from the earth strap.

71 Disconnect the row of ECM wiring plugs along the base of the module.

72 Remove the two ECM mounting bracket bolts, and remove the module from the car **(see illustration)**. The module can be separated from the mounting bracket by removing the two bolts either side.

73 Refitting is a reversal of removal. Make sure the battery is still disconnected before reconnecting the ECM wiring plugs.

Fuel shut-off (inertia) switch

74 The fuel shut-off switch is a safety device which automatically cuts off the fuel supply in the event of a sudden impact or collision. The switch may occasionally be triggered in normal driving, for example when driving over badly-maintained roads.

75 The switch is located behind the glovebox, on the right-hand side. To access it, open

the glovebox, then press the glovebox sides inwards to allow the glovebox to open past its stops. For the best access, remove the glovebox completely, as described in Chapter 11, Section 27.

76 To reset the switch after an impact or shock, depress the button on the top of the switch.

77 To remove the switch, disconnect the wiring plug on the base, then remove the mounting bolts and withdraw the switch from behind the glovebox **(see illustration)**.

78 Refitting is a reversal of removal.

Brake pedal position switch

79 The brake pedal position switch is fitted above and behind the top of the brake pedal itself – access is from the driver's footwell.

80 Reach up under the facia to the switch mounting bracket, and disconnect the wiring plug from the top of the switch.

81 Turn the switch body anti-clockwise to remove it from the bracket.

82 To refit and set the switch, offer the switch into its bracket, so that the switch plunger touches the pedal. Without moving the switch in or out, turn it clockwise to lock it.

83 Reconnect the switch wiring plug to complete.

Clutch pedal position switch

84 The clutch pedal position switch is fitted above the clutch pedal (note that some models do not have this switch, and a bolt is fitted in its place).

85 Reach up under the facia to the switch mounting bracket, and disconnect the wiring plug from the top of the switch.

86 Unscrew the switch locknut, then unscrew and remove it from the bracket.

87 Refitting is a reversal of removal. Turn the switch clockwise until it just contacts the pedal arm, then turn it in an additional 3/4 to 1 turn. Tighten the locknut.

EPS torque sensor

88 The UK Civic is equipped with electric power steering (refer to Chapter 10 for more details). The steering system's torque sensor signals the engine management ECM when the steering load is high, as the resultant electrical load on the engine could cause the idle speed to drop.

11.72 Unscrew the ECM mounting bracket bolts

11.77 Fuel shut-off inertia switch inside glovebox aperture

12.5 Unbolt and remove the fuel rail centre support bracket

12.8a Unscrew the two bolts . . .

12.8b . . . and lift off the heater hose support bracket

12.9a Release the hose clip using pliers . . .

12.9b . . . then disconnect the brake servo vacuum hose

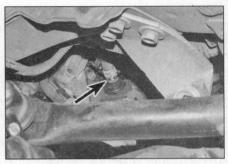

12.11 Crankcase breather hose connection to inlet manifold – seen from below

12 Inlet manifold – removal and refitting

Removal

1 Remove the air cleaner and inlet air resonator as described in Section 6.

2 Using the information in Section 4, disconnect the accelerator cable from the throttle body.

3 The throttle body can be removed with the inlet manifold, rather than removed separately as described in Section 11, but all the wiring plugs and hoses listed in the Section 11 removal procedure must be disconnected from it first.

4 Remove the fuel rail and injectors as described in Section 11.

5 At the rear of the cylinder head, remove the two bolts securing a square cast metal support bracket for the fuel rail, and remove the bracket **(see illustration)**.

6 Disconnect the MAP sensor wiring plug (refer to Section 11 if necessary).

7 Unclip the two heater hoses from the side of the manifold, and move them clear.

8 Unscrew the two bolts on top of the manifold securing the heater hose support bracket, and lift it off **(see illustrations)**.

9 At the rear of the manifold in the centre, use pliers to release the hose clip, and pull off the brake servo vacuum hose **(see illustrations)**.

10 Jack up the front of the car, and support it on axle stands (see *Jacking and vehicle support*).

11 Disconnect the crankcase breather pipe from the left-hand side of the manifold – this is easier from below. If necessary, pull out the

flame trap itself, rather than try to disconnect the pipe **(see illustration)**.

12 Working from below, unscrew the three inlet manifold support bracket bolts – leave the brackets attached to the rear of the engine **(see illustration)**. Access to these bolts is hampered by the driveshaft – note that there are washers between the brackets and the manifold.

13 The manifold is secured from below by three centre nuts, and a bolt at either end – on top, there is a centre bolt and two elongated nuts. Unscrew the nuts/bolts **(see illustrations)**.

14 Hold the injector plate against the engine, and withdraw the manifold rearwards on its studs. When it is clear of the studs, remove it from the engine compartment **(see illustration)**. Treat the manifold with care – do not drop it, as it is made of plastic.

12.12 Unscrew the three inlet manifold support bracket bolts

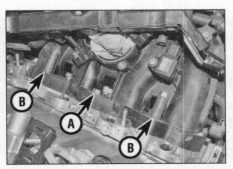

12.13a On top, the manifold is secured by a centre bolt (A), and two elongated nuts (B)

12.13b Removing the centre bolt . . .

12.13c ... and one of the elongated nuts

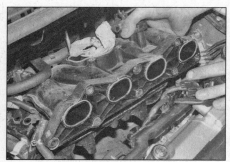

12.14 Hold the injector plate against the head, and withdraw the manifold

12.15 The inlet manifold port seals must be renewed

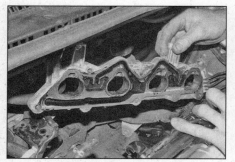

12.16a Withdraw the injector plate from the mounting studs ...

12.16b ... and recover the gasket

15 Recover the four rubber port seals from the manifold, and discard them – new ones **must** be used when refitting **(see illustration)**.
16 The injector plate should also be removed from the manifold studs, so that a new plate-to-head gasket can be fitted (this should always be renewed when the manifold has been disturbed) **(see illustrations)**.
17 Clean all mating faces prior to refitting, and wipe them dry.
18 Check the manifold for any signs of splitting or cracking – this may be most evident around the mounting holes. If the manifold is damaged, a new one will be needed, although small isolated cracks may be repairable, either with sealant or with the help of a plastics repair specialist.

Refitting

19 Fit a new injector plate-to-head gasket over the studs, then slide on the injector plate.

20 Fit four new port seals to the inlet manifold, then slide it onto the studs and up to the injector plate.
21 Refit the manifold nuts and bolts, and tighten them fully by hand. Once they are hand-tight, tighten the manifold nuts and bolts by a quarter-turn each at a time to the specified torque.
22 Further refitting is a reversal of removal.

13 Exhaust manifold – removal and refitting

⚠️ **Warning: Inspection and repair of exhaust system components should be done only after the system has cooled completely. Apart from the catalytic converter, the manifold is potentially the hottest part of the exhaust.**

Removal

1 The exhaust manifold heat shield is secured by three bolts – two above and one below. The two upper bolts also secure the manifold itself – unscrew and remove them **(see illustration)**. These bolts often suffer from corrosion, and may be difficult to remove. Use a wire brush and plenty of penetrating oil first if they appear to be rusty. If the bolts are in less-than-perfect condition, new ones should be obtained for reassembly.
2 Jack up the front of the car, and support it on axle stands (see *Jacking and vehicle support*). Remove the engine undertray.
3 Unscrew the remaining bolt from below, then remove the heat shield **(see illustration)**.
4 Have a support (such as an axle stand or a small jack) ready to rest the front pipe on.
5 Undo the two bolts securing the front pipe to the manifold **(see illustration 14.11)**. Recover the springs and the 'olive' gasket – it is recommended that new bolts, springs and a new gasket are used when refitting (these should be available as part of a fitting kit from dealers and parts suppliers).
6 Do not let the front pipe hang down unsupported, as this will strain the oxygen sensor wiring (as well as the pipe itself). Place an axle stand or another jack under the pipe.
7 Unscrew and remove the three nuts securing the manifold to the cylinder head **(see illustration)**. Use a wire brush and plenty of penetrating oil first if they appear to be rusty.

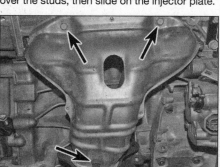

13.1 Manifold heat shield bolts

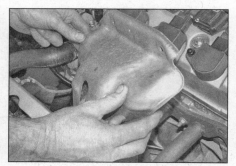

13.3 Removing the heat shield

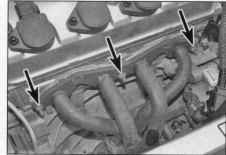

13.7 Unscrew the three manifold mounting nuts

13.8a Withdraw the manifold from the engine . . .

13.8b . . . and recover the gasket

HAYNES HiNT *If a nut appears to be sticking, do not try to force it; tighten the nut back half a turn, apply some more penetrating oil to the stud threads, wait several seconds for it to soak in, then gradually unscrew the nut by one turn. Repeat this process until the nut is free. It doesn't matter if some of the studs are removed with the nuts.*

8 Withdraw the manifold off the studs, and remove it from the engine compartment. Recover the manifold gasket – a new one should always be used when refitting **(see illustrations)**.

Refitting

9 Refitting is a reversal of removal, noting the following points:
  a) *Clean the manifold and cylinder head mating faces, and fit a new gasket.*
  b) *It is recommended that new nuts are used as a matter of course – even if the old ones came off without difficulty, they may not stand being retightened. New components will be much easier to remove in future, should this be necessary.*
  c) *If some of the manifold studs were removed, it's best to obtain a set of new studs and nuts, rather than try to separate the old ones. The new studs can be fitted by tightening two nuts against each other on the stud, then using them to screw the stud into place – once this is done, the nuts can be unscrewed from each other, and removed.*
  d) *If the old studs and bolts are re-used, clean the threads thoroughly to remove all traces of rust.*
  e) *Apply anti-seize compound (copper grease will do) to the manifold studs before fitting the nuts.*
  f) *Tighten the manifold nuts (and the two heat shield upper bolts) to the specified torque.*

  g) *Reconnect the front pipe, using a new gasket, springs and bolts. Tighten the bolts fully by hand, then by a quarter-turn each at a time to the specified torque.*

14 Exhaust system – general information, removal and refitting

Warning: Inspection and repair of exhaust system components should be done only after the system has cooled completely. This applies particularly to the catalytic converter, which runs at very high temperatures.

General information

1 The exhaust system consists of three sections: the front pipe and catalytic converter, the centre pipe and silencer, and the rear silencer.
2 The system is suspended throughout its entire length by rubber mountings.
3 If any section of the exhaust is damaged or deteriorated, excessive noise and vibration will occur.
4 Carry out regular inspections of the exhaust system, to check security and condition. Look for any damaged or bent parts, open seams, holes, loose connections, excessive corrosion, or other defects which could allow exhaust fumes to enter the car. Deteriorated sections of the exhaust system should be renewed.
5 If the exhaust system components are extremely corroded or rusted together, it may not be possible to separate them. This often happens with the rear silencer, which rusts to the centre section – try twisting the pipes to separate them. Cut off the old components carefully with a hacksaw, and see if any corroded pipe can be removed (perhaps with a chisel) without damaging the remaining exhaust section. Wear safety glasses to protect your eyes, and wear gloves to protect your hands.

6 Here are some simple guidelines to follow when repairing the exhaust system:
  a) *Work from the back to the front when removing exhaust system components.*
  b) *Apply penetrating fluid to the flange nuts before unscrewing them. If possible, wire-brush any exposed threads to remove corrosion and dirt before trying to loosen the nuts.*
  c) *Use new gaskets and rubber mountings when installing exhaust system components.*
  d) *Apply anti-seize compound (copper grease will do) to the threads of all exhaust system studs during reassembly.*
  e) *The downpipe is secured to the manifold, and the rear silencer to the centre section, by two coil springs and bolts. When the bolts are tightened to the specified torque, the pressure of the springs will then be sufficient to make a leak-proof connection. Do not over-tighten the bolts to cure a leak, or they may shear. Renew the gasket and the springs if a leak is found.*
  f) *Be sure to allow sufficient clearance between newly-installed parts and all points on the underbody, to avoid overheating the floorpan, and possibly damaging the interior carpet and insulation. Pay particularly close attention to the catalytic converter and its heat shield.*

Removal

7 Each exhaust section can be removed individually, or the complete system can be removed as a unit **(see illustration)**. Even if only one part of the system needs attention, in some cases it will be easier to remove the whole system and separate the sections on the bench.
8 To remove the system or part of the system, first jack up the front or rear of the car, and support it on axle stands. Alternatively, position the car over an inspection pit, or on car ramps. Where necessary, undo the

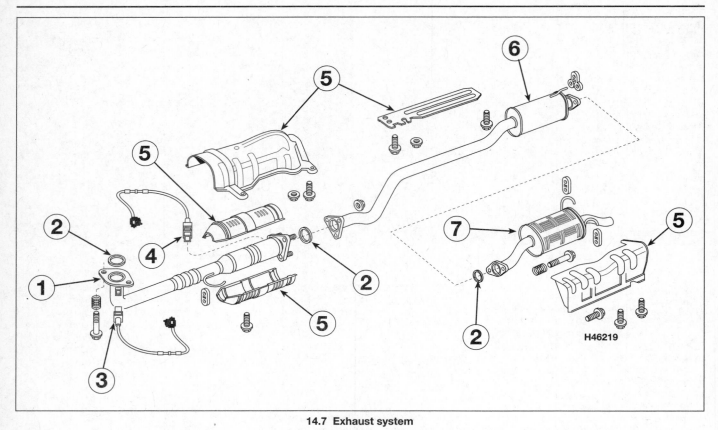

14.7 Exhaust system

1 Front pipe and catalytic converter	4 Secondary oxygen sensor	6 Centre pipe and silencer
2 Gasket	5 Heat shield	7 Rear silencer
3 Primary oxygen sensor		

14.11 Remove the two manifold-to-downpipe bolts

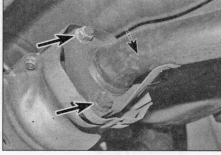

14.12 Unscrew the three nuts (one hidden) from the converter flange

14.13a Unhook the rubber mounting . . .

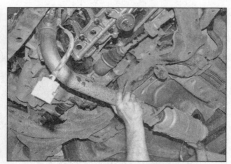

14.13b . . . and remove the front pipe/catalytic converter

retaining bolts and remove the undertray from beneath the engine/transmission.

Front pipe and catalytic converter

9 Trace the wiring from both oxygen sensors to their in-line wiring plugs, and disconnect them. Release the wiring from any clips or ties, so that it is free to be removed with the exhaust system.

10 Have a support (such as an axle stand or a small jack) ready to rest the front pipe on as required during removal.

11 Undo the two bolts securing the front pipe to the manifold (see illustration). Recover the springs and the 'olive' gasket – it is recommended that new bolts, springs and a new gasket are used when refitting (these should be available as part of a fitting kit from dealers and parts suppliers).

12 Unscrew the three flange nuts from the joint behind the catalytic converter, and separate the converter flange from the centre section (see illustration). Recover the gasket and discard it – this and the flange nuts should be renewed, and they may also be part of an exhaust fitting kit.

13 Unhook the pipe from the rubber mounting by pulling it forwards, then remove it from underneath the car (see illustrations). Take care that the converter is not dropped or roughly handled.

Centre pipe and silencer

14 Slacken and remove the three flange nuts securing the centre pipe to the catalytic converter, and separate the joint. Recover and discard the 'olive' gasket – a new one must be used when refitting.

15 Undo the two bolts securing the rear silencer to the centre section **(see illustration)**. Recover the springs and the 'olive' gasket – it is recommended that new bolts, springs and a new gasket are used when refitting (these should be available as part of a fitting kit from dealers and parts suppliers).

16 Release the centre section from its mounting rubbers by pulling it forwards, then remove it from underneath the car.

Rear silencer

17 Undo the two bolts securing the rear silencer to the centre section. Recover the springs and the 'olive' gasket – it is recommended that new bolts, springs and a new gasket are used when refitting (these should be available as part of a fitting kit from dealers and parts suppliers).

18 Unhook the rear silencer from its mounting rubbers, and free it from the centre pipe **(see illustration)**.

Complete system

19 Trace the wiring from both oxygen sensors to their in-line wiring plugs, and disconnect them. Release the wiring from any clips or ties, so that it is free to be removed with the exhaust system.

20 Have a support (such as an axle stand or a small jack) ready to rest the front pipe on as required during removal.

21 Undo the two bolts securing the front pipe to the manifold. Recover the springs and the 'olive' gasket – it is recommended that new bolts, springs and a new gasket are used when refitting (these should be available as part of a fitting kit from dealers and parts suppliers).

22 Free the system from its mounting rubbers, then remove it from underneath the car.

Heat shields

23 The heat shields are secured to the under-

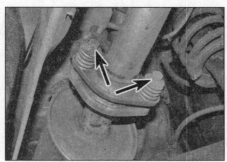

14.15 Remove the two centre section-to-silencer bolts

14.18 Unhook the rear silencer from its mounting rubbers

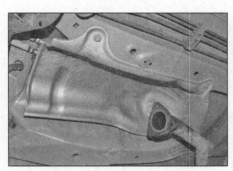

14.23 Exhaust front heat shield (with front pipe removed)

14.25 Fitting a new gasket at the rear of the catalytic converter

side of the body by various nuts and bolts. Each shield can be removed once the relevant exhaust section has been removed **(see illustration)**. If a shield is being removed to gain access to a component located behind it, it may prove sufficient in some cases to remove the retaining nuts and/or bolts, and simply lower the shield, without disturbing the exhaust system.

24 The catalytic converter has a two-part clam-shell shield around it, with a further shield above attached to the floor.

Refitting

25 Each section is refitted by reversing the removal sequence, noting the following points:

a) Ensure that all traces of corrosion have been removed from the flanges, and renew all necessary gaskets, bolts and springs as applicable **(see illustration)**.

b) The exhaust system flange nuts are all of self-locking type, and new ones should be used when refitting.

c) Inspect the rubber mountings for signs of damage or deterioration, and renew as necessary.

d) Prior to tightening the exhaust system fasteners, ensure that all rubber mountings are correctly located, and that there is adequate clearance between the exhaust system and underbody.

e) Tighten all flange bolts and nuts fully by hand, then by a quarter-turn each at a time to the specified torque.

Chapter 4 Part B:
Fuel and exhaust systems – diesel models

Contents

Degrees of difficulty

| **Easy,** suitable for novice with little experience | | **Fairly easy,** suitable for beginner with some experience | | **Fairly difficult,** suitable for competent DIY mechanic | | **Difficult,** suitable for experienced DIY mechanic | | **Very difficult,** suitable for expert DIY or professional | |

Specifications

General

System type . . . . Common-rail direct injection system incorporating a high-pressure pump and fuel supply rail. Diesel engine electronic management system. Turbocharger and intercooler fitted to all models

Idle speed. . . . . 850 ± 50 rpm – controlled by ECM

Accelerator cable deflection. . . . . 10 to 12 mm

Torque wrench settings

	Nm	lbf ft
Catalytic converter flange nuts*	33	24
Coolant temperature sensor	12	9
Dipstick tube upper bolt to engine	50	37
EGR pipe-to-exhaust manifold flange bolts	25	18
EGR pipe union nut	25	18
Exhaust front pipe support bracket:		
Pipe-to-bracket nuts*	18	13
Pipe-to-underbody nuts*	33	24
Exhaust front pipe-to-turbo nuts*	54	40
Exhaust heat shield nuts/bolts	12	9
Exhaust manifold nuts	36	27
Exhaust rear silencer flange nuts*	54	40
Fuel high-pressure pump mounting nuts	20	15
Fuel high-pressure pump supply pipe unions	23	17
Fuel supply (common) rail mounting bolts	25	18
Fuel tank support frame bolts	38	28
Injector front retaining plate nuts	22	16
Injector locating plate bolts:		
Inner pair of bolts	17	13
Outer pair of bolts	22	16
Single rear bolt (oiled)	27	20
Injector pipes to injectors	23	17
Injector pipes to supply rail	30	22
Turbocharger:		
Heat shield bolts	12	9
Oil feed pipe-to-engine union bolt	28	21
Oil feed pipe-to-turbo union bolt	17	12
Oil return pipe flange bolts	10	7
Turbocharger-to-exhaust elbow nuts	17	13
Turbocharger-to-manifold nuts*:		
Stage 1	39	29
Stage 2	78	58

Use new nuts

1 General information and precautions

General information

The fuel system consists of a fuel tank (mounted under the body, beneath the rear seats), fuel gauge sender unit mounted in the fuel tank, fuel filter, high-pressure fuel injection pump, fuel supply rail, fuel pipes, injectors, and the engine management electronic control module (ECM).

Fuel is fed from the tank via a combined lift pump and gauge sender unit mounted inside the tank, and it then passes through the fuel filter located in the engine bay, where foreign matter and water are removed. The high-pressure injection pump is driven from the crankshaft via the timing belt, but unlike previous distributor-type pumps, the high-pressure pump has no timing function; the pump supplies fuel at high pressure to a common rail supplying all four injectors, which are then opened as signalled by the ECM.

On reaching the high-pressure pump, the fuel is pressurised according to demand, via an ECM-controlled fuel metering unit built into the pump. The fuel accumulates in the injection common rail, which acts as a fuel reservoir for all four injectors – the pressure in the rail is accurately maintained using a pressure sensor in the end of the rail. The ECM controls the injectors directly, and determines the exact timing and duration of the injection period according to engine operating conditions. The four fuel injectors operate sequentially according to the firing order of the cylinders.

There are four pipes from the fuel supply manifold (one for each of the injectors), as well as the main supply pipe from the pump. Unusually for a modern engine, there is a fuel leak-off pipe from each injector, and excess fuel is returned to the tank. Each injector disperses the fuel evenly, and sprays fuel directly into the combustion chamber as its piston approaches TDC on the compression stroke. This system is known as direct injection. The pistons have a recess machined into their crowns, the shape of which has been calculated to improve 'swirl' (fuel/air mixing). In addition, the inlet manifold contains vacuum-operated plates which are used to improve the swirl under different operating conditions – this under ECM control, via the variable swirl control valve (VSCV).

The engine is very much a 'state-of-the-art' unit, in that it features a full electronic engine management system. An extensive array of sensors are fitted, which supply information on many different parameters to the ECM.

a) Throttle position sensor – informs the ECM of the accelerator pedal position, and rate of change.
b) Coolant temperature sensor – informs the ECM of engine temperature.
c) Mass airflow/inlet air temperature sensor – informs the ECM of the amount and temperature of air passing through the inlet duct into the engine.
d) Crankshaft and camshaft position sensors – inform the ECM of engine speed and crankshaft position, allowing fine control of injection timing.
e) Manifold absolute pressure (MAP) sensor – informs ECM of the pressure in the inlet manifold.
f) Vehicle speed sensor – informs the ECM of the vehicle speed.
g) Fuel rail pressure sensor – informs the ECM of the fuel pressure in the common rail.
h) Barometric pressure sensor – built into the ECM itself, this is primarily used to refine operation as altitude changes.
i) Brake pedal position switch – used by the ECM to indicate when the brakes are applied, confirming that the throttle has been released.

All the above information is analysed by the ECM and, based on this, the ECM determine the appropriate injection requirements for the engine. The engine ECM controls the injection timing directly at the injectors, to provide the best setting for cranking, starting (with either a hot or cold engine), warm-up, idle, cruising, and acceleration.

The engine ECM also controls the exhaust gas recirculation (EGR) system (see Chapter 4C) and the preheating system (see Chapter 5A).

The inlet manifold is a two-part assembly sealed by a metal gasket. The EGR (exhaust gas recirculation) valve and charge pressure sensor are mounted to the upper part of the manifold.

A turbocharger is fitted to increase engine efficiency by raising the pressure in the inlet manifold above atmospheric pressure. Instead of the air simply being sucked into the cylinders, it is forced in. Additional fuel is supplied by the injection pump in proportion to the increased air intake.

Energy for the operation of the turbocharger comes from the exhaust gas. The gas flows through a specially-shaped housing (the turbine housing) and in so doing, spins the turbine wheel. The turbine wheel is attached to a shaft, at the end of which is another vaned wheel known as the compressor wheel. The compressor wheel spins in its own housing, and compresses the inlet air on the way to the inlet manifold.

Between the turbocharger and the inlet manifold the compressed air passes through an intercooler. This is an air-to-air heat exchanger is mounted next to the radiator, and supplied with cooling air from the front of the car. The purpose of the intercooler is to remove some of the heat gained in being compressed from the inlet air. Because cooler air is denser, removal of this heat further increases engine efficiency.

Charge pressure (the pressure in the inlet manifold) is limited by a wastegate, which diverts the exhaust gas away from the turbine wheel in response to a pressure-sensitive actuator. A pressure-operated switch operates a warning light on the instrument panel in the event of excessive charge pressure developing.

The turbo shaft is pressure-lubricated by an oil feed pipe from the engine main oil so that the shaft 'floats' on a cushion of oil. A drain pipe returns the oil to the sump.

The charge pressure wastegate is controlled by the ECM via a solenoid valve.

If there is an abnormality in any of the readings obtained from any sensor, the ECM enters its back-up mode. In this event, the ECM ignores the abnormal sensor signal, and assumes a preprogrammed value which will allow the engine to continue running (albeit

2.2a Unclip the wiring harness from the back . . .

at reduced efficiency). If the ECM enters this back-up mode, the warning light on the instrument panel will come on, and the relevant fault code will be stored in the ECM memory.

If the warning light comes on, the car should be taken to a Honda dealer at the earliest opportunity. A complete test of the injection system can then be carried out, using a special electronic diagnostic test unit which is simply plugged into the system's diagnostic connector. The connector is located under the driver's side of the facia.

Precautions

⚠️ **Warning: It is necessary to take certain precautions when working on the fuel system components, particularly the fuel injectors. Before carrying out any operations on the fuel system, refer to the precautions given in Safety first! at the beginning of this manual, and to any additional warning notes at the start of the relevant Sections.**

Caution: Do not operate the engine if any of air inlet ducts are disconnected or the filter element is removed. Any debris entering the engine will cause severe damage to the turbocharger.

Caution: To prevent damage to the turbocharger, do not race the engine immediately after start-up, especially if it is cold. Allow it to idle smoothly to give the oil a few seconds to circulate around the turbocharger bearings. Always allow the engine to return to idle speed before

2.2b . . . and from the side of the air cleaner

switching it off – do not blip the throttle and switch off, as this will leave the turbo spinning without lubrication.
Caution: Observe the recommended intervals for oil and filter changing, and use a reputable oil of the specified quality. Neglect of oil changing, or use of inferior oil, can cause carbon formation on the turbo shaft, leading to subsequent failure.

---

2 Air cleaner assembly and inlet ducts – removal and refitting

Note: *Refer to the warnings and cautions in Section 1 before proceeding.*

Removal

1 The air cleaner is located at the rear of the engine compartment, between the coolant expansion tank and the battery. To improve access, remove the battery as described in Chapter 5A.

2 The air cleaner housing has two sections of wiring harness clipped across the back and side – lift the harness out of the plastic clips, noting how it is routed (see illustrations).

3 Similarly, unclip the hose lower down on the side of the housing, then pull off the small vacuum hose from its pipe stub on the housing (see illustrations).

4 The engine compartment fusebox is also clipped to the air cleaner cover – lift it upwards a little to release it (see illustration).

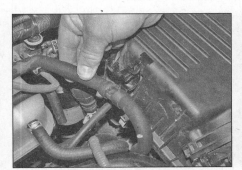

2.3a Unclip the hose from the side . . .

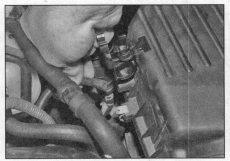

2.3b . . . then pull off the vacuum hose

2.4 Unclip the auxiliary fusebox

2.5 Disconnect the airflow sensor wiring plug

2.6 Loosen the air inlet duct hose clip

2.7a Unscrew the air cleaner front mounting bolt . . .

2.7b . . . and the inlet air duct nut . . .

2.7c . . . then remove the inlet duct

2.8 Removing the air cleaner

5 Disconnect the wiring plug from the mass airflow sensor **(see illustration)**.

6 Loosen the hose clip and disconnect the air inlet duct from the front of the air cleaner **(see illustration)**.

7 Unscrew the air cleaner front mounting bolt, and the nut which secures the inlet air duct to the inner wing. Remove the inlet duct, which fits over a stud and is a sliding fit into the side of the air cleaner **(see illustrations)**.

8 Make sure there is nothing still attached to the air cleaner, then lift it off its two remaining push-fit mounting pegs, at the side and rear. Remove it from the engine compartment **(see illustration)**.

9 The remaining ducts linking the turbocharger, intercooler and inlet manifold can be removed once their hose clips and (where necessary) bolts have been slackened. Note that the inlet duct from the air cleaner housing to the turbocharger incorporates the mass airflow sensor.

Refitting

10 Refitting is the reverse of removal, ensuring that all inlet ducts are properly reconnected and their retaining clips securely tightened.

---

3 Accelerator pedal – removal and refitting

Refer to Chapter 4A.

---

4 Accelerator cable – removal, refitting and adjustment

Removal

1 First, disconnect the cable from the throttle position sensor, which is located at the rear of the engine compartment, next to the fuel filter (access is improved by removing the air cleaner as described in Section 2). Unclip the plastic cover, then open the throttle quadrant, and unhook the accelerator cable end fitting from it. Loosen the cable locknut, then lift the cable from the bracket and move it to one side **(see illustrations)**.

2 Trace the cable back round the engine compartment, freeing it from any clips, and noting how it is routed.

3 Remove the driver's side facia closing panel to gain access to the accelerator pedal (see Chapter 11, Section 27).

4 Working in the driver's footwell, operate the accelerator pedal by hand, and unhook the cable end fitting from the top of the pedal, by sliding the fitting out of the pedal to the right. Feed the cable back into the

4.1a Unclip the plastic cover fitted over the throttle quadrant

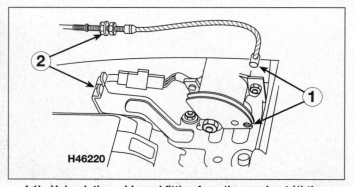

4.1b Unhook the cable end fitting from the quadrant (1) then remove the cable outer (2)

engine compartment, releasing the bulkhead grommet.

5 Withdraw the cable from the engine side, and remove it.

Refitting

6 Refitting is a reversal of removal. On completion, adjust the cable as described later in this Section.

Adjustment

7 The cable adjustment is measured in terms of its total sideways deflection, measured at the throttle quadrant. Push the cable fully one way, then the other, and assess the amount of deflection present – if this is outside the specified range, adjust the cable as follows.

8 Loosen the cable locknut on one side of the cable outer mounting bracket, then turn the adjuster nut on the other side until the deflection is correct **(see illustration)**. Tighten the locknut on completion.

9 Without starting the engine, have an assistant depress the accelerator pedal fully, and check that the throttle quadrant opens fully. Similarly check that the quadrant returns to the idle position when the pedal is released.

5 Fuel system – priming and bleeding

1 It is not always necessary to manually prime and bleed the fuel system after working on the system components. Just starting the engine may be sufficient (this may take longer than usual). Operate the starter in ten-second bursts **only**, with five seconds rest in between each operation. When the engine starts, run it at fast idle speed for a minute or so to purge any trapped air from the fuel lines. After this time, the engine should idle smoothly at a constant speed.

2 If a significant amount of work has been carried out on the fuel system, and the engine either won't start or idles roughly, then there is still some air trapped in the fuel system.

3 The easiest way to bleed the system is to use the hand-priming bulb, clipped in front of the fuel filter, at the rear of the engine compartment. The bulb is (just) accessible without any dismantling – ideally, have an

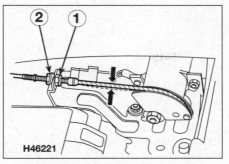

4.8 If the cable deflection is not as specified, loosen locknut (1) and turn adjuster nut (2)

assistant on hand to operate the bulb, while you try to start the engine. The bulb should first be squeezed a few times until it becomes hard. Try to start the engine, while continuing to squeeze the bulb **(see illustration)**. Once the engine starts, stop squeezing, and let the engine run at a fast idle for a few minutes.

4 If this does not work, remove the air cleaner as described in Section 2.

5 A bleed bolt is provided on top of the fuel filter in the engine compartment **(see illustration)**. Clean around the bolt, then unscrew it completely and fit a **new** sealing washer – this is essential, to avoid air being drawn into the system after bleeding.

6 Refit the bleed bolt loosely, leaving the cutaway section of its threads visible. Wrap some clean absorbent towel around the filter, to soak up the fuel which will be lost – remember that no dirt must be allowed to enter the system.

7 Release the hand-priming bulb from its two storage clips on the filter mounting bracket **(see illustration)**. Squeeze the bulb several times, and fuel containing air bubbles will emerge from the bleed bolt hole.

8 When no more bubbles are seen in the escaping fuel, tighten the bleed bolt securely. Wipe up the spilt fuel.

9 With the bleed bolt tightened, squeeze the hand-priming bulb again until it becomes hard, then try to start the engine, bearing in mind the points made in paragraph 1. If the engine does not start after a couple of attempts, squeeze the bulb again until it becomes hard, and try again.

6 Fuel lift pump/ gauge sender unit – removal and refitting

Refer to Chapter 4A, Section 7. There is no need to depressurise the fuel system, and there will be two fuel hoses to disconnect – note their fitted positions. On completion, bleed the system if necessary, as described in Section 5.

7 Fuel tank – removal and refitting

Refer to Chapter 4A, Section 8. There will be two fuel hoses to disconnect from the sender unit – note their fitted positions. No EVAP system is fitted to diesel models. On completion, bleed the system if necessary, as described in Section 5.

8 Fuel filler flap and cable – removal and refitting

Refer to Chapter 4A, Section 9.

9 Diesel injection system – checking and fault code clearing

1 If a fault appears in the diesel injection system, first ensure that all the system wiring connectors are securely connected and free of corrosion. Then ensure that the fault is not due to poor maintenance; ie, check that the air cleaner filter element is clean, the valve clearances are correct, the cylinder compression pressures are correct, the fuel filter has been drained (or changed) and the engine breather hoses are clear and undamaged, referring to Chapter 1B or Chapter 2B.

2 If these checks fail to reveal the cause of the problem, the car should be taken to a suitably-equipped Honda dealer for testing. A diagnostic connector is incorporated in the engine management system wiring harness,

5.3 Squeeze the hand-priming bulb until it becomes hard

5.5 Unscrew the fuel filter bleed bolt

5.7 Unclip the hand-priming bulb from its bracket

10.1 Disconnect the airflow sensor wiring plug

10.3 Remove the two airflow sensor bolts (one hidden)

into which dedicated electronic test equipment can be plugged – the connector is located under the steering column. The test equipment is capable of 'interrogating' the engine control module (ECM) electronically and accessing its internal fault log (reading fault codes).

3 Fault codes can only be extracted from the ECM using a dedicated fault code reader. A Honda dealer will obviously have such a reader, but they are also available from other suppliers. It is unlikely to be cost-effective for the private owner to purchase a fault code reader, but a well-equipped local garage or auto-electrical specialist will have one.

4 Using this equipment, faults can be pinpointed quickly and simply, even if their occurrence is intermittent. Testing all the system components individually in an attempt to locate the fault by elimination is a time-consuming operation that is unlikely to be fruitful (particularly if the fault occurs dynamically), and carries a high risk of damage to the ECM's internal components.

5 Experienced home mechanics equipped with a diesel tachometer or other diagnostic equipment may be able to check the engine idle speed; if found to be out of specification, the car must be taken to a suitably-equipped Honda dealer for assessment. The engine idle

speed is not manually adjustable; incorrect test results indicate the need for maintenance (possibly injector cleaning or recalibration) or a fault within the injection system.

6 If excessive smoking or knocking is evident, it may be due to a problem with the fuel injectors. Proprietary treatments are available which can be added to the fuel to clean the injectors. Injectors deteriorate with prolonged use, however, and it is reasonable to expect them to need reconditioning or renewal after 100 000 miles or so. Accurate testing, overhaul and calibration of the injectors must be left to a specialist.

Clearing fault codes

7 Most of the components and sensors which make up the engine management system will log a fault code in the ECM memory in the event of a fault. When this happens, the engine management warning light on the instrument panel will come on. In some cases, the ECM will substitute its own default value instead of the correct sensor reading, and although it can still be driven safely, the car will suffer driveability problems, often especially noticeable when cold.

8 Once the faulty component has been identified and the problem corrected (usually by fitting a new component), the fault code must be cleared. In some cases, this will happen automatically once the ignition has been switched on and off enough times – if the fault does not recur, it may clear itself.

9 To clear fault codes manually requires the use of a fault code reader tool as described at the start of this Section. However, codes

may also be cleared by the DIY mechanic, as follows.

10 With the ignition off, remove fuse No 6 from the engine compartment fusebox for at least 10 seconds, then refit it. Switch the ignition on, and the fault should have cleared.

11 If the engine management light remains on (or comes back on later), either the same fault still exists, or there is another faulty component triggering a different fault code. Check that any new components have been correctly fitted, and especially that their wiring plugs are clean and secure.

10 Diesel injection system electrical components – removal and refitting

Mass airflow sensor

Note: *The inlet air temperature sensor is built into the airflow meter.*

1 Ensure the ignition is switched off, and disconnect the wiring plug from the airflow sensor **(see illustration)**.

2 Release the hose clip, and pull off the inlet air duct at the front of the air cleaner.

3 Remove the two bolts securing the airflow sensor to the air cleaner, and remove it from the engine compartment **(see illustration)**.

4 Refitting is the reverse of removal, ensuring the air ducts is securely refitted, and the sensor mounting bolts fully tightened.

Throttle position sensor

5 The throttle position sensor is located at the rear of the engine compartment, on the passenger's side – unclip and remove the plastic cover for access.

6 Open the throttle quadrant, and unhook the accelerator cable end fitting from it. Loosen the cable locknut, then lift the cable from the bracket and move it to one side.

7 Unscrew the two mounting bolts, and lift the position sensor assembly up for access to the wiring plug **(see illustration)**. Disconnect the wiring plug from the sensor, and remove it from the car.

8 Refitting is a reversal of removal. Tighten the mounting bolts securely, and adjust the accelerator cable as described in Section 4.

Crankshaft sensor

9 Firmly apply the handbrake, then jack up the front of the car and support it on axle stands (see *Jacking and vehicle support*). Where necessary, undo the retaining bolts/clips and remove the undertray from beneath the engine.

10 The sensor is located on the rear of the cylinder block, at the flywheel end underneath the starter motor. Working from under the car, disconnect the wiring plug from the sensor.

11 Undo the retaining bolt and remove the sensor. Recover the sealing ring **(see illustration)**. If required, a second bolt can be removed, which retains the sensor's spacer.

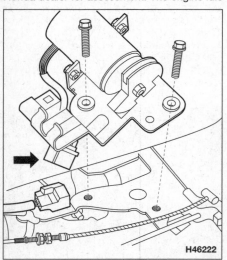

10.7 Throttle position sensor removal details – wiring plug arrowed

10.11 Crankshaft position sensor removal – recover the sealing ring

12 Refitting is a reversal of removal. Renew the sealing ring if necessary, and tighten the sensor retaining bolt securely

Coolant temperature sensor

13 Either drain the cooling system as described in Chapter 1B or, if the new switch can be fitted immediately, anticipate some small loss of coolant when the old switch is removed.

14 The coolant temperature sensor is located in the front of the thermostat housing at the transmission end of the cylinder head. To access the sensor, loosen the hose clips and remove the large intercooler air duct above the thermostat housing **(see illustration)**.

15 Disconnect the wiring plug from the sensor, then unscrew the sensor from the thermostat housing, and recover the sealing washer/O-ring. Mop-up any spilled coolant.

16 Check the condition of the sensor's sealing washer/O-ring before fitting. Apply a little locking compound to the threads of the sensor, and refit the sensor to the housing.

17 Tighten the sensor to the specified torque, then reconnect the wiring plug.

18 Either refill or top-up the cooling system, as applicable (see Chapter 1B or *Weekly checks*). Refit the intercooler air duct, and tighten the hose clip securely.

Manifold absolute pressure (MAP) sensor

19 The MAP sensor is located on the rear of the inlet manifold, next to the vacuum capsule for the variable swirl system **(see illustration)**.

20 Disconnect the wiring plug from the sensor.

21 Remove the sensor mounting bolt, and pull it out from its location – there may be some resistance, as there is an O-ring on the sensor stem.

22 Refitting is a reversal of removal. Check the condition of the O-ring, and renew if necessary.

Vehicle speed sensor

23 The vehicle speed sensor is mounted on top of the transmission. The sensor is driven by a gear, in much the same way as the older speedometer drive, and provides an electronic signal of the vehicle speed. This information is used by the engine management ECM, electric power steering system (EPS) and anti-lock braking system (ABS), besides the speedometer itself.

24 Remove the battery as described in Chapter 5A, and the air cleaner as described in Section 2.

25 Disconnect the wiring plug from the speed sensor – do not confuse the sensor with the reversing light switch which, unlike the sensor, does not have a separate mounting bolt.

26 Unscrew the sensor mounting bolt, then withdraw the sensor from the transmission – there may be some resistance, both from the O-ring seal and from the sensor drive gear.

10.14 Loosen the hose clip and disconnect the air duct

27 Refitting is a reversal of removal, noting the following points:

  a) *Clean the mating faces of the sensor and transmission, and use a new O-ring if necessary. Expect the sensor to twist as it meshes with the transmission gear, then turn it to align the mounting bolt hole.*

  b) *Tighten the sensor mounting bolt securely, and ensure that the wiring plug is securely reconnected.*

Exhaust gas recirculation valve

28 Refer to Chapter 4C.

Fuel rail pressure sensor

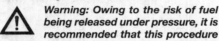 *Warning: Owing to the risk of fuel being released under pressure, it is recommended that this procedure only be carried out after the engine has been switched off for several hours.*

29 The fuel rail pressure sensor is located in the middle of the fuel supply rail.

30 Disconnect the wiring plug from the sensor.

31 Position a container underneath the sensor to catch the fuel which will be lost from the rail when the sensor is removed. In addition, if possible, wrap some clean towel around the sensor-to-rail joint, as the fuel released may still be under pressure (refer to the warning at the start of this procedure).

32 Loosen the sensor slowly, to allow time for any stored fuel pressure to be released, then unscrew it fully and remove it from the fuel rail. If the sensor will be removed for some time, either plug or tape over the opening in the fuel rail – no dirt must enter the system.

33 Refitting is a reversal of removal, noting the following points:

  a) *Ensure that no dirt enters the system.*

  b) *Fit a new sealing washer, where applicable.*

  c) *Tighten the sensor securely.*

  d) *On completion, bleed the system as described in Section 5, then run the engine and check for leaks.*

Camshaft position sensor

34 The camshaft position sensor is fitted in front of the inlet camshaft sprocket, at the timing belt end. To access the sensor, first remove the timing belt upper cover, as described in Chapter 2B.

10.19 MAP sensor location – arrowed

35 Disconnect the wiring plug from the sensor, then unscrew the mounting bolt and withdraw it from the engine **(see illustration)**.

36 Refitting is a reversal of removal. Refit the timing belt upper cover as described in Chapter 2B.

Brake pedal position switch

37 The brake pedal position switch is fitted above and behind the top of the brake pedal itself – access is from the driver's footwell.

38 Reach up under the facia to the switch mounting bracket, and disconnect the wiring plug from the top of the switch.

39 Turn the switch body anti-clockwise to remove it from the bracket.

40 To refit and set the switch, offer the switch into its bracket, so that the switch plunger touches the pedal. Without moving the switch in or out, turn it clockwise to lock it.

41 Reconnect the switch wiring plug to complete.

Clutch pedal position switch

42 The clutch pedal position switch is fitted above the clutch pedal (note that some models do not have this switch, and a bolt is fitted in its place).

43 Reach up under the facia to the switch mounting bracket, and disconnect the wiring plug from the top of the switch.

44 Unscrew the switch locknut, then unscrew and remove it from the bracket.

45 Refitting is a reversal of removal. Turn the switch clockwise until it just contacts the pedal arm, then turn it in an additional 3/4 to 1 turn. Tighten the locknut.

10.35 Disconnect the camshaft position sensor wiring plug – mounting bolt arrowed

10.55 Fuel shut-off inertia switch inside glovebox aperture

Electronic control module (ECM)

Note: *The ECM contains the immobiliser coding which was programmed into it when the car was new. If a new ECM is fitted, the immobiliser coding will have to be programmed into it by a Honda dealer before the car will start.*

46 Disconnect the battery negative lead, and position the lead away from the battery (also see *Disconnecting the battery*). This is **essential** when working on the ECM – if the module's wiring connector is unplugged when the battery is still connected, this will almost certainly damage the module.

47 The module is located inside the car, behind the glovebox. Remove the lower facia panel from the passenger side, and the glovebox, as described in Chapter 11.

48 Above the ECM, remove the relay mounting nut and the nut from the earth strap.

49 Remove the two ECM mounting bolts, then separate the module from the mounting bracket by removing the two bolts either side.

50 Disconnect the ECM wiring plug, and remove the module from the car.

51 Refitting is a reversal of removal. Make sure the battery is still disconnected before reconnecting the ECM wiring plug.

Fuel shut-off (inertia) switch

52 The fuel shut-off switch is a safety device which automatically cuts off the fuel supply

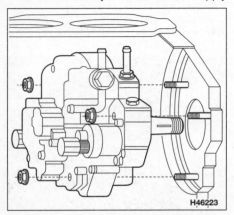

11.6 Fuel high-pressure pump removal details

in the event of a sudden impact or collision. The switch may occasionally be triggered in normal driving, for example when driving over badly-maintained roads.

53 The switch is located behind the glovebox, on the left-hand side. To access it, open the glovebox, then press the glovebox sides inwards to allow the glovebox to open past its stops. For the best access, remove the glovebox completely, as described in Chapter 11, Section 27.

54 To reset the switch after an impact or shock, depress the button on the top of the switch.

55 To remove the switch, disconnect the wiring plug on the base, then remove the mounting bolt and withdraw the switch from behind the glovebox **(see illustration)**.

56 Refitting is a reversal of removal.

EPS torque sensor

57 The UK Civic is equipped with electric power steering (refer to Chapter 10 for more details). The steering system's torque sensor signals the engine management ECM when the steering load is high, as the resultant electrical load on the engine could cause the idle speed to drop.

---

11 Fuel high-pressure pump – removal and refitting

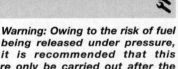

> ⚠ **Warning: Owing to the risk of fuel being released under pressure, it is recommended that this procedure only be carried out after the engine has been switched off for several hours. Also, be careful not to allow dirt into the pump or pipes during this procedure.**

Removal

1 Disconnect the battery negative lead, and position the lead away from the battery (also see *Disconnecting the battery*).

2 With reference to Chapter 2B, remove the timing belt and the pump sprocket – note that a puller will be required to remove the sprocket..

3 Disconnect the fuel supply and return hoses on top of the pump. Note the hoses' fitted positions, and either plug or tape over the open connections – no dirt must enter the system.

4 Loosen the union at either end, then remove the fuel pump-to-supply rail pipe. If necessary, hold the pipe itself, so that the pipe is not unduly strained as the unions are loosened.

5 Recover the supply rail pipe sealing washers, where applicable. Either plug or tape over the open connections – no dirt must enter the system. Note that Honda recommend a new pipe must always be used when refitting.

6 Support the pump, then loosen and remove the three pump mounting nuts. Slide the pump off its three mounting studs, and remove it from the engine **(see illustration)**.

7 Store the pump in clean conditions – take care that no dirt enters the pipe unions.

8 It appears at the time of writing that no spare parts are available for the pump, though reconditioned pumps may be available – check with your parts supplier.

Refitting

9 Refitting is a reversal of removal, noting the following points:
a) *Tighten the pump mounting nuts to the specified torque.*
b) *Fit the pump-to-supply rail fuel pipe, ensuring that no dirt enters the system. New sealing washers should be supplied with a new pipe. Tighten the pipe unions to the specified torque – hold the pipe if necessary, to prevent the pipe being strained.*
c) *Again ensuring that dirt is kept out, reconnect the fuel supply and return hoses to the top of the pump.*
d) *Refit the pump sprocket and the timing belt as described in Chapter 2B.*
e) *On completion, bleed the fuel system as described in Section 5, then start the engine and check for leaks.*

---

12 Injector pipes – removal and refitting

> ⚠ **Warning: Owing to the risk of fuel being released under pressure, it is recommended that this procedure only be carried out after the engine has been switched off for several hours. Also, be careful not to allow dirt into the system during this procedure.**

Removal

1 The fuel injection pipes should be removed as a set. At the time of writing, it is not clear whether individual pipes are available.

2 Disconnect the battery negative (earth) lead (refer to *Disconnecting the battery* at the end of this manual).

3 Remove the cylinder head cover as described in Chapter 2B.

4 Wrap some clean towel around each union, as the fuel released may still be under pressure (refer to the warning at the start of this procedure). If absorbent towel is used, this will soak away any dirt which might otherwise enter.

5 Loosen the four pipe unions at the supply (common) rail first, then loosen the unions at each injector. If necessary, hold the pipes themselves, so that the pipes are not unduly strained as the unions are loosened.

6 Remove each pair of pipes, noting their fitted positions **(see illustration)**. Recover the sealing washers.

7 Either plug or tape over the open connections – no dirt must enter the system.

8 Honda recommend that new pipes must always be used when refitting.

Refitting

9 Refitting is a reversal of removal, noting the following points:

a) *Use new sealing washers – these should be supplied with a new set of pipes.*

b) *Fit the pipes in pairs, using the original ones as a pattern. The pipes should be set at the correct angle, relative to the supply rail, before tightening the unions (see illustration).*

c) *Tighten the pipe unions at all four injectors first, then at the fuel supply rail.*

d) *Refit the cylinder head cover as described in Chapter 2B.*

e) *On completion, bleed the fuel system as described in Section 5, then start the engine and check for leaks.*

13 Fuel supply (common) rail – removal and refitting

⚠️ **Warning: Owing to the risk of fuel being released under pressure, it is recommended that this procedure only be carried out after the engine has been switched off for several hours. Also, be careful not to allow dirt into the system during this procedure.**

Removal

1 Remove the injector pipes as described in Section 12.

2 Loosen the union at either end, then remove the fuel pump-to-supply rail pipe. If necessary, hold the pipe itself, so that the pipe is not unduly strained as the unions are loosened. Recover the supply rail pipe sealing washers, where applicable. Either plug or tape over the open connections – no dirt must enter the system. Note that Honda recommend a new pipe must always be used when refitting.

3 Disconnect the wiring plug from the fuel rail pressure sensor.

4 Unscrew and remove the two fuel supply rail mounting bolts, and withdraw the rail from the back of the engine **(see illustration)**.

5 Store the fuel rail in clean conditions – take care that no dirt enters the pipe unions.

Refitting

6 Refitting is a reversal of removal, noting the following points:

a) *Offer the supply rail into position, then fit and tighten the two mounting bolts to the specified torque..*

b) *Refit the injector pipes as described in Section 12.*

c) *Fit the pump-to-supply rail fuel pipe, ensuring that no dirt enters the system. New sealing washers should be supplied with a new pipe. Tighten the pipe unions to the specified torque – hold the pipe if necessary, to prevent the pipe being strained.*

d) *On completion, bleed the fuel system as described in Section 5, then start the engine and check for leaks.*

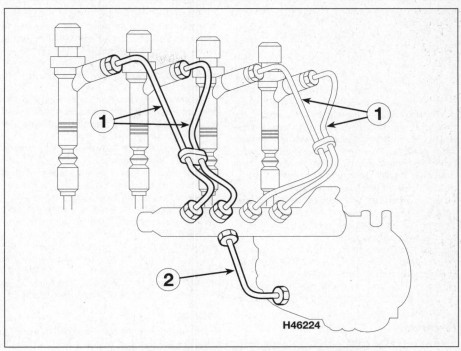

12.6 Fuel injector pipes (1) and fuel supply pipe (2)

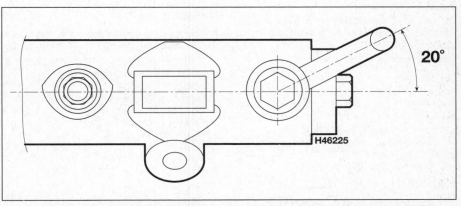

12.9 The pipes should be set at the correct angle, relative to the common rail

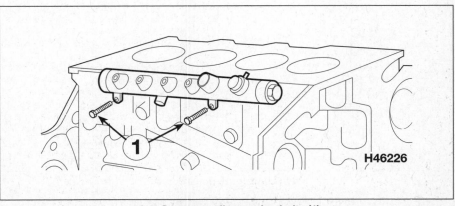

13.4 Common rail mounting bolts (1)

14 Injectors –
removal, testing and refitting

⚠️ **Warning: Exercise extreme caution when working on the fuel injectors. Never expose the hands or any part of the body to injector spray, as the high working pressure can cause the fuel to penetrate the skin, with possibly fatal results. You are strongly advised to have any work which involves testing the injectors under pressure carried out by a dealer or fuel injection specialist.**

⚠️ **Warning: Owing to the risk of fuel being released under pressure, it is recommended that this procedure only be carried out after the engine has been switched off for several hours. Also, be careful not to allow dirt into the system during this procedure.**

Note: *Honda special tools will be required for the refitting procedure of the fuel injectors – see text.*

Removal

1 Disconnect the battery negative (earth) lead (refer to *Disconnecting the battery* at the end of this manual).
2 Remove the cylinder head cover as described in Chapter 2B.
3 The injectors are located in position in pairs, by two locating plates, each secured with five bolts.

4 Loosen the four smaller bolts at the front of each injector locating plate, then loosen the larger single bolt and lift off the two plates. Below each plate is a further retaining 'finger' for each of the four injectors – the fingers are still trapped at the front by the retaining plate at this stage.
5 Unscrew three further nuts securing the long front retaining plate, and lift off the plate, noting how it is fitted **(see illustration)**. Lift off the injector fingers, keeping them in their fitted order, to match with their injectors when removed.
6 Label each injector to indicate its fitted position, then carefully pull upwards to remove the injector assembly from the cylinder head – there will be some resistance, as the injectors have an O-ring seal. Recover the copper washers from the base of each injector – new seals and washers must be used when refitting. **Do not** attempt to dismantle the injectors any further.
7 Take care not to drop the injectors, nor allow the needles at their tips to become damaged.

Testing

8 Testing of the injectors requires the use of special equipment. If any injector is thought to be faulty have it tested and, if necessary, reconditioned by a diesel engine specialist or Honda dealer.

Refitting

9 Commence reassembly by ensuring that the injector and cylinder head mating faces are clean, and fitting new copper sealing washers/rubber seals to each injector.
10 Carefully fit each injector into its original location in the cylinder head, and loosely retain them in position by refitting the four fingers and the front retaining plate.
11 The injector fitted angle must now be set, using a special Honda tool (5-86751-052-0) **(see illustration)**. Unfortunately, it is unlikely that a DIY alternative could be fabricate with enough accuracy, so this tool (or a pattern equivalent) will have to be obtained. However, all this tool appears to do is hold all four injectors equally spaced, and at right-angles to the head – if this can be assured by eye as the injector bolts are tightened the tool may not be needed.
12 With the setting tool in place (where available), refit the two injector locating plates, and secure them with the five bolts, tightened by hand only. Note that the locating plate's larger single bolt should be oiled prior to fitting.
13 Tighten the front retaining bracket nuts to the specified torque.
14 Progressively tighten the five locating plate bolts to their respective specified torques, in several stages so that the injectors are pulled into position gradually and evenly. On completion, remove the special setting tool.
15 Refit the cylinder head cover as described in Chapter 2B.
16 On completion, bleed the fuel system as described in Section 5, then start the engine and check for leaks.

15 Turbocharger –
removal and refitting

Removal

1 Remove the exhaust manifold and turbocharger assembly as described in Section 18.
2 With the assembly on the bench, undo the three retaining nuts and remove the exhaust connection elbow and gasket from the turbocharger.
3 Slacken and remove the three mounting nuts, then remove the turbocharger and gasket from the manifold **(see illustration)**.

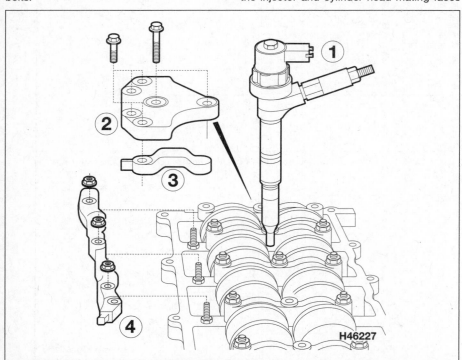

14.5 Injector removal details

1 *Injector*
2 *Locating plate*
3 *Retaining finger*
4 *Front retaining plate*

14.11 Injector holding special tool

4 Do not attempt to dismantle the turbocharger any further. If the unit is thought to be faulty, take it to a turbo specialist or Honda dealer for testing and examination. They will be able to inform you if the unit can be overhauled or will need renewing.

Refitting

5 Refitting is the reverse of removal, using new gaskets, and tightening the nuts to their specified torque settings. Refit the manifold

and turbocharger assembly as described in Section 18.

16 Intercooler – removal and refitting

Removal

1 The intercooler is mounted to the left of

the radiator (left as seen from the driver's seat). To access the intercooler, the engine compartment front crossmember (or 'slam panel') must first be removed.

2 Work along the crossmember, disconnecting the following wiring plugs (as applicable):

  a) *Radiator cooling fan.*
  b) *Bonnet lock alarm switch.*
  c) *Air conditioning compressor clutch.*
  d) *Air conditioning condenser fan.*

3 Carefully release or cut through the cable-

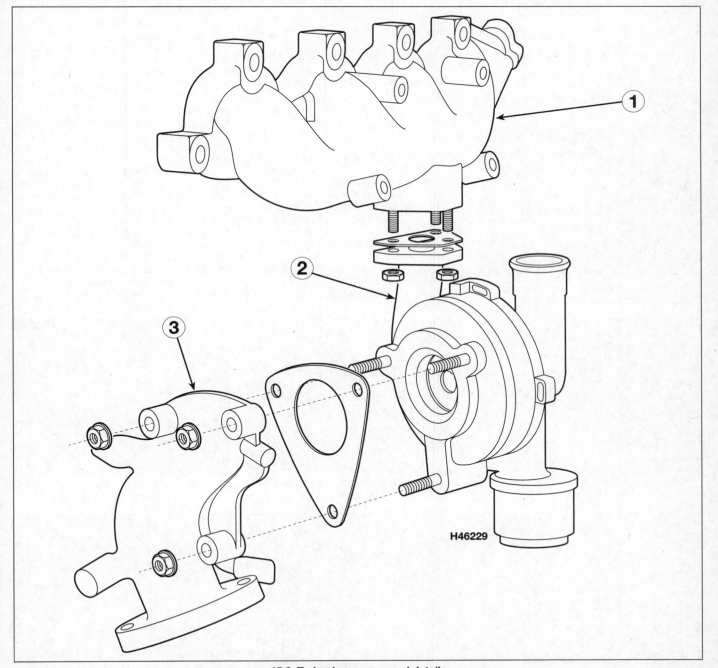

H46229

15.3 Turbocharger removal details

1 *Exhaust manifold*   2 *Turbocharger*   3 *Exhaust connection elbow*

16.7 Intercooler removal details

1 Turbocharger outlet hose
2 Intercooler outlet hose
3 Intercooler
4 Radiator

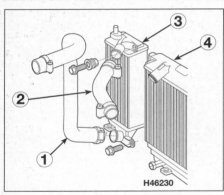

17.3a Unclip the harnesses from the bracket on the EGR valve . . .

ties securing the wiring harness to the cross-member.

4 Unscrew the bolts along the crossmember securing the upper support brackets for the radiator and air conditioning condenser (where fitted). As the bolts and brackets are removed, note their fitted positions for refitting.

5 Remove a further bolt at each end of the crossmember, and one at the base of the panel's central support. Carefully lift out the crossmember (refer to Chapter 3, Section 5, for more information).

6 Loosen the hose clips and disconnect the two air hoses from the intercooler, noting their fitted positions.

7 Support the intercooler, then remove the upper and lower mounting bolt. Recover the spacer collar from the upper bolt **(see illustration)**.

8 Lift out the intercooler, taking care not to damage the fins.

Refitting

9 Before refitting the intercooler, check inside the duct connection stubs for significant amounts of oil. If present, this can be cleaned out with a suitable solvent – if contamination is bad, the whole intercooler should be washed out. The presence of oil indicates that the turbocharger oil seals have failed – the turbo should be removed for inspection as described in Section 15.

10 Refitting is a reversal of removal, noting the following points:

a) Tighten the hose clips securely, to avoid air leaks.

b) Tighten the intercooler mounting bolts securely.

c) Once the crossmember has been refitted, reconnect the wiring plugs and re-attach the wiring harness.

17 Inlet manifold – removal, inspection and refitting

Removal

1 Remove the engine top cover, which is secured by four bolts.

2 Remove the air cleaner as described in Section 2.

3 Unclip the wiring harness from the bracket on top of the EGR valve, then unscrew the two bolts and take off the bracket **(see illustrations)**.

4 The rigid pipe supplying the inlet manifold with air from the intercooler must be removed. Loosen the hose clip at the side of the engine, and pull off the large-diameter air hose from the intercooler. At the inlet manifold, unscrew the two pipe flange bolts, and release the flange from the EGR valve **(see illustrations)**. Unbolt the pipe support bolts (where applicable), and withdraw the pipe from the engine.

5 Unscrew the EGR union pipe nut and disconnect the pipe from the valve – if necessary, trace the pipe back to the exhaust manifold and unbolt it from there (a new gasket will be needed when refitting) **(see illustrations)**.

6 Disconnect the vacuum hose from the EGR valve – now the valve can be removed with the

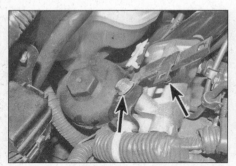

17.3b . . . then remove the two bolts . . .

17.3c . . . and take off the wiring harness bracket

17.4a Loosen the hose clip and disconnect the air hose from the rigid pipe

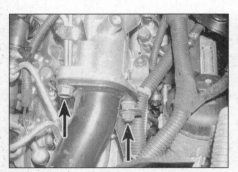

17.4b Unbolt the intercooler pipe flange from the EGR valve

17.5a Unscrew the EGR pipe union nut, and disconnect the pipe

17.5b If necessary, unbolt the EGR pipe from the exhaust manifold, and recover the gasket

manifold, avoiding the need for a new EGR valve gasket when refitting.

7 Remove the oil cooler as described in Chapter 2B.

8 Remove the injector pipes as described in Section 12.

9 Unscrew the three bolts securing the injector wiring harness, then disconnect the injector wiring plugs, labelling the plugs if necessary to ensure correct refitting.

10 Remove the three bolts securing the injector fuel return pipe to the engine.

11 Pull out the securing clips from the four return pipe connections to the injectors, then lift off the return 'rail' from the injectors by pulling squarely upwards. Recover the O-ring seal from each injector – new seals should be used when refitting.

12 Disconnect the vacuum hose from the variable swirl valve.

13 The inlet manifold is secured to the back of the cylinder head by a total of seven bolts and two nuts. Remove the nuts and bolts, then withdraw the manifold from the two studs and remove it. The variable swirl valve has a bead of gasket sealant, which may stick as the manifold is removed.

Inspection

14 The variable swirl valve can be checked for smooth operation by operating it with your finger – likewise the swirl plates fitted in the manifold ports. However, apart from careful cleaning, little else can be done to the swirl system components.

Refitting

15 Clean the mating surfaces of the head, manifold and swirl valve, taking care not to damage the alloy material, as this will lead to air leaks and rough running on reassembly.

16 Apply a bead of sealant to the variable swirl valve.

17 Fit a new manifold gasket, then offer the manifold into position over the two studs, and secure with the two nuts and seven bolts.

18 Tighten the nuts and bolts securely.

19 Further refitting is a reversal of removal, noting the following points:

 a) *Use new O-rings when refitting the fuel return 'rail' to the four injectors.*

 b) *Reconnect the injector wiring plugs correctly and securely.*

 c) *Fit the injector pipes as described in Section 12. Honda recommend that new pipes are used whenever the old ones are removed.*

 d) *Refit the oil cooler as described in Chapter 2B.*

 e) *Tighten the EGR pipe union nut securely (use the specified torque as a guide). If the other end of the pipe was disconnected from the exhaust manifold, use a new gasket when refitting, and tighten the flange bolts to the specified torque.*

 e) *On completion, bleed the fuel system as described in Section 5, then start the engine and check for leaks.*

18.11 Exhaust manifold heat shield bolts (one hidden)

18 Exhaust manifold – removal and refitting

Removal

1 The exhaust manifold is at the front of the engine, and should be removed with the turbo.

2 Firmly apply the handbrake, then jack up the front of the car so access can be gained both from above and below (see *Jacking and vehicle support*). Unbolt the undertray and remove it from beneath the engine/ transmission.

3 Remove the four bolts securing the engine top cover, and lift it off.

4 Release the cable-tie securing the wiring harness to the engine lifting eye above the turbo, and move the wiring to one side.

5 Loosen the hose clip and disconnect the intercooler inlet hose from the turbo.

6 Under the car, disconnect the air conditioning compressor wiring plug, then remove the bolt securing the compressor wiring harness. Support the compressor, then remove the three mounting bolts and move the compressor clear of the engine, **without** disconnecting or straining any of the pipework. Tie the compressor up to a convenient point – do not leave it hanging.

7 Remove the three bolts securing the compressor mounting bracket, and remove the bracket from the engine.

8 Release the hose clip and disconnect the turbo oil return hose from the engine.

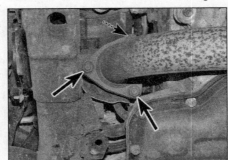

18.14a Exhaust downpipe-to-turbo nuts (one hidden)

18.13 Unbolt the EGR pipe flange

Anticipate a small amount of oil spillage as this is done.

9 Remove the alternator as described in Chapter 5A.

10 Unscrew the bolt securing the oil dipstick guide tube bracket to the cylinder block, and the two bolts securing the guide tube to the sump. Withdraw the dipstick tube, noting the O-ring seal at its base – a new seal should be obtained for reassembly.

11 Undo the retaining bolts and remove the turbocharger and exhaust manifold heat shields – each shield has four bolts. If the bolts are in poor condition, new ones should be obtained for reassembly **(see illustration)**.

12 Release the hose clips at the air cleaner and turbo, then detach the inlet air duct at both ends. Pull off the smaller hose attached to the crankcase ventilation (PCV) valve on top of the engine, and remove the inlet air duct completely.

13 Unscrew the two bolts from the EGR supply pipe flange on top of the exhaust manifold, and detach the pipe **(see illustration)**. Recover the gasket – a new one should be used on reassembly.

14 Unscrew the three flange nuts, and separate the exhaust front pipe from the turbo – to do this, it may be necessary to remove the nuts from the front pipe support bracket under the car **(see illustrations)**. A new turbo-to-front pipe gasket and flange nuts should be obtained for refitting. For maximum working room, it is preferable to remove the front pipe completely, as described in Section 19.

15 Remove the two flange bolts, and disconnect the oil return pipe from the base

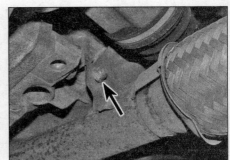

18.14b One of the front pipe support bracket nuts

of the turbo. Recover the gasket – a new one should be used on reassembly.

16 Unscrew the union bolt and disconnect the oil feed pipe from the top of the turbo. Recover the sealing washers – new ones should be used when refitting. Similarly unbolt the feed pipe union on the engine – this is not strictly necessary, but does move the feed pipe clear to allow removal of the manifold and turbo assembly.

17 Unscrew the manifold mounting nuts, then slide the manifold/turbo rearwards off its studs, and remove it from the engine compartment. Recover the manifold gasket – a new one should be used on reassembly. If

the manifold nuts are in poor condition, obtain new ones **(see illustration)**.

18 If required, the turbocharger can now be separated from the manifold as described in Section 15.

Refitting

19 Refitting is the reverse of removal, noting the following points:
a) *Ensure all mating surfaces are clean and dry, and renew all gaskets/sealing washers.*
b) *Tighten the manifold nuts, turbo pipe fittings, exhaust front pipe nuts, etc, to their specified torque settings.*

c) *Securely reconnect the turbocharger air ducts.*
d) *Refit the alternator as described in Chapter 5A, and the air conditioning compressor as described in Chapter 3.*
e) *On completion check and, if necessary, top-up the oil level as described in Weekly checks, then start the engine and check for oil and exhaust gas leaks.*

19 Exhaust system – general information, removal and refitting

Warning: Inspection and repair of exhaust system components should be done only after the system has cooled completely. This applies particularly to the catalytic converter, which runs at very high temperatures.

General information

1 The exhaust system consists of four sections: the front pipe, catalytic converter, the intermediate pipe and silencer, and the rear silencer.

2 The system is suspended throughout its entire length by rubber mountings, though the front pipe is rigidly mounted to the underbody via a square bracket.

3 If any section of the exhaust is damaged or deteriorated, excessive noise and vibration will occur.

4 Carry out regular inspections of the exhaust system, to check security and condition. Look for any damaged or bent parts, open seams, holes, loose connections, excessive corrosion, or other defects which could allow exhaust fumes to enter the car. Deteriorated sections of the exhaust system should be renewed.

5 If the exhaust system components are extremely corroded or rusted together, it may not be possible to separate them. This often happens with the rear silencer, which rusts to the centre section – try twisting the pipes to separate them. Cut off the old components carefully with a hacksaw, and see if any corroded pipe can be removed (perhaps with a chisel) without damaging the remaining exhaust section. Wear safety glasses to protect your eyes, and wear gloves to protect your hands.

6 Here are some simple guidelines to follow when repairing the exhaust system:
a) *Work from the back to the front when removing exhaust system components.*
b) *Apply penetrating fluid to the flange nuts before unscrewing them. If possible, wire-brush any exposed threads to remove corrosion and dirt before trying to loosen the nuts.*
c) *Use new gaskets and rubber mountings when installing exhaust system components.*
d) *Apply anti-seize compound (copper grease will do) to the threads of all exhaust system studs during reassembly.*

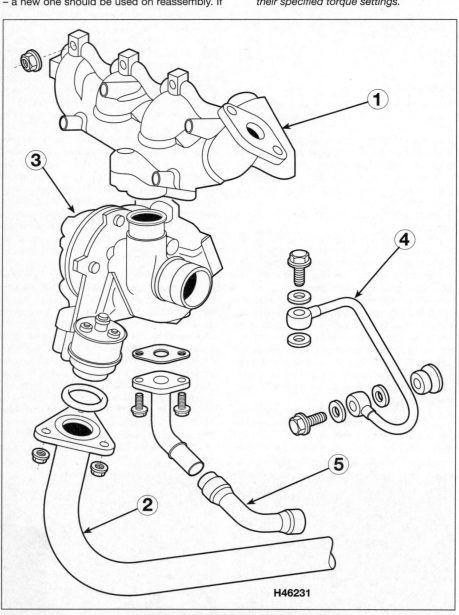

18.17 Exhaust manifold removal details

1	Exhaust manifold	3	Turbocharger	5	Turbo oil return
2	Exhaust front pipe	4	Turbo oil feed pipe		pipe

H46231

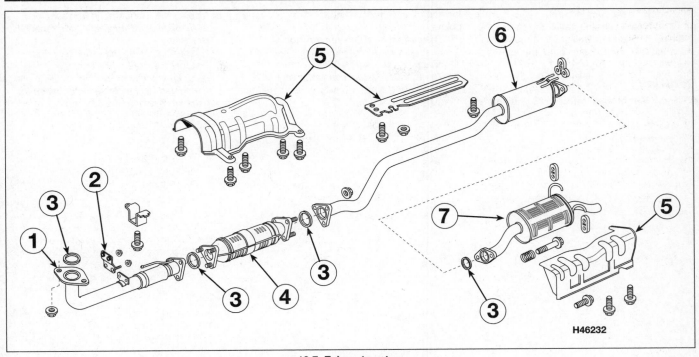

19.7 Exhaust system

1 Front pipe	3 Gasket	5 Heat shield	7 Rear silencer
2 Front pipe support bracket	4 Catalytic converter	6 Centre pipe/silencer	

e) Be sure to allow sufficient clearance between newly-installed parts and all points on the underbody, to avoid overheating the floorpan, and possibly damaging the interior carpet and insulation. Pay particularly close attention to the catalytic converter and its heat shield.

Removal

7 Each exhaust section can be removed individually, or the complete system can be removed as a unit **(see illustration)**. Even if only one part of the system needs attention, in some cases it will be easier to remove the whole system and separate the sections on the bench.

8 To remove the system or part of the system, first jack up the front or rear of the car, and support it on axle stands. Alternatively, position the car over an inspection pit, or on car ramps. Where necessary, undo the retaining bolts and remove the undertray from beneath the engine/transmission.

Front pipe

9 Undo the three flange nuts securing the front pipe to the turbocharger. Slacken and remove the nuts securing the front pipe to the catalytic converter **(see illustration)**.

10 Unscrew the two lower nuts from the front pipe support bracket, and unhook the pipe from the rubber mounting.

11 Free the front pipe from the turbocharger (recover the gasket) and catalytic converter, then remove it from underneath the car.

Catalytic converter

12 Unscrew the three flange nuts at either end of the catalytic converter, then separate the joints at either end, and lower the converter out **(see illustration)**. Recover the gasket from each end.

Centre pipe and silencer

13 Slacken and remove the three flange nuts securing the centre pipe to the catalytic converter, and to the rear silencer.

14 Release the centre pipe from its mounting rubbers. Disengage the centre pipe from the converter and rear silencer, and remove it from underneath the car. Recover the gaskets fitted to the front and rear joints.

Rear silencer

15 Slacken and remove the two flange nuts securing the rear silencer to the centre pipe joint.

16 Unhook the rear silencer from its mounting rubbers, and free it from the centre pipe. Recover the gasket from the joint.

Complete system

17 Slacken and remove the nuts securing the front pipe flange joint to the turbocharger.

18 Free the system from its mounting rubbers, then remove the two nuts from the front support bracket and remove it from underneath the car. Recover the gasket from the front pipe joint.

Heat shields

19 The heat shields are secured to the underside of the body by various nuts and bolts. Each shield can be removed once the relevant exhaust section has been removed. If a shield is being removed to gain access

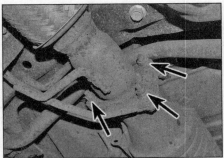

19.9 Front pipe-to-catalytic converter nuts

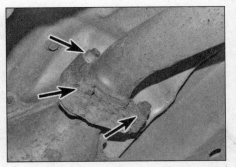

19.12 Catalytic converter rear flange nuts

to a component located behind it, it may prove sufficient in some cases to remove the retaining nuts and/or bolts, and simply lower the shield, without disturbing the exhaust system.

Refitting

20 Each section is refitted by reversing the removal sequence, noting the following points:

a) *Ensure that all traces of corrosion have been removed from the flanges, and renew all necessary gaskets.*

b) *The exhaust system flange nuts are all of self-locking type, and new ones should be used when refitting.*

c) *Inspect the rubber mountings for signs of damage or deterioration, and renew as necessary.*

d) *Prior to tightening the exhaust system fasteners, ensure that all rubber mountings are correctly located, and that there is adequate clearance between the exhaust system and underbody.*

Chapter 4 Part C:
Emission control systems

Contents

Degrees of difficulty

Easy, suitable for novice with little experience	**Fairly easy,** suitable for beginner with some experience 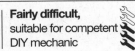	**Fairly difficult,** suitable for competent DIY mechanic 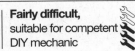	**Difficult,** suitable for experienced DIY mechanic	**Very difficult,** suitable for expert DIY or professional

Specifications

Torque wrench settings

	Nm	lbf ft
EGR components (diesel models):		
EGR pipe union nut	25	18
EGR pipe to exhaust manifold	25	18
EGR valve nut and bolt.	25	18
Oxygen sensors	44	32

1 General information

Petrol models

1 All petrol engines are designed to use unleaded petrol, and are controlled by the engine management system to give the best compromise between driveability, fuel consumption and exhaust emission production. In addition, a number of systems are fitted that help to minimise other harmful emissions.

2 A positive crankcase ventilation (PCV) control system is fitted, which reduces the release of pollutants from the engine's lubrication system, and a catalytic converter is fitted which reduces exhaust gas pollutants.

3 An exhaust gas recirculation (EGR) system is fitted, to further reduce emissions. Also an evaporative emission control system is fitted which reduces the release of gaseous hydrocarbons from the fuel tank.

Crankcase emissions control

4 The positive crankcase ventilation (PCV or 'breather') system reduces hydrocarbon emissions by scavenging crankcase vapours. It does this by circulating fresh air from the air cleaner through the crankcase, where it mixes with blow-by gases and is then rerouted through a PCV valve to the inlet manifold.

5 The main components of the PCV system are the PCV valve, a blow-by filter and the vacuum hoses connecting these two components with the engine.

6 To maintain idle quality, the PCV valve restricts the flow when the inlet manifold vacuum is high. If abnormal operating conditions (such as piston ring problems) arise, the system is designed to allow excessive amounts of blow-by gases to flow back through the crankcase vent tube into the air cleaner to be consumed by normal combustion.

7 The PCV valve is inside the cylinder head cover, with the breather hose attached to the cover, next to the oil filler cap. Petrol engines have an oil separator at the back of the engine, on the left-hand side of the inlet manifold **(see illustration)**.

8 The most common reason for problems with the PCV system is blocked or damaged hoses, or a blocked valve. Disconnect the hose at one end, and see whether it can be blown through. If the pipe is blocked with oil sludge, it must be removed and cleaned, or for preference, renewed. Hoses which have perished, been crushed, or which have split ends, should also be renewed.

9 With the engine idling at normal operating temperature, pull off the PCV hose.

10 Place your finger over the hose. If there is no vacuum, check for a blocked hose, manifold port, or the valve itself. Renew any blocked or deteriorated hoses.

Exhaust emissions control

11 To minimise the amount of pollutants which escape into the atmosphere, all models are fitted with a catalytic converter in the exhaust system. The system is of the closed-loop type, in which two oxygen sensors in the exhaust system provide the ECM with constant feedback, enabling the ECM to adjust the mixture to provide the best possible conditions for the converter to operate. One oxygen sensor is located ahead of the catalytic converter, with the second downstream of it, to monitor the converter's efficiency.

12 The oxygen (lambda) sensor has a heating element built-in that is controlled by the ECM through the sensor relay to bring the sensor's tip to an efficient operating temperature quickly. The sensor's tip is sensitive to oxygen and sends the ECM a varying voltage depending on the amount of oxygen in the exhaust gases; if the inlet air/fuel mixture is too rich, the exhaust gases are low in oxygen, so the sensor sends a low voltage signal, the voltage rising as the mixture weakens and the amount of oxygen rises in the exhaust gases.

13 Peak conversion efficiency of all major pollutants occurs if the inlet air/fuel mixture

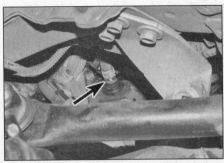

1.7 Crankcase breather hose connection to inlet manifold – seen from below

1.23 Diesel engine PCV valve location

is maintained at the chemically correct ratio for the complete combustion of petrol of 14.7 parts (by weight) of air to 1 part of fuel (the 'stoichiometric' ratio). The sensor output voltage alters in a large step at this point, the ECM using the signal change as a reference point and correcting the inlet air/fuel mixture accordingly by altering the fuel injector pulse width.

Evaporative emissions control

14 Only fitted to petrol models, the fuel evaporative emissions control system absorbs fuel vapours and, during engine operation, releases them into the inlet manifold where they mix with the incoming air/fuel mixture.

15 The fuel filler cap is fitted with a two-way valve as a safety device. The valve vents fuel vapours to the atmosphere if the evaporative control system fails.

16 Another fuel cut-off valve (two-way valve), mounted behind the fuel tank, regulates fuel vapour flow from the fuel tank to the charcoal canister, based on the pressure or vacuum caused by temperature changes. A vapour separator is fitted to some models, to ensure that no liquid fuel is passed into the EVAP system.

17 After passing through the two-way valve, fuel vapour passes to the charcoal canister behind the fuel tank. The activated charcoal in the canister absorbs and stores these vapours.

18 When the engine is running and warmed to a preset temperature, a solenoid valve (known as the canister purge solenoid valve) on the throttle body closes, allowing a diaphragm

valve in the charcoal canister to be opened by inlet manifold vacuum. Fuel vapours from the canister are then drawn through by inlet manifold vacuum, and burned in the engine.

19 Always check the hoses first. A disconnected, damaged or missing hose is the most likely cause of a malfunctioning EVAP system. Repair any damaged hoses or renew any missing hoses as necessary.

Exhaust gas recirculation

20 To reduce oxides of nitrogen (NOx) emissions, some of the exhaust gases are recirculated through the EGR valve to the inlet manifold. This has the effect of lowering combustion temperatures.

21 The EGR system consists of the EGR valve (which is supplied with coolant from the engine's cooling system), the EGR control solenoid valve, and the Electronic Control Module (ECM). The ECM regulates the amount of exhaust gas which is recycled into the engine, via the solenoid valve. Unusually, the exhaust gas is fed from the exhaust side of the head to the inlet side via an internal passage, meaning there is no external pipework.

Diesel models

22 All diesel engine models are designed to meet strict emission requirements, and are also equipped with a crankcase emissions control system. In addition to this, all models are fitted with an unregulated catalytic converter to reduce harmful exhaust emissions. To further reduce emissions, an exhaust gas recirculation (EGR) system is also fitted.

Crankcase emissions control

23 To reduce the emission of unburned hydrocarbons from the crankcase into the atmosphere, the engine is sealed. Blow-by gases and oil vapour are drawn from inside the crankcase, through the cylinder head cover, then through a pressure-sensitive recirculation valve into the turbocharger **(see illustration)**. From the turbocharger, the gases enter the inlet manifold to be burned by the engine during normal combustion.

24 There are no restrictors in the system hoses, since the minimal depression in the inlet manifold remains constant during all engine operating conditions.

Exhaust emissions control

25 To minimise the amount of pollutants which escape into the atmosphere, an unregulated (reduction) catalytic converter is fitted in the exhaust system. The catalytic converter consists of a canister containing a fine mesh impregnated with a catalyst material, over which the exhaust gases pass. The catalyst speeds up the oxidation of harmful carbon monoxide, unburnt hydrocarbons and soot, effectively reducing the quantity of harmful products reaching the atmosphere. The catalytic converter operates remotely in the exhaust system, and there is no oxygen sensor as fitted to the petrol engines.

Exhaust gas recirculation

26 The EGR valve used on diesel engines is similar in principle to that used on petrol engines. The valve is mounted on the inlet manifold, and is piped a supply of exhaust gas from the exhaust manifold. The valve is switched via an ECM-controlled solenoid, known as the EVRV (electronic vacuum regulating valve).

2 Exhaust gas recirculation (EGR) system – component renewal

Petrol models

EGR valve

1 The EGR valve is fitted to the coolant housing on the right-hand end of the cylinder head (right as seen from the driver's seat). Disconnect the wiring plug from the top of the valve **(see illustration)**.

2 Drain the cooling system as described in Chapter 1A, or be prepared for coolant loss when the EGR valve is removed.

3 Remove the two 12 mm nuts that secure the EGR valve to the inlet manifold, and detach the EGR valve **(see illustrations)**. We found that a cranked spanner was the only way to access one of the nuts. Recover the gasket – a new one should be used when refitting.

4 Clean the mating surfaces of the EGR valve and housing.

2.1 Disconnect the EGR valve wiring plug

2.3a Unscrew the two EGR valve mounting nuts (one hidden) . . .

2.3b . . . and lift off the valve

2.5 Use a new gasket when refitting the valve

2.9a Unclip the harnesses from the bracket . . .

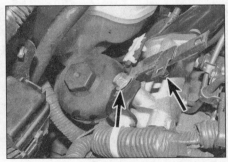

2.9b . . . then remove the two bolts . . .

2.9c . . . and take off the wiring harness bracket

2.10a Undo the two intercooler air pipe bolts (one is a stud with a nut attached) . . .

2.10b . . . then unscrew the EGR pipe union nut, and disconnect the pipe

2.10c If unbolting the EGR pipe from the exhaust manifold, recover the gasket

2.11 Disconnect the vacuum hose from the EGR valve

2.12a Removing the EGR valve (diesel models)

5 Fit the EGR valve, using a new gasket **(see illustration)**. Tighten the nuts securely.
6 Reconnect the sensor wiring plug to complete.

EGR control solenoid

7 The EGR control solenoid is integral with the valve, and cannot be renewed separately.

Diesel models

EGR valve

8 Remove the engine top cover, which is secured by four bolts.
9 The EGR valve has a wiring harness bracket bolted to the top of it, which must be removed first. Unclip the wiring harness from the bracket, then unscrew the two bolts and take off the bracket **(see illustrations)**.
10 Unscrew the two flange bolts and disconnect the intercooler air pipe from the valve. Unscrew the EGR union pipe nut

and disconnect the pipe from the valve – if necessary, trace the pipe back to the exhaust manifold and unbolt it from there (a new gasket will be needed when refitting) **(see illustrations)**.
11 Detach the vacuum hose from the valve's vacuum capsule **(see illustration)**.
12 Remove the two bolts that secure the EGR valve to the inlet manifold, and detach the EGR valve **(see illustrations)**. Recover the gasket and discard it – obtain a new gasket for refitting.
13 Clean the mating surfaces of the EGR valve and inlet manifold.
14 Fit the EGR valve, using a new gasket. Tighten the nut and bolt to the specified torque.
15 Reconnect the EGR pipe and intercooler pipe, tightening the pipe union nut securely (use the specified torque as a guide). If the EGR pipe was disconnected from the exhaust

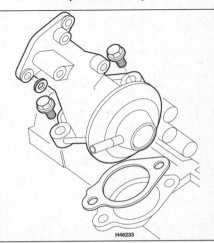

2.12b EGR valve removal details (diesel models)

3.4a Disconnect the solenoid wiring plug . . .

3.4b . . . then release the hose at the front . . .

3.4c . . . and the one at the rear

3.5a Remove the two upper screws . . .

3.5b . . . and remove the bracket from the throttle body

3.7 The charcoal canister and two-way valve are behind the fuel tank

manifold, use a new gasket and tighten the bolts to the specified torque.

16 Refit the wiring harness bracket, and clip the harness securely to it.

17 Reconnect the vacuum hose and refit the engine top cover to complete.

EGR control solenoid (EVRV)

18 The EVRV which regulates the EGR valve is mounted on the front of the engine at the transmission end, below the turbocharger.

19 Disconnect the various vacuum hoses from the valve, labelling them as they are removed to ensure correct refitting.

20 Disconnect the EVRV wiring plug.

21 Unscrew the upper mounting bolt, loosen the lower bolt, and withdraw the EVRV from the engine – the mounting bracket is slotted, to make removal and refitting easier.

22 Refitting is a reversal of removal, noting the following points:

a) *Ensure that the vacuum hoses are reconnected to their original positions.*

b) *If any of the hoses show signs of perishing, split ends or other damage, new hoses should be obtained and fitted.*

3 Evaporative emissions (EVAP) system – component renewal

Canister purge solenoid valve

1 The purge control solenoid valve allows inlet manifold vacuum to purge vapours from the canister when the engine is warm, and cuts

off vacuum to the canister when the engine is cold.

2 Remove the air cleaner as described in Chapter 4A.

3 The canister purge solenoid is mounted on the left-hand side of the throttle body (left as seen from the driver's seat).

4 Disconnect the wiring plug from the front of the solenoid, then release the hose clips and disconnect the two hoses from the front and rear of the valve. Label the hoses to avoid confusion when refitting **(see illustrations)**.

5 Unscrew the two upper mounting screws and remove the solenoid bracket from the throttle body **(see illustrations)**.

6 Refitting is a reversal of removal, noting the following points:

a) *Ensure that the wiring plug and hoses are correctly and securely refitted.*

b) *If the hoses show signs of perishing, or split ends, new ones should be fitted.*

Charcoal canister

7 The charcoal canister and two-way valve are mounted as an assembly at the rear of the car, behind the fuel tank **(see illustration)**.

8 Label all hoses before disconnecting, to ensure correct refitting. Once the hoses have been disconnected, the canister can be unbolted and removed.

9 Refitting is a reversal of removal, noting the following points:

a) *Ensure that the hoses are correctly and securely refitted.*

b) *If the hoses show signs of perishing, or split ends, new ones should be fitted.*

4 Catalytic converter – general information and precautions

General information

1 The catalytic converter reduces harmful exhaust emissions by chemically converting the more poisonous gases to ones which (in theory at least) are less harmful. The chemical reaction is known as an 'oxidising' reaction, or one where oxygen is 'added'.

2 Inside the converter is a honeycomb structure, made of ceramic material and coated with the precious metals palladium, platinum and rhodium (the 'catalyst' which promotes the chemical reaction). The chemical reaction generates heat, which itself promotes the reaction – therefore, once the car has been driven several miles, the body of the converter will be very hot.

3 The ceramic structure contained within the converter is understandably fragile, and will not withstand rough treatment. Since the converter runs at a high temperature, driving through deep standing water (in flood conditions, for example) is to be avoided, since the thermal stresses imposed when plunging the hot converter into cold water may well cause the ceramic internals to fracture, resulting in a 'blocked' converter – a common cause of failure. A converter which has been damaged in this way can be checked by shaking it (do not strike it) – if a rattling noise is heard, this indicates probable failure.

Precautions

4 The catalytic converter is a reliable and simple device which needs no maintenance in itself, but there are some facts of which an owner should be aware if the converter is to function properly for its full service life.

Petrol models

a) *DO NOT use leaded petrol (or lead-replacement petrol, LRP) in a car equipped with a catalytic converter – the lead (or other additives) will coat the precious metals, reducing their converting efficiency and will eventually destroy the converter.*

b) *Always keep the ignition and fuel systems well-maintained in accordance with the manufacturer's schedule (see Chapter 1A).*

c) *If the engine develops a misfire, do not drive the car at all (or at least as little as possible) until the fault is cured.*

d) *DO NOT push or tow start the car – this will soak the catalytic converter in unburned fuel, causing it to overheat when the engine does start.*

e) *DO NOT switch off the ignition at high engine speeds – ie, do not 'blip' the throttle immediately before switching off the engine.*

f) *DO NOT use fuel or engine oil additives – these may contain substances harmful to the catalytic converter.*

g) *DO NOT continue to use the car if the engine burns oil to the extent of leaving a visible trail of blue smoke.*

h) *Remember that the catalytic converter operates at very high temperatures. DO NOT, therefore, park the car on dry undergrowth, over long grass or piles of dead leaves after a long run.*

i) *As mentioned above, driving through deep water should be avoided if possible. The sudden cooling effect may fracture the ceramic honeycomb, damaging it beyond repair.*

j) *Remember that the catalytic converter is FRAGILE – do not strike it with tools during servicing work, and take care handling it when removing it from the car for any reason.*

k) *In some cases, a sulphurous smell (like that of rotten eggs) may be noticed from the exhaust. This is common to many catalytic converter-equipped cars, and has more to do with the sulphur content of the brand of fuel being used than the converter itself.*

l) *If a substantial loss of power is experienced, remember that this could be due to the converter being blocked. This can occur simply as a result of contamination after a high mileage, but may be due to the ceramic element having fractured and collapsed internally (see paragraph 3). A new converter is the only cure in this instance.*

m) *The catalytic converter, used on a well-maintained and well-driven car, should last at least 100 000 miles – if the converter is no longer effective, it must be renewed.*

Diesel models

5 The catalytic converter fitted to diesel models is simpler than that fitted to petrol models, but it still needs to be treated with respect to avoid problems:

a) *DO NOT use fuel or engine oil additives – these may contain substances harmful to the catalytic converter.*

b) *DO NOT continue to use the car if the engine burns (engine) oil to the extent of leaving a visible trail of blue smoke.*

c) *Remember that the catalytic converter operates at very high temperatures. DO NOT, therefore, park the car in dry undergrowth, over long grass or piles of dead leaves after a long run.*

d) *As mentioned above, driving through deep water should be avoided if possible. The sudden cooling effect will fracture the ceramic honeycomb, damaging it beyond repair.*

e) *Remember that the catalytic converter is FRAGILE – do not strike it with tools during servicing work, and take care handling it when removing it from the car for any reason.*

f) *If a substantial loss of power is experienced, remember that this could be due to the converter being blocked. This can occur simply as a result of contamination after a high mileage, but may be due to the ceramic element having fractured and collapsed internally (see paragraph 3). A new converter is the only cure in this instance.*

g) *The catalytic converter, used on a well-maintained and well-driven car, should last at least 100 000 miles – if the converter is no longer effective, it must be renewed.*

5 Catalytic converter – removal and refitting

Refer to Chapter 4A or 4B. The converter is either part of the exhaust system front pipe (petrol models), or is fitted separately between the front pipe and centre section (diesel models).

6 Oxygen sensors – testing and renewal

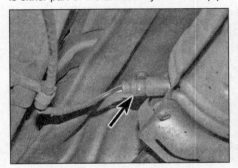

6.4 Access to the secondary sensor is hampered by the heat shields

Testing

1 Testing the oxygen sensor is only possible by connecting special diagnostic equipment to the sensor wiring, and checking that the voltage varies from low to high values when the engine is running. **Do not** attempt to 'test' any part of the system with anything other than the correct test equipment. This is beyond the scope of the DIY mechanic, and should be left to a Honda dealer. **Note:** *All models are fitted with two sensors – one before and one after the catalytic converter. This enables more efficient monitoring of the exhaust gas, allowing a faster response time. The overall efficiency of the converter itself can also be checked. The sensors before and after the converter are known as the 'primary' and 'secondary' sensors respectively.*

Renewal

Note: *The sensor is delicate, and will not work if it is dropped or knocked, or if unsuitable cleaning materials are used on it.*

2 Jack up the front of the car, and support it on axle stands (see *Jacking and vehicle support*).

3 Trace the wiring from the sensor body back to its wiring plug, and disconnect it. The wiring attached to the sensor must be released form any securing clips or ties. Note how the wiring is routed, as it must not come into contact with hot exhaust components.

4 If working on the secondary sensor, note that it is accessible without removing the heat shield fitted around the converter, but take care, as the shield edges may be sharp **(see illustration)**.

5 Unscrew the sensor from the exhaust system – it will be very tight, so be sure to use a good-quality, close-fitting spanner to remove it **(see illustration)**. The secondary sensor is harder to unscrew, as the heat shields limit access, and the sensor wiring prevents the

6.5 Unscrew the primary sensor from the front downpipe

use of a conventional deep socket. Special slotted sockets are available for this task from tool companies and suppliers.

6 It may be beneficial to wipe the sensor clean before refitting it, especially if the sensor tip appears to be contaminated. However, great care must be exercised, as the tip will be damaged by any abrasives, and by certain solvents. Seek the advice of a Honda dealer before cleaning the sensor with any products.

7 Refitting is a reversal of removal, noting the following points:

  a) *Apply a little anti-seize compound to the* sensor threads, taking care not to allow any on the sensor tip, and tighten the sensor to the specified torque.

  b) *If the special slotted socket is not available, the sensor will have to be tightened securely with just a spanner – use the specified torque as a guide to tightening.*

  c) *Reconnect the wiring, ensuring that it is routed clear of any hot exhaust components, and securely clipped in place as required.*

  d) *If required, proof that the sensor is* working can be gained by having the exhaust emissions checked by a Honda dealer or MoT test station. Remember that a faulty sensor may have generated a fault code. It is sometimes possible to clear these codes as follows. With the ignition off, remove fuse No 6 from the engine compartment fusebox for at least 10 seconds, then refit it. If the code is still logged in the ECM electronic memory, a Honda dealer or engine management specialist will have to erase the fault code from the memory.

Chapter 5 Part A:
Starting and charging systems

Contents

Degrees of difficulty

Easy, suitable for novice with little experience	**Fairly easy,** suitable for beginner with some experience	**Fairly difficult,** suitable for competent DIY mechanic	**Difficult,** suitable for experienced DIY mechanic	**Very difficult,** suitable for expert DIY or professional

Specifications

General
System type . . . . 12 volt, negative-earth

Starter motor
Output:
1.4 litre and 1.6 litre engines with manual transmission	0.8 kW or 1.0 kW
1.6 litre engine with automatic transmission	1.0 kW or 1.2 kW
Diesel engine	1.4 kW

Minimum brush length:
0.8 kW starter (Denso)	6.0 mm
1.0 kW starters:	
Denso	9.0 mm
Valeo	5.0 mm
1.2 kW starters	N/A
1.4 kW starters	10.5 mm

Battery
Ratings . . . . 36, 38, 45 or 47 Ah (depending on model)

Alternator
Output:
Petrol models	70A
Diesel models	80A or 100A

Minimum brush length:
Petrol models	5 mm
Diesel models	6.5 mm

Torque wrench settings

	Nm	lbf ft
Alternator mounting bolts:		
Petrol models:		
Lower bolt/lockbolt	24	18
Upper bolt	44	32
Diesel models:		
Lower bolt/nut	46	34
Upper bolt	19	14
Glow plugs	20	15
Starter motor mounting bolts:		
Petrol models	44	32
Diesel models:		
Lower bolt	38	28
Upper bolt	98	72

1 General information and precautions

General information

The engine electrical system consists mainly of the charging and starting systems, and includes the diesel engine preheating (glow plug) system. Because of their engine-related functions, these are covered separately from the body electrical devices such as the lights, instruments, etc, which are covered in Chapter 12. On petrol models, refer to Part B of this Chapter for information on the ignition system.

The electrical system is of the 12 volt negative-earth type.

The battery may be of the low maintenance or maintenance-free (sealed for life) type and is charged by the alternator, which is belt-driven from the crankshaft pulley.

Charging system

The charging system includes the alternator, an internal voltage regulator, a charge indicator light, the battery, a fusible link and the wiring between all the components. The charging system supplies electrical power for the ignition system, the lights, the radio, etc. The alternator is driven by a drivebelt at the timing belt end of the engine.

The alternator control system within the ECM controls the voltage generated at the alternator in accordance with driving conditions. Depending upon electric load, vehicle speed, engine coolant temperature, accessories (air conditioning system, radio, cruise control, etc) and the inlet air temperature, the system will adjust the amount of voltage generated, creating less load on the engine.

The purpose of the voltage regulator is to limit the alternator's voltage to a preset value. This prevents power surges, circuit overloads, etc, during peak voltage output.

The charging system doesn't ordinarily require periodic maintenance. However, the auxiliary drivebelt, battery and wires and connections should be inspected at the intervals outlined in Chapter 1A or 1B.

The instrument panel warning light should come on when the ignition key is turned to the second position, but it should go off immediately after the engine is started. If it is slow to go out, or remains on, there is a malfunction in the charging system (see Section 4).

Starting system

The starting system consists of the battery, the starter motor, the starter solenoid and the wires connecting them. The solenoid is mounted directly on the starter motor.

The solenoid/starter motor assembly is installed at the rear of the engine, next to the transmission bellhousing.

When the ignition key is turned to the Start position, the starter solenoid is actuated through the starter control circuit. The starter solenoid then connects the battery to the starter. The battery supplies the electrical energy to the starter motor, which does the actual work of cranking the engine.

The starter on models equipped with automatic transmissions can only be operated when the selector lever is in P or N.

Further details of the various systems are given in the relevant Sections of this Chapter. While some repair procedures are given, the usual course of action is to renew the component concerned.

Preheating system (diesel engines)

On diesel engines, each cylinder has a heater plug (commonly called a glow plug) screwed into it. The plugs are electrically-operated before and during start-up when the engine is cold. Electrical feed to the glow plugs is controlled via a glow plug relay, through the injection system ECM.

A warning light in the instrument panel tells the driver that preheating is taking place. When the light goes out, the engine is ready to be started. The voltage supply to the glow plugs continues for several seconds after the light goes out. If no attempt is made to start, the timer then cuts off the supply, in order to avoid draining the battery and overheating the glow plugs.

The glow plugs also provide a 'post-heating' function, whereby the glow plugs remain switched on for a period after the engine has started. The length of time 'post-heating' takes place for is also determined by the control unit, and is anything up to six minutes, depending on engine temperature.

To further assist with engine warm-up, a heating element (known by Honda as a 'water glow plug') is mounted in the thermostat housing. Its purpose is to heat the coolant (which initially will bypass the closed thermostat when the engine is cold) – refer to Chapter 3, Section 8, for more details.

Precautions

Always observe the following precautions when working on the electrical system:

a) *Be extremely careful when servicing engine electrical components. They are easily damaged if checked, connected or handled improperly.*
b) *Never leave the ignition switched on for long periods of time when the engine is not running.*
c) *Don't disconnect the battery leads while the engine is running.*
d) *Maintain correct polarity when connecting a battery lead from another vehicle during jump starting – see the Jump starting Section at the front of this manual.*
e) *Always disconnect the negative lead first, and reconnect it last, or the battery may be shorted by the tool being used to loosen the lead clamps.*

It's also a good idea to review the safety-related information regarding the engine electrical systems shown in the *Safety first!* section at the front of this manual, before beginning any operation included in this Chapter.

Battery disconnection

Refer to *Disconnecting the battery* at the end of this manual.

2 Battery – testing and charging

Testing

1 The simplest way to test a battery is with a voltmeter (or multimeter set to voltage testing) – connect the voltmeter across the battery terminals, observing the correct polarity. The test is only accurate if the battery has not been subjected to any kind of charge for the previous six hours. If this is not the case, switch on the headlights for 30 seconds, then wait four to five minutes before testing the battery after switching off the headlights. All other electrical circuits must be switched off, so check that the doors and tailgate are fully shut when making the test.

2 If the voltage reading is less than 12.0 volts, then the battery is less than healthy. Under 11.5 volts, and the battery needs charging. However, as little as 11.0 volts will still usually be enough to start the engine, though a battery in this condition could not be relied on. A reading of around 10.0 volts suggests that one of the six battery cells has died – a common way for modern batteries to fail.

3 If the battery is to be charged, remove it from the car (Section 3) and charge it as described later in this Section.

Low-maintenance battery

4 If the car covers a small annual mileage, it is worthwhile checking the specific gravity of the electrolyte every three months to determine the state of charge of the battery. Use a hydrometer to make the check, and compare the results with the tool maker's instructions (typically, there will be a colour-coded scale on hydrometers sold for battery testing).

5 If the battery condition is suspect, first check the specific gravity of electrolyte in each cell. A significant variation between any cells indicates loss of electrolyte, or deterioration of the internal plates.

6 If the cell variation is satisfactory but the battery is discharged, it should be charged as described later in this Section.

Maintenance-free battery

7 In cases where a 'sealed for life' maintenance-free battery is fitted, topping-up and testing of the electrolyte in each cell is not possible. The condition of the battery can therefore only be tested using a battery condition indicator or a voltmeter.

3.2 Battery location – diesel models

3.4 Disconnecting the battery positive lead

3.5a Unscrew the battery hold-down clamp bolt, and loosen the nut . . .

Charging

Note: *The following is intended as a guide only. Always refer to the manufacturer's recommendations (often printed on a label attached to the battery), and always disconnect both terminal leads before charging a battery.*

Low-maintenance battery

8 It is advisable to remove the cell caps or covers if possible during charging, but note that the battery will be giving off potentially-explosive hydrogen gas while it is being charged. Small amounts of acidic electrolyte may also escape as the battery nears full charge – keep your face and hands clear. Removing the cell caps will allow you to check whether all six cells are receiving charge – after a while, the electrolyte should start to bubble. If any cell does not bubble, this may indicate that it has failed, and the battery is no longer fit for use.

9 Charge the battery at a rate of 3.5 to 4 amps, and continue to charge the battery at this rate until no further rise in specific gravity is noted over a four-hour period.

10 Alternatively, a trickle charger charging at the rate of 1.5 amps can safely be used overnight.

11 Specially rapid 'boost' charges which are claimed to restore the power of the battery in 1 to 2 hours are not recommended, as they can cause serious damage to the battery plates through overheating.

12 While charging the battery, note that the temperature of the electrolyte should never exceed 38°C.

Maintenance-free battery

13 This battery type takes considerably longer to fully recharge than the standard type, the time taken being dependent on the extent of discharge, but it can take anything up to three days.

14 A constant-voltage type charger is required, to be set, when connected, to 13.9 to 14.9 volts with a charger current below 25 amps. Using this method, the battery should be usable within three hours, giving a voltage reading of 12.5 volts, but this is for a partially-discharged battery and, as mentioned, full charging can take considerably longer.

15 If the battery is to be charged from a fully-

3.5b . . . unhook the clamp bolt from the tray . . .

discharged state (condition reading less than 12.2 volts), have it recharged by your local automotive electrician, as the charge rate is higher and constant supervision during charging is necessary.

3	Battery – removal and refitting

Removal

1 Before removing the battery, refer to *Disconnecting the battery* in the reference section of this manual.

2 The battery is located at the right-hand side of the engine compartment on petrol models, and on the left on diesels **(see illustration)**.

3 Loosen the clamp nut and disconnect the battery negative (–) lead from the terminal.

4 Lift the plastic flap where fitted, then loosen

3.6 Pull the battery box upwards off the battery

3.5c . . . then remove the hold-down clamp and bolt

the clamp nut and disconnect the battery positive (+) lead from the terminal **(see illustration)**.

5 Unscrew the bolt at the front of the hold-down clamp, then loosen the nut at the rear, sufficient to unhook the clamp bolt from the battery tray. Lift off the hold-down clamp and bolt **(see illustrations)**.

6 Slide off the plastic battery box, where fitted **(see illustration)**.

7 Lift out the battery and withdraw it from the engine compartment **(see illustration)**.

8 If required, the battery tray can be removed as follows. With the battery removed, first unclip the wiring harness from it – unscrew the earth strap bolt and move the sections of harness clear of the tray. The tray itself is secured by four bolts – two on top, and two underneath into the chassis leg (the two underneath need only be loosened, as the tray has slotted lower mountings). Remove the bolts and lift out the tray **(see illustrations)**.

3.7 Removing the battery

3.8a Unclip the wiring harness from the battery tray

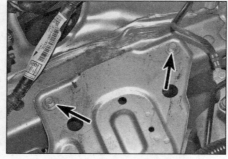

3.8b Unscrew the two bolts on top . . .

3.8c . . . then loosen the two underneath . . .

3.8d . . . and lift out the battery tray

Refitting

9 Refitting is a reversal of removal, noting the following points:

- a) *Clean the battery tray if necessary.*
- b) *Tighten the battery hold-down clamp securely.*
- c) *Reconnect the battery leads, positive first, negative last.*
- d) *Re-activate the radio, reprogram the electric windows, etc, as described in Disconnecting the battery.*

4 Alternator/charging system – testing

Note: *Refer to Section 1 of this Chapter before starting work.*

1 If the charge warning light fails to illuminate when the ignition is switched on, first check

the alternator wiring connections for security. If the light still fails to illuminate, check the continuity of the warning light feed wire from the alternator to the instrument panel. Check the condition of the auxiliary drivebelt. Check the condition of the regulator within the alternator as described in Section 6 of this Chapter. If all is satisfactory, the alternator is at fault and should be renewed or taken to an auto-electrician for testing and repair.

2 Similarly, if the charge warning light comes on with the ignition, but is then slow to go out when the engine is started, this may indicate an impending alternator problem. Check all the items listed in the preceding paragraph, and refer to an auto-electrical specialist if no obvious faults are found.

3 If the charge warning light illuminates when the engine is running, stop the engine and check that the drivebelt is correctly tensioned (see Chapter 1A or 1B) and that the alternator

connections are secure. If all is so far satisfactory, check the alternator brushes and slip-rings as described in Section 6. If the fault persists, the alternator should be renewed, or taken to an auto-electrician for testing and repair.

4 If the alternator output is suspect even though the warning light functions correctly, the regulated voltage may be checked as follows.

5 Connect a voltmeter across the battery terminals, and start the engine.

6 Increase the engine speed until the voltmeter reading remains steady; the reading should be approximately 12 to 13 volts, and no more than 14 volts.

7 Switch on as many electrical accessories (such as the headlights, heated rear window and heater blower) as possible, and check that the alternator maintains the regulated voltage at around 13 to 14 volts.

8 If the regulated voltage is not as stated, this may be due to worn brushes, weak brush springs, a faulty voltage regulator, a faulty diode, a severed phase winding or worn or damaged slip-rings. The brushes and slip-rings may be checked (see Section 6), but if the fault persists, the alternator should be renewed or taken to an auto-electrician.

5 Alternator – removal and refitting

Removal

1 Disconnect the battery negative and positive leads, and position the leads away from the battery (also see *Disconnecting the battery*). This is **essential** before disconnecting the alternator wiring.

2 Remove the auxiliary drivebelt as described in Chapter 1A or 1B.

3 On diesel models, remove the condenser fan as described in Chapter 3. Also undo the four retaining bolts and remove the turbocharger heat shield – if the bolts are in poor condition, new ones should be obtained for reassembly.

4 Unclip the wiring harness, then unscrew the nut and disconnect the battery supply lead. Disconnect the main alternator wiring plug **(see illustrations)**.

5.4a Unclip the alternator wiring harness . . .

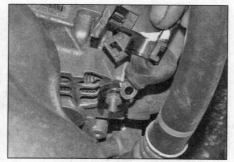

5.4b . . . then pull back the boot and unscrew the nut securing the battery lead

5.4c Disconnect the alternator wiring plug

5 On diesel models, disconnect the vacuum hoses and oil supply union from the brake vacuum pump **(see illustration)**. Label the vacuum hoses for position, to ensure correct refitting.

6 Loosen the alternator upper mounting bolt, and slide it out as far as possible (on petrol models, note that the bolt will not come out, as it hits the wing).

7 Remove the lower mounting bolt, then withdraw the alternator from its mounting bracket (note that it may have to be prised out of the upper mounting) and out of the engine compartment **(see illustrations)**. On diesel models, anticipate a small amount of oil spillage from the brake vacuum pump.

8 On diesel models, the brake vacuum pump may be removed if required – check first that this is available separately. The pump is secured by three 6 mm bolts – unscrew the bolts and withdraw the pump, recovering the O-ring seal, which should be renewed when refitting.

Refitting

9 Refitting is a reversal of removal, noting the following points:

a) On diesel models, if the vacuum pump was removed, refit using a new O-ring, and tighten the bolts securely. Also ensure that the vacuum and oil feed hoses are correctly and securely refitted. If any of the hoses show signs of damage, or split ends, new hoses should be fitted.

b) Refit and adjust the auxiliary drivebelt as described in Chapter 1A or 1B.

c) On diesel models, check and if necessary top-up the engine oil (see Weekly checks).

d) Check the charging voltage to verify proper operation of the alternator (see Section 4).

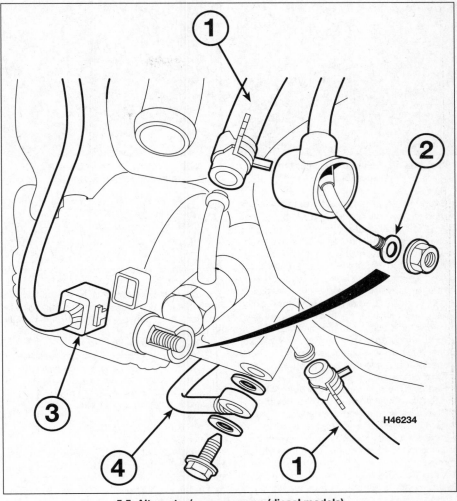

5.5 Alternator/vacuum pump (diesel models)

1 Vacuum hoses
2 Battery supply lead

3 Alternator wiring plug
4 Vacuum pump oil supply union

---

6 Alternator – overhaul

Note: *Some models use Mitsubishi alternators. Renewing the brushes and regulator on these alternators requires major dismantling, and should be done by a suitable auto-electrical repair specialist. It's practical to renew the brushes and regulator on a Denso or Bosch alternator, but don't attempt to completely overhaul the alternator. If renewing the brushes and regulator does not solve the alternator problem, take the alternator to a dealer service department or specialist and have it rebuilt or exchange it for a rebuilt unit.*

1 Remove the alternator as described in Section 5.

2 It is strongly recommended that the alternator is taken to an auto-electrical specialist for assessment. It's likely that a Honda dealer will only offer a new or exchange unit, while a specialist may be able to supply spare parts for DIY repair. In any case, there's little point dismantling the alternator if it then turns out spares aren't available after all.

5.7a Remove the lower mounting bolt . . .

5.7b . . . unscrew and slide across the upper bolt, prise the alternator free . . .

5.7c . . . then remove it from the engine

8.3a Pull off the spade terminal from the solenoid . . .

8.3b . . . then unscrew the nut and disconnect the main wire

3 Examine the alternator to determine the work necessary to remove the brushes. On a typical unit, look where the main wiring plug socket is – the brush holder will be part of the housing which contains the plug socket.

4 If the brush holder is removable without major dismantling, the retaining screws will be visible, or at most, an easily-removed plastic end cover will be covering them. If the brush holder is not visible, it's better to consult an auto-electrical specialist for advice.

5 Assuming spare parts are available, proceed as follows. The following is a general procedure, but should be broadly applicable to most alternator types.

6 Remove the rear cover nuts/bolts, the nut and terminal insulator and the rear cover.

7 Remove the brush holder retaining screws. **Note:** *On Bosch alternators, the brush holder is integral with the voltage regulator module.*

8 Remove the brush holder from the rear end frame.

9 Measure the exposed length of the brush and compare it to the minimum length in this Chapter's Specifications. If the length of the brush is less than specified, renew the brush.

10 Make sure that each brush moves smoothly in the brush holder.

11 To remove the voltage regulator on Denso alternators, remove the brushes as described above, then remove the mounting screws and take the regulator off.

12 Refitting is the reverse of removal. Fit the brush holder by depressing the brush with a small screwdriver to clear the shaft.

7 Starting system – testing

Note: *Refer to Section 1 of this Chapter before starting work.*

1 If the starter motor fails to operate when the ignition key is turned to the appropriate position, the following possible causes may be to blame:
  a) *The battery is faulty.*
  b) *The electrical connections between the switch, solenoid, battery and starter motor are somewhere failing to pass the necessary current from the battery through the starter to earth.*
  c) *The solenoid is faulty.*
  d) *The starter motor is mechanically or electrically defective.*

2 To check the battery, switch on the headlights. If they dim after a few seconds, this indicates that the battery is discharged – recharge (see Section 2) or renew the battery. If the headlights glow brightly, operate the ignition switch and observe the lights. If they dim, then this indicates that current is reaching the starter motor, therefore the fault must lie in the starter motor. If the lights continue to glow brightly (and no clicking sound can be heard from the starter motor solenoid), this indicates that there is a fault in the circuit or solenoid – see following paragraphs. If the starter motor turns slowly when operated, but the battery is in good condition, then this indicates that either the starter motor is faulty, or there is considerable resistance somewhere in the circuit.

3 If a fault in the circuit is suspected, disconnect the battery leads (including the earth connection to the body), the starter/solenoid wiring and the engine/transmission earth strap. Thoroughly clean the connections, and reconnect the leads and wiring, then use a voltmeter or test light to check that full battery voltage is available at the battery positive lead connection to the solenoid, and that the earth is sound. Smear petroleum jelly around the battery terminals to prevent corrosion – corroded connections are amongst the most frequent causes of electrical system faults.

4 If the battery and all connections are in good condition, check the circuit by disconnecting the wire from the solenoid blade terminal. Connect a voltmeter or test light between the wire end and a good earth (such as the battery negative terminal), and check that the wire is live when the ignition switch is turned to the start position. If it is, then the circuit is sound – if not the circuit wiring can be checked as described in Chapter 12.

5 The solenoid contacts can be checked by connecting a voltmeter or test light between the battery positive feed connection on the starter side of the solenoid, and earth. When the ignition switch is turned to the start position, there should be a reading or lighted bulb, as applicable. If there is no reading or lighted bulb, the solenoid is faulty and should be renewed.

6 If the circuit and solenoid are proved sound, the fault must lie in the starter motor. Begin checking the starter motor by removing it (see Section 8), and having the brushes checked. If the fault does not lie in the brushes, the motor windings must be faulty. In this event, it may be possible to have the starter motor overhauled by a specialist, but check on the availability and cost of spares before proceeding, as it may prove more economical to obtain a new or exchange motor.

8 Starter motor – removal and refitting

Removal

1 Disconnect the battery negative and positive leads, and position the leads away from the battery (also see *Disconnecting the battery*). This is **essential** before disconnecting the starter wiring.

Petrol models

2 On petrol models, the starter motor is mounted on the front of the transmission. To improve access, remove the inlet air resonator and inlet air duct as described in Chapter 4A.

3 Disconnect the (spade type) wiring plug from the solenoid, then unscrew the nut and take off the main starter wire **(see illustrations)**.

4 Unclip the starter wiring loom from the support bracket on the motor **(see illustration)**.

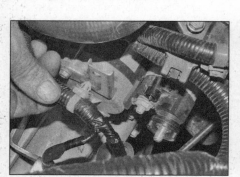

8.4 Unclip the starter motor wiring harness from its bracket

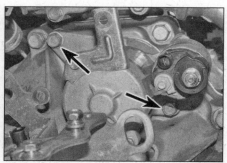

8.5a Unscrew the two bolts . . .

5 Unscrew and remove the two mounting bolts, withdraw the starter motor from the transmission, and remove it from the engine compartment **(see illustrations)**. Note that the lower (front) mounting bolt is longer than the upper (rear) one.

Diesel models

6 The diesel starter motor is located on the rear of the transmission. To access the upper mounting bolt, first remove the air cleaner as described in Chapter 4B.

7 Unscrew the starter motor upper mounting bolt, which is located next to the gearchange cable support bracket.

8 Jack up the front of the car, and support it on axle stands (see *Jacking and vehicle support*). Remove the engine undertray (Chapter 11, Section 23).

9 Pull back the rubber cover, then unscrew the nut securing the starter main wire, and disconnect it, noting which way round the ring terminal fits.

10 Unscrew the small retaining bolt, then disconnect the smaller solenoid wire from the starter.

11 Unscrew the single bolt securing the wiring support bracket in front of the starter, and remove it.

12 Unscrew and remove the starter lower mounting bolt, then withdraw the starter motor from the transmission and out from under the car **(see illustration)**.

Refitting

13 Refitting is a reversal of removal, noting the following points:

 a) *Tighten the starter mounting bolts to the specified torque.*
 b) *Ensure that the wiring connections are correctly and securely remade.*

9 Starter motor – overhaul

If the starter motor is thought to be defective, it should be removed from the car and taken to an auto-electrician for assessment. In the majority of cases, new starter motor brushes can be fitted at a reasonable cost. However, check the cost of repairs first, as it may

8.5b . . . and remove the starter motor

prove more economical to purchase a new or exchange motor.

10 Glow plugs (diesel models) – testing, removal and refitting

Testing

1 If the system malfunctions, testing is ultimately by substitution of known good units, but some preliminary checks may be made as follows.

2 Connect a voltmeter or 12 volt test light between the glow plug supply cable and earth (engine or vehicle metal). Make sure that the live connection is kept clear of the engine and bodywork.

3 Have an assistant switch on the ignition, and check that voltage is applied to the glow plugs. Note the time for which the warning light is lit, and the total time for which voltage is applied before the system cuts out. Switch off the ignition.

4 At an underbonnet temperature of 20°C, typical times noted should be approximately 3 seconds for warning light operation.

Warning light time will increase with lower temperatures and decrease with higher temperatures.

5 If there is no supply at all, the relay or associated wiring is at fault.

6 To locate a defective glow plug, pull off the wiring connector from each plug.

7 Use a continuity tester, or a 12 volt test light connected to the battery positive terminal, to check for continuity between each glow plug terminal and earth. The resistance of a glow plug in good condition is very low (less than 1 ohm), so if the test light does not come on or the continuity tester shows a high resistance, the glow plug is certainly defective.

8 If an ammeter is available, the current draw of each glow plug can be checked. After an initial surge of 15 to 20 amps, each plug should draw 12 amps. Any plug which draws much more or less than this is probably defective.

9 As a final check, the glow plugs can be removed and inspected.

Removal

10 Disconnect the battery negative lead, and position the lead away from the battery (also see *Disconnecting the battery*).

11 Remove the engine top cover, which is

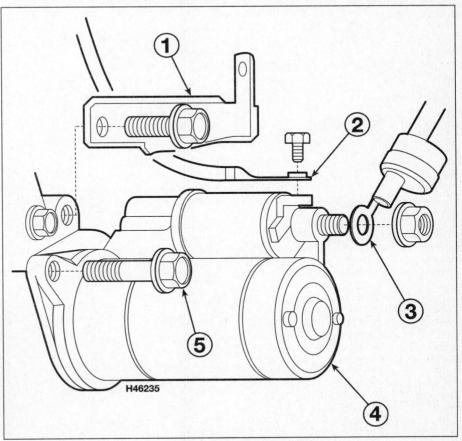

8.12 Starter motor (diesel models)

1 *Wiring support bracket*	3 *Starter main wire*	5 *Starter lower mounting bolt*
2 *Solenoid wire*	4 *Starter motor*	

H46235

10.11 The glow plug connectors are on the rear of the head

10.12 Pulling off a glow plug connector

secured by four bolts. The glow plugs are screwed into the rear of the cylinder head **(see illustration)**.

12 Disconnect the glow plugs by squeezing the connectors with thumb and forefinger, and pulling the connectors from the plugs **(see illustration)**.

⚠️ *Warning: If the glow plug (preheating) system has just been energised, or if the engine has recently been running, the glow plugs may be extremely hot.*

13 Unscrew the glow plugs and remove them from the cylinder head.

14 Inspect the glow plug stems for signs of damage. A badly burned or charred stem may be an indication of a faulty fuel injector – consult a diesel specialist for advice if necessary. Otherwise, if one plug is found to be faulty and the engine has completed a high mileage, it is probably worth renewing all four plugs as a set.

Refitting

15 Refitting is a reversal of removal, noting the following points:

a) Apply a little anti-seize compound (or copper brake grease) to the glow plug threads.

b) Tighten the glow plugs to the specified torque.

c) Make sure when remaking the glow plug wiring connections that the contact surfaces are clean.

Chapter 5 Part B:
Ignition system – petrol models

Contents

Degrees of difficulty

Easy, suitable for novice with little experience	Fairly easy, suitable for beginner with some experience	Fairly difficult, suitable for competent DIY mechanic	Difficult, suitable for experienced DIY mechanic	Very difficult, suitable for expert DIY or professional

Specifications

System type
All models. . . . . Fully-electronic under ECM control, four individual ignition coils mounted directly on spark plugs (distributorless direct ignition)

Firing order . . . . 1-3-4-2 (No 1 cylinder at timing belt end)

Ignition timing
All models. . . . . 8° ± 2° at idle (red pulley mark)

Torque wrench setting

	Nm	lbf ft
Knock sensor mounting bolt	22	16

1 General information

The PGM-FI engine management system provides complete control of the ignition timing by determining the optimum timing in response to engine speed, coolant temperature, throttle position and vacuum pressure in the intake manifold. These parameters are relayed to the engine control module (ECM) by the crankshaft position and TDC sensors, throttle position sensor, coolant temperature sensor and the MAP sensor. Ignition timing is altered during warm-up, idling and warm running conditions by the ECM. This electronic ignition system also consists of the ignition switch, battery, four direct-ignition coils, and spark plugs.

The knock sensor is mounted on the cylinder block to inform the ECM when the engine is 'pinking'. Its sensitivity to a particular frequency of vibration allows it to detect the impulses which are caused by the shock waves set up when the engine starts to pink (pre-ignite). The knock sensor sends an electrical signal to the ECM which retards the ignition advance setting until the pinking ceases – the ignition timing is then gradually returned to the 'normal' setting. This maintains the ignition timing as close to the knock threshold as possible – the most efficient setting for the engine under normal running conditions.

The ignition system uses one coil for each cylinder, with each coil mounted on the relevant spark plug. The coils are fed individually in firing order.

Precautions

The following precautions must be observed, to prevent damage to the ignition system components and to reduce risk of personal injury.

a) Ensure the ignition is switched off before disconnecting any of the ignition wiring.

b) Ensure that the ignition is switched off before connecting or disconnecting any ignition test equipment, such as a timing light.

c) Do not earth the coil primary or secondary circuits.

 Warning: Voltages produced by an electronic ignition system are considerably higher than those produced by conventional ignition systems. Extreme care must be taken when working on the system with the ignition switched on. Persons with surgically-implanted cardiac pacemaker devices should keep well clear of the ignition circuits, components and test equipment

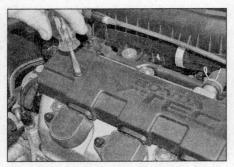

3.2a Release the cover fasteners with a screwdriver . . .

3.2b . . . and lift the cover off the ignition coils

3.3 Unscrew the ignition coil mounting nut

3.4 Lift the coil off the spark plug . . .

2 Ignition system – testing

1 The components of ignition systems are normally very reliable; most faults are far more likely to be due to loose or dirty connections, or to 'tracking' of HT voltage due to dirt, dampness or damaged insulation than to the failure of any of the system's components. Always check all wiring thoroughly before condemning an electrical component and work methodically to eliminate all other possibilities before deciding that a particular component is faulty.

Engine will not start

2 If the engine either will not turn over at all, or only turns very slowly, first check the battery and starter motor as described in Chapter 5A.

3.5 . . . then disconnect the wiring plug at the rear . . .

3 The anti-theft immobiliser system disables the fuel system when in operation, meaning that the engine will turn over as normal, but will not start. The immobiliser should be deactivated when a properly-coded ignition key is inserted into the ignition switch. If possible, substitute a spare key and recheck.

4 Ordinarily, it would be possible to check the ignition coil resistances, but Honda do not publish resistance specifications.

5 Ultimately, the car should be referred to a Honda dealer or diagnostic specialist for testing. A diagnostic connector is incorporated in the engine management system wiring harness, into which dedicated electronic test equipment can be plugged – the connector is located under the steering column. The tester will locate the fault quickly and simply, alleviating the need to test all the system components individually, which is a time-consuming operation that carries a high risk of

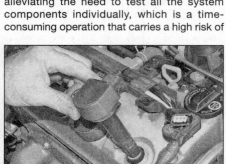

3.6 . . . and lift it out completely

damaging the ECM. If necessary, the system wiring and wiring connectors can be checked as described in Chapter 12, ensuring that the ECM wiring connector is only unplugged with the battery disconnected.

Engine misfires

6 An irregular misfire suggests either a loose connection or intermittent fault in the primary circuit, or an HT fault between the coils and spark plugs.

7 With the ignition switched off, check carefully through the system, ensuring that all connections are clean and securely fastened.

8 Check that the HT coils and their associated wiring connections are clean and dry.

9 Regular misfiring of one spark plug may be due to a faulty spark plug, faulty injector, a faulty coil or loss of compression in the relevant cylinder. Regular misfiring of all the cylinders suggests a fuel supply fault, such as a clogged fuel filter or faulty fuel pump, especially if it occurs in conditions where fuel demand is high.

3 Ignition coils – removal and refitting

Removal

1 Ensure that the ignition is switched off (take out the key).

2 Remove the plastic cover which sits over the ignition coil connectors on top of the engine, by turning the two quick-release fasteners a quarter-turn anti-clockwise using a flat-bladed screwdriver. Lift the cover off (see illustrations).

3 Unscrew the nut securing each ignition coil to the top of the engine (see illustration).

4 Lift the first coil slightly to detach it from the spark plug, but note that it is still plugged in at this point (see illustration).

5 Press the locking tab on the first coil's wiring connector, and slide the connector back to disconnect it from the coil (see illustration).

6 Lift the coil out of the engine (see illustration).

7 Repeat this process and remove the remaining three coils. Though it appears that all four coils are identical, it may be advisable to mark them for position, so that they can be refitted in their original locations.

Refitting

8 Offer the ignition coil into the engine so that the hole in the coil mounting plate aligns with the stud on the engine, and fit it over the plug. Reconnect the coil wiring plug, ensuring that a good connection is made, then press the coil firmly down over the mounting stud and onto the plug. Fit the coil mounting nut, and tighten it securely.

9 Repeat the procedure for the remaining coils and spark plugs. It is advisable to work on one coil and plug at a time, to avoid mixing up the coils, though they appear to be identical.

10 On completion, refit the plastic cover over the coils, and secure by turning the fasteners a quarter-turn clockwise.

4 Ignition timing – checking and adjustment

It is possible to check the ignition timing, but the service check connector inside the car has to be bridged, and a timing light suitable for connection to the No 1 direct-ignition coil will be needed (there are no conventional HT leads). Even if all this is done/available, the ignition timing cannot be adjusted, and if a check reveals it to be out of specification, a new engine control module (ECM) will be needed.

If the timing is felt to be incorrect because the engine can be heard pinking, the knock sensor may be faulty (see Section 5).

If performance in general is down, carry out the primary operations listed in Chapter 1A, Section 2, before having the engine management system checked by a Honda dealer or diagnostic specialist. The principal engine management sensors (described in Chapter 4A) having the most direct bearing on ignition timing are the crankshaft position sensor, TDC sensor and MAP sensor.

If a new timing belt has recently been fitted, note that engine performance will suffer if the belt is incorrectly fitted (one or more teeth 'out').

5 Knock sensor – removal and refitting

1 The knock sensor is mounted on the back of the engine, just below the inlet manifold. Realistically, access is only possible with the inlet manifold removed as described in Chapter 4A, though it may just be possible from below **(see illustration)**.
2 Trace the sensor wiring to the in-line plug, which is clipped to a bracket to the left of the sensor. Unclip the plug from the bracket, and disconnect it.

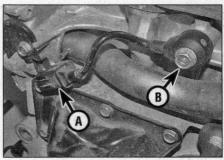

5.1 Knock sensor wiring plug (A) and mounting bolt (B) – inlet manifold removed

3 Unscrew the mounting bolt in the centre of the sensor, then withdraw the sensor from the back of the engine.
4 Clean the sensor and engine block mating faces before fitting.
5 Refitting is a reversal of removal. It is critical for the correct operation of the sensor that its mounting bolt is tightened to the specified torque.

Notes

Chapter 6
Clutch

Contents

Degrees of difficulty

Easy, suitable for novice with little experience	**Fairly easy,** suitable for beginner with some experience	**Fairly difficult,** suitable for competent DIY mechanic	**Difficult,** suitable for experienced DIY mechanic	**Very difficult,** suitable for expert DIY or professional

Specifications

General

Type	Single dry plate, diaphragm spring with spring-loaded hub
Operation	Hydraulic
Clutch pedal:	
Minimum disengagement height from floor	113 mm
Pedal free play	8 to 18 mm
Pedal stroke:	
Petrol models	130 to 140 mm
Diesel models	140 to 150 mm
Standard height	198 mm
Friction disc thickness:	
Petrol models:	
Nominal	8.3 to 9.0 mm
Wear limit	5.7 mm
Diesel models	N/A (friction material above rivets)

Torque wrench settings

	Nm	lbf ft
Clutch slave cylinder mounting bolts	22	16
Master cylinder mounting nuts	13	10
Pressure plate-to-flywheel bolts:		
Petrol models	25	18
Diesel models	19	14

1 General information and precautions

All manual transmission models use a single dry-plate, diaphragm-spring type clutch. The clutch friction disc has a splined hub which allows it to slide along the splines of the transmission input shaft. The friction disc is held in contact with the flywheel by spring pressure exerted by the diaphragm in the pressure plate.

The clutch release system is operated by hydraulic pressure. The hydraulic release system consists of the clutch pedal, a master cylinder and fluid reservoir, the hydraulic pipe, a slave (release) cylinder which actuates the clutch release lever and the clutch release bearing.

When pressure is applied to the clutch pedal to release the clutch, hydraulic pressure is exerted against the outer end of the clutch release lever. As the lever pivots the shaft, fingers push against the release bearing. The bearing pushes against the fingers of the diaphragm spring of the pressure plate assembly, which in turn releases the clutch friction disc.

When the pedal is released, the diaphragm spring forces the pressure plate back into contact with the linings on the clutch friction disc. The disc is now firmly held between the pressure plate and the flywheel, thus transmitting engine power to the transmission.

The hydraulic system requires no adjustment, since the quantity of hydraulic fluid in the circuit automatically compensates for wear every time the clutch pedal is operated.

Other than to renew components with obvious damage, some preliminary checks should be performed to diagnose clutch problems. These checks assume that the transmission is in good working condition.

a) *The first check should be the fluid level in the clutch master cylinder (see Weekly checks). If the fluid level is low, add fluid as necessary and inspect the hydraulic system for leaks. If the master cylinder reservoir has run dry, bleed the system as described in Section 4 and retest the clutch operation.*

b) *To check 'clutch spin-down time,' run the engine at normal idle speed with the transmission in neutral (clutch pedal up – engaged). Disengage the clutch (pedal down), wait several seconds and select reverse. No grinding noise should be heard. A grinding noise would most likely*

2.3 Access to the master cylinder is hindered by pipes and hoses

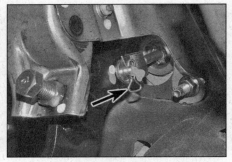

2.4 Remove the spring clip from the right-hand side, and pull out the clevis pin to the left

2.5 Master cylinder mounting nuts in front of brake pedal

indicate a problem in the pressure plate or the clutch friction disc.

c) Visually inspect the pivot bushing at the top of the clutch pedal to make sure there is no binding or excessive play.

d) Check under the car that the clutch release lever is solidly mounted on the ball-stud.

⚠ **Warning: The fluid used in the system is brake hydraulic fluid, which is poisonous. Take care to keep it off bare skin, and in particular not to get splashes in your eyes. The fluid also attacks paintwork, and may discolour carpets, etc – keep spillages to a minimum, and wash any off immediately with cold water. Finally, hydraulic fluid is highly flammable, and should be handled with the same care as petrol.**

⚠ **Warning: Dust produced by clutch wear and deposited on clutch components may be hazardous to your health. DO NOT blow it out with compressed air and DO NOT inhale it. DO NOT use petrol or petroleum-based solvents to remove the dust. Brake system cleaner should be used to flush the dust into a drain pan.**

2 Master cylinder – removal, overhaul and refitting

Note: Refer to the hydraulic fluid warning in Section 1 before proceeding.

Removal

1 Clamp the fluid supply hose from the reservoir, then release the spring clip, and pull off the hose – quickly turn the hose end upwards, to reduce fluid spillage. Take care not to drip hydraulic fluid onto paintwork or hot engine components.

2 Unscrew the bolt securing the fluid reservoir support bracket to the side of the master cylinder, and remove the reservoir with its hose still attached.

3 Access to the master cylinder in the engine compartment is limited by various hydraulic pipes and coolant hoses – where possible, unclip them to improve matters **(see illustration)**. Unscrew the union nut and

disconnect the fluid pipe from the front of the master cylinder. Either plug or tape over the open connections.

4 Working under the facia, remove the spring clip from the master cylinder pushrod clevis pin **(see illustration)**. Pull out the clevis pin to the left, to disconnect the pushrod from the pedal.

5 Unscrew the two master cylinder mounting nuts in front of the pedal **(see illustration)**, then return to the engine compartment and withdraw the master cylinder from the bulkhead. Recover the gasket fitted behind the cylinder, and the O-ring fitted inside the fluid pipe connection – new ones should be used when refitting.

Overhaul

Note: Check availability of overhaul kits prior to dismantling the cylinder.

6 Remove the nut from the end of the cylinder, hold the pushrod into the cylinder body, and prise out the circlip.

7 Remove the stopper, then ease out the pushrod, and pull out the piston assembly. If necessary, use compressed air to force the piston from the cylinder body.

8 Carefully examine the bore of the cylinder for rust, scratches, gouges and general wear. If the bore is damaged, the complete cylinder must be renewed. If the bore is in good condition, thoroughly clean the assembly, and renew the seals as described below.

9 Take note of the seal orientation on the piston, and using a small screwdriver, lever the seals from the grooves on the piston.

10 Fit the new seals to the piston, ensuring

3.5a Slave cylinder location – diesel models

the seal lips point towards the spring end of the piston. Smear the seals with the assembly grease supplied in the overhaul kit.

11 Insert the piston assembly into the cylinder, spring end first. Ensure the seal lips enter the cylinder bore without catching or folding back.

12 Compress the piston with the pushrod, fit the stopper, then secure with the circlip. Refit and tighten the nut to complete.

Refitting

13 Refitting is a reversal of removal, noting the following points:

a) Use a new bulkhead gasket and pipe connection O-ring.

b) Tighten the mounting nuts and pipe union securely.

c) Where the reservoir is clipped into place, use a new clip, and splay the clip ends open to retain the clip securely.

d) Use a new spring clip to secure the pedal clevis pin.

e) Top-up the reservoir, then bleed the system as described in Section 4.

3 Slave cylinder – removal, overhaul and refitting

Note: Refer to the hydraulic fluid warning in Section 1 before proceeding.

Removal

1 On petrol models, remove the inlet air resonator and inlet air duct as described in Chapter 4A.

2 On diesel models, remove the air cleaner as described in Chapter 4B. Access to the slave cylinder is also hampered by the battery and its tray, which can be removed as described in Chapter 5A.

3 Pull out the two roll-pins from the front of the cylinder, at the bleed screw end.

4 Anticipating some fluid spillage, disconnect the fluid pipe union and recover the O-ring – a new one must be used when refitting. Either plug or tape over the open connections.

5 Unscrew and remove the two mounting bolts, then withdraw the cylinder from the transmission **(see illustrations)**.

Overhaul

Note: *Check availability of overhaul kits prior to dismantling the cylinder.*

6 Unclip the dust boot from the cylinder body, and pull the pushrod out. Extract the piston and spring. If necessary, use compressed air to force the piston from the bore. Recover the piston spring.

7 Carefully examine the bore of the cylinder for rust, scratches, gouges and general wear. If the bore is damaged, the complete cylinder must be renewed. If the bore is in good condition, thoroughly clean the assembly, and renew the seals as described below.

8 Note their fitted locations, then using a small screwdriver, prise the seals from the piston.

9 Fit the new seals to the piston, ensuring they are fitted as noted on removal. Coat the seals with assembly grease (supplied in the overhaul kit).

10 Insert the spring, large diameter end towards the cylinder bleed nipple, followed by the piston. Ensure the seals lips enter the cylinder bore without catching or folding back.

11 Squeeze some assembly grease into the dust boot, then refit the boot and pushrod.

Refitting

12 Refitting is a reversal of removal, noting the following points:
  a) *Use a new pipe connection O-ring.*
  b) *Apply a little grease to the end of the slave cylinder pushrod where it contacts the clutch release lever.*
  c) *Tighten the mounting bolts and pipe union securely.*
  d) *Top-up the fluid reservoir, and bleed the system as described in Section 4.*

4 Hydraulic system – bleeding

Note: *Refer to the hydraulic fluid warning in Section 1 before proceeding.*

1 The correct operation of any hydraulic system is only possible after removing all air from the components and circuit; this is achieved by bleeding the system.

2 During the bleeding procedure, add only clean, unused hydraulic fluid of the recommended type; never re-use fluid that has already been bled from the system. Ensure that sufficient fluid is available before starting work.

3 If there is any possibility of incorrect fluid being already in the system, the hydraulic circuit must be flushed completely with uncontaminated, correct fluid.

4 If hydraulic fluid has been lost from the system, or air has entered because of a leak, ensure that the fault is cured before continuing further.

5 Check that all pipes and hoses are secure, unions tight and the bleed screw is closed. The bleed screw is located on the end of

3.5b Removing the slave cylinder – petrol models

the release cylinder, on the front of the transmission casing. It should be possible to access the bleed screw without removing any components, but for improved access, remove the air cleaner or related parts as necessary (see Chapter 4A or 4B).

6 Unscrew the master cylinder fluid reservoir cap, and top the reservoir up to the upper (MAX) level line. Refit the cap loosely, and remember to maintain the fluid level at least above the lower (MIN) level line throughout the procedure, or there is a risk of further air entering the system.

7 Clean any dirt from around the bleed screw (which is on the slave cylinder), and remove the dust cap **(see illustration)**.

8 The procedure for bleeding is much the same as that for bleeding the brakes as described in Chapter 9. It is recommended that either the basic (two-man) or one-way valve method is used, for simplicity.

9 When bleeding is complete, and correct pedal feel is restored, tighten the bleed screw securely and wash off any spilt fluid. Refit the dust cap to the bleed screw. Refit any components removed for access.

10 Check the hydraulic fluid level in the master cylinder reservoir, and top-up if necessary (see *Weekly checks*).

11 Discard any hydraulic fluid that has been bled from the system; it will not be fit for re-use.

12 Check the operation of the clutch pedal. If the clutch is still not operating correctly, air may still be present in the system, and further bleeding is required. Failure to bleed

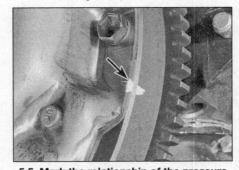

5.5 Mark the relationship of the pressure plate to the flywheel

4.7 Remove the clutch bleed screw dust cap

satisfactorily after a reasonable repetition of the bleeding procedure may be due to worn master cylinder/slave cylinder seals.

5 Clutch components – removal, inspection and refitting

Note: *Refer to the clutch dust warning in Section 1 before proceeding.*

Removal

1 Access to the clutch components is normally accomplished by removing the transmission, leaving the engine in the car. However, note that this does not actually save much work over removing the engine and transmission together.

2 If the engine is being removed for major overhaul, check the clutch for wear and renew worn components as necessary. However, the relatively low cost of the clutch components compared to the time and trouble spent gaining access to them warrants their renewal anytime the engine or transmission is removed, unless they are new or in near-perfect condition. The following procedures are based on the assumption the engine will stay in place.

3 Remove the transmission from the car (see Chapter 7A). Support the engine while the transmission is out. Preferably, an engine hoist should be used to support it from above. However, if a jack is used underneath the engine, make sure a piece of wood is positioned between the jack and engine sump to spread the load.

4 The clutch fork and release bearing can remain attached to the transmission housing for the time being.

5 If the pressure plate is to be refitted, scribe or paint marks so the pressure plate and the flywheel will be in the same alignment during refitting **(see illustration)**.

6 Turning each bolt a little at a time, loosen the pressure plate-to-flywheel bolts (note that they have bi-hex heads – an ordinary splined socket will undo them). Work in a diagonal pattern until all spring pressure is relieved. Then hold the pressure plate securely and completely remove the bolts, followed by

5.6a Remove the pressure plate bolts (arrowed) gradually and evenly in a diagonal pattern

5.6b Removing the pressure plate and friction disc

the pressure plate and friction disc **(see illustrations)**.

Inspection

7 Ordinarily, when a problem occurs in the clutch, it can be attributed to wear of the clutch friction disc. However, all components should be inspected at this time.

8 Inspect the flywheel for cracks, heat distortion, grooves and other obvious defects. If the imperfections are slight, a engineering workshop can machine the surface flat and smooth, which is highly recommended regardless of the surface appearance. Refer to Chapter 2A or 2B for the flywheel removal and refitting procedure.

9 Inspect the lining on the clutch disc. There should be at least 1.5 mm of lining above the rivet heads. Check for loose rivets, distortion, cracks, broken springs and other obvious damage **(see illustration)**. As mentioned above, ordinarily the clutch friction disc is routinely renewed, so if in doubt about the condition, renew it.

10 The release bearing should also be renewed along with the clutch friction disc (see Section 7). Typically, the release bearing, friction disc and pressure plate will be available as a three-part clutch 'kit' from dealers and other parts suppliers. This is also a good time to check the condition of the pilot bearing, where applicable (see Section 6).

11 Check the machined surfaces and the diaphragm spring fingers of the pressure plate **(see illustrations)**. If the surface is grooved or otherwise damaged, renew the pressure plate. Also check for obvious damage, distortion, cracking, etc. Light glazing can be removed with emery cloth or sandpaper. If a new pressure plate is required, new and reconditioned units are available.

Refitting

12 Before refitting, clean the flywheel and pressure plate machined surfaces with brake cleaner or degreaser. It's important that no oil or grease is on these surfaces or the lining of

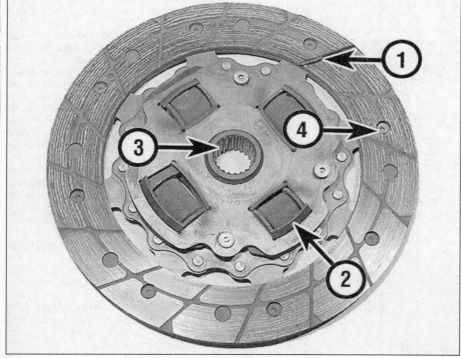

5.9 Examining the clutch disc

1 *Lining – this will wear down in use*
2 *Springs or dampers – check for cracking and deformation*
3 *Splined hub – the splines must not be worn and should slide smoothly on the input shaft splines*
4 *Rivets – these secure the lining and will damage the flywheel or pressure plate if allowed to contact the surfaces*

5.11a Inspect the pressure plate friction surface for score marks, cracks and signs of overheating

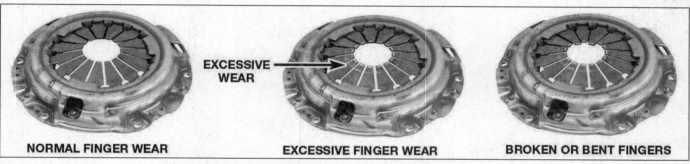

NORMAL FINGER WEAR   EXCESSIVE FINGER WEAR   BROKEN OR BENT FINGERS

5.11b Renew the pressure plate if any of these conditions are noted

5.14 Centre the clutch disc with a clutch alignment tool . . .

5.15 . . . then fit the pressure plate over it

the clutch friction disc. Handle the parts with clean hands only.

13 Position the clutch friction disc against the flywheel. Make sure the disc is installed properly (most renewal clutch discs will be marked 'flywheel side' or something similar – if not marked, fit the clutch friction disc with the damper springs towards the transmission).

14 Centre the clutch disc by ensuring the alignment tool extends through the splined hub and into the pocket in the crankshaft **(see illustration)**. Wiggle the tool up, down or side-to-side as needed to centre the disc.

15 Offer the pressure plate into position over the tool, and tighten the pressure plate-to-flywheel bolts a little at a time, working in a criss-cross pattern to prevent distorting the cover **(see illustration)**. When all of the bolts are snug, tighten them to the torque listed in this Chapter's Specifications. Remove the alignment tool.

16 Using clutch assembly grease (copper grease will do as a substitute), lubricate the inner groove of the release bearing. Also apply a little grease on the release lever contact areas and the transmission input shaft bearing retainer.

17 Fit the clutch release bearing (see Section 7).

18 Fit the transmission and all components removed previously.

6 Pilot bearing – inspection and renewal

1 The clutch pilot bearing is a ball-bearing which is pressed into the rear of the flywheel (it appears to be only fitted to petrol models). It's greased at the factory, and doesn't require additional lubrication. Its primary purpose is to support the front of the transmission input shaft. The pilot bearing should be inspected whenever the clutch components are removed from the engine. Because of its inaccessibility, renew it if you have any doubt about its condition.

2 Remove the clutch components (see Section 5).

3 Using an electric torch, inspect the bearing for excessive wear, scoring, dryness, roughness and any other obvious damage. If any of these conditions are noted, renew the bearing.

4 Remove the flywheel (see Chapter 2A). Using hammer and drift, drive the bearing out of the flywheel, from the front to the rear **(see illustration)**.

5 To fit a new bearing, lightly lubricate the outside surface with grease, then drive it into the recess with a bearing driver or a socket which is slightly smaller than the bearing **(see illustration)**.

6.4 Use a small slide-hammer puller to remove the pilot bearing

6.5 Tap the bearing into place with a suitable socket

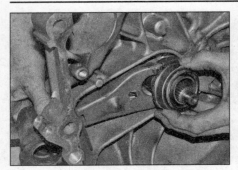

7.3a Unclip the release bearing from the release fork

7.3b Pull the release fork to release the spring clip from the ball-stud

7.4 If the bearing doesn't turn smoothly or is noisy, renew it

7.6 Apply grease to the surface of the release bearing guide

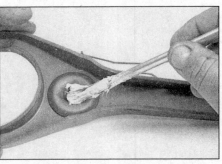

7.7a Apply grease to the ball-stud socket in the rear of the release lever . . .

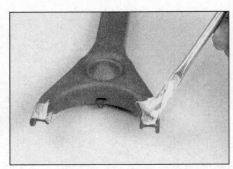

7.7b . . . the lever ends, the depression for the slave cylinder pushrod . . .

6 Fit the flywheel, if removed (see Chapter 2A). Fit the clutch components, transmission and other components removed previously. Tighten all fasteners to the recommended torque values where given.

7 Release bearing and fork – removal, inspection and refitting

Removal

1 Unbolt the clutch slave cylinder (see Section 3), but don't disconnect the fluid line. Suspend the release cylinder out of the way with a piece of wire or string.
2 Remove the transmission (see Chapter 7A). Slide out the release fork dust boot, noting how it is fitted.
3 Slide the release bearing off the input shaft

and unclip it from the release fork. Pull the clutch release fork to release the retention spring from the ball-stud and remove the fork **(see illustrations)**.

Inspection

4 Hold the bearing by the outer race and rotate the inner race while applying pressure. If the bearing doesn't turn smoothly or if it's noisy, renew the bearing/hub assembly **(see illustration)**.
5 Wipe the bearing with a clean rag and inspect it for damage, wear and cracks. It's common practice to renew the bearing whenever a clutch overhaul is performed, to decrease the possibility of a bearing failure in the future. Don't immerse the bearing in solvent – it's sealed for life and to do so would ruin it. Also check the release lever for cracks and bends.

Refitting

6 Fill the inner groove of the release bearing with clutch assembly grease (copper grease will suffice). Also apply a light coat of the same grease to the transmission input shaft splines and release bearing guide **(see illustration)**.
7 Lubricate the release fork ball socket, fork ends and slave cylinder pushrod socket with clutch assembly grease **(see illustrations)**.
8 Attach the release bearing to the release fork.
9 Slide the release bearing onto the transmission input shaft front bearing retainer while passing the end of the release fork through the opening in the clutch housing **(see illustration)**. Push the clutch release fork onto the ball-stud until it's firmly seated.
10 Apply a light coat of clutch assembly grease to the face of the release bearing where it contacts the pressure plate diaphragm fingers.
11 The remainder of refitting is the reverse of the removal procedure.

8 Clutch pedal adjustment

Pedal height

1 The height of the clutch pedal is the distance the pedal sits off the floor, measured from the top surface of the pedal **(see illustration)**. If the pedal height is not as specified, it must be adjusted.

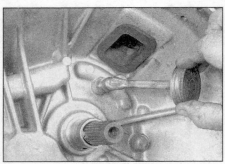

7.7c . . . and the ball-stud

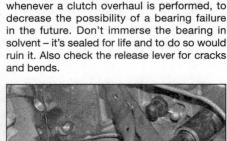

7.9 Refitting the release fork and bearing

8.1 Pedal height is the distance between the pedal pad and the floor

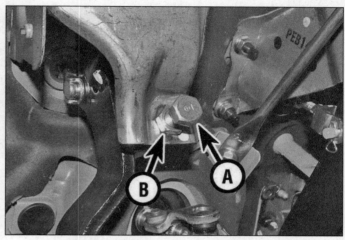

8.2 Clutch pedal adjuster bolt (A) and locknut (B)

2 To adjust the clutch pedal, loosen the locknut on the clutch switch (or the adjuster bolt) and back the switch/bolt out until it no longer touches the pedal, then loosen the locknut on the clutch pushrod **(see illustration)**. Turn the pushrod to adjust the pedal height. Also check the pedal stroke, which is the distance from the fully-depressed to fully-released position. When both adjustments are correct, tighten the locknut.

3 Turn the switch/bolt clockwise until it just contacts the pedal arm, then turn it in an additional 3/4 to 1 turn. Tighten the locknut.

Pedal free play

4 The free play is the pedal slack, or the distance the pedal can be depressed before it begins to have any effect on the clutch system **(see illustration)**. If the pedal free play is not within the specified range, it must be adjusted.

5 To adjust the pedal free play, loosen the locknut on the clutch pushrod. Back off the pushrod to adjust the pedal free play to the specified range, and retighten the locknut.

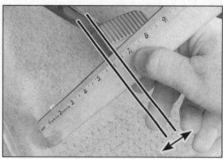

8.4 Pedal freeplay is the distance the pedal travels before resistance is felt

Chapter 7 Part A:
Manual transmission

Contents

Degrees of difficulty

Easy, suitable for novice with little experience	Fairly easy, suitable for beginner with some experience	Fairly difficult, suitable for competent DIY mechanic	Difficult, suitable for experienced DIY mechanic	Very difficult, suitable for expert DIY or professional

Specifications

General

Type	Manual, five forward speeds and reverse. Synchromesh on all forward speeds
Transmission code/designation:	
Petrol models	SLW
Diesel models	MD4

Gear ratios (typical)

Petrol engine models:	
1st	3.461
2nd	1.869
3rd	1.241
4th	0.969
5th	0.805
Reverse	3.230
Final drive	4.411
Diesel engine models:	
1st	3.545
2nd	2.055
3rd	1.333
4th	0.923
5th	0.744
Reverse	3.583
Final drive	3.578

Lubrication

Oil type	See *Lubricants and fluids*
Oil capacity	See Chapter 1A or 1B

Torque wrench settings

	Nm	lbf ft
Clutch semi-circular cover plate bolts:		
1.4 litre engine models	24	18
1.6 litre engine models	10	7
Engine-to-transmission bolts:		
Petrol models	64	47
Diesel models:		
M10 bolts	40	30
M12 bolts	60	44
Engine/transmission mountings (petrol):		
Front mounting:		
Bracket-to-engine bolts:		
M10 bolt	54	40
M12 bolts	64	47
Through-bolt*	64	47
Left-hand mounting:		
Side bracket-to-engine bolts	44	32
Upper bracket nuts	54	40
Rear mounting:		
Bracket-to-mounting through-bolt	64	47
Bracket-to-transmission bolts	64	47
Mounting-to-subframe bolts	59	44
Right-hand mounting:		
Mounting-to-transmission nuts, bolt and through-bolt	54	40
Engine/transmission mountings (diesel):		
Front mounting:		
Bracket-to-engine bolts	91	67
Through-bolt	64	47
Left-hand mounting:		
Mounting-to-transmission nuts, bolt and through-bolt	54	40
Rear mounting:		
Bracket-to-transmission bolts	69	51
Mounting-to-subframe bolts	59	44
Front subframe bolts:		
M10 bolts	59	44
M14 bolts	103	76
Gearchange cable mounting bracket bolts	27	20
Gearchange mechanism mounting bolts	22	16
Reversing light switch:		
Petrol models	25	18
Diesel models	39	29
Roadwheel nuts	108	80
Starter motor mounting bolts:		
Petrol models	44	32
Diesel models:		
Lower bolt	38	28
Upper bolt	98	72
Transmission-to-sump stiffener bracket bolts:		
M8 bolts	24	18
M10 bolts	44	32

* Use new bolt

---

1 General information

The transmission is contained in a cast-aluminium alloy casing bolted to the engine's right-hand end (petrol models) or left-hand end (diesel models), and consists of the gearbox and final drive differential. The transmissions fitted to petrol and diesel models are clearly different in detail, but similar enough in practice to be treated the same in this Chapter. However, their differences should be borne in mind when sourcing parts.

Drive is transmitted from the crankshaft via the clutch to the input shaft, which has a splined extension to accept the clutch friction disc, and rotates in tapered roller bearings. From the input shaft, drive is transmitted to the output shaft, which also rotates in tapered roller bearings. From the output shaft, the drive is transmitted to the differential crownwheel, which rotates with the differential case and planetary gears, thus driving the sun gears and driveshafts. The rotation of the planetary gears on their shaft allows the inner roadwheel to rotate at a slower speed than the outer roadwheel when the car is cornering.

The input and output shafts are arranged side-by-side, parallel to the crankshaft and driveshafts, so that their gear pinion teeth are in constant mesh. In the neutral position, the output shaft gear pinions rotate freely, so that drive cannot be transmitted to the crownwheel.

Gear selection is via a facia-mounted lever with a cable linkage. The selector linkage causes the appropriate selector fork to move its respective synchro-sleeve along the shaft, to lock the gear pinion to the synchro-hub. Since the synchro-hubs are splined to the output shaft, this locks the pinion to the shaft, so that drive can be transmitted. To ensure that gearchanging can be made quickly and quietly, a synchromesh system is fitted to all gears, consisting of baulk rings and spring-loaded fingers, as well as the gear pinions and synchro-hubs. The synchromesh cones are formed on the mating faces of the baulk rings and gear pinions.

2 Driveshaft oil seals – renewal

1 Oil leaks frequently occur due to wear of the driveshaft oil seals. Renewal of these seals is relatively easy, since the repair can usually be performed without removing the transmission from the car.
2 Driveshaft oil seals are located at the sides of the transmission, where the driveshafts are attached. If leakage at the seal is suspected, raise the car and support it securely on axle stands (see *Jacking and vehicle support*). If the seal is leaking, lubricant will be found on the sides of the transmission, below the seals.
3 Refer to Chapter 8 and remove the driveshaft(s).
4 Use a screwdriver or lever bar to carefully prise the oil seal out of the transmission casing **(see illustration)**.
5 Using a large section of pipe or a large deep socket (slightly smaller than the outside diameter of the seal) as a drift, fit the new oil seal **(see illustration)**. Ensure that the spring side of the seal faces into the transmission casing. Drive it into the bore squarely and make sure it's completely seated. Coat the seal lip with transmission lubricant.

2.4 Insert the tip of a large screwdriver behind the oil seal and carefully lever it out

6 Refit the driveshaft(s). Be careful not to damage the lip of the new seal.

3 Gearchange mechanism and cables – removal and refitting

Removal

1 Unscrew the gear lever knob **(see illustration)**.
2 Remove the gear lever trim panel, facia lower centre section (or the centre console) as described in Chapter 11. We also found it was necessary to remove the heater control panel, as described in Chapter 3, to allow the gearchange mechanism enough room to be removed.
3 The two gearchange cables must now be detached. Each inner cable is secured by

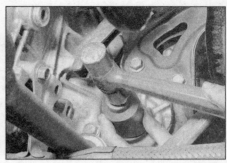

2.5 Using a large socket or a section of pipe, drive the new seal squarely into the bore

a spring clip – note how all components are arranged, then unhook the clips, and separate the inner cables from the ball fittings **(see illustrations)**.
4 Remove the screws securing the mechanism's lower cover, and remove it **(see illustration)**.
5 Each cable outer has a moulded fitting which locates sideways into the front of the gearchange mechanism. Twist the cable outer anti-clockwise, and pull it out to the side, noting how the moulded fitting locates in the bracket **(see illustration)**.
6 Unscrew the four gearchange mechanism bolts, then detach the facia wiring loom from the assembly as required. Manipulate the assembly out of the facia, and remove it **(see illustrations)**.
7 Raise the front of the car and place it securely on axle stands (see *Jacking and*

3.1 Unscrew the gear lever knob

3.3a Using a small screwdriver, prise the spring clip sideways . . .

3.3b . . . and detach the cable ends from the ball fittings

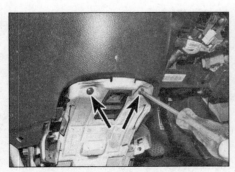

3.4 Remove the screws from the lower cover

3.5 Push the cable fittings sideways to detach them

3.6a Remove the four gearchange mechanism mounting bolts . . .

3.6b . . . then detach the facia wiring harness . . .

3.6c . . . and withdraw the mechanism through the facia

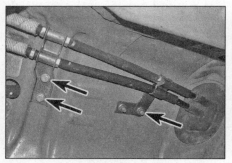

3.8 Gearchange cable support bracket bolts/nut under the car

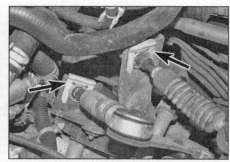

3.11 Slide the 'horse-shoe' clips upwards to release the cables

vehicle support). Trace the gearchange cables under the car, to the point where they enter through the floorpan – depending on model, it may be necessary to unbolt and remove the exhaust system heat shields for access.
8 Two cable support/guides are fitted – one secured with a single nut, the other with two bolts **(see illustration)**. Remove the support/ guides, noting how they are fitted. Pull the cables through the floor grommet under the car.
9 In the engine compartment, gain access to the cables by removing the inlet air resonator and air duct (petrol models) or the air cleaner (diesel models) as described in Chapter 4A or 4B.
10 The shift and selector cable end fittings are secured to the transmission levers by a split pin and washers. Noting how these components are arranged, remove the pins and disconnect the cable ends **(see illustrations 5.7a to 5.7c).**

11 The cables are further secured to a mounting bracket on top of the transmission, by two metal 'horse-shoe' clips **(see illustration)**. Pull these clips upwards to remove, then unhook the cables and withdraw them completely from the car. Mark the cables for identification purposes, if they are to be refitted.

Refitting

12 Refitting is a reversal of removal, noting the following points:
a) *Lightly grease the cable end fittings, at the transmission and gearchange mechanism ends, when refitting.*
b) *Honda state that, at the transmission end, new split pins and horse-shoe clips should be used when refitting the cables.*
c) *Ensure that the cables are correctly refitted, and routed as before, with no sharp bends. Refit the support/guides under the car.*

4.5 Reversing light switch (A) and wiring plug (B) – diesel models

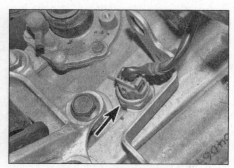

4.10 Reversing light switch – petrol models

d) *Tighten the gearchange mechanism mounting bolts to the specified torque.*
e) *On completion, check that all gears can be selected properly before taking the car out on the road.*

4 Reversing light switch – testing and renewal

Testing

1 Before testing the reversing light switch, check the fuse in the passenger compartment fuse/relay box (refer to the wiring diagrams in Chapter 12).
2 Put the gear lever in reverse, and turn the ignition switch to the On position (warning lights on). The reversing lights should go on. Turn off the ignition switch.
3 If the reversing lights don't go on, check the light bulbs in the tail light assembly (see Chapter 12). It's unlikely that both bulbs would fail at once, but it's still a possibility.
4 If the fuse and bulbs are both okay, the reversing light switch on top of the transmission should be checked. As required, gain access to the switch by removing the inlet air resonator and air duct (petrol models) or the air cleaner (diesel models) as described in Chapter 4A or 4B.
5 The reversing light switch should not be confused with the vehicle speed sensor, which is also screwed into the top of the transmission, but unlike the reversing light switch, has a separate mounting bolt. Disconnect the switch wiring plug (on diesel models, trace the wire from the switch to its in-line connector) **(see illustration)**.
6 With the gear lever in reverse, there should be continuity; with the lever in any other gear, there should be no continuity.
7 If the switch fails this test, renew it (see below).
8 If the switch is OK, but the reversing lights aren't coming on, check for power to the switch. If voltage is not available, trace the circuit between the switch and the fusebox. If power is present, trace the circuit between the switch and the reversing lights for an open-circuit condition.

Renewal

9 If not already done, gain access to the switch by removing the inlet air resonator and air duct (petrol models) or the air cleaner (diesel models) as described in Chapter 4A or 4B.
10 The reversing light switch should not be confused with the vehicle speed sensor, which is also screwed into the top of the transmission, but unlike the reversing light switch, has a separate mounting bolt. Disconnect the switch wiring plug (on diesel models, trace the wire from the switch to its in-line connector) **(see illustration)**.
11 A large deep socket or spanner will be

4.11 Unscrew the switch, and recover the sealing washer

5.3 Unbolt the transmission earth strap – clutch fluid pipe bracket bolt arrowed

5.4a Unbolt the clutch pipe bracket . . .

5.4b . . . then unbolt the slave cylinder, and move it clear

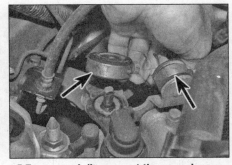

5.7a Pull out the split pin . . .

needed to unscrew the switch – recover the sealing washer **(see illustration)**.

12 Refitting is a reversal of removal. Use a new sealing washer, and tighten the switch to the specified torque. Test the operation of the lights on completion.

5 Transmission – removal and refitting

Removal

Petrol models

1 Remove the battery as described in Chapter 5A.
2 Remove the inlet air resonator and inlet air duct as described in Chapter 4A.
3 Unbolt the earth strap next to the transmission mounting **(see illustration)**.
4 Trace the clutch slave cylinder fluid pipe back from the cylinder to the fluid hose union, and unbolt the pipe/union support bracket. Remove the two slave cylinder mounting bolts, and move it clear of the transmission, if possible without opening the pipe union **(see illustrations)**.
Caution: Be careful not to bend or kink the clutch hydraulic pipe, and don't depress the clutch pedal while the slave cylinder is removed.
5 Disconnect the wiring plugs from the reversing light switch and vehicle speed sensor.
6 Remove the starter motor as described in Chapter 5A.
7 Remove the split pin and washers securing the cable ends to the transmission levers, and disconnect the cables. Unscrew the three bolts securing the gearchange cable bracket to the top of the transmission, then move the whole assembly to one side, taking care not to bend the cables **(see illustrations)**.
8 Support the transmission end of the engine. Preferably, this should be done from above, either with an engine hoist/crane or an engine support bar – supporting from below will be awkward, as the front subframe must be removed later.
9 Remove the two uppermost transmission-to-engine bolts.
10 Ensuring the engine is securely supported,

unscrew the right-hand mounting through-bolt, then remove the two upper nuts and bolt, and take off the upper bracket from the transmission **(see illustrations)**.
11 Unscrew the through-bolt from the engine

5.7b . . . then take off the washer . . .

5.7c . . . and disconnect the gearchange cables

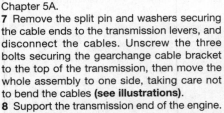

5.7d Unbolt the gearchange cable bracket, and lift it clear

front mounting (note that the nut is 'captive'). Unscrew the three bolts securing the front mounting to the engine/transmission, and remove it completely **(see illustrations)**.
12 Loosen the front wheel nuts, and if

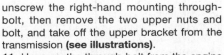

5.10a Unscrew the right-hand mounting through-bolt . . .

5.10b ... then unbolt and remove the upper bracket

5.11a Unscrew the front mounting through-bolt, and recover the 'captive' nut

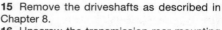

5.11b Unscrew the three bolts ...

5.11c ... and take off the front mounting

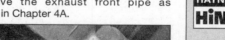

5.16 Unscrew the rear mounting through-bolt (note the damper weight)

15 Remove the driveshafts as described in Chapter 8.

16 Unscrew the transmission rear mounting through-bolt (noting that it has a damper weight attached) – if preferred, the rest of the rear mounting can also be unbolted, but we found this wasn't necessary (see illustration).

17 Remove the front subframe as described in Chapter 10.

18 Unbolt and remove the stiffener brackets fitted between the engine sump and transmission. Also unbolt and remove the semi-circular clutch cover (see illustrations).

19 Support the transmission from below, using a jack and a flat piece of wood (see illustration). Have an assistant ready to support the transmission as the jack is lowered.

possible, also loosen both driveshaft nuts while the car is still on the ground. Jack up the front of the car, and support it on axle stands (see *Jacking and vehicle support*). Note that the car must be raised sufficiently high for the transmission to be lowered out and withdrawn from underneath. Remove the front wheels and the engine undertray.

13 Drain the transmission fluid as described in Chapter 1A.

14 Remove the exhaust front pipe as described in Chapter 4A.

> **HAYNES HiNT** *Paint or scribe an alignment mark across the transmission and engine faces. This is simply to make refitting easier – the transmission has two locating dowels, but an alignment mark will be helpful in eliminating guesswork when offering the unit into position.*

20 Unscrew the remaining transmission-to-engine bolts, then carefully pull the transmission away from the engine until the transmission shaft is clear of the clutch pressure plate. If necessary, carefully prise the transmission away at first, to release the alignment dowels (see illustration).

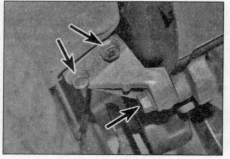

5.18a Remove the bolts ...

5.18b ... and take off the stiffener brackets on the sump

5.18c Remove the clutch cover/splash shield

5.19 Support the transmission from below, with a jack and block of wood

5.20 Separate the transmission by carefully prising with a screwdriver

21 Check round the transmission that everything has been disconnected from it, and that there is nothing in the way which might hinder its removal.

22 With the help of an assistant to guide the unit out, lower the transmission on the jack until it can be removed from under the car **(see illustration)**. Recover the two dowel pins, noting their fitted locations, and store them for safekeeping.

Diesel models

23 Remove the battery and its tray as described in Chapter 5A.

24 Remove the air cleaner and inlet air duct as described in Chapter 4B.

25 Referring to Chapter 6 if necessary, unbolt the slave cylinder, and move it clear of the transmission, if possible without opening the pipe union.

Caution: Be careful not to bend or kink the clutch hydraulic pipe, and don't depress the clutch pedal while the slave cylinder is removed.

26 Disconnect the wiring plugs from the reversing light switch and vehicle speed sensor.

27 Next to the reversing light wiring plug, unscrew the single bolt securing the coolant pipe support bracket, and move the bracket clear **(see illustration)**.

28 Disconnect the shift and selector cables from their levers on the transmission – each is secured by a split pin, and there are two washers. Unhook the cables, then pull up the metal 'horse-shoe' clips securing the cables to the mounting bracket, and place the cables to one side, taking care not to bend them **(see illustrations)**.

29 Remove the three bolts and take off the gearchange cable mounting bracket.

30 Remove the starter motor as described in Chapter 5A.

31 Support the transmission end of the engine. Preferably, this should be done from above, either with an engine hoist/crane or an engine support bar – supporting from below will be awkward, as the front subframe must be removed later.

32 Ensuring the engine is securely supported, unscrew the left-hand mounting through-bolt, then remove the two upper nuts and bolt, and take off the upper bracket from the transmission **(see illustration)**.

33 Remove the three uppermost transmission-to-engine bolts.

34 Loosen the front wheel nuts, and if possible, also loosen both driveshaft nuts while the car is still on the ground. Jack up the front of the car, and support it on axle stands (see *Jacking and vehicle support*). Note that the car must be raised sufficiently high for the transmission to be lowered out and withdrawn from underneath. Remove the front wheels and the engine undertray.

35 Drain the transmission fluid as described in Chapter 1B.

36 Remove the exhaust front pipe as described in Chapter 4B.

5.22 Removing the transmission

37 Remove the driveshafts as described in Chapter 8.

38 Unscrew and remove the three lower bolts from the transmission rear mounting.

39 Unscrew the through-bolt from the engine front mounting – note that the nut is 'captive' **(see illustration)**.

40 Referring to Chapter 10 if necessary, remove the front subframe.

41 Unscrew the three bolts securing the front mounting to the engine/transmission, and remove it completely.

42 Unscrew the rear mounting's through-bolt, then remove the three further bolts securing the bracket to the transmission.

43 Support the transmission from below, using a jack and a flat piece of wood. Have an assistant ready to support the transmission as the jack is lowered.

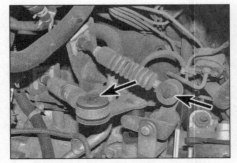

5.28a Gearchange cable split pins/ washers . . .

5.32 Left-hand mounting through-bolt

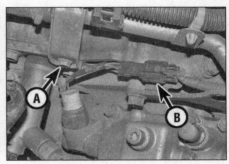

5.27 Coolant pipe bracket (A) and reversing light switch wiring plug (B)

> **HAYNES HiNT** *Paint or scribe an alignment mark across the transmission and engine faces. This is simply to make refitting easier – the transmission has two locating dowels, but an alignment mark will be helpful in eliminating guesswork when offering the unit into position.*

44 Unscrew the remaining transmission-to-engine bolts, then carefully pull the transmission away from the engine until the transmission shaft is clear of the clutch pressure plate.

45 Check round the transmission that everything has been disconnected from it, and that there is nothing in the way which might hinder its removal.

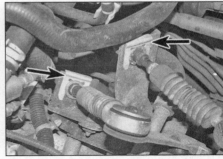

5.28b . . . and horse-shoe clips

5.39 Unscrew the front mounting through-bolt

46 With the help of an assistant to guide the unit out, lower the transmission on the jack until it can be removed from under the car. Recover the adapter plate, and also two dowel pins, noting their fitted locations, and store them for safe-keeping.

Refitting

47 If removed, fit the clutch components (see Chapter 6). It is recommended that the clutch components are at least inspected, if not renewed, while the transmission is removed.

48 Make sure the two locating dowels are installed in the transmission mating face. On diesel models, make sure the adapter plate is fitted between the engine and transmission.

49 Raise the transmission on the jack, then use the alignment marks made on dismantling to align it with the engine.

50 Make sure the transmission is at the right height, then slide it onto the engine so that the transmission shaft enters the clutch. It may be necessary to 'wiggle' the transmission slightly, to align the shaft splines with those of the clutch – if great difficulty is experienced when new clutch components have been fitted, it may mean that the clutch disc has not been centred (see Chapter 6). With the splines aligned, the transmission should slide onto the two dowels, and fully up to the engine.

51 While your assistant holds the transmission in place, insert two or three transmission-to-engine bolts initially, and tighten them fully by hand to hold the unit fully onto the dowels.

52 Further refitting is a reversal of removal, noting the following points:

a) *As far as possible, fit all engine/transmission mounting bolts hand-tight only at first. Delay fully tightening the engine/transmission mounting bolts until the weight of the engine is resting on its mountings.*

b) *Tighten all nuts/bolts to the specified torque.*

c) *Lightly grease the gearchange cable end fittings and slave cylinder pushrod end when refitting.*

d) *Honda state that new split pins and horse-shoe clips should be used when refitting the cables.*

e) *Refill the transmission with fluid as described in Chapter 1A or 1B.*

f) *Check the operation of the clutch, and bleed the system if necessary as described in Chapter 6.*

g) *As the front subframe was removed, have the front wheel alignment checked at the earliest opportunity.*

6 Transmission overhaul – general information

Overhauling a manual transmission is a difficult and involved job for the DIY home mechanic. In addition to dismantling and reassembling many small parts, clearances must be precisely measured and, if necessary, changed by selecting shims and spacers. Internal transmission components are also often difficult to obtain, and in many instances, extremely expensive. Because of this, if the transmission develops a fault or becomes noisy, the best course of action is to have the unit overhauled by a specialist repairer, or to obtain an exchange reconditioned unit.

Nevertheless, it is not impossible for the more experienced mechanic to overhaul the transmission, provided the special tools are available, and the job is done in a deliberate step-by-step manner, so that nothing is overlooked.

The tools necessary for an overhaul include internal and external circlip pliers, bearing pullers, a slide hammer, a set of pin punches, a dial test indicator, and possibly a hydraulic press. In addition, a large, sturdy workbench and a vice will be required.

During dismantling of the transmission, make careful notes of how each component is fitted, to make reassembly easier and more accurate.

Before dismantling the transmission, it will help if you have some idea what area is malfunctioning. Certain problems can be closely related to specific areas in the transmission, which can make component examination and renewal easier. Refer to the *Fault finding* Section of this manual for more information.

Chapter 7 Part B:
Automatic transmission

Contents

Degrees of difficulty

Easy, suitable for novice with little experience	Fairly easy, suitable for beginner with some experience	Fairly difficult, suitable for competent DIY mechanic	Difficult, suitable for experienced DIY mechanic	Very difficult, suitable for expert DIY or professional

Specifications

General

Type	Automatic transmission, 4 forward speeds, 1 reverse, electronic control by powertrain control module (PCM), torque converter lockup in two top gears
Transmission code/designation	SLXA

Gear ratios (typical)

1st	2.722
2nd	1.468
3rd	0.975
4th	0.674
Reverse	1.955
Final drive	4.357

Torque wrench settings

	Nm	lbf ft
Driveplate-to-torque converter bolts	12	9
Driveplate/torque converter cover plate bolts	12	9
Engine-to-transmission bolts	64	47
Engine/transmission mountings:		
Front mounting:		
Bracket-to-engine bolts:		
M10 bolt	54	40
M12 bolts	64	47
Through-bolt*	64	47
Left-hand mounting:		
Side bracket-to-engine bolts	44	32
Upper bracket nuts	54	40
Rear mounting:		
Bracket-to-mounting through-bolt	64	47
Bracket-to-transmission bolts	64	47
Mounting-to-subframe bolts	59	44
Right-hand mounting:		
Mounting-to-transmission nuts, bolt and through-bolt	54	40
Front subframe bolts:		
M10 bolts	59	44
M14 bolts	103	76
Roadwheel nuts	108	80
Selector cable lockbolt	14	10
Selector lever mounting bolts	22	16
Starter motor bolts	44	32
Transmission-to-sump stiffener bracket bolts:		
M8 bolts	24	18
M10 bolts	44	32

Use new bolt

1 General information

The automatic transmission fitted to the Civic has four forward speeds (and one reverse). The automatic gearchanges are controlled electronically, including the kickdown function, which allows a lower gear to be selected when full acceleration is required. The transmission's powertrain control module (PCM) employs 'fuzzy logic' to determine the gear up-shift and down-shift points. Instead of these being preset to different vehicle speeds, the PCM takes into account several influencing factors before deciding to shift up or down. These factors include engine and vehicle speed, engine load, brake pedal position, throttle position, and the rate at which the throttle pedal position is changed. This results in an almost infinite number of shift points, which the PCM can tailor to match the driving style, from sporting to economical. The PCM on automatic transmission models is, however, all but identical to the ECM used on other petrol engine models, and differs only in its transmission control functions.

The automatic transmission consists of three main assemblies, these being the torque converter, which is directly coupled to the engine; the final drive unit, which incorporates the differential unit; and the planetary gearbox, with its multi-disc clutches and brake bands. The transmission is lubricated with automatic transmission fluid (ATF), which should be changed at regular intervals as described in Chapter 1A.

The torque converter incorporates a lock-up feature, which eliminates any possibility of converter slip in the top two gears, to the benefit of performance and economy.

The selector lever features both D and D3 positions, with the latter offering automatic shifting using only the first three gears. When driving in D with the engine cold, the transmission may delay up-shifts to help the engine warm up more quickly.

A safety interlock system is fitted, which requires that the transmission is placed in P before leaving the car – the system prevents the ignition key being removed until P is selected. On next entering the car, the transmission cannot be shifted out of P unless the brake pedal is pressed (the accelerator pedal must be completely released), and the ignition switch is in positions II or III. Similarly, a reverse interlock prevents R being selected at speeds above 9 mph. An emergency override procedure is provided in the car's handbook.

Because of the need for special test equipment, the complexity of some of the parts, and the need for scrupulous cleanliness when servicing the transmission, the amount which the owner can do is limited. Repairs to the final drive differential are also not recommended. Most major repairs and overhaul operations should be left to a Honda dealer or specialist, who will have the necessary equipment for fault diagnosis and repair. The information in this Chapter is therefore limited to removal and refitting of the transmission as a complete unit.

In the event of a transmission problem occurring, consult a Honda dealer or transmission specialist before removing the transmission from the car, since the majority of fault diagnosis is carried out with the transmission *in situ*.

2 Fault finding – general

Note: *Automatic transmission malfunctions may be caused by five general conditions: poor engine performance, improper adjustments, hydraulic malfunctions, mechanical malfunctions or malfunctions in the computer or its signal network. Diagnosis of these problems should always begin with a check of the easily-repaired items: fluid level and condition (see Chapter 1A), and selector cable adjustment (Section 3). Next, perform a road test to determine if the problem has been corrected or if more diagnosis is necessary. If the problem persists after the preliminary tests and corrections are completed, additional diagnosis should be done by a dealer service department or transmission specialist.*

Preliminary checks

1 Drive the car to warm the transmission to normal operating temperature.
2 Check the fluid level as described in Chapter 1A:
  a) *If the fluid level is unusually low, add enough fluid to bring the level within the designated area of the dipstick, then check for external leaks (see below).*
  b) *If the fluid level is abnormally high, drain off the excess, then check the drained fluid for contamination by coolant. The presence of engine coolant in the automatic transmission fluid indicates that a failure has occurred in the internal radiator walls that separate the coolant from the transmission fluid.*
  c) *If the fluid is foaming, drain it and refill the transmission, then check for coolant in the fluid, or a high fluid level.*
3 Check the engine idle speed. **Note:** *If the engine is malfunctioning, do not proceed with the preliminary checks until it has been repaired and runs normally.*
4 Inspect the selector cable linkage (see Section 3). Make sure that it's properly adjusted and that the linkage operates smoothly.

Fluid leak diagnosis

5 Most fluid leaks are easy to locate visually. Repair usually consists of renewing a seal or gasket. If a leak is difficult to find, the following procedure may help.

6 Identify the fluid. Make sure it's transmission fluid and not engine oil or brake fluid (automatic transmission fluid is typically a deep red colour).
7 Try to pinpoint the source of the leak. Drive the car several miles, then park it over a large sheet of cardboard. After a minute or two, you should be able to locate the leak by determining the source of the fluid dripping onto the cardboard.
8 Make a careful visual inspection of the suspected component and the area immediately around it. Pay particular attention to gasket mating surfaces. A mirror is often helpful for finding leaks in areas that are hard to see.
9 If the leak still cannot be found, clean the suspected area thoroughly with a degreaser, then dry it.
10 Drive the car for several miles at normal operating temperature and varying speeds. After driving the car, visually inspect the suspected component again.
11 Once the leak has been located, the cause must be determined before it can be properly repaired. If a gasket is renewed but the sealing flange is bent, the new gasket will not stop the leak. The bent flange must be straightened.
12 Before attempting to repair a leak, check to make sure that the following conditions are corrected or they may cause another leak. **Note:** *Some of the following conditions cannot be fixed without highly specialised tools and expertise. Such problems must be referred to a transmission specialist or a dealer service department.*

Gasket leaks

13 Check the right-hand side cover periodically. Make sure the bolts are tight, no bolts are missing, the gasket is in good condition and the cover is not damaged.
14 If the leak is from the right-hand side cover area, the bolts may be too tight, the sealing surface of the transmission housing may be damaged, the gasket may be damaged or the transmission casting may be cracked or porous. If sealant instead of gasket material has been used to form a seal between the cover and the transmission housing, it may be the wrong sealant.

Seal leaks

15 If a transmission seal is leaking, the fluid level or pressure may be too high, the vent may be blocked, the seal bore may be damaged, the seal itself may be damaged or improperly installed, the surface of the shaft protruding through the seal may be damaged or a loose bearing may be causing excessive shaft movement.
16 Make sure the dipstick tube seal is in good condition and the tube is properly seated. Periodically check the area around the vehicle speed sensor for leakage. If transmission fluid is evident, check the O-ring for damage.

Housing leaks

17 If the housing itself appears to be leaking,

the casting is porous and will have to be repaired or renewed.

18 Make sure the fluid cooler hose fittings are tight and in good condition.

Fluid comes out vent pipe or filler tube

19 If this condition occurs, the transmission is overfilled, there is coolant in the fluid, the housing is porous, the dipstick is incorrect, the vent is blocked or the drain-back holes are blocked.

Fault diagnosis

20 Should a fault be recognised by the PCM, a fault code will be generated and stored in the module's memory, and the D warning light on the instrument panel's transmission display will flash.

21 First ensure that all the system wiring connectors are securely connected and free of corrosion.

22 If these checks fail to reveal the cause of the problem, the car should be taken to a suitably-equipped Honda dealer for testing. A diagnostic connector is incorporated in the wiring harness, into which dedicated electronic test equipment can be plugged – the connector is located under the steering column. The test equipment is capable of 'interrogating' the PCM electronically and accessing its internal fault log (reading fault codes).

23 Fault codes can only be extracted from the PCM using a dedicated fault code reader. A Honda dealer will obviously have such a reader, but they are also available from other suppliers. It is unlikely to be cost-effective for the private owner to purchase a fault code reader, but a well-equipped local garage or auto-electrical specialist will have one.

24 Using this equipment, faults can be pinpointed quickly and simply, even if their occurrence is intermittent. Testing all the system components individually in an attempt to locate the fault by elimination is a time-consuming operation that is unlikely to be fruitful (particularly if the fault occurs dynamically), and carries a high risk of damage to the PCM's internal components.

Clearing fault codes

25 Once the fault has been identified and the problem corrected (usually by fitting a new component), the fault code must be cleared. In some cases, this will happen automatically once the ignition has been switched on and off enough times – if the fault does not recur, it may clear itself.

26 To clear fault codes manually requires the use of a fault code reader tool as described at the start of this Section. However, codes may also be cleared by the DIY mechanic, as follows.

27 With the ignition off, remove fuse No 6 from the engine compartment fusebox for at least 10 seconds, then refit it. Switch the ignition on, and the fault should have cleared.

28 If the engine management light remains on (or comes back on later), either the same fault still exists, or there is another faulty component triggering a different fault code. Check that any new components have been correctly fitted, and especially that their wiring plugs are clean and secure.

| 3 | Selector cable –
renewal and adjustment | |

Renewal

1 Remove the selector lever surround

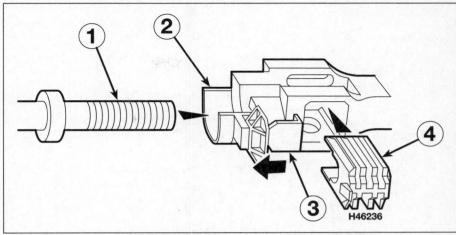

3.3 Disconnecting the selector cable end fitting

| 1 Cable end fitting | 2 Cable end holder | 3 Plastic locktab | 4 Locking clip |

panel, facia lower centre section (and where applicable, the centre console) as described in Chapter 11.

2 Move the selector lever to the R position.

3 Slide down the plastic locktab on the selector cable end holder. Pull out the ribbed horseshoe-shaped locking clip from the cable end holder **(see illustration)**.

4 Move the selector lever to the N position, then unhook the cable end fitting from the end holder.

5 Further down the cable, twist the moulded fitting anti-clockwise so that the projecting tab is at the front, then slide it forwards out of the selector cable mounting bracket **(see illustration)**.

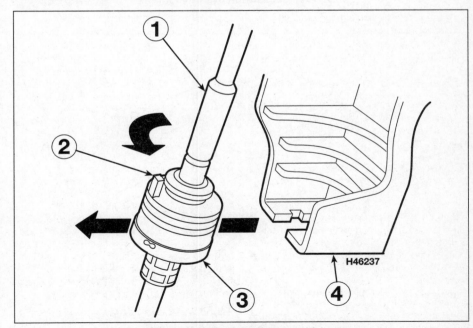

3.5 Disconnecting the selector cable outer

| 1 Cable guide – do not twist here | 3 Moulded fitting – twist here |
| 2 Projecting tab | 4 Cable mounting bracket |

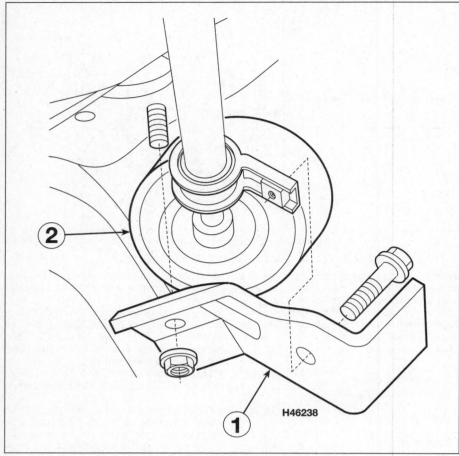

3.6 Selector cable removal at floor level

1 Cable guide bracket   2 Cable grommet

6 Just above the floor, remove the nut and bolt, and take off the selector cable guide bracket **(see illustration)**.

7 Raise the front of the car and support it securely on axle stands (see *Jacking and vehicle support*). Remove the engine undertray.

8 Unclip the selector cable grommet from the floor – note that it may be necessary to unbolt and remove one or more of the exhaust heat shields to gain access.

9 Trace the cable through to the front of the car, freeing it from any clips or ties, and noting how it is routed.

10 Unbolt and remove the two covers fitted over the transmission end of the cable, then unbolt the cable support plate **(see illustration)**.

11 Bend back the lockwasher tabs, then unscrew the lockbolt from the base of the transmission selector lever (recover the lockwasher). Remove the cable and the lever, sliding it from the transmission control shaft – take care not to bend the cable more than necessary.

12 Refitting is a reversal of removal, noting the following points:

a) *Refit the cable at the transmission end, starting with the transmission selector lever in the R position.*

b) *Use a new lockwasher on the transmission selector lever, tighten the lockbolt to the specified torque, then bend over the lockwasher tabs to secure it.*

c) *Once the cable is fully refitted at the transmission end, refit the covers, and feed the cable back into the car.*

d) *Adjust the cable as described later in this Section.*

Adjustment

13 If not already done, proceed as described in paragraphs 1 to 5.

14 Switch on the ignition and check that the instrument panel is displaying R selected. If this is not the case, push the cable downwards, then pull it back into the car one 'click' until R is displayed. Turn off the ignition.

15 Offer the cable's moulded fitting into the cable mounting bracket, with the projecting tab at the front. When the cable is slotted in correctly, twist the moulded fitting a quarter-turn clockwise to secure it.

16 Move the selector lever to the N position, slot the cable end fitting into the end holder, then move the selector lever to the R position.

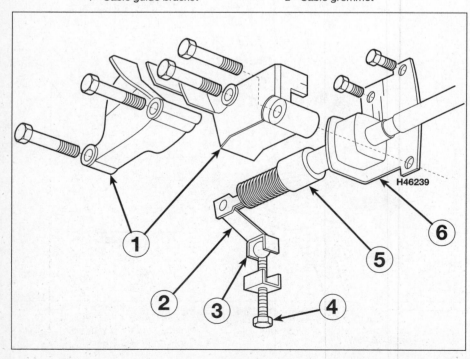

3.10 Selector cable removal at transmission

1 Cable covers
2 Transmission selector lever
3 Lockwasher
4 Lockbolt
5 Selector cable
6 Cable support plate

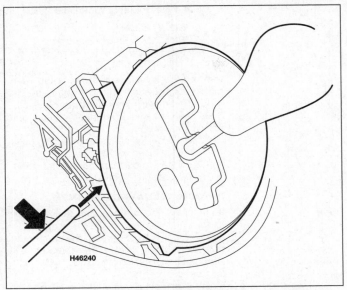

3.17 Insert a 6.0 mm drill bit into the selector housing hole

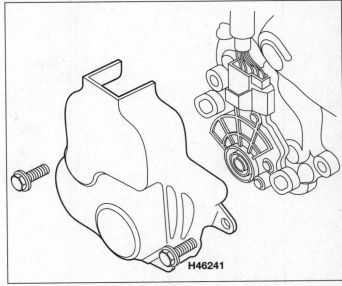

4.3 Transmission range switch and cover

17 Insert a 6.0 mm pin (such as a drill bit) into the hole on the left-hand side at the base of the selector lever housing, to lock the selector lever in the R position **(see illustration)**.

18 Refit the horseshoe-shaped locking clip into the cable end holder, then push up the plastic locktab to secure it.

19 Remove the 6.0 mm pin or drill bit from the selector lever housing, then switch on the ignition and check that the instrument panel display follows the selected gear.

20 On completion, refit all removed components, then take the car for a road test.

4 Transmission range switch – renewal and adjustment

Renewal

1 Raise the front of the car and support it securely on axle stands (see *Jacking and vehicle support*). Remove the engine undertray.

2 Move the selector lever to the N position.

3 On the right-hand end of the transmission, remove the two bolts and take off the cover from the transmission range switch **(see illustration)**.

4 Disconnect the wiring plug on top of the switch, then unscrew the two mounting bolts and slide the switch off its shaft.

5 Before refitting the switch, ensure that the shaft on the transmission is in the N position – this should be the case if the selector lever inside the car is also in the N position.

6 The switch has to be 'aligned with itself' before fitting – the centre part (which turns) has to align with the switch body. Using a 2.0 mm thick feeler blade across the face of the switch, align the two slots in the centre of the switch with the slot on the edge of the

switch body, just below the wiring plug socket **(see illustration)**.

7 Keeping the switch aligned in this position, offer it carefully onto the transmission shaft.

8 With the feeler blade still holding the switch aligned, tighten the two switch mounting bolts securely.

9 Reconnect the wiring plug, then refit the switch cover, and secure with the two bolts. Refit the engine undertray, then lower the car to the ground.

10 Turn the ignition on, then move the selector lever through all positions, and check that the instrument panel display follows the selected gear.

11 Check that the engine can only be started in positions P or N, and that the reversing lights come on when R is selected.

Adjustment

12 To adjust the switch, follow the renewal

procedure, with the exception that the switch does not have to be removed – for adjustment only, the switch mounting bolts need only be loosened.

5 Selector lever and related components – removal and refitting

Selector lever

1 Proceed as described in Section 3, paragraphs 1 to 5 inclusive.

2 Remove the metal bracket fitted in front of the lever base, which is secured by two screws.

3 Also at the front of the lever base, disconnect the shift lock solenoid wiring plug.

4 Unscrew the four lever mounting bolts, then, taking care not to scratch any surrounding

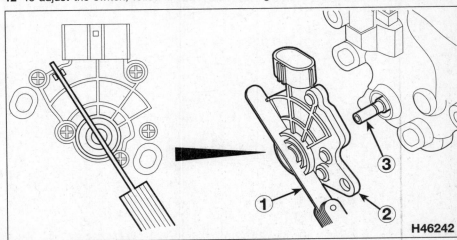

4.6 Align switch centre with tab on switch body, and refit

1 2.0 mm feeler blade   *2 Transmission range switch*   *3 Transmission shaft*

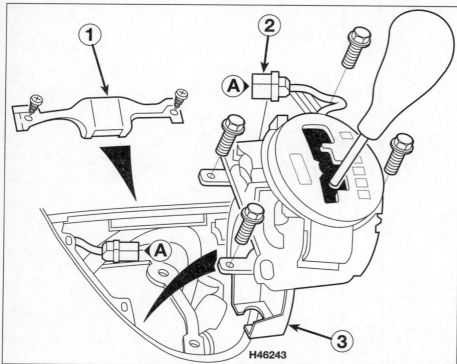

H46243

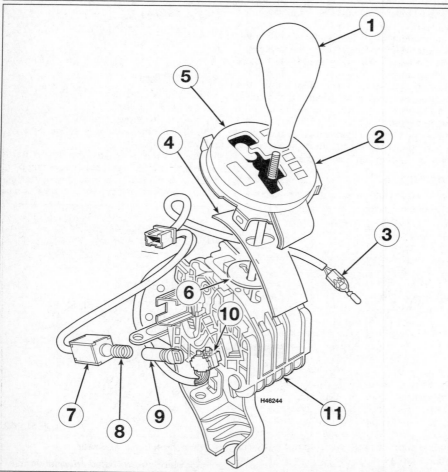

H46244

5.4 Selector lever removal details

1 Metal bracket
2 Shift lock solenoid wiring plug
3 Selector cable mounting bracket

trim, lift the lever assembly past the wiring harnesses, twisting it anti-clockwise a quarter-turn, and remove it **(see illustration)**.

5 Refitting is a reversal of removal, noting the following points:

a) Tighten the selector lever mounting bolts to the specified torque.

b) Reconnect and adjust the selector cable as described in Section 3.

Selector illumination bulb

6 Unscrew and remove the selector lever knob.

7 Taking care not to scratch the surrounding trim, carefully prise up the selector lever surround panel, which is secured by four clips (one at each 'corner').

8 The illumination bulbholder is clipped into the underside of the lever surround panel **(see illustration)**. Pull out the bulbholder, then withdraw the wedge-base bulb.

9 Fit the new bulb, then clip the bulbholder back into place.

10 Refit the selector lever surround panel, ensuring that it is fully seated all round.

11 Screw the selector lever knob fully back on to complete.

Selector D3 switch

12 Remove the selector lever assembly as described previously in this Section.

13 The D3 switch is clipped into the left-hand side of the selector lever assembly. However, the switch is part of the selector lever wiring harness, which means that all the related electrical components on the lever must be removed with it.

14 Unclip the selector illumination bulbholder from the surround panel, and the D3 switch from the left-hand side of the lever, then remove the shift lock solenoid as described in Section 6. Release the wiring harness from any clips or ties, noting how it is arranged, and remove all three components together.

15 It appears at the time of writing that the D3 switch is only available with the shift lock solenoid and selector illumination bulbholder, as it shares a common wiring harness and wiring connector plug with these components.

5.8 Selector lever and related components

1 Knob
2 Surround panel
3 Illumination bulb
4 Lever cover
5 Gear indicator window
6 Gear indicator slider cover
7 Shift lock solenoid
8 Solenoid plunger spring
9 Solenoid plunger
10 D3 switch
11 Selector lever housing

If a new (or secondhand) D3 switch can be obtained separately, it will be necessary to splice the switch wires into the existing ones – ensure that good soldered connections are made, and that the wires are properly insulated afterwards.

16 Refitting is a reversal of removal.

6 Interlock system – component renewal

1 The main components of the interlock system are as follows:

a) *The powertrain control module (PCM) – see Chapter 4A, where this component is referred to as the ECM. Through its control of the ignition system, it is able to prevent the engine being started when this is inappropriate. The information it receives from the vehicle speed sensor enables it to control the reverse gear interlock, and it also receives a signal from the brake pedal position switch for the Park interlock system.*

b) *The brake pedal position switch – see Chapter 4A. This informs the PCM when the brake pedal is being pressed, for the Park interlock system.*

c) *The ignition switch/steering lock assembly – see Chapter 10. This contains the ignition key interlock and solenoid, which prevents the key being removed, and which only allows the selector lever to be moved out of P in switch positions II and III.*

d) *The shift lock solenoid – see later in this Section. Fitted to the selector lever assembly, this is what physically prevents the lever being moved into or out of positions P and R.*

Shift lock solenoid

2 Remove the selector lever assembly as described in Section 5.

3 The solenoid is fitted to the left-hand side of the selector lever assembly. However, the solenoid is part of the selector lever wiring harness, which means that all the related electrical components on the lever must be removed with it.

4 Unclip the selector illumination bulbholder from the surround panel, and the D3 switch from the left-hand side of the lever.

5 Lift up the locktab on the left-hand side of the lever, then slide the solenoid out sideways, noting how the plunger end fits over the lock operating lever pin (see illustration).

6 Release the wiring harness from any clips or ties, noting how it is arranged, and remove the solenoid with the bulbholder and D3 switch.

7 It appears at the time of writing that the solenoid is only available with the D3 switch and selector illumination bulbholder, as it shares a common wiring harness and wiring connector plug with these components. If a new (or secondhand) solenoid can be obtained separately, it will be necessary to splice the

solenoid wires into the existing ones – ensure that good soldered connections are made, and that the wires are properly insulated afterwards.

8 Refitting is a reversal of removal. Ensure that the solenoid plunger end engages correctly with the lock operating lever pin.

7 Powertrain control module (PCM) – removal and refitting

The procedure is identical to that for the engine control module (ECM), described in Chapter 4A, Section 11.

8 Automatic transmission – removal and refitting

Removal

1 Remove the battery and its tray as described in Chapter 5A.

2 Remove the inlet air resonator and inlet air duct as described in Chapter 4A.

3 Loosen the front wheel nuts, and if possible, also loosen both driveshaft nuts while the car is still on the ground. Jack up the front of the car, and support it on axle stands (see *Jacking and vehicle support*). Note that the car must be raised sufficiently high for the transmission to be lowered out and withdrawn from underneath. Remove the front wheels and the engine undertray.

4 Drain the transmission fluid as described in Chapter 1A.

5 Disconnect the starter motor wiring – the motor does not have to be removed (unless a new transmission is being fitted, in which case the motor must be transferred over).

6 Remove the earth strap bolt on top of the transmission, and move the strap clear.

7 Work methodically round the transmission, and disconnect approximately ten wiring plugs, labelling each one to ensure correct refitting. These plugs are for the various transmission control solenoids, vehicle speed sensor, transmission range switch, and the two oxygen sensors. Unclip the wiring harness from the transmission as the plugs are disconnected, noting how the harness is routed.

8 Remove the exhaust front pipe as described in Chapter 4A.

9 At the front of the transmission, release the hose clips and disconnect the fluid hoses from the pipes. Anticipate some fluid spillage as this is done – keep the hose ends turned upwards to reduce this, and either plug or tape over the open connections.

10 Support the transmission end of the engine. Preferably, this should be done from above, either with an engine hoist/crane or an engine support bar – supporting from below will be awkward, as the front subframe must be removed later.

11 Unscrew the nut and withdraw the through-bolt from the engine front mounting. Unscrew the two bolts securing the front mounting to the engine/transmission, and remove it completely.

12 Remove the driveshafts as described in Chapter 8.

13 Unbolt and remove the stiffener plates fitted between the engine sump and transmission. Also unbolt and remove the semi-circular torque converter cover.

14 With the torque converter cover removed, unscrew and remove the eight torque converter bolts, turning the engine using a socket on the crankshaft pulley bolt to bring each of the bolts into view.

15 Unscrew and remove the three lower bolts from the transmission rear mounting.

16 Referring to Chapter 10 if necessary, remove the front subframe.

17 Remove the four bolts securing the rear mounting bracket to the transmission, and withdraw it from under the car.

18 Remove the four uppermost transmission-to-engine bolts at the front.

19 Ensuring the engine is securely supported, unscrew the two upper nuts, and then the through-bolt, from the engine/transmission right-hand mounting.

20 Support the transmission from below, using a jack and a flat piece of wood. Have an assistant ready to support the transmission as the jack is lowered.

> **HAYNES HINT** *Paint or scribe an alignment mark across the transmission and engine faces. This is simply to make refitting easier – the transmission has two locating dowels, but an alignment mark will be helpful in eliminating guesswork when offering the unit into position.*

21 Unscrew the remaining transmission-to-engine bolts, then carefully pull the transmission away from the engine until the transmission is clear of the locating dowels. If necessary, push the torque converter back into the transmission – take care that it does not fall out as the transmission is lowered.

22 Check round the transmission that

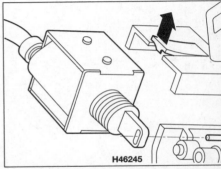

6.5 Shift lock solenoid removal details

everything has been disconnected from it, and that there is nothing in the way which might hinder its removal.

23 With the help of an assistant to guide the unit out, lower the transmission on the jack until it can be removed from under the car. Recover the two dowel pins, noting their fitted locations, and store them for safekeeping. Either remove the torque converter, or devise a method of keeping it inside the housing (such as bolting a metal strip across its face, secured through the transmission mounting bolt holes).

Refitting

24 If the torque converter was removed, refit it using a new O-ring seal. Have an assistant ready to keep the converter pressed into the housing as the transmission is refitted.

25 If a new transmission is being fitted, unbolt the starter motor from the old one, and fit it to the new unit.

26 Make sure the two locating dowels are installed in the transmission mating face.

27 Raise the transmission on the jack, then use the alignment marks made on dismantling to align it with the engine.

28 Make sure the transmission is at the right height, then slide it onto the two dowels, and fully up to the engine.

29 While your assistant holds the transmission in place, insert two or three transmission-to-engine bolts initially, and tighten them fully by hand to hold the unit fully onto the dowels.

30 Further refitting is a reversal of removal, noting the following points:

a) *As far as possible, fit all engine/ transmission mounting bolts hand-tight only at first. Delay fully tightening the engine/transmission mounting bolts until the weight of the engine is resting on its mountings.*

b) *Tighten all nuts/bolts to the specified torque.*

c) *Refer to Section 3 when reconnecting the selector cable at the transmission end, and adjust the cable if necessary.*

d) *Refill the transmission with fluid as described in Chapter 1A. Note that the transmission may require more fluid than in a normal fluid and filter change, since the torque converter may be empty (the converter is not drained during a fluid change).*

e) *On completion, start the engine. Allow the engine to reach its proper operating temperature with the transmission in P or N, then switch it off and check the fluid level. Road test the car and check for fluid leaks.*

f) *As the front subframe was removed, have the front wheel alignment checked at the earliest opportunity.*

Chapter 8
Driveshafts

Contents

Degrees of difficulty

Easy, suitable for novice with little experience	**Fairly easy,** suitable for beginner with some experience	**Fairly difficult,** suitable for competent DIY mechanic	**Difficult,** suitable for experienced DIY mechanic	**Very difficult,** suitable for expert DIY or professional

Specifications

General

Driveshaft type . . . . Unequal-length, solid shaft, ball-and-cage outer CV joint, tripod inner joint, dynamic damper fitted to longer driveshaft

Driveshaft 'length' (from the outer ends of the CV joints):
   Petrol models:
      Left driveshaft:
         Manual transmission models . . . . 788 to 793 mm
         Automatic transmission models . . . . 792 to 797 mm
      Right driveshaft . . . . 502 to 507 mm
   Diesel models:
      Left driveshaft . . . . 495 to 500 mm
      Right driveshaft . . . . 790 to 795 mm
Dynamic damper fitted position (from outer end of outer CV joint):
   Longer driveshaft . . . . 478 to 482 mm
   Shorter driveshaft . . . . 262 to 267 mm

Torque wrench settings

	Nm	lbf ft
Anti-roll bar drop link nut*	39	29
Bottom balljoint nut:		
Stage 1 (or minimum setting)	49	36
Stage 2 (or maximum setting)	59	44
Driveshaft hub nut*	181	134
Roadwheel nuts	108	80

* Use a new nut

---

1 General information

Drive is transmitted from the differential to the front wheels by means of two steel driveshafts of solid construction. Both driveshafts are splined at their outer ends, to accept the wheel hubs, and are secured to the hub by a large nut. The inner end of each driveshaft is a push fit, secured by a circlip.

Constant velocity (CV) joints are fitted to each end of the driveshafts, to ensure the smooth and efficient transmission of drive at all the angles possible as the roadwheels move up-and-down with the suspension, and as they turn from side-to-side under steering. On all models, the outer joint is of the ball-and-cage type, but the inner joint is of the tripod type.

Rubber or plastic gaiters are secured over both CV joints with steel clips. The gaiters contain the grease which lubricates the joints, and also protect the joints from the entry of dirt and debris.

2 Driveshafts – removal and refitting

Removal

1 The driveshaft nut is tightened to an extremely high torque, and for this reason, it is preferable if possible to loosen the nut with the wheel on the ground. However, on Civics with steel wheels, the wheel nuts are used to secure the wheel trim, which covers the driveshaft nut.

2.3 Slacken the driveshaft nut with a long breaker bar

2.9 Prise down the lower arm, and separate the balljoint

2.12 Swing the hub assembly out and pull the driveshaft from the hub

This means loosening the wheel nuts, jacking up the car, taking off the wheel nuts and wheel trim, then refitting the wheel and nuts before lowering the car to undo the driveshaft nut.

2 The driveshaft nut has a locking tab (or a raised collar) which is punched into the driveshaft groove to stop the nut loosening accidentally. Using a sturdy flat-bladed screwdriver, or preferably a punch or chisel, bend the tab/collar back so the nut can be unscrewed.

3 Significant force will be required to loosen the nut, so be sure to use only good-quality, close-fitting tools. A long-handled 'breaker bar' will be needed, to provide the necessary leverage – if this is not available, slip a strong piece of metal pipe over the end of the socket handle **(see illustration)**. Wear gloves to protect your hands, should something slip.

4 Chock the front wheel, and have an assistant apply the footbrake firmly, while

you slacken the nut. It is not necessary at this stage to remove the nut completely.

5 If the nut has to be loosened with the car raised, ensure that it is very well supported, using well-placed, good-quality axle stands (see *Jacking and vehicle support*). Have an assistant firmly depress the brake pedal to prevent the disc from turning, whilst you slacken and remove the driveshaft retaining nut. Alternatively, a tool can be fabricated from two lengths of steel strip (one long, one short) and a nut and bolt; the nut and bolt forming the pivot of a forked tool which fits over the wheel studs.

6 Once the nut has been loosened, (if not already done) jack up the front of the car and support it on axle stands (see *Jacking and vehicle support*). Remove the front wheel.

7 Drain the transmission fluid as described in Chapter 1A or 1B. If this is not done, be prepared for significant fluid spillage when the driveshafts are removed.

8 Unscrew the nut securing the anti-roll bar drop link to the suspension lower arm – use an Allen key to stop the drop link balljoint turning as this is done. Unhook the drop link from the lower arm. Discard the nut – a new one should be used when refitting.

9 Extract the locking pin (note which way round it is fitted), then unscrew the bottom balljoint nut. Using a balljoint separator tool (or a suitable lever to prise down the arm) disconnect the lower arm from the swivel hub **(see illustration)**. Note that a new locking pin will be needed for refitting.

10 The splined end of the driveshaft now has to be released from its location in the hub. It's likely that the splines will be very tight (corrosion may even be a factor, if the driveshaft has not been disturbed for some time), and considerable force may be needed. Tap the end of the shaft with a plastic or hide mallet only – if an ordinary hammer is used, place a small piece of wood over the end of the driveshaft – and leave the old nut loosely in place on the end to avoid damaging the splines.

11 Once the splines have been released, remove the driveshaft nut and discard it – the nut is only intended to be used once.

12 Pull the disc/hub outwards, and turn it to allow the driveshaft to be withdrawn through the hub. It's helpful to have an assistant on hand here, to pull the hub outwards, while you slide out the driveshaft **(see illustration)**.

13 Carefully lever the inner end of the driveshaft from the transmission, using a large screwdriver or lever bar positioned between the transmission and the CV joint housing. The inner end of the shaft is secured with a circlip, which must be released – do not pull on the shaft, as the inner joint may separate. Support the CV joints and carefully remove the driveshaft from the car. To prevent damage to the driveshaft oil seal, hold the inner CV joint horizontal until the driveshaft is clear of the transmission **(see illustrations)**.

14 Lever the old circlip from the inner end of the driveshaft, and fit a new one **(see illustrations)**.

Refitting

15 Lubricate the differential with multi-purpose grease, and raise the driveshaft into position while supporting the CV joints.

16 Insert the splined end of the inner CV joint

2.13a Lever the inner end of the driveshaft out of the transmission

2.13b Keep the driveshaft horizontal as it is removed – do not bend the joints

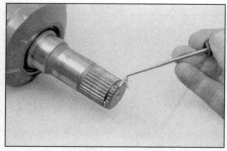

2.14a Prise the old circlip from the inner end of the driveshaft with a small screwdriver

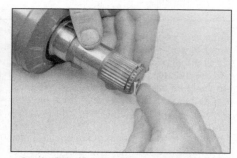

2.14b Start one end of the circlip in the groove, then work it over the end of the shaft

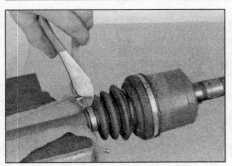

3.3a Cut off the gaiter clamps and discard them

3.3b Slide the gaiter towards the centre of the driveshaft

3.10 Slide the inner gaiter onto the driveshaft

into the differential side gear, and make sure the circlip locks in its groove. Grasp the inner CV joint housing (not the driveshaft) and pull out to make sure the driveshaft has seated securely in the transmission.

17 Apply a light coat of multi-purpose grease to the outer CV joint splines, then pull the strut/swivel hub outwards and refit the driveshaft into the hub – it may be necessary to turn the shaft to align the splines. Lightly oil the new hub nut, then screw it on hand-tight only at this stage.

18 Clean the balljoint and its seat in the lower arm before fitting – it must be fitted dry.

19 Lever the lower arm downwards, then hook the outer end over the swivel hub balljoint stud. Refit the bottom balljoint nut, and tighten it initially to the Stage 1 (minimum) setting. From this point, tighten the nut as required to align the locking pin holes (do not loosen to align), then fit a new pin to secure.

20 Reconnect the anti-roll bar drop link to the lower arm, and fit a new nut. Tighten the nut to the specified torque, holding the drop link balljoint with an Allen key as for removal.

21 Refit the roadwheel and nuts, then lower the car to the ground.

22 Chock the wheel, and have an assistant apply the footbrake. Tighten the driveshaft hub nut to the specified torque. Using a hammer and punch, stake the nut to the groove in the driveshaft. If the hub nut uses a locking tab, be sure to bend the tabs against the nut.

23 Refill the transmission with the recommended type and amount of lubricant (see Chapter 1A or 1B).

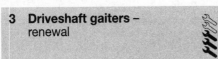

3 Driveshaft gaiters – renewal

1 Remove the driveshaft from the car (see Section 2).

2 Mount the driveshaft in a vice. The jaws of the vice should be lined with wood or rags to prevent damage to the driveshaft.

Inner CV joint and gaiter

Dismantling

3 If you have any doubts about the condition of the outer gaiter, this would be a good time

to renew it as well. Cut off both gaiter clamps, and slide the gaiter towards the centre of the driveshaft **(see illustrations)**.

4 Scribe or paint alignment marks on the outer race and the tripod bearing assembly so they can be returned to their original position, then slide the outer race off the tripod bearing assembly.

5 Remove the circlip from the end of the driveshaft.

6 Secure the bearing rollers with tape, then remove the tripod bearing assembly from the driveshaft with a brass drift and a hammer. Remove the tape, but don't let the rollers fall off and get mixed up.

7 Remove the stop ring (if equipped), slide the old gaiter off the driveshaft and discard it.

Inspection

8 Clean the old grease from the outer race and the tripod bearing assembly. Carefully dismantle each section of the tripod assembly,

3.11a Slide the tripod onto the shaft . . .

3.12 Fit the outer circlip

one at a time so as not to mix up the parts, and clean the needle bearings with degreaser.

9 Inspect the rollers, tripod, bearings and outer race for scoring, pitting or other signs of abnormal wear, which will warrant the renewal of the inner CV joint.

Reassembly

10 Wrap the splines of the driveshaft with tape to avoid damaging the new gaiter, then slide the gaiter onto the driveshaft. Remove the tape and slide the inner stop ring (if equipped) into place **(see illustration)**.

11 Slide the tripod assembly onto the driveshaft, and tap it home with a soft-faced mallet **(see illustrations)**.

12 Fit the outer circlip **(see illustration)**.

13 Apply a little CV joint grease to the inner bearing surfaces to hold the needle bearings in place when reassembling the tripod assembly **(see illustration)**. Make sure each roller is refitted on the same post as before.

3.11b . . . and tap it home on the splines

3.13 Use grease to hold the roller's needle bearings in place during fitting

3.14a Fill the outer race with half the supplied grease . . .

3.14b . . . then fit the shaft into the outer race

3.15 Fit the gaiter into its grooves, then lift the edge to equalise pressure

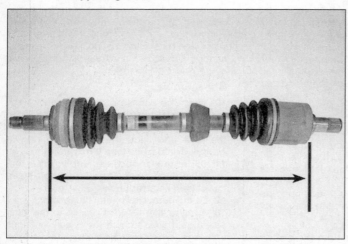

3.16a Adjust the driveshaft length to that specified before tightening the gaiter clips

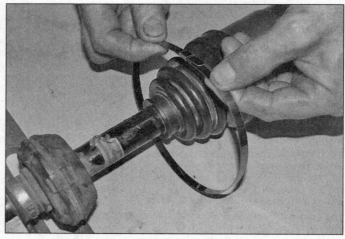

3.16b Fit the clip, and thread the end through the loop . . .

3.16c . . . then pull tight using pliers and a screwdriver as shown . . .

3.16d . . . fold over the end . . .

Note: *If the rollers are equipped with a flat, rectangular-shaped surface, make sure the flat sides are positioned closest to the driveshaft.*

14 Pack the outer race with half of the grease supplied with the new gaiter, and place the remainder in the gaiter. Refit the outer race – we found it easier to fit the outer race in a vice, and offer in the shaft **(see illustrations)**. Make sure the marks you made on the tripod assembly and the outer race are aligned.

15 Seat the gaiter in the grooves in the outer race and the driveshaft, then lift the gaiter edges to release any trapped air **(see illustration)**.

16 Fit and tighten the new gaiter clamps **(see illustrations)**.

3.16e . . . and flatten down to secure

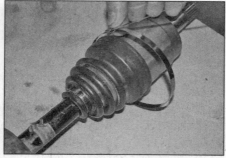

3.16f Repeat the process on the larger clip

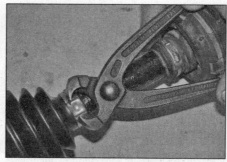

3.16g Some clips need special crimping pliers, but side-cutters can be used with care

17 Refit the driveshaft assembly (see Section 2).

Outer CV joint and gaiter

Dismantling

18 Cut the gaiter clamps from the outer CV joint. Slide the gaiter back down the shaft.

19 The outer joint is secured on the shaft by a small circlip at the outer end. Mount the shaft in a vice, then, using a soft-headed mallet (or a hammer and block of wood), tap the outer joint off the shaft. Remove the old gaiter.

20 If the driveshaft is equipped with a dynamic damper, it should not need to be removed for this operation. However, if the shaft is being stripped, scribe or paint a location mark on the driveshaft along the outer edge of the damper (the side facing the outer CV joint), cut the retaining clamp and slide the damper off.

21 Remove the circlip from the driveshaft outer groove – a new one should always be used when refitting (and will probably be supplied in the gaiter repair kit).

Inspection

22 Thoroughly wash the inner and outer CV joints in degreaser and blow them dry with compressed air, if available. **Note:** *Because the outer joint can't be dismantled, it is difficult to wash away all the old grease and to rid the bearing of degreaser once it's clean. But it is imperative that the job be done thoroughly.*

 Warning: Wear eye protection when using compressed air.

23 Bend the outer CV joint housing at an angle to the driveshaft to expose the bearings, inner race and cage. Inspect the bearing surfaces for signs of wear **(see illustration)**. If the bearings are damaged or worn, a new driveshaft will probably be needed – check the availability of spare parts, or try to source a good secondhand item.

Reassembly

24 Slide the dynamic damper, if removed, onto the shaft. Make sure its outer edge is aligned with the previously-applied mark. Fit a new retaining clamp.

25 Slide the inner clip, then the new outer gaiter, onto the driveshaft **(see illustrations)**. It's a good idea to wrap tape around the splines of the shaft to prevent damage to the gaiter.

26 Fit a new circlip into the groove at the end of the shaft, and fit the larger gaiter clip to the boot **(see illustrations)**.

27 Add the grease from the repair kit to the outer joint – try to 'squirt' the grease into the centre, as this will distribute it around the ball-bearings. Work the grease around the joint's insides. Put most of the grease into the joint, and any left over into the gaiter **(see illustrations)**.

28 Slide the joint on to the end of the

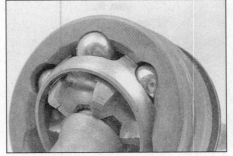
3.23 Inspect the bearing surfaces for signs of wear

3.25b . . . then the new gaiter onto the shaft

3.26b . . . and the larger clip to the gaiter

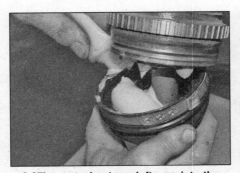
3.27b . . . and out any left over into the gaiter

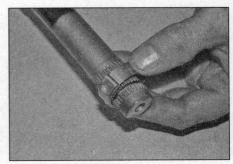
3.25a Slide the inner clip . . .

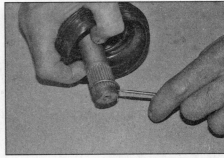
3.26a Fit a new circlip into the driveshaft groove . . .

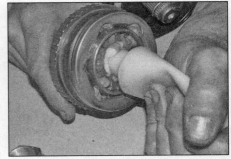
3.27a Squirt the grease into the centre of the outer joint . . .

3.28 Slide the outer joint onto the shaft, and locate onto the circlip

driveshaft, and locate it onto the circlip **(see illustration)**. When the joint is secure on the shaft, fit the gaiter onto the joint, and sit it into the grooves.

29 Tighten the gaiter clips as described in paragraph 16.

30 Refit the driveshaft assembly (see Section 2).

Chapter 9
Braking system

Contents

Degrees of difficulty

Easy, suitable for novice with little experience 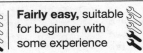	**Fairly easy,** suitable for beginner with some experience	**Fairly difficult,** suitable for competent DIY mechanic	**Difficult,** suitable for experienced DIY mechanic	**Very difficult,** suitable for expert DIY or professional

Specifications

General

Brake pedal:	
Freeplay	0.4 to 3.0 mm
Height (with carpet pulled back):	
Manual transmission models	180 mm
Automatic transmission models	184 mm
Handbrake lever travel	7 to 9 clicks
Brake pad minimum thickness (excluding backing plate)	1.6 mm
Brake shoe lining minimum thickness	2.0 mm
Brake disc minimum thickness:	
Front	19.0 mm
Rear	8.0 mm
Disc thickness variation (parallelism)	0.015 mm
Disc run-out limit	0.10 mm
Drum inside diameter:	
New	219.9 to 220 mm
Wear limit	221 mm

Torque wrench settings

	Nm	lbf ft
ABS wheel sensor retaining bolt	10	7
Brake disc retaining screws	10	7
Brake pipe unions to master cylinder	15	11
Front caliper:		
Brake hose union bolt	34	25
Guide pin bolts:		
Petrol models	22	16
Diesel models	27	20
Mounting bracket bolts	108	80
Master cylinder mounting nuts	15	11
Rear backplate bolts (drum brake models)	64	47
Rear caliper:		
Brake hose union bolt	34	25
Guide pin bolts	23	17
Handbrake cable support bracket bolts	22	16
Handbrake linkage retaining nut	27	20
Mounting bracket bolts	55	41
Rear hub nut*	181	134
Rear wheel cylinder mounting bolts	9	7
Roadwheel nuts	108	80
Servo mounting nuts	22	16

Use new nut

1 General information

The braking system is of the servo-assisted, dual circuit hydraulic type. Most models are fitted with front and rear disc brakes, with the front discs being of ventilated type, but some models use rear drum brakes. An anti-lock braking system (ABS) is fitted to all models as standard. Refer to Section 20 for further information on ABS operation.

The front and rear disc brakes are actuated by single-piston sliding type calipers, which ensure that equal pressure is applied to each disc pad.

The rear disc brake calipers incorporate mechanical handbrake mechanisms, providing an independent mechanical means of rear brake application.

The rear drums are of standard type, with leading and trailing shoes operated by a hydraulic wheel cylinder. The handbrake cable is attached to the trailing shoe.

The vacuum servo unit uses inlet manifold depression (generated only when a petrol engine is running) to boost the effort applied

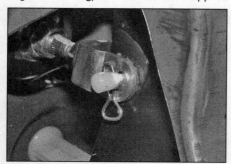

2.2 Pull out the spring clip on the left of the pedal

by the driver at the brake pedal and transmits this increased effort to the master cylinder pistons. Because there is no throttling of the inlet manifold on a diesel engine, it is not a suitable source of vacuum for brake servo operation. Vacuum is therefore derived from a separate vacuum pump, which is attached to the alternator, and is effectively driven from it.

Precautions

The car's braking system is one of its most important safety features. When working on the brakes, there are a number of points to be aware of, to ensure that your health (or even your life) is not being put at risk.

⚠️ *Warning: Brake fluid is poisonous. Take care to keep it off bare skin, and in particular not to get splashes in your eyes. The fluid also attacks paintwork and plastics – wash off spillages immediately with cold water. Finally, brake fluid is highly flammable, and should be handled with the same care as petrol.*

• *Make sure the ignition is off (take out the key) before disconnecting any braking system hydraulic union, and do not switch it on until after the hydraulic system has been bled. Failure to do this could lead to air entering the ABS hydraulic unit. If air enters the hydraulic unit pump, it will prove very difficult (in some cases impossible) to bleed the unit (see Section 5).*

• *When servicing any part of the system, work carefully and methodically – do not take short-cuts; also observe scrupulous cleanliness when overhauling any part of the hydraulic system.*

• *Always renew components in axle sets, where applicable – this means renewing brake pads, shoes, etc, on BOTH sides, even if only one set of pads is worn, or one wheel cylinder is leaking (for example). In*

the instance of uneven brake wear, the cause should be investigated and fixed (on front brakes, sticking caliper pistons is a likely problem).

• *Use only genuine Honda parts, or at least those of known good quality.*

• *Although genuine Honda brake pads and shoes are asbestos-free, the dust created by wear of non-genuine parts may contain asbestos, which is a health hazard. Never blow it out with compressed air, and don't inhale any of it.*

• *DO NOT use petroleum-based solvents to clean brake parts; use brake cleaner or methylated spirit only.*

• *DO NOT allow any brake fluid, oil or grease to contact the brake pads or disc.*

2 Brake pedal – removal, refitting and adjustment

Removal

1 Remove the pedal position switch as described in Section 18.

2 On the left-hand side of the pedal, pull out the spring clip, then withdraw the clevis pin from the right-hand side **(see illustration)**.

3 Unhook the return spring from the top of the pedal, and remove it **(see illustration)**.

4 If required, the pedal bracket can also be removed, by unscrewing the two mounting nuts either side **(see illustrations 3.14a and 3.14b)**. Note that these are also the mounting nuts for the brake servo – take care when removing the bracket that the servo is not disturbed.

5 Check the condition of the clevis pin and its spring clip – these are vital components connecting the brake pedal to the master cylinder, and if their condition is at all suspect, new parts should be fitted.

Refitting

6 Refitting is a reversal of removal, noting the following points:

 a) *If removed, tighten the pedal mounting bracket nuts .*

 b) *Ensure that the pedal-to-cross-shaft clevis pin's spring clip is securely refitted.*

 c) *Check the operation of the brakes before taking the car out on the road.*

Adjustment

Pedal height

7 The height of the brake pedal is the distance the pedal sits off the floor, measured from the top surface of the pedal. If the pedal height is not as specified, it must be adjusted.

8 To adjust the brake pedal, twist the pedal position switch anti-clockwise and back the switch out until it no longer touches the pedal, then loosen the locknut on the brake pushrod (note that this is a special splined nut, and in the absence of a proper tool, pliers may have to be used). Turn the adjuster nut behind to adjust the pedal height. When the adjustment is correct, tighten the locknut against the adjuster nut to lock it **(see illustration)**.

9 Push the switch up to the pedal until it just contacts the pedal arm, then turn it clockwise to lock it in position.

Pedal freeplay

10 The freeplay is the pedal slack, or the distance the pedal can be depressed before it begins to have any effect on the brake system. If the pedal freeplay is not within the specified range, it must be adjusted.

11 Pedal freeplay is adjusted using the brake pedal position switch. Turn the switch anti-clockwise to unlock it, then slide it up to the pedal until it just contacts it. Without moving the switch in or out, turn it clockwise to lock it.

---

3 Vacuum servo unit – testing, removal and refitting

Testing

1 To test the operation of the servo unit, depress the footbrake several times to exhaust the vacuum, then start the engine whilst keeping the pedal firmly depressed.

2 As the engine starts, there should be a noticeable 'give' in the brake pedal as the vacuum builds-up. Allow the engine to run for at least two minutes, then switch it off. If the brake pedal is now depressed it should feel normal, but further applications should result in the pedal feeling firmer, with the pedal stroke decreasing with each application.

3 If the servo does not operate as described, inspect the servo unit check valve as described in Section 4.

4 If the servo unit still fails to operate satisfactorily, the fault lies within the unit itself. Apart from external components, no spares are available, so a defective servo must be renewed.

2.3 Unhook the return spring on top of the pedal

Removal

5 Servo units should not be dismantled. They require special tools not normally found in most repair workshops. They are fairly complex and because of their critical relationship to brake performance it is best to renew a defective servo unit or fit a rebuilt one.

6 To remove the servo, first remove the brake master cylinder as described in Section 7.

7 On petrol models, remove the inlet air resonator as described in Chapter 4A.

8 On diesel models, where necessary, unbolt and remove the air cleaner mounting bracket.

9 Trace the servo vacuum hose from the servo to the fitting on the engine, and disconnect it – this is simpler, and less likely to cause damage, than trying to prise out the hose fitting from the servo itself. On petrol models, the hose runs to the centre on the inlet manifold, at the rear, while on diesel models, it is fitted to the

3.9 Disconnecting the servo hose from the inlet manifold – petrol models

3.14a Unscrew the two pedal mounting bracket nuts on the left . . .

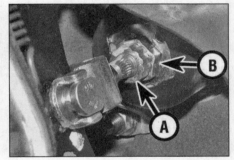

2.8 Brake pedal pushrod locknut (A) and adjuster nut (B)

vacuum pump on the back of the alternator **(see illustration)**.

10 Remove the driver's side facia lower trim panels as described in Chapter 11.

11 To gain access, the fusebox must be removed from under the facia. First disconnect the battery negative lead, and position the lead away from the battery (also see *Disconnecting the battery*) – this is essential before continuing.

12 The fusebox is secured by one main bolt at the top, and one more at the base, in front **(see illustration)**. There are also a number of wiring plugs to disconnect – try to disturb the fusebox wiring as little as possible.

13 Locate the pushrod clevis pin connecting the servo to the brake pedal. Remove the spring clip with pliers and pull out the clevis pin **(see illustration 2.2)**.

14 Remove the four nuts in front of the brake pedal holding the brake servo to the bulkhead **(see illustrations)**.

3.12 Unbolt the fusebox at the top, and in front

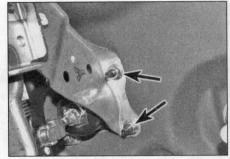

3.14b . . . and the two on the right

15 Slide the servo straight out from the bulkhead until the studs clear the holes and pull the servo, brackets and gaskets from the engine compartment area.

Refitting

16 If a new servo is being installed, the servo pushrod clearance must be set. This requires the use of special tools, so should be entrusted to a Honda dealer. If the same servo is being refitted, it can be assumed that the pushrod clearance is still correct.
17 Refitting is a reversal of removal, noting the following points:
   a) Tighten the servo mounting nuts to the specified torque.
   b) Use a new split pin when reconnecting the servo pushrod to the brake pedal.
   c) After the final refitting of the master cylinder and brake hoses and pipes, bleed the brakes as described in Section 5.
   d) Check and if necessary adjust the brake pedal height as described in Section 2.

4 Vacuum servo unit check valve – removal, testing and refitting

Removal

1 On petrol models, remove the inlet air resonator as described in Chapter 4A.
2 Trace the servo vacuum hose from the servo to the fitting on the engine, and disconnect it. On petrol models, the hose runs to the centre on the inlet manifold, at the rear, while on diesel models, it is fitted to the vacuum pump on the back of the alternator. Be careful not to damage the hose when removing it from the servo fitting.
3 The check valve is an integral part of the hose. Trace the hose to its connection on the inlet manifold (petrol models) or to the alternator/vacuum pump (diesel models) and disconnect it. Remove the hose from the engine compartment, freeing it from any securing clips, and noting how it is routed.

Testing

4 Examine the hose for signs of damage, such as splits at the ends, and renew if necessary. The valve may be tested by blowing through it in both directions. Air should flow through the valve in one direction only – when blown through from the servo unit end of the valve. Renew the valve if this is not the case.

Refitting

5 Refitting is a reversal of removal. Ensure that the hose clips are secure, to prevent leaks. Check the operation of the brakes before taking the car onto the road.

5 Hydraulic system – bleeding

Note: Refer to the precautions in Section 1 before proceeding.
Caution: Make sure the ignition is off (take out the key) before bleeding the system.

General

1 The correct operation of any hydraulic system is only possible after removing all air from the components and circuit; this is achieved by bleeding the system.
2 During the bleeding procedure, add only clean, unused hydraulic fluid of the recommended type; never re-use fluid that has already been bled from the system. Ensure that sufficient fluid is available before starting work.
3 If there is any possibility of incorrect fluid being already in the system, the system must be flushed completely with uncontaminated, correct fluid, and new seals should be fitted to the various components.
4 If air has entered the hydraulic system because of a leak, ensure that the fault is cured before proceeding further.
5 Park the car on level ground, switch off the engine, remove the key, and select first or reverse gear (or P on automatic transmission models). Chock the wheels and release the handbrake.
6 Check that all pipes and hoses are secure, unions tight and bleed screws closed. Clean any dirt from around the bleed screws – if they have not been opened for some time, use a small wire brush to clean the threads, then apply a maintenance spray such as WD-40, and allow time for it to soak in. If a bleed screw has seized, do not apply heat to it, as brake fluid is highly flammable.
7 Unscrew the master cylinder reservoir cap and top the master cylinder reservoir up to the MAX level line; refit the cap loosely. Remember to maintain the fluid level at least above the MIN level line throughout the procedure, or there is a risk of further air entering the system.
8 There is a number of one-man, do-it-yourself brake bleeding kits currently available from motor accessory shops. It is recommended that one of these kits is used whenever possible, as they greatly simplify the bleeding operation, and also reduce the risk of expelled air and fluid being drawn back into the system. If such a kit is not available, the basic (two-man) method must be used, which is described in detail below.
9 If a kit is to be used, prepare the car as described previously, and follow the kit manufacturer's instructions. The procedure may vary slightly according to the type of kit being used; general procedures are as outlined below in the relevant sub-section.
10 Whichever method is used, the same sequence must be followed (paragraphs 11 and 12) to ensure the removal of all air from the system.

Bleeding sequence

11 If the system has been only partially disconnected, and the correct precautions were taken to minimise fluid loss, it should be necessary only to bleed that part of the system (ie, the primary or secondary circuit).
12 If the complete system is to be bled, then it should be done working in the following sequence:
   a) Left-hand front brake.
   b) Right-hand front brake.
   c) Right-hand rear brake.
   d) Left-hand rear brake.

Bleeding

Basic (two-man) method

13 Collect a clean glass jar, a length of plastic or rubber tubing which is a tight fit over the bleed screw, and a ring spanner to fit the screw. The help of an assistant will also be required.
14 Remove the dust cap from the first screw in the sequence. Fit the spanner and tube to the screw, place the other end of the tube in the jar, and pour in sufficient fluid to cover the end of the tube.
15 Ensure that the master cylinder reservoir fluid level is maintained at least above the MIN level line throughout the procedure.
16 Have the assistant fully depress the brake pedal several times to build-up pressure, then maintain it on the final stroke.
17 While pedal pressure is maintained, unscrew the bleed screw (approximately one turn) and allow the compressed fluid and air to flow into the jar. The assistant should maintain pedal pressure, following it down to the floor if necessary, and should not release it until instructed to do so. When the flow stops, tighten the bleed screw again. Have the assistant release the pedal slowly.
18 Repeat the steps given in paragraphs 16 and 17 until the fluid emerging from the bleed screw is free from air bubbles. Remember to recheck the fluid level in the master cylinder reservoir every five strokes or so. If the master cylinder has been drained and refilled, and air is being bled from the first screw in the sequence, allow approximately five seconds between strokes for the master cylinder passages to refill.
19 When no more air bubbles appear, tighten the bleed screw securely, remove the tube and spanner, and refit the dust cap. Do not overtighten the bleed screw.
20 Repeat the procedure on the remaining screws in the sequence until all air is removed from the system and the brake pedal feels firm.

Using a one-way valve kit

21 As their name implies, these kits consist of a length of tubing with a one-way valve fitted to prevent expelled air and fluid being drawn back into the system; some kits include a translucent container, which can be positioned so that the air bubbles can be more easily seen flowing from the end of the tube.

22 The kit is connected to the bleed screw, which is then opened **(see illustration)**. The user returns to the driver's seat and depresses the brake pedal with a smooth, steady stroke and slowly releases it; this is repeated until the expelled fluid is clear of air bubbles.

23 Note that these kits simplify work so much that it is easy to forget the master cylinder reservoir fluid level; ensure that this is maintained at least above the MIN level line at all times.

Using a pressure-bleeding kit

24 These kits are usually operated by the reservoir of pressurised air contained in the spare tyre, although it may be necessary to reduce the pressure in the tyre to lower than normal; refer to the instructions supplied with the kit.

25 By connecting a pressurised, fluid-filled container to the master cylinder reservoir, bleeding can be carried out simply by opening each screw in turn (in the specified sequence) and allowing the fluid to flow out until no more air bubbles can be seen in the expelled fluid.

26 This method has the advantage that the large reservoir of fluid provides an additional safeguard against air being drawn into the system during bleeding.

27 Pressure-bleeding is particularly effective when bleeding 'difficult' systems, or when bleeding the complete system at the time of routine fluid renewal.

All methods

28 When bleeding is complete and firm pedal feel is restored, wash off any spilt fluid, tighten the bleed screws securely and refit their dust caps.

29 Check the hydraulic fluid level, and top-up if necessary (see *Weekly checks*).

30 Discard any hydraulic fluid that has been bled from the system; it will not be fit for re-use.

31 Check the feel of the brake pedal. If it feels at all spongy, air must still be present in the system, and further bleeding is required. Failure to bleed satisfactorily after several repetitions of the bleeding procedure may be due to worn master cylinder seals.

6 Brake pipes and hoses – renewal

Note: *Refer to the precautions in Section 1 before proceeding.*

1 If any pipe or hose is to be renewed, minimise fluid loss by removing the master cylinder reservoir cap and then tightening it down onto a piece of polythene (taking care not to damage the sender unit) to obtain an airtight seal. Alternatively, flexible hoses can be sealed, if required, using a proprietary brake hose clamp; metal brake pipe unions

5.22 Bleeding the brakes with a one-way valve kit

can be plugged (if care is taken not to allow dirt into the system) or capped immediately they are disconnected. Place a wad of rag under any union that is to be disconnected, to catch any spilt fluid.

2 If a flexible hose is to be disconnected, unscrew the brake pipe union nut before removing the horse-shoe clip which secures the hose to its mounting bracket **(see illustrations)**.

3 To unscrew the union nuts, it is preferable to obtain a brake pipe spanner of the correct size (split ring); these are available from motor accessory shops. Failing this, a close-fitting open-ended spanner will be required, though if the nuts are tight or corroded, their flats may be rounded off if the spanner slips. In such a case, a self-locking wrench is often the only way to unscrew a stubborn union, but it follows that the pipe and the damaged nuts must be renewed on reassembly. Always clean a union and surrounding area before disconnecting it. If disconnecting a component with more than one union, make a careful note of the connections before disturbing any of them.

4 If a brake pipe is to be renewed, it can be obtained, cut to length and with the union nuts and end flares in place, from Honda dealers. All that is then necessary is to bend it to shape, following the line of the original, before fitting it to the car. Alternatively, most motor accessory shops can make up brake pipes from kits, but this requires very careful measurement of the original to ensure that the new pipe is of the correct length. The safest

answer is usually to take the original to the shop as a pattern.

5 On refitting, do not over-tighten the union nuts – it is not necessary to exercise brute force to obtain a sound joint.

6 Ensure that the pipes and hoses are correctly routed with no kinks, and that they are secured in the clips or brackets provided. In the case of flexible hoses, make sure that they cannot contact other components during movement of the steering and/or suspension assemblies.

7 After fitting, remove the polythene from the reservoir (or remove the plugs or clamps, as applicable), and bleed the hydraulic system as described in Section 5. Wash off any spilt fluid, and check carefully for fluid leaks.

7 Master cylinder – removal, overhaul and refitting

Note: *Refer to the precautions in Section 1 before proceeding.*

Removal

1 The master cylinder is located on the driver's side of the engine compartment, mounted to the servo unit.

2 Remove as much fluid as you can from the reservoir before starting, using a syringe. If a syringe is not available, the fluid can be soaked out with clean paper towel. Take care not to drip hydraulic fluid onto paintwork or hot engine components.

3 Disconnect the brake fluid level sensor wiring plug at the side of the reservoir, next to the reservoir mounting bolt.

4 Loosen the two brake pipe union nuts on the side of the master cylinder. To prevent rounding off the corners on these nuts, the use of a brake pipe nut spanner which wraps around the nut is preferred. Place some absorbent rag or towel underneath, pull the brake pipes away slightly from the master cylinder. Either plug or tape over the open connections to prevent contamination.

5 Unscrew and remove the two nuts attaching the master cylinder to the servo **(see illustration)**. Pull the master cylinder off the studs and out of the engine compartment.

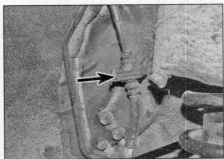

6.2a Rear brake pipe-to-hose connection and mounting bracket – locking clip arrowed

6.2b Note that the hoses have a support bracket on the strut or hub

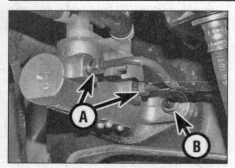

7.5 Master cylinder fluid unions (A) and mounting nuts (B – one hidden)

Again, be careful not to spill the fluid as this is done. Recover the master cylinder pushrod seal – a new one should be obtained for refitting.

Overhaul

Note: *Check availability of overhaul kits prior to dismantling the cylinder.*

6 Unscrew the reservoir front mounting bolt. Wrap some clean rag or paper towel around the reservoir, then release the hose clips, disconnect the two hoses, and remove the reservoir from the cylinder.

7 Hold the rear piston into the cylinder body, and extract the circlip.

8 Remove the screw which secures the reservoir pipe union assembly to the top of the cylinder, and withdraw the assembly. Recover the two grommets – new ones must be used on reassembly.

9 Push the rear piston inwards, then extract the stop pin through the cylinder front port.

8.4 Unbolt the caliper brake hose from the strut

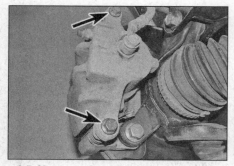

8.5 Unscrew the caliper guide pin bolts

10 Remove the stopper, then ease out the piston assemblies. If necessary, use compressed air to force the piston from the cylinder body.

11 Carefully examine the bore of the cylinder for rust, scratches, gouges and general wear. If the bore is damaged, the complete cylinder must be renewed. If the bore is in good condition, thoroughly clean the assembly, and renew the seals as described below.

12 Take note of the seal orientation on the piston, and using a small screwdriver, lever the seals from the grooves on the piston.

13 Smear the new seals with clean brake fluid, then fit them to the piston as noted on removal.

14 Apply a little of the assembly grease (which should be supplied in the overhaul kit) to the piston bodies and O-rings.

15 Insert the primary piston assembly into the cylinder, spring end first. Ensure the seal lips enter the cylinder bore without catching or folding back. Align the piston slot with the stop pin hole at the top of the cylinder.

16 Fit the secondary piston, and use it to push the primary piston in far enough to refit the stop pin, though the cylinder front port.

17 Push the rear piston inwards, fit the stopper, then secure with the circlip.

18 Using two new grommets, refit the reservoir pipe union assembly, and secure with the screw. Reconnect the two hoses, ensuring that the clips are secure.

Refitting

19 Apply some of the overhaul kit's assembly grease to a new pushrod seal, and fit it to the rear of the cylinder.

20 Fit the master cylinder over the studs on the servo, and tighten the attaching nuts only finger-tight at this stage.

21 Thread the brake pipe fittings into the master cylinder. Since the master cylinder is still loose, it can be moved slightly in order for the fittings to thread in easily. Do not strip the threads as the fittings are tightened.

22 Fully tighten the mounting nuts and pipe unions to the specified torque.

23 Fill the master cylinder reservoir with fluid, then bleed the master cylinder and the brake system as described in Section 5. Check the operation of the brakes before taking the car out on the road.

8.6a Unclip the shim from the caliper piston

8 Brake pads – renewal

Note: *Refer to the precautions in Section 1 before proceeding.*

Front pads

1 Loosen the roadwheel nuts, then raise the front of the car and support it securely on axle stands (see *Jacking and vehicle support*).

2 Remove the front wheels. Work on one brake assembly at a time, using the assembled brake for reference if necessary.

3 First, inspect the brake disc carefully as outlined in Section 10. If renewal is necessary, follow the information in that Section to remove the disc, at which time the calipers and pads can be removed as well.

4 Trace the brake hose back from the caliper, and remove the single bolt securing the hose support bracket to the strut **(see illustration)**.

5 Unscrew and remove both caliper guide pin bolts, then lift the caliper off the pads **(see illustration)**. Support the caliper by resting it on a nearby component, or hang it up on a piece of wire.

6 Noting their order of fitting, unclip and remove the pad shims. On early petrol models, two shims are used on the inner pad (the larger one fits next to the pad), with one shim on the outer pad. Diesel and later petrol models only have one shim per pad, but have a circular shim clipped to the caliper piston **(see illustrations)**.

7 Unclip the pads from the caliper mounting bracket, and remove them **(see illustration)**.

> **HAYNES HINT** *If the pads are wearing unevenly, the calipers are probably seized, which will also wear the discs prematurely. Just removing the pads and pushing the piston fully back into its bore (see paragraph 11) may unseize the piston enough to restore correct operation. If not, remove and overhaul the calipers as described in Section 9.*

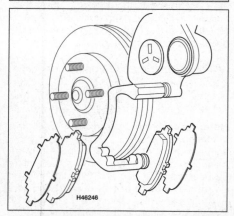

H46246

8.6b Front brake pad and shim arrangement – diesel and later petrol models

8 Release the pad retaining clips from the top and bottom of the caliper bracket, noting how they are fitted. If the clips are in poor condition, it is recommended that new clips are used when refitting.

9 While the pads are removed, clean the caliper and mounting bracket. This is best done using a brush together with spray or liquid brake cleaner, rather than dry brushing, which carries a greater risk of inhaling brake dust. Though the chance of any pads containing harmful asbestos is greatly reduced nowadays, it still pays to take care on this point.

10 Check the disc and caliper, brake hose, piston dust seals and guide pin boots for any signs of damage. Caliper overhaul is covered in Section 9.

11 The caliper piston must be pushed back into the caliper to make room for the new pads – this may require considerable effort. Either use a G-clamp, sliding-jaw (water pump) pliers, or suitable pieces of wood as levers **(see illustration)**.

Caution: Pushing back the piston causes a reverse-flow of brake fluid, which has been known to 'flip' the master cylinder rubber seals, resulting in a total loss of braking. To avoid this, clamp the caliper flexible hose and open the bleed screw – as the piston is pushed back, the fluid can be directed into a suitable container using a hose attached to the bleed screw. Close the screw just before the piston is pushed fully back, to ensure no air enters the system.

12 If the recommended method of opening a bleed screw before pushing back the piston is not used, the fluid level in the reservoir will rise, and possibly overflow. Make sure that there is sufficient space in the brake fluid reservoir to accept the displaced fluid, and if necessary, syphon some off first. Any brake fluid spilt on paintwork should be washed off with clean water, without delay – brake fluid is also a highly-effective paint-stripper.

13 Begin refitting by applying a little copper brake grease to the mating surfaces of the pad retaining clips, before clipping them into the caliper bracket.

14 Apply a little of the same grease to the edges of the brake pad backing plates, and in particular the 'ears' which locate in the caliper bracket – don't get any grease on the pad friction material **(see illustration)**.

15 Fit the pads into the caliper mounting bracket, clipping them firmly into place, with the friction material facing the disc.

16 Smear a little grease on both sides of the pad (and caliper piston) shims, then clip them into place.

17 Slide the caliper over the pads, then refit and tighten the guide pin bolts to the specified torque **(see illustration)**. If the caliper will not fit over the new pads, the caliper piston has not been pushed back far enough – see paragraph 11.

18 Refit the brake hose support bracket to the swivel hub/strut, and tighten the bolt securely.

19 Depress the brake pedal several times to

8.7 Unclip the pads from the caliper bracket

8.14 Apply copper grease to the edges of the pad backplates

bring the pads into firm contact with the brake disc.

20 Repeat the above procedure on the other front brake caliper.

21 Refit the roadwheels, then lower the car to the ground and tighten the wheel nuts to the specified torque.

22 Check the hydraulic fluid level as described in *Weekly checks*.

23 If new pads have been fitted, full braking efficiency will not be obtained until the linings have bedded-in. Be prepared for longer stopping distances, and avoid harsh braking as far as possible for the first hundred miles or so after fitting new pads.

Rear pads

24 Chock the front wheels, loosen the roadwheel nuts, then raise the rear of the car and support it securely on axle stands (see *Jacking and vehicle support*).

8.28 Unbolt the brake hose support bracket from the hub

8.11 Retracting the caliper piston with the hose clamped and bleed screw open

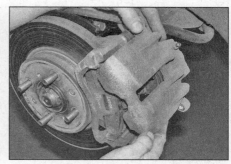

8.17 Refit the caliper over the pads

25 Remove the rear wheels. Work on one brake assembly at a time, using the assembled brake for reference if necessary.

26 Release the handbrake fully.

27 First, inspect the brake disc carefully as outlined in Section 10. If renewal is necessary, follow the information in that Section to remove the disc, at which time the calipers and pads can be removed as well.

28 Trace the brake hose back from the caliper, and remove the single bolt securing the hose support bracket to the hub **(see illustration)**.

29 Unscrew and remove the two caliper guide pin bolts, and remove the caliper body from its mounting bracket for access to the pads **(see illustrations)**. Support the caliper while it is removed, either by suspending it on a piece of wire, or by resting it on an axle stand – do not let it hang down on its brake hose. Also, do not bend the handbrake cable excessively.

8.29a Unscrew the caliper guide pin bolts . . .

8.29b ... and slide the caliper off the pads

8.31 Unclip and remove the pads

30 Where applicable, unclip and remove the pad shims – different shims are used on the inner and outer pads.

31 Unclip the pads from the caliper mounting bracket, and remove them **(see illustration)**.

32 Release the pad retaining clips from the top and bottom of the caliper bracket, noting how they are fitted. If the clips are in poor condition, it is recommended that new clips are used when refitting.

33 While the pads are removed, clean the caliper and mounting bracket. This is best done using a brush together with spray or liquid brake cleaner, rather than dry brushing, which carries a greater risk of inhaling brake dust. Though the chance of any pads containing harmful asbestos is greatly reduced nowadays, it still pays to take care on this point.

34 Check the disc and caliper, brake hose, piston dust seals and guide pin boots for any

signs of damage. Caliper overhaul is covered in Section 9.

35 If new brake pads are to be fitted, it will be necessary to retract the piston fully into the caliper bore by rotating it in a clockwise direction. This can be achieved using sturdy circlip pliers, but note that as well as being turned, the piston has to be pressed in very firmly. Special tools are available from companies such as Draper to achieve this with less effort **(see illustration)**.

Caution: Pushing back the piston causes a reverse-flow of brake fluid, which has been known to 'flip' the master cylinder rubber seals, resulting in a total loss of braking. To avoid this, clamp the caliper flexible hose and open the bleed screw – as the piston is pushed back, the fluid can be directed into a suitable container using a hose attached to the bleed screw. Close the screw just before the piston is pushed fully back, to ensure no air enters the system.

36 Lubricate the piston dust seal with rubber grease (a little washing-up liquid will serve as a substitute) before turning the piston. If the seal gets twisted, turn the piston the opposite way to un-twist the seal, then try again. When the piston is fully retracted, turn it so that one of its grooves is vertical in the caliper body, to accept the raised tab on the back of the inner pad **(see illustration)**.

37 If the recommended method of opening a bleed screw before pushing back the piston is not used, the fluid level in the reservoir will rise, and possibly overflow. Make sure that there is sufficient space in the brake fluid reservoir to accept the displaced fluid, and if necessary, syphon some off first. Any brake fluid spilt on paintwork should be washed off with clean water, without delay – brake fluid is also a highly-effective paint-stripper.

38 Begin refitting by applying a little copper brake grease to the mating surfaces of the pad retaining clips, before clipping them into the caliper bracket.

39 Apply a little of the same grease to the edges of the brake pad backing plates, and in particular the 'ears' which locate in the caliper bracket – don't get any grease on the pad friction material. Fit the pads into the caliper mounting bracket, clipping them firmly into place, with the friction material facing the disc. Where applicable, the pad with a wear indicator should be the inner pad. The inner pad should also have a raised tab on its backplate, to engage the caliper piston **(see illustrations)**.

40 Where applicable, smear a little grease on both sides of the pad (and caliper piston) shims, then clip them into place.

41 Offer the caliper into position over the pads, then refit and tighten the guide pin bolts to the specified torque. If the caliper will not fit over the new pads, the caliper piston has either not been retracted far enough, or the piston's groove is not in the correct alignment – see paragraphs 35 and 36.

42 Refit the brake hose support bracket to the hub, and tighten the bolt securely.

43 Depress the brake pedal, and operate the handbrake, several times to bring the pads into firm contact with the brake disc.

44 Repeat the above procedure on the other rear brake caliper.

45 Refit the roadwheels, then lower the car to the ground and tighten the wheel nuts to the specified torque.

46 Check the hydraulic fluid level as described in *Weekly checks*.

47 Check the handbrake operation as described in Chapter 1A or 1B, and adjust if necessary as described in Section 15.

48 If new pads have been fitted, full braking efficiency will not be obtained until the linings have bedded-in. Be prepared for longer stopping distances, and avoid harsh braking as far as possible for the first hundred miles or so after fitting new pads.

8.35 Retracting the caliper piston with the hose clamped and bleed screw open

8.36 Turn the piston so that one of its grooves is vertical in the caliper body

8.39a Apply copper brake grease to the pad backing plates

8.39b Showing how the inner pad's raised tab engages with the piston groove

9 Brake caliper –
removal, overhaul and refitting

Note: *Refer to the precautions in Section 1 before proceeding.*

Front caliper

Removal

1 Loosen the roadwheel nuts, then raise the front of the car and support it securely on axle stands (see *Jacking and vehicle support*). Remove the front wheel.

2 Trace the brake hose back from the caliper, and remove the single bolt securing the hose support bracket to the strut **(see illustration)**.

3 Clamp the brake hose, using a proper brake hose clamp if available (these are not expensive, and greatly reduce the risk of damaging the hose). In the absence of a proper clamp, use some self-locking pliers, but protect the hose by placing a couple of pieces of card in the plier jaws.

4 Wrap some clean rag or paper towel around the brake hose union on the caliper, then just loosen the bolt.

5 Unscrew and remove both caliper guide pin bolts, then lift the caliper off the pads **(see illustration)**.

6 Fully unscrew the union bolt, and disconnect the brake hose from the caliper – anticipate a small amount of fluid spillage as this is done. Recover the copper sealing washers fitted either side of the hose end fitting – new washers should be used when reassembling.

Overhaul

Note: *Ensure that an appropriate caliper overhaul kit is obtained before starting work.*

7 With the caliper on the bench, wipe away all traces of dust and dirt, but avoid inhaling the dust, as it is may be a health hazard.

8 Using a small flat-bladed screwdriver, carefully prise the dust seal retaining clip out of the caliper bore **(see illustration)**.

9 Withdraw the partially-ejected piston from the caliper body and remove the dust seal. The piston can be withdrawn by hand, or if necessary forced out by applying compressed air to the union bolt hole.

Caution: The piston may be ejected with some force. Only low pressure should be required, such as is generated by a foot pump.

10 Extract the piston hydraulic seal using a blunt instrument such as a knitting needle or a crochet hook, taking care not to damage the caliper bore.

11 Withdraw the guide sleeves or pins from the caliper body or mounting bracket (as applicable) and remove the rubber gaiters.

12 Thoroughly clean all components, using only methylated spirit, isopropyl alcohol or clean hydraulic fluid as a cleaning medium. Never use mineral-based solvents, such as petrol or paraffin, which will attack the hydraulic system rubber components.

9.2 Unbolt the caliper brake hose from the strut

Dry the components immediately, using compressed air or a clean, lint-free cloth. Use compressed air to blow clear the fluid passages.

13 Check all components and renew any that are worn or damaged. Check particularly the cylinder bore and piston; if they are scratched, worn or corroded in any way, they must be renewed (note that this means the renewal of the complete body assembly). Similarly check the condition of the guide sleeves or pins and their bores; they should be undamaged and (when cleaned) a reasonably tight sliding fit in the body or mounting bracket bores. If there is any doubt about the condition of a component, renew it.

14 If the assembly is fit for further use, obtain the appropriate repair kit.

15 Renew all rubber seals, dust covers and caps disturbed on dismantling as a matter of course; these should never be re-used.

16 Before commencing reassembly, ensure that all components are absolutely clean and dry.

17 Dip the piston and the new piston (fluid)

9.5 Unscrew the guide pin bolts, and remove the caliper

seal in clean hydraulic fluid. Smear clean fluid on the cylinder bore surface.

18 Fit the new piston (fluid) seal, using only the fingers to manipulate it into the cylinder bore groove. Fit the new dust seal to the piston. Refit the piston to the cylinder bore using a twisting motion, ensuring that the piston enters squarely into the bore. Press the piston fully into the bore, then press the dust seal into the caliper body.

19 Install the dust seal retaining clip, ensuring that it is correctly seated in the caliper groove.

20 Apply the grease supplied in the repair kit (or copper brake grease) to the guide sleeves or pins. Fit the sleeves or pins to the caliper body or mounting bracket. Fit the new rubber gaiters, ensuring that they are correctly located in the grooves on both the sleeve or pin, and body or mounting bracket (as applicable).

21 As with all other work on the braking system, it is recommended that the calipers are overhauled in axle pairs – in other words, it is not advisable to only overhaul one caliper at a time, as this may result in uneven braking.

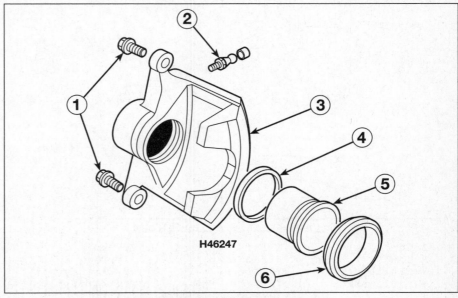

H46247

9.8 Front brake caliper exploded view

1 *Guide pin bolts*	3 *Caliper body*	5 *Piston*
2 *Bleed screw*	4 *Piston seal*	6 *Dust seal*

9.29 Unbolt the brake hose support bracket from the hub

9.30a Turn the handbrake lever, and unhook the cable end fitting

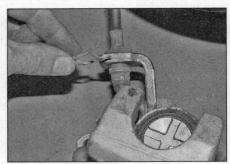

9.30b Pull out the horse-shoe clip . . .

9.30c . . . and slide out the cable from the caliper mounting bracket

9.33 Slide the rear caliper off the pads

Refitting

22 Using new copper sealing washers either side of the hose end fitting, reconnect the brake hose to the caliper, tightening the bolt only hand-tight at this stage.

23 Offer the caliper into position over the pads, then refit the guide pin bolts and tighten them to the specified torque.

24 Tighten the brake hose union bolt to the specified torque, then remove the brake hose clamp.

25 Refit the brake hose support bracket to the swivel hub/strut, and tighten the bolt securely.

26 Bleed the brakes as described in Section 5. If the brake hose was clamped throughout, then only the disturbed caliper should require bleeding.

27 On completion, refit the wheel and lower the car to the ground. Tighten the wheel nuts to the specified torque.

Rear caliper

Removal

28 Chock the front wheels, loosen the roadwheel nuts, then raise the rear of the car and support it securely on axle stands (see *Jacking and vehicle support*). Remove the rear wheel.

29 Trace the brake hose back from the caliper, and remove the single bolt securing the hose support bracket to the hub **(see illustration)**.

30 Turn the caliper handbrake lever using pliers, and unhook the handbrake cable end fitting from it. Pull out the horse-shoe clip securing the outer cable to its bracket on the caliper body **(see illustrations)**.

31 Clamp the brake hose, using a proper brake hose clamp if available (these are not expensive, and greatly reduce the risk of damaging the hose). In the absence of a proper clamp, use some self-locking pliers, but protect the hose by placing a couple of pieces of card in the plier jaws.

32 Wrap some clean rag or paper towel around the brake hose union on the caliper, then just loosen the bolt.

33 Unscrew and remove both caliper guide pin bolts, then slide the caliper off the pads **(see illustration)**.

34 Fully unscrew the union bolt, and disconnect

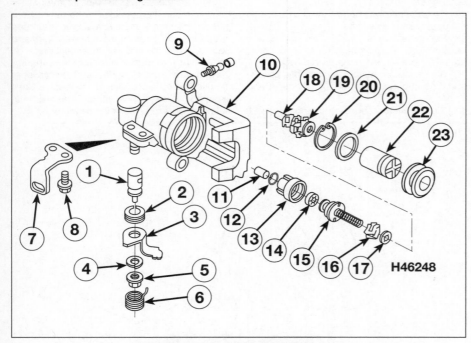

9.37 Rear brake caliper exploded view

1 Cam	8 Bolt	16 Bearing
2 Boot	9 Bleed screw	17 Spacer
3 Cam lever	10 Caliper body	18 Adjusting spring
4 Spring washer	11 Pin	19 Spring cover
5 Nut	12 O-ring	20 Circlip
6 Return spring	13 Slave piston	21 Piston seal
7 Handbrake cable	14 Clip	22 Piston
support bracket	15 Adjusting bolt	23 Dust seal

the brake hose from the caliper – anticipate a small amount of fluid spillage as this is done. Recover the copper sealing washers fitted either side of the hose end fitting – new washers should be used when reassembling.

Overhaul

Note: *Ensure the correct caliper overhaul kit is obtained before starting work.*

35 With the caliper on the bench, wipe away all traces of dust and dirt, but avoid inhaling the dust, as it is may be a health hazard.

36 Using a small screwdriver, carefully prise out the dust seal from the caliper bore, taking care not to damage the piston.

37 Remove the piston from the caliper bore by rotating it in an anti-clockwise direction **(see illustration opposite)**. This can be achieved by using a square-section bar, such as the shaft of a screwdriver, which locates snugly in the caliper piston slots. Once the piston turns freely but does not come out any further, the piston can be withdrawn by hand, or if necessary pushed out by applying compressed air to the union bolt hole.

Caution: The piston may be ejected with some force – only low pressure should be required, such as is generated by a foot pump.

38 Using a blunt instrument such as a knitting needle or a crochet hook, extract the piston hydraulic seal, taking care not to damage the caliper bore.

39 Withdraw the guide sleeves from the caliper body, and remove the guide sleeve gaiters.

40 Inspect the caliper components as described previously in this Section for the front calipers. Renew as necessary, noting that the inside of the caliper piston must not be dismantled. If necessary, the handbrake mechanism can be overhauled as described in the following paragraphs. If it is not wished to overhaul the handbrake mechanism, proceed to paragraph 46.

41 Before dismantling the handbrake mechanism, note carefully how it is assembled. If possible, take some digital photos from various angles, as a guide for refitting – the other rear caliper may also be used for guidance.

42 Remove the nut and bolt securing the handbrake cable support bracket, and take off the bracket. Recover the washer fitted under the nut.

43 Take off the return spring, cam lever, boot and the cam, noting their fitted sequence.

44 Clean all the handbrake components in brake cleaner or methylated spirit, and examine them for wear. If there is any sign of wear or damage, the complete handbrake mechanism assembly should be renewed.

45 Ensure that all components are clean and dry. Apply some copper brake grease to the cam and its boot, then fit them, followed by the cam lever and return spring. Refit the cable support bracket, secured with the washer, nut and bolt – tighten the nut and bolt to the specified torque.

46 Soak the piston and the new piston (fluid) seal in clean hydraulic fluid. Smear clean fluid on the cylinder bore surface.

47 Fit the new piston (fluid) seal, using only the fingers to manipulate it into the cylinder bore groove, and refit the piston assembly. Turn the piston in a clockwise direction, using the method employed on dismantling, until it is fully retracted into the caliper bore. When the piston is fully retracted, turn it so that its tapered cut-out will align with the raised tab on the back of the inner pad, when both are refitted.

48 Fit the dust seal to the caliper, ensuring that it is correctly located in the caliper and also the groove on the piston.

49 Apply the grease supplied in the repair kit (or copper brake grease) to the guide sleeves or pins. Fit the sleeves or pins to the caliper body or mounting bracket. Fit the new rubber gaiters, ensuring that they are correctly located in the grooves on both the sleeve or pin, and body or mounting bracket (as applicable).

50 As with all other work on the braking system, it is recommended that the calipers are overhauled in axle pairs – in other words, it is not advisable to only overhaul one caliper at a time, as this may result in uneven braking.

Refitting

51 Using new copper sealing washers either side of the hose end fitting, reconnect the brake hose to the caliper, tightening the bolt only hand-tight at this stage.

52 Offer the caliper into position over the pads, then refit the guide pin bolts and tighten them to the specified torque.

53 Tighten the brake hose union bolt to the specified torque, then remove the brake hose clamp.

54 Refit the brake hose support bracket to the swivel hub/strut, and tighten the bolt securely.

55 Hook the handbrake inner cable into the caliper handbrake operating lever, then clip the outer cable into its bracket on the caliper body.

56 Bleed the brakes as described in Section 5. If the brake hose was clamped throughout, then only the disturbed caliper should require bleeding.

57 On completion, refit the wheel and lower the car to the ground. Tighten the wheel nuts to the specified torque.

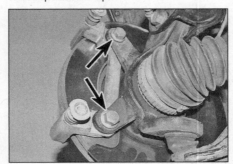

10.8a Unscrew the caliper bracket bolts . . .

10 Brake discs – inspection, removal and refitting

Note: *Refer to the precautions in Section 1 before proceeding.*

Inspection

1 Loosen the relevant wheel nuts, chock the wheels, then jack up either the front or rear of the car and support on axle stands (see *Jacking and vehicle support*). Remove the appropriate roadwheel.

2 Slowly rotate the brake disc so that the full area of both sides can be checked; remove the brake pads, as described in Section 8, if better access is required to the inboard surface. Light scoring is normal in the area swept by the brake pads, but if heavy scoring is found, the disc must be renewed.

3 It is normal to find a lip of rust and brake dust around the disc's perimeter; this can be scraped off if required. If, however, a lip has formed due to wear of the brake pad swept area, the disc thickness must be measured using a micrometer. Take measurements at several places around the disc at the inside and outside of the pad swept area; if the disc has worn at any point to the specified minimum thickness or less, it must be renewed.

4 If the disc is thought to be warped, it can be checked for run-out, ideally by using a dial gauge mounted on any convenient fixed point, while the disc is slowly rotated. In the absence of a dial gauge, use feeler blades to measure (at several points all around the disc) the clearance between the disc and a fixed point such as the caliper mounting bracket.

5 If the measurements obtained are at the specified maximum or beyond, the disc is excessively warped, and must be renewed; however, it is worth checking first that the wheel bearing is in good condition (Chapters 1A or 1B and 10). Also try the effect of removing the disc and turning it through 180° to reposition it on the hub; if run-out is still excessive, the disc must be renewed.

6 Check the disc for cracks, and for any other wear or damage. Renew the disc if necessary.

Removal

7 Remove the brake caliper and pads as described in Sections 8 and 9.

8 Unscrew the two bolts securing the brake caliper mounting bracket to the hub, and slide the bracket off the disc **(see illustrations)**.

9 If the same disc is to be refitted, use chalk or paint to mark the relationship of the disc to the hub.

10 Remove the two disc retaining screws – these may be tight, due to corrosion. If available, use an impact driver to remove the screws, or try tapping the end of the screwdriver to break the screw free **(see illustration)**. Sometimes, using a close-fitting

10.8b . . . and withdraw the bracket from the disc

10.10 Using an impact driver to loosen the two brake disc screws

10.11 Removing a rear disc

screwdriver bit in a socket handle can provide greater leverage on a difficult screw than a screwdriver will.

11 With the screws removed, pull the brake disc from the hub – if it is tight, lightly tap its rear face with a hide or plastic mallet **(see illustration)**. If the disc is stuck, two M8 threaded holes are provided in the disc face – screw two M8 bolts into these, and tighten them evenly to draw off the disc.

Refitting

12 Refitting is the reverse of the removal procedure, noting the following points:
  a) *Ensure that the mating surfaces of the disc and hub are clean and flat. To reduce the risk of corrosion, apply copper grease to the hub before fitting the disc (ensure that the grease does not get on the disc friction surfaces).*
  b) *If applicable, align the marks made on removal.*
  c) *If a new disc has been fitted, use a suitable solvent to wipe any preservative coating from the disc before refitting the caliper.*
  d) *If the disc retaining screws suffered damage during removal, use new ones when reassembling. Apply a little copper grease to their threads, to prevent future corrosion problems.*
  e) *Tighten the brake caliper mounting bracket bolts to the specified torque.*
  f) *Refit the pads and caliper as described in Sections 8 and 9.*
  g) *Refit the roadwheel, then lower the car to the ground and tighten the wheel nuts*

to the specified torque. On completion, depress the brake pedal several times to bring the brake pads into contact with the disc.

11 Rear brake drum –
removal, inspection
and refitting

Note: *Refer to the precautions in Section 1 before proceeding.*

Removal

1 Loosen the relevant wheel nuts, chock the wheels, then jack up either the front or rear of the car and support on axle stands (see *Jacking and vehicle support*). Remove the appropriate roadwheel.

2 Remove the brake drum. It should simply pull straight off the hub, but if necessary, a few sharp blows with a soft-faced mallet may be required to free it **(see illustration)**.

3 If the drum is tight, screw a couple of 8.0 mm bolts into the tapped holes, and tighten them to free the drum **(see illustration)**.

4 If the drum is catching on the shoes, it may be possible to get the drum off by repeatedly pushing the drum back on, turning it a little, and carefully trying to withdraw it squarely over the shoes – getting the 'alignment' right is critical, and can only be achieved by trial-and-error.

5 In the worst case, the shoes will have to be retracted, which can be a fiddly operation. Remove the rubber plug at the top of the backplate. Use one screwdriver inserted through the hole in the backing plate to hold

the self-adjuster lever away from the adjuster bolt, then use another screwdriver to rotate the adjuster bolt until the drum can be removed.

Inspection

6 Brush the dirt and dust from the drum, taking care not to inhale it.

7 Examine the internal friction surface of the drum. If deeply scored, or so worn that the drum has become ridged to the width of the shoes, then both drums must be renewed.

8 Regrinding of the friction surface may be possible, provided the maximum diameter given in the Specifications is not exceeded, but note that both rear drums should be reground to the identical diameter.

9 While the drum is removed, check the condition of the shoes. Also look for signs of fluid leakage from the wheel cylinder – one sign is a build-up of brake dust on either end of the cylinder body (gently pull back the cylinder rubber boots, and look for wetness) **(see illustration)**.

Refitting

10 If necessary, back off the adjuster wheel on the strut until the drum will pass over the shoes, then slip the drum into position.

11 Adjust the brakes by operating the footbrake a number of times. A clicking noise will be heard at the drum as the automatic adjuster operates. When the clicking stops, adjustment is complete.

12 Check the operation of the handbrake, then refit the roadwheel and lower the car to the ground. Tighten the wheel nuts to the specified torque.

11.2 Removing the brake drum

11.3 Use a pair of 8 mm bolts into the holes provided to press the drum off

11.9 Lift the wheel cylinder boots and check for wetness

12.3a Turn the end of each shoe retainer pin with pliers . . .

12.3b . . . then withdraw the pin from the rear, and take off the spring

12.3c Pull out the shoes from the anchor plate . . .

12.3d . . . and unhook the return spring

12.3e Remove the shoes from the backplate . . .

12.3f . . . then pull back the spring and unhook the handbrake cable

12 Rear brake shoes – renewal

Note 1: *Refer to the precautions in Section 1 before proceeding.*
Note 2: *All four rear brake shoes must be renewed at the same time, but to avoid mixing up parts, work on only one brake assembly at a time.*

1 Remove the brake drum on the side concerned, as described in Section 11. Since both sets of shoes must be renewed, it is helpful to remove both drums, so that the undisturbed shoes can be referred to as a guide.
2 Renewing the shoes is a lot easier if you remove the rear wheel hub as described in Chapter 10. However, this is not absolutely necessary.
3 Follow **illustrations 12.3a to 12.3r** for the brake shoe renewal procedure. Be sure to stay in order and read the caption under each illustration.
4 If removed, refit the hub as described in Chapter 10 – note that a new hub nut must be used.

5 When refitting the brake drum, adjust the brake shoes by turning the star wheel on the adjuster bolt until the drum just slips over the shoes. When turning the drum, the shoes should not rub; if they do, remove the drum and back off the star wheel a little bit so they don't.
6 Refit the drum as described in Section 11.
7 Check the brake operation before taking the car out on the road – remember that the new shoes will need several hundred miles before they bed-in fully and give proper performance.

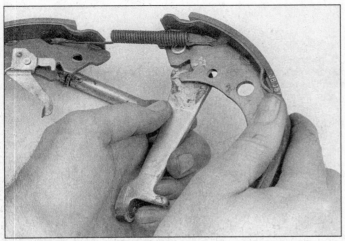

12.3g Swing the handbrake lever away from the trailing shoe, which will force the adjuster bolt clevis out of its groove in the shoe; the two shoes can now be separated

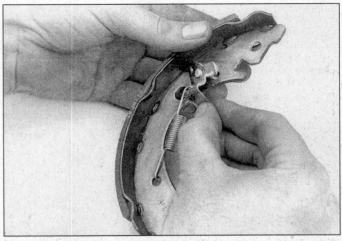

12.3h Remove the self-adjuster lever and spring from the leading shoe

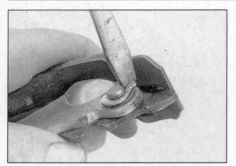

12.3i Prise open the handbrake lever retaining clip and separate the lever from the shoe; don't lose the wave washer under the clip

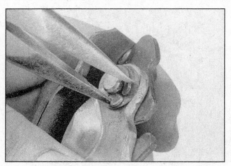

12.3j Put the new trailing shoe on the lever, place the wave washer over the pin, then fit the retaining clip; crimp the ends of the clip together with thin-nose pliers

12.3k Clean the adjuster bolt and clevis, then apply copper grease to the threads and ends

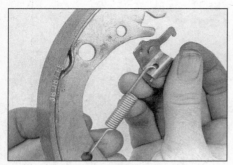

12.3l Connect the self-adjuster lever spring to the leading brake shoe, then insert the pin on the lever into its hole in the shoe

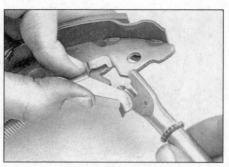

12.3m Insert the short clevis of the adjuster bolt into its slot in the leading shoe, making sure it catches the self-adjuster lever

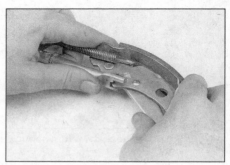

12.3n Connect the upper return spring, prise the shoe lower ends apart, and fit the adjuster into the other shoe; note how the clevis stepped portion fits

12.3o Lubricate the brake shoe contact areas on the backplate with copper grease

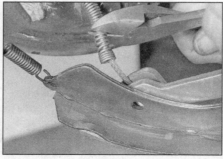

12.3p Compress the handbrake cable spring, hold it in position and connect the cable end to the handbrake lever

12.3q Offer up the brake shoes to the backplate, engaging the shoe upper ends in the wheel cylinder piston slots. Connect the shoe lower return spring

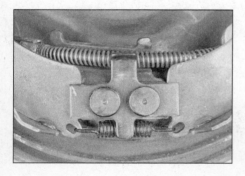

12.3r Secure the shoes with the retainer pins and spring plates – make sure the handbrake cable spring and lower return spring are behind the anchor plate

13 Rear brake backplate (drum brake models) – removal and refitting

Removal

1 Remove the brake drum as described in Section 11.
2 Remove the rear hub assembly as described in Chapter 10.
3 If the backplate is being removed purely for access to the rear suspension, and no work is

required on the brake shoes or wheel cylinder, the backplate can be removed with the shoes and cylinder attached, which makes less work when refitting; otherwise, remove the shoes as described in Section 12.

4 Clamp the rear brake hose, then unscrew the brake pipe union from the rear wheel cylinder – anticipate a small amount of brake fluid loss as this is done.

5 Trace the wiring back from the ABS wheel sensor, and disconnect it at the plug.

6 If the brake shoes have been removed, and the backplate is to be removed completely, unscrew the two small bolts securing the handbrake cable to the backplate, and withdraw the cable through it.

7 Remove the four brake backplate mounting bolts, and withdraw the backplate from the stub axle.

Refitting

8 Refitting is a reversal of removal, noting the following points:

a) Before refitting the backplate, clean up the stub axle and backplate mating surfaces.

b) Tighten the backplate mounting bolts to the specified torque.

c) Tighten the wheel cylinder pipe union securely.

d) If removed, refit the shoes as described in Section 12.

e) Refit the rear hub as described in Chapter 10.

f) On completion, once the drum has been refitted, bleed the brakes as described in Section 5, and if necessary adjust the handbrake as described in Section 15.

14 Rear wheel cylinder (drum brake models) – renewal

1 Remove the brake backplate as described in Section 13. This is necessary, since with the backplate in place, one of the wheel cylinder

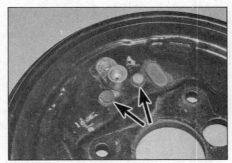

14.2a Wheel cylinder mounting bolts

bolts is obscured by the rear suspension knuckle.

2 Unscrew the two wheel cylinder bolts, and withdraw the cylinder from the backplate – if the shoes are still fitted, gently pull the shoes apart at the top **(see illustrations)**.

3 If a wheel cylinder is leaking, usually the only course of action is to fit a new one complete, though repair kits may be available – check with your Honda dealer or parts supplier. Unlike other brake components, it is not essential to renew both rear cylinders at the same time, but if one has gone, it is likely the other will soon follow, and it may be wise to renew them in pairs for peace of mind.

4 When refitting, check that the mating faces are clean, and tighten the wheel cylinder mounting bolts to the specified torque.

5 Refit the brake backplate as described in Section 13.

15 Handbrake – adjustment

1 If the handbrake check in Chapter 1A or 1B reveals a need for handbrake adjustment, proceed as follows.

2 Chock the front wheels, then jack up the rear of the car, and support it on axle stands (see *Jacking and vehicle support*).

14.2b Removing the wheel cylinder from the backplate

3 Release the handbrake lever fully.

4 On rear disc brake models, check to see whether the rear brake caliper's handbrake lever is in contact with the caliper stop pin **(see illustration)**. If not, this suggests that the cable on that side may be seized (not releasing properly), or that the handbrake is over-adjusted (being held off the rest position).

5 Remove the centre console (or handbrake lever cover) as described in Chapter 11, Section 28.

6 Apply the handbrake lever by one click.

7 Tighten the handbrake adjuster nut at the rear of the handbrake lever, until the rear wheels just start to drag **(see illustration)**.

8 Release the handbrake lever completely, and verify that the rear wheels are free to turn. Reset the adjuster nut accordingly if this is not the case.

9 Ensure that, by the time the handbrake lever is applied by 7 to 9 clicks, the rear wheels are completely locked.

10 Failure to adjust properly suggests that one or more of the handbrake cables may be binding. Examine and lubricate the cables and linkages as far as possible first. If necessary, new cables should be fitted as described in Section 16.

11 On completion, refit the centre console (or handbrake lever cover). Refit the rear wheels (if applicable) then lower the car to the ground and tighten the wheel nuts to the specified torque.

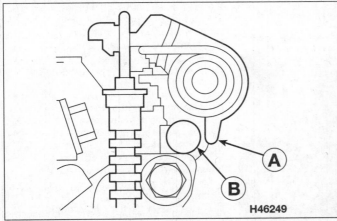

15.4 When fully released, handbrake lever (A) should contact caliper stop pin (B)

15.7 Adjusting the handbrake

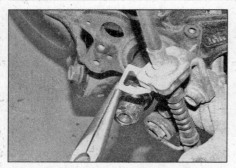

16.5a Pull off the spring clip securing the handbrake cable outer . . .

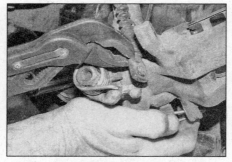

16.5b . . . then use pliers to unhook the cable inner from the caliper

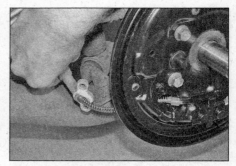

16.6 Unbolt the cable from the backplate, and feed it through

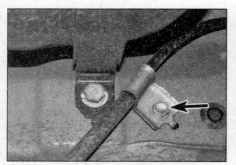

16.7 Unbolt the handbrake cable support brackets

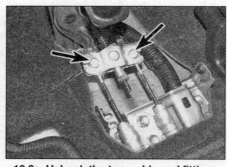

16.8a Unhook the two cable end fittings from the equaliser plate . . .

16.8b . . . then feed the cables down through the floor and remove them

16 Handbrake cables – renewal

1 Chock the front wheels, loosen the rear wheel nuts, then jack up the rear of the car, and support it on axle stands (see *Jacking and vehicle support*). Remove the rear wheels.
2 Release the handbrake lever fully.
3 Remove the centre console (or handbrake lever cover) as described in Chapter 11, Section 28.
4 Fully slacken the handbrake adjuster nut at the rear of the handbrake lever (**see illustration 15.7**).
5 On rear disc brake models, pull off the spring clip securing each outer cable to its bracket on the caliper body, then unhook the handbrake inner cable from each caliper handbrake operating lever (**see illustrations**).

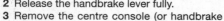
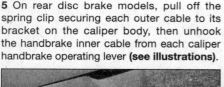

17.4 Measure the length of exposed thread behind the adjuster nut

6 On rear drum brake models, remove the brake shoes as described in Section 12. With the handbrake cable unhooked from the shoe, unscrew the two small bolts securing the cable to the backplate, and feed the cable through the backplate (**see illustration**).
7 Working from the rear of the car forwards, trace the cables along the underside, unbolting the support brackets and releasing the cables from any clips or ties (**see illustration**). Note how the cables are arranged and routed, for refitting.
8 Inside the car, unhook the cable ends from the equaliser plate at the rear of the handbrake lever. Feed the cables down through the floor grommet, and remove them from under the car (**see illustrations**).
9 Refitting is a reversal of removal, noting the following points:
   a) Apply grease to all accessible handbrake pivots and linkages.

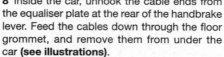
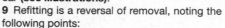

17.5 Disconnect the handbrake warning light switch

   b) Ensure that the cables are correctly routed, and secured using all of the support brackets to the underside of the car.
   c) On rear drum brake models, refit the brake shoes as described in Section 12.
   c) Adjust the handbrake as described in Section 15.

17 Handbrake lever – removal and refitting

Removal

1 For preference, park the car on level ground before starting. Chock the front wheels, engage a gear (or P) and release the handbrake.
2 Though not essential, access to the handbrake is greatly improved by removing one of the front seats (see Chapter 11).
3 Remove the centre console (or handbrake lever cover) as described in Chapter 11, Section 28.
4 To make adjusting the handbrake easier, measure and note down the length of adjuster bolt behind the adjuster nut – on completion, the nut can be tightened to the same position (**see illustration**). Loosen the handbrake adjuster nut until both handbrake cables can be unhooked from the equaliser bar.
5 On the right-hand side of the lever, disconnect the wiring plug from the handbrake warning light switch (**see illustration**).
6 Unscrew the three handbrake lever mounting bolts, and lift the lever assembly out of the car.

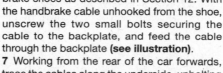
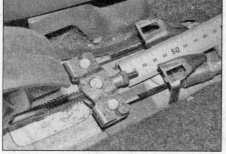
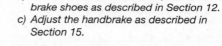

Refitting

7 Refitting is a reversal of removal. Adjust the handbrake as described in Section 15. Check the operation of the handbrake warning light switch before refitting the handbrake lever cover.

18 Brake pedal position switch
– testing and renewal

1 The brake pedal position switch has a dual role – it informs the engine management ECM when the brakes are applied (which among other things, allows the ECM to implement fuel injection cut-off, where applicable), and also switches on the brake lights.

Testing

2 To check the brake light switch, push on the brake pedal and verify that the brake lights come on.
3 If they don't, check the brake light fuse (refer to the wiring diagrams at the end of Chapter 12). Also check the brake light bulbs in both tail light assemblies – don't forget to check the high-mounted brake light (also Chapter 12).
4 If the fuse and the bulbs are okay, locate the brake light switch at the top of the brake pedal.
5 Disconnect the switch wiring plug.
6 Check for continuity across the switch terminals. When the brake pedal is depressed, there should be continuity; when it's released, there should be no continuity. If the switch doesn't operate as described, renew it.

Renewal

7 The brake pedal position switch is fitted above and behind the top of the brake pedal itself – access is from the driver's footwell.
8 Reach up under the facia to the switch mounting bracket, and disconnect the wiring plug from the top of the switch **(see illustration)**.
9 Turn the switch body anti-clockwise to remove it from the bracket **(see illustration)**.
10 To refit and set the switch, offer the switch into its bracket, so that the switch plunger touches the pedal. Without moving the switch in or out, turn it clockwise to lock it.
11 Reconnect the switch wiring plug to complete.

19 Brake fluid level switch
– testing and renewal

Testing

1 Disconnect the wiring plug from the switch, which is located next to the reservoir mounting bolt.
2 Unscrew the reservoir cap for access to the fluid level float.

18.8 Disconnect the wiring plug from the switch

3 Connect a multimeter across the switch terminals, and check for continuity.
4 When the float is up, there should be no continuity. Now press the float down – continuity should be indicated. If this is not the case, the switch is faulty.
5 The brake fluid level float and switch are integral with the brake fluid reservoir, and are not available separately.

Renewal

6 Remove as much fluid as you can from the reservoir before starting, using a syringe. If a syringe is not available, the fluid can be soaked out with clean paper towel. Take care not to drip hydraulic fluid onto paintwork or hot engine components.
7 If not already done, disconnect the brake fluid level sensor wiring plug at the side of the reservoir, next to the reservoir mounting bolt.
8 Unscrew the reservoir front mounting bolt. Wrap some clean rag or paper towel around the reservoir, then release the hose clips, disconnect the two hoses, and remove the reservoir from the cylinder.
9 Refitting is a reversal of removal, noting the following points:
a) Ensure the reservoir hose connections are securely remade.
b) On completion, refill the reservoir with fresh fluid, and bleed the brakes as described in Section 5.

20 Anti-lock braking system (ABS) –
general information

Virtually all Civic models are equipped with ABS. The purpose of the system is to prevent the wheel(s) locking during heavy braking. This is achieved by automatic release of the brake on the relevant wheel before it can lock up, followed by rapid reapplication of the brake.

The main components of the system are four wheel sensors (one per wheel), and a modulator block which contains the ABS computer, the hydraulic solenoid valves and accumulators, and an electrically-driven return pump.

The solenoids are controlled by the computer, which receives signals from the

18.9 Twist the switch anti-clockwise to remove it from the pedal bracket

wheel sensors. The sensors detect the speed of rotation of a reluctor ring, attached to the wheel hub. By comparing the speed signals from the four wheels, the computer can determine when a wheel is decelerating at an abnormal rate, and can therefore predict when a wheel is about to lock. During normal operation, the system functions in the same way as a non-ABS braking system does.

If the computer senses that a wheel is about to lock, the ABS system enters the 'pressure-maintain' phase. The computer operates the relevant solenoid valve in the modulator block; this isolates the brake on the wheel in question from the master cylinder, effectively sealing-in the hydraulic pressure.

If the speed of rotation of the wheel continues to decrease at an abnormal rate, the ABS system then enters the 'pressure-decrease' phase. The return pump operates and pumps the hydraulic fluid back into the master cylinder, releasing pressure on the brake. When the speed of rotation of the wheel returns to an acceptable rate, the pump stops and the solenoid valve opens, allowing hydraulic pressure to return and reapply the brake. This cycle can be carried out at up to 10 times a second.

The action of the solenoid valves and return pump creates pulses in the hydraulic circuit. When the ABS system is functioning, these pulses can be felt through the brake pedal.

The Civic is also equipped with an additional safety feature built into the ABS system, called EBD (Electronic Brake force Distribution), which automatically apportions braking effort between the front and rear wheels. On any car, whether fitted with ABS or not, 90% of the actual braking is done by the front wheels, and under heavy braking, there is significant weight transfer to the front wheels. This situation is compounded if the car is lightly loaded (without rear seat passengers or luggage), as the rear wheels will have very little weight over them. The EBD function is built into the system's software, and the intention is to limit braking effort (fluid pressure) to the rear wheels, to prevent them locking prematurely under heavy braking, which might otherwise lead to the driver losing control of the rear of the car.

Certain models also feature Brake Assist,

which monitors how rapidly the brake pedal is pressed, and determines whether an emergency stop is required – in this case, maximum braking effort is applied more quickly than the driver would normally be able to, unaided.

The operation of the ABS system is entirely dependent on electrical signals. To prevent the system responding to any inaccurate signals, a built-in safety circuit monitors all signals received by the computer. If an inaccurate signal or low battery voltage is detected, the ABS system is automatically shut down, and the warning light on the instrument panel is illuminated to inform the driver that the ABS system is not operational. Normal braking is unaffected, apart from the loss of the Electronic Brake force Distribution function (which may result in premature rear wheel lock-up under braking).

If a fault does develop in the ABS system, the car must be taken to a Honda dealer for fault diagnosis and repair. Check first, however, that the problem is not due to loose or damaged wiring connections, or badly-routed wiring picking up spurious signals from the ignition system.

21 Anti-lock braking system (ABS) components – removal and refitting

Note: Refer to the precautions in Section 1 before proceeding.

21.1a ABS hydraulic unit is on the left, on petrol models . . .

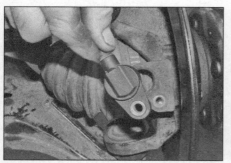

21.13 Unscrew the single bolt, and release the sensor from the hub

Hydraulic unit

Removal

1 The hydraulic unit is located in front of the suspension strut mounting (on petrol models, it is on the left, while diesels have the unit on the right – as seen from the driver's seat) **(see illustrations)**.

2 Disconnect the battery negative lead (refer to *Disconnecting the battery* in the Reference Section).

3 Unscrew the nut and disconnect the hydraulic unit's earth lead from the inner wing.

4 Release the unit's wiring connector plug, then disconnect the plug and move the harness to one side.

5 Before removing the hydraulic unions from the unit, it may be advisable to mark them for position, perhaps by attaching labels, or marked pieces of tape, to each pipe.

6 Loosen the hydraulic unions, then disconnect and unclip the pipes from the unit – avoid bending the pipes at all costs.

7 Unscrew the two upper nuts securing the unit to its mounting bracket, and lift it out.

Caution: Do not attempt to dismantle the hydraulic unit assembly. Overhaul of the unit is a complex job, and should be entrusted to a Honda dealer.

Refitting

8 Refitting is the reverse of the removal procedure, noting the following points:
 a) *Tighten the hydraulic unit mounting bolts securely.*
 b) *Refit the brake pipes to the correct*

21.1b . . . while diesels have the unit on the right

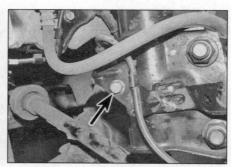

21.14a Unbolt the wiring support bracket on the strut . . .

unions, and tighten the union nuts securely.
 c) *Reconnect the wiring plug securely.*
 d) *Before reconnecting the battery, bleed the complete braking system as described in Section 5. Ensure the system is bled in the correct order, to prevent air entering the return pump.*

ABS computer

9 The computer is an integral part of the hydraulic unit assembly, and cannot be renewed separately. If renewal is necessary, the hydraulic unit must be renewed as a complete assembly, as described in this Section.

Wheel sensors

10 The wheel sensors are subject to extreme operating conditions, and many faults are due to corrosion resulting from water ingress. In the event of a fault arising with a sensor, its wiring plug should first be disconnected and sprayed with a maintenance spray such as WD-40 (the wiring to the sensor should also be checked for damage).

11 If there is any evidence of corrosion (which will typically appear as a green or white powdery deposit), it may be possible to clean the terminals carefully with a narrow file, or a folded piece of emery paper.

Front wheel sensor

12 Loosen the front wheel nuts, then jack up the front of the car and support it on axle stands (see *Jacking and vehicle support*). Remove the front wheel.

13 The wheel sensor is located at the front of the swivel hub assembly. Unscrew the single mounting bolt, and carefully release the sensor from the hub **(see illustration)**. It is likely that the sensor and its mounting bolt will have suffered from its exposed position – use plenty of penetrating fluid, and clean around the bolt and sensor before attempting removal. If the sensor is being re-used, take care when removing it, or it will suffer damage

14 Trace the sensor wiring back from the hub, freeing the wiring from any clips or ties. There's a wiring support bracket bolted to the strut, and another on the inner wheel arch, to which the sensor wiring plug is clipped **(see illustrations)**. Note how the wiring is routed,

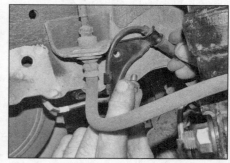

21.14b . . . unbolt a similar bracket on the inner arch . . .

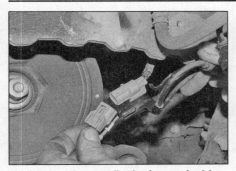

21.14c ...then unclip the (orange) wiring plug and disconnect it

21.17 Removing the brake disc splash shield

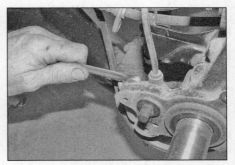

21.18a Unscrew the sensor mounting bolt on the inside of the knuckle

21.18b If the sensor has seized in the knuckle, fit a washer . . .

21.18c . . . and a deep socket over it, and use a soft-faced mallet . . .

21.18d . . . to tap it out

for refitting. Once all the wiring has been detached, disconnect the wiring plug and remove the sensor.

15 Refitting is a reversal of removal, noting the following points:

a) *Clean the sensor location in the hub, and apply a little copper grease to make future removal easier.*

b) *Ensure that the wiring is routed as noted before removal, and secured with all necessary brackets, clips and ties.*

c) *Reconnect the wiring plug securely.*

Rear wheel sensor

16 Chock the front wheels, loosen the rear wheel nuts, then jack up the rear of the car and support it on axle stands (see *Jacking and vehicle support*). Remove the rear wheel.

17 The wheel sensor is located on the inside of the knuckle assembly, at the front. To improve access, remove the rear hub as described in Chapter 10, then remove either the brake disc (Section 10) and splash shield (three bolts) or the brake backplate (Section 13) **(see illustration)**.

18 Unscrew the single mounting bolt, and carefully release the sensor from the knuckle. It is likely that the sensor and its mounting bolt will have suffered from its exposed position – use plenty of penetrating fluid, and clean around the bolt and sensor before attempting

removal. If the sensor is being re-used, take care when removing it, or it will suffer damage **(see illustrations)**.

19 Trace the sensor wiring back from the knuckle, freeing the wiring from any clips or ties. Unbolt the wiring support brackets as necessary. On the driver's side, the wiring plug is located above the exhaust heat shield, but access is not easy on either side. Once all the wiring has been detached, disconnect the wiring plug and remove the sensor.

20 Refitting is a reversal of removal, noting the following points:

a) *Clean the sensor location in the knuckle, and apply a little copper grease to make future removal easier* **(see illustration)**.

b) *Ensure that the wiring is routed as noted before removal, and secured with all necessary brackets, clips and ties.*

c) *Reconnect the wiring plug securely.*

22 Vacuum pump (diesel engines) – removal and refitting

The vacuum pump is attached to the alternator, and is removed with it, as described in Chapter 5A.

23 Vacuum pump (diesel engines) – testing and overhaul

The operation of the braking system vacuum pump can be checked using a vacuum gauge. However, a suitable oil supply must be provided to the pump if it is being tested off the car. The pump should be capable of generating a vacuum of approximately 400 mm Hg.

Pump overhaul procedures are not given by Honda, which suggests that this may not be possible. Check for availability of spare parts before attempting to dismantle the pump.

21.20 Apply a little copper grease to the sensor when refitting

Chapter 10
Suspension and steering

Contents

Degrees of difficulty

Easy, suitable for novice with little experience 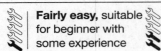	**Fairly easy,** suitable for beginner with some experience	**Fairly difficult,** suitable for competent DIY mechanic	**Difficult,** suitable for experienced DIY mechanic	**Very difficult,** suitable for expert DIY or professional

Specifications

Front suspension
Type . . . . Independent with shock absorber/coil spring, lower control arm, anti-roll bar

Rear suspension
Type . . . . Independent with tubular lower arm, upper control arm, coil spring/shock absorber unit, anti-roll bar

Steering
Type . . . . Rack and pinion, electrically power-assisted

Wheel alignment and steering angles
Total toe:
    Front . . . . 0 ± 3.0 mm
    Rear:
        Inspection values (toe-in) . . . . 2.0 ± 3.0 mm
        Setting values (toe-in) . . . . 2.0 +2.0 -1.0 mm
Camber angle:
    Front . . . . 0° 00' ± 45'
    Rear . . . . -0° 45' ± 45'
Castor angle . . . . 1° 33' ± 1°

Roadwheels
Type . . . . Pressed-steel or aluminium alloy

Tyres
Pressures . . . . Refer to the label on the driver's door aperture

Torque wrench settings	Nm	lbf ft
Front suspension		
Anti-roll bar clamp bolts and drop link nuts*	39	29
Bottom balljoint nut:		
Stage 1 (or minimum setting)	49	36
Stage 2 (or maximum setting).	59	44
Driveshaft/hub nut*	181	134
Front subframe bolts:		
M10 bolts	59	44
M14 bolts*	103	76
Lower arm pivot and inner mounting bolts	83	61
Strut piston rod nut*	44	32
Strut-to-hub pinch-bolt/nut	103	76
Strut upper mounting nuts	44	32
Rear suspension		
Anti-roll bar:		
Clamp bolts	22	16
Drop link nuts*	38	28
Hub nut*	181	134
Knuckle:		
Adjuster bolt/nut*	59	44
Lower mounting bolt.	59	44
Lower arm:		
Front mounting bolts (to floor)	108	80
Rear mounting bolt (to crossmember)	59	44
Strut lower mounting bolt.	61	45
Strut piston rod nut*	29	21
Upper control arm bolts	59	44
Steering		
Steering column mounting nuts/bolts	16	12
Steering column pinch-bolts	29	21
Steering motor mounting bolts.	20	15
Steering rack mounting bolts:		
To bulkhead	61	45
To subframe	28	21
Steering rack front mounting nut	61	45
Steering wheel	39	29
Track rod end balljoint nut	43	32
Roadwheels		
Wheel nuts	108	80

* Use new nuts/bolts

1   General information

The front suspension is of independent type, with a subframe, MacPherson struts (with integral steering arms), lower arms, and an anti-roll bar. The struts, which incorporate coil springs and integral shock absorbers, are attached at their upper ends to the reinforced strut mountings on the body shell. The lower end of each strut is bolted to the top of a cast swivel hub, which carries the hub, and the brake disc and caliper. The hubs run within non-adjustable bearings in the swivel hubs. The lower end of each swivel hub is attached, via a balljoint, to a pressed-steel lower arm assembly. The bottom balljoint is integral with the swivel hub. Each lower arm is attached at its inboard end to the subframe, via flexible rubber bushes, and controls both lateral and fore-and-aft movement of the front wheels.

An anti-roll bar is fitted to all models. The anti-roll bar is mounted on the subframe, and is connected to the lower arms via vertical drop links.

The rear suspension is semi-independent, with a rigid crossmember and two tubular lower arms. The lower arms pivot on three mountings, on the underbody, the crossmember, and the cast rear knuckle assembly. Compact rear suspension struts are bolted to the lower arm at the base, and to the body housings at the top. An upper control arm is mounted to the crossmember on the inner end, and to the rear knuckle at the outer end. The rear hubs run on stub axles which are part of the rear knuckle assembly.

All models have power-assisted rack-and-pinion steering. The Civic differs from previous models in that it has an electric motor at the base of the steering column to provide the turning assistance, rather than an engine-driven hydraulic system. The advantage of the EPS (electric power steering) system is that it only operates when the wheels are turned – a torque sensor signals the motor – whereas on the older system, the pump was running at all times, taking power from the engine. Not having an engine-driven power steering pump also simplifies the auxiliary drivebelt arrangement and engine installation. The system has an electronic control unit mounted in the passenger footwell. The vehicle speed sensor (see Chapter 4A or 4B) signals the steering system to provide extra assistance at low speeds.

Seized nuts/bolts

When working on the suspension or steering system components, you may come across fasteners which seem impossible to loosen. These fasteners on the underside of the car are continually subjected to water, road grime, mud, etc, and can become rusted or 'seized,' making them extremely difficult to remove.

In order to unscrew these stubborn fasteners without damaging them (or other components), first use a wire brush to clean exposed threads. Afterwards, use lots of penetrating oil or a maintenance spray such as WD-40, and allow it to soak in for a while.

On stubborn screws, using a close-fitting screwdriver bit in a socket handle can provide greater leverage on a difficult screw than a screwdriver will, reducing the chance of chewing-up the screw head.

With nuts or bolts, hex sockets (ones with six 'sides') are preferable to bi-hex ones, as they are less likely to round off the corners – 'surface-drive' sockets are also available, which grip on the flats, not the corners. With spanners, use the open end rather than the ring end, for the same reason. In any case, don't use any tool which isn't a close fit, as it will slip if enough force is applied. If the nut/bolt corners have already gone, it can help to use a socket one size smaller (or try an imperial size), and tap it on using a hammer, to make a tight fit – in this case, a new nut or bolt will clearly be needed.

Try turning the nut or bolt in the tightening (usually clockwise) direction first – this will help to break it loose. If this produces a little movement, loosen then tighten the nut or bolt several times, and slowly try to increase the range of movement, until it will unscrew completely. Beware, however, that this approach may cause the nut or bolt to shear off.

Sometimes a sharp blow with a hammer and punch is effective in breaking the bond between a nut and bolt threads, but care must be taken to prevent the punch from slipping off the fastener and ruining the threads. Impact drivers can also be successful in freeing a stubborn fastener, but make sure a close-fitting socket is used.

Heating the stuck fastener and surrounding area sometimes helps too, but isn't always recommended because of the obvious dangers associated with fire – take care if rubber or plastic components, or fuel/brake pipes, are close by. Heat may also ignite the penetrating oil or maintenance spray.

Long breaker bars and extension pipes will increase leverage (an extension pipe is any strong piece of metal tube, slipped over a socket handle, to make it 'longer'). Don't use an extension pipe on a ratchet handle – the ratchet mechanism could be damaged. Wear gloves if a great amount of force is being applied – these will protect your hands if something 'lets go'.

In extreme cases, the nut or bolt head may have to be cut off, if there's sufficient access. Fasteners that require drastic measures to remove should always be renewed.

⚠️ *Warning: Since most of the procedures that are dealt with in this Chapter involve jacking up the car and working underneath it, a good pair of axle stands will be needed. A trolley jack is the preferred type of jack to lift the car, and it can also be used to support other components during certain operations. Do*

2.8 Unscrew the nut securing the anti-roll bar drop link to the lower arm

2.9 Unbolt and remove the ABS wheel sensor

not rely on a trolley jack alone to support the car, as they can 'creep' down – once the car is raised on the jack, place at least one axle stand underneath as a precaution.

2 Front swivel hub –
removal and refitting

Removal

1 To remove the hub, the driveshaft nut first has to be loosened. The nut is tightened to an extremely high torque, and for this reason, it is preferable if possible to loosen the nut with the wheel on the ground. However, on Civics with steel wheels, the wheel nuts are used to secure the wheel trim, which covers the driveshaft nut. This means loosening the wheel nuts, jacking up the car, taking off the wheel nuts and wheel trim, then refitting the wheel and nuts before lowering the car to undo the driveshaft nut.

2 The driveshaft nut has a locking tab (or a raised collar) which is punched into the driveshaft groove to stop the nut loosening accidentally. Using a sturdy flat-bladed screwdriver, or preferably a punch or chisel, bend the tab/collar back so the nut can be unscrewed.

3 Significant force will be required to loosen the nut, so be sure to use only good-quality, close-fitting tools. A long-handled 'breaker bar' will be needed, to provide the necessary leverage – if this is not available, slip a strong

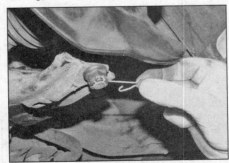

2.10a Extract the locking clip . . .

piece of metal pipe over the end of the socket handle. Wear gloves to protect your hands, should something slip.

4 Chock the front wheel, and ·have an assistant apply the footbrake firmly, while you slacken the nut. It is not necessary at this stage to remove the nut completely.

5 If the nut has to be loosened with the car raised, ensure that it is very well supported, using well-placed, good-quality axle stands (see *Jacking and vehicle support*). Have an assistant firmly depress the brake pedal to prevent the disc from turning, whilst you slacken and remove the driveshaft retaining nut. Alternatively, a tool can be fabricated from two lengths of steel strip (one long, one short) and a nut and bolt; the nut and bolt forming the pivot of a forked tool which fits over the wheel studs.

6 Once the nut has been loosened, (if not already done) jack up the front of the car and support it on axle stands (see *Jacking and vehicle support*). Remove the front wheel.

7 Remove the brake disc as described in Chapter 9.

8 It is helpful, though not essential, to disconnect the anti-roll bar drop link from the lower arm at this stage – this will make it easier to prise down the lower arm to separate the bottom balljoint (we managed without doing this, however). Unscrew the nut securing the anti-roll bar drop link to the suspension lower arm – use an Allen key to stop the drop link balljoint turning as this is done **(see illustration)**. Unhook the drop link from the lower arm. Discard the nut – a new one should be used when refitting.

9 Unscrew the ABS wheel sensor mounting bolt, and carefully remove the wheel sensor from the front of the hub **(see illustration)**. Move the sensor clear of the hub – unclip the wiring harness as necessary, but it should not be necessary to disconnect it.

10 Extract the locking pin (note which way round it is fitted), then unscrew the bottom balljoint nut **(see illustrations)**. Note that a new locking pin will be needed for refitting.

11 The balljoint's taper can be released using a balljoint separator tool, but this carries the risk of damaging the balljoint's rubber boot – often, it is possible to release the taper by tapping the end of the lower arm with a

2.10b ... then unscrew and remove the bottom balljoint nut

2.11a Tap the end of the lower arm to release the balljoint ...

2.11b ... then lever the lower arm down, and separate it from the hub

hammer. Use a suitable lever to prise down the arm, and disconnect the lower arm from the swivel hub **(see illustrations)**.

12 The splined end of the driveshaft now has to be released from its location in the hub. It's likely that the splines will be very tight (corrosion may even be a factor, if the driveshaft has not been disturbed for some time), and considerable force may be needed. Tap the end of the shaft with a plastic or hide mallet only – if an ordinary hammer is used, place a small piece of wood over the end of the driveshaft – and leave the old nut loosely in place on the end to avoid damaging the splines.

13 Once the splines have been released, remove the driveshaft nut and discard it – the nut is only intended to be used once **(see illustration)**.

14 Pull the disc/hub outwards, and turn it to allow the driveshaft to be withdrawn through the hub **(see illustration)**. It's helpful to have

an assistant on hand here, to pull the hub outwards, while you slide out the driveshaft.

15 Unscrew the two nuts from the pinch-bolts securing the lower end of the suspension strut to the hub. Support the hub, then tap the bolts through using a pin punch, noting that they are fitted from the rear. Remove the hub from under the car **(see illustrations)**.

Refitting

16 Refitting is a reversal of removal, bearing in mind the following points:

a) *Use a new driveshaft nut and anti-roll bar drop link nut, and a new balljoint locking pin. Lightly oil the driveshaft nut before fitting.*

b) *Clean the balljoint and its seat in the lower arm before fitting – it must be fitted dry. Tighten the bottom balljoint nut initially to the Stage 1 (minimum) setting. From this point, tighten the nut as required to align the locking pin holes (do not loosen to align), then fit a new pin to secure.*

c) *Do not fully tighten the hub nut until the car is resting on its wheels. Stake the nut collar into the driveshaft groove (or bend over the locktabs).*

d) *Tighten all fixings to the specified torque.*

3 Front wheel bearings – renewal

Note: *A press, a suitable puller, or a selection of large bolts, washers and other improvised tools will be required for this operation. Obtain a bearing kit before proceeding.*

1 With the swivel hub removed as described in Section 2, proceed as follows.

2 Securely support the hub carrier, on two metal bars for instance, with the inner face uppermost then, using a metal bar or tube of suitable diameter, press or drive out the hub flange – we used a large nut (the same diameter as the end of the hub's splined end) and a hammer **(see illustrations)**. Alternatively, use the puller to separate the hub from the bearing. Note that the bearing inner race will remain on the hub. Take care not to damage the brake disc splash shield.

3 With the hub flange removed, take off the disc shield, which is secured by three screws **(see illustrations)**.

4 Preferably using circlip pliers (two small screwdrivers could be used as a substitute), extract the bearing circlip **(see illustrations)**.

5 Now the bearing itself must be removed. After applying a generous amount of spray lubricant, we were able to drive the

2.13 Unscrew and remove the driveshaft nut

2.14 Pull out the disc/hub, and withdraw the driveshaft from the inside

2.15a Remove the two strut-to-hub pinch-bolts ...

2.15b ... separate the top of the hub from the base of the strut ...

2.15c ... and remove the swivel hub

3.2a Using a hammer and large nut . . .

3.2b . . . drive out the hub flange

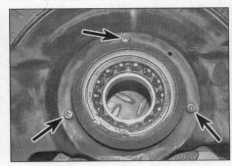

3.3a Remove the three small screws . . .

3.3b . . . and take off the disc splash shield

3.4a Using circlip pliers . . .

3.4b . . . extract the bearing circlip from its groove

bearing out, using another old bearing **(see illustration)**. Mount the swivel hub across two large blocks of wood (or even bricks) – putting it across the open jaws of a vice might result in damage to the vice, owing to the amount of force which will be necessary.

6 The bearing inner race left on the hub flange must now be removed. To do this, grip the edge of the flange in a vice, and drive the race off with a chisel, then a punch **(see illustrations)**. Tap the race at the top and both sides (even turn the flange over in the vice) to

stop it jamming as it comes off. Take care not to mark the hub flange bearing surface.
7 Using emery paper, clean off any burrs or raised edges from the hub flange and hub carrier, which might stop the components going back together **(see illustrations)**.

3.5 Driving out the bearing, using an old bearing

3.6a Start removing the inner race from the hub flange with a chisel . . .

3.6b . . . then use a punch . . .

3.6c . . . to drive the flange off

3.7a Use emery paper to clean up the hub flange . . .

3.7b . . . and the hub carrier

3.8 Lightly tap the bearing in all round to start fitting

3.9a Mount the hub in a vice, with threaded rod, washers, large nuts, etc . . .

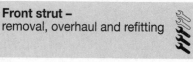

3.9b . . . then tighten the nuts to press in the new bearing

3.10 Fit the new retaining circlip

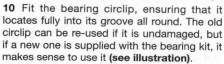

3.12 Refit the disc shield, then use the nut-and-rod method to press on the hub flange

4 Front strut –
removal, overhaul and refitting

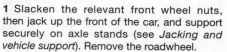

Removal

1 Slacken the relevant front wheel nuts, then jack up the front of the car, and support securely on axle stands (see *Jacking and vehicle support*). Remove the roadwheel.

2 Extract the split pin from the steering track rod end balljoint nut (a new one will be needed when refitting) **(see illustration)**. Unscrew the nut, but leave it attached by a couple of threads for now.

3 Disconnect the track rod end from the strut, either using a balljoint separator tool, or by tapping the end of the balljoint stud (use a block of wood and the still-fitted nut to protect the threads). When the balljoint separates, unscrew the nut completely, and move the track rod clear **(see illustration)**.

4 Unscrew the two bolts securing the ABS wiring harness and brake hose support brackets, and move the harness and hose clear of the strut **(see illustration)**.

5 Unscrew the two nuts from the pinch-bolts securing the lower end of the suspension strut to the hub. Support the hub, then tap the bolts through using a pin punch, noting that they are fitted from the rear. Tilt the hub outwards on the bottom balljoint, to separate it from the base of the strut **(see illustrations)**.

6 Ensure that the strut is supported from below, then working in the engine

8 Apply a light coat of lubricant to the inside of the hub carrier, and to the outside of the new bearing. Start fitting the bearing by offering it squarely into the carrier, then give it a few light taps with the hammer all round to locate it – keep the bearing square as this is done, or it will jam **(see illustration)**.

9 Fitting the bearing by tapping it in all the way with a hammer will likely damage it. We used a length of threaded bar (available from motor factors, DIY stores, etc), with a nut, some large washers and a drilled plate on the inside of the hub carrier. With the old bearing, another washer, and a nut on the outside, the whole assembly was mounted in a vice, and the nut tightened to press the new bearing in place. The actual method was to tighten the nut slightly, give the old bearing a few taps round its edge, tighten the nut some more, and so on until the bearing was fully home **(see illustrations)**.

10 Fit the bearing circlip, ensuring that it locates fully into its groove all round. The old circlip can be re-used if it is undamaged, but if a new one is supplied with the bearing kit, it makes sense to use it **(see illustration)**.

11 Refit the brake disc shield, tightening its three screws securely.

12 The hub flange can be pressed into the new bearing using a very similar method to the one just used for the bearing **(see illustration)**.

> **HAYNES HINT** *There is a distinct change in the sound produced by the hammer when the bearing and flange are fully home – this may otherwise be hard to judge.*

13 On completion, refit the swivel hub as described in Section 2.

4.2 Extract the split pin from the track rod end balljoint nut

4.3 Disconnect the track rod end from the hub

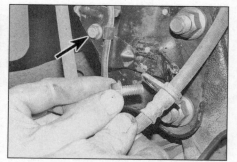

4.4 Unbolt the brake hose from the strut (ABS wiring support bracket bolt arrowed)

4.5a Unscrew the two nuts at the front . . .

4.5b . . . and remove the strut-to-hub pinch-bolts from the rear

4.5c Tilt the hub outwards to free it from the strut

compartment, loosen and remove the three suspension strut top mounting nuts. **Do not** loosen the strut centre nut. Lower the strut (if necessary, press the lower arm down slightly) and withdraw it from under the wheel arch **(see illustrations)**.

Overhaul

Note: *A spring compressor tool will be required for this operation.*

7 With the suspension strut resting on a bench, or clamped in a vice, fit a spring compressor tool, and compress the coil spring to relieve the pressure on the spring seats. Ensure that the compressor tool is securely located on the spring, in accordance with the tool manufacturer's instructions **(see illustration)**.

8 Counterhold the strut piston rod with the Allen key or hexagon bit used during removal, and unscrew the piston rod nut. This nut is of self-locking type, so a new one must be obtained for reassembly.

9 Remove the piston rod nut, followed by the top mounting, strut bearing, spring upper seat, the spring (with compressor tool still fitted), and finally the rubber bump stop **(see illustration)**. **Note:** *On petrol models, do not remove the rubber cushion from the top of the spring, unless a new spring is being fitted.*

10 With the strut assembly now completely dismantled, examine all the components for wear, damage or deformation, and check the strut bearing for smoothness of operation. Renew any of the components as necessary.

11 Examine the strut for signs of fluid

4.6a Unscrew and remove the three strut upper mounting nuts . . .

leakage. Check the strut piston for signs of pitting along its entire length, and check the strut body for signs of damage. While holding it in an upright position, test the operation of the strut by moving the piston through a full stroke, and then through short strokes of 50 to 100 mm. In both cases, the resistance felt should be smooth and continuous. If the resistance is jerky or uneven or if there is any visible sign of wear or damage to the strut, renewal is necessary.

12 If any doubt exists as to the condition of the coil spring, carefully remove the spring compressors and check the spring for distortion and signs of cracking. Renew the spring if it is damaged or distorted, or if there is any doubt as to its condition.

13 Inspect all other components for damage or deterioration, and renew any that are suspect.

4.6b . . . and lower out the strut

14 On petrol models, if a new spring is being fitted, or if a new upper rubber cushion is required due to wear, fit the new cushion as follows (where applicable, carefully remove the spring compressors first). The old cushion is secured by metal tangs, which must be bent back to remove it. Fit the new cushion in place, positioning it to leave a small gap between the spring end and the projection on the inside of the cushion. To secure the cushion, bend over only the three tangs marked with a triangle.

15 Slide the rubber bump stop onto the strut piston.

16 If the spring compressor tool has been removed from the spring, refit it and compress the spring sufficiently to enable it to be refitted to the strut.

17 Slide the spring over the strut, and position it so that the lower end of the spring

4.7a Fitting the coil spring compressor – try to 'catch' as many coils as possible . . .

4.7b . . . then tighten the clamps slowly and evenly, making sure they don't slip round

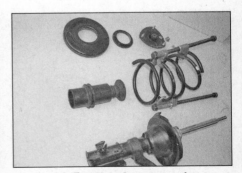

4.9 Front strut components

4.17 Fit the spring over the strut, and engage the spring end with the stop

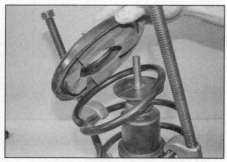

4.18a Fit the spring upper seat onto the spring, ensuring it locates properly . . .

4.18b . . . then fit the bearing

4.19 Fitting the top mounting plate

4.20a Fit a new piston rod nut . . .

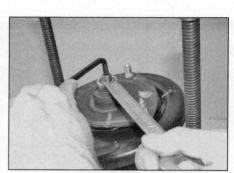

4.20b . . . and tighten it, using an Allen key to hold the piston rod

is resting against the stop on the lower seat **(see illustration)**.

18 Refit the spring upper seat, making sure it is aligned on the spring end correctly, and then fit the bearing **(see illustrations)**.

19 Refit the top mounting plate **(see illustration)**, noting the following:

a) *On petrol models, the small hole in the plate's outer edge must face to the inside (towards the engine) when the strut is refitted.*

b) *On diesel models, the cut-out in the side of the upper spring seat must face to the inside (towards the engine) when the strut is refitted.*

20 Fit a new piston rod nut, and tighten it securely, using the specified torque as a guide. Counterhold the piston rod using an Allen key or hexagon bit as during removal **(see illustrations)**.

21 Slowly slacken the spring compressor tool to relieve the tension in the spring. Check that the ends of the spring locate correctly against the stops on the spring seats. If necessary, turn the spring and the upper seat so that the components locate correctly before the compressor tool is removed. Remove the compressor tool when the spring is fully seated.

Refitting

22 Refitting is a reversal of removal, bearing in mind the following points:

a) *Clean the track rod balljoint and its seat in the strut before fitting – it must be fitted dry. Tighten the balljoint nut to the specified torque. From this point, tighten the nut slightly as required to align the split pin holes (do not loosen to align), then fit a new pin to secure.*

b) *Tighten all fixings to the specified torque.*

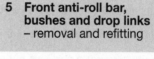

5 Front anti-roll bar, bushes and drop links
– removal and refitting

1 Loosen the front wheel nuts, then jack up the front of the car, and support it on axle stands (see *Jacking and vehicle support*). Remove the front wheels.

Bushes

2 If the bushes alone are to be renewed, working on one side at a time, unscrew the two bolts and remove the anti-roll bar mounting clamp **(see illustration)**. The bar can then be lowered slightly, and the bush removed (the bush is split for easy removal).

3 Slip the new bush into place around the roll bar – if necessary, lubricate the bush with a little washing-up liquid first. Also note that the roll bar has a painted mark to indicate the fitted position of the bushes, to make initial fitting more accurate.

4 Refit the clamp, noting that it has an arrow marking which indicates the front of the car. Slide the bush along the bar slightly if required, to bring the clamp bolt holes into alignment. Tighten the clamp bolts to the specified torque, then repeat the procedure on the other side.

5 On completion, refit the wheels, then lower the car to the ground and tighten the wheel nuts to the specified torque.

Drop links

6 Unscrew the nut at each end of the link – use an Allen key to stop the drop link balljoints turning as this is done **(see illustration)**.

5.2 Front anti-roll bar mounting clamp

5.6 Front anti-roll bar drop link

Remove the drop link from the lower arm and anti-roll bar, noting how it is fitted. Discard the nuts – new ones should be used when refitting.

7 Refitting is a reversal of removal, noting the following points:

  a) *Use new self-locking nuts on the anti-roll bar drop links.*

  b) *Position a jack under the bottom balljoint, and raise it to load the front suspension before tightening the nuts to the specified torque.*

  c) *Wait 5 minutes, then recheck that the nuts are properly tightened.*

  d) *On completion, refit the wheels, then lower the car to the ground and tighten the wheel nuts to the specified torque.*

Anti-roll bar

8 Unscrew the nut securing each of the two anti-roll bar drop links to the suspension lower arm – use an Allen key to stop the drop link balljoint turning as this is done. Unhook the drop links from the lower arm. Discard the two nuts – new ones should be used when refitting.

9 Unscrew the two bolts from each of the two anti-roll bar outer clamps, then remove the clamps and lower out the roll bar. Withdraw the bar from under the car.

10 If wished, the drop links can be removed from the anti-roll bar after unscrewing the securing nuts. If necessary, counterhold the drop link pins using an Allen key. Discard the drop link nuts – new ones should be used when refitting.

11 Refitting is a reversal of removal, noting the following points:

  a) *Ensure that the clamps are refitted with their arrow markings facing forwards, and tighten the bolts to the specified torque.*

  b) *If the drop links were removed, refit them as described in paragraph 7.*

  c) *On completion, refit the wheels, then lower the car to the ground and tighten the wheel nuts to the specified torque.*

6   Front lower arm – removal and refitting

Removal

1 Slacken the front wheel nuts on the side concerned, then apply the handbrake, jack up the front of the car, and support securely on axle stands (see *Jacking and vehicle support*). Remove the wheel.

2 Unscrew the nut securing the anti-roll bar drop link to the suspension lower arm – use an Allen key to stop the drop link balljoint turning as this is done. Unhook the drop link from the lower arm. Discard the nut – a new one should be used when refitting.

3 Extract the locking pin (note which way round it is fitted), then unscrew the bottom balljoint nut. Using a balljoint separator tool (or a suitable lever to prise down the arm) disconnect the lower arm from the swivel hub. Note that a new locking pin will be needed for refitting.

4 Unscrew and remove the lower arm pivot bolt and the front mounting bolt, then remove the arm from under the car (**see illustration**).

Overhaul

5 Examine the rubber bushes for wear and damage, and check the arm for straightness, as it could have been bent by careless jacking-up. At the time of writing, the rubber bushes could not be renewed separately. Renew the complete lower arm if there is any wear or damage.

Refitting

6 Check the bottom balljoint rubber boot condition while the lower arm is removed (see Section 7).

7 Clean the balljoint and its seat in the lower arm before fitting – it must be fitted dry. Offer the lower arm into position, taking care not to damage the balljoint boot as the lower arm is refitted.

8 Refit the two lower arm bolts, and tighten them by hand only at this stage.

9 Tighten the bottom balljoint nut initially to the Stage 1 (minimum) setting. From this point, tighten the nut as required to align the locking pin holes (do not loosen to align), then fit a new pin to secure.

10 Refit the wheel, and lower the car to the ground. Tighten the wheel nuts to the specified torque.

11 With the car resting on its wheels, tighten the two lower arm bolts to the specified torque.

7   Front bottom balljoint – renewal

If the bottom balljoint rubber boot is damaged, a new one can be obtained from Honda dealers. Once the lower arm has been disconnected (refer to Section 6 for details), the old boot can be unclipped. Wipe the balljoint clean (do not use excessive amounts of solvent), then pack it with fresh grease and fit the new boot. However, bear in mind that if the boot has been damaged for some time, it is likely that dirt will have got into the balljoint, and a new balljoint may soon be needed.

If the bottom balljoint itself is worn, the balljoint is available separately, but a press and various special tools are needed. If possible, remove the swivel hub as described in Section 2, and take it to a Honda dealer for the new balljoint to be fitted.

6.4 Lower arm front mounting bolt

8   Front subframe – removal and refitting

Removal

1 Loosen the front wheel nuts, then jack up the front of the car, and support it on axle stands (see *Jacking and vehicle support*). Remove the front wheels.

2 Unbolt and remove the engine undertray.

3 Remove the front lower arms as described in Section 6.

4 Remove the exhaust front pipe (and catalytic converter) as described in Chapter 4A or 4B.

5 Referring to Chapter 2A or 2B as applicable, unbolt the engine front and rear mountings. As long as the engine remains supported on the left- and right-hand mountings, it will be secure, though there will be increased movement.

6 Check around the subframe to ensure that there are no brackets, hoses or harnesses still attached, or anything in the way which would prevent it from being lowered.

7 The subframe is secured to the body by a total of six bolts. By the two rear bolts, there are alignment markings to indicate the subframe's relative position to the body – if these are not clear, clean the area and make your own subframe-to-body marks with paint (**see illustration**). However, there appears to be no requirement to align the subframe during refitting.

8 Support the subframe, either with two jacks, or (preferably) with the help of an assistant, then progressively loosen and remove the

8.7 The subframe has alignment marks by the rear bolts

8.8a Removing a subframe front mounting bolt

8.8b The subframe 'side' bolts are on slotted mountings

8.9 Lowering out the subframe

bolts. Note that the two 'side' bolts are on slotted mountings, so need only be loosened **(see illustrations)**.

9 Lower the subframe to clear the engine front and rear mountings, then manoeuvre it past the exhaust at the rear, and withdraw it from under the car **(see illustration)**.

10 Note that the four larger subframe bolts are only intended to be used once, and new ones should be obtained for refitting.

Refitting

11 With the help of an assistant, position the subframe on the jacks, then raise the jack to lift the subframe into position under the car. Ensure that the subframe is securely supported.

12 Where applicable, align the marks made prior to removal. Fit and tighten the subframe bolts (including the four new larger bolts), and tighten them all to their specified torques.

13 The remainder of refitting is a reversal of removal, noting the following points:
  a) *Tighten all fixings to the specified torque.*
  b) *Refit the front lower arms as described in Section 6.*
  c) *Have the front wheel alignment checked on completion.*

9	**Rear knuckle and wheel bearing** – inspection and renewal

Inspection

1 The rear wheel bearings are non-adjustable.

2 To check the bearings for excessive wear, chock the front wheels, then jack up the rear of the car and support it on axle stands. Fully release the handbrake.

3 Grip the rear wheel at the top and bottom, and attempt to rock it. If excessive movement is noted, or if there is any roughness or vibration felt when the wheel is spun, it is indicative that the wheel bearings are worn.

Renewal

Rear hub/bearing

4 The rear hub nut first has to be loosened. The nut is tightened to an extremely high torque, and for this reason, it is preferable if possible to loosen the nut with the wheel on the ground. However, on Civics with steel wheels, the wheel nuts are used to secure the wheel trim, which covers the hub nut. This means loosening the wheel nuts, jacking up the car, taking off the wheel nuts and wheel trim, then refitting the wheel and nuts before lowering the car to undo the hub nut.

5 Tap off the dust cap to access the hub nut **(see illustration)**. Note that Honda recommend a new dust cap is used when refitting, though in practice, provided the old cap is in good condition and still a tight fit, it can be re-used.

6 The hub nut has a locking tab (or a raised collar) which is punched into the stub axle groove to stop the nut loosening accidentally. Using a sturdy flat-bladed screwdriver, or preferably a punch or chisel, bend the tab/collar back so the nut can be unscrewed **(see illustration)**.

7 Significant force will be required to loosen the nut, so be sure to use only good-quality, close-fitting tools. A long-handled 'breaker bar' will be needed, to provide the necessary leverage – if this is not available, slip a strong piece of metal pipe over the end of the socket handle. Wear gloves to protect your hands, should something slip.

8 Chock the rear wheel, and have an assistant apply the footbrake firmly, while you slacken the nut. It is not necessary at this stage to remove the nut completely.

9 If the nut has to be loosened with the car raised, ensure that it is very well supported, using well-placed, good-quality axle stands (see *Jacking and vehicle support*). Have an assistant firmly depress the brake pedal to prevent the disc from turning, whilst you slacken and remove the hub nut. Alternatively, a tool can be fabricated from two lengths of steel strip (one long, one short) and a nut and bolt; the nut and bolt forming the pivot of a forked tool which fits over the wheel studs.

10 Once the nut has been loosened, (if not already done) jack up the rear of the car and support it on axle stands (see *Jacking and vehicle support*). Remove the rear wheel.

11 Remove the brake disc or drum as described in Chapter 9.

12 Remove the hub nut and withdraw the hub flange from the stub axle **(see illustration)**. Note that the wheel bearing is an integral part of the hub flange, and is not available separately – to renew the wheel bearing, a new hub flange will have to be fitted. A new hub nut will also be required for refitting.

9.5 Tap off the dust cap fitted over the rear hub nut

9.6 Relieve the hub nut staking with a hammer and punch

9.12 Removing the rear hub/bearing

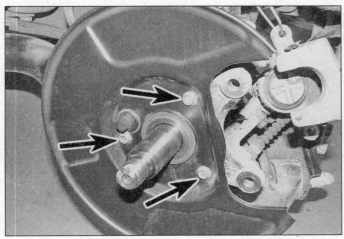

9.14 On disc brake models, remove the splash shield

9.17 On rear disc brake models, unbolt and remove the handbrake cable bracket

Rear knuckle

13 Remove the rear hub and bearing as described previously in this Section.

14 On disc brake models, unscrew the three bolts securing the brake disc splash shield, and withdraw it over the stub axle **(see illustration)**.

15 On drum brake models, remove the brake backplate as described in Chapter 9.

16 Remove the rear wheel ABS sensor from the hub, with reference to Chapter 9. Move the sensor clear – unclip the wiring harness as necessary, but it should not be necessary to disconnect it.

17 As applicable, unbolt and remove the brake hose and handbrake cable support brackets from the inside of the knuckle, and move them clear **(see illustration)**.

18 Position a jack under the end of the lower arm (avoid the blade section), and raise the arm just slightly, so that its weight is supported – do not compress the suspension significantly.

19 Unscrew and withdraw the bolt securing the upper control arm to the knuckle, and separate the arm. For information, the other end of the control arm is secured to the floor at its inner end by two bolts **(see illustrations)**.

20 The rear wheel camber is adjustable, by means of an adjuster bolt and cam arrangement. To preserve the rear wheel alignment, clean the hub in the area of the adjuster bolt and cam, and mark their positions relative to the knuckle with paint **(see illustrations)**.

21 Unscrew the nut from the adjuster bolt, then remove the cam and withdraw the adjuster bolt from the knuckle. Note that a new self-locking nut must be used when refitting the adjuster bolt.

22 Support the knuckle, then unscrew and withdraw the knuckle lower mounting bolt. Remove the knuckle from under the car.

Refitting

Rear knuckle

23 Offer the knuckle into position, then refit the lower mounting bolt, adjuster bolt/cam

and upper control arm bolt (use a new self-locking nut on the adjuster bolt). Tighten all three by hand only at this stage.

24 Position a jack under the end of the lower arm (avoid the blade section), and raise the arm so that the suspension is compressed, approximately the same as if the car were resting on its wheels.

25 Align the adjuster bolt and cam with their previously-made marks, and tighten the adjuster nut/bolt to the specified torque.

26 Tighten the lower mounting bolt and upper control arm bolt to the specified torque.

27 Refit the upper control arm to the knuckle, then insert the bolt and tighten to the specified

torque. Lower the jack so that the lower arm is hanging free.

28 Lightly grease and refit the ABS wheel sensor.

29 As applicable, refit the brake hose and handbrake cable support brackets.

30 On disc brake models, refit the splash shield, and secure with the three bolts, tightened securely.

31 On drum brake models, refit the brake backplate as described in Chapter 9.

32 Refit the hub flange as described in paragraph 34 onwards.

33 On completion, have the rear wheel alignment checked and if necessary adjusted.

9.19a Upper control arm-to-knuckle bolt

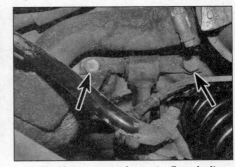

9.19b Upper control arm-to-floor bolts

9.20a Cleaning reveals that the bolt and knuckle have several graduated marks

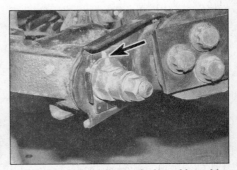

9.20b Mark the adjuster bolt and knuckle with paint before removal

9.37a Tighten the rear hub nut to the specified torque . . .

9.37b . . . then using a hammer and punch . . .

9.37c . . . stake the rear hub nut into the stub axle groove

Rear hub/bearing

34 Slide the hub flange into position on the stub axle and secure with a new hub nut, lightly oiled, and tightened by hand only at this stage.

35 Refit the brake disc or drum as described in Chapter 9.

36 Refit the wheel, then lower the car to the ground and tighten the wheel nuts to the specified torque.

37 Tighten the hub nut to the specified torque when the car is resting on its wheels. Stake the nut collar into the stub axle groove (or bend over the locktabs), then refit the dust cap, tapping it squarely into place **(see illustrations)**.

10 Rear strut – removal, overhaul and refitting

Removal

1 Slacken the relevant rear wheel nuts. Chock the front wheels, select 1st gear, then jack up the rear of the car, and support securely on axle stands (see *Jacking and vehicle support*). Remove the rear roadwheel.

2 Unscrew the strut lower mounting bolt, and separate the base of the unit from the lower arm **(see illustration)**.

3 Inside the boot, on 3-door models, fold the backrest forwards and unclip the access cover in the side trim panel for access to the two strut upper mounting nuts – on 5-door models, remove the luggage area side carpet as described in Chapter 11, Section 27. Support the strut, then unscrew the two upper nuts, and withdraw the unit into the rear wheel arch **(see illustrations)**.

Overhaul

Note: *A spring compressor tool will be required for this operation.*

4 With the suspension strut resting on a bench, or clamped in a vice, fit a spring compressor tool, and compress the coil spring to relieve the pressure on the spring seats. Ensure that the compressor tool is securely located on the spring, in accordance with the tool manufacturer's instructions **(see illustration)**.

5 Counterhold the strut piston rod with the Allen key or hexagon bit used during removal, and unscrew the piston rod nut **(see illustration)**. This nut is of self-locking type, so a new one must be obtained for reassembly.

6 Remove the piston rod nut, followed by the top washer, top mounting plate and bush, mounting collar, spring upper seat, spacer washer, dust cover, another spacer washer,

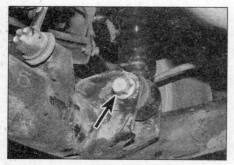

10.2 Unscrew the strut lower mounting bolt

10.3a On 3-door models, unclip the access cover in the rear side trim panel

10.3b Unscrew the two upper mounting nuts . . .

10.3c . . . and lower out the rear strut

10.4 Fit a coil spring compressor, 'catching' as many coils as possible

10.5 Hold the piston rod with an Allen key, and unscrew the nut

10.6 Rear strut components

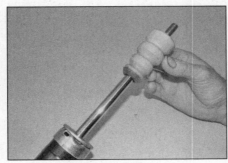

10.11a Slide on the bump stop . . .

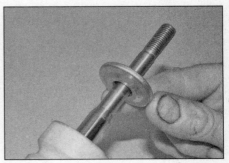

10.11b . . . and the first spacer washer

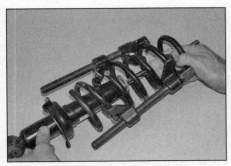

10.13 Refit the compressed spring over the strut

10.14a Refit the dust cover over the bump stop/spacer . . .

10.14b . . . followed by the second spacer washer

the bump stop and finally the spring (with compressor tool still fitted) **(see illustration)**. **Note:** *The top mounting plate has a rubber bush in the top, which is actually separate, but usually remains attached during overhaul.*

7 With the strut assembly now completely dismantled, examine all the components for wear, damage or deformation. Renew any of the components as necessary.

8 Examine the strut for signs of fluid leakage. Check the strut piston for signs of pitting along its entire length, and check the strut body for signs of damage. While holding it in an upright position, test the operation of the strut by moving the piston through a full stroke, and then through short strokes of 50 to 100 mm. In both cases, the resistance felt should be smooth and continuous. If the resistance is jerky or uneven or if there is any visible sign

of wear or damage to the strut, renewal is necessary.

9 If any doubt exists as to the condition of the coil spring, carefully remove the spring compressors and check the spring for distortion and signs of cracking. Renew the spring if it is damaged or distorted, or if there is any doubt as to its condition.

10 Inspect all other components for damage or deterioration, and renew any that are suspect.

11 Slide the bump stop onto the strut piston, followed by the first spacer washer **(see illustrations)**.

12 If the spring compressor tool has been removed from the spring, refit it and compress the spring sufficiently to enable it to be refitted to the strut.

13 Slide the spring over the strut, and

position it so that the lower spring end is resting against the stop on the lower seat **(see illustration)**.

14 Refit the dust cover and second spacer washer **(see illustrations)**.

15 Refit the spring upper seat, ensuring that the spring end sits against the projection on the underside of the seat (though on our car, this projection was barely visible) **(see illustration)**.

16 Fit the mounting collar over the strut, noting that it has a semi-circular moulding on its underside, which should sit in a corresponding recess on the spring upper seat **(see illustrations)**.

17 Fit the top mounting plate and upper bush, noting that there is a round peg on the underside of the plate, which locates in a recess on top of the mounting collar **(see**

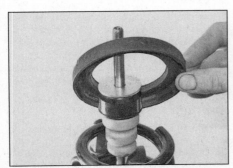

10.15 Refit the spring upper seat, and align with the spring end

10.16a Noting the semi-circular alignment moulding and recess . . .

10.16b . . . fit the mounting collar over the strut

10.17a Note the peg under the top plate, and the recess in the collar . . .

10.17b . . . then fit the top plate (and bush) over the strut

10.18 Refit the top washer, using a new piston rod nut

10.19 Tighten the nut securely, holding the piston rod with an Allen key

illustrations). Also, the small hole in the plate's outer edge should face to the inside of the car when the strut is refitted.

18 Refit the top washer and a new piston rod nut **(see illustration)**.

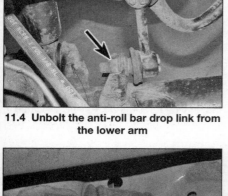

11.4 Unbolt the anti-roll bar drop link from the lower arm

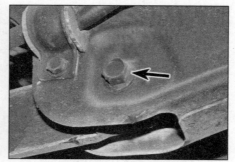

11.6 Unscrew the two lower arm front mounting bolts

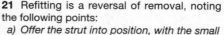

11.7 Unscrew the pivot bolt securing the arm to the crossmember

19 Tighten the piston rod nut securely, using the specified torque as a guide. Counterhold the piston rod using an Allen key or hexagon bit as during removal **(see illustration)**.

20 Slowly and evenly slacken the spring compressor tool to relieve the tension in the spring. Check that the ends of the spring locate correctly against the stops on the spring seats. If necessary, turn the spring and the upper seat so that the components locate correctly before the compressor tool is removed. Remove the compressor tool when the spring is fully seated.

Refitting

21 Refitting is a reversal of removal, noting the following points:

a) Offer the strut into position, with the small hole in the top mounting plate facing the inside of the car, and loosely refit the two upper mounting nuts. Guide the lower

end of the strut into position on the lower arm, then loosely refit the lower mounting bolt.

b) Position a jack under the end of the lower arm (avoid the blade section), and raise the arm so that the suspension is compressed, approximately the same as if the car were resting on its wheels.

c) Tighten the lower mounting bolt and the two upper mounting nuts, then lower the jack under the lower arm.

d) Refit the rear wheel, then lower the car to the ground and tighten the wheel nuts to the specified torque.

11 Rear lower arm – removal, overhaul and refitting

Removal

1 Slacken the rear wheel nuts. Chock the front wheels, select 1st gear, then jack up the rear of the car, and support securely on axle stands (see *Jacking and vehicle support*). Remove the rear roadwheels.

2 Remove the rear knuckle as described in Section 9.

3 Ensure that the lower arm is supported at its outer end on a jack – the jack should be just taking its weight, not compressing the suspension. Avoid the blade section of the arm when jacking up.

4 Unscrew the nut securing the anti-roll bar drop link to the lower arm – use an Allen key to stop the drop link balljoint turning as this is done **(see illustration)**. Unhook the drop link from the arm. Discard the nut – a new one should be used when refitting.

5 Unscrew the strut lower mounting bolt, and separate the base of the unit from the lower arm.

6 Unscrew and remove the two lower arm front mounting bolts from the floor **(see illustration)**.

7 Unscrew the pivot bolt securing the rear of the lower arm to the crossmember **(see illustration)**, then lower the arm on the jack and remove it from under the car.

Overhaul

8 Examine the rubber bushes for wear and damage, and check the arm for straightness, as it could have been bent by careless jacking-up. At the time of writing, it does not appear that the lower arm bushes are available separately, and therefore overhaul of the lower arm is not possible.

Refitting

9 Refitting is a reversal of removal, noting the following points:

a) Offer the arm into position, and loosely refit the three mounting bolts. Guide the lower end of the strut into position on the lower arm, then loosely refit the

lower mounting bolt. Reconnect the anti-roll bar drop link to the arm, using a new nut, tightened hand-tight at this stage.
b) Position a jack under the end of the lower arm (avoid the blade section), and raise the arm so that the suspension is compressed, approximately the same as if the car were resting on its wheels.
c) Tighten all nuts and bolts to the specified torque.
d) Refit the knuckle as described in Section 9.
e) Refit the rear wheel, then lower the car to the ground and tighten the wheel nuts to the specified torque.

12 Rear anti-roll bar, bushes and drop links – removal and refitting

1 Loosen the rear wheel nuts. Chock the front wheels, then jack up the rear of the car, and support it on axle stands (see *Jacking and vehicle support*). Remove the rear wheels.

Bushes

2 If the bushes alone are to be renewed, working on one side at a time, unscrew the two bolts and remove the anti-roll bar mounting clamp **(see illustration)**. The bar can then be pulled away slightly, and the bush removed (the bush is split for easy removal).
3 Slip the new bush into place around the roll bar – if necessary, lubricate the bush with a little washing-up liquid first. Also note that the roll bar has a painted mark to indicate the fitted position of the bushes, to make initial fitting more accurate.
4 Refit the clamp, noting that it has an arrow marking which should face upwards, and an L or R for left or right. Slide the bush along the bar slightly if required, to bring the clamp bolt holes into alignment. Tighten the clamp bolts to the specified torque, then repeat the procedure on the other side.
5 On completion, refit the wheels, then lower the car to the ground and tighten the wheel nuts to the specified torque.

Drop links

6 Unscrew the nut at each end of the link – use an Allen key to stop the drop link balljoints turning as this is done **(see illustration)**. Remove the drop link from the lower arm and anti-roll bar, noting how it is fitted. Discard the nuts – new ones should be used when refitting.
7 Refitting is a reversal of removal, noting the following points:
a) Use new self-locking nuts on the anti-roll bar drop links.
b) Position a jack under the end of the lower arm (avoid the blade section), and raise it to load the rear suspension before tightening the nuts to the specified torque.

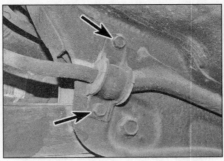
12.2 Unscrew the anti-roll bar mounting clamp bolts to change the bushes

c) Wait 5 minutes, then recheck that the nuts are properly tightened.
d) On completion, refit the wheels, then lower the car to the ground and tighten the wheel nuts to the specified torque.

Anti-roll bar

8 Unscrew the nut securing each of the two anti-roll bar drop links to the lower arm – use an Allen key to stop the drop link balljoint turning as this is done. Unhook the drop links from the lower arm. Discard the two nuts – new ones should be used when refitting.
9 Unscrew the two bolts from each of the two anti-roll bar outer clamps, then remove the clamps and lower out the roll bar. Withdraw the bar from under the car.
10 If wished, the drop links can be removed from the anti-roll bar after unscrewing the securing nuts. If necessary, counterhold the drop link pins using an Allen key. Discard the drop link nuts – new ones should be used when refitting.
11 Refitting is a reversal of removal, noting the following points:
a) Ensure that the clamps are refitted with their arrow markings facing upwards (also note the L and R markings for left and right), and tighten the bolts to the specified torque.
b) If the drop links were removed, refit them as described in paragraph 7.
c) On completion, refit the wheels, then lower the car to the ground and tighten the wheel nuts to the specified torque.

13.4 Loosen the steering wheel nut, while holding the wheel rim

12.6 Unscrew the nut securing the drop link to the anti-roll bar

13 Steering wheel – removal and refitting

Removal

1 Disconnect the battery negative lead, and position the lead away from the battery (also see *Disconnecting the battery*). Wait at least one minute before proceeding. If this waiting period is not observed, there is a danger of accidentally activating the airbag(s).
2 Remove the airbag unit from the steering wheel as described in Chapter 12.
3 Ensure that the front wheels are pointing in the straight-ahead position.
4 Prevent the steering wheel turning by grasping the rim firmly, then unscrew and remove the steering wheel securing nut. Do not rely on the steering column lock to prevent the wheel turning, as this may damage the lock **(see illustration)**.
5 Disconnect the horn wiring connector on the left-hand side of the wheel **(see illustration)**. Where applicable, also disconnect the switch wiring on the right-hand side of the wheel.
6 If one is not already present, make an alignment mark between the steering wheel and the column, to make refitting easier.

HAYNES HINT *Before pulling off the wheel, refit the wheel bolt by a couple of threads. This way, if excess effort is needed to pull the wheel off its splines, the wheel won't suddenly fly off and cause injury.*

13.5 Disconnect the horn wiring plug from the wheel

13.7 Removing the steering wheel

13.8 Using the bolt holes provided to make a home-made puller

7 Grip the steering wheel on each side (or top and bottom), then pull and withdraw it from the splines on the end of the column **(see illustration)**. If it was refitted, remove the securing nut completely.

8 If the wheel proves difficult to remove, use a puller to release it from the splines. Two threaded holes are provided, which may be used with two bolts, a strong metal plate and a socket as a spacer, to free the wheel **(see illustration)**.

Refitting

9 Make sure that the front wheels are pointing in the straight-ahead position.

10 If not already done, set the airbag clock spring to its central position, as described in Chapter 12.

11 The two direction indicator self-cancelling tabs should be in the vertical position, and the airbag clock spring's two locating pins should be horizontal.

12 Offer the steering wheel into position, ensuring that the recesses on the back of the wheel fit over the airbag clock spring's two pins.

13 Refit the steering wheel securing nut, and tighten to the specified torque – again, do not rely on the steering column lock to hold the wheel as the nut is tightened.

14 The remainder of the refitting procedure is a reversal of removal. Ensure that the battery is still disconnected before refitting the airbag unit as described in Chapter 12.

---

14 Steering column –
removal and refitting

Removal

1 Disconnect the battery negative lead, and

position the lead away from the battery (also see *Disconnecting the battery*). Wait at least one minute before proceeding. If this waiting period is not observed, there is a danger of accidentally activating the airbag(s).

2 Remove the steering wheel as described in Section 13.

3 Move the driver's seat fully to the rear, to allow maximum working area.

4 Remove the steering column switch assembly, and disconnect the three wiring plugs from the ignition switch and related components, as described in Chapter 12, Section 4.

5 Remove the driver's side lower facia panels as described in Chapter 11, Section 27.

6 Working in the footwell, unscrew the upper pinch-bolt securing the column shaft to the universal joint **(see illustrations)**. The bolt has a master spline, so it will only fit in one position.

7 Detach the wiring harness from the column, noting how it is routed **(see illustration)**.

8 Unscrew the steering column's two upper mounting nuts and two lower mounting bolts, and lower the column assembly into the footwell. Pull the column rearwards to separate it from the universal joint, and it can be removed from the car **(see illustrations)**.

Inspection

9 Check the column for obvious signs of damage, then check the upper and lower bearings for play. Check the condition of the sliding bushes on the column adjustment linkage. The column is only available as a complete assembly.

Refitting

10 Refitting is a reversal of removal, noting the following points:
  a) *Align the previously-made marks when refitting the column to the universal joint.*
  b) *Tighten all fixings to the specified torque.*
  c) *Ensure that the column wiring harness is routed correctly, and securely re-attached. Also ensure that all wiring connections are properly remade.*
  d) *Refit the steering wheel as described in Section 13.*

14.6a The pinch-bolt securing the column to the universal joint . . .

14.6b . . . can be unscrewed from the fusebox side of the column

14.7 Unclip the wiring harness from the column

14.8a Unscrew the upper nut and lower bolt each side . . .

14.8b . . . then lower the column, and pull it into the car

15 Steering rack – removal and refitting

Removal

1 Set the front wheels to the straight-ahead position, and engage the steering lock. The lock must be engaged, to prevent the column from turning during rack removal – which might otherwise cause damage to the airbag clock spring.
2 Remove the electric power steering motor as described in Section 19.
3 Move the driver's seat fully to the rear, to allow maximum working area.
4 Remove the driver's side lower facia panels as described in Chapter 11.
5 Working in the footwell, make alignment marks at either end of the universal joint for easier refitting. Unscrew the upper and lower pinch-bolt from the universal joint, then pull the joint back into the car, to free it from the rack pinion.
6 Loosen the front wheel nuts, then jack up the front of the car, and support it on axle stands (see *Jacking and vehicle support*). Remove the front wheels.
7 Extract the split pin from each steering track rod end balljoint nut (new split pins will be needed when refitting). Unscrew the nut, but leave it attached by a couple of threads for now.
8 Disconnect the track rod end from each strut, either using a balljoint separator tool, or by tapping the end of the balljoint stud (use a block of wood and the still-fitted nut to protect the threads). When the balljoint separates, unscrew the nut completely, and move the track rod clear.
9 On manual transmission models, unscrew the bolt securing the clutch fluid reservoir support bracket to the side of the master cylinder, and move the reservoir to one side without disconnecting its hose.
10 Remove the single bolt securing the wiring harness support bracket to the centre of the bulkhead.
11 Unbolt the earth strap located under the pinion end of the steering rack.
12 Unscrew the two steering rack-to-bulkhead bolts, and recover the clamp and washers **(see illustration)**. Move the rack forwards to clear the bulkhead.
13 At the passenger end of the rack, unscrew the three rack-to-inner wing bolts **(see illustration)**. Unscrew and remove the mounting nut on the front of the rack, and recover the large washer behind it, then move the rack forwards to free it from the mounting stud.
14 Lower the rack at the pinion end, to free the grommet (the grommet can also be 'helped' out from inside the car, if necessary). When the pinion is free of the bulkhead, twist the rack round so that the pinion points vertically upwards.

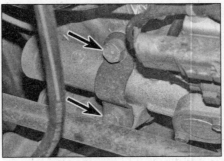

15.12 Steering rack-to-bulkhead bolts and clamp

15 As the rack is being removed, take great care not to damage the gaiters. Slide the rack over into the passenger wheel arch. When the driver's end is clear, lift it upwards and withdraw it from the back of the engine compartment, taking care not to catch the heater hoses.

Refitting

16 Refitting is a reversal of removal, noting the following points:
a) Offer the rack carefully into position, again taking care not to damage any of the bulkhead hoses or components. Feed the pinion into the car, and engage the grommet.
b) Tighten all fasteners to the specified torque.
c) Use new split pins when reconnecting the track rod ends.
d) Align the previously-made marks when reconnecting the column universal joint, and tighten the pinch-bolts to the specified torque.
e) Refit the electric power steering motor as described in Section 19.
f) On completion, have the wheel alignment checked, and if necessary, adjusted.

16 Steering rack rubber gaiters – renewal

The rubber gaiters are in one piece, and can only be removed once the rack has been removed. In addition, the rack must be

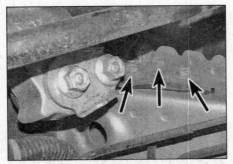

15.13 Unscrew the three rack-to-inner wing bolts

dismantled before the gaiter 'assembly' can be slid off one end. Dismantling the rack requires tools which will not be readily available to the DIY mechanic, so this work must be entrusted to a Honda dealer. Depending on the 'mileage' on the rack, it might be worth investigating the cost of a new or exchange rack in the event of new gaiters being needed.

17 Steering rack guide – adjustment

The Civic has an adjustable guide (sometimes known as the 'slipper') fitted below the steering rack. If any unusual rattling or vibration is felt through the steering wheel when travelling over rough roads, it is possible that the noise could be the rack, rattling up and down inside the steering rack housing. The rack guide can be adjusted, to take out this vertical movement. This is not in itself a difficult operation, but special tools are required, and the job must be performed to a high level of accuracy – over-tightening the adjuster will lead to stiff steering, which could be dangerous. It is therefore recommended that this job is entrusted to a Honda dealer.

18 Track rod end – removal and refitting

1 If the track rod end rubber boot is damaged, a new one can be obtained from Honda dealers. Once the track rod end has been disconnected (as described later in this Section), the old boot can be unclipped. Wipe the balljoint clean (do not use excessive amounts of solvent), then pack it with fresh grease and fit the new boot. However, bear in mind that if the boot has been damaged for some time, it is likely that dirt will have got into the balljoint, and a new track rod end may soon be needed.
2 If the complete track rod end is to be renewed, proceed as follows:

Removal

3 Slacken the relevant front wheel nuts. Apply the handbrake, then jack up the front of the car, and support securely on axle stands (see *Jacking and vehicle support*). Remove the wheel.
4 Extract the split pin from the track rod balljoint nut (a new split pin will be needed when refitting) **(see illustration)**. Unscrew the nut, but leave it attached by a couple of threads for now.
5 Disconnect the track rod end from the strut, either using a balljoint separator tool, or by tapping the end of the balljoint stud (use a block of wood and the still-fitted nut to protect the threads). When the balljoint separates, unscrew the nut completely, and move the track rod clear **(see illustration)**.

18.4 Extract the split pin from the balljoint nut

18.5 With the balljoint separated, unscrew the nut and move the track rod clear

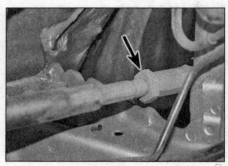

18.6 Track rod end locknut (seen from engine compartment)

6 Slacken the track rod end locknut, then unscrew the track rod end from the track rod, counting the number of turns necessary to remove it **(see illustration)**.

Refitting

7 Screw the track rod end onto the track rod the number of turns noted during removal, then tighten the locknut while holding the track rod in position (the track rod has flats to accept a spanner).
8 Clean the balljoint and its seat in the steering arm before fitting – it must be fitted dry. Offer the balljoint into position, taking care not to damage the boot.
9 Tighten the balljoint nut to the specified torque. From this point, tighten the nut slightly as required to align the split pin holes (do not loosen to align), then fit a new pin to secure.
10 Refit the roadwheel, then lower the car to the ground, and tighten the wheel nuts to the specified torque.
11 Have the front wheel alignment checked (see Section 20) at the earliest opportunity.

19 Electric power steering components – removal and refitting

Motor

1 Disconnect the battery negative lead, and position the lead away from the battery (also see *Disconnecting the battery*).
2 The motor is located in the engine

compartment, at the pinion end (driver's side) of the steering rack.
3 On petrol models, remove the inlet air resonator as described in Chapter 4A.
4 On diesel models, access to the motor is more difficult. Depending on model and equipment, it may be easier to access the motor from below.
5 Unbolt the heater control valve support bracket from the bulkhead, and move it clear without disconnecting the hoses.
6 As necessary for access, unclip the brake servo vacuum hose, brake pipes and wiring harness from the bulkhead.
7 Disconnect the two wiring plugs from the motor. Trace the wiring harness back, and unbolt the harness support bracket from the steering rack housing.
8 Remove the two mounting bolts, and withdraw the motor from the steering rack **(see illustration)**. Recover the large O-ring – a new one should be used when refitting.
9 Clean the mating surfaces of the motor and steering rack.
10 Lightly grease the steering motor drive components on the motor and inside the steering rack.
11 Apply a little silicone grease to the new motor O-ring, then fit it to the motor. Offer the motor into position, ensuring it is the right way round (with its wiring harness pointing forwards). Fit the mounting bolts, and tighten them to the specified torque.
12 Reconnect the motor wiring plugs, and secure the harness support bracket.
13 Further refitting is a reversal of removal.

19.8 Power steering motor mounting bolts

19.18 EPS control unit mounting nuts

On completion, start the engine and let it idle. Turn the steering from lock-to-lock several times, and make sure that the EPS warning light on the instrument panel does not come on.

EPS torque sensor

14 The torque sensor is part of the steering rack housing, and is not available separately.

Control unit

15 Disconnect the battery negative lead, and position the lead away from the battery (also see *Disconnecting the battery*). It is **essential** that this is done, to prevent possible damage to the EPS control unit when its plug is disconnected.
16 The control unit is located at the front of the passenger's footwell – release any clips as necessary, and fold back the carpeting for access.
17 Noting their fitted locations, disconnect the wiring plugs from the control unit,
18 Unscrew the two bracket mounting nuts, and pull the control unit and its bracket off the mounting studs **(see illustration)**.
19 If required, the control unit can be separated from the mounting bracket after removing the two bolts.
20 Refitting is a reversal of removal, noting the following points:
a) Ensure that the control unit wiring plugs are correctly and securely refitted.
b) On completion, start the engine and let it idle. Turn the steering from lock-to-lock several times, and make sure that the EPS warning light on the instrument panel does not come on.

20 Wheel alignment and steering angles – general information

Definitions

1 A car's steering and suspension geometry is defined in four basic settings – all angles are expressed in degrees; the steering axis is defined as an imaginary line drawn through the axis of the suspension strut, extended where necessary to contact the ground.
2 Camber is the angle between each

roadwheel and a vertical line drawn through its centre and tyre contact patch, when viewed from the front or rear of the car. Positive camber is when the roadwheels are tilted outwards from the vertical at the top; negative camber is when they are tilted inwards.

3 The front camber angle is not adjustable, and is given for reference only (see paragraph 5). The rear camber angle is adjustable, using a camber angle gauge.

4 **Castor** is the angle between the steering axis and a vertical line drawn through each roadwheel's centre and tyre contact patch, when viewed from the side of the car. Positive castor is when the steering axis is tilted so that it contacts the ground ahead of the vertical; negative castor is when it contacts the ground behind the vertical.

5 Castor is not adjustable, and is given for reference only; while it can be checked using a castor checking gauge, if the figure obtained is significantly different from that specified, the car must be taken for careful checking by a professional, as the fault can only be caused by wear or damage to the body or suspension components.

6 **Steering axis inclination/SAI** – also known as **kingpin inclination/KPI** – is the angle between the steering axis and a vertical line drawn through each roadwheel's centre and tyre contact patch, when viewed from the front or rear of the car.

7 SAI/KPI is not adjustable, and is given for reference only.

8 **Toe** is the difference, viewed from above, between lines drawn through the roadwheel centres and the car's centre-line. 'Toe-in' is when the roadwheels point inwards, towards each other at the front, while 'toe-out' is when they splay outwards from each other at the front.

9 The front wheel toe setting is adjusted by screwing the track rods in or out of their balljoint, to alter the effective length of the track rod assembly.

10 Rear wheel toe setting is also adjustable at the rear knuckle (see Section 9), but only by changing the rear knuckle bolts to move the rear wheel.

Checking – general

11 Due to the special measuring equipment necessary to check the wheel alignment, and the skill required to use it properly, the checking and adjustment of these settings is best left to an expert. Most tyre-fitting centres now possess sophisticated checking equipment.

12 For accurate checking, the car must be at the kerb weight specified in *Dimensions and weights* in the Reference Section.

13 Before starting work, check first that the

tyre sizes and types are as specified, then check tyre pressures and tread wear. Also check roadwheel run-out, the condition of the hub bearings, the steering wheel free play and the condition of the front suspension components (Chapter 1A or 1B). Correct any faults.

14 Park the car on level ground, with the front roadwheels in the straight-ahead position. Rock both ends to settle the suspension. Release the handbrake and roll the car backwards 1 metre (3 feet), then forwards again, to relieve any stresses in the steering and suspension components.

Front wheel toe setting

Checking

15 Two methods are available to the home mechanic for checking the front wheel toe setting. One method is to use a gauge to measure the distance between the front and rear inside edges of the roadwheels. The other method is to use a scuff plate, in which each front wheel is rolled across a movable plate which records any deviation, or scuff, of the tyre from the straight-ahead position as it moves across the plate. Such gauges are available in relatively-inexpensive form from accessory outlets. It is up to the owner to decide whether the expense is justified, in view of the small amount of use such equipment would normally receive. Also note that Honda only quote the toe setting in millimetres, so ensure that there is some means of converting the angle recorded into a measurement.

16 Prepare the car as described previously in paragraphs 12 to 14.

17 If the measurement procedure is being used, carefully measure the distance between the front edges of the roadwheel rims and the rear edges of the rims. Subtract the rear measurement from the front measurement, and check that the result is within the specified range. If not, adjust the toe setting as described in paragraph 19.

18 If scuff plates are to be used, roll the car backwards, check that the roadwheels are in the straight-ahead position, then roll it across the scuff plates so that each front roadwheel passes squarely over the centre of its respective plate. Note the angle recorded by the scuff plates. To ensure accuracy, repeat the check three times, and take the average of the three readings. If the roadwheels are running parallel, there will of course be no angle recorded; if a deviation value is shown on the scuff plates, compare the reading obtained for each wheel with that specified. If the value recorded is outside the specified tolerance, the toe setting is incorrect, and must be adjusted as follows.

Adjustment

19 Apply the handbrake, jack up the front of the car and support it securely on axle stands (see *Jacking and vehicle support*). Turn the steering wheel onto full-left lock, and record the number of exposed threads on the right-hand track rod end. Now turn the steering onto full-right lock, and record the number of threads on the left-hand side. If there are the same number of threads visible on both sides, then subsequent adjustment should be made equally on both sides. If there are more threads visible on one side than the other, it will be necessary to compensate for this during adjustment. **Note:** *It is important that, after adjustment, the same number of threads be visible on each track rod end.*

20 First clean the track rod threads; if they are corroded, apply penetrating fluid before starting adjustment.

21 Use a straight-edge and a scriber or similar to mark the relationship of each track rod to its balljoint. Holding each track rod in turn, unscrew its locknut fully.

22 Alter the length of the track rods, bearing in mind the note in paragraph 19, by screwing them into or out of the balljoints. Rotate the track rod using an open-ended spanner fitted to the flats provided. Shortening the track rods (screwing them onto their balljoints) will reduce toe-in and increase toe-out. Each complete turn of the track rod effectively adjusts the toe setting by 30' or 3 mm (depending on the method being used).

23 When the setting is correct, hold the track rods and securely tighten the balljoint locknuts. Count the exposed threads – if the number of threads exposed is not the same on both sides, then the adjustment has not been made equally, and problems will be encountered with tyre scrubbing in turns; also, the steering wheel will no longer sit straight when the wheels are in the straight-ahead position.

24 When the track rod lengths are the same, lower the car to the ground and recheck the toe setting; readjust if necessary.

Rear wheel toe setting

25 The rear wheel toe setting can be checked as described for the front wheels. However, adjustment involves changing the rear knuckle bolts (see Section 9) – seek the advice of a Honda dealer.

Rear wheel camber

26 Adjusting the rear camber involves loosening the rear knuckle bolts (see Section 9), and moving the adjuster cam to reset the rear wheel position. This is not considered a DIY operation, and should only be attempted if the proper tools are available.

Chapter 11
Bodywork and fittings

Contents

Degrees of difficulty

Easy, suitable for novice with little experience	**Fairly easy,** suitable for beginner with some experience	**Fairly difficult,** suitable for competent DIY mechanic	**Difficult,** suitable for experienced DIY mechanic	**Very difficult,** suitable for expert DIY or professional

Specifications

Torque wrench settings	Nm	lbf ft
Door hinge bolts (all)*	29	21
Facia mounting bolts	22	16
Front seat bolts	34	25
Rear seat hinge bolts	22	16
Seat belt bolts:		
Front seat belt height adjuster bolts.	22	16
Front seat belt inertia reel upper mounting bolt (5-door)	10	7
All other seat belt mounting bolts.	32	24
Tailgate hinge nuts/bolts	22	16
Tailgate lock striker bolts	18	13

* Use new bolts

1 General information

The body shell is made of pressed-steel sections, and is available in three- and five-door Hatchback versions. Most body panel components are welded together. The front wings are bolted on, for easier accident repair.

Though the body is not 'fully' galvanised, all the outer panels and floor are, and high-strength steel is used extensively, giving a high degree of strength to the shell. Extensive use is made of plastic materials, mainly in the interior, but also in exterior components. The front and rear bumpers, and front grille, are injection-moulded from a synthetic material that is very strong and yet light. Plastic components such as wheel arch liners are fitted to the underside of the car, to improve the body's resistance to corrosion.

2 Maintenance –
bodywork and underside

The general condition of a car's bodywork is the one thing that significantly affects its value. Maintenance is easy, but needs to be regular. Neglect, particularly after minor damage, can lead quickly to further deterioration and costly repair bills. It is important also to keep watch on those parts of the car not immediately visible, for instance the underside, inside all the wheel arches, and the lower part of the engine compartment.

The basic maintenance routine for the bodywork is washing – preferably with a lot of water, from a hose. This will remove all the loose solids which may have stuck to the car. It is important to flush these off in such a way as to prevent grit from scratching the finish. The wheel arches and underside need washing in the same way, to remove any accumulated mud which will retain moisture and tend to encourage rust. Strange as it sounds, the best time to clean the underside and wheel arches is in wet weather, when the mud is thoroughly wet and soft. In very wet weather, the underside is usually cleaned of large accumulations automatically, and this is a good time for inspection.

Periodically, except on cars with a wax-based underbody protective coating, it is a good idea to have the whole of the underside of the car steam-cleaned, engine compartment included, so that a thorough inspection can be carried out to see what minor repairs are necessary. Steam-cleaning is available at many garages, and is necessary for the removal of the accumulation of oily grime, which sometimes is allowed to become thick in certain areas. If steam-cleaning facilities are not available, grease solvents are available which can be brush-applied; the dirt can then be simply hosed off. Note that these methods should not be used on cars with wax-based underbody protective coating, or the coating will be removed. Such cars should be inspected annually, preferably just prior to Winter, when the underbody should be washed down, and any damage to the wax coating repaired. Ideally, a completely fresh coat should be applied. It would also be worth considering the use of such wax-based protection for injection into door panels, sills, box sections, etc, as an additional safeguard against rust damage, where such protection is not provided by the car manufacturer.

After washing the paintwork, wipe off with a chamois leather to give an unspotted clear finish. A coat of clear protective wax polish will give added protection against chemical pollutants in the air. If the paintwork sheen has dulled or oxidised, use a cleaner/polisher combination to restore the brilliance of the shine. This requires a little effort, but such dulling is usually caused because regular washing has been neglected. Care needs to be taken with metallic paintwork, as special non-abrasive cleaner/polisher is required to avoid damage to the lacquer finish – also note that many 'solid' colours are in fact lacquered ('clear over base') these days. Always check that the door and ventilator opening drain holes and pipes are completely clear, so that water can be drained out. Brightwork should be treated in the same way as paintwork. Windscreens and windows can be kept clear of the smeary film which often appears, by the use of proprietary glass cleaner. Never use wax polish on the windscreen.

3 Maintenance –
upholstery and carpets

Mats and carpets should be brushed or vacuum-cleaned regularly, to keep them free of grit. If they are badly stained, remove them from the car for scrubbing or sponging, and make quite sure they are dry before refitting.

Cloth or velour seats and interior trim panels can be kept clean by wiping with a damp cloth. If they do become stained (which can be more apparent on light-coloured cloth or velour upholstery), use a little liquid detergent and a soft nail brush to scour the grime out of the grain of the material. Keep the headlining clean in the same way as the upholstery

In the case of leather upholstery, a whole range of different products exist to clean, feed and generally restore the leather, and it is recommended that these are used exclusively. Ordinary detergents should be avoided, as they will prematurely dry out leather, causing it to crack and split.

When using liquid cleaners inside the car, do not over-wet the surfaces being cleaned. Excessive damp could get into the seams and padded interior, causing stains, offensive odours or even rot. If the inside of the car gets wet accidentally, it is worthwhile taking some trouble to dry it out properly, particularly where carpets are involved. *Do not leave oil or electric heaters inside the car for this purpose.*

4 Minor body damage –
repair

Minor scratches

If the scratch is very superficial, and does not penetrate to the metal of the bodywork, repair is very simple. Lightly rub the area of the scratch with a paintwork renovator, or a very fine cutting paste, to remove loose paint from the scratch, and to clear the surrounding bodywork of wax polish. Rinse the area with clean water.

In the case of metallic paint, the most commonly-found scratches are not in the paint, but in the lacquer top coat, and appear white. If care is taken, these can sometimes be rendered less obvious by very careful use of paintwork renovator (which would otherwise not be used on metallic paintwork); otherwise, repair of these scratches can be achieved by applying lacquer with a fine brush. Also note that damage to the lacquer coat will show up worse if (white) polish residue collects in the chip or scratch – clean any suspected area thoroughly.

Apply touch-up paint to the scratch using a fine paint brush; continue to apply fine layers of paint (allowing each one time to dry) until the surface of the paint in the scratch is level with the surrounding paintwork. Allow the new paint at least two weeks to harden, then blend it into the surrounding paintwork by rubbing the scratch area with a paintwork renovator or a very fine cutting paste. Finally, apply wax polish.

Where the scratch has penetrated right through to the metal of the bodywork, causing the metal to rust, a different repair technique is required. Remove any loose rust from the bottom of the scratch with a penknife, then apply rust-inhibiting paint, to prevent the formation of rust in the future. Using a rubber or nylon applicator, fill the scratch with bodystopper paste. If required, this paste can be mixed with cellulose thinners, to provide a very thin paste which is ideal for filling narrow scratches. Before the stopper-paste in the scratch hardens, wrap a piece of smooth cotton rag around the top of a finger. Dip the finger in cellulose thinners, and quickly sweep it across the surface of the stopper-paste in the scratch; this will ensure that the surface of the stopper-paste is slightly hollowed. The scratch can now be painted over as described earlier in this Section.

Dents

If the dent is shallow, and the paint has not been broken, it may be possible to have the dent repaired professionally, by one of the specialist mobile dent repair companies.

When deep denting of the car's bodywork has taken place, the first task is to pull the dent out, until the affected bodywork almost attains its original shape. There is little point in trying to restore the original shape completely, as the metal in the damaged area will have stretched on impact, and cannot be reshaped fully to its original contour. It is better to bring the level of the dent up to a point which is about 3 mm below the level of the surrounding bodywork. In cases where the dent is very shallow anyway, it is not worth trying to pull it out at all. If the underside of the dent is accessible, it can be hammered out gently from behind, using a mallet with a wooden or plastic head. Whilst doing this, hold a block of wood firmly against the outside of the panel, to absorb the impact from the hammer blows and thus prevent a large area of the bodywork from being 'belled-out'.

Should the dent be in a section of the bodywork which has a double skin, or some other factor making it inaccessible from behind, a different technique is called for. Drill several small holes through the metal inside the area – particularly in the deeper section. Then screw long self-tapping screws into the holes, just sufficiently for them to gain a good purchase in the metal. Now the dent can be pulled out by pulling on the protruding heads of the screws with a pair of pliers.

The next stage of the repair is the removal of the paint from the damaged area, and from an inch or so of the surrounding 'sound' bodywork. This is accomplished most easily by using a wire brush or abrasive pad on a power drill, although it can be done just as effectively by hand, using sheets of abrasive paper. To complete the preparation for filling, score the surface of the bare metal with a screwdriver or the tang of a file, or alternatively, drill small holes in the affected area. This will provide a really good 'key' for the filler paste.

To complete the repair, see the Section on filling and respraying.

Rust holes or gashes

Remove all paint from the affected area, and from an inch or so of the surrounding 'sound' bodywork, using an abrasive pad or a wire brush on a power drill. If these are not available, a few sheets of abrasive paper will do the job most effectively. With the paint removed, you will be able to judge the severity of the corrosion, and therefore decide whether to renew the whole panel (if this is possible) or to repair the affected area. New body panels are not as expensive as most people think, and it is often quicker and more satisfactory to fit a new panel than to attempt to repair large areas of corrosion.

Remove all fittings from the affected area, except those which will act as a guide to the original shape of the damaged bodywork (e.g. light units). Then, using tin snips or a hacksaw blade, remove all loose metal and any other metal badly affected by corrosion. Hammer the edges of the hole inwards, in order to create a slight depression for the filler paste.

Wire-brush the affected area to remove the powdery rust from the surface of the remaining metal. Paint the affected area with rust-inhibiting paint; if the back of the rusted area is accessible, treat this also.

Before filling can take place, it will be necessary to block the hole in some way. This can be achieved by the use of aluminium or plastic mesh, or aluminium tape.

Aluminium or plastic mesh, or glass-fibre matting is probably the best material to use for a large hole. Cut a piece to the approximate size and shape of the hole to be filled, then position it in the hole so that its edges are below the level of the surrounding bodywork. It can be retained in position by several blobs of filler paste around its periphery.

Aluminium tape should be used for small or very narrow holes. Pull a piece off the roll, trim it to the approximate size and shape required, then pull off the backing paper (if used) and stick the tape over the hole; it can be overlapped if the thickness of one piece is insufficient. Burnish down the edges of the tape with the handle of a screwdriver or similar, to ensure that the tape is securely attached to the metal underneath.

Filling and respraying

Before using this Section, see the Sections on dent, deep scratch, rust holes and gash repairs.

Many types of bodyfiller are available, but generally speaking, those proprietary kits which contain a tin of filler paste and a tube of resin hardener are best for this type of repair. A wide, flexible plastic or nylon applicator will be found invaluable for imparting a smooth and well-contoured finish to the surface of the filler.

Mix up a little filler on a clean piece of card or board – measure the hardener carefully (follow the maker's instructions on the pack), otherwise the filler will set too rapidly or too slowly. Using the applicator, apply the filler paste to the prepared area; draw the applicator across the surface of the filler to achieve the correct contour and to level the surface. As soon as a contour that approximates to the correct one is achieved, stop working the paste – if you carry on too long, the paste will become sticky and begin to 'pick-up' on the applicator. Continue to add thin layers of filler paste at 20-minute intervals, until the level of the filler is just proud of the surrounding bodywork.

Once the filler has hardened, the excess can be removed using a metal plane or file. From then on, progressively-finer grades of abrasive paper should be used, starting with a 40-grade production paper, and finishing with a 400-grade wet-and-dry paper. Always wrap the abrasive paper around a flat rubber, cork, or wooden block – otherwise the surface of the filler will not be completely flat. During the smoothing of the filler surface, the wet-and-dry paper should be periodically rinsed in water. This will ensure that a very smooth finish is imparted to the filler at the final stage.

At this stage, the 'dent' should be surrounded by a ring of bare metal, which in turn should be encircled by the finely 'feathered' edge of the good paintwork. Rinse the repair area with clean water, until all of the dust produced by the rubbing-down operation has gone.

Spray the whole area with a light coat of primer – this will show up any imperfections in the surface of the filler. Repair these imperfections with fresh filler paste or bodystopper, and once more smooth the surface with abrasive paper. If bodystopper is used, it can be mixed with cellulose thinners, to form a really thin paste which is ideal for filling small holes. Repeat this spray-and-repair procedure until you are satisfied that the surface of the filler, and the feathered edge of the paintwork, are perfect. Clean the repair area with clean water, and allow to dry fully.

The repair area is now ready for final spraying. Paint spraying must be carried out in a warm, dry, windless and dust-free atmosphere. This condition can be created artificially if you have access to a large indoor working area, but if you are forced to work in the open, you will have to pick your day very carefully. If you are working indoors, dousing the floor in the work area with water will help to settle the dust which would otherwise be in the atmosphere. If the repair area is confined to one body panel, mask off the surrounding panels; this will help to minimise the effects of a slight mis-match in paint colours. Bodywork fittings (e.g. chrome strips, door handles etc) will also need to be masked off. Use genuine masking tape, and several thicknesses of newspaper, for the masking operations.

Before commencing to spray, agitate the aerosol can thoroughly, then spray a test area (an old tin, or similar) until the technique is mastered. Cover the repair area with a thick coat of primer; the thickness should be built up using several thin layers of paint, rather than one thick one. Using 400-grade wet-and-dry paper, rub down the surface of the primer until it is really smooth. While doing this, the work area should be thoroughly doused with water, and the wet-and-dry paper periodically rinsed in water. Allow to dry before spraying on more paint.

Spray on the top coat, again building up the thickness by using several thin layers of paint. Start spraying at the top of the repair area, and then, using a side-to-side motion, work downwards until the whole repair area and about 2 inches of the surrounding original paintwork is covered. Remove all masking material 10 to 15 minutes after spraying on the final coat of paint.

Allow the new paint at least two weeks to harden, then, using a paintwork renovator or a very fine cutting paste, blend the edges of the paint into the existing paintwork. Finally, apply wax polish.

Plastic components

With the use of more and more plastic body components by the car manufacturers (e.g. bumpers, spoilers, and in some cases major body panels), rectification of more serious damage to such items has become

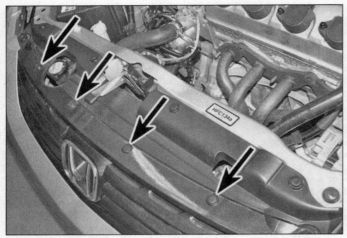

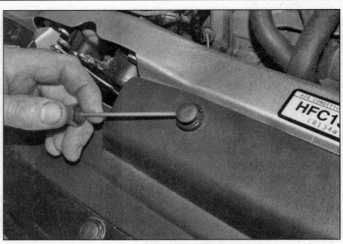

6.1a The top edge of the bumper is secured with four clips . . .

6.1b . . . which are prised out . . .

a matter of either entrusting repair work to a specialist in this field, or renewing complete components. Repair of such damage by the DIY owner is not really feasible, owing to the cost of the equipment and materials required for effecting such repairs. The basic technique involves making a groove along the line of the crack in the plastic, using a rotary burr in a power drill. The damaged part is then welded back together, using a hot-air gun to heat up and fuse a plastic filler rod into the groove. Any excess plastic is then removed, and the area rubbed down to a smooth finish. It is important that a filler rod of the correct plastic is used, as body components can be made of a variety of different types (e.g. polycarbonate, ABS, polypropylene).

Damage of a less serious nature (abrasions, minor cracks etc) can be repaired by the DIY owner using a two-part epoxy filler repair. Once mixed in equal, this is used in similar fashion to the bodywork filler used on metal panels. The filler is usually cured in twenty to thirty minutes, ready for sanding and painting.

If the owner is renewing a complete component himself, or if he has repaired it with epoxy filler, he will be left with the problem of finding a suitable paint for finishing which is compatible with the type of plastic used. At one time, the use of a universal paint was not possible, owing to the complex range

of plastics encountered in body component applications. Standard paints, generally speaking, will not bond to plastic or rubber satisfactorily, but suitable paints to match any plastic or rubber finish, can be obtained from dealers. However, it is now possible to obtain a plastic body parts finishing kit which consists of a pre-primer treatment, a primer and coloured top coat. Full instructions are normally supplied with a kit, but basically, the method of use is to first apply the pre-primer to the component concerned, and allow it to dry for up to 30 minutes. Then the primer is applied, and left to dry for about an hour before finally applying the special-coloured top coat. The result is a correctly-coloured component, where the paint will flex with the plastic or rubber, a property that standard paint does not normally possess.

5 Major body damage – repair

Where serious damage has occurred, or large areas need renewal due to neglect, it means that complete new panels will need welding-in, and this is best left to professionals. If the damage is due to impact, it will also be necessary to check completely the alignment

of the body shell, and this can only be carried out accurately by a Honda dealer using special jigs. If the body is left misaligned, it is primarily dangerous, as the car will not handle properly, and secondly, uneven stresses will be imposed on the steering, suspension and possibly transmission, causing abnormal wear, or complete failure, particularly to such items as the tyres.

6 Front bumper and crossmember – removal and refitting

Front bumper

Removal

1 Open the bonnet, and carefully prise out the four clips securing the top edge of the grille to the front crossmember ('slam panel') **(see illustrations)**.
2 Remove the single bumper retaining screw at the front of each front wheel arch **(see illustration)**.
3 On the underside of the bumper, remove two screws and eight clips along the bottom edge **(see illustrations)**.
4 Where applicable, disconnect the wiring plugs from the front foglights.
5 With the help of an assistant, unclip the ends of the bumper (the clips are stiff to release, and a small screwdriver may help), then slide it forwards to release the clips under the headlights, and remove it **(see illustrations)**.
6 On models with headlight washers, disconnect the washer tubes from the headlight washer jets. Some models may have a quick-release fitting on the hose, released by pulling the small plastic locking clip upwards. Where this is not the case, it is likely that the hose will be a very tight fit – removal will be easier if the hose end can be warmed, and careful prising with a small screwdriver may also help.

Refitting

7 Refitting is a reversal of removal. Again, the

6.1c . . . and removed

6.2 Removing the bumper screw from the wheel arch

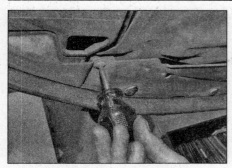

6.3a Remove a screw at each end ...

6.3b ... and eight clips from the centre, along the bottom edge

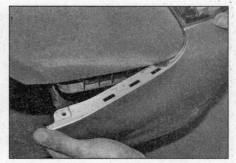

6.5a Pull the bumper ends outwards to unclip ...

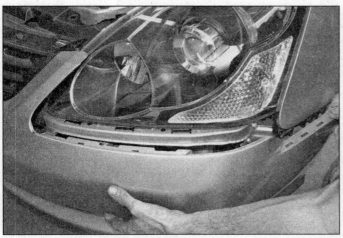

6.5b ... then slide the bumper forwards to release the headlight clips ...

6.5c ... and remove it from the car

help of an assistant will be required, to line up the bumper clips as the bumper is refitted.

Front bumper crossmember

Removal

8 Remove the front bumper as described previously in this Section.

9 Disconnect the wiring from the horn unit(s), then release the clips securing the horn wiring to the underside of the crossmember **(see illustrations)**.

10 At each end of the crossmember, remove the single bolt underneath, and two on top. Withdraw the crossmember from the front of the car **(see illustrations)**.

6.9a Disconnect the horn wiring ...

6.9b ... then release the clips securing it to the crossmember

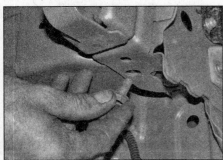

6.10a Remove the bolt underneath ...

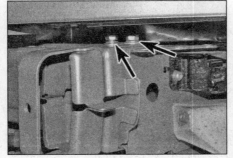

6.10b ... and two more on top at each end ...

6.10c ... then withdraw the crossmember

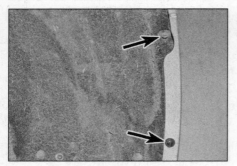

7.1a There are two screws to remove inside the wheel arch . . .

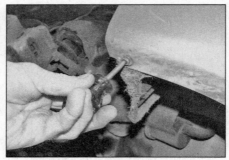

7.1b . . . and a further one underneath

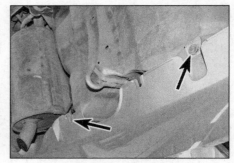

7.2 Prise out the two clips on the underside

7 Rear bumper – removal and refitting

Removal

1 Remove the three bumper retaining screws at the rear of each rear wheel arch **(see illustrations)**.

2 Working underneath, carefully prise out the two clips on the bottom edge of the bumper, either side of the centre **(see illustration)**.

3 Open the tailgate, then carefully prise out the two bolt covers from the 'tailgate aperture' at the top of the bumper – take care not to damage the paint. Remove the bolt behind each cover **(see illustrations)**.

4 With the help of an assistant, unclip the bumper ends by pulling them slightly outwards (the clips are stiff to release), and withdraw the bumper from the car **(see illustrations)**.

Refitting

5 Refitting is a reversal of removal. Again, the help of an assistant will be required, to line up the bumper clips as the bumper is refitted.

8 Radiator grille – removal and refitting

The radiator grille is part of the front bumper assembly – refer to Section 6.

9 Bonnet – removal, refitting and adjustment

Removal

1 Open the bonnet, then trace the windscreen washer tubing up to the T-piece connector, and disconnect it. Feed the washer tube back through the clips, and remove it from the bonnet, so that the bonnet is free to be removed **(see illustrations)**.

2 Using a pencil or felt tip pen, mark the outline of each bonnet hinge relative to the bonnet, to use as a guide on refitting.

3 Have an assistant support the bonnet in its open position.

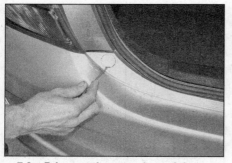

7.3a Prise out the cover in each lower corner of the tailgate aperture . . .

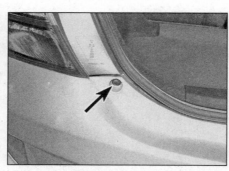

7.3b . . . and remove the bolt underneath

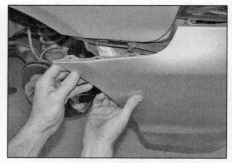

7.4a Pull the bumper end outwards to release the clips . . .

7.4b . . . then withdraw the bumper from the car

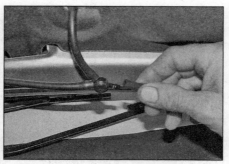

9.1a Disconnect the washer tube at the T-piece . . .

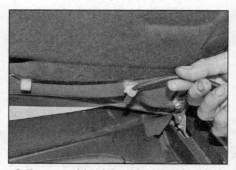

9.1b . . . and feed the tube back through the clips

4 Unscrew the bonnet retaining bolts and carefully lift the bonnet clear **(see illustration)**. Store the bonnet out of the way in a safe place.

5 Inspect the bonnet hinges for signs of wear and free play at the pivots, and if necessary renew them. Each hinge is secured to the body by two bolts; mark the position of the hinge on the body then undo the retaining bolts and remove it from the car.

Refitting and adjustment

6 Where removed, refit the bonnet hinges, and align them with the previously-made marks. Tighten the bolts securely.

7 With the aid of an assistant, offer up the bonnet and loosely fit the retaining bolts. Align the hinges with the marks made on removal, then tighten the retaining bolts securely.

8 Close the bonnet, and check for alignment with the adjacent panels. If necessary, slacken the hinge bolts and re-align the bonnet. Adjust the height of the bonnet so that it is level with the surrounding front wings, by turning the rubber buffer at each front corner of the bonnet. Once the bonnet is correctly aligned, tighten the hinge bolts. Check that the bonnet fastens and releases satisfactorily.

9.4 Unscrew the bonnet retaining bolts

10.7 Unbolt the bonnet release lever

10 Bonnet release cable – removal and refitting

Removal

1 Remove the front bumper as described in Section 6.

2 Loosen the right-hand front wheel nuts. Jack up the front of the car, and support it on axle stands (see *Jacking and vehicle support*). Remove the right-hand front wheel.

3 Remove the wheel arch liner as described in Section 23.

4 Remove the kick panel from the driver's footwell as described in Section 27.

5 At the bonnet lock, lift the cable to release it from the locating slot, then unhook the cable end fitting. Take care not to bend the cable as this is done.

6 Trace the cable back from the bonnet lock, releasing it from its retaining clips and ties, and noting how it is routed.

7 Inside the car, remove the two mounting bolts and detach the bonnet release lever **(see illustration)**. Unhook the cable end fitting from the lever.

8 Release the bulkhead grommet around the cable, then withdraw the cable into the car and remove it.

Refitting

9 Refitting is a reversal of removal. Ensure the cable is correctly routed and secured to all the relevant retaining clips. Before closing the bonnet, check the operation of the release lever and cable.

11 Bonnet lock – removal and refitting

Removal

1 Open the bonnet, and carefully prise out the four clips securing the top edge of the grille to the front crossmember ('slam panel'). Release the top of the radiator grille for access to the bonnet lock.

2 Disconnect the alarm switch wiring plug from the bonnet lock, then unclip the alarm wiring harness from the back of the lock assembly.

3 Lift the bonnet release cable to free it from the locating slot, then unhook the cable end fitting. Take care not to bend the cable as this is done.

4 If possible, make alignment marks between the lock and the body, to make refitting easier.

5 Unscrew and remove the three bonnet lock mounting bolts, and withdraw the lock assembly from the car **(see illustration)**.

Refitting

6 Refitting is a reversal of removal. Align the lock using the marks made on removal, and tighten the three bolts securely. Before closing the bonnet fully, check that the bonnet striker appears to be entering the lock centrally, and if necessary, adjust the lock position (by loosening the three mounting bolts) to achieve satisfactory bonnet closing

11.5 Bonnet lock mounting bolts

12 Door – removal, refitting and adjustment

Removal

Front door

1 Remove the front wheel arch liner on the side concerned, as described in Section 23.

2 Working from outside the car, through the gap at the front of the open front door, prise out the upper and lower clips securing the narrow front wing rear trim panel. From inside the wheel arch, prise out another upper and lower clip, then withdraw the trim panel into the wheel arch, freeing from the indicator side repeater wiring.

3 Locate the door wiring plug, then twist and disconnect it.

4 Unbolt the door check strap from the door pillar **(see illustration)**.

5 Have an assistant support the door, or rest it on an axle stand – pad the top of the stand with cloth, to prevent damage to the paint.

6 Unscrew the two upper and lower door-to-hinge bolts, and remove the door from the car **(see illustration)**. Unclip the door wiring boot as the door is removed. Discard the hinge bolts – new ones should be used when refitting.

7 Examine the hinges for signs of wear or damage. If renewal is necessary, mark the position of the hinge, then unscrew the

12.4 Unbolt the door check strap

12.6 Door hinge bolts

12.12 Unclip the door wiring rubber boot as the door is removed

12.15 Loosen the bolts and adjust the door lock striker slightly if necessary

retaining bolts and remove the hinge from the car. Fit the new hinge, aligning it with the marks made before removal, then tighten the retaining bolts to the specified torque.

Rear door

8 Remove the front seat belt as described in Section 26.
9 Locate the door wiring plug, then twist and disconnect it.
10 Unbolt the door check strap from the door pillar.
11 Have an assistant support the door, or rest it on an axle stand – pad the top of the stand with cloth, to prevent damage to the paint.
12 Unscrew the two upper and lower door-to-hinge bolts, and remove the door from the car. Unclip the door wiring boot as the door is removed **(see illustration)**. Discard the hinge bolts – new ones should be used when refitting.

13 Examine the hinges for signs of wear or damage. If renewal is necessary, mark the position of the hinge, then unscrew the retaining bolts and remove the hinge from the car. Fit the new hinge, aligning it with the marks made before removal, then tighten the retaining bolts to the specified torque.

Refitting

14 Refitting is a reversal of removal, noting the following points:
   a) *Use new hinge bolts, and tighten them to the specified torque.*
   b) *Check the door alignment and if necessary adjust as described later in this Section.*
   c) *If the paintwork around the hinges has been damaged, paint the area with a suitable touch-in brush to prevent corrosion.*

Adjustment

15 To adjust the door to compensate for general wear in the hinges, this is best done by adjusting the position of the lock striker **(see illustration)**.
16 If adjusting the door after removal, close the door and check that the gap between the door and surrounding bodywork is equal around the complete perimeter. If necessary, slight adjustment of the door position can be made by slackening the hinge retaining bolts and repositioning the hinge/door as necessary. Once the door is correctly positioned, tighten the hinge bolts to their specified torque. Check that the door striker engages centrally with the lock, and if necessary, adjust the position of the striker.

13 Door trim panel – removal and refitting

Removal

Front door – 3-door models

1 Lower the window glass fully.
2 Carefully pull off the mirror inner trim panel by hand – pull the panel out at the front edge, then lift it up to disengage the lower mounting lug **(see illustration)**.
3 Insert the shorter end of an Allen key in through the hole on the inside of the door pull handle, and use it to push out the handle cover from behind. When the cover starts to come free at the bottom, pull the cover panel out from the front **(see illustration)**.
4 Carefully prise off the side cover from below the armrest, starting at the front, then working along the underside **(see illustrations)**.
5 Remove a total of eight screws (note their positions, as they are of two different lengths) from the door pull handle/armrest, then remove the handle from the door **(see illustrations)**. **Note:** *Only seven of the eight screws actually hold on the armrest, but the last screw still has to be removed, to take off the door trim panel.*
6 Pull out the window switch panel to release the hooked tab from the door trim panel, and disconnect its wiring plug **(see illustration)**.
7 Starting at the bottom of the door trim

13.2 Unclip and remove the mirror trim panel

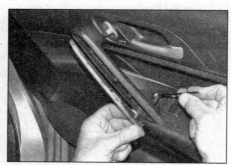

13.3 Push the door pull handle cover out with an Allen key, then remove it

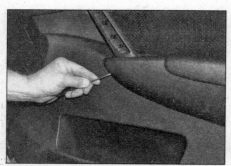

13.4a Starting at the front, unclip . . .

13.4b . . . and remove the armrest side cover

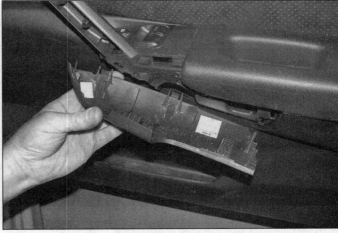

13.5a Remove the eight screws . . .

13.5b . . . and take off the armrest

panel, either prise behind it or simply pull the panel itself, to release the clips holding it to the door (there are four clips along the base, two at the rear edge, and three up the front). Take care – the clips have a nasty habit of not releasing, which breaks their locations in the panel itself. A hot-glue gun is a very handy tool to have, for putting this right.

8 When the panel is free, it must be pulled upwards, to disengage the window channel sealing strip – this is best done by lifting the panel at the rear, and working the strip out gradually (see illustration).

9 Reach behind the panel, unclip the interior handle operating cable, then twist the small plastic clip further forward, and unhook the cable end fitting. Where applicable, disconnect the wiring plug from the central locking switch, and detach the wiring harness from the panel (see illustrations).

Front door – 5-door models

10 Lower the window glass fully.

11 Carefully pull off the mirror inner trim panel by hand – pull the panel out at the front edge, then lift it up to disengage the lower mounting lug (see illustration).

12 Carefully prise out the rectangular panel in the centre of the door lock handle (see illustration).

13 Remove the two screws now exposed, then slide the whole handle forwards, and unhook it by pulling out the rear edge. Unhook the door lock operating rod, noting how it fits (see illustrations).

14 Carefully prise off the side cover from the door pull/armrest, starting at the top, then working down the pull handle itself (see illustration).

15 Remove the six screws from the door pull

13.6 Disconnect the window switch wiring plug (driver's switch shown)

13.8 Unclip and lift the panel over the door lock knob

13.9a Disconnect the central locking switch . . .

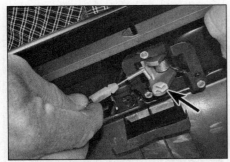

13.9b . . . then release the clip and unhook the interior handle cable

13.11 Unclip the mirror inner trim panel

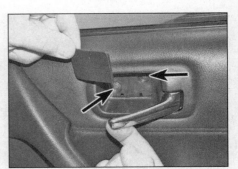

13.12 Prise out the panel from the lock handle, to access the two screws behind

13.13a Slide out the handle . . .

13.13b . . . then release the rod clip and lift out the door lock rod

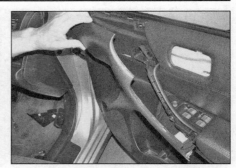

13.14 Prise off the door pull handle cover

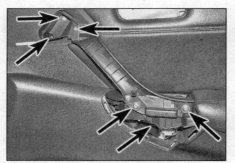

13.15a Remove a total of six screws . . .

13.15b . . . and take off the door pull handle

panel itself, to release the clips holding it to the door (there are three clips along the base, and two up each side). Take care – the clips have a nasty habit of not releasing, which breaks their locations in the panel itself (a hot-glue gun is a very handy tool to have, for putting this right). When the panel is free, it must be pulled upwards, to disengage the window channel sealing strip – this is best done by lifting the panel at the rear, and working the strip out gradually. Remove the panel from the car, over the door lock knob **(see illustrations)**.

Rear door

18 On models with manual rear windows, use a hooked piece of wire or a commercially-available tool to release the window regulator handle securing clip from the shaft – if neither of these is available, see the **Haynes Hint** opposite. Pull off the regulator handle, and recover the spring clip and the trim disc.

handle (note that they are of different lengths), and remove the handle from the door **(see illustrations)**.
16 Remove a further screw at the front of the window switch, then disconnect the switch

wiring plug and remove the switch assembly **(see illustrations)**.
17 Remove a single screw at the front of the panel. Starting at the bottom of the door trim panel, either prise behind it or simply pull the

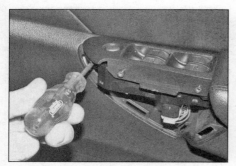

13.16a Remove a screw at the front . . .

13.16b . . . then take off the window switch panel . . .

13.16c . . . and disconnect the wiring plug

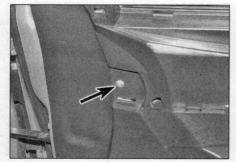

13.17a Remove the single screw at the front of the panel . . .

13.17b . . . then release the panel clips around the edges . . .

13.17c . . . and lift the panel to remove it

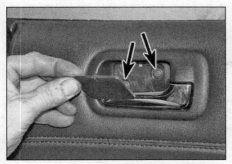

13.19 Prise out the panel from the interior handle, to access the two screws behind

13.20a Slide out the handle . . .

13.20b . . . then release the rod clip and lift out the door lock rod

---

> **HAYNES HINT**
>
> *Prise the regulator handle to open a gap between it and the circular disc behind. Work the edge of a piece of (clean) cloth/rag into the gap behind the handle, either from the top or underneath. Using a 'sawing' action, work the cloth side-to-side, and also pull the ends of the cloth up (or down). It may take some time, but what you're trying to do is snag the ends of the spring clip holding the handle in place – when you do, the sawing action should work the clip off, allowing the handle to be pulled from the splines. A little patience is required, but it will work. Keep an eye on where the spring clip goes, though – it will release with some force.*

19 Carefully prise out the rectangular panel in the centre of the door lock handle **(see illustration)**.

20 Remove the two screws now exposed, then slide the whole handle forwards, and unhook it by pulling out the rear edge. Unhook the door lock operating rod, noting how it fits **(see illustrations)**.

21 Carefully prise off the side cover from the door pull/armrest, working along the top edge from the front **(see illustration)**.

22 Remove the five screws from the armrest, then (where applicable) disconnect the window switch wiring plug and remove the armrest from the door **(see illustrations)**.

23 Remove the triangular trim panel at the rear of the door by unhooking its front edge first, then slide it forwards to release the locating lugs **(see illustration)**.

24 Starting at the bottom of the door trim panel, either prise behind it or simply pull the panel itself, to release the clips holding it to the door (there are two clips along the base, and two more up each side) **(see illustration)**. Take care – two of the clips on our car refused to release, and this broke their locations in the panel itself. A hot-glue gun is a very handy tool to have, for putting this right.

25 When the panel is free, it must be pulled upwards, to disengage the window channel sealing strip – this is best done by lifting the panel at the rear, and working the strip out gradually. Remove the panel from the car, over the door lock knob **(see illustration)**.

Door membrane

26 To access the door internal components, the plastic membrane must be removed.

27 On models with deadlocking ('super-locking'), disconnect the wiring plug then remove the screw securing the deadlocking

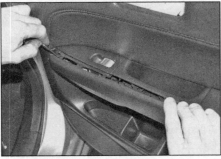

13.21 Prise off the armrest cover . . .

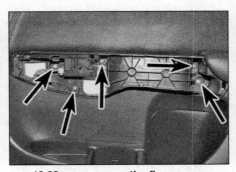

13.22a . . . remove the five screws behind . . .

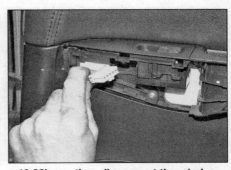

13.22b . . . then disconnect the window switch wiring plug . . .

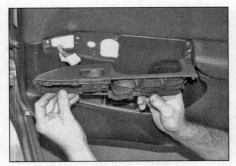

13.22c . . . and remove the armrest

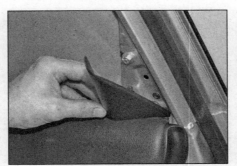

13.23 Unclip the triangular trim panel at the rear of the door

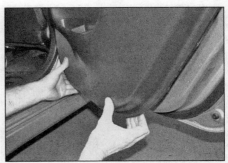

13.24 Release the clips securing the panel to the door

13.25 Lift the panel out of the window channel, and remove it

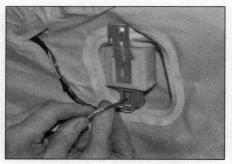

13.27a Disconnect the wiring plug . . .

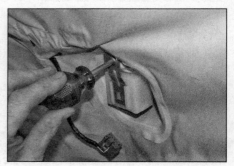

13.27b . . . then remove the screw and take off the deadlocking unit

13.28a Prise out the clips at the corners . . .

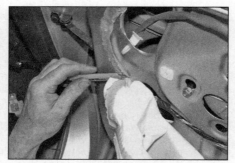

13.28b . . . then slice through the mastic with a sharp knife . . .

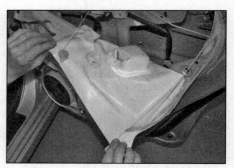

13.28c . . . and remove the membrane

control unit from the centre of the panel (see illustrations).

28 Prise out the clips, then carefully peel back the membrane. This sheet will be stuck on with a bead of mastic, which can be sliced though

'vertically' with a sharp knife, so that the membrane can be re-attached afterwards (see illustrations). Pull off the membrane and move it to a safe place, where it can be kept clean.

Refitting

29 Refitting is a reversal of removal, noting the following points:

a) Check the door for any trim clips which might have been left behind by the panel as it was removed. If necessary, carefully prise these clips out of the door, and refit them to the panel – if this is not done, they will not re-engage properly when refitting the panel. If any clips have been broken, obtain new ones for refitting – take one of the good clips along to the dealer for matching.

b) Once the trim panel wiring has been reconnected, check the operation of the door electrical equipment as applicable, before clipping the panel back in place.

c) Similarly, check the operation of the interior lock handle, once the operating rod has been reconnected.

d) On models with manual rear windows, refit the regulator handle trim disc, then slot the spring clip into the handle. With the window fully closed, offer the handle onto the splines – the handle should be set to face forwards and horizontal. Push the handle home until the spring clip clicks into place.

14 Door handle and lock components – removal and refitting

Removal

Interior door handle

1 On 5-door models, the interior door handle is removed as part of the door trim panel procedure – refer to Section 13. On 3-door models, the handle is part of the door trim panel.

Front door handle and lock cylinder

2 Remove the door trim panel and membrane as described in Section 13, then temporarily reconnect the door window switch and close the window.

3 Where applicable, remove the single screw at the top of the lock operating rod's plastic cover, then unhook the cover's lower end from the lock assembly, and remove it.

4 Unscrew the bolt at the base of the window glass rear guide channel, then pull out the channel trim, and pull it downwards to remove it (see illustrations).

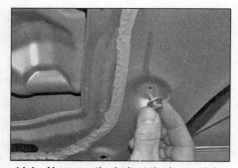

14.4a Unscrew the bolt at the base of the window guide channel . . .

14.4b . . . then pull out the trim . . .

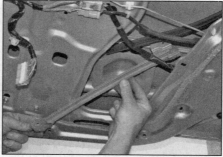

14.4c . . . and remove the guide channel

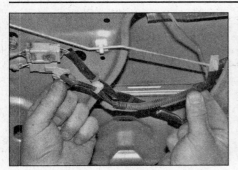

14.5 Disconnect the lock wiring plug, and unclip the wiring

14.6 Unclip the long plastic anti-theft cover – seen with lock/handle removed

14.7a Prise out the plastic cap, then . . .

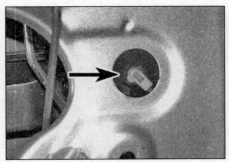
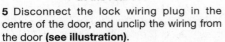

14.7b . . . working through the access hole at the rear . . .

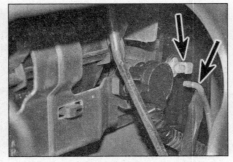

14.7c . . . release the clip and unhook the lock operating rod

14.8 Remove the screw and take off the lock cylinder switch

5 Disconnect the lock wiring plug in the centre of the door, and unclip the wiring from the door **(see illustration)**.

6 Reach inside to the rear edge of the door, and unclip the lock barrel operating rod's plastic cover, which is attached to the door handle at the top, and the lock itself at the bottom **(see illustration)**.

7 Unclip the lock barrel operating rod from the door, then reach inside and release the clip securing the rod end behind the lock barrel – there is a capped access hole in the door panel for this **(see illustrations)**.

8 Remove the screw and take off the actuator switch from the back of the lock cylinder **(see illustration)**.

9 Unclip the operating rod from the door handle by sliding it sideways out of the arm **(see illustration)**.

10 Unscrew the bolt front and rear, and take out the metal plate from the inside of the door

handle, noting that it has three locating tabs along its bottom edge **(see illustration)**.

11 Remove the handle from the outside of the door **(see illustrations)**.

12 The lock cylinder is secured to the handle

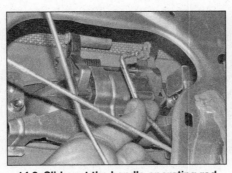

14.9 Slide out the handle operating rod

by a U-shaped spring clip, which must be pulled down to release it **(see illustration)**.

Rear door handle

13 Remove the door trim panel and membrane

14.10 Unscrew the two bolts and take off the handle plate

14.11a Removing the door handle

14.11b Door handle, plate and anti-theft cover removed and assembled

14.12 The lock cylinder is secured to the handle with a U-shaped spring clip

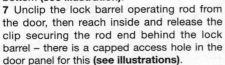
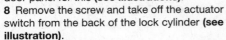
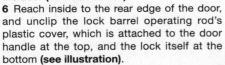

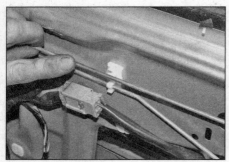

14.14a Unclip the lock rods from the door holder . . .

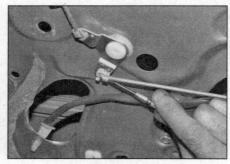

14.14b . . . and detach the rod from the lock knob linkage

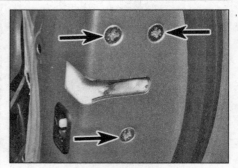

14.15 Remove the lock screws at the rear edge of the door

14.16a The door handle front mounting bolt is easy to access . . .

14.16b . . . while the rear one is reached through the lock aperture

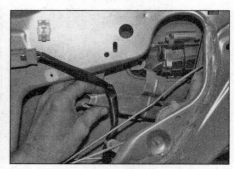

14.16c Lift out the handle's metal plate

as described in Section 13, then temporarily reconnect the door window switch (or refit the regulator handle) and close the window.

14 Noting their fitted positions, unclip the

two lock operating rods from the holder on the door (also unhook the longer rod from the door lock knob linkage) **(see illustrations)**. Where applicable, remove the single front screw from

the plastic cover fitted behind the door lock rods, then unclip it at the rear and withdraw it.

15 Unscrew and remove the three lock securing screws at the rear of the door, then move the lock down slightly, without bending any of the operating rods **(see illustration)**.

16 Unscrew the two door handle retaining bolts – where applicable, take off the metal plate from the inside of the handle, noting that it has three lower locating tabs **(see illustrations)**.

17 From outside the car, lift the handle and pull it outwards to remove **(see illustration)**.

Front door lock

18 Proceed as described in paragraphs 2 to 5 inclusive.

19 Disconnect the lock motor wiring plug in the centre of the door, then trace the wiring back to the motor, unclipping it from the door **(see illustrations)**.

20 Unclip the interior handle operating rod from the rod holder on the door **(see illustration)**.

21 Remove the three lock securing screws from the rear edge of the door, then move the lock assembly forwards and withdraw it from the door, taking care not to bend the still-attached operating rods **(see illustrations)**.

Rear door lock

22 Proceed as described in paragraphs 13 to 15 inclusive.

23 Disconnect the lock motor wiring plug in the centre of the door, then trace the wiring back to the motor, unclipping it from the door **(see illustrations)**.

24 Carefully unhook the two operating rods

14.17 Removing the door handle

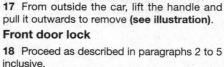

14.19a Disconnect the lock wiring plug, and unclip it from the door . . .

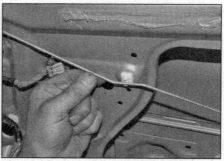

14.19b . . . then trace the wiring back and release it also

14.20 Unclip the lock operating rods from the door

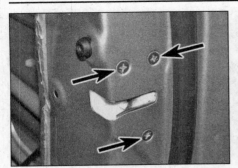

14.21a Remove the three screws from the rear edge of the door . . .

14.21b . . . then withdraw the lock assembly from the door

14.23a Disconnect the lock motor wiring plug, and unclip it from the door . . .

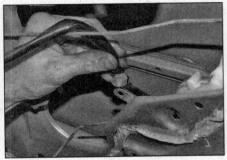

14.23b . . . then trace the wiring back, and unclip it also

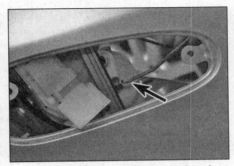

14.24a Disconnect the first lock rod through the door handle aperture . . .

14.24b . . . and the second from inside the door

from the door lock, noting how they are fitted **(see illustrations)**.

25 Unscrew and remove the bolt at the base of the window rear guide channel (this is on the rear edge of the door itself, underneath) **(see illustration)**.

26 Withdraw the lock assembly between the window guide channel and the door, twisting it horizontally through 90° to swing it around the guide channel **(see illustration)**.

Refitting

27 Refitting is a reversal of removal, noting the following points:
a) Ensure that all operating rods and wiring plugs are correctly and securely reconnected.
b) Lightly grease the operating rod sliding surfaces and pivots as necessary.
c) Check the operation of all components before refitting the membrane and door trim panel.

---

15 Door window glass and regulator – removal and refitting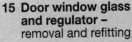

Removal

1 Remove the door trim panel and membrane as described in Section 13.

Front glass

2 Temporarily reconnect the window switch, and lower the glass until the two securing bolts are visible in the door frame **(see illustration)**.

3 Have an assistant support the glass (take care – it's heavy), then unscrew and remove the bolts. Tilt the glass forwards, then lift and withdraw it from the door **(see illustration)**.

Front regulator/motor

4 To remove the regulator, first disconnect the motor wiring plug. Trace the wiring back

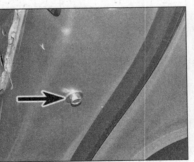

14.25 Unscrew the window guide channel bolt under the door rear edge

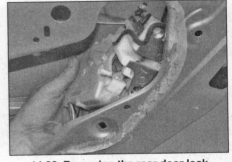

14.26 Removing the rear door lock assembly

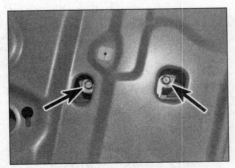

15.2 Door glass securing bolts, seen through the door access holes

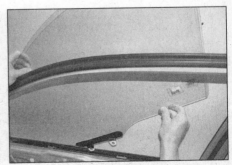

15.3 Removing the door glass

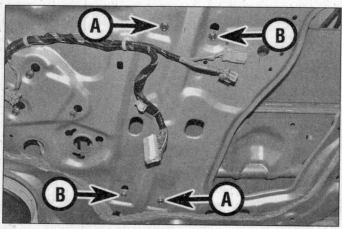

15.5 Remove two of the regulator mounting bolts (A), and loosen the other two (B)

15.6a Loosen the three motor mounting bolts . . .

towards the motor, and release the harness clip.

5 Unscrew and remove the two of the regulator bolts – the other two bolts are on slotted mountings, and need only be loosened **(see illustration)**.

6 Similarly, the three motor mounting bolts need only be loosened, as they sit in slotted mountings. Withdraw the regulator and motor assembly through the door frame **(see illustrations)**.

Rear glass

7 Temporarily reconnect the window handle or switch, and fully lower the glass.

8 Starting at the front, carefully pull up and remove the door glass outer weatherstrip **(see illustration)**. Take care to ease the strip out slowly, as it can be bent if too much force is used, and the plastic clips are fragile. Also take care not to scratch the paint (it may be wise to apply a strip or two of masking tape along the top of the door first).

9 Remove the screw in the centre of the triangular plate at the rear of the door frame – this secures the door's rear outer trim panel. From the outside of the door, pull forwards then upwards on the door's rear trim panel, and remove it **(see illustrations)**.

10 Now raise the glass until the two securing bolts are visible in the door frame **(see illustration)**.

11 Have an assistant support the glass (take care – it's heavy), then unscrew and remove the bolts. Lower the glass as far as it will go, noting that it cannot be removed for the moment.

12 Unscrew the guide channel's upper nut and lower bolt – the nut is on the triangular plate at the rear of the door frame, while the bolt is on the rear edge of the door itself, underneath. Pull the channel forward to free the top end from the door frame, then carefully twist it to release it from the glass at the base, and slide the channel up out of the door **(see illustrations)**.

13 Lift the glass from the bottom of the door, and withdraw it completely **(see illustration)**.

15.6b . . . and remove the motor/regulator assembly from the door

15.8 Unclip the door glass outer weatherstrip, working from the front

15.9a Remove the screw from the triangular panel at the rear . . .

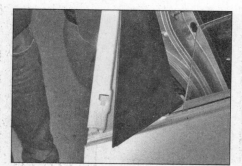

15.9b . . . and take off the door rear trim panel from outside

15.10 Raise the glass until both glass-to-regulator bolts can be seen

15.12a Remove the window guide channel upper nut . . .

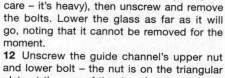

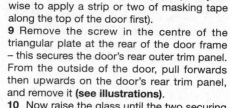

15.12b ... and lower bolt, under the rear edge of the door ...

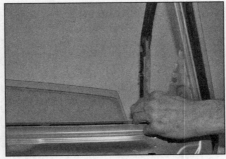

15.12c ... then pull the channel forwards and lift it out

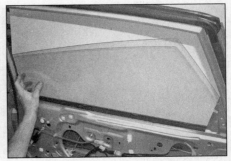

15.13 Lift the glass out of the door

Rear regulator/motor

14 To remove the regulator, where applicable first disconnect the motor wiring plug, which is at the top of the regulator. Unclip the wiring harness from the door **(see illustrations)**.

15 Unscrew and remove the regulator's single lower bolt, and the forward one of the two upper bolts – the rearward bolt is on a slotted mounting, and need only be loosened. Similarly, the three regulator spindle (or motor) mounting bolts need only be loosened, as they sit in slotted mountings **(see illustrations)**.

16 Withdraw the regulator and spindle/motor assembly through the door frame **(see illustrations)**.

Refitting

17 Refitting is a reversal of removal, noting the following points:

  a) *Tighten all mounting bolts securely.*
  b) *Lightly grease the regulator sliding surfaces as necessary.*
  c) *Check the operation of all components before refitting the membrane and door trim panel.*

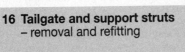

16 Tailgate and support struts – removal and refitting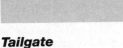

Tailgate

Removal

1 Remove all the tailgate trim panels, the C-

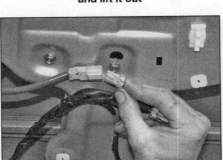

15.14a Disconnect the window motor wiring plug ...

pillar trim panels, and the rear grab handles, as described in Section 27.

2 Disconnect all wiring connectors from inside the tailgate, and disconnect the washer tube from the rear wiper motor (refer to Chapter 12

15.15a Window regulator mounting bolts (rearward one on slotted mounting)

15.14b ... then unclip the wiring from the door

if necessary). Also, prise the washer tube and wiring grommets from the tailgate **(see illustrations)**.

3 Tie a piece of string to each end of the wiring then, noting the correct routing of the

15.15b All the motor bolts are on slotted mountings

15.16a Withdraw the motor through to the inside ...

15.16b ... then lift out the motor and regulator

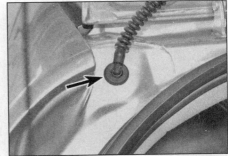

16.2a Prise out the washer tube grommet on the left ...

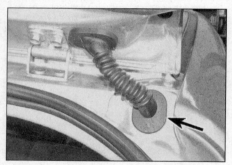

16.2b . . . and the wiring grommet on the right

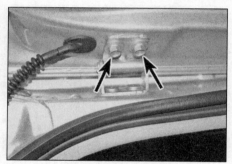

16.7 Unscrew the tailgate mounting bolts

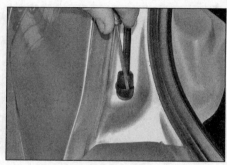

16.11 Prise off the support strut lower locking clip

wiring harness, release the harness rubber grommets from the tailgate and withdraw the wiring. When the end of the wiring appears, untie the string and leave it in position in the tailgate; it can then be used on refitting to draw the wiring into position.

4 Release the headlining at the rear edge, and carefully pull it down for access to the tailgate hinges.

5 Using a suitable marker pen, draw around the outline of each hinge, marking its correct position on the tailgate. Protect the paintwork surrounding the hinges with masking tape.

6 With the help of an assistant to support the tailgate, remove the support struts as described below.

7 With the tailgate still supported, unscrew the two nuts and bolts from each hinge, then lift the tailgate from the car (see illustration).

8 Inspect the hinges for signs of wear or damage and renew if necessary.

Refitting

9 Refitting is a reversal of removal, but tighten the tailgate mounting nuts and bolts to the specified torque. Check the tailgate alignment with the surrounding panels. If necessary, slight adjustment can be made by slackening the hinge fasteners and repositioning the tailgate on its hinges – adjustable tailgate rubbers are also fitted on either side, and the tailgate lock striker is also adjustable.

Support struts

⚠️ *Warning: The support struts are filled with gas, and must be disposed of safely.*

Removal

10 With the help of an assistant (or a suitable wooden prop), support the tailgate in the open position.

11 Using a small screwdriver, prise out the

centre cap/locking clip from the lower end of the strut, and pull the strut off its ball-stud fitting on the tailgate aperture (see illustration). The strut can now be removed with the tailgate if required.

12 To remove the strut completely, unscrew the upper ball-stud fitting from the tailgate, using an open-ended spanner.

Refitting

13 Refitting is a reversal of removal. Ensure that the locking clip is properly refitted, to secure the bottom of the strut in place. Where removed, tighten the ball-stud securely.

17 Tailgate lock components – removal and refitting

Removal

1 Remove the tailgate main trim panel as described in Section 27.

Lock

2 Unscrew the three lock mounting bolts, and withdraw the lock from the tailgate (see illustrations).

3 Disconnect the operating cable from the tailgate handle, by sliding the cable end fitting sideways out of the arm on the inside of the handle (see illustrations).

4 Trace the two wiring harnesses from either side of the lock, and disconnect the wiring plugs (these are for the lock motor and lock switch). Release the wiring from the tailgate (see illustrations).

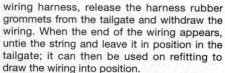

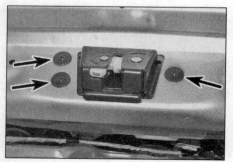

17.2a Unscrew the three tailgate lock mounting bolts . . .

17.2b . . . and withdraw the lock from its location

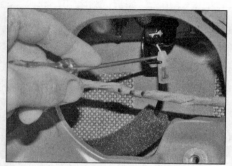

17.3a Use a small screwdriver . . .

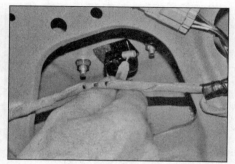

17.3b . . . to slide the lock cable out of the handle

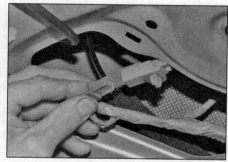

17.4a Disconnect the two lock wiring plugs . . .

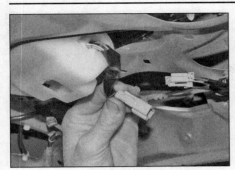

17.4b ... and detach the wiring from the tailgate

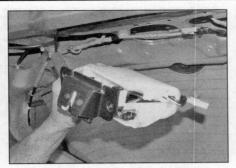

17.5a Removing the tailgate lock

17.5b Removing the operating cable from the lock

5 Withdraw the lock assembly from the tailgate. If required, remove the single screw and take off the lock cover – this allows access to the tailgate handle operating cable, which can then be detached from the lock if necessary **(see illustrations)**.

6 Refitting is a reversal of removal. Check the operation of the lock before refitting the tailgate trim panel.

Lock cylinder

Note: *Not all models have a separate lock cylinder – typically, on models with remote locking, the lock cylinder is omitted.*

7 Remove the tailgate outer trim panel as described in Section 27.

8 Unhook the lock cylinder operating rod, then disconnect the cylinder switch wiring plug and detach the wiring from the tailgate.

9 Remove the lock cylinder mounting bolt on the outside of the tailgate, then pull the lock cylinder from the inside to release its retaining clip, and remove it.

10 Refitting is a reversal of removal. Check the operation of the lock before refitting the tailgate outer trim panel.

Tailgate handle

11 Disconnect the operating cable from the tailgate handle, by sliding the cable end fitting sideways out of the arm on the inside of the handle **(see illustrations 17.3a and 17.3b)**.

12 Remove the tailgate outer trim panel as described in Section 27.

13 Unscrew the two handle mounting nuts from the inside, then withdraw the handle from the outside of the tailgate **(see illustrations)**.

14 Refitting is a reversal of removal. Check the operation of the handle before refitting the tailgate trim panels.

Lock striker

15 Remove the luggage area rear trim panel as described in Section 27.

16 Mark around the striker with paint (such as typist's correction fluid) to ensure it is accurately refitted.

17 Unscrew the two mounting bolts, and withdraw the striker from the tailgate aperture.

18 Refitting is a reversal of removal. Align the striker with the previously-made marks, and tighten the bolts to the specified torque.

18 Central locking components – general

1 The operation of the central locking is integrated into the door locks, and is controlled by the multiplex control unit. If a fault occurs in the system, the car should be taken to a Honda dealer who will have the special diagnostic equipment necessary to find the fault quickly.

Central locking switches

2 The central locking switches fitted to the two front door lock cylinders are removed as described in Section 14. The lock switches fitted to the rear doors and tailgate are part of the lock assemblies themselves. The central locking system switch fitted on 3-door model front door trim panels can be removed after taking off the door trim panel as described in Section 13 – the switch is screwed to the inside of the panel.

Remote receiver

3 The remote central locking receiver unit is mounted on the facia between the instrument panel and radio unit – remove the radio unit as described in Chapter 12 for access. Disconnect the wiring plug, then unscrew the mounting bolt and remove the receiver unit from the facia.

Deadlocking control units

4 Each of the doors has a separate dead-locking (or 'superlocking') control unit fitted. When the deadlocking feature is activated, the interior door handles are effectively disconnected, meaning that a thief will still not be able to open a door, even after breaking a window. Remove the door trim panel as described in Section 13, then disconnect the deadlocking control unit wiring plug and remove the single mounting screw.

19 Electric window components – removal and refitting

Window switch

1 Refer to Chapter 12.

Window motor

2 The window motor is removed with the regulator assembly, as described in Section 15.

20 Mirrors and associated components – removal and refitting

Interior mirror

1 See Section 27.

Door mirror assembly

2 Lower the window glass fully.

3 Carefully pull off the mirror inner trim panel by hand – pull the panel out at the front edge,

17.13a Unscrew the handle mounting nuts inside ...

17.13b ... then withdraw the handle from outside

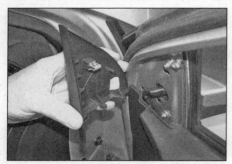

20.3 Unclip the mirror trim panel at the front of the door

20.5a Unclip the wiring harness from the door . . .

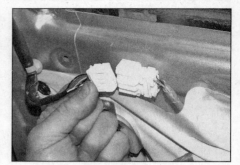

20.5b . . . then disconnect the mirror wiring plug

20.6a Remove the three mounting nuts . . .

20.6b . . . then withdraw the mirror from the outside

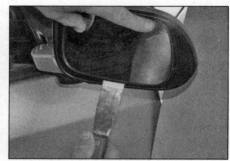

20.8a Release the glass from below, with a wide-bladed tool . . .

then lift it up to disengage the lower mounting lug (see illustration).

4 Remove the door trim panel as described in Section 13.

5 Disconnect the mirror wiring plug at the top of the door – unclip the wiring harness from the door frame first, to make this easier (see illustrations).

6 Support the mirror, then unscrew the three mounting nuts and withdraw the mirror from the outside of the door (see illustrations).

7 Refitting is a reversal of removal. Check the mirror operation before refitting the door and mirror trim panels.

Door mirror glass

8 Push the glass fully into the housing at the top, so that the lower edge is sticking out. Insert a wide, flat-bladed tool (wrapped with tape to protect the housing) into the gap between the glass and mirror housing, and release the glass, which is secured to the centre pivot plate with two clips and a little mastic (see illustrations).

9 Disconnect the wiring connector from the mirror heating element, and remove the glass (see illustration).

10 When refitting, align the glass with the two mounting clips, and push it evenly onto them

– use a wad of cloth, and take care not to use excessive force, as the glass is easily broken.

Door mirror switch

11 Refer to Chapter 12.

Door mirror motor

12 With the mirror removed, separate the mirror body from the mounting plate by removing the three screws underneath.

13 The motor wiring plug will have to be cut off, to feed it back through the mirror body – leave plenty of wire attached to the plug, to reconnect the new motor to.

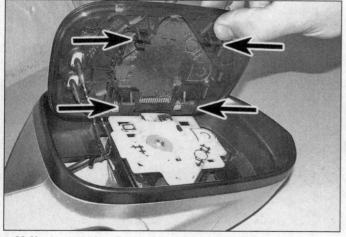

20.8b . . . note the clips and mastic used to hold it to the pivot plate

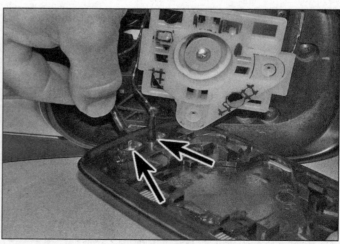

20.9 Disconnect the wiring connectors for the heating element

14 Unscrew the three motor mounting screws, then remove the motor, withdrawing the wiring through the mirror body.

15 Refitting is a reversal of removal. Feed the wiring through, then reconnect the wiring plug – it is recommended that the wires are soldered and properly insulated.

21 Windscreen, tailgate and fixed side window glass – general information

These areas of glass are bonded in position with a special adhesive. Renewal of such fixed glass is a difficult, messy and time-consuming task, which is beyond the scope of the home mechanic. It is difficult, unless one has plenty of practice, to obtain a secure, waterproof fit. In view of this, owners are strongly advised to have this work carried out by one of the many specialist windscreen fitters.

22 Sunroof – general information

Due to the complexity of the sunroof mechanism, considerable expertise is needed to repair, renew or adjust the sunroof components successfully. Removal of the roof first requires the headlining to be removed, which is a complex and tedious operation, and not a task to be undertaken lightly. Therefore, any problems with the sunroof should be referred to a Honda dealer.

On models with an electric sunroof, if the sunroof motor fails to operate, first check the relevant fuse. If the fault cannot be traced and rectified, the sunroof can be opened and closed manually using a special cranked tool to turn the motor spindle (this tool is supplied with the car, in the toolkit which is in the boot). To gain access to the motor, unclip the small round trim cover in front of the rear interior light. Insert the tool fully into the motor opening, and turn it to open or close the sunroof.

23 Exterior fittings – removal and refitting

Engine undertray

1 Jack up the front of the car, and support it on axle stands (see *Jacking and vehicle support*).
2 The undertray is secured by a number of bolts around the edge – remove the bolts and lower out the panel (note that diesel engine models have a second smaller undertray panel in addition to the main one) **(see illustrations)**.
3 Refitting is a reversal of removal.

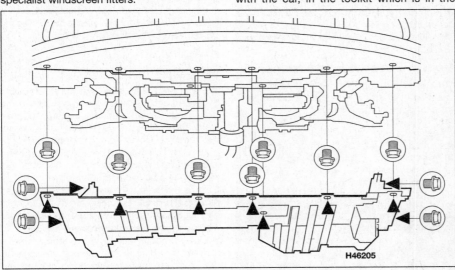

23.2a Engine undertray removal details – petrol models

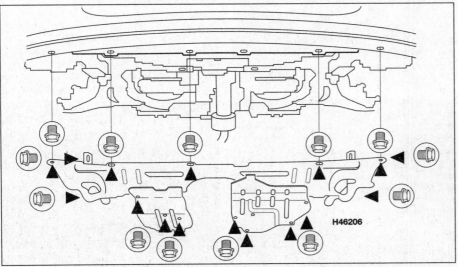

23.2b Engine undertray removal details – diesel models

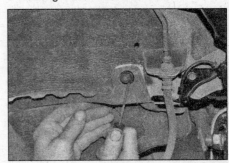

23.2c The engine undertray is secured by a number of clips . . .

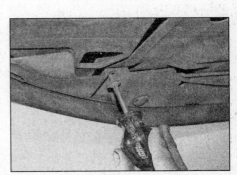

23.2d . . . and screws . . .

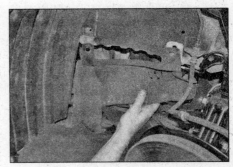

23.2e . . . and is removed in one piece

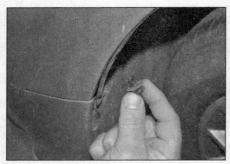

23.6 Remove the liner clips and screws . . .

23.7 . . . then free the liner from the edges of the wing, and remove it

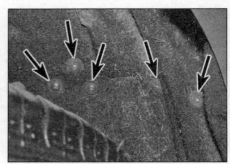

23.9 The rear liners are of carpet type, secured by screws and clips

Wheel arch liners

4 Removing the wheel arch liners is much easier with the relevant wheel removed. Loosen the relevant wheel nuts, then jack up the front or rear of the car, and support it on axle stands (see *Jacking and vehicle support*). Remove the wheel.

Front

5 Remove the three screws from the mudflap at the rear of the wheel arch, and a further single screw underneath at the front.
6 Work around the inside of the arch liner, and prise out the clips (approximately ten in total) securing the liner to the wheel arch. It may be necessary to wipe the liner clean, to see them clearly **(see illustration)**. Take care, as the clips are easily broken – special forked tools are available for removing these clips, and these are preferable to a flat-bladed screwdriver.
7 With all the clips removed, release the liner

and withdraw it from under the wheel arch **(see illustration)**.
8 On refitting, renew any retaining clips that may have been broken on removal, and ensure that the panel is securely retained.

Rear

9 Material-type liners are used at the rear, secured by a combination of screws and clips **(see illustration)**. Removal is therefore very similar to the front liners.

Body trim strips and badges

10 The various body trim strips and badges are held in position with a special adhesive tape and locating lugs. Removal requires the trim/badge to be heated, to soften the adhesive, and then carefully lifted away from the surface. Due to the high risk of damage to the paintwork during this operation, it is recommended that this task should be entrusted to a Honda dealer.

24 Seats – removal and refitting

Note: *Refer to the airbag warnings in Chapter 12 if removing front seats with side airbags. Before disconnecting the battery, refer to Disconnecting the battery at the rear of this manual.*

Removal

Front seats

1 On models with side airbags (identifiable by having an AIRBAG label on the side of the front seat), disconnect the battery negative lead, and wait for at least 3 minutes before proceeding (refer to *Disconnecting the battery*). If this precaution is not taken, there is a risk that the side airbags will fire when the seat wiring plug is disconnected.
2 Slide the seat fully to the rear. Unclip and remove the plastic end caps from the front of each seat rail, then remove the two seat front mounting bolts **(see illustration)**.
3 Slide the seat fully forwards, then remove the plastic end caps from the rear of each seat rail. Unscrew and remove the two seat rear mounting bolts **(see illustration)**.
4 Tilt the seat backwards and disconnect the wiring plugs underneath for the side airbag, seat heating and seat belt buckle signalling, as applicable **(see illustrations)**.
5 Carefully remove the seat from inside the car, taking care not to damage the surrounding trim panels. The help of an assistant may be necessary, as the seat is heavy **(see illustration)**.

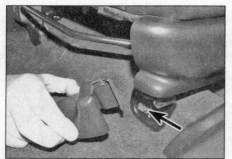

24.2 Unclip the seat rail front covers, and remove the seat bolts

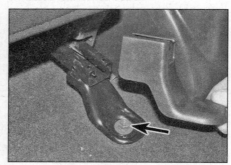

24.3 Similarly, at the rear, unclip the covers and remove the seat bolts

24.4a Tilt the seat backwards to access the wiring plugs

24.4b The side airbag wiring plug has a spring-loaded locking sleeve

24.5 When removing a front seat, take care the seat rails don't scratch the trim

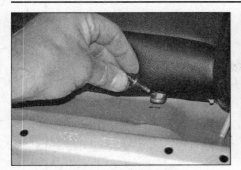

24.7a Remove the single bolt from the loop at the rear . . .

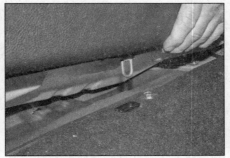

24.7b . . . then lift the front edge of the seat to free the two catches

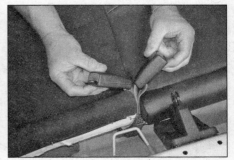

24.7c Free the seat belt buckles from the cushion . . .

24.7d . . . and lift it out of the car

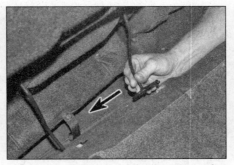

24.8a Press the two spring legs towards the outside of the car . . .

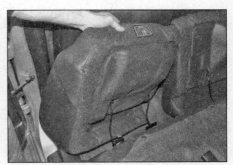

24.8b . . . and lift out the seat cushion

Rear seat cushion

6 Lift the rear of the seat cushion, and fold the cushion forwards.

7 Where a one-piece cushion is fitted, remove the single bolt in the centre at the rear, then unclip the two front catches by pulling sharply upwards (when refitting, these catches need a firm downward push to re-engage). Free the seat belt buckles from the cushion and remove it **(see illustrations)**.

8 On models with separate cushions, release the two spring legs securing the seat to the pivots on the floor, by pressing the legs towards the outer side of the car. Remove the cushion from the car **(see illustrations)**.

Rear seat backrest

9 Lift the rear of the seat cushions, and fold them forwards.

10 Where an inertia reel centre seat belt is fitted in the right-hand backrest, unscrew the belt lower anchor bolt from the floor **(see illustration)**.

11 Release the catches and fold both the backrests forwards.

12 In the centre of the seats, unclip and remove the plastic cover from the central hinge **(see illustration)**.

13 Remove the two bolts securing the hinge to the right-hand backrest, then slide the backrest forwards slightly, off the hinge. Slide the backrest sideways into the car, to release the outer pivot pin, and remove it **(see illustrations)**.

14 The left-hand backrest can now be removed, by unscrewing the hinge through-

bolt and removing the hinge. As with the right-hand backrest, slide it inwards off the outer pivot pin to remove. On 3-door models, the

backrest has to be pushed hard to the left, and prised out to free the pivot from the centre hinge **(see illustrations)**.

24.10 On models with the centre rear belt, unbolt the lower anchor

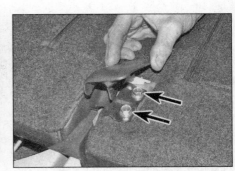

24.12 Unclip the cover from the central hinge, and remove the two bolts

24.13a Separate the backrest from the hinge, then slide into the car . . .

24.13b . . . to release it from the outer pivot pin

24.14a Unscrew the hinge through-bolt, and take it off . . .

24.14b . . . then slide the left-hand backrest inwards, and remove

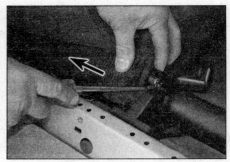

24.14c On 3-door models, the backrest must be forced sideways to free it

Refitting

15 Refitting is a reversal of removal, noting the following points:

a) *Before reconnecting the front seat wiring, on models with side airbags, ensure that the battery is still disconnected.*

b) *Tighten the front seat mounting bolts to the specified torque.*

c) *Where removed, tighten the rear seat hinge bolts and seat belt lower anchor bolt to the specified torques.*

25 Front seat belt tensioners – general information and precautions

The front seat belt inertia reels are fitted with integral automatic belt tensioners (the rear seat belt inertia reels are not fitted with tensioners). The system is designed to instantaneously take up any slack in the seat belt in the case of a sudden frontal impact, therefore reducing the possibility of injury to the front seat occupants.

The seat belt tensioner is triggered by a frontal impact above a predetermined force. Lesser impacts, including impacts from behind, will not trigger the system. If the impact is sufficient to trigger the airbags, the seat belt tensioners will also be deployed.

When the system is triggered, the explosive gas in the tensioner mechanism retracts and locks the seat belt through a cable which acts on the inertia reel. This prevents the seat belt moving and keeps the occupant firmly

in position in the seat. Once the tensioner has been triggered, the seat belt will be permanently locked and the assembly must be renewed.

Note the following warnings before contemplating any work on the front seat belts.

 Warning: Do not expose the tensioner mechanism to temperatures in excess of 100°C.

• *If the tensioner mechanism is dropped, it must be renewed, even it has suffered no apparent damage.*

• *Do not allow any solvents to come into contact with the tensioner mechanism.*

• *Do not attempt to open the tensioner mechanism as it contains explosive gas.*

• *Tensioners must be discharged before they are disposed of, but this task should be entrusted to a Honda dealer.*

• *Before removing the front seat belt inertia reels, the battery negative lead must be disconnected. Once disconnected, wait at least 3 minutes before proceeding, otherwise there is a risk that the tensioners will fire when the inertia reel wiring plug is disconnected. The battery must remain disconnected until after the tensioner wiring plug is reconnected.*

26 Seat belt components – removal and refitting

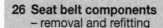

Front seat belt

Note: *Refer to the warnings in Section 25.*

1 Disconnect the battery negative lead (refer to *Disconnecting the battery* in the *Reference* Chapter at the end of this manual). Wait at least 3 minutes before proceeding.

2 Slide the front seat fully forwards.

3-door models

3 Remove the bolt from each end of the seat belt lower anchor rail, then slide the looped end of the belt off the rail **(see illustrations)**.

4 Unclip the seat belt upper anchor's plastic cover by spreading it apart at the rear. Unscrew and remove the upper anchor bolt, noting carefully how the washers and bushes are arranged.

5 Remove the rear side trim panel as described in Section 27.

6 Disconnect the tensioner wiring plug from the inertia reel. Unscrew the lower mounting bolt and upper screw, then unhook and remove the inertia reel and belt from the car **(see illustration)**.

7 Refitting is a reversal of removal, noting the following points:

a) *Apply thread-locking fluid to the upper anchor bolt.*

b) *Tighten all bolts to the specified torque, where given.*

c) *Ensure that the battery is still disconnected before reconnecting the tensioner wiring plug.*

5-door models

8 Unclip the seat belt lower anchor trim cover for access to the lower anchor bolt. Unscrew and remove the bolt, noting carefully how

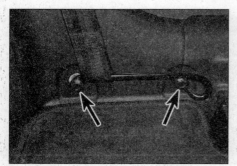

26.3a Remove the two bolts . . .

26.3b . . . then unhook and remove the anchor rail

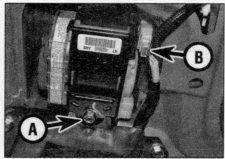

26.6 Seat belt front inertia reel lower bolt (A) and tensioner plug (B)

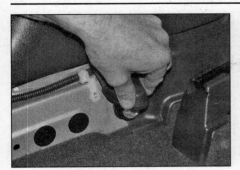

26.8a Unclip the trim cover . . .

26.8b . . . then unscrew the belt lower anchor bolt

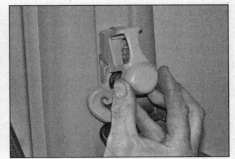

26.9a Unclip the upper anchor trim cover . . .

26.9b . . . then unscrew the bolt and remove the upper anchor

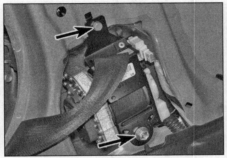

26.11a Remove the upper and lower mounting bolts . . .

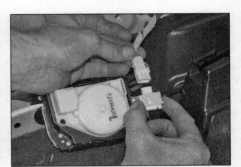

26.11b . . . then disconnect the tensioner wiring plug and remove the belt

the washers and bushes are arranged (**see illustrations**).

9 Unclip the seat belt upper anchor's plastic cover by spreading it apart at the rear. Unscrew and remove the upper anchor bolt, again noting carefully how the washers and bushes are arranged (**see illustrations**).

10 Remove the rear sill and B-pillar lower trim panels as described in Section 27.

11 Unscrew the upper mounting bolt and (larger) lower bolt, then disconnect the tensioner wiring plug (note that this has a spring-loaded locking collar) and remove the inertia reel and belt from the car (**see illustrations**).

12 Refitting is a reversal of removal, noting the following points:

a) Apply thread-locking fluid to the upper anchor bolt.

b) Tighten all bolts to the specified torque, where given.

c) Ensure that the battery is still disconnected before reconnecting the tensioner wiring plug.

Front height adjuster

13 Unclip the seat belt upper anchor's plastic cover by spreading it apart at the rear. Unscrew and remove the upper anchor bolt, again noting carefully how the washers and bushes are arranged.

14 Remove the B-pillar upper trim panel as described in Section 27.

15 Unscrew the height adjuster upper and lower mounting bolts, and remove the adjuster from the B-pillar (**see illustration**).

16 Refitting is a reversal of removal, noting the following points:

a) Apply thread-locking fluid to the upper anchor bolt.

b) Tighten all bolts to the specified torque, where given.

Front belt stalk

17 Remove the front seat as described in Section 24.

18 Unclip and remove the plastic cover from the inner side of the seat.

19 Disconnect the wiring from the seat occupancy monitor and stalk buckle indicator (where applicable), and unclip the wiring from under the seat.

20 Unscrew the stalk mounting bolt, noting carefully how the washers are arranged, and remove the stalk from the seat.

21 Refitting is a reversal of removal. Engage the stalk's mounting lug into the hole on the

seat frame, and tighten the mounting bolt to the specified torque.

Rear side belts

22 Fold the rear seat cushion and backrest forwards.

23 Remove the parcel shelf support panel, and the C-pillar trim panel, as described in Section 27. On 3-door models, also remove the rear side trim panel, while on 5-door models, the rear door aperture trim panel must also be removed.

24 Unscrew and remove the rear belt lower anchor bolt from the floor, noting how the lug on the anchor plate fits into the hole in the floor. Feed the end of the belt through the parcel shelf support panel (**see illustrations**).

25 Unscrew the inertia reel's two mounting bolts, and remove the seat belt from the car (**see illustrations**).

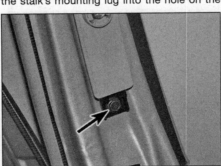

26.15 Height adjuster lower mounting bolt

26.24a Unbolt the lower anchor from the floor . . .

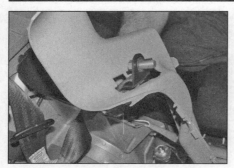

26.24b . . . and feed the belt through the parcel shelf support panel

26.25a Remove the inertia reel's upper . . .

26.25b . . . and lower mounting bolt . . .

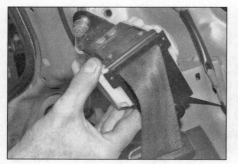

26.25c . . . and remove the seat belt

26.28 Unbolt the rear belt buckles from the floor

26 Refitting is a reversal of removal. Tighten all bolts to the specified torque.

Rear belt buckles

27 Fold the rear seat cushions forwards.
28 Unscrew the buckle mounting bolts as required, and remove the buckles from the car **(see illustration)**.
29 Refitting is a reversal of removal. Tighten all bolts to the specified torque.

Rear centre belt

30 The belt's inertia reel is contained inside the rear seat right-hand backrest, which can be removed as described in Section 24. However, accessing the reel itself requires that the backrest is dismantled, which is not considered a DIY operation, For this reason, take the backrest to a Honda dealer (or car upholstery specialist) for work on the centre belt.

27 Interior trim and fittings – removal and refitting

General

1 The interior trim panels are secured by a combination of clips and screws, with plastic clips featuring heavily – these clips often get 'left behind' in the bodywork when the panels are removed, and should be prised out for refitting to the panels. Removal and refitting is generally self-explanatory, noting that it may be necessary to remove or loosen surrounding panels to allow a particular panel to be removed. The following paragraphs describe the removal and refitting of the major panels in more detail.

Door trim panels

2 Refer to Section 13.

Steering column shrouds

3 Working in the driver's footwell, remove the three screws from the lower shroud **(see illustration)**.
4 Unclip the upper shroud from the lower one, and withdraw it.
5 Remove the lower shroud, manoeuvring it out past the column height adjuster lever, and over the ignition switch **(see illustration)**.
6 Refitting is a reversal of removal.

Driver's lower facia trim panels

Left-hand panel

7 Release the turn-buckle fasteners on either side of the panel by turning them through 45°.
8 Pull the shorter edge of the panel outwards, and slide it out sideways to free the clips on the longer edge **(see illustration)**.
9 Refitting is a reversal of removal.

Right-hand panel/cubby

10 Remove the facia closing panel as described later in this Section.
11 Remove the two screws at the top of the panel **(see illustration)**.
12 Reach in from below, and push the panel out from behind to release the two lower clips.
13 Unhook the panel at the top, and remove it from the facia **(see illustration)**.
14 Refitting is a reversal of removal.

Facia closing panel

15 Release the turn-buckle fastener on the left side of the panel by turning it through 45°.
16 Pull the front edge of the panel down on

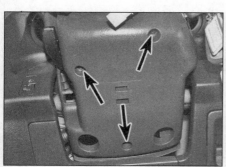

27.3 Unscrew the three lower shroud screws under the steering column

27.5 Unclip the upper shroud, then remove the lower shroud

27.8 Removing the driver's lower left-hand trim panel

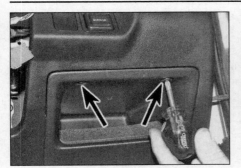

27.11 Remove the two screws at the top of the cubby holder . . .

27.13 . . . then release it from behind and at the top edge

27.16 Removing the driver's side facia closing panel

27.23 Unscrew and remove the gear knob

27.25a Release the panel clips from behind, or prise carefully from the front . . .

27.25b . . . and withdraw the panel

the right-hand side to release the clip, then pull the panel away from the facia, to release the rear clip from its guide (see illustration).

17 Refitting is a reversal of removal.

Facia centre lower panel

Note: *This panel is only fitted on models without a centre console.*

18 Open the ashtray, then press down on the metal plate inside, and slide it out completely.

19 Remove the three screws securing the ashtray holder to the facia, and remove it.

20 Disconnect the ashtray illumination bulbholder.

21 Remove the two screws at the top, then release the two side clips, and slide the floor panel rearwards to release the side locating tabs.

22 Refitting is a reversal of removal.

Gear/selector lever trim panel

23 On manual transmission models, unscrew and remove the gear lever knob **(see illustration)**.

24 Remove the glovebox as described later in this Section.

25 Working through the glovebox aperture, use a screwdriver to push out the left-hand side of the trim panel, from behind. There is a clip at each 'corner' of the panel (two on top, and two below), but they are very stiff to release – the top two corners seem especially prone to damage if care is not taken **(see illustrations)**.

26 Reach in behind the panel and disconnect the hazard warning light switch and cigarette lighter wiring plugs, then remove the panel over the gear/selector lever. If required, the gear lever gaiter can be removed from the

panel, by unscrewing the three collar retaining screws on the inside **(see illustrations)**.

27 Refitting is a reversal of removal.

Facia centre control panel

28 Refer to the heater control panel removal procedure, in Chapter 3, Section 9.

Passenger's facia closing panel

29 Pull the panel down at the front to release the three clips securing it to the facia, then pull the panel away from the facia, to release the two rear clips from their guides **(see illustration)**.

30 Refitting is a reversal of removal.

Glovebox

31 Remove the passenger's facia closing panel as described previously in this Section.

27.26a Disconnect the wiring plugs from the back of the panel

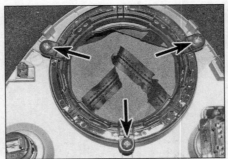

27.26b The gear lever gaiter collar is secured by three screws

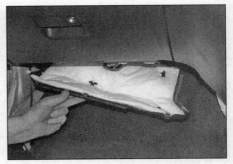

27.29 Removing the passenger's facia closing panel

27.32 Unscrew the two glovebox hinge bolts . . .

27.33 . . . then lower out the glovebox

27.35 Removing one of the A-pillar trim panels

32 Unscrew and remove the two glovebox hinge bolts from below **(see illustration)**.
33 Lower out the glovebox and remove it from the facia **(see illustration)**.
34 Refitting is a reversal of removal.

A-pillar trim panels

35 The A-pillar trim panels are held in place by two clips along their length, and there are locating lugs at the top and bottom. Start at the top of the panel, and pull the panel towards the facia to release the clips **(see illustration)**.
36 Lift the panel to free the lugs at the base from the facia, and remove it.
37 Refitting is a reversal of removal. Transfer any clips back onto the panel as necessary before refitting.

Front footwell kick panels

38 The panel is secured by three clips (two

on 3-door models) – starting at the rear, pull the panel into the car to release them **(see illustration)**.
39 If working on the driver's side, twist the panel to free it from the bonnet release lever, and withdraw it from the car **(see illustration)**.
40 Refitting is a reversal of removal. Transfer any clips back onto the panel as necessary before refitting.

Sill trim panels

3-door models

41 The front sill trim panel is 'trapped' at each end, by the footwell kick panel and rear side trim panel. It is recommended that the footwell kick panel is removed first, as described previously in this Section.
42 If working on the driver's front sill panel, prise up the square cover behind the fuel

filler release lever, and remove the screw underneath.
43 Unscrew and remove the front bolt securing the seat belt lower anchor rail – to improve access, it may be as well to remove the rear bolt too, and take off the rail completely.
44 Starting at the front, pull upwards on the sill panel to release the four clips, then slide the panel forwards to free the lug at the rear, and remove the panel from the car.
45 Refitting is a reversal of removal. Tighten the seat belt rail bolt(s) to the specified torque.

5-door models – front

46 The front sill trim panel is 'trapped' at each end by the footwell kick panel and B-pillar trim panel. Though it should not normally be necessary to remove these other panels first, it may be useful to at least loosen them where they overlap the sill panels.
47 If working on the driver's front sill panel, prise up the square cover behind the fuel filler release lever, and remove the screw underneath **(see illustrations)**.
48 Starting at one end, pull upwards on the sill panel to release the three clips, and remove the panel from the car **(see illustrations)**.
49 Refitting is a reversal of removal. Where the surrounding panels were not removed, tuck the sill panel under them before re-engaging the clips.

5-door models – rear

50 Remove the rear wheel arch trim panel as described later in this Section. The B-pillar

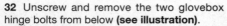

27.38 Unclip and remove the footwell trim on the passenger's side

27.39 On the driver's side, work the panel round the bonnet release lever

27.47a On the driver's side, unclip the square cover . . .

27.47b . . . and remove the screw underneath

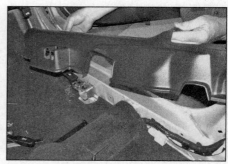

27.48a Removing the front sill panel on the driver's . . .

27.48b . . . and on the passenger's side

27.52a Taking care not to mark the paint, prise up . . .

27.52b . . . and remove the sill rear trim panel

trim panel overlaps the rear sill panel, but it should not be necessary to remove it first.

51 The sill trim panel hooks around the lower anchor points for the front and rear seat belts, but it is not necessary to disturb them. However, the trim cover for the front lower anchor bolt may be dislodged during removal.

52 Carefully prise up the sill panel to release the two clips, and remove the panel from the car **(see illustrations)**.

53 Refitting is a reversal of removal.

B-pillar trim panels

54 Detach the rubber weatherstrip from the B-pillar as necessary to free the edges of the trim panel.

Upper panel – 3-door models

55 Unclip the seat belt upper anchor's plastic cover by spreading it apart at the rear. Unscrew and remove the upper anchor bolt, noting carefully how the washers and bushes are arranged.

56 Pull the trim panel out to release the clip at the top. To free the bottom of the panel, pull out the rear side trim panel slightly where it overlaps.

57 Refitting is a reversal of removal. Apply thread-locking fluid to the seat belt upper anchor bolt, then tighten it to the specified torque.

Upper panel – 5-door models

58 Unclip the seat belt upper anchor's plastic cover by spreading it apart at the rear. Unscrew and remove the upper anchor bolt, noting carefully how the washers and bushes are arranged.

59 Pull the panel out at the top to release the clip, then lift it to free the lower mounting lugs, and remove it from the car **(see illustration)**.

60 Refitting is a reversal of removal. Apply thread-locking fluid to the seat belt upper anchor bolt, then tighten it to the specified torque.

Lower panel – 5-door models

61 At the top of the panel, pull both sides outwards to release them.

62 Lift the panel, and pull it into the car at the top **(see illustration)**.

63 Refitting is a reversal of removal.

Rear trim panels – 3-door models

Parcel shelf support panel

64 Remove the parcel shelf.

65 The support panel is secured by two

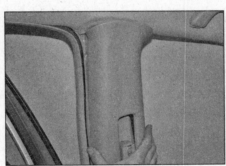

27.59 Removing the B-pillar upper trim panel

27.65a Unclip and hinge down the cover, then remove the rear screw . . .

screws – one at the back, under a cover which hinges down, and one at the front, accessed from the side **(see illustrations)**.

66 Unclip the panel, and remove it from the car. At the front, it wraps around the C-pillar trim – unclip it by pulling the corner forwards, then slide it off sideways. Alternatively, unclip the C-pillar trim panel itself, and remove both panels together. Slide the seat belt out through the slot at the side of the panel, and remove the panel completely **(see illustration)**.

67 Refitting is a reversal of removal. Tighten the screws securely – if the original screws will no longer 'bite' sufficiently, use screws which are slightly larger instead (these are available from Honda dealers, if required).

C-pillar trim panel

68 Remove the parcel shelf support panel as described previously in this Section.

69 The panel is secured by a clip at each

27.62 Removing the B-pillar lower trim panel

27.65b . . . and the one at the front

27.66 Removing the parcel shelf support panel

27.72a Remove the side trim panel screw at the rear . . .

27.72b . . . and one more, in front of the seat belt reel

27.74 Unclip and remove the access panel for the rear suspension

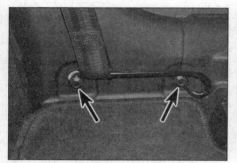

27.75a Remove the two bolts . . .

27.75b . . . and take off the front seat belt anchor rail

27.75c It's also useful to unbolt the rear seat belt lower anchor

corner – starting at the top, pull the panel into the car to release the clips, and remove it.

70 Refitting is a reversal of removal.

Rear side trim panel

71 This is a very large panel, covering as it does the whole side of the car, from the B-pillar rearwards, in one piece. First remove the rear seat (cushion and backrest) as described in Section 24.

72 Remove the parcel shelf support panel as described previously in this Section. There are two side trim panel screws to remove from this area – one at the rear, the other in front of the rear seat belt inertia reel **(see illustrations)**.

73 In the boot, remove the floor carpet, spare tyre cover panel, and the luggage area rear trim panel as described later in this Section.

74 Starting at the top, unclip and remove the curved trim panel which fits over the rear suspension mounting (about halfway along the side trim panel) **(see illustration)**.

75 Unscrew and remove the bolt from each end of the front seat belt lower anchor rail, and take off the rail completely. Though not essential, it is helpful to unbolt the rear side seat belt lower anchor, and move it clear **(see illustrations)**.

76 Prise out the two plastic clips securing the panel to the floor **(see illustrations)**.

77 Unclip the 'grommet' from the panel which surrounds the rear seat backrest catch **(see illustration)**.

78 The rear speaker is mounted through the panel, and so must be removed. Taking care not to scratch the main panel, prise out the speaker grille. Remove the three speaker mounting screws, then withdraw the speaker and disconnect its wiring plug **(see illustrations)**.

79 Detach the rubber weatherstrip from the B-pillar and tailgate aperture as necessary to free the edges of the trim panel.

27.76a Prise out the floor-level clip behind the suspension mount . . .

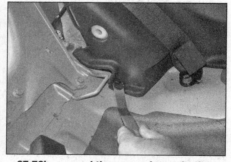

27.76b . . . and the second one, further forward

27.77 Unclip the 'grommet' from the backrest catch

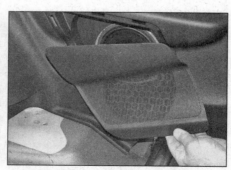

27.78a Prise out the speaker grille . . .

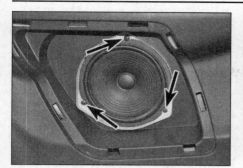

27.78b ... then remove the speaker, which has three screws ...

27.78c ... and disconnect the wiring plug

27.80 Removing the rear side trim panel

27.88 Removing the rear wheel arch trim panel

27.90a Starting at the rear, unclip the panel from the C-pillar trim ...

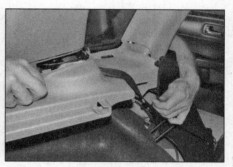

27.90b ... then free it at the front and pull away with the seat belt

80 Starting at the front of the panel, unclip it from the sill panel and release the front edge. The panel has a clip above and below the speaker hole, and a row of four clips under the side window. Work around the panel, releasing the clips and freeing it from the carpet (see illustration).

81 If working on the driver's side panel, disconnect the boot light wiring plug.

82 When the panel is ready to come out, lift it over the rear seat backrest catch, and remove it.

83 Refitting is a reversal of removal. Tighten the seat belt mounting bolts to the specified torque.

Luggage area rear panel

84 Detach the rubber weatherstrip from the tailgate aperture as necessary to free the edges of the trim panel.

85 The trim panel has a row of four clips

along its top edge, and two hooked lugs at each side, further down. Starting at one end, carefully prise the panel upwards to free the clips, then lift it off the two hooked lugs and remove it (see illustration 27.101).

86 Refitting is a reversal of removal.

Rear trim panels – 5-door models

Rear wheel arch trim panel

87 Fold forward the rear seat cushion and backrest.

88 Starting at the bottom, release the panel from the sill trim panel, then release the two clips higher up, and unclip it from the panel above (see illustration).

89 Refitting is a reversal of removal.

Parcel shelf support panel

90 The parcel shelf support panel is clipped

to the base of the C-pillar trim panel. Start at the rear corner, and release the clips along its length. To free the front of the panel, it may be necessary to pull out the wheel arch trim panel slightly (see illustrations). Note that the parcel shelf support panel 'traps' the luggage area side carpet between it and the C-pillar trim panel.

91 To remove the panel completely, unbolt the rear seat belt lower anchor, then unclip the seat belt guide from the main panel, and feed the belt through (see illustrations).

92 Refitting is a reversal of removal.

C-pillar trim panel

93 Remove the parcel shelf support panel, as described previously in this Section.

94 Remove the two screws at the base of the panel (see illustration).

95 The panel is secured by four clips at the 'corners', with three further clips securing it

27.91a Unbolt the seat belt lower anchor ...

27.91b ... then unclip the belt guide, and feed the belt through

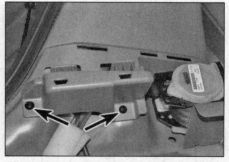

27.94 Remove the two screws at the base of the C-pillar trim panel

27.95a Start releasing the clips at the rear . . .

27.95b . . . then work round the panel and remove it

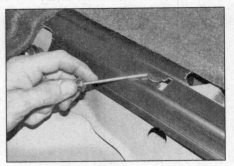

27.97 Prise up the clips from the boot carpet securing strip

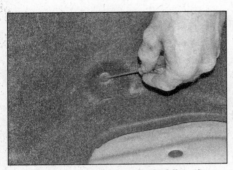

27.99a Prise out the clip holding the carpet to the side at the rear . . .

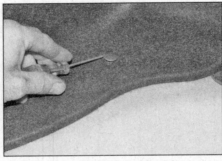

27.99b . . . and the clip holding the carpet to the floor . . .

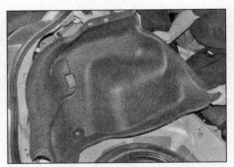

27.99c . . . then release the carpet edges and remove it

around the side window. Open the tailgate and peel back the rubber weatherstrip to free the panel's rear edge. Release the clips and remove the panel **(see illustrations)**.

96 Refitting is a reversal of removal.

Luggage area side carpet

97 Remove the floor carpet (this is secured at the front edge by two clips), the spare tyre cover panel and the parcel shelf **(see illustration)**. Fold forwards the rear seat backrest on the side concerned.

98 Remove the parcel shelf support panel and the luggage area rear panel as described elsewhere in this Section.

99 Prise out the two clips at the base of the panel, then release the edges of the carpet, and remove it **(see illustrations)**.

100 Refitting is a reversal of removal.

Luggage area rear panel

101 The trim panel has a row of four clips along its top edge, and two hooked lugs at each side, further down. Starting at one end, carefully prise the panel upwards to free the clips, then lift it off the two hooked lugs and remove it **(see illustration)**.

102 Refitting is a reversal of removal.

Tailgate trim panels

Upper trim panel

103 Open the tailgate, and taking care not to scratch the panels, prise one end of the tailgate upper trim panel to start releasing it. The panel has four clips along its length – once the end is free, gradually pull the panel down to release the clips and remove it **(see illustrations)**.

104 Refitting is a reversal of removal. Note that the tailgate side trim panels (where removed) must be refitted before the upper trim panel.

Side trim panels

105 Remove the upper trim panel as described previously in this Section.

106 Starting at the bottom, carefully prise the trim panel away, and separate it from the main panel. The side trim panel is secured by two clips along its length – ease the panel away from the tailgate until both clips are released, and remove it **(see illustration)**.

107 Refitting is a reversal of removal. Note that the side trim panels should be fitted after the main panel, but before the upper trim panel.

27.101 Removing the luggage area rear trim panel

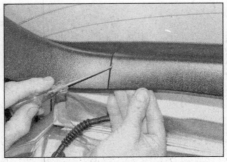

27.103a Starting at one end, unclip the tailgate upper trim panel . . .

27.103b . . . and remove it

27.106 Removing a tailgate side trim panel

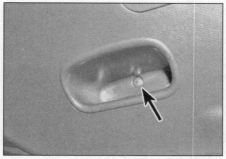

27.109 Remove the screw from the handle

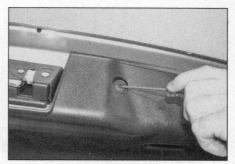

27.110a Push in the central pin . . .

27.110b . . . then withdraw the clip body from the base of the panel

27.111 Release the clips and withdraw the tailgate main trim panel

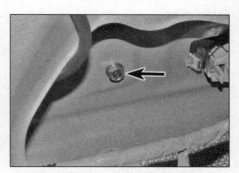

27.114a Remove the bolt at each end, inside . . .

Main trim panel

108 Because the tailgate side and upper trim panels overlap each other, to remove the main trim panel without risk of damage, the upper and side trim panels must be removed first, as described previously in this Section .

109 With the tailgate open, remove the screw inside the handle on the panel's bottom edge **(see illustration)**.

110 Release the two clips either side of the tailgate lock by pushing their centre pins in, then prise out the outer body of the clip – if pushed right through, the pins must be recovered from inside the tailgate for refitting **(see illustrations)**.

111 Working from the loosened bottom edge of the panel, carefully ease it away from the tailgate to release nine more clips, arranged in two rows across the panel **(see illustration)**.

Withdraw the panel from the tailgate, and recover the pins for the two lower trim clips.

112 Refitting is a reversal of removal, noting the following points:

a) *Fit the main panel first, then the side and upper panels.*

b) *To refit the two lower clips, press the outer part of the clip into the hole, then insert the expander pin in the centre, and tap the pin in until it is just flush.*

Outer trim panel (handle cover)

113 Remove the main trim panel from the inside of the tailgate, as described previously in this Section.

114 Working inside the tailgate, remove the two outer trim panel bolts (one at each end), then squeeze together and release the four panel retaining clips, and withdraw the panel from the outside **(see illustrations)**.

115 Refitting is a reversal of removal.

Carpets

116 The passenger compartment floor carpet is in several pieces, and is secured along the edges by various types of clips.

117 Carpet removal and refitting is reasonably straightforward, but time-consuming, due to the fact that all adjoining trim panels must be released, and the seats and centre console (where applicable) must be removed.

Grab handles

118 Fold the grab handle down, away from the roof, then carefully prise off the screw covers using a small screwdriver **(see illustration)**.

119 Unscrew and remove the single screw at each end of the handle, and remove it from the roof **(see illustration)**.

120 Refitting is a reversal of removal.

27.114b . . . then release the four clips and take off the panel

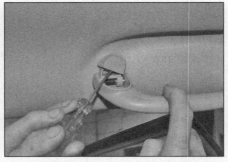

27.118 Prise off the cover at each end of the grab handle . . .

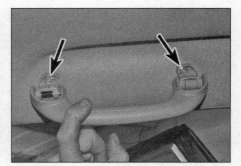

27.119 . . . for access to the mounting screws

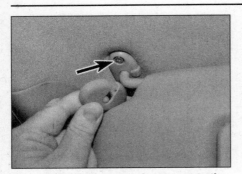

27.122 Unclip the cover for access to the sunvisor screws

Sunvisors

121 Unclip the visor from the inner support, then move it for the best access to the outer mounting.
122 Carefully prise off the cover from the outer mounting, then remove the two screws underneath and remove the visor from the headlining **(see illustration)**.
123 If required, the inner support can be removed by twisting it anti-clockwise.
124 Refitting is a reversal of removal.

Headlining

125 The headlining is clipped to the roof, and can be withdrawn only once all fittings such as the grab handles, sunvisors, sunroof, A, B- and C-pillar trim panels, and associated components have been removed. The door, tailgate and sunroof aperture weatherseals will also have to be prised clear.
126 Note that headlining removal requires

considerable skill and experience if it is to be carried out without damage, and is therefore best entrusted to an expert.

Interior mirror

127 According to Honda, the mirror is removed by sliding the base downwards to release it from the base, which is bonded to the windscreen. Take care not to unbond the base from the windscreen, however.
128 Refitting is a reversal of removal. Offer the mirror up to the base, twisted round approximately 90° clockwise. Engage the mirror onto the base, then twist it 90° anti-clockwise to secure.

Cup holder

129 To remove the facia cup holder, the facia panel must be removed first, as described in Section 29.
130 Remove the two screws from the inside of the facia panel, and take off the cup holder.
131 Refitting is a reversal of removal. Refit the facia panel as described in Section 29.

28 Centre console – removal and refitting

Note: *Not all models have a centre console, but there is a cover fitted over the handbrake lever, which may be removed as follows. At the front of the cover on the passenger side, release the side clip by pushing the centre pin inwards slightly, then prise out the larger main body of the clip. (To reset the clip for refitting, push the*

pin out slightly so that it stands proud – when the clip is refitted, push the pin flush to secure it.) Lift the handbrake lever cover at the rear to release the two clips, then pivot it forwards off the handbrake lever (see illustrations). Where applicable, reach inside and disconnect the heated switch wiring plugs, which will allow the cover to be removed.

Removal

1 The console is comprised of two sections – the rear section must be removed first.
2 Slide both front seats fully forwards. Although not essential, access is greatly improved if one or both front seats are removed as described in Section 24.
3 On models with heated seats, prise out and disconnect the switch, referring if necessary to Chapter 12.
4 Remove the mounting screw on each side of the console, at the rear **(see illustration)**.
5 If they are still fitted, slide the front seats fully forwards.
6 Pull the front of the rear section of console upwards to release the clips, and free it from the front section of the console by pulling it rearwards – there are two clips on top, and two more tabs down each side, where the console sections join.
7 Lift the rear section off the mounting bracket at the rear, then lift it over the handbrake lever **(see illustration)**.
8 Open the ashtray at the front of the console, then press the metal plate inside to release it, and slide the ashtray upwards to remove **(see illustration)**.

28.0a Push in the centre pin, then prise out the clip body at the front

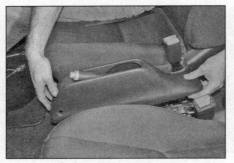

28.0b Lift the cover to release the rear clips, and remove it

28.0c Refit the front clip with the pin pulled out

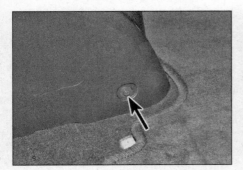

28.4 Remove the console rear section mounting screw either side

28.7 With the console rear section released, lift it over the handbrake lever

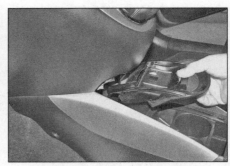

28.8 Removing the ashtray

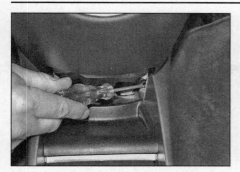

28.9 Remove the two screws at the front of the ashtray aperture

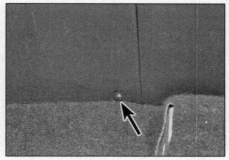

28.10a Remove the screw at the rear, at floor level . . .

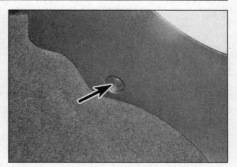

28.10b . . . then prise out the front clip each side

9 Remove the two screws inside the ashtray aperture, at the front corners **(see illustration)**.
10 Remove the screw at the rear of the front section, at floor level. Taking care not to mark the trim, prise out the front securing clip on each side of the front section **(see illustrations)**.
11 Remove the two bolts visible through the top of the console at the rear **(see illustration)**.
12 Pull the console front section rearwards from the facia, to release the two hooks each side and the two tabs on top. When the console is free, lift it at the rear and withdraw it completely **(see illustration)**.

Refitting

13 Refitting is a reversal of removal. Take care that the console's locating tabs slot together properly when the front and rear sections are each offered in place.

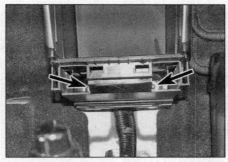

28.11 Remove the two rear mounting bolts

28.12 Removing the console front section

29 Facia panel assembly
– removal and refitting

Note: *This is a complicated procedure – it is strongly recommended that this Section is read through thoroughly before starting work. The plastic facia panel is removed WITH the metal crossmember underneath it – if required, the panel can be separated from the crossmember after removal.*

⚠ **Warning: Remove the ignition key, disconnect both battery leads, negative first (see Disconnecting**

the battery). Wait at least 3 minutes before starting work. If this precaution is not observed, there is danger of activating the airbags and seat belt tensioners.

Removal

Facia panel

1 Disconnect the battery negative lead (refer to *Disconnecting the battery* in the *Reference* Chapter at the end of this manual).
2 Remove the steering wheel as described in Chapter 10.
3 Remove the steering column switches as described in Chapter 12.
4 Where applicable, remove the centre console as described in Section 28. On models without a centre console, remove the facia centre lower panel.
5 Referring to Section 27, remove the following trim panels:
 a) Driver's lower facia panels.

 b) Glovebox.
 c) A-pillar trim panels.
 d) Front footwell kick panels.
6 Remove the gear/selector lever as described in Chapter 7A or 7B.
7 Remove the steering column as described in Chapter 10.
8 Working in the driver's footwell, look up under the facia, and disconnect the following (if necessary, attach labels for easier refitting):
 a) All the wiring harness plugs at the right-hand end.
 b) Brake pedal position switch **(see illustration)**.
 c) Clutch switch, where applicable (manual transmission models).
 d) Fusebox wiring plugs, as required (unbolt the fusebox for easier access) **(see illustrations)**.
 e) Mirror and headlight adjuster switches **(see illustrations)**.

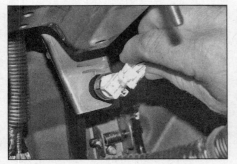

29.8a Disconnect the brake pedal position switch

29.8b Unbolt the fusebox at the front, and on top . . .

29.8c . . . and disconnect the wiring plugs

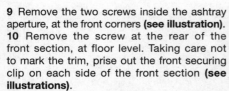

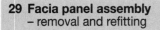

29.8d Disconnect the mirror switch . . .

29.8e . . . and the headlight adjuster switch

29.8f Disconnect the cabin temperature sensor . . .

29.8g . . . and pull off the air hose behind its grille

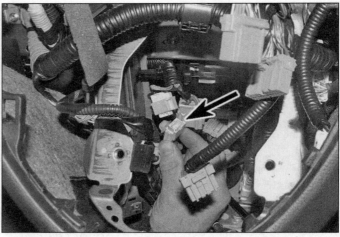

29.9 Disconnect and detach the wiring in the centre part of the facia

29.10a Disconnect the wiring plugs at the passenger end . . .

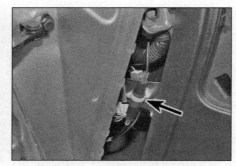

29.10b . . . including the aerial lead

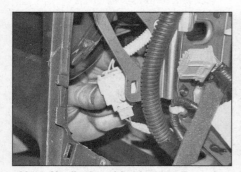

29.11 Unclip the wiring harness from the crossmember

29.12 Unscrew the three facia mounting bolts on the driver's side

f) *On models with automatic air conditioning, disconnect the cabin temperature sensor, and pull off the air hose from the small facia grille (see illustrations).*

9 Working around the centre part of the facia, at floor level, disconnect the following:
a) *All accessible wiring harness plugs (depending on model and equipment, there may be up to eight of these) (see illustration).*
b) *On models with manual air conditioning, detach the distribution and temperature control cables.*

10 From the passenger footwell, disconnect all the wiring harness plugs, including the aerial lead, where applicable **(see illustrations)**.

11 Release all the disconnected wiring harnesses from its securing clips and ties – note how it is routed, for refitting **(see illustration)**.

12 Open the driver's door, and (where applicable) prise off the caps from the three bolts above the door check strap. Unscrew and remove the three bolts **(see illustration)**.

13 Remove the facia mounting bolt on either side of the central part of the facia, at floor level. Unclip the wiring harness from the floor bracket, then remove it completely **(see illustrations)**.

14 Behind the floor bracket, reach in and

29.13a Unscrew the bolt on either side . . .

29.13b . . . then unclip the wiring harness on the left . . .

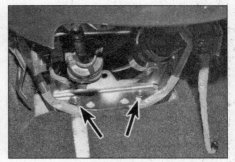

29.13c . . . unscrew the two bracket-to-floor bolts . . .

unclip the floor-level ventilation duct from the base of the facia (see illustration).

15 Open the passenger front door, and pull out the end cover from the facia panel – this gives access to the two facia end bolts, which should now be unscrewed (see illustrations).

16 Make a final check that all the wiring has been disconnected, and that the facia panel is free to be removed.

17 With the help of an assistant, lift the facia at both ends to free it from the guide pins, and remove it from the car (see illustration).

Crossmember

18 With the facia removed, the metal crossmember can be separated from the facia panel if required, as follows.

19 Remove the instrument panel and passenger airbag as described in Chapter 12.

20 On models with automatic air conditioning, remove the sun sensor as described in Chapter 3, Section 11.

21 Remove the row of four screws securing the glovebox catch/striker plate. Where applicable, also disconnect the glovebox bulbholder.

22 Loosen the fusebox two upper bolts, then remove the lower bolt, and slide the fusebox downwards to release it from the mounting bracket.

23 Where applicable, detach the air

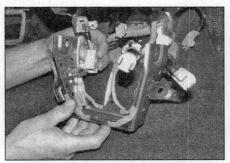

29.13d . . . and the floor bracket can be removed completely

29.14 Pull off the ventilation duct at the base of the facia

29.15a Unclip the facia end cover on the passenger's side . . .

29.15b . . . then remove the end mounting bolt at the top . . .

29.15c . . . and the one lower down

29.17 Lifting out the facia and crossmember assembly

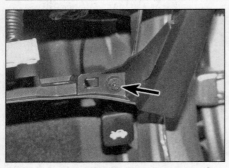

29.24a Remove the facia-to-crossmember bolt on the driver's side . . .

29.24b . . . and two more below the glovebox aperture

29.25a The smaller facia-to-crossmember screws . . .

29.25b . . . can only be accessed from behind

conditioning sun sensor wiring harness from the crossmember.

24 From the facia side ('front'), remove the four bolts securing the facia to the crossmember – one at each end, low down, and two more in the centre, top and bottom **(see illustrations)**.

25 From the crossmember side ('rear'), remove a total of eight screws **(see illustrations)**.

26 With the help of an assistant, and ensuring that the facia panel does not get damaged, separate the crossmember from the facia panel.

Refitting

27 Refitting is a reversal of the removal procedure, noting the following points:

a) *Make sure the wiring is correctly routed and connected, and secure where necessary with cable-ties. Do not allow the wiring harness to get trapped or pinched during refitting.*

b) *Refit all the facia fasteners, and tighten them securely. The facia mounting bolts should be coated with thread-locking fluid, before tightening them to the specified torque.*

c) *On completion, check that all the electrical components and switches function correctly. As a precaution against the airbags being activated, make sure no one is sitting in the car as the battery is being reconnected.*

Chapter 12
Body electrical system

Contents

Degrees of difficulty

Easy, suitable for novice with little experience	**Fairly easy,** suitable for beginner with some experience	**Fairly difficult,** suitable for competent DIY mechanic	**Difficult,** suitable for experienced DIY mechanic	**Very difficult,** suitable for expert DIY or professional

Specifications

General
System type . . . . 12 volt, negative earth

Fuses
Refer to labels on fusebox lids

Bulbs

	Type	Wattage
Headlight:		
Models up to 2003	H4	60/55
Models from 2004 onwards:		
Dipped beam	H1 or HB4	51
Main beam	HB3	60
Front sidelight.	Push-fit	5
Front direction indicator light:*		
Models up to 2003	Bayonet-fit	21
Models from 2004 onwards	Push-fit	21
Front direction indicator side repeater light*	Push-fit	5
Front foglight	H11	55
Stop/tail light	Bayonet-fit	21/5
High-level stop-light	Push-fit	5
Rear direction indicator light:*		
Models up to 2003	Bayonet-fit	21
Models from 2004 onwards	Push-fit	21
Reversing light	Bayonet-fit	21
Rear foglight.	Bayonet-fit	21
Number plate light	Push-fit	5
Courtesy light:		
Front	Push-fit	5
Centre.	Festoon	8
Map reading lights	Push-fit or festoon	5 or 8
Luggage compartment light.	Push-fit	5
Glovebox light	Festoon	3.4

* Amber bulb used on later models with 'clear' lights

1 General information and precautions

⚠️ **Warning: Before carrying out any work on the electrical system, read through the precautions given in Safety first! at the beginning of this manual.**

The electrical system is of 12 volt negative-earth type. Power for the lights and all electrical accessories is supplied by a lead-acid battery which is charged by the alternator.

This Chapter covers repair and service procedures for the various electrical components not associated with the engine. Information on the battery, alternator, and starter motor can be found in Chapter 5A; the ignition system is covered in Chapter 5B.

All UK models are fitted with an alarm system incorporating an engine immobiliser. The system protects the doors, bonnet and tailgate, and certain models may also have ultrasonic protection for the whole interior, meaning that the alarm will sound if a thief breaks a window to gain entry. A transponder chip fitted to the ignition key automatically disarms the immobiliser when it is inserted into the ignition switch. For more information, refer to Section 19.

All models are fitted with airbags for the driver and front seat passenger, which are designed to prevent serious chest and head injuries during a frontal accident. Most Civics also have side airbags, fitted into the front seat side cushions. For more information, refer to Section 20.

All models are fitted with a manually-controlled headlight levelling system, with a facia-mounted control. On position 0, the headlights are in their base (normal) position – from here, turn the control to lower the aim of the headlights according to the load being carried.

It should be noted that, when portions of the electrical system are serviced, the lead should be disconnected from the battery negative terminal, to prevent electrical shorts and fires (refer to *Disconnecting the battery* at the end of this manual).

2 Electrical fault finding – general information

Note: *Refer to the precautions given in* Safety first! *and at the beginning of Chapter 5A before starting work. The following tests relate to testing of the main electrical circuits, and should not be used to test delicate electronic circuits (such as anti-lock braking systems), particularly where an electronic control module is used.*

General

1 A typical electrical circuit consists of an electrical component, any switches, relays, motors, fuses, fusible links or circuit breakers related to that component, and the wiring and connectors which link the component to both the battery and the chassis. To help to pinpoint a problem in an electrical circuit, wiring diagrams are included at the end of this Chapter.

2 Before attempting to diagnose an electrical fault, first study the appropriate wiring diagram to obtain a more complete understanding of the components included in the particular circuit concerned. The possible sources of a fault can be narrowed down by noting whether other components related to the circuit are operating properly. If several components or circuits fail at one time, the problem is likely to be related to a shared fuse or earth connection.

3 The multiplex wiring system fitted to this car makes electrical fault finding less straightforward than on previous models. The multiplex module 'talks' to other parts of the car's wiring, meaning that the same wire might be carrying different signals at any time – this can produce confusing test results, and there is even a risk of damage to the module itself through careless testing. For more information, see Section 3.

4 Electrical problems usually stem from simple causes, such as loose or corroded connections, a faulty earth connection, a blown fuse, a melted fusible link, or a faulty relay (refer to Section 3 for details of testing relays). Visually inspect the condition of all fuses, wires and connections in a problem circuit before testing the components. Use the wiring diagrams to determine which terminal connections will need to be checked, in order to pinpoint the trouble-spot.

5 The basic tools required for electrical fault finding include a circuit tester or voltmeter (a 12 volt bulb with a set of test leads can also be used for certain tests); a self-powered test light (sometimes known as a continuity tester); an ohmmeter (to measure resistance); a battery and set of test leads; and a jumper wire, preferably with a circuit breaker or fuse incorporated, which can be used to bypass suspect wires or electrical components. Before attempting to locate a problem with test instruments, use the wiring diagram to determine where to make the connections.

6 To find the source of an intermittent wiring fault (usually due to a poor or dirty connection, or damaged wiring insulation), a 'wiggle' test can be performed on the wiring. This involves wiggling the wiring by hand, to see if the fault occurs as the wiring is moved. It should be possible to narrow down the source of the fault to a particular section of wiring. This method of testing can be used in conjunction with any of the tests described in the following sub-Sections.

7 Apart from problems due to poor connections, two basic types of fault can occur in an electrical circuit – open-circuit, or short-circuit.

8 Open-circuit faults are caused by a break somewhere in the circuit, which prevents current from flowing. An open-circuit fault will prevent a component from working, but will not cause the relevant circuit fuse to blow.

9 Short-circuit faults are caused by a 'short' somewhere in the circuit, which allows the current flowing in the circuit to 'escape' along an alternative route, usually to earth. Short-circuit faults are normally caused by a breakdown in wiring insulation, which allows a feed wire to touch either another wire, or an earthed component such as the bodyshell. A short-circuit fault will normally cause the relevant circuit fuse to blow.

Finding an open-circuit

10 To check for an open-circuit, connect one lead of a circuit tester or voltmeter to either the negative battery terminal or a known good earth.

11 Connect the other lead to a connector in the circuit being tested, preferably nearest to the battery or fuse.

12 Switch on the circuit, bearing in mind that some circuits are live only when the ignition switch is moved to a particular position.

13 If voltage is present (indicated either by the tester bulb lighting or a voltmeter reading, as applicable), this means that the section of the circuit between the relevant connector and the battery is problem-free.

14 Continue to check the remainder of the circuit in the same fashion.

15 When a point is reached at which no voltage is present, the problem must lie between that point and the previous test point with voltage. Most problems can be traced to a broken, corroded or loose connection.

Finding a short-circuit

16 To check for a short-circuit, first disconnect the load(s) from the circuit (loads are the components which draw current from a circuit, such as bulbs, motors, heating elements, etc).

17 Remove the relevant fuse from the circuit, and connect a circuit tester or voltmeter to the fuse connections.

18 Switch on the circuit, bearing in mind that some circuits are live only when the ignition switch is moved to a particular position.

19 If voltage is present (indicated either by the tester bulb lighting or a voltmeter reading, as applicable), this means that there is a short-circuit.

20 If no voltage is present, but the fuse still blows with the load(s) connected, this indicates an internal fault in the load(s).

Finding an earth fault

21 The battery negative terminal is connected to 'earth' – the metal of the engine/transmission unit and the car body – and most systems are wired so that they only receive a positive feed, the current returning via the metal of the car body. This means that the component mounting and the body form part of that circuit. Loose or corroded mountings can therefore cause a range

of electrical faults, ranging from total failure of a circuit, to a puzzling partial fault.

22 In particular, lights may shine dimly (especially when another circuit sharing the same earth point is in operation), motors (eg, wiper motors or the radiator cooling fan motor) may run slowly, and the operation of one circuit may have an apparently-unrelated effect on another.

23 Note that on many vehicles, earth straps are used between certain components, such as the engine/transmission and the body, usually where there is no metal-to-metal contact between components, due to flexible rubber mountings, etc.

24 To check whether a component is properly earthed, disconnect the battery, and connect one lead of an ohmmeter to a known good earth point. Connect the other lead to the wire or earth connection being tested. The resistance reading should be zero; if not, check the connection as follows.

25 If an earth connection is thought to be faulty, dismantle the connection, and clean back to bare metal both the bodyshell and the wire terminal or the component earth connection mating surface. Be careful to remove all traces of dirt and corrosion, then use a knife to trim away any paint, so that a clean metal-to-metal joint is made.

26 On reassembly, tighten the joint fasteners securely; if a wire terminal is being refitted, use serrated washers between the terminal and the bodyshell, to ensure a clean and secure connection.

27 When the connection is remade, prevent the onset of corrosion in the future by applying a coat of petroleum jelly or silicone-based grease, or by spraying on (at regular intervals) a proprietary maintenance spray such as WD-40.

3 Fuses, relays and multiplex module – general information

Fuses

1 Fuses are designed to break a circuit when a predetermined current is reached, in order to protect the components and wiring which could be damaged by excessive current flow. Any excessive current flow will be due to a fault in the circuit, usually a short-circuit (see Section 2).

2 The main fuses are located in the fusebox, below and to the left of the steering column.

3 Release the turn-buckle fasteners on either side of the panel by turning them through 45°. Pull the shorter edge of the panel outwards, and slide it out sideways to free the clips on the longer edge **(see illustration)**.

4 A blown fuse can be recognised from its melted or broken wire.

5 To remove a fuse, first ensure that the relevant circuit is switched off – for maximum safety, disconnect the battery (see *Disconnecting the battery*).

3.3 Removing the fusebox cover panel

6 Pull the fuse from its location, using thin-nosed pliers if necessary **(see illustration)**.

7 Before renewing a blown fuse, trace and rectify the cause, and always use a fuse of the correct rating. Never substitute a fuse of a higher rating, or make temporary repairs using wire or metal foil; more serious damage, or even fire, could result.

8 Note that the fuses are colour-coded as follows. Refer to the markings on the back of the glovebox for details of the circuits protected. Also note that the Civic uses the later-type 'mini' fuses.

Colour	Rating
Orange	5A
Red	10A
Blue	15A
Yellow	20A
Clear or white	25A
Green	30A

9 Additional fuses are located the engine

3.9a Unclip and remove the engine fusebox cover . . .

3.9c . . . or on the outside, on the diesel auxiliary fusebox

3.6 Pull out the fuse

fusebox, behind the battery in the engine compartment **(see illustrations)**. Some of these are rated at 60 amps – if any of these have blown, it indicates a serious wiring fault, which should be investigated. Just fitting a new fuse may cause further problems.

Relays

10 A relay is an electrically-operated switch, which is used for the following reasons:

a) A relay can switch a heavy current remotely from the circuit in which the current is flowing, allowing the use of lighter-gauge wiring and switch contacts.

b) A relay can receive more than one control input, unlike a mechanical switch.

c) A relay can have a timer function – for example, the intermittent wiper relay.

11 Most of the relays are located under the facia, either above the main fusebox or behind the glovebox. Additional relays are located in

3.9b . . . and the fuse information is printed inside . . .

3.9d Removing a fuse from the engine compartment fusebox

4.2a Remove the screw from behind . . .

4.2b . . . take off the immobiliser reader coil unit . . .

4.2c . . . and disconnect the wiring plug

4.3a Disconnect the wiring plug, then remove the screw (arrowed) . . .

4.3b . . . and take off the ignition key switch

17 Because the module is part of virtually every circuit on the car, it must be considered during any diagnosis of a non-functioning electrical item. A Honda dealer can interrogate the module to determine the nature of most electrical faults, using a special tool.

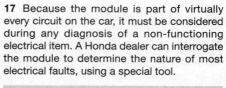

4 Switches – removal and refitting

Note: *Before removing any switch, disconnect the battery negative lead, and position the lead away from the battery (also see Disconnecting the battery).*

Ignition switch/steering lock

Ignition switch

1 Remove the three screws from the steering column lower shroud, unclip the upper shroud from it, then work off the lower shroud (refer to Chapter 11, Section 27, if necessary).
2 Remove the screw from behind, take off the immobiliser reader coil, and disconnect the (green) wiring plug **(see illustrations)**.
3 Disconnect the second (green) wiring plug, then remove the screw in front and take off the ignition key switch **(see illustrations)**.
4 Disconnect the (brown) wiring plug from underneath the ignition switch **(see illustration)**.
5 Remove the two mounting screws (one either side) and withdraw the ignition switch **(see illustrations)**.
6 Refitting is a reversal of removal.

the engine fusebox, behind the battery in the engine compartment.
12 To access the relays behind the glovebox, open the glovebox and press the sides of the glovebox inwards, then open the glovebox past its stops.
13 If a circuit or system controlled by a relay develops a fault, and the relay is suspect, operate the system. If the relay is functioning, it should be possible to hear it 'click' as it is energised. If this is the case, the fault lies with the components or wiring of the system. If the relay is not being energised, then either the relay is not receiving a main supply or a switching voltage, or the relay itself is faulty. Testing is by the substitution of a known good unit, but be careful – while some relays are identical in appearance and in operation, others look similar but perform different functions.
14 To remove a relay, first ensure that the relevant circuit is switched off. The relay can

then simply be pulled out from the socket, and pushed back into position.

Multiplex module

15 This module, which is part of the fusebox fitted behind the facia to the left of the steering wheel, directly controls some of the car's electrical functions:
a) *Interior lighting, including battery saver function (the interior lights and chimes are automatically shut off after a predetermined period of inactivity).*
b) *Wipers and washers.*
c) *Lights-on, door-ajar and ignition key-in warnings.*
d) *Central locking.*
16 However, the module also communicates with the engine management's ECM, the instrument panel, air conditioning system, exterior lighting system and ABS – in fact, with most of the car's major electrical systems.

4.4 Disconnect the ignition switch wiring plug

4.5a Remove the ignition switch screw on the right . . .

4.5b . . . and the one on the left . . .

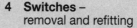
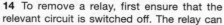

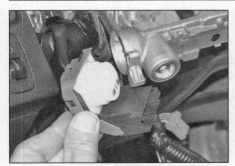

4.5c . . . and remove the ignition switch

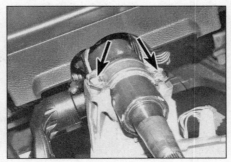

4.9 The steering column lock is secured by two shear-bolts

4.15 Disconnect the wiring plugs from the steering column switch assembly

4.16a Loosen the clamp screw on top . . .

4.16b . . . then withdraw the switch assembly from the column

4.19 Hazard warning light switch screws

Steering column lock

7 Remove the ignition switch as described previously in this Section.

8 Referring to Chapter 10, unscrew the steering column mounting nuts/bolts, and lower the column into the driver's footwell.

9 The lock assembly is clamped to the column by two shear-bolts, which must be drilled out using a 5 mm drill bit, after centre-punching them **(see illustration)**.

10 Place the new lock assembly in position without the key inserted and tighten the bolts until they are snug.

11 Insert the key and check the lock cylinder for proper operation.

12 Tighten the bolts until their heads break off.

13 Refit the steering column as described in Chapter 10, then refit the ignition switch as described previously in this Section.

Steering column switches

14 Remove the driver's airbag and clockspring as described in Section 21.

15 Disconnect the wiring plugs from the back of the switch assembly **(see illustration)**.

16 Loosen the clamp screw on top of the switch assembly, then slide the assembly off the steering column **(see illustrations)**.

17 Refitting is a reversal of removal.

Hazard warning light switch

18 Remove the gear/selector lever trim panel, as described in Chapter 11, Section 27.

19 Unscrew and remove the two switch retaining screws, and remove the switch from the panel **(see illustration)**.

20 Refitting is a reversal of removal.

Fuel filler release

21 Refer to Chapter 4A.

Heated rear window switch

22 Remove the heater control panel as described in Chapter 3, Section 9.

23 Unscrew and remove the screw at each end of the switch assembly, and remove it from the back of the heater control panel.

24 It appears that the switch panel is only available as a complete assembly.

25 Refitting is a reversal of removal.

Air conditioning and recirculation switches

26 Remove the heater control panel as described in Chapter 3, Section 9.

27 Unscrew and remove the screw at each end of the switch panel, and remove it from the back of the heater control panel.

28 It appears that the switch panel is only available as a complete assembly.

29 Refitting is a reversal of removal.

Blower motor switch

30 Remove the heater control panel as described in Chapter 3, Section 9.

31 Taking care not to damage the trim, carefully prise off the three control knobs from the front of the panel.

32 Unscrew and remove the three screws securing the switch/control assembly to the panel, and remove it.

33 It appears that the switch is only available as a complete assembly with the other switches/controls.

34 Refitting is a reversal of removal.

Electric sunroof switch

35 With care, it may be possible to prise the switch from the headlining, starting at the front edge – however, if this proves

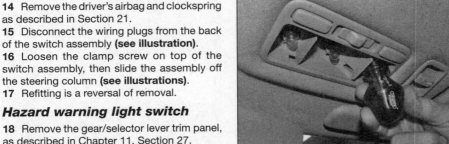

4.35a With the lens unclipped, remove the two screws . . .

4.35b . . . and take out the interior light

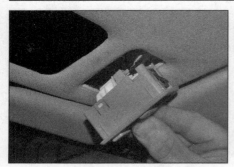

4.36a Remove the switch from the headlining . . .

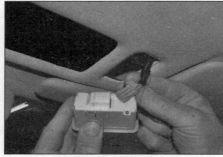

4.36b . . . and disconnect the wiring plug

4.41 Prise out the heated seat switch . . .

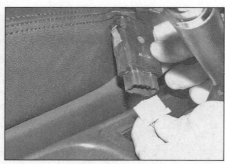

4.42 . . . and disconnect the wiring plug

difficult, we suggest trying the following. Working as described in Section 6, remove the interior light lens for access to the light unit mounting bolts. Unscrew the bolts, remove the light from the headlining, and disconnect its wiring plugs. Working

through the hole left by the interior light, push the sunroof switch out from behind **(see illustrations)**.
36 Disconnect the wiring plug, and remove the switch completely **(see illustrations)**.
37 Refitting is a reversal of removal.

Heated seat switches

Without centre console

38 Lift the handbrake lever cover at the rear to release the two clips, then pivot it forwards off the handbrake lever. Where applicable, reach inside and disconnect the heated switch wiring plugs, which will allow the cover to be removed.
39 Push each switch out of the handbrake cover from behind.
40 Refitting is a reversal of removal.

With centre console

41 Taking care not to mark the trim, prise the switch out of the centre console **(see illustration)**.
42 Disconnect the wiring plug from the switch, and remove it completely **(see illustration)**.
43 Refitting is a reversal of removal.

Electric window switches

3-door models

44 Insert the shorter end of an Allen key in through the hole on the inside of the door pull handle, and use it to push out the handle cover from behind. When the cover starts to come free at the bottom, pull the cover panel out from the front.
45 Carefully prise off the side cover from the armrest, starting at the front, then working along the underside.
46 Remove a total of eight screws (note their positions, as they are of two different lengths) the door pull handle/armrest, then remove the handle from the door.
47 Pull out the window switch panel to release the hooked tab from the door trim panel, and disconnect its wiring plug **(see illustration)**.
48 The switch itself can be removed from the trim panel on top by removing the three screws underneath **(see illustration)**.
49 Refitting is a reversal of removal.

Front door switches – 5-door

50 Carefully prise off the side cover from the door pull/armrest, starting at the top, then working down the pull handle itself **(see illustration)**.
51 Remove the six screws from the door pull handle (note that they are of different lengths), and remove the handle from the door **(see illustrations)**.

4.47 Disconnect the window switch wiring plug

4.48 The switch has three mounting screws underneath

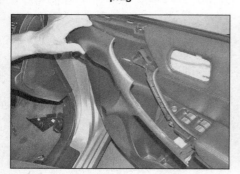

4.50 Prise off the door pull side cover

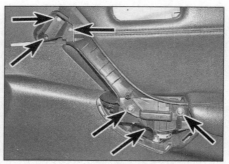

4.51a Remove the six screws behind the cover . . .

4.51b . . . and take off the door pull

52 Remove a further screw at the front of the window switch, then disconnect the switch wiring plug and remove the switch assembly **(see illustrations)**.

53 The switch itself can be removed from the trim panel on top by removing the screws underneath.

54 Refitting is a reversal of removal.

Rear door switches – 5-door

55 Carefully prise out the side cover from the door pull/armrest, working along the top edge from the front **(see illustration)**.

56 Remove the five screws from the armrest, then disconnect the window switch wiring plug and remove the armrest from the door **(see illustrations)**.

57 The switch itself can be removed from the trim panel on top by removing the screws underneath.

58 Refitting is a reversal of removal.

Electric mirror switch

59 Remove the driver's lower right-hand cubby panel as described in Chapter 11, Section 27.

60 Working through the hole in the facia, disconnect the wiring plug, then push the mirror switch out from behind **(see illustration)**. The switch is very well located, and attempting to prise it out from the front is not recommended.

61 Refitting is a reversal of removal.

Headlight adjuster switch

62 Release the turn-buckle fastener, then unclip and remove the fusebox cover.

63 Reach in behind the switch, disconnect

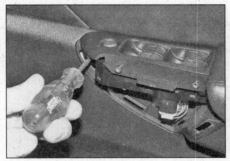

4.52a Remove the screw at the front of the switch panel . . .

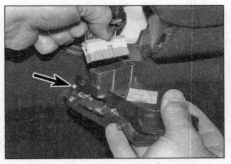

4.52c . . . and disconnect the wiring plug – one of the screws is arrowed

the wiring plug, then release the upper and lower clips, and push it out from behind **(see illustrations)**. The switch is very well located, and attempting to prise it out from the front is not recommended.

4.52b . . . then withdraw it from the door . . .

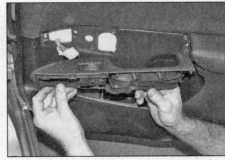

4.55 Prise off the armrest side cover, starting at the front

64 Refitting is a reversal of removal.

Handbrake-on warning switch

Note: *Although not absolutely necessary, access to the handbrake switch is greatly*

4.56a Remove the five screws behind the cover . . .

4.60 Push out the mirror switch from behind, and disconnect it

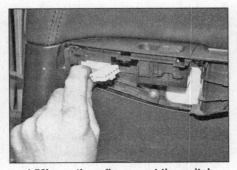

4.56b . . . then disconnect the switch wiring plug . . .

4.63a Disconnect the headlight adjuster switch wiring plug . . .

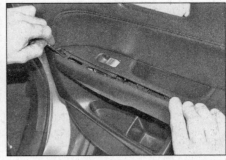

4.56c . . . and remove the armrest – the switch screws are underneath

4.63b . . . then use a screwdriver to release the switch from behind

4.67a Disconnect the switch wiring plug . . .

4.67b . . . then remove the screw on the other side of the lever

4.72 Fuel shut-off inertia switch inside glovebox aperture

4.74 Prise open the screw cap . . .

4.75 . . . then remove the mounting screw . . .

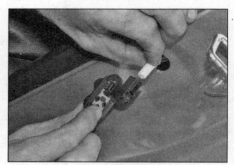

4.76 . . . withdraw the switch and disconnect the plug

improved if the driver's seat is removed as described in Chapter 11.

65 On models without a centre console, lift the handbrake lever cover at the rear to release the two clips, then pivot it forwards off the handbrake lever. Where applicable, reach inside and disconnect the heated switch wiring plugs, which will allow the cover to be removed.

66 On models with a centre console, remove the console as described in Chapter 11, Section 28.

67 Disconnect the wiring plug from the switch, then remove the securing screw and withdraw the switch (see illustrations).

68 The switch is a simple plunger-type design. If the switch has not been operating properly, it may be possible to restore its proper function by soaking it with lubricant (such as WD-40) and working the plunger several times.

69 Refitting is a reversal of removal.

Fuel cut-off (inertia) switch

70 The inertia switch is located on the left-hand side of the passenger footwell.

71 Open the glovebox, and press the sides inwards to release the stops, which allows the glovebox to be opened further than normal. For best access, remove the glovebox completely, as described in Chapter 11, Section 27.

72 Disconnect the wiring plug from the base of the switch, then remove the mounting bolt and withdraw the switch from the car (see illustration).

73 Refitting is a reversal of removal.

Interior (courtesy) light switch

74 Open the relevant door, then prise back the screw cap from the switch (see illustration).

75 Remove the mounting screw, and withdraw the switch from the door pillar (see illustration).

76 Disconnect the switch wiring plug, and remove the switch (see illustration).

> **HAYNES HINT** There is a danger of the wiring plug slipping back inside the door pillar – have a piece of tape ready to stick it to the pillar while the switch is removed.

77 These switches are simple 'plunger' types, and can sometimes suffer from corrosion, which causes them to stick, or have a bad contact. It is worth applying a maintenance spray such as WD-40 to a defective switch, as this may be enough to restore its operation.

78 Note that the interior light switches itself off after a time, to save the battery – it will only 'reset' once the doors have been shut.

79 Refitting is a reversal of removal. Reconnect the switch wiring plug, and test the operation of the interior light before fitting the switch back into position.

Central locking switch

80 Remove the door trim panel as described in Chapter 11. Remove the screws securing the switch to the inside of the panel, and remove it.

81 Refitting is a reversal of removal.

Glovebox light switch

82 Refer to the bulb renewal procedure in Section 6.

Boot light switch

83 The boot light switch is built into the tailgate lock assembly, which is removed as described in Chapter 11. Note that the boot light switches itself off after a time, to save the battery – it will only 'reset' once the tailgate has been shut.

Brake pedal position (stop-light) switch

84 Refer to Chapter 9.

5 Bulbs (exterior lights) – renewal

1 Whenever a bulb is renewed, note the following points:

a) *Ensure that the light is switched off, and also switch off the ignition (take out the key). For maximum safety, and particularly when changing the headlight bulbs, disconnect the battery negative lead (see Disconnecting the battery).*

b) *Remember that, if the light has just been in use, the bulb may be extremely hot.*

c) *Always check the bulb contacts and holder, ensuring that there is clean metal-to metal contact between the bulb and its live(s) and earth. Clean off any corrosion or dirt before fitting a new bulb.*

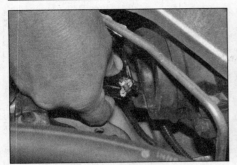

5.5 Pull off the headlight bulb wiring plug in the centre of the rubber cover

5.6 Peel off the rubber cover

5.7 Release the spring clip securing the bulb, and remove it

d) *Wherever bayonet-type bulbs are fitted (see Specifications), ensure that the live contact(s) bear firmly against the bulb contact.*

e) *Always ensure that the new bulb is of the correct rating, and that it is completely clean before fitting it; this applies particularly to headlight/foglight bulbs (see below).*

Headlight

2 Models up to the end of 2003 had 'normal' headlight bulbs, with a single headlight bulb containing both main and dipped beam filaments. From 2004 onwards, 'projector-style' headlights were fitted, using separate main and dipped beam bulbs. Since the later bulbs are of less-conventional type, it is recommended that the old bulb is removed and taken with you for reference when buying a new one.

3 When handling the new bulb, try and grip it only by the terminals at the rear. Avoid touching the glass with your fingers, as moisture and grease from the skin can cause blackening and rapid failure of this type of bulb. If the glass is accidentally touched, wipe it clean using methylated spirit.

4 If working on the bulb on the same side as the battery, it may be helpful to loosen the battery clamp, and slide the battery over in its tray slightly, to improve access. Ultimately, if required, remove the battery completely, as described in Chapter 5A.

Up to 2003

5 Open the bonnet, identify the headlight bulb (it has a large round rubber cover on the back), then pull the wiring plug in the centre straight back to disconnect it **(see illustration)**.

6 Pull off the round rubber cover, using the tab provided (note that the cover is also marked with the word TOP, or an arrow) **(see illustration)**.

7 Release the bulb's wire retaining clip by unhooking it sideways at the top, then pivot the clip down. Withdraw the bulb **(see illustration)**.

8 Install the new bulb, ensuring that its three locating tabs are correctly seated in the light cut-outs. Secure the bulb in position with the spring clip.

9 Refit the cover, then reconnect the wiring plug securely to complete.

10 Switch on the headlights, and check the operation on main and dipped beam.

2004 onwards – main beam

11 Open the bonnet, and identify the main beam bulb (it will be the inner one of the two, and does not have a rubber cover).

12 Squeeze the wiring plug to release the tab, and pull the wiring plug downwards to disconnect it **(see illustration)**.

13 Loosen the three screws, then twist the bulb a quarter-turn anti-clockwise, and withdraw it from the back of the headlight **(see illustrations)**. Note that the bulb and holder are one unit.

14 To fit the new bulb, offer it into the back of the headlight, then turn a quarter-turn clockwise to secure it.

15 Push the wiring plug securely onto the new bulb to complete.

16 Switch on the headlights, and check the main beam operation.

2004 onwards – dipped beam

17 Open the bonnet, identify the headlight bulb (it has a large round rubber cover on the back), then pull the wiring plug in the centre straight back to disconnect it **(see illustration)**.

18 Pull off the round rubber cover (note that the cover is also marked with an arrow at the top, though the alignment does not appear to be critical) **(see illustration)**.

19 Release the bulb's wire retaining clip by unhooking it sideways at the top, then pivot the clip down. Withdraw the bulbholder, then pull out the bulb **(see illustrations)**.

20 Fit the new bulb into the holder, then offer

5.12 Disconnect the main beam bulbholder wiring plug

5.13a Loosen the three bulb retaining screws . . .

5.13b . . . then turn the bulb anti-clockwise and remove it

5.17 Pull off the dipped beam wiring plug

5.18 Pull off the rubber cover from the dipped beam bulb

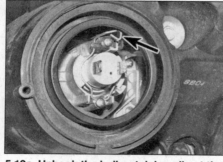

5.19a Unhook the bulb retaining clip at the top . . .

with its own small wiring plug and bulbholder).

24 Twist the wiring plug and bulbholder a quarter-turn anti-clockwise, and withdraw it from the headlight **(see illustration)**.

25 Pull out the wedge-base bulb, then fit the new one by pushing it firmly into the bulbholder **(see illustration)**.

26 Offer the bulbholder into the headlight, then twist it a quarter-turn clockwise to secure.

27 Check the operation of the sidelights on completion.

2004 onwards

28 The sidelight bulb is most easily accessed through a panel in the front wheel arch liner. However, with care, the bulb can be reached from within the engine compartment.

29 If using the wheel arch access method, refer to paragraph 36.

30 Twist the bulbholder a quarter-turn anti-clockwise, and withdraw it from the headlight **(see illustration)**.

31 Pull out the wedge-base bulb, then fit the new one by pushing it firmly into the bulbholder **(see illustration)**.

32 Offer the bulbholder into the headlight, then twist it a quarter-turn clockwise to secure.

33 Fold the access panel back into place, and secure with the two clips.

34 Check the operation of the sidelights on completion.

Front direction indicator

35 The indicator bulb is most easily accessed through a panel in the front wheel arch liner. However, with care, the bulb can be reached from within the engine compartment.

36 If using the wheel arch access method, turn the front wheel fully inwards on the side being worked on (run the engine temporarily to make this easier). We couldn't find the special access panel in our wheel arch liner, so we just removed the clips at the outer edge, and folded the whole panel down **(see illustrations)**.

37 Twist the bulbholder a quarter-turn anti-clockwise, and withdraw it from the headlight **(see illustration)**.

38 Models up to 2003 have a bayonet-fit bulb, which is removed by pressing and

5.19b . . . then swing the clip down and pull out the bulb

in the bulbholder, and secure with the spring clip.

21 Refit the cover, then reconnect the wiring plug securely to complete.

22 Switch on the headlights, and check the operation on main and dipped beam.

5.19c Pull the bulb out of the holder – don't touch the glass

Front sidelight

Up to 2003

23 Open the bonnet, and identify the sidelight bulb (it is above the headlight bulb,

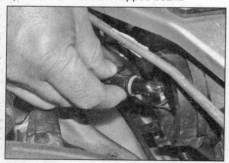

5.24 Remove the sidelight bulbholder . . .

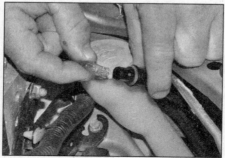

5.25 . . . then pull out the wedge-base bulb

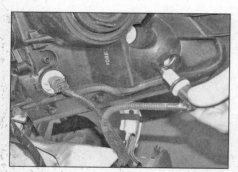

5.30 Twist and remove the sidelight bulbholder . . .

5.31 . . . then pull out the wedge-base bulb

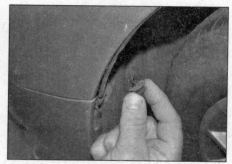

5.36a Remove the clips from the edge of the wheel arch liner . . .

5.36b ... then fold the liner down to access the back of the headlight

5.37 Twist and remove the indicator bulbholder ...

5.38 ... then push and twist to remove the bayonet-fit bulb

turning anti-clockwise (see illustration) – the new bulb is fitted by turning clockwise.

39 On models from 2004, pull out the wedge-base bulb, then fit the new one by pushing it firmly into the bulbholder (see illustration).

40 Offer the bulbholder into the headlight, then twist it a quarter-turn clockwise to secure.

41 Where applicable, fold the wheel arch access panel back into place, and secure with the clip(s).

42 Check the operation of the indicators on completion.

Front foglight

43 Unscrew and remove the crosshead screw on the inner side of the light which secures the surround panel. Pull the surround away at the inside, then unhook the tab at the outer side and remove the surround completely.

44 Remove the crosshead mounting screw on the inner side of the light, then loosen the screw next to the foglight reflector (this screw sits in a slotted mounting, so does not have to be removed).

45 Withdraw the light assembly from the bumper, and separate the reflector from the mounting plate, noting how the screw sits in its slotted mounting.

46 Squeeze the wiring plug to release the tab, and pull the wiring plug downwards to disconnect it.

47 Twist the bulb a quarter-turn anti-clockwise, and withdraw it from the back of the foglight.

48 When handling the new bulb, try and

grip it only by the plug socket at the rear. Avoid touching the glass with your fingers, as moisture and grease from the skin can cause blackening and rapid failure of this type of bulb. If the glass is accidentally touched, wipe it clean using methylated spirit.

49 To fit the new bulb, offer it into the back of the foglight, then turn a quarter-turn clockwise to secure it. Push the wiring plug securely onto the new bulb to complete.

50 Fit the reflector onto its mounting plate, then offer the assembly into the bumper, and secure with the mounting screw.

51 Check the operation of the foglights, then refit the surround, hooking it in on the outer side, and securing with the inner screw.

Indicator side repeater

Wing-mounted – method 1

52 Push the light unit rearwards to compress

5.39 Models from 2004 have a wedge-base bulb which pulls out

its rear clip, then unhook the front end from the wing and withdraw it (see illustration). Don't use any tools for this, otherwise there is a risk of damaging the paint – if tools must be used, it's worth applying some masking tape around the light first.

Wing-mounted – method 2

53 If the light unit is difficult to move, this method is easier, and carries less risk of damaging the wing. Remove the screws securing the lower part of the wheel arch liner, then reach inside and release the light unit from behind (see illustrations).

Wing-mounted – both methods

54 Twist the bulbholder anti-clockwise to release it, and pull out the wedge-base bulb (see illustrations). Make sure that the bulbholder does not disappear back through the hole in the wing – tape it in place temporarily if necessary.

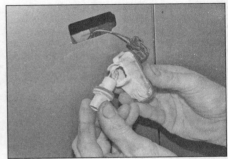

5.52 Removing the wing-mounted side repeater – note rear clip

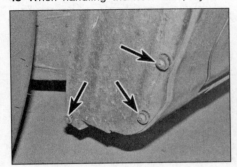

5.53a Remove the screws from the arch liner ...

5.53b ... then reach inside, and release the light unit from behind

5.54a Twist and remove the bulbholder ...

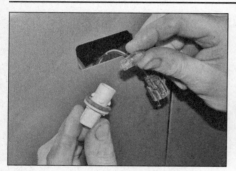

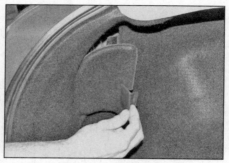

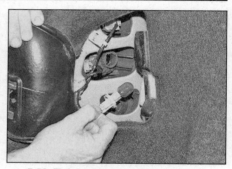

5.54b ... then pull out the wedge-base bulb

5.57 Unclip the front edge of the bulb access panel

5.58 Twist and remove the relevant bulbholder ...

55 Refitting is a reversal of removal. Make sure that the light unit is refitted with the clip facing rearwards, and that it is clipped securely in place.

Mirror-mounted

56 Where the side repeater lights are built into the mirrors, they are non-renewable LEDs. It appears that the light unit is not available separately, and that if damaged, a new mirror assembly would be needed – check with a Honda dealer.

Rear lights

57 Open the tailgate and unclip the front edge of the bulb access panel inside the boot **(see illustration)**. The access panel's rear edge can then be unhooked and the panel removed, if required.
58 Remove the relevant bulbholder by turning it a quarter-turn anti-clockwise **(see illustration)**.

59 Any of the bayonet-fitting bulbs can now be removed by pressing and turning them anti-clockwise. Note that later models with 'clear' rear lights have a push-fit indicator bulb **(see illustration)**.
60 Fit the new bulb, then refit the bulbholder securely, and clip the access panel back into place inside the boot.
61 Check the operation of the lights on completion.

Number plate lights

62 Open the tailgate and prise out the rectangular access panel from the main trim panel **(see illustration)**.
63 Reach inside, then squeeze together the retaining legs and withdraw the bulbholder **(see illustration)**.
64 Pull out the wedge-base bulb, then fit the new one by pushing it firmly into the bulbholder **(see illustration)**.

65 Check that the light is working, then clip the bulbholder back into place. Refit the access panel to complete.

High-level stop-light

66 Open the tailgate, and taking care not to scratch the panels, prise one end of the tailgate upper trim panel to start releasing it. The panel has four clips along its length – once the end is free, gradually pull the panel down to release the clips and remove it.
67 Unclip the bulbholder by pressing the retaining tabs at either end inwards, and withdraw it from the light – take care, as the wiring between the light and bulbholder is short **(see illustration)**.
68 There are five bulbs in total – pull out the blown bulb, then fit the new one by pushing it firmly into the bulbholder **(see illustration)**.
69 Clip the bulbholder firmly back onto the light, then refit the tailgate trim panel to complete.

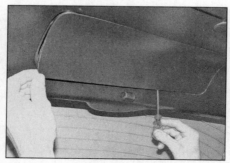

5.59 ... and remove the bulb (later-type push-fit indicator bulb shown)

5.62 Prise out the access panel inside the tailgate

5.63 Squeeze together the 'legs' on the bulbholder, and withdraw it

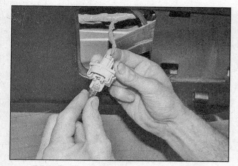

5.64 Pull out the wedge-base bulb

5.67 Release the bulbholder from the high-level stop-light

5.68 Pull out the blown bulb – there are five in total

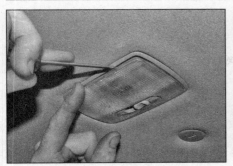

6.2 Prise out the lens for access to the bulb

6.4a Removing a wedge-base bulb (from the front interior light)

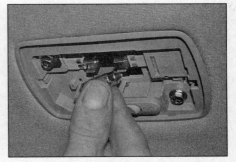

6.4b Removing a festoon-type bulb (from the centre interior light)

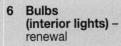

6 Bulbs (interior lights) – renewal

General

1 Refer to Section 5, paragraph 1.

Interior light and map reading lights

2 On lights which have visible switches, carefully prise out the light lens at the front or side (see illustration).

3 On lights which are switched on by pressing the lens, press the outer end of the lens, then prise out the inner end with a small screwdriver and remove the lens. If required, the other half of the lens can also be prised out.

4 The bulb will either be a push-fit wedge-base type, or a festoon bulb which is held between two spring contacts. Pull out the bulb (note that the wedge-base bulbs are often a tight fit), and fit a new one, ensuring that it is securely refitted (see illustrations).

5 Clip the light lens (or lenses) back into place to complete.

Luggage compartment light

6 Carefully prise the light unit out from the trim panel, at the front edge (see illustration). If required, the bulbholder can

6.6 Unclip the luggage compartment light at the front edge

be disconnected, and the light removed completely.

7 Release the legs holding the bulbholder to the lens, using a small screwdriver. Pull out the wedge-base bulb, then fit the new one by pushing it firmly into the bulbholder (see illustrations).

8 Clip the light unit back into the trim panel to complete.

Instrument panel illumination bulbs

9 Remove the instrument panel as described in Section 10.

10 Twist the relevant bulbholder anti-clockwise and remove it from the rear of the panel. Pull

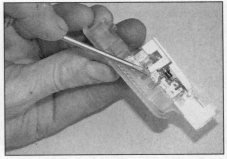

6.7a Release the bulbholder legs with a screwdriver . . .

out the wedge-base bulb, and fit a new one firmly into place. Note: On models from 2004, there are no renewable bulbs fitted.

11 Refit the instrument panel as described in Section 10.

Switch illumination

12 The bulbs are integral with the switches, and cannot be renewed separately.

Glovebox illumination

13 Remove the glovebox as described in Chapter 11, Section 27.

14 The bulb is part of the switch assembly at the top of the glovebox aperture. Remove the two switch screws, then withdraw it and disconnect the wiring plug (see illustrations).

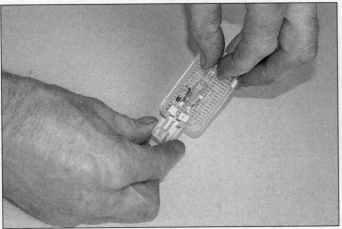

6.7b . . . then pull out the wedge-base bulb

6.14a Remove the two mounting screws, withdraw the switch . . .

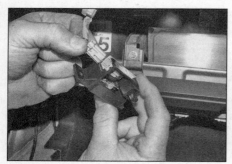

6.14b . . . and disconnect its wiring plug

15 Prise the festoon-type bulb from its spring contacts, and renew it **(see illustration)**.
16 Refitting is a reversal of removal.

Heater control unit illumination

17 Remove the heater control unit as

7.2a The offside headlight may have a rubber cover . . .

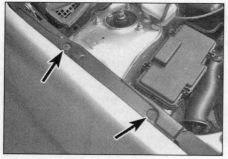

7.3a Remove the two screws . . .

7.4a Remove the bolt on the outer corner . . .

6.15 Prise the glovebox light bulb from the switch

described in Chapter 3, Section 9.
18 To renew a bulb, twist the relevant bulbholder anti-clockwise and remove it from the rear of the panel. The ones on our car appear to be one-piece items (ie, bulb and holder are supplied together) **(see illustration)**.

7.2b . . . which is removed after taking out the two clips

7.3b . . . and take off the side plastic cover

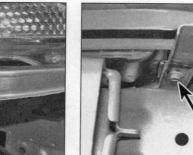

7.4b . . . and one underneath, on the inner end

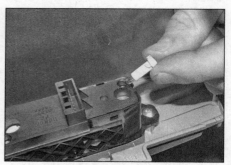

6.18 Removing a bulbholder from the heater control switch panel

19 Refit the heater control unit as described in Chapter 3, Section 9.

Automatic transmission selector illumination

20 Refer to Chapter 7B, Section 5.

7   Exterior light units –
    removal and refitting

Headlight

1 Remove the front bumper as described in Chapter 11 – this is necessary for access to the lower mounting bolts.
2 On our project car, the offside headlight had a rubber cover fitted over one of the upper bolts, secured by two screw-type clips – turn each clip with a screwdriver, then prise it out and remove the cover **(see illustrations)**.
3 Similarly, the second upper bolt may be hidden under a plastic cover fitted to the inner wing channel, secured by two screws – remove the screws and take off the side cover panel **(see illustrations)**.
4 Remove the headlight lower mounting bolts first – note that these also secure the metal bracket underneath the light. There is one bolt on the outer corner, and another on the inner end of the bracket, which is tricky to access **(see illustrations)**.
5 Remove the two upper bolts and withdraw the headlight – note that the metal bracket will also be loose, and this could also be removed if preferred **(see illustrations)**.

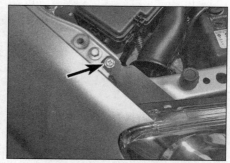

7.5a Remove the upper bolt at the inner corner . . .

7.5b . . . and the one in the centre . . .

7.5c . . . then withdraw the headlight

7.6a Disconnect the wiring plugs and bulbholders . . .

7.6b . . . and detach the wiring harness, then remove the headlight

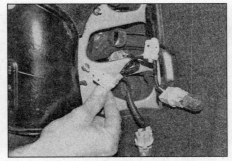

7.14 Pull off the bulbholder wiring from the mounting studs

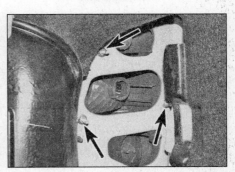

7.15a Unscrew the three inner mounting nuts . . .

6 Disconnect the wiring plugs and bulbholders, and the wiring harness, from the back of the light, and remove it completely **(see illustrations)**.

7 Refitting is a reversal of removal. On completion, check the light operation, and if necessary have the headlight beam alignment checked (see Section 8).

Front direction indicator

8 The front indicator is integral with the headlight.

Front foglight

9 The foglight is removed as part of the bulb renewal procedure, in Section 5.

Indicator side repeater light

10 Remove the light as described in the bulb renewal procedure in Section 5.

11 Disconnect the wiring plug from the bulbholder, and remove the light completely.

12 Refitting is a reversal of removal.

Rear lights

13 Remove the rear bumper as described in Chapter 11.

14 Remove all the bulbholders from the inside, as described in Section 5. Pull off the bulbholder wiring from the light unit mounting studs **(see illustration)**.

15 The light unit is secured with three nuts which are removed from the inside. In addition, there is a further bracket underneath, accessible from the outside (which is why the bumper has to be removed). It is simplest to unscrew the two bracket nuts for removal – if a new light is being fitted, remove the centre screw, and transfer the bracket to the new unit **(see illustrations)**.

16 When all the fasteners have been removed, withdraw the light from the car, and recover the foam seal **(see illustration)**. If the seal is in poor condition, a new one should be used when refitting.

17 Refitting is a reversal of removal.

7.15b . . . and the two nuts from the bracket underneath (also note the centre screw)

7.16 Removing the light unit (and mounting bracket)

7.22 Withdraw the bulbholder from the high-level stop-light

7.23a Remove the mounting bolt at either end . . .

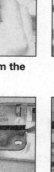

7.23b . . . release the clips along the bottom . . .

7.23c . . . then disconnect the wiring plug and remove the light unit

Rear number plate light

18 Remove the bulbholder as described in the bulb renewal procedure in Section 5, and disconnect the wiring plug from it.

19 If the lens must also be removed, remove the tailgate outer trim panel as described in Chapter 11, Section 27. Unclip the lens by prising at one end with a small screwdriver, and remove it.

20 Refitting is a reversal of removal.

High-level stop-light

21 Open the tailgate, and taking care not to scratch the panels, prise one end of the tailgate upper trim panel to start releasing it. The panel has four clips along its length – once the end is free, gradually pull the panel down to release the clips and remove it.

22 Release the catch at either end, and withdraw the bulbholder **(see illustration)**.

23 Remove the mounting bolt at each end of the light unit, then release the clips along the lower edge, and withdraw it from the tailgate. Disconnect the wiring plug, and remove the light completely **(see illustrations)**.

24 Refitting is a reversal of removal.

8 Headlight beam alignment – general information

All models are equipped with an electrical vertical beam adjuster unit – this can be used to adjust the headlight beam, to compensate for the relevant load which the car is carrying. An adjuster wheel is provided on the facia – refer to the car's handbook for further information.

Accurate adjustment of the headlight beam is only possible using optical beam-setting equipment, and this work should therefore be carried out by a Honda dealer or suitably-equipped workshop. Note that the headlight adjuster wheel should be set to its lowest position (0) before any adjustments are made.

For reference, the headlights can be finely adjusted by rotating the adjuster screws fitted to the top of each light unit, using a cross-head screwdriver. The screws are accessible through the top of the body front panel. The vertical adjustment screw is mounted at the inner end of the headlight. The horizontal adjustment screw is mounted at the outer end of the headlight **(see illustrations)**.

9 Headlight adjuster components – removal and refitting

Adjuster switch

1 Refer to Section 4.

Adjuster motor

2 Removing the motor is possible without removing the headlight, but refitting it will be much easier if the headlight is removed as described in Section 7.

3 Disconnect the wiring plug from the motor **(see illustration)**.

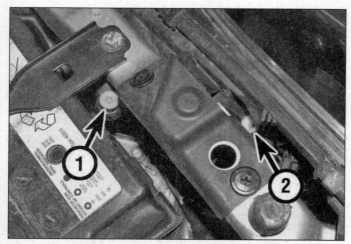

8.3a Up to 2004 model headlight adjusters – vertical (1) and horizontal (2)

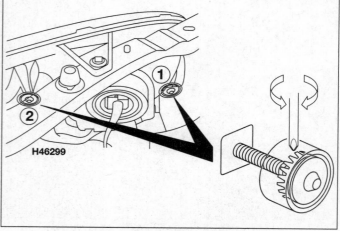

H46299

8.3b 2004-on headlight adjuster locations – vertical (1) and horizontal (2) – nearside shown

9.3 Disconnect the adjuster motor wiring plug

9.4 Removing the headlight adjuster motor – note the balljoint

9.5 Hold the adjuster mechanism with a finger through the bulb hole when refitting

4 Twist the motor to free it, then gently pull it from the headlight, to release the ball-and-socket joint **(see illustration)**.
5 When refitting, remove the headlight bulb (or the main beam bulb on 2004-on models) and hold the adjuster mechanism with a finger as the ball-and-socket joint is reconnected **(see illustration)**.

10 Instrument panel – removal and refitting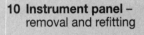

Removal

1 Ensure that the ignition is switched off (take out the key).
2 Remove the three screws from the steering column lower shroud, unclip the upper shroud from it, then work off the lower shroud (refer to Chapter 11, Section 27, if necessary).
3 Adjust the steering column to its lowest setting, using the lever underneath the steering wheel.
4 The instrument panel surround must now be removed. Some models have two upper screws which must be removed, but on our project car, the surround had no screws, and was released by gently pulling at the corners **(see illustration)**.
5 Remove the three instrument panel retaining screws (one at the top, and one on each front corner), and withdraw the panel from the facia. Disconnect the two wiring plugs, and remove the panel completely **(see illustrations)**.

Refitting

6 Refitting is a reversal of removal.

Bulb renewal

7 Bulb renewal is covered in Section 6.

11 Horn(s) – removal and refitting

Removal

1 All models have a horn unit mounted directly below the left-hand headlight. Some models have a second horn unit (with a higher tone) located below the other headlight.
2 Remove the front bumper as described in Chapter 11.
3 Disconnect the wiring plug from the horn **(see illustrations)**.

10.4 Unclip and remove the instrument panel surround

4 Unscrew the mounting bolt, and remove the horn from the front of the car.

Refitting

5 Refitting is a reversal of removal.

12 Wiper arms – removal and refitting

Removal

1 Operate the wiper motor, then switch it off so that the wiper arm returns to the park position **(see Haynes Hint overleaf)**.

Windscreen wiper arm

2 Prise off the wiper arm spindle nut cover (note that a different cover is fitted to each arm), then slacken and remove the spindle nut

10.5a Remove the three mounting screws . . .

10.5b . . . then withdraw the panel and disconnect the two wiring plugs

11.3a Twin horns – with bumper removed

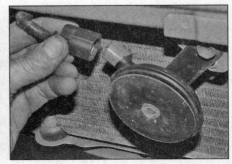

11.3b Disconnecting the wiring plug from a horn unit

Stick a piece of masking tape along the edge of the wiper blade, to use as an alignment aid on refitting.

12.2a Prise off the wiper arm nut cover . . .

12.2b . . . and remove the nut underneath

12.3 Pull the wiper arm off its splines

12.4a Lift up the hinged cover . . .

12.4b . . . and unscrew the wiper arm nut

(see illustrations). Recover the washer, where applicable.

3 Lift the blade off the glass, and pull the wiper arm off its spindle **(see illustration)**. Note that on some models, the wiper arms may be very tight on the spindle splines – it should be possible to lever the arm off the spindle, using a flat-bladed screwdriver (take care not to damage the scuttle cover panel). In extreme cases, it may even be necessary to use a small puller to free the arm.

Tailgate wiper arm

4 Lift up the hinged cover, then unscrew the nut **(see illustrations)**.

5 Lift the blade off the glass, and pull the wiper arm off its spindle. It should be possible to lever the arm off the spindle, using a flat-bladed screwdriver, but in extreme cases, it may even be necessary to use a small puller to free the arm. If a puller is used, take care to protect the washer jet from damage (we used a small socket over the jet to protect it) **(see illustrations)**.

Refitting

6 Ensure that the wiper arm and spindle splines are clean and dry, then refit the arm to the spindle. Where applicable, align the wiper blade with the tape fitted on removal.

7 Refit the spindle nut (and washer), tightening it securely, and clip the nut cover back into position.

13 Windscreen wiper motor and linkage –
removal and refitting

Removal

1 Remove the wiper arms as described in Section 12.

2 Peel off the rubber weatherstrip along the

12.5a Using a puller to remove the wiper arm (note the small socket over the washer jet)

12.5b Removing the tailgate wiper arm

13.2 Pull off the cowl panel rubber strip

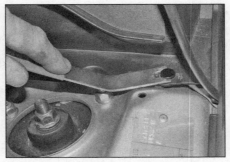

13.3 Prise out the three cowl panel clips on the front edge

13.5a Lift the panel in the centre to bend it, and release the ends . . .

13.5b . . . then with the rear clips released, remove the panel completely

13.6a The wiper motor assembly has three mounting bolts – one on the driver's side . . .

13.6b . . . and two more in the centre of the car

edge of the windscreen scuttle panel **(see illustration)**.

3 Carefully prise out the three clips from the front edge of the windscreen cowl panel **(see illustration)**.

4 The cowl panel's rear edge is secured under the windscreen by a row of eight clips – starting at one end, pull the panel forwards to release them.

5 At each end of the panel, a rubber trim seals the panel to the windscreen and the wing – note how this rubber is fitted under the wing before removal. Lift the cowl panel slightly in the centre, to bend it a little, and the end rubbers will release, allowing the panel to be removed **(see illustrations)**.

6 The motor and linkage assembly is secured by three bolts – unscrew them and lift out the assembly **(see illustrations)**.

7 Disconnect the wiring plug from the wiper motor, then unclip the wiring harness and remove it **(see illustrations)**.

8 Before separating the motor from the linkage, make an alignment mark between the linkage and the cranked arm attached to the motor, to show its parked position (typically, it will be horizontally aligned, along the axis of the motor frame).

9 Remove the spindle nut and washer, and separate the cranked arm from the motor. The other end of the cranked arm need not be detached, but for reference, it is on a ball fitting, which can be prised off if required.

10 Remove the three motor mounting bolts, and withdraw the motor from the wiper frame.

13.7a Disconnect the wiper motor wiring plug . . .

Refitting

11 Refitting is a reversal of removal, bearing in mind the following points:

a) Ensure that the motor arm is aligned in the 'parked' position (see paragraph 8) when refitting.

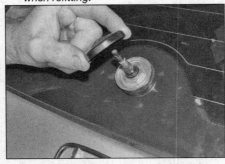

14.2 Lift off the trim cover behind the wiper arm

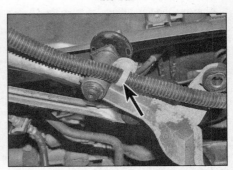

13.7b . . . then release the wiring from its clips, and remove the assembly

b) Where they have been disturbed, lightly grease the wiper linkage pivots.

c) Tighten all nuts and bolts securely.

d) Ensure that the cowl panel is clipped back into place, and that the rubber trims at each end are tucked back under the wing correctly.

e) Test the motor's operation before refitting the wiper arms as described in Section 12.

14 Tailgate wiper motor – removal and refitting

Removal

1 Remove the tailgate wiper arm as described in Section 12.

2 Lift off the outer trim cover from the wiper spindle **(see illustration)**.

14.3 Unscrew the flat nut and remove the spacer washer

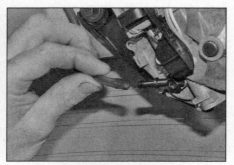

14.5a Pull off the washer tube . . .

14.5b . . . and disconnect the wiring plug

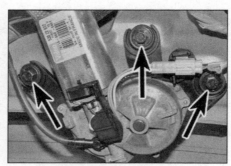

14.6a Wiper motor mounting bolts

3 Unscrew the flat nut and remove the spacer washer behind it **(see illustration)**.
4 Remove the tailgate main trim panel as described in Chapter 11, Section 27.
5 Carefully pull off the washer tube from the stub on the motor, and disconnect the motor wiring plug **(see illustrations)**.
6 Remove the three motor mounting bolts, and withdraw the motor from the tailgate **(see illustrations)**.

Refitting

7 Refitting is a reversal of removal. Ensure that the wiper motor spindle grommet stays in place in the tailgate glass as the spindle is fitted back through.

---

15 Windscreen/tailgate washer system components – removal and refitting

Washer fluid reservoir

Note: *Petrol and diesel engine models have the reservoir on different sides – petrol models have it on the left, diesels on the right (left and right as seen from the driver's seat).*

Removal

1 Remove the front wheel arch liner as described in Chapter 11, Section 23. Alternatively, for the best access, remove

---

the front bumper as described in Chapter 11, Section 6.
2 Disconnect the wiring plug and washer tube from each of the two washer pumps – anticipate a small amount of fluid loss when the tubes are disconnected. Note the location of each washer tube, as they must be refitted to the correct pump.
3 Alternatively, the two pumps can be prised out of the reservoir, which means they can be left behind on the car – however, the contents of the reservoir will be lost when the pumps are removed. Recover the rubber sealing grommet from each pump, and refit them to the reservoir.
4 Remove the three reservoir mounting bolts, and lower the reservoir into the wheel arch to remove it **(see illustration)**.

Refitting

5 Refitting is a reversal of removal, noting the following points:
a) *If the pumps were removed, it may be helpful to apply a little washing-up liquid to the rubber sealing grommets to make refitting easier.*
b) *Make sure the washer hoses are securely reconnected to their original positions.*
c) *Refill the reservoir, then check the operation of the washers before refitting the wheel arch liner.*

Washer fluid pumps

Removal

6 Refer to the note at the start of this Section – the pumps are fitted into the washer reservoir. Remove the front wheel arch liner as described in Chapter 11, Section 23. Alternatively, for the best access, remove the front bumper as described in Chapter 11, Section 6.
7 All models have two pumps – the front one is for the windscreen, with the rear one for the tailgate **(see illustration)**. Where headlight washers are fitted, the pump is larger, and fitted on its own at the front of the reservoir.
8 Disconnect the wiring plug and washer tube from the pump – anticipate a small amount

---

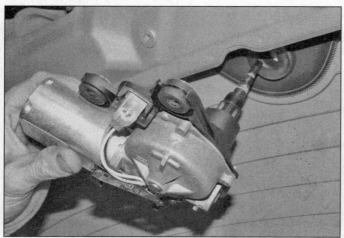

14.6b Removing the wiper motor

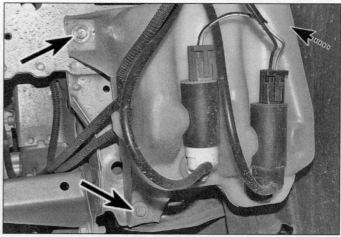

15.4 Unscrew the three reservoir mounting bolts (one hidden)

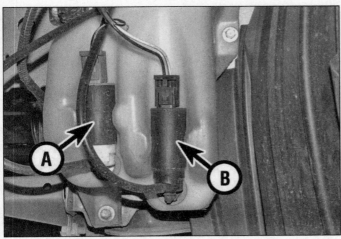

15.7 Windscreen washer pump (A) and tailgate washer pump (B)

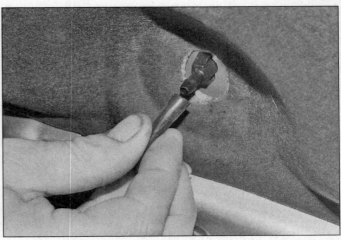

15.11 Pull off the washer tube from the base of the jet

of fluid loss when the tube is disconnected. If both pumps are being removed, note the location of each washer tube, as they must be refitted to the correct pump.

9 Prise the pump out of the reservoir, and remove it. If the rubber sealing grommet came out with the pump, refit it to the reservoir.

Refitting

10 Refitting is a reversal of removal, noting the following points:

a) *It may be helpful to apply a little washing-up liquid to the rubber sealing grommets to make refitting easier.*

b) *Make sure the washer hoses are securely reconnected to their original positions.*

c) *Refill the reservoir, then check the operation of the washers before refitting the wheel arch liner.*

Windscreen washer jet

Removal

11 Working under the bonnet, unclip the washer hoses as necessary, then disconnect the tube from the washer jet **(see illustration)**. Some models may have a quick-release fitting on the tube, released by pulling the small plastic clip upwards. Where this is not the case, it is likely that the tube will be a very

tight fit – removal will be easier if the tube end can be warmed, and careful prising with a small screwdriver may also help.

12 Use a small screwdriver to release the washer jet from inside the bonnet, then remove it from the outside **(see illustrations)**.

Refitting

13 Refitting is a reversal of removal, but make sure that the fluid hose connections are securely remade. It may be helpful to apply a little washing-up liquid to the jet, to make fitting the tube easier.

Tailgate washer jet

Removal

14 The washer jet is part of the sealing grommet fitted around the tailgate wiper spindle – to remove it, the tailgate wiper motor must first be removed, as described in Section 14.

15 From inside the tailgate, unclip the washer hose as necessary, then disconnect the hose from the washer jet. Some models may have a quick-release fitting on the hose, released by pulling the small plastic clip upwards. Where this is not the case, it is likely that the hose will be a very tight fit – removal will be easier if the hose end can be warmed, and

careful prising with a small screwdriver may also help.

16 Taking care not to scratch the glass, prise out the jet/grommet from the tailgate window.

17 The tailgate washer tube is routed down the passenger side of the car, and up the C-pillar. To gain access, remove the C-pillar and luggage area side trim panels as described in Chapter 11 **(see illustration)**.

Refitting

18 Refitting is a reversal of removal. Refit the wiper motor as described in Section 14.

Headlight washer jet

Removal

19 Remove the front bumper as described in Chapter 11.

20 Apply masking tape to the bumper, around the top part of the washer jet. Taking care not to damage the bumper or the cover, prise off the jet's top cover (which has two mounting legs) and remove it.

21 Remove the two jet body retaining screws now exposed in the bumper, and withdraw the jet body from inside.

Refitting

22 Refitting is a reversal of removal.

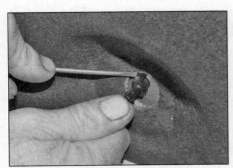

15.12a Use a small screwdriver to release the jet clips . . .

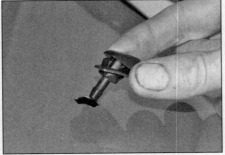

15.12b . . . then withdraw it from the bonnet

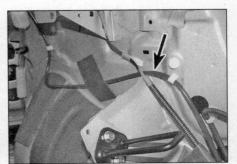

15.17 The tailgate washer tube is routed around and up the C-pillar

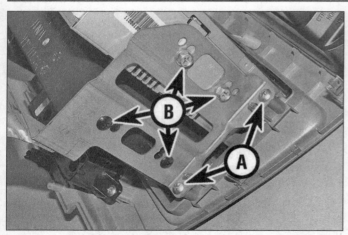

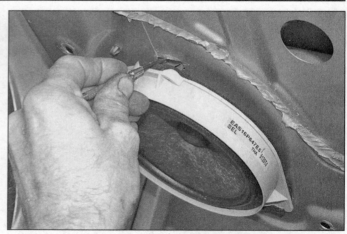

16.2 Remove the mounting frame screws (A) or the unit side screws (B)

17.2a Use a small screwdriver to release the upper clip . . .

16 Radio unit –
removal and refitting

Removal

1 Remove the heater control panel as described in Chapter 3, Section 9.
2 The whole unit can be removed by removing the four screws securing the metal mounting frame to the back of the heater control panel. Alternatively, the unit(s) can be removed individually, by removing the two screws on either side, and sliding the unit(s) out of the frame **(see illustration)**.

Refitting

3 Refitting is a reversal of removal. Refit the heater control panel as described in Chapter 3, Section 9.

17 Speakers –
removal and refitting

Removal

Front speakers

1 Remove the relevant door trim panel as described in Chapter 11, Section 13.

2 The speakers are clipped into the door. Insert a small screwdriver at the top to release the upper clip, then lift the speaker to unhook the two lower legs **(see illustrations)**.
3 Withdraw the speaker from the door, and disconnect the wiring plug **(see illustration)**.

Rear speakers – 3-door

4 Taking care not to scratch the main panel, prise out the speaker grille from the rear side trim panel **(see illustration)**.
5 Remove the three speaker mounting screws, then withdraw the speaker and disconnect its wiring plug **(see illustrations)**.

Rear speakers – 5-door

6 The rear speakers on 5-door models are removed in the same way as the front speakers.

Refitting

7 Refitting is a reversal of removal. Ensure that the speakers are securely clipped or screwed in place.

18 Radio aerial –
removal and refitting

Note: *The aerial mast can be unscrewed from the base, from outside. For good reception (and to discourage theft) always ensure the mast is fully tightened when refitting.*

17.2b . . . then lift the speaker to unhook the lower legs

17.3 Disconnect the wiring plug, and remove the speaker

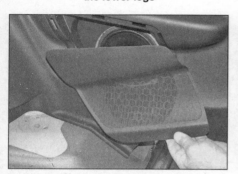

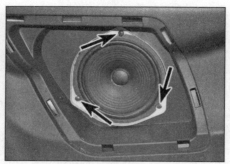

17.4 Prise out the speaker grille . . .

17.5a . . . then remove the speaker, which has three screws . . .

17.5b . . . and disconnect the wiring plug

Removal

1 On models with the ultrasonic alarm, access to the roof aerial is gained by removing the ultrasonic transmitter from the headlining, as follows (models without an alarm may still have a trim panel fitted in the same location). Prise off the trim covers, remove the screw above each, then withdraw the unit and disconnect the wiring plug **(see illustrations)**.
2 On models without an alarm (or an access panel in the headlining), remove the C-pillar trim panels and rear grab handles as described in Chapter 11, Section 27. Release the headlining at the rear edge, and carefully pull it down for access to the aerial.
3 Disconnect the earth terminal spade connector, then pull the aerial lead from the base of the aerial **(see illustrations)**.
4 Unscrew the mounting nut, and withdraw the aerial from the roof **(see illustration)**. Recover the rubber seal – if this has perished, use a new one when refitting.

Refitting

5 Refitting is a reversal of removal. Ensure that there is a good seal between the aerial and the roof, and good electrical connections on the base of the aerial, or reception will suffer.

19 Immobiliser system and alarm – general information

Immobiliser system

An engine immobiliser system is fitted as standard to all models, and the system is operated automatically every time the ignition key is inserted/removed.

The immobiliser system ensures that the car can only be started using the original Honda ignition key. The key contains an electronic chip (transponder) which is programmed with a code. When the key is inserted into the ignition switch, it uses the current present in the reader coil (which is fitted around the switch) to send a signal to the immobiliser electronic control unit (ECU). The ECU checks this code every time the ignition is switched on. If the key code does not match the ECU code, the ECU will disable the fuel pump circuit (lift pump circuit on diesel models) to prevent the engine being started.

If the ignition key is lost, a new one can be obtained from a Honda dealer. They have access to the correct key code for the immobiliser system of your car, and will be able to supply a new coded key.

If you have any spare keys cut, if they are not coded correctly, they will only open the doors, etc, and will not be capable of starting the engine. For this reason, it may be best to have any spare keys supplied by your Honda dealer, who will also be able to advise you on coding the keys.

Alarm system

Certain models are equipped with an anti-theft alarm system, in addition to the engine immobiliser. Various types of system may be fitted, depending on specification and market.

The anti-theft alarm system is automatically activated by the central locking system (manually, or via the remote control, where applicable). The alarm system uses the door lock cylinder/lock knob switches, and the tailgate and bonnet lock switches, to detect whether any of them is opened with the alarm set. A security control unit under the facia constantly monitors the switches – if any switch receives an earth signal, the alarm siren will be activated, and the indicators will flash.

This system (sometimes referred to as a 'perimetric' alarm, as it only protects the 'perimeter' of the car) does not prevent a thief from gaining access to the inside of the car by breaking a window – provided the doors, etc, are not opened, the alarm will not go off.

Later models may be fitted with an alarm featuring ultrasonic scanning of the whole inside of the car – with this system, if the ultrasonic beam is broken by any movement inside the car, the alarm will sound. Models with an ultrasonic alarm can be identified by the ultrasonic emitter and receiver grilles in the rear interior light unit.

Any faults with the system will most likely be related to the lock switches or associated wiring, which are covered in the relevant parts of Chapter 11. False alarms may also occur if the doors, bonnet or tailgate are not closing properly for any reason. On an ultrasonic alarm system, not closing a window or the sunroof properly may also set off the alarm, especially in windy conditions. Any persistent problems not explained by the above should be referred to a Honda dealer for diagnosis – for obvious security reasons, a more detailed description of the system is not included in this manual.

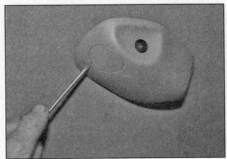
18.1a Prise out the trim covers . . .

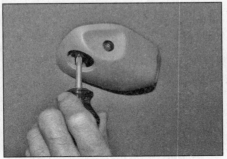
18.1b . . . remove the screws above . . .

18.1c . . . then withdraw the ultrasonic unit and disconnect it

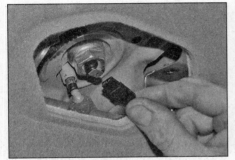
18.3a Disconnect the earth terminal . . .

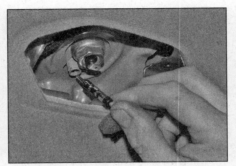
18.3b . . . then pull out the aerial lead

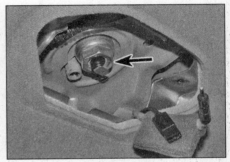
18.4 Unscrew the mounting nut to remove the aerial

20.1 Side airbag crash sensor on the front inner sill

20 Airbag system –
general information
and precautions

General information

All models are fitted with a driver's airbag mounted in the steering wheel, and a similar airbag for the front seat passenger, mounted in the facia panel. These are designed to prevent serious chest and head injuries during a frontal accident (of sufficient force) within 30° from the left or right of the car centre-line. Most Civics also have side airbags, fitted into the front seat side cushions, which are triggered if there is an impact from the side of the car. The control unit for the airbag system is located under the centre of the facia, and performs continual system diagnostics. Two crash sensors are located at the front of the car, and a side impact sensor is located on the inner sill, in front of each B-pillar **(see illustration)**.

The airbag system on the Civic has an adaptive capability – it can adjust the level of protection according to circumstances, and to the number of passengers (or lack of them). If the system's crash sensors detect a less-severe impact, the front airbags may not fire at all. A seat occupancy sensor is fitted to the passenger seat, so the system knows when a front seat passenger is present – when the seat is empty, the passenger front and side airbags are disabled. The occupancy sensor forms part of the seat side cushion, and cannot be renewed separately.

The seat belt tensioners (described in Chapter 11) are also deployed in the event of an accident, and in fact can deploy independently at lower impact levels than the airbags.

The front seat side airbags offer greater passenger protection in a side impact. Although the side airbags are linked to the 'front' airbags, the side airbags will only deploy if the car is struck from the side.

The airbags are inflated by a gas generator, which forces the bag out of the cover in the steering wheel, facia panel, or seat cushion. On the driver's airbag (which turns with the steering wheel) a 'clock spring' rotary connector ensures that a good electrical connection is maintained with the airbag at all times.

⚠️ *Warning: When working on the airbag system, always wait at least 3 minutes after disconnecting the battery, as a precaution against accidental deployment of the airbag unit. This period ensures that any stored energy in the back-up capacitor is dissipated. Do not use battery-operated radio key code savers, as this may cause the airbag to be deployed, with the possibility of personal injury.*

Precautions

⚠️ *Warning: The following precautions must be observed when working on cars equipped with an airbag system, to prevent the possibility of personal injury.*

General precautions

The following precautions **must** be observed when carrying out work on a car equipped with an airbag:
a) *Do not disconnect the battery with the engine running.*
b) *Before carrying out any work in the vicinity of the airbag, removal of any of the airbag components, or any welding work on the car, de-activate the system as described in the following sub-Section.*
c) *Do not attempt to test any of the airbag system circuits using test meters or any other test equipment.*
d) *If the airbag warning light comes on, or any fault in the system is suspected, consult a Honda dealer without delay. Do*

not attempt to carry out fault diagnosis, or any dismantling of the components.

Precautions when handling an airbag
a) *Transport the airbag by itself, bag upward.*
b) *Do not put your arms around the airbag.*
c) *Carry the airbag close to the body, bag outward.*
d) *Do not drop the airbag or expose it to impacts.*
e) *Do not attempt to dismantle the airbag unit.*
f) *Do not connect any form of electrical equipment to any part of the airbag circuit.*

Precautions when storing an airbag
a) *Store the unit in a cupboard with the airbag upward.*
b) *Do not expose the airbag to temperatures above 80°C.*
c) *Do not expose the airbag to flames.*
d) *Do not attempt to dispose of the airbag – consult a Honda dealer.*
e) *Never refit an airbag which is known to be faulty or damaged.*

De-activation of airbag system

The system must be de-activated as follows, before carrying out any work on the airbag components or surrounding area.
a) *Remove the ignition key.*
b) *Switch off all electrical equipment.*
c) *Disconnect the battery negative lead (see Disconnecting the battery).*
d) *Insulate the battery negative terminal and the end of the battery negative lead to prevent any possibility of contact.*
e) ***Wait for at least 3 minutes*** *before carrying out any further work.*
f) *Ensure that the battery is still disconnected, before reconnecting any airbag wiring.*

21 Airbag system components
– removal and refitting

⚠️ *Warning: Refer to the precautions given in Section 20 before attempting to carry out work on the airbag components.*

Driver's airbag

Removal

1 De-activate the airbag system as described in Section 20. The airbag unit is an integral part of the steering wheel centre pad.
2 On models with the three-spoke steering wheel, prise off the two side covers from the back of the wheel – one is larger than the other, and hides the airbag wiring plug. Behind each cover is an airbag retaining bolt **(see illustrations)**.
3 On four-spoke steering wheels, prise off the rectangular cover at the base/back of the steering wheel **(see illustration)**.
4 Disconnect the (yellow) airbag wiring plug

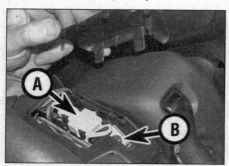

21.2a Prise off the large cover to access the airbag plug (A) and one bolt (B) . . .

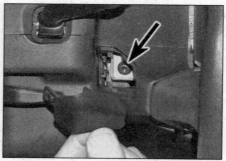

21.2b . . . on the other side, a smaller cover hides the other airbag bolt

21.3 Prise off the airbag wiring connector cover at the base of the wheel

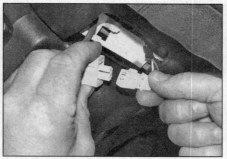

21.4 Slide back the locking sleeve, and disconnect the plug

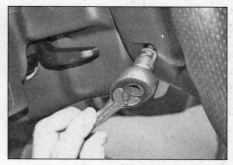

21.5 Unscrew the airbag bolt on either side of the wheel

by sliding back the spring-loaded locking sleeve **(see illustration)**.

5 Unscrew the two airbag mounting Torx bolts, using a T30 Torx bit. On four-spoke wheels, the bolts are located either side of the wheel, and are deeply recessed – look around the wheel rim to see them **(see illustration)**. The bolts may be quite tight – ensure that the right size of Torx bit is used.

6 When the bolts are loose, lift the airbag unit out of the steering wheel, feeding the wiring plug through as it is removed **(see illustration)**. Move the airbag to a safe place, and always keep the front facing upwards.

Refitting

7 Refitting is a reversal of removal. Feed the wiring back through the wheel, and (with the battery still off) connect the plug securely. Tighten the airbag mounting bolts, and clip on the wheel's lower cover to complete. Reconnect the battery and check for correct operation of the airbag warning light by switching on the ignition.

Passenger's airbag

Removal

8 De-activate the airbag system as described in Section 20.

9 Remove the glovebox as described in Chapter 11, Section 27.

10 Disconnect the (yellow) airbag wiring plug by sliding back the spring-loaded locking sleeve **(see illustration)**.

11 Remove the three mounting nuts securing the airbag unit to its mounting bracket **(see illustration)**.

12 Protect the top of the facia with strips of masking tape or some cloth. Using a wide-bladed tool, carefully prise the airbag at the sides to release the retaining tabs, and lift the unit out of the facia.

13 Move the airbag to a safe place, and always keep the front facing upwards.

Refitting

14 Refitting is a reversal of removal. Tighten the mounting nuts securely, and (with the battery still off) reconnect the airbag wiring plug. On completion, reconnect the battery and check for correct operation of the airbag warning light by switching on the ignition.

Airbag control unit

Removal

15 When a car is involved in a heavy enough impact to set off the airbags, the event is logged in the airbag control unit. On some cars, even after new airbags are fitted, the 'event code' cannot be cleared from the airbag control unit (so the airbag warning light stays on), and a new control unit has to be fitted. Consult a Honda dealer for advice on this point.

16 Honda state that, before the control unit is removed, as well as disconnecting the battery and waiting three minutes, **all** the airbag and seat belt tensioner wiring plugs must be disconnected. This means disconnecting the driver's and passenger's airbags, the front seat wiring (models with side airbags), and the wiring plugs to the front seat belt inertia reels (refer to Chapter 11 for the last two).

21.6 Removing the driver's airbag

21.11 Remove the three airbag unit mounting nuts

17 Remove the centre console as described in Chapter 11. On models without a centre console, remove the facia centre lower panel as described in Chapter 11, Section 27.

18 Fold down the carpet for access to the unit. Disconnect the three wiring plugs, noting their fitted locations, then remove the three Torx screws and withdraw the unit from the floor location **(see illustration)**.

Refitting

19 Refitting is a reversal of removal, bearing in mind the following points:

a) The battery must still be disconnected when reconnecting the airbag and seat belt tensioner wiring.

b) Make sure that the wiring connectors are securely reconnected.

c) Tighten the mounting screws securely.

d) On completion, reconnect the battery and check for correct operation of the airbag warning light by switching on the ignition.

21.10 Disconnect the passenger airbag wiring plug

21.18 Disconnect the airbag control unit wiring plugs

21.23a Disconnect the clockspring wiring plug on top . . .

21.23b . . . and the yellow plug underneath

21.24 Note the arrow marking on the clockspring front face

21.25 Release the upper and lower tabs, and remove the clockspring

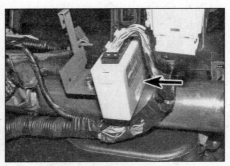

22.3 The central locking remote receiver is bolted to the facia crossmember

Airbag clockspring (rotary connector)

20 Remove the driver's airbag as described previously in this Section.

21 Remove the steering wheel as described in Chapter 10.

22 Remove the steering column shrouds as described in Chapter 11, Section 27.

23 Trace the wiring harness from the front of the clockspring to the wiring plugs below at the top and bottom of the steering wheel – on most models, there will be two plugs to disconnect. The yellow plug underneath has a spring-loaded locking sleeve (see illustrations).

24 Before removing the clockspring, note that it has an arrow marking on its front face – this should face upwards (see illustration). If the same clockspring will be refitted, tape the unit so that it cannot turn once removed.

25 When the wiring has been disconnected, carefully release the upper and lower tabs, and slide the clockspring off the steering column – feed its wiring through as it is removed, noting how it is routed (see illustration).

26 Before fitting the clockspring, it must

first be centred. If a new unit is being fitted, note that they are supplied set in the centre position. Similarly, if the old clockspring has not been turned while it was removed, this procedure can be omitted.

27 To centre the unit, gently turn the front face clockwise until it stops. Now turn the front face anti-clockwise by about 2 1/2 turns, and the arrow mark on its face should point straight up – this is the centre position. As a further reference, the two steering wheel locating pins on the front face should be horizontal.

28 With the front wheels still pointing straight ahead, offer the clockspring onto the steering column. Note that the direction indicator self-cancelling sleeve's two tabs should be aligned vertically.

29 Feed the clockspring wiring into position, making sure it is routed as before, and connect the wiring plugs. Secure the unit in place by pressing it home so that its upper and lower tabs locate properly.

30 Further refitting is a reversal of removal. On completion, reconnect the battery and check for correct operation of the airbag warning light by switching on the ignition.

Side airbags

31 The side airbags are located internally within the front seat backrest, and no attempt should be made to remove them. Any suspected problems with the side airbag system should be referred to a Honda dealer.

---

22 Central locking system components – removal and refitting

Door actuator switches

1 The actuator switches are fitted to the lock cylinders on the front door locks, and can be removed as described in Chapter 11, Section 14.

Deadlocking units

2 The deadlocking (or 'superlocking') control units are fitted to each door, and are accessible after removing the door trim panel as described in Chapter 11, Section 13. Removing the units themselves is covered in the door membrane removal procedure, in the same Section.

Remote receiver

3 The receiver unit for the remote locking function is fitted behind the facia, to the left of centre, and is accessible after removing the heater control panel as described in Chapter 3, Section 9. Disconnect the wiring plug, then unbolt and remove the unit from the facia crossmember (see illustration).

Control unit

4 Overall control of the central locking system is via the multiplex module, which is fitted behind the fusebox – refer to Section 3.

HONDA CIVIC wiring diagrams

Diagram 1

Key to symbols

Bulb	—⊗—	Solenoid actuator		Item no.	2	
Flashing bulb	—⊗—	Heating element		Pump/motor	Ⓜ	
Switch	—o— o—	Wire splice or soldered joint		Gauge/meter	⊘	
Multiple contact switch (ganged)		Resistor	—▭—	Earth point & location		E4
Fuse/fusible link and current rating	F5 30A	Variable resistor		Diode	—▷|—	
Connecting wires		Variable resistor		Light emitting diode (LED)		

Wire colour (brown with yellow tracer), bracket denotes alternative wiring.   ▬▬▬ Bn/Ye ▬▬▬

Dashed outline denotes part of a larger item, containing in this case an electronic or solid state device.

Engine compartment fuses 3

Fuse	Rating	Circuit protected
F1	20A	Condenser fan
F2	15A	Sidelights
F3	7.5A	Interior light
F4	20A	Cooling fan
F5	10A	Hazard warning lights
F6	15A	Fuel injection control unit
F7	15A	Horn, stoplights
F8	20A	ABS
F9	10A	Wash/wipe, instrument cluster, central locking, audio system
F10	40A	ABS pump
F11	30A	Heated rear window
F12	40A	Heater blower motor
F13	40A	Electric windows, sunroof
F14	40A	Option
F15	15A	LH headlight
F16	20A	Central locking
F17	15A	RH headlight
F18	60A	Electric power steering
F19	80A	Main fuse battery
F20	50A	Main fuse ignition
F21	Spare	
F22	Spare	
F23	Spare	
F24	Spare	
F25	Spare	

Passenger compartment fuses 4

Fuse	Rating	Circuit protected
F1	15A	Ignition coil
F2	-	Not used
F3	20A	Front foglights
F4	10A	ACG (IG)
F5	-	Not used
F6	7.5A	Electric window relay, sunroof
F7	20A	Sunroof
F8	7.5A	ACC radio
F9	-	Not used
F10	7.5A	Meter, reversing lights, central locking
F11	7.5A	ABS
F12	7.5A	Daytime running lights
F13	10A	SRS
F14	10A	Electric mirrors, cooling fan, heater blower, heated rear window, heated mirrors
F15	30A	Headlight washer
F16	20A	Heated seats
F17	15A	Fuel pump
F18	15A	ACC cigar lighter
F19	7.5A	Direction indicators
F20	30A	Front wiper
F21	-	Not used
F22	20A	LH front electric window
F23	20A	RH front electric window
F24	20A	LH rear electric window
F25	20A	RH rear electric window

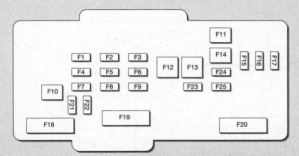

H33630

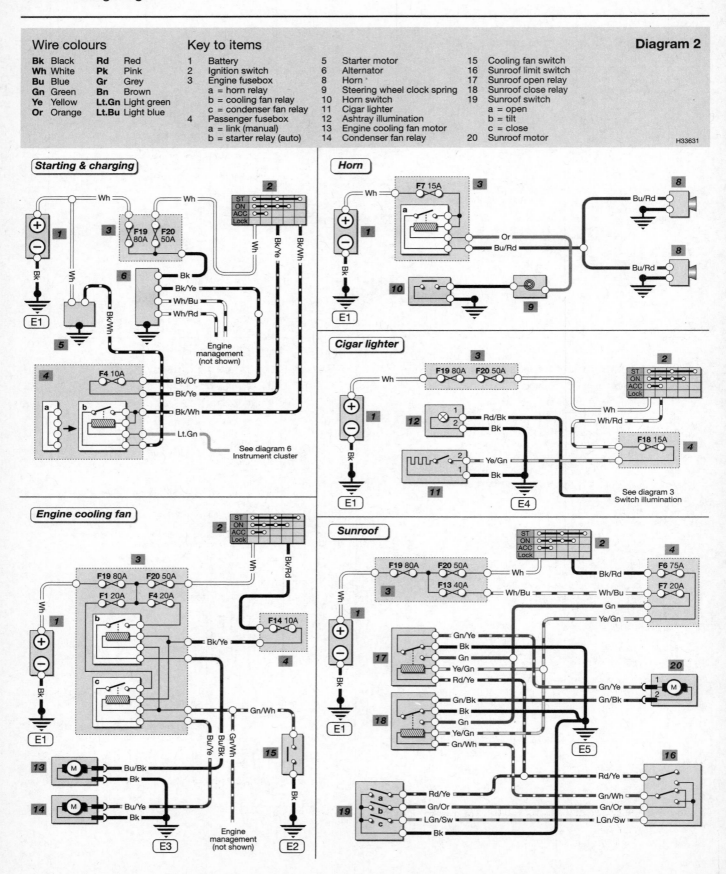

Wire colours

Bk	Black	**Rd**	Red
Wh	White	**Pk**	Pink
Bu	Blue	**Gr**	Grey
Gn	Green	**Bn**	Brown
Ye	Yellow	**Lt.Gn**	Light green
Or	Orange	**Lt.Bu**	Light blue

Key to items

1 Battery
2 Ignition switch
3 Engine fusebox
  a = horn relay
  b = cooling fan relay
  c = condenser fan relay
4 Passenger fusebox
  a = link (manual)
  b = starter relay (auto)

5 Starter motor
6 Alternator
8 Horn
9 Steering wheel clock spring
10 Horn switch
11 Cigar lighter
12 Ashtray illumination
13 Engine cooling fan motor
14 Condenser fan relay

15 Cooling fan switch
16 Sunroof limit switch
17 Sunroof open relay
18 Sunroof close relay
19 Sunroof switch
  a = open
  b = tilt
  c = close
20 Sunroof motor

Diagram 2

H33631

Starting & charging

Horn

Engine cooling fan

Cigar lighter

Sunroof

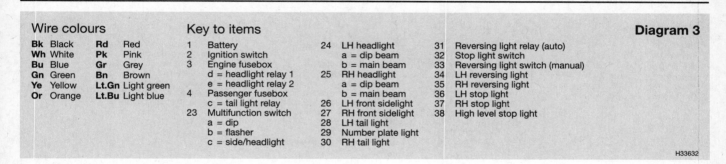

Wire colours

Bk Black **Rd** Red
Wh White **Pk** Pink
Bu Blue **Gr** Grey
Gn Green **Bn** Brown
Ye Yellow **Lt.Gn** Light green
Or Orange **Lt.Bu** Light blue

Key to items

1 Battery
2 Ignition switch
3 Engine fusebox
   d = headlight relay 1
   e = headlight relay 2
4 Passenger fusebox
   c = tail light relay
23 Multifunction switch
   a = dip
   b = flasher
   c = side/headlight

24 LH headlight
   a = dip beam
   b = main beam
25 RH headlight
   a = dip beam
   b = main beam
26 LH front sidelight
27 RH front sidelight
28 LH tail light
29 Number plate light
30 RH tail light

31 Reversing light relay (auto)
32 Stop light switch
33 Reversing light switch (manual)
34 LH reversing light
35 RH reversing light
36 LH stop light
37 RH stop light
38 High level stop light

Diagram 3

H33632

Side, tail, no. plate & headlights

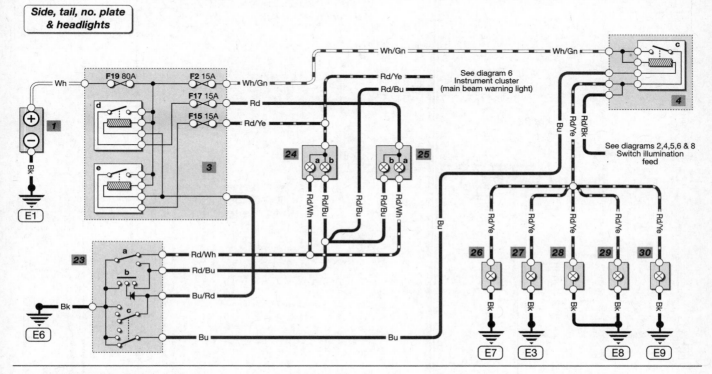

Stop & reversing lights

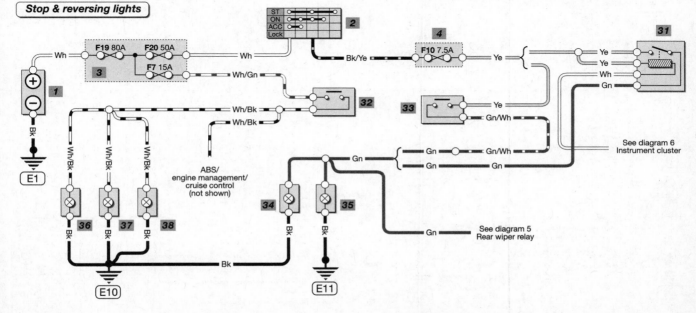

Wire colours

Bk	Black	**Rd**	Red
Wh	White	**Pk**	Pink
Bu	Blue	**Gr**	Grey
Gn	Green	**Bn**	Brown
Ye	Yellow	**Lt.Gn**	Light green
Or	Orange	**Lt.Bu**	Light blue

Key to items

1 Battery
2 Ignition switch
3 Engine fusebox
4 Passenger fusebox
  c = tail light relay
  d = multiplex control unit
23 Multifunction switch
  c = side/headlight
  d = rear foglight
  e = front foglight
  f = indicator

40 Front foglight relay
41 Multiplex control unit
42 LH front foglight
43 RH front foglight
44 Rear foglight
45 Hazard warning switch
46 Direction indicator flasher relay
47 LH rear direction indicator
48 LH indicator side repeater
49 LH front direction indicator
50 RH rear direction indicator

51 RH indicator side repeater
52 RH front direction indicator
53 Front interior map reading lights
54 Rear interior light
55 Luggage compartment light
56 Luggage compartment light switch
57 Glove box light/switch

Diagram 4

H33633

Fog lights

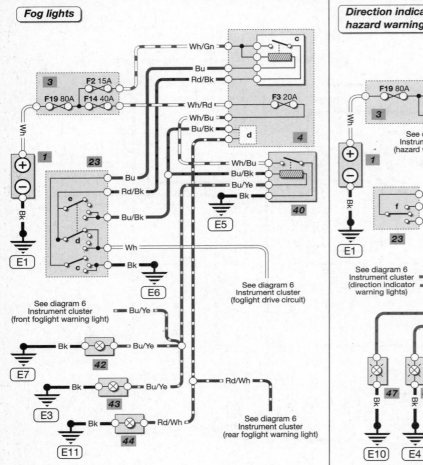

Direction indicators & hazard warning lights

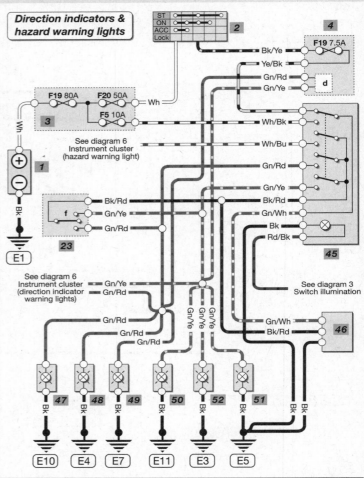

Interior lighting

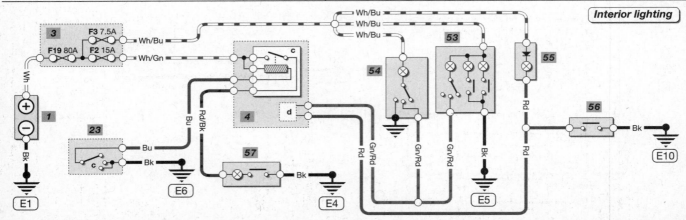

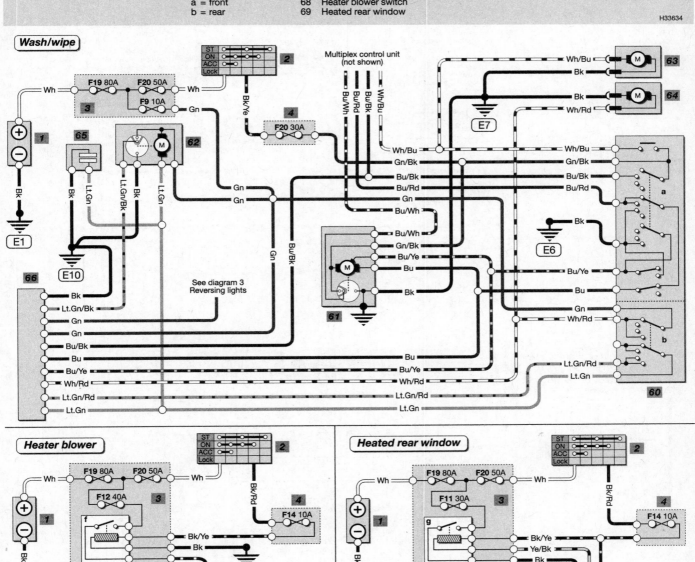
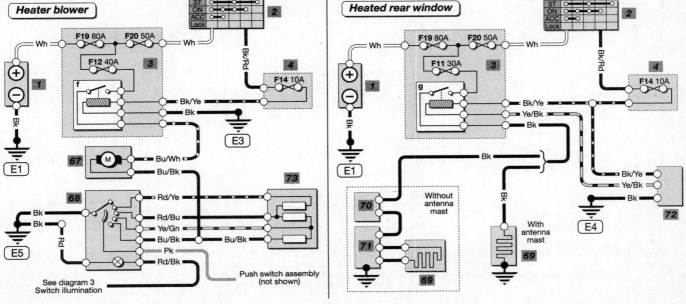

Wire colours

Bk	Black	Rd	Red
Wh	White	Pk	Pink
Bu	Blue	Gr	Grey
Gn	Green	Bn	Brown
Ye	Yellow	Lt.Gn	Light green
Or	Orange	Lt.Bu	Light blue

Key to items

1 = Battery
2 = Ignition switch
3 = Engine fusebox
4 = Passenger fusebox
d = multiplex control unit
75 Instrument cluster
a = control unit
b = speedometer
c = tachometer
d = fuel gauge
e = coolant temp. gauge
f = drive circuit
g = power circuit
h = odo/trip/temp. display
i = LCD backlight
j = odo/trip/temp. power circuit
k = alarm sounder
l = seatbelt warning
m = brake system warning

n = door ajar warning
o = tailgate open warning
p = alternator warning
q = low fuel warning
r = maintenance warning
s = ABS indicator circuit
t = SRS indicator circuit
u = cruise control warning
v = cruise control warning
w = hazard warning indicator
x = side airbag warning
y = ABS warning
z = SRS warning
a1 = alarm warning
b1 = A/T 'D' warning
c1 = A/T 'D3' warning
d1 = A/T '2' warning
e1 = A/T '1' warning
f1 = A/T 'P' warning

g1 = A/T 'R' warning
h1 = A/T 'N' warning
i1 = main beam warning
j1 = trip/reset switch
k1 = dimmer circuit
l1 = instrument illumination
m1 = rear foglight warning
n1 = front foglight warning
o1 = LH indicator warning
p1 = RH indicator warning
q1 = multifunction warning
r1 = low oil pressure warning
s1 = EPS warning
76 Vehicle speed sensor
77 Fuel gauge sender unit
78 Outside air temperature sensor
79 Transmission range switch
80 Oil pressure switch

Diagram 6

H33635

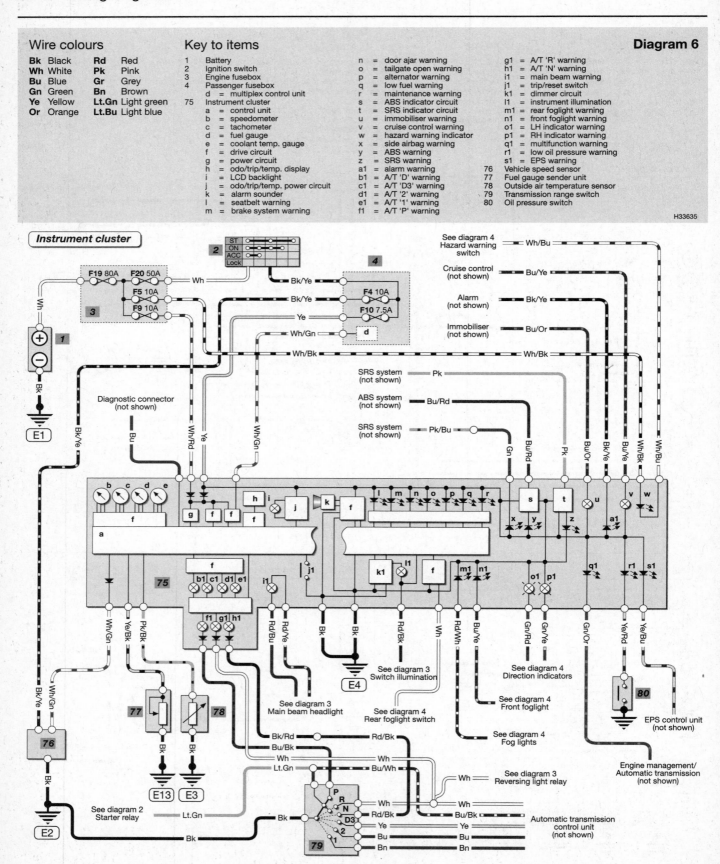

Diagram 7

Wire colours

Bk	Black	Rd	Red
Wh	White	Pk	Pink
Bu	Blue	Gr	Grey
Gn	Green	Bn	Brown
Ye	Yellow	Lt.Gn	Light green
Or	Orange	Lt.Bu	Light blue

Key to items

1 Battery
2 Ignition switch
3 Engine fusebox
4 Passenger fusebox
   d = multiplex control unit
85 Remote receiver unit
86 Driver's locking control unit
87 Driver's door lock
88 LH front locking control unit
89 LH front door lock

90 LH rear locking control unit
91 LH rear door lock
92 RH rear locking control unit
93 RH rear door lock
94 Driver's door switch
95 LH front door switch
96 LH rear door switch
97 RH rear door switch
98 Driver's door key switch
99 LH front door key switch

100 Tailgate key switch
101 Diode
102 Driver's door lock switch
103 LH front door lock switch
104 LH rear door lock switch
105 RH rear door lock switch
106 Tailgate lock switch
107 Test connector

H33636

Central locking

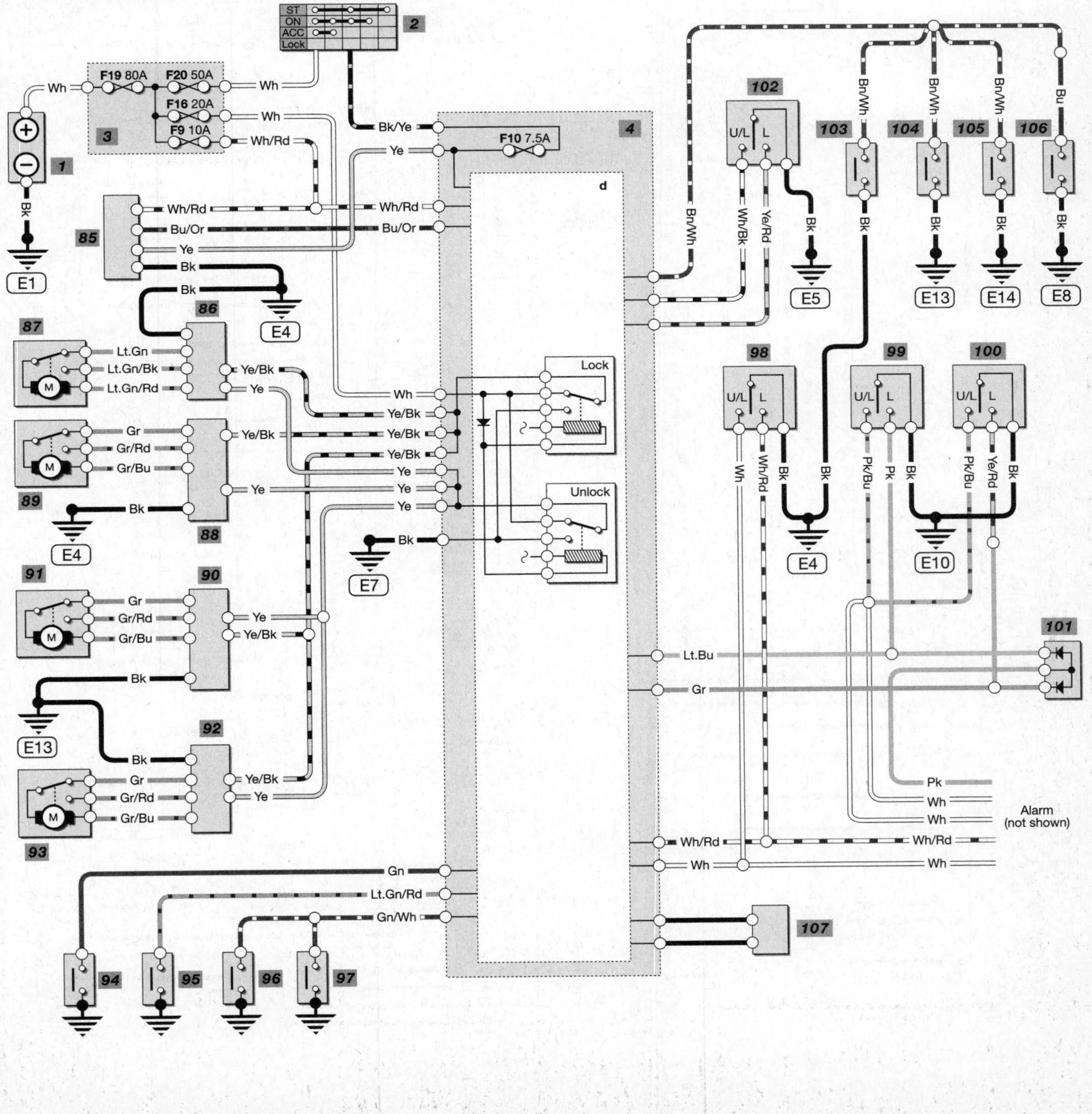

Wire colours

Bk	Black	Rd	Red
Wh	White	Pk	Pink
Bu	Blue	Gr	Grey
Gn	Green	Bn	Brown
Ye	Yellow	Lt.Gn	Light green
Or	Orange	Lt.Bu	Light blue

Key to items

1 Battery
2 Ignition switch
3 Engine fusebox
4 Passenger fusebox
  e = electric window relay
110 Driver's window motor
111 LH front window motor
112 LH rear window motor
113 RH rear window motor

114 Driver's door switch
  a = illumination
  b = driver's switch
  c = LH front door switch
  d = LH rear door switch
  e = RH rear door switch
  f = main switch
115 LH front window switch
116 LH rear window switch

117 RH rear window switch
118 Mirror control switch
119 LH mirror assembly
120 RH mirror assembly
121 Audio unit
122 LH front speaker
123 RH front speaker
124 LH rear speaker
125 RH rear speaker

Diagram 8

H33637

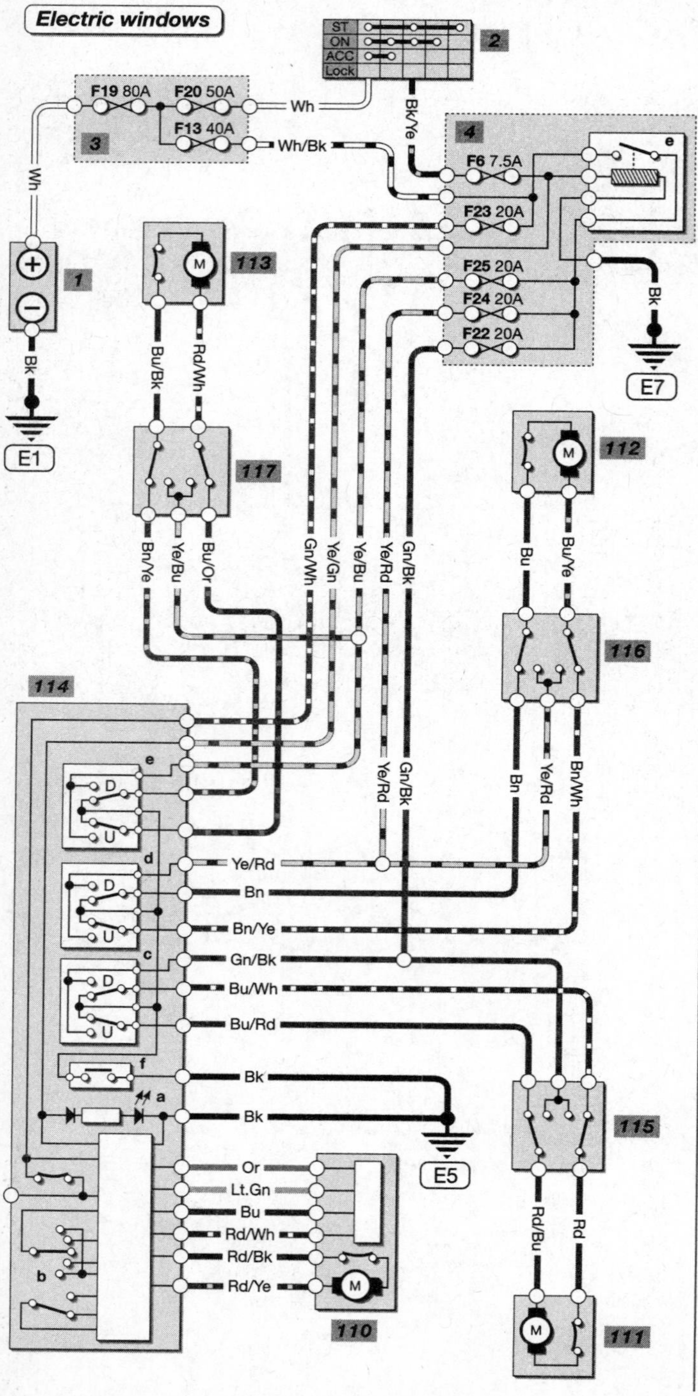

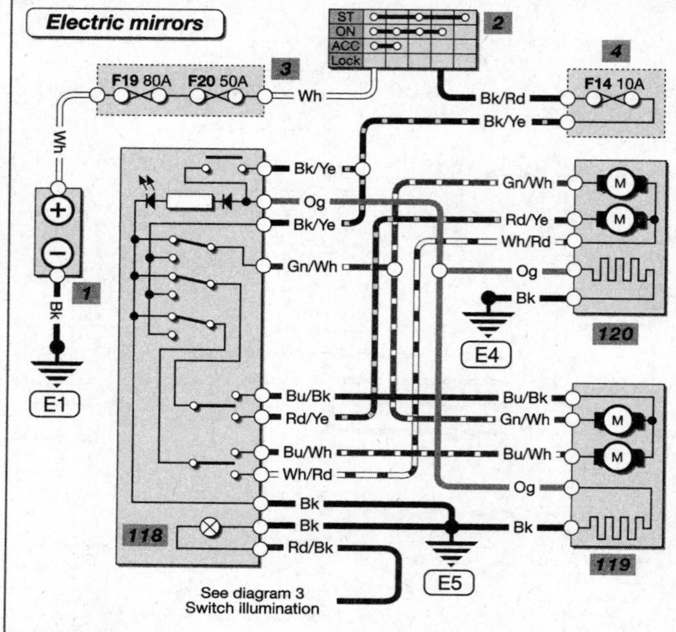

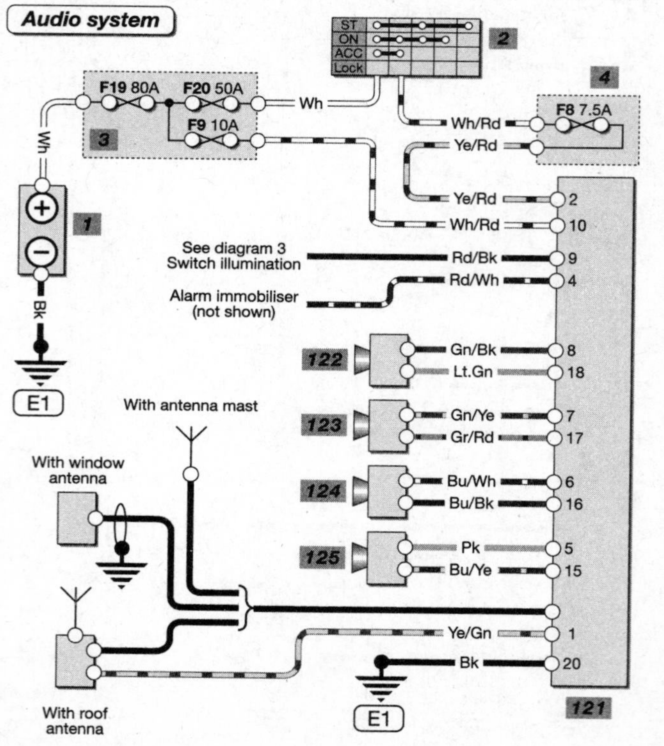

Electric windows

Electric mirrors

Audio system

Dimensions and weights

Note: *All figures are approximate, and vary according to model. Refer to manufacturer's data for exact figures*

Dimensions

Overall length:
  3-door. . . . . 4140 mm
  5-door. . . . . 4285 mm
Overall width. . . . . 1695 mm
Overall height – at kerb weight (excluding roof aerial):
  3-door:
    Except Sport. . . . . 1440 mm
    Sport. . . . . 1430 mm
  5-door. . . . . 1495 mm

Weights

	3-door models	5-door models
Kerb weight:		
Petrol engine:		
Manual transmission.	1096 to 1208 kg	1125 to 1274 kg
Automatic transmission	1123 to 1208 kg	1160 to 1230 kg
Diesel engine	1261 to 1312 kg	1288 to 1323 kg
Towing weight:	**Braked**	**Unbraked**
Manual transmission.	1000 kg	500 kg
Automatic transmission:		
With optional fluid cooler	1000 kg	500 kg
Without optional fluid cooler.	500 kg	500 kg

Length (distance)

Inches (in)	x 25.4	= Millimetres (mm)	x 0.0394	=	Inches (in)
Feet (ft)	x 0.305	= Metres (m)	x 3.281	=	Feet (ft)
Miles	x 1.609	= Kilometres (km)	x 0.621	=	Miles

Volume (capacity)

Cubic inches (cu in; in³)	x 16.387	= Cubic centimetres (cc; cm³)	x 0.061	=	Cubic inches (cu in; in³)
Imperial pints (Imp pt)	x 0.568	= Litres (l)	x 1.76	=	Imperial pints (Imp pt)
Imperial quarts (Imp qt)	x 1.137	= Litres (l)	x 0.88	=	Imperial quarts (Imp qt)
Imperial quarts (Imp qt)	x 1.201	= US quarts (US qt)	x 0.833	=	Imperial quarts (Imp qt)
US quarts (US qt)	x 0.946	= Litres (l)	x 1.057	=	US quarts (US qt)
Imperial gallons (Imp gal)	x 4.546	= Litres (l)	x 0.22	=	Imperial gallons (Imp gal)
Imperial gallons (Imp gal)	x 1.201	= US gallons (US gal)	x 0.833	=	Imperial gallons (Imp gal)
US gallons (US gal)	x 3.785	= Litres (l)	x 0.264	=	US gallons (US gal)

Mass (weight)

Ounces (oz)	x 28.35	= Grams (g)	x 0.035	=	Ounces (oz)
Pounds (lb)	x 0.454	= Kilograms (kg)	x 2.205	=	Pounds (lb)

Force

Ounces-force (ozf; oz)	x 0.278	= Newtons (N)	x 3.6	=	Ounces-force (ozf; oz)
Pounds-force (lbf; lb)	x 4.448	= Newtons (N)	x 0.225	=	Pounds-force (lbf; lb)
Newtons (N)	x 0.1	= Kilograms-force (kgf; kg)	x 9.81	=	Newtons (N)

Pressure

Pounds-force per square inch (psi; lbf/in²; lb/in²)	x 0.070	= Kilograms-force per square centimetre (kgf/cm²; kg/cm²)	x 14.223	=	Pounds-force per square inch (psi; lbf/in²; lb/in²)
Pounds-force per square inch (psi; lbf/in²; lb/in²)	x 0.068	= Atmospheres (atm)	x 14.696	=	Pounds-force per square inch (psi; lbf/in²; lb/in²)
Pounds-force per square inch (psi; lbf/in²; lb/in²)	x 0.069	= Bars	x 14.5	=	Pounds-force per square inch (psi; lbf/in²; lb/in²)
Pounds-force per square inch (psi; lbf/in²; lb/in²)	x 6.895	= Kilopascals (kPa)	x 0.145	=	Pounds-force per square inch (psi; lbf/in²; lb/in²)
Kilopascals (kPa)	x 0.01	= Kilograms-force per square centimetre (kgf/cm²; kg/cm²)	x 98.1	=	Kilopascals (kPa)
Millibar (mbar)	x 100	= Pascals (Pa)	x 0.01	=	Millibar (mbar)
Millibar (mbar)	x 0.0145	= Pounds-force per square inch (psi; lbf/in²; lb/in²)	x 68.947	=	Millibar (mbar)
Millibar (mbar)	x 0.75	= Millimetres of mercury (mmHg)	x 1.333	=	Millibar (mbar)
Millibar (mbar)	x 0.401	= Inches of water (inH₂O)	x 2.491	=	Millibar (mbar)
Millimetres of mercury (mmHg)	x 0.535	= Inches of water (inH₂O)	x 1.868	=	Millimetres of mercury (mmHg)
Inches of water (inH₂O)	x 0.036	= Pounds-force per square inch (psi; lbf/in²; lb/in²)	x 27.68	=	Inches of water (inH₂O)

Torque (moment of force)

Pounds-force inches (lbf in; lb in)	x 1.152	= Kilograms-force centimetre (kgf cm; kg cm)	x 0.868	=	Pounds-force inches (lbf in; lb in)
Pounds-force inches (lbf in; lb in)	x 0.113	= Newton metres (Nm)	x 8.85	=	Pounds-force inches (lbf in; lb in)
Pounds-force inches (lbf in; lb in)	x 0.083	= Pounds-force feet (lbf ft; lb ft)	x 12	=	Pounds-force inches (lbf in; lb in)
Pounds-force feet (lbf ft; lb ft)	x 0.138	= Kilograms-force metres (kgf m; kg m)	x 7.233	=	Pounds-force feet (lbf ft; lb ft)
Pounds-force feet (lbf ft; lb ft)	x 1.356	= Newton metres (Nm)	x 0.738	=	Pounds-force feet (lbf ft; lb ft)
Newton metres (Nm)	x 0.102	= Kilograms-force metres (kgf m; kg m)	x 9.804	=	Newton metres (Nm)

Power

Horsepower (hp)	x 745.7	= Watts (W)	x 0.0013	=	Horsepower (hp)

Velocity (speed)

Miles per hour (miles/hr; mph)	x 1.609	= Kilometres per hour (km/hr; kph)	x 0.621	=	Miles per hour (miles/hr; mph)

Fuel consumption*

Miles per gallon, Imperial (mpg)	x 0.354	= Kilometres per litre (km/l)	x 2.825	=	Miles per gallon, Imperial (mpg)
Miles per gallon, US (mpg)	x 0.425	= Kilometres per litre (km/l)	x 2.352	=	Miles per gallon, US (mpg)

Temperature

Degrees Fahrenheit = (°C x 1.8) + 32

Degrees Celsius (Degrees Centigrade; °C) = (°F - 32) x 0.56

It is common practice to convert from miles per gallon (mpg) to litres/100 kilometres (l/100km), where mpg x l/100 km = 282

Spare parts are available from many sources, including maker's appointed garages, accessory shops, and motor factors. To be sure of obtaining the correct parts, it will sometimes be necessary to quote the vehicle identification number (see *Vehicle identification*). If possible, it can also be useful to take the old parts along for positive identification. Items such as starter motors and alternators may be available under a service exchange scheme – any parts returned should always be clean.

Our advice regarding spare part sources is as follows.

Officially-appointed garages

This is the best source of parts which are peculiar to your car, and which are not otherwise generally available (eg, badges, interior trim, certain body panels, etc). It is also the only place at which you should buy parts if the car is still under warranty.

Accessory shops

These are very good places to buy materials and components needed for the maintenance of your car (oil, air and fuel filters, light bulbs, drivebelts, greases, brake pads, touch-up paint, etc). Components of this nature sold by a reputable shop are of the same standard as those used by the car manufacturer.

Besides components, these shops also sell tools and general accessories, usually have convenient opening hours, charge lower prices, and can often be found close to home. Some accessory shops have parts counters where components needed for almost any repair job can be purchased or ordered.

Motor factors

Good factors will stock all the more important components which wear out comparatively quickly, and can sometimes supply individual components needed for the overhaul of a larger assembly (eg, brake seals and hydraulic parts, bearing shells, pistons, valves). They may also handle work such as cylinder block reboring, crankshaft regrinding, etc.

Tyre and exhaust specialists

These outlets may be independent, or members of a local or national chain. They frequently offer competitive prices when compared with a main dealer or local garage, but it will pay to obtain several quotes before making a decision. When researching prices, also ask what 'extras' may be added – for instance fitting a new valve and balancing the wheel are both commonly charged on top of the price of a new tyre.

Other sources

Beware of parts or materials obtained from market stalls, car boot sales or similar outlets. Such items are not invariably sub-standard, but there is little chance of compensation if they do prove unsatisfactory. In the case of safety-critical components such as brake pads, there is the risk not only of financial loss, but also of an accident causing injury or death.

Second-hand components or assemblies obtained from a car breaker can be a good buy in some circumstances, but his sort of purchase is best made by the experienced DIY mechanic.

Jacking and vehicle support

The jack supplied with the car's tool kit should only be used for changing the roadwheels – see *Wheel changing* at the front of this book. When carrying out any other kind of work, raise the car using a hydraulic (or 'trolley') jack, and always supplement the jack with axle stands positioned under the jacking/support points. If the roadwheels do not have to be removed, consider using wheel ramps – if wished, these can be placed under the wheels once the car has been raised using a hydraulic jack, and then lowered onto the ramps so that it is resting on its wheels.

Only ever jack the car up on a solid, level surface. If there is even a slight slope, take great care that the car cannot move as the wheels are lifted off the ground. Jacking up on an uneven or gravelled surface is not recommended, as the weight of the car will not be evenly distributed, and the jack may slip as the car is raised.

As far as possible, do not leave the car unattended once it has been raised, particularly if children are playing nearby.

Before jacking up the front of the car, ensure

that the handbrake is firmly applied – it is also advisable to chock behind the rear wheels. Place the jack head under the front jacking points on the door sill (these are indicated by an arrow marking) **(see illustration)**. If the vehicle jack is not being used, place a block of wood between the jack head and the sill to prevent damage. Honda also suggest using the front centre-point on the front subframe as a support point – in fact, if care is taken, most places on the front subframe make an acceptable support point **(see illustration)**. Alternatively, there are square-section chassis rails on the floorpan, which should make adequate support points **(see illustration)**. Always place a flat piece of wood on the jack head, to spread the load and prevent underbody damage.

To raise the rear of the car, chock the front wheels and engage a gear (or select P). Use the two rear jacking points on the door sill, with a block of wood to prevent damage. Rear support points are less easy to find – the rear axle must not be used, and there are brake and fuel pipes to avoid also. There is a support point inboard of the sill jacking points, just in

front of the fuel tank which can be used, but care should be taken, as the 'target area' is quite small **(see illustration)**. Honda provide a support point in the centre of the car, just inside the bottom edge of the rear bumper – any jack used here must be substantial, as the weight of the whole rear end is being lifted (there is also a danger of the car tipping sideways). Also, the bottom surface of this central jacking point is not flat – the rear towing eye is incorporated into it – so care must be taken when positioning the jack head **(see illustration)**. The only alternative is to jack up on the rear sill points, and place axle stands as close to these points as possible.

To raise the side of the car, prepare the car as described for front AND rear lifting. Place the jack head under the appropriate points.

Do not jack the car under any other part of the sill, sump, floor pan, or directly under any of the steering or suspension components.

Never work under, around, or near a raised car, unless it is adequately supported on stands. Do not rely on a jack alone, as even a hydraulic jack could fail under load.

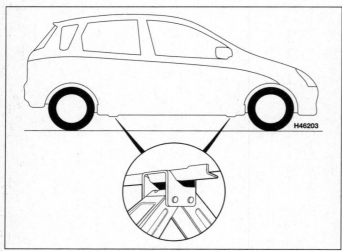

Door sill jacking points

The raised boss at the front of the subframe is a jacking point

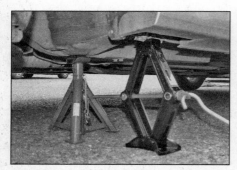

Using the vehicle jack with an axle stand on the chassis rail

Using the vehicle jack and a rear support point

The rear central jacking point must be used with care

Several systems fitted to the car require battery power to be available at all times, either to ensure their continued operation (such as the clock), or to maintain electronic memory settings which would otherwise be erased. Whenever the battery is to be disconnected, first note the following points, to ensure there are no unforeseen consequences:

a) *First, on any car with central door locking, it is a wise precaution to remove the key from the ignition, and to keep it with you, so that it does not get locked in if the central locking engages when the battery is reconnected.*

b) *During normal operation, the car's engine control module (ECM) learns and stores idling and other engine operating values in its memory. Whenever the battery is disconnected, this information is lost, and has to be re-learned. The ECM does this by itself, but until then, there may be surging, hesitation, erratic idle and a generally inferior level of performance. To allow the ECM to re-learn these values, start the engine and let it run as close to idle speed as possible until it reaches* its normal operating temperature, then run it for approximately two minutes at 1200 rpm. Next, drive the car as far as necessary – approximately 5 miles of varied driving conditions is usually sufficient – to complete the re-learning process.

c) *If the battery is disconnected while the alarm system is armed or activated, the alarm will remain in the same state when the battery is reconnected. The same applies to the engine immobiliser system. In some cases, the alarm may sound on reconnecting the battery – have the remote control ready to disarm the system.*

d) *If work is being carried out on the car's airbag or seat belt tensioner systems, the battery should be reconnected last – ie, **after** all the airbag and belt tensioner wiring has been reconnected.*

e) *Where electric windows with 'one-touch' or 'auto' operation are fitted, this function may not work correctly until each window has been reset. This is done by fully opening the window, keeping the button* pressed for a few seconds after opening so the system can 'learn' the fully-open position. Close the window, again keeping the button pressed for a second or two.

Devices known as 'memory-savers' or 'code-savers' can be used to avoid some of the above problems. Precise details of use vary according to the device used. Typically, it is plugged into the cigar lighter socket, and is connected by its own wiring to a spare battery; the car's battery is then disconnected from the electrical system, leaving the memory-saver to pass sufficient current to maintain audio unit security codes and other memory values, and also to run permanently-live circuits such as the clock.

⚠ **Warning: Some of these devices allow a considerable amount of current to pass, which can mean that many of the car's systems are still operational when the main battery is disconnected. If a 'memory-saver' is used, ensure that the circuit concerned is actually 'dead' before carrying out any work on it!**

Whenever servicing, repair or overhaul work is carried out on the car or its components, observe the following procedures and instructions. This will assist in carrying out the operation efficiently and to a professional standard of workmanship.

Joint mating faces and gaskets

When separating components at their mating faces, never insert screwdrivers or similar implements into the joint between the faces in order to prise them apart. This can cause severe damage which results in oil leaks, coolant leaks, etc upon reassembly. Separation is usually achieved by tapping along the joint with a soft-faced hammer in order to break the seal. However, note that this method may not be suitable where dowels are used for component location.

Where a gasket is used between the mating faces of two components, a new one must be fitted on reassembly; fit it dry unless otherwise stated in the repair procedure. Make sure that the mating faces are clean and dry, with all traces of old gasket removed. When cleaning a joint face, use a tool which is unlikely to score or damage the face, and remove any burrs or nicks with an oilstone or fine file.

Make sure that tapped holes are cleaned with a pipe cleaner, and keep them free of jointing compound, if this is being used, unless specifically instructed otherwise.

Ensure that all orifices, channels or pipes are clear, and blow through them, preferably using compressed air.

Oil seals

Oil seals can be removed by levering them out with a wide flat-bladed screwdriver or similar implement. Alternatively, a number of self-tapping screws may be screwed into the seal, and these used as a purchase for pliers or some similar device in order to pull the seal free.

Whenever an oil seal is removed from its working location, either individually or as part of an assembly, it should be renewed.

The very fine sealing lip of the seal is easily damaged, and will not seal if the surface it contacts is not completely clean and free from scratches, nicks or grooves. If the original sealing surface of the component cannot be restored, and the manufacturer has not made provision for slight relocation of the seal relative to the sealing surface, the component should be renewed.

Protect the lips of the seal from any surface which may damage them in the course of fitting. Use tape or a conical sleeve where possible. Lubricate the seal lips with oil before fitting and, on dual-lipped seals, fill the space between the lips with grease.

Unless otherwise stated, oil seals must be fitted with their sealing lips toward the lubricant to be sealed.

Use a tubular drift or block of wood of the appropriate size to install the seal and, if the seal housing is shouldered, drive the seal down to the shoulder. If the seal housing is unshouldered, the seal should be fitted with its face flush with the housing top face (unless otherwise instructed).

Screw threads and fastenings

Seized nuts, bolts and screws are quite a common occurrence where corrosion has set in, and the use of penetrating oil or releasing fluid will often overcome this problem if the offending item is soaked for a while before attempting to release it. The use of an impact driver may also provide a means of releasing such stubborn fastening devices, when used in conjunction with the appropriate screwdriver bit or socket. If none of these methods works, it may be necessary to resort to the careful application of heat, or the use of a hacksaw or nut splitter device.

Studs are usually removed by locking two nuts together on the threaded part, and then using a spanner on the lower nut to unscrew the stud. Studs or bolts which have broken off below the surface of the component in which they are mounted can sometimes be removed using a stud extractor. Always ensure that a blind tapped hole is completely free from oil, grease, water or other fluid before installing the bolt or stud. Failure to do this could cause the housing to crack due to the hydraulic action of the bolt or stud as it is screwed in.

When tightening a castellated nut to accept a split pin, tighten the nut to the specified torque, where applicable, and then tighten further to the next split pin hole. Never slacken the nut to align the split pin hole, unless stated in the repair procedure.

When checking or retightening a nut or bolt to a specified torque setting, slacken the nut or bolt by a quarter of a turn, and then retighten to the specified setting. However, this should not be attempted where angular tightening has been used.

For some screw fastenings, notably cylinder head bolts or nuts, torque wrench settings are no longer specified for the latter stages of tightening, "angle-tightening" being called up instead. Typically, a fairly low torque wrench setting will be applied to the bolts/nuts in the correct sequence, followed by one or more stages of tightening through specified angles.

Locknuts, locktabs and washers

Any fastening which will rotate against a component or housing during tightening should always have a washer between it and the relevant component or housing.

Spring or split washers should always be renewed when they are used to lock a critical component such as a big-end bearing retaining bolt or nut. Locktabs which are folded over to retain a nut or bolt should always be renewed.

Self-locking nuts can be re-used in non-critical areas, providing resistance can be felt when the locking portion passes over the bolt or stud thread. However, it should be noted that self-locking stiffnuts tend to lose their effectiveness after long periods of use, and should then be renewed as a matter of course.

Split pins must always be replaced with new ones of the correct size for the hole.

When thread-locking compound is found on the threads of a fastener which is to be re-used, it should be cleaned off with a wire brush and solvent, and fresh compound applied on reassembly.

Special tools

Some repair procedures in this manual entail the use of special tools such as a press, two or three-legged pullers, spring compressors, etc. Wherever possible, suitable readily-available alternatives to the manufacturer's special tools are described, and are shown in use. In some instances, where no alternative is possible, it has been necessary to resort to the use of a manufacturer's tool, and this has been done for reasons of safety as well as the efficient completion of the repair operation. Unless you are highly-skilled and have a thorough understanding of the procedures described, never attempt to bypass the use of any special tool when the procedure described specifies its use. Not only is there a very great risk of personal injury, but expensive damage could be caused to the components involved.

Environmental considerations

When disposing of used engine oil, brake fluid, antifreeze, etc, give due consideration to any detrimental environmental effects. Do not, for instance, pour any of the above liquids down drains into the general sewage system, or onto the ground to soak away. Many local council refuse tips provide a facility for waste oil disposal, as do some garages. If none of these facilities are available, consult your local Environmental Health Department, or the National Rivers Authority, for further advice.

With the universal tightening-up of legislation regarding the emission of environmentally-harmful substances from motor vehicles, most vehicles have tamperproof devices fitted to the main adjustment points of the fuel system. These devices are primarily designed to prevent unqualified persons from adjusting the fuel/air mixture, with the chance of a consequent increase in toxic emissions. If such devices are found during servicing or overhaul, they should, wherever possible, be renewed or refitted in accordance with the manufacturer's requirements or current legislation.

OIL CARE
FOLLOW THE CODE

OIL BANK LINE
0800 66 33 66
www.oilbankline.org.uk

Note: It is antisocial and illegal to dump oil down the drain. To find the location of your local oil recycling bank, call this number free.

Modifications are a continuing and unpublicised process in vehicle manufacture, quite apart from major model changes. Spare parts manuals and lists are compiled upon a numerical basis, the individual vehicle identification numbers being essential to correct identification of the component concerned.

When ordering spare parts, always give as much information as possible. Quote the car model, year of manufacture, body and engine numbers as appropriate.

The *vehicle identification plate* is located under the bonnet, on the left-hand front suspension strut mounting (left as seen from the driver's seat) **(see illustration)**. In addition to many other details, it carries the Vehicle Identification Number (VIN), maximum vehicle weight information, and codes for interior trim and body colours.

The *Vehicle Identification Number (VIN)* is given on the vehicle identification plate. It is also stamped into the bulkhead at the rear of the engine compartment, and appears on a tag on the left-hand side of the facia, so that it can be seen through the bottom left-hand corner of the windscreen **(see illustrations)**.

The *engine number* is stamped on the cylinder block/crankcase, just below the cylinder head. On petrol engines, it is found at the transmission end of the block, next to the exhaust manifold, with the engine type code on a square area lower down **(see illustrations)**. On diesel engines, it is at the timing belt end, at the rear.

The vehicle identification plate is on the left-hand suspension strut mounting

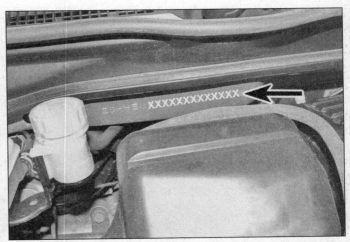

The vehicle identification number (VIN) is stamped into the bulkhead

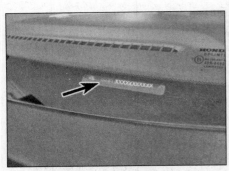

The VIN is also visible through the windscreen

The engine number is stamped vertically, next to the exhaust manifold

The engine type code is on a square area, lower down

Introduction

A selection of good tools is a fundamental requirement for anyone contemplating the maintenance and repair of a motor vehicle. For the owner who does not possess any, their purchase will prove a considerable expense, offsetting some of the savings made by doing-it-yourself. However, provided that the tools purchased meet the relevant national safety standards and are of good quality, they will last for many years and prove an extremely worthwhile investment.

To help the average owner to decide which tools are needed to carry out the various tasks detailed in this manual, we have compiled three lists of tools under the following headings: *Maintenance and minor repair, Repair and overhaul*, and *Special*. Newcomers to practical mechanics should start off with the *Maintenance and minor repair* tool kit, and confine themselves to the simpler jobs around the vehicle. Then, as confidence and experience grow, more difficult tasks can be undertaken, with extra tools being purchased as, and when, they are needed. In this way, a *Maintenance and minor repair* tool kit can be built up into a *Repair and overhaul* tool kit over a considerable period of time, without any major cash outlays. The experienced do-it-yourselfer will have a tool kit good enough for most repair and overhaul procedures, and will add tools from the *Special* category when it is felt that the expense is justified by the amount of use to which these tools will be put.

Maintenance and minor repair tool kit

The tools given in this list should be considered as a minimum requirement if routine maintenance, servicing and minor repair operations are to be undertaken. We recommend the purchase of combination spanners (ring one end, open-ended the other); although more expensive than open-ended ones, they do give the advantages of both types of spanner.

☐ *Combination spanners:*
Metric - 8 to 19 mm inclusive
☐ *Adjustable spanner - 35 mm jaw (approx.)*
☐ *Spark plug spanner (with rubber insert) - petrol models*
☐ *Spark plug gap adjustment tool - petrol models*
☐ *Set of feeler gauges*
☐ *Brake bleed nipple spanner*
☐ *Screwdrivers:*
Flat blade - 100 mm long x 6 mm dia
Cross blade - 100 mm long x 6 mm dia
Torx - various sizes (not all vehicles)
☐ *Combination pliers*
☐ *Hacksaw (junior)*
☐ *Tyre pump*
☐ *Tyre pressure gauge*
☐ *Oil can*
☐ *Oil filter removal tool*
☐ *Fine emery cloth*
☐ *Wire brush (small)*
☐ *Funnel (medium size)*
☐ *Sump drain plug key (not all vehicles)*

Repair and overhaul tool kit

These tools are virtually essential for anyone undertaking any major repairs to a motor vehicle, and are additional to those given in the *Maintenance and minor repair* list. Included in this list is a comprehensive set of sockets. Although these are expensive, they will be found invaluable as they are so versatile - particularly if various drives are included in the set. We recommend the half-inch square-drive type, as this can be used with most proprietary torque wrenches.

The tools in this list will sometimes need to be supplemented by tools from the *Special* list:

☐ *Sockets (or box spanners) to cover range in previous list (including Torx sockets)*
☐ *Reversible ratchet drive (for use with sockets)*
☐ *Extension piece, 250 mm (for use with sockets)*
☐ *Universal joint (for use with sockets)*
☐ *Flexible handle or sliding T "breaker bar" (for use with sockets)*
☐ *Torque wrench (for use with sockets)*
☐ *Self-locking grips*
☐ *Ball pein hammer*
☐ *Soft-faced mallet (plastic or rubber)*
☐ *Screwdrivers:*
Flat blade - long & sturdy, short (chubby), and narrow (electrician's) types
Cross blade – long & sturdy, and short (chubby) types
☐ *Pliers:*
Long-nosed
Side cutters (electrician's)
Circlip (internal and external)
☐ *Cold chisel - 25 mm*
☐ *Scriber*
☐ *Scraper*
☐ *Centre-punch*
☐ *Pin punch*
☐ *Hacksaw*
☐ *Brake hose clamp*
☐ *Brake/clutch bleeding kit*
☐ *Selection of twist drills*
☐ *Steel rule/straight-edge*
☐ *Allen keys (inc. splined/Torx type)*
☐ *Selection of files*
☐ *Wire brush*
☐ *Axle stands*
☐ *Jack (strong trolley or hydraulic type)*
☐ *Light with extension lead*
☐ *Universal electrical multi-meter*

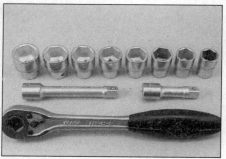

Sockets and reversible ratchet drive

Brake bleeding kit

Torx key, socket and bit

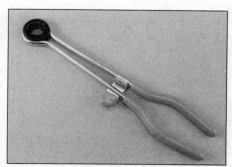

Hose clamp

Angular-tightening gauge

Special tools

The tools in this list are those which are not used regularly, are expensive to buy, or which need to be used in accordance with their manufacturers' instructions. Unless relatively difficult mechanical jobs are undertaken frequently, it will not be economic to buy many of these tools. Where this is the case, you could consider clubbing together with friends (or joining a motorists' club) to make a joint purchase, or borrowing the tools against a deposit from a local garage or tool hire specialist. It is worth noting that many of the larger DIY superstores now carry a large range of special tools for hire at modest rates.

The following list contains only those tools and instruments freely available to the public, and not those special tools produced by the vehicle manufacturer specifically for its dealer network. You will find occasional references to these manufacturers' special tools in the text of this manual. Generally, an alternative method of doing the job without the vehicle manufacturers' special tool is given. However, sometimes there is no alternative to using them. Where this is the case and the relevant tool cannot be bought or borrowed, you will have to entrust the work to a dealer.

- ☐ *Angular-tightening gauge*
- ☐ *Valve spring compressor*
- ☐ *Valve grinding tool*
- ☐ *Piston ring compressor*
- ☐ *Piston ring removal/installation tool*
- ☐ *Cylinder bore hone*
- ☐ *Balljoint separator*
- ☐ *Coil spring compressors (where applicable)*
- ☐ *Two/three-legged hub and bearing puller*
- ☐ *Impact screwdriver*
- ☐ *Micrometer and/or vernier calipers*
- ☐ *Dial gauge*
- ☐ *Stroboscopic timing light*
- ☐ *Dwell angle meter/tachometer*
- ☐ *Fault code reader*
- ☐ *Cylinder compression gauge*
- ☐ *Hand-operated vacuum pump and gauge*
- ☐ *Clutch plate alignment set*
- ☐ *Brake shoe steady spring cup removal tool*
- ☐ *Bush and bearing removal/installation set*
- ☐ *Stud extractors*
- ☐ *Tap and die set*
- ☐ *Lifting tackle*
- ☐ *Trolley jack*

Buying tools

Reputable motor accessory shops and superstores often offer excellent quality tools at discount prices, so it pays to shop around.

Remember, you don't have to buy the most expensive items on the shelf, but it is always advisable to steer clear of the very cheap tools. Beware of 'bargains' offered on market stalls or at car boot sales. There are plenty of good tools around at reasonable prices, but always aim to purchase items which meet the relevant national safety standards. If in doubt, ask the proprietor or manager of the shop for advice before making a purchase.

Care and maintenance of tools

Having purchased a reasonable tool kit, it is necessary to keep the tools in a clean and serviceable condition. After use, always wipe off any dirt, grease and metal particles using a clean, dry cloth, before putting the tools away. Never leave them lying around after they have been used. A simple tool rack on the garage or workshop wall for items such as screwdrivers and pliers is a good idea. Store all normal spanners and sockets in a metal box. Any measuring instruments, gauges, meters, etc, must be carefully stored where they cannot be damaged or become rusty.

Take a little care when tools are used. Hammer heads inevitably become marked, and screwdrivers lose the keen edge on their blades from time to time. A little timely attention with emery cloth or a file will soon restore items like this to a good finish.

Working facilities

Not to be forgotten when discussing tools is the workshop itself. If anything more than routine maintenance is to be carried out, a suitable working area becomes essential.

It is appreciated that many an owner-mechanic is forced by circumstances to remove an engine or similar item without the benefit of a garage or workshop. Having done this, any repairs should always be done under the cover of a roof.

Wherever possible, any dismantling should be done on a clean, flat workbench or table at a suitable working height.

Any workbench needs a vice; one with a jaw opening of 100 mm is suitable for most jobs. As mentioned previously, some clean dry storage space is also required for tools, as well as for any lubricants, cleaning fluids, touch-up paints etc, which become necessary.

Another item which may be required, and which has a much more general usage, is an electric drill with a chuck capacity of at least 8 mm. This, together with a good range of twist drills, is virtually essential for fitting accessories.

Last, but not least, always keep a supply of old newspapers and clean, lint-free rags available, and try to keep any working area as clean as possible.

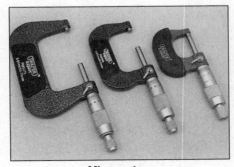

Micrometers

Dial test indicator ("dial gauge")

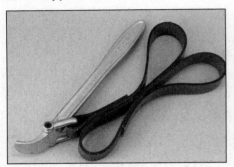

Strap wrench

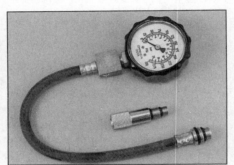

Compression tester

Fault code reader

This is a guide to getting your vehicle through the MOT test. Obviously it will not be possible to examine the vehicle to the same standard as the professional MOT tester. However, working through the following checks will enable you to identify any problem areas before submitting the vehicle for the test.

Where a testable component is in borderline condition, the tester has discretion in deciding whether to pass or fail it. The basis of such discretion is whether the tester would be happy for a close relative or friend to use the vehicle with the component in that condition. If the vehicle presented is clean and evidently well cared for, the tester may be more inclined to pass a borderline component than if the vehicle is scruffy and apparently neglected.

It has only been possible to summarise the test requirements here, based on the regulations in force at the time of printing. Test standards are becoming increasingly stringent, although there are some exemptions for older vehicles.

An assistant will be needed to help carry out some of these checks.

The checks have been sub-divided into four categories, as follows:

1 Checks carried out **FROM THE DRIVER'S SEAT**

2 Checks carried out **WITH THE VEHICLE ON THE GROUND**

3 Checks carried out **WITH THE VEHICLE RAISED AND THE WHEELS FREE TO TURN**

4 Checks carried out on **YOUR VEHICLE'S EXHAUST EMISSION SYSTEM**

1 Checks carried out **FROM THE DRIVER'S SEAT**

Handbrake

☐ Test the operation of the handbrake. Excessive travel (too many clicks) indicates incorrect brake or cable adjustment.
☐ Check that the handbrake cannot be released by tapping the lever sideways. Check the security of the lever mountings.

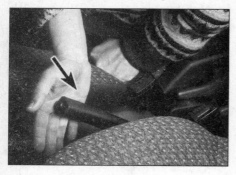

Footbrake

☐ Depress the brake pedal and check that it does not creep down to the floor, indicating a master cylinder fault. Release the pedal, wait a few seconds, then depress it again. If the pedal travels nearly to the floor before firm resistance is felt, brake adjustment or repair is necessary. If the pedal feels spongy, there is air in the hydraulic system which must be removed by bleeding.

☐ Check that the brake pedal is secure and in good condition. Check also for signs of fluid leaks on the pedal, floor or carpets, which would indicate failed seals in the brake master cylinder.
☐ Check the servo unit (when applicable) by operating the brake pedal several times, then keeping the pedal depressed and starting the engine. As the engine starts, the pedal will move down slightly. If not, the vacuum hose or the servo itself may be faulty.

Steering wheel and column

☐ Examine the steering wheel for fractures or looseness of the hub, spokes or rim.
☐ Move the steering wheel from side to side and then up and down. Check that the steering wheel is not loose on the column, indicating wear or a loose retaining nut. Continue moving the steering wheel as before, but also turn it slightly from left to right.
☐ Check that the steering wheel is not loose on the column, and that there is no abnormal

movement of the steering wheel, indicating wear in the column support bearings or couplings.

Windscreen, mirrors and sunvisor

☐ The windscreen must be free of cracks or other significant damage within the driver's field of view. (Small stone chips are acceptable.) Rear view mirrors must be secure, intact, and capable of being adjusted.

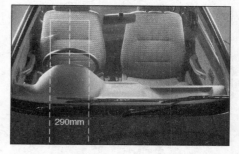

☐ The driver's sunvisor must be capable of being stored in the "up" position.

Seat belts and seats

Note: *The following checks are applicable to all seat belts, front and rear.*

☐ Examine the webbing of all the belts (including rear belts if fitted) for cuts, serious fraying or deterioration. Fasten and unfasten each belt to check the buckles. If applicable, check the retracting mechanism. Check the security of all seat belt mountings accessible from inside the vehicle.

☐ Seat belts with pre-tensioners, once activated, have a "flag" or similar showing on the seat belt stalk. This, in itself, is not a reason for test failure.

☐ The front seats themselves must be securely attached and the backrests must lock in the upright position.

Doors

☐ Both front doors must be able to be opened and closed from outside and inside, and must latch securely when closed.

2 Checks carried out WITH THE VEHICLE ON THE GROUND

Vehicle identification

☐ Number plates must be in good condition, secure and legible, with letters and numbers correctly spaced – spacing at (**A**) should be at least twice that at (**B**).

☐ The VIN plate and/or homologation plate must be legible.

Electrical equipment

☐ Switch on the ignition and check the operation of the horn.

☐ Check the windscreen washers and wipers, examining the wiper blades; renew damaged or perished blades. Also check the operation of the stop-lights.

☐ Check the operation of the sidelights and number plate lights. The lenses and reflectors must be secure, clean and undamaged.

☐ Check the operation and alignment of the headlights. The headlight reflectors must not be tarnished and the lenses must be undamaged.

☐ Switch on the ignition and check the operation of the direction indicators (including the instrument panel tell-tale) and the hazard warning lights. Operation of the sidelights and stop-lights must not affect the indicators - if it does, the cause is usually a bad earth at the rear light cluster.

☐ Check the operation of the rear foglight(s), including the warning light on the instrument panel or in the switch.

☐ The ABS warning light must illuminate in accordance with the manufacturers' design. For most vehicles, the ABS warning light should illuminate when the ignition is switched on, and (if the system is operating properly) extinguish after a few seconds. Refer to the owner's handbook.

Footbrake

☐ Examine the master cylinder, brake pipes and servo unit for leaks, loose mountings, corrosion or other damage.

☐ The fluid reservoir must be secure and the fluid level must be between the upper (**A**) and lower (**B**) markings.

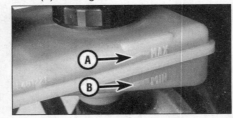

☐ Inspect both front brake flexible hoses for cracks or deterioration of the rubber. Turn the steering from lock to lock, and ensure that the hoses do not contact the wheel, tyre, or any part of the steering or suspension mechanism. With the brake pedal firmly depressed, check the hoses for bulges or leaks under pressure.

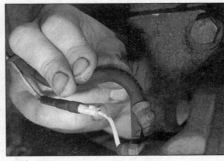

Steering and suspension

☐ Have your assistant turn the steering wheel from side to side slightly, up to the point where the steering gear just begins to transmit this movement to the roadwheels. Check for excessive free play between the steering wheel and the steering gear, indicating wear or insecurity of the steering column joints, the column-to-steering gear coupling, or the steering gear itself.

☐ Have your assistant turn the steering wheel more vigorously in each direction, so that the roadwheels just begin to turn. As this is done, examine all the steering joints, linkages, fittings and attachments. Renew any component that shows signs of wear or damage. On vehicles with power steering, check the security and condition of the steering pump, drivebelt and hoses.

☐ Check that the vehicle is standing level, and at approximately the correct ride height.

Shock absorbers

☐ Depress each corner of the vehicle in turn, then release it. The vehicle should rise and then settle in its normal position. If the vehicle continues to rise and fall, the shock absorber is defective. A shock absorber which has seized will also cause the vehicle to fail.

Exhaust system

☐ Start the engine. With your assistant holding a rag over the tailpipe, check the entire system for leaks. Repair or renew leaking sections.

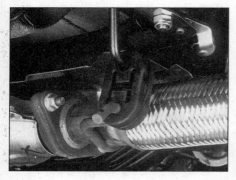

3 Checks carried out **WITH THE VEHICLE RAISED AND THE WHEELS FREE TO TURN**

Jack up the front and rear of the vehicle, and securely support it on axle stands. Position the stands clear of the suspension assemblies. Ensure that the wheels are clear of the ground and that the steering can be turned from lock to lock.

Steering mechanism

☐ Have your assistant turn the steering from lock to lock. Check that the steering turns smoothly, and that no part of the steering mechanism, including a wheel or tyre, fouls any brake hose or pipe or any part of the body structure.
☐ Examine the steering rack rubber gaiters for damage or insecurity of the retaining clips. If power steering is fitted, check for signs of damage or leakage of the fluid hoses, pipes or connections. Also check for excessive stiffness or binding of the steering, a missing split pin or locking device, or severe corrosion of the body structure within 30 cm of any steering component attachment point.

Front and rear suspension and wheel bearings

☐ Starting at the front right-hand side, grasp the roadwheel at the 3 o'clock and 9 o'clock positions and rock gently but firmly. Check for free play or insecurity at the wheel bearings, suspension balljoints, or suspension mountings, pivots and attachments.
☐ Now grasp the wheel at the 12 o'clock and 6 o'clock positions and repeat the previous inspection. Spin the wheel, and check for roughness or tightness of the front wheel bearing.

☐ If excess free play is suspected at a component pivot point, this can be confirmed by using a large screwdriver or similar tool and levering between the mounting and the component attachment. This will confirm whether the wear is in the pivot bush, its retaining bolt, or in the mounting itself (the bolt holes can often become elongated).

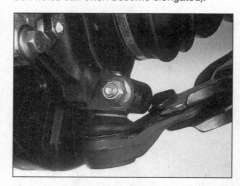

☐ Carry out all the above checks at the other front wheel, and then at both rear wheels.

Springs and shock absorbers

☐ Examine the suspension struts (when applicable) for serious fluid leakage, corrosion, or damage to the casing. Also check the security of the mounting points.
☐ If coil springs are fitted, check that the spring ends locate in their seats, and that the spring is not corroded, cracked or broken.
☐ If leaf springs are fitted, check that all leaves are intact, that the axle is securely attached to each spring, and that there is no deterioration of the spring eye mountings, bushes, and shackles.

☐ The same general checks apply to vehicles fitted with other suspension types, such as torsion bars, hydraulic displacer units, etc. Ensure that all mountings and attachments are secure, that there are no signs of excessive wear, corrosion or damage, and (on hydraulic types) that there are no fluid leaks or damaged pipes.
☐ Inspect the shock absorbers for signs of serious fluid leakage. Check for wear of the mounting bushes or attachments, or damage to the body of the unit.

Driveshafts (fwd vehicles only)

☐ Rotate each front wheel in turn and inspect the constant velocity joint gaiters for splits or damage. Also check that each driveshaft is straight and undamaged.

Braking system

☐ If possible without dismantling, check brake pad wear and disc condition. Ensure that the friction lining material has not worn excessively, (A) and that the discs are not fractured, pitted, scored or badly worn (B).

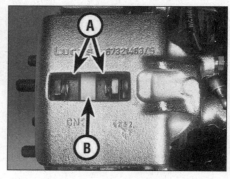

☐ Examine all the rigid brake pipes underneath the vehicle, and the flexible hose(s) at the rear. Look for corrosion, chafing or insecurity of the pipes, and for signs of bulging under pressure, chafing, splits or deterioration of the flexible hoses.
☐ Look for signs of fluid leaks at the brake calipers or on the brake backplates. Repair or renew leaking components.
☐ Slowly spin each wheel, while your assistant depresses and releases the footbrake. Ensure that each brake is operating and does not bind when the pedal is released.

□ Examine the handbrake mechanism, checking for frayed or broken cables, excessive corrosion, or wear or insecurity of the linkage. Check that the mechanism works on each relevant wheel, and releases fully, without binding.

□ It is not possible to test brake efficiency without special equipment, but a road test can be carried out later to check that the vehicle pulls up in a straight line.

Fuel and exhaust systems

□ Inspect the fuel tank (including the filler cap), fuel pipes, hoses and unions. All components must be secure and free from leaks.

□ Examine the exhaust system over its entire length, checking for any damaged, broken or missing mountings, security of the retaining clamps and rust or corrosion.

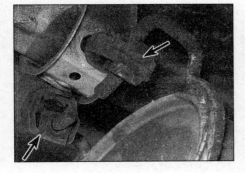

Wheels and tyres

□ Examine the sidewalls and tread area of each tyre in turn. Check for cuts, tears, lumps, bulges, separation of the tread, and exposure of the ply or cord due to wear or damage. Check that the tyre bead is correctly seated on the wheel rim, that the valve is sound and properly seated, and that the wheel is not distorted or damaged.

□ Check that the tyres are of the correct size for the vehicle, that they are of the same size

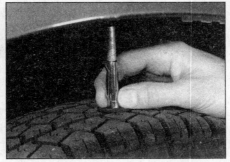

and type on each axle, and that the pressures are correct.

□ Check the tyre tread depth. The legal minimum at the time of writing is 1.6 mm over at least three-quarters of the tread width. Abnormal tread wear may indicate incorrect front wheel alignment.

Body corrosion

□ Check the condition of the entire vehicle structure for signs of corrosion in load-bearing areas. (These include chassis box sections, side sills, cross-members, pillars, and all suspension, steering, braking system and seat belt mountings and anchorages.) Any corrosion which has seriously reduced the thickness of a load-bearing area is likely to cause the vehicle to fail. In this case professional repairs are likely to be needed.

□ Damage or corrosion which causes sharp or otherwise dangerous edges to be exposed will also cause the vehicle to fail.

4 Checks carried out on **YOUR VEHICLE'S EXHAUST EMISSION SYSTEM**

Petrol models

□ The engine should be warmed up, and running well (ignition system in good order, air filter element clean, etc).

□ Before testing, run the engine at around 2500 rpm for 20 seconds. Let the engine drop to idle, and watch for smoke from the exhaust. If the idle speed is too high, or if dense blue or black smoke emerges for more than 5 seconds, the vehicle will fail. Typically, blue smoke signifies oil burning (engine wear); black smoke means unburnt fuel (dirty air cleaner element, or other fuel system fault).

□ An exhaust gas analyser for measuring carbon monoxide (CO) and hydrocarbons (HC) is now needed. If one cannot be hired or borrowed, have a local garage perform the check.

CO emissions (mixture)

□ The MOT tester has access to the CO limits for all vehicles. The CO level is measured at idle speed, and at 'fast idle' (2500 to 3000 rpm). The following limits are given as a general guide:
At idle speed – Less than 0.5% CO
At 'fast idle' – Less than 0.3% CO
Lambda reading – 0.97 to 1.03
□ If the CO level is too high, this may point to poor maintenance, a fuel injection system problem, faulty lambda (oxygen) sensor or catalytic converter. Try an injector cleaning treatment, and check the vehicle's ECU for fault codes.

HC emissions

□ The MOT tester has access to HC limits for all vehicles. The HC level is measured at 'fast idle' (2500 to 3000 rpm). The following limits are given as a general guide:
At 'fast idle' – Less then 200 ppm
□ Excessive HC emissions are typically caused by oil being burnt (worn engine), or by a blocked crankcase ventilation system ('breather'). If the engine oil is old and thin, an oil change may help. If the engine is running badly, check the vehicle's ECU for fault codes.

Diesel models

□ The only emission test for diesel engines is measuring exhaust smoke density, using a calibrated smoke meter. The test involves accelerating the engine at least 3 times to its maximum unloaded speed.

Note: *On engines with a timing belt, it is VITAL that the belt is in good condition before the test is carried out.*

□ With the engine warmed up, it is first purged by running at around 2500 rpm for 20 seconds. A governor check is then carried out, by slowly accelerating the engine to its maximum speed. After this, the smoke meter is connected, and the engine is accelerated quickly to maximum speed three times. If the smoke density is less than the limits given below, the vehicle will pass:
Non-turbo vehicles: 2.5m-1
Turbocharged vehicles: 3.0m-1
□ If excess smoke is produced, try fitting a new air cleaner element, or using an injector cleaning treatment. If the engine is running badly, where applicable, check the vehicle's ECU for fault codes. Also check the vehicle's EGR system, where applicable. At high mileages, the injectors may require professional attention.

Fault finding

Engine

- ☐ Engine fails to rotate when attempting to start
- ☐ Engine rotates, but will not start
- ☐ Engine difficult to start when cold
- ☐ Engine difficult to start when hot
- ☐ Starter motor noisy or excessively-rough in engagement
- ☐ Engine starts, but stops immediately
- ☐ Engine idles erratically
- ☐ Engine misfires at idle speed
- ☐ Engine misfires throughout the driving speed range
- ☐ Engine hesitates on acceleration
- ☐ Engine stalls
- ☐ Engine lacks power
- ☐ Engine backfires
- ☐ Oil pressure warning light illuminated with engine running
- ☐ Engine runs-on after switching off
- ☐ Engine noises

Cooling system

- ☐ Overheating
- ☐ Overcooling
- ☐ External coolant leakage
- ☐ Internal coolant leakage
- ☐ Corrosion

Fuel and exhaust systems

- ☐ Excessive fuel consumption
- ☐ Fuel leakage and/or fuel odour
- ☐ Excessive noise or fumes from exhaust system

Clutch

- ☐ Pedal travels to floor – no pressure or very little resistance
- ☐ Clutch fails to disengage (unable to select gears)
- ☐ Clutch slips (engine speed increases, with no increase in vehicle speed)
- ☐ Judder as clutch is engaged
- ☐ Noise when depressing or releasing clutch pedal

Manual transmission

- ☐ Noisy in neutral with engine running
- ☐ Noisy in one particular gear
- ☐ Difficulty engaging gears
- ☐ Jumps out of gear
- ☐ Vibration
- ☐ Lubricant leaks

Automatic transmission

- ☐ Fluid leakage
- ☐ Transmission fluid brown, or has burned smell
- ☐ General gear selection problems
- ☐ Transmission will not downshift (kickdown) with accelerator pedal fully depressed
- ☐ Engine will not start in any gear, or starts in gears other than Park or Neutral
- ☐ Transmission slips, shifts roughly, is noisy, or has no drive in forward or reverse gears

Driveshafts

- ☐ Vibration when accelerating or decelerating
- ☐ Clicking or knocking noise on turns (at slow speed on full-lock)

Braking system

- ☐ Car pulls to one side under braking
- ☐ Noise (grinding or high-pitched squeal) when brakes applied
- ☐ Excessive brake pedal travel
- ☐ Brake pedal feels spongy when depressed
- ☐ Excessive brake pedal effort required to stop car
- ☐ Judder felt through brake pedal or steering wheel when braking
- ☐ Brakes binding
- ☐ Rear wheels locking under normal braking
- ☐ ABS warning light stays on

Suspension and steering

- ☐ Car pulls to one side
- ☐ Wheel wobble and vibration
- ☐ Excessive pitching and/or rolling around corners, or during braking
- ☐ Wandering or general instability
- ☐ Excessively-stiff steering
- ☐ Excessive play in steering
- ☐ Lack of power assistance
- ☐ Tyre wear excessive

Electrical system

- ☐ Battery will not hold a charge for more than a few days
- ☐ Ignition/no-charge warning light remains illuminated with engine running
- ☐ Ignition/no-charge warning light fails to come on
- ☐ Lights inoperative
- ☐ Instrument readings inaccurate or erratic
- ☐ Horn inoperative, or unsatisfactory in operation
- ☐ Windscreen wipers inoperative, or unsatisfactory in operation
- ☐ Windscreen washers inoperative, or unsatisfactory in operation
- ☐ Electric windows inoperative, or unsatisfactory in operation
- ☐ Central locking system inoperative, or unsatisfactory in operation

Introduction

The car owner who does his or her own maintenance according to the recommended service schedules should not have to use this section of the manual very often. Modern component reliability is such that, provided those items subject to wear or deterioration are inspected or renewed at the specified intervals, sudden failure is comparatively rare. Faults do not usually just happen as a result of sudden failure, but develop over a period of time. Major mechanical failures in particular are usually preceded by characteristic symptoms over hundreds or even thousands of miles. Those components which do occasionally fail without warning are often small and easily carried in the car.

With any fault-finding, the first step is to decide where to begin investigations. Sometimes this is obvious, but on other occasions, a little detective work will be necessary. The owner who makes half a dozen haphazard adjustments or replacements may be successful in curing a fault (or its symptoms), but will be none the wiser if the fault recurs, and ultimately may have spent more time and money than was necessary. A calm and logical approach will be found to be more satisfactory in the long run. Always take into account any warning signs or abnormalities that may have been noticed in the period preceding the fault – power loss, high or low gauge readings, unusual smells, etc – and remember that failure of components such as fuses or spark plugs may only be pointers to some underlying fault.

The pages which follow provide an easy-reference guide to the more common problems which may occur during the operation of the car. These problems and their possible causes are grouped under headings denoting various components or systems, such as Engine, Cooling system, etc. The general Chapter which deals with the problem is also shown in brackets; refer to the relevant part of that Chapter for system-specific information. Whatever the fault, certain basic principles apply. These are as follows:

Verify the fault. This is simply a matter of being sure that you know what the symptoms are before starting work. This is particularly important if you are investigating a fault for someone else, who may not have described it very accurately.

Don't overlook the obvious. For example, if the car won't start, is there fuel in the tank? (Don't take anyone else's word on this particular point, and don't trust the fuel gauge either!) If an electrical fault is indicated, look for loose or broken wires before digging out the test gear.

Cure the disease, not the symptom. Substituting a flat battery with a fully-charged one will get you off the hard shoulder, but if the underlying cause is not attended to, the new battery will go the same way. Similarly, changing oil-fouled spark plugs for a new set will get you moving again, but remember that the reason for the fouling (if it wasn't simply an incorrect grade of plug) will have to be established and corrected.

Don't take anything for granted. Particularly, don't forget that a 'new' component may itself be defective (especially if it's been rattling around in the boot for months), and don't leave components out of a fault diagnosis sequence just because they are new or recently-fitted. When you do finally diagnose a difficult fault, you'll probably realise that all the evidence was there from the start.

Consider what work, if any, has recently been carried out. Many faults arise through careless or hurried work. For instance, if any work has been performed under the bonnet, could some of the wiring have been dislodged or incorrectly routed, or a hose trapped? Have all the fasteners been properly tightened? Were new, genuine parts and new gaskets used? There is often a certain amount of detective work to be done in this case, as an apparently-unrelated task can have far-reaching consequences.

Diesel fault diagnosis

The majority of starting problems on small diesel engines are electrical in origin. The mechanic who is familiar with petrol engines but less so with diesel may be inclined to view the diesel's injectors and pump in the same light as the spark plugs and distributor, but this is generally a mistake.

When investigating complaints of difficult starting for someone else, make sure that the correct starting procedure is understood and is being followed. Some drivers are unaware of the significance of the preheating warning light – many modern engines are sufficiently forgiving for this not to matter in mild weather, but with the onset of winter, problems begin. Glow plugs in particular are often neglected – just one faulty plug will make cold-weather starting very difficult.

As a rule of thumb, if the engine is difficult to start but runs well when it has finally got going, the problem is electrical (battery, starter motor or preheating system). If poor performance is combined with difficult starting, the problem is likely to be in the fuel system. The low-pressure (supply) side of the fuel system should be checked before suspecting the injectors and high-pressure pump. The most common fuel supply problem is air getting into the system, and any pipe from the fuel tank forwards must be scrutinised if air leakage is suspected.

Engine

Engine fails to rotate when attempting to start

- ☐ Battery discharged or faulty (Chapter 5A)
- ☐ Battery terminal connections loose or corroded (see *Weekly checks*)
- ☐ Broken, loose or disconnected wiring in the starting circuit (Chapter 5A)
- ☐ Engine earth strap broken or disconnected (Chapter 5A)
- ☐ Defective starter solenoid or ignition switch (Chapter 5A or 12)
- ☐ Defective starter motor (Chapter 5A)
- ☐ Starter pinion or flywheel ring gear teeth loose or broken (Chapter 2 or 5A)
- ☐ Engine suffering 'hydraulic lock' (eg, from water ingested after driving through a flood, or from a serious internal coolant leak) – consult a Honda dealer for advice
- ☐ Automatic transmission not in position P or N (Chapter 7B)

Engine rotates, but will not start

- ☐ Fuel shut-off (inertia) switch energised – after impact or shock (Chapter 4A or 4B)
- ☐ Fuel tank empty
- ☐ Battery discharged (engine rotates slowly) (Chapter 5A)
- ☐ Battery terminal connections loose or corroded (see *Weekly checks*)
- ☐ Ignition components damp or damaged – petrol models (Chapter 1A or 5B)
- ☐ Immobiliser fault, or 'uncoded' ignition key being used (Chapter 12 or *Roadside repairs*)

- ☐ Crankshaft sensor fault (Chapter 4A or 4B)
- ☐ Broken, loose or disconnected wiring in the ignition circuit – petrol models (Chapter 1A or 5B)
- ☐ Worn, faulty or incorrectly-gapped spark plugs – petrol models (Chapter 1A)
- ☐ Preheating system faulty – diesel models (Chapter 5A)
- ☐ Fuel injection system fault (Chapter 4A or 4B)
- ☐ Air in fuel system – diesel models (Chapter 4B)
- ☐ Major mechanical failure (eg, timing belt snapped) (Chapter 2A, 2B or 2C)

Engine difficult to start when cold

- ☐ Battery discharged (Chapter 5A)
- ☐ Battery terminal connections loose or corroded (see *Weekly checks*)
- ☐ Worn, faulty or incorrectly-gapped spark plugs – petrol models (Chapter 1A)
- ☐ Other ignition system fault – petrol models (Chapter 1A or 5B)
- ☐ Preheating system faulty – diesel models (Chapter 5A)
- ☐ Fuel injection system fault (Chapter 4A or 4B)
- ☐ Wrong grade of engine oil used (*Weekly checks*, Chapter 1A or 1B)
- ☐ Low cylinder compressions (Chapter 2A, 2B or 2C)

Engine difficult to start when hot

- ☐ Air filter element dirty or clogged (Chapter 1A or 1B)
- ☐ Fuel injection system fault (Chapter 4A or 4B)
- ☐ Low cylinder compressions (Chapter 2A, 2B or 2C)

Engine (continued)

Starter motor noisy or excessively-rough in engagement

☐ Starter pinion or flywheel ring gear teeth loose or broken (Chapter 2 or 5A)
☐ Starter motor mounting bolts loose or missing (Chapter 5A)
☐ Starter motor internal components worn or damaged (Chapter 5A)

Engine starts, but stops immediately

☐ Low fuel pressure – or low fuel level in tank (Chapter 4A or 4B)
☐ Loose or faulty electrical connections in the ignition circuit – petrol models (Chapter 1A or 5B)
☐ Vacuum leak at the throttle body or inlet manifold – petrol models (Chapter 4A)
☐ Blocked injectors/fuel injection system fault (Chapter 4A or 4B)
☐ EGR valve or control solenoid (Chapter 4C)
☐ Air in fuel, possibly due to loose fuel line connection – diesel models (Chapter 4B)

Engine idles erratically

☐ Air filter element clogged (Chapter 1A or 1B)
☐ Vacuum leak at the throttle body, inlet manifold or associated hoses – petrol models (Chapter 4A)
☐ Worn, faulty or incorrectly-gapped spark plugs – petrol models (Chapter 1A)
☐ Valve clearances incorrect (Chapter 2A, 2B or 2C)
☐ Uneven or low cylinder compressions (Chapter 2A, 2B or 2C)
☐ Camshaft lobes worn (Chapter 2A, 2B or 2C)
☐ Blocked injectors/fuel injection system fault (Chapter 4A or 4B)
☐ Air in fuel, possibly due to damaged or loose fuel line connection – diesel models (Chapter 1B or 4B)

Engine misfires at idle speed

☐ Worn, faulty or incorrectly-gapped spark plugs – petrol models (Chapter 1A)
☐ Faulty ignition coil(s) – petrol models (Chapter 5B)
☐ Vacuum leak at the throttle body, inlet manifold or associated hoses – petrol models (Chapter 4A)
☐ Blocked injectors/fuel injection system fault (Chapter 4A or 4B)
☐ Faulty injector(s) – diesel models (Chapter 4B)
☐ Uneven or low cylinder compressions (Chapter 2A, 2B or 2C)
☐ Disconnected, leaking, or perished crankcase ventilation hoses (Chapter 4C)

Engine misfires throughout the driving speed range

☐ Fuel pump faulty, or delivery pressure low – petrol models (Chapter 4A)
☐ Fuel filter choked – diesel models (Chapter 1B)
☐ Fuel tank vent blocked, or fuel pipes restricted (Chapter 4A or 4B)
☐ Vacuum leak at the throttle body, inlet manifold or associated hoses – petrol models (Chapter 4A)
☐ Worn, faulty or incorrectly-gapped spark plugs – petrol models (Chapter 1A)
☐ Faulty ignition coil(s) – petrol models (Chapter 5B)
☐ Faulty injector(s) – diesel models (Chapter 4B)
☐ Uneven or low cylinder compressions (Chapter 2A, 2B or 2C)
☐ Blocked injector/fuel injection system fault (Chapter 4A or 4B)
☐ EGR valve or control solenoid (Chapter 4C)
☐ Blocked catalytic converter (Chapter 4A or 4B)
☐ High engine operating temperature (Chapter 3)

Engine hesitates on acceleration

☐ Worn, faulty or incorrectly-gapped spark plugs – petrol models (Chapter 1A)
☐ Vacuum leak at the throttle body, inlet manifold or associated hoses – petrol models (Chapter 4A)
☐ Blocked injectors/fuel injection system fault (Chapter 4A or 4B)
☐ EGR valve or control solenoid (Chapter 4C)
☐ Faulty injector(s) – diesel models (Chapter 4B)

Engine stalls

☐ Vacuum leak at the throttle body, inlet manifold or associated hoses – petrol models (Chapter 4A)
☐ Fuel pump faulty, or delivery pressure low – petrol models (Chapter 4A)
☐ Fuel filter choked – diesel models (Chapter 1B)
☐ Fuel tank vent blocked, or fuel pipes restricted (Chapter 4A or 4B)
☐ Blocked injectors/fuel injection system fault (Chapter 4A or 4B)
☐ Faulty injector(s) – diesel models (Chapter 4B)

Engine lacks power

☐ Air filter element blocked (Chapter 1A or 1B)
☐ Fuel filter choked – diesel models (Chapter 1B)
☐ Fuel pipes blocked or restricted (Chapter 4A or 4B)
☐ Valve clearances incorrect (Chapter 2A or 2B)
☐ Worn, faulty or incorrectly-gapped spark plugs – petrol models (Chapter 1A)
☐ Fault with VTEC system, or low engine oil level – 1.6 litre petrol models (Chapter 2A)
☐ High engine operating temperature (Chapter 3)
☐ Accelerator cable problem (Chapter 4A or 4B)
☐ Accelerator position sensor faulty – diesel models (Chapter 4B)
☐ Vacuum leak at the throttle body, inlet manifold or associated hoses – petrol models (Chapter 4A)
☐ Blocked injectors/fuel injection system fault (Chapter 4A or 4B)
☐ Faulty injector(s) – diesel models (Chapter 4B)
☐ Fuel pump faulty, or delivery pressure low – petrol models (Chapter 4A)
☐ EGR valve or control solenoid (Chapter 4C)
☐ Uneven or low cylinder compressions (Chapter 2A, 2B or 2C)
☐ Blocked catalytic converter (Chapter 4A, 4B or 4C)
☐ Brakes binding (Chapter 1A, 1B or 9)
☐ Clutch slipping (Chapter 6)

Engine backfires

☐ Vacuum leak at the throttle body, inlet manifold or associated hoses – petrol models (Chapter 4A)
☐ Blocked injectors/fuel injection system fault (Chapter 4A or 4B)
☐ Blocked catalytic converter (Chapter 4A, 4B or 4C)
☐ Faulty ignition coil(s) – petrol models (Chapter 5B)

Oil pressure warning light illuminated with engine running

☐ Low oil level, or incorrect oil grade (see *Weekly checks*)
☐ Faulty oil pressure sensor, or wiring damaged (Chapter 5A)
☐ Worn engine bearings and/or oil pump (Chapter 2A, 2B or 2C)
☐ High engine operating temperature (Chapter 3)
☐ Oil pump pressure relief valve defective (Chapter 2A or 2B)
☐ Oil pump pick-up strainer clogged (Chapter 2A or 2B)

Engine runs-on after switching off

☐ Excessive carbon build-up in engine (Chapter 2A, 2B or 2C)
☐ High engine operating temperature (Chapter 3)
☐ Fuel injection system fault (Chapter 4A or 4B)

Engine (continued)

Engine noises

Pre-ignition (pinking) or knocking during acceleration or under load

- [ ] Ignition timing incorrect/ignition system fault – petrol models (Chapter 1A or 5B)
- [ ] Incorrect grade of spark plug – petrol models (Chapter 1A)
- [ ] Incorrect grade of fuel – petrol models (Chapter 4A)
- [ ] Knock sensor faulty – petrol models (Chapter 5B)
- [ ] Vacuum leak at the throttle body, inlet manifold or associated hoses – petrol models (Chapter 4A)
- [ ] Excessive carbon build-up in engine (Chapter 2A, 2B or 2C)
- [ ] Blocked injector/fuel injection system fault (Chapter 4A or 4B)
- [ ] Faulty injector(s) – diesel models (Chapter 4B)

Whistling or wheezing noises

- [ ] Leaking inlet manifold or throttle body gasket – petrol models (Chapter 4A)
- [ ] Leaking exhaust manifold gasket or pipe-to-manifold joint (Chapter 4A or 4B)
- [ ] Leaking vacuum hose (Chapter 4, 5 or 9)

- [ ] Blowing cylinder head gasket (Chapter 2A or 2B)
- [ ] Partially blocked or leaking crankcase ventilation system (Chapter 4C)

Tapping or rattling noises

- [ ] Valve clearances incorrect (Chapter 2A or 2B)
- [ ] Worn valve gear or camshaft(s) (Chapter 2A or 2B)
- [ ] Ancillary component fault (water pump, alternator, etc) (Chapter 3, 5A, etc)

Knocking or thumping noises

- [ ] Worn big-end bearings (regular heavy knocking, perhaps less under load) (Chapter 2C)
- [ ] Worn main bearings (rumbling and knocking, perhaps worsening under load) (Chapter 2C)
- [ ] Piston slap – most noticeable when cold, caused by piston/bore wear (Chapter 2C)
- [ ] Ancillary component fault (water pump, alternator, etc) (Chapter 3, 5A, etc)
- [ ] Engine mountings worn or defective (Chapter 2A or 2B)
- [ ] Front suspension or steering components worn (Chapter 10)

Cooling system

Overheating

- [ ] Insufficient coolant in system (see *Weekly checks*)
- [ ] Thermostat faulty (Chapter 3)
- [ ] Radiator core blocked, or grille restricted (Chapter 3)
- [ ] Cooling fan/switch faulty (Chapter 3)
- [ ] Inaccurate coolant temperature sensor (Chapter 3, 4A or 4B)
- [ ] Airlock in cooling system – typically after coolant refilling, or due to a leak (Chapter 1A or 1B)
- [ ] Expansion tank pressure cap faulty (Chapter 3)
- [ ] Engine management system fault (Chapter 4A or 4B)

Overcooling

- [ ] Thermostat faulty (Chapter 3)
- [ ] Inaccurate cylinder head temperature sender (Chapter 3, 4A or 4B)
- [ ] Cooling fan/switch faulty (Chapter 3)
- [ ] Engine management system fault (Chapter 4A or 4B)

External coolant leakage

- [ ] Deteriorated or damaged hoses or hose clips (Chapter 1A or 1B)
- [ ] Radiator core or heater matrix leaking (Chapter 3)
- [ ] Expansion tank pressure cap faulty (Chapter 1A or 1B)
- [ ] Water pump internal seal leaking (Chapter 3)
- [ ] Water pump gasket leaking (Chapter 3)
- [ ] Boiling due to overheating (Chapter 3)
- [ ] Cylinder block core plug leaking (Chapter 2C)

Internal coolant leakage

- [ ] Leaking cylinder head gasket (Chapter 2A or 2B)
- [ ] Cracked cylinder head or cylinder block (Chapter 2A, 2B or 2C)

Corrosion

- [ ] Infrequent draining and flushing (Chapter 1A or 1B)
- [ ] Incorrect coolant mixture or inappropriate coolant type (see *Weekly checks*)

Fuel and exhaust systems

Excessive fuel consumption

☐ Air filter element dirty or clogged (Chapter 1A or 1B)
☐ Fuel injection system fault (Chapter 4A or 4B)
☐ Engine management system fault (Chapter 4A or 4B)
☐ Crankcase ventilation system blocked (Chapter 4C)
☐ Tyres under-inflated (see *Weekly checks*)
☐ Brakes binding (Chapter 1A, 1B or 9)
☐ Fuel leak, causing apparent high consumption (Chapter 1A, 1B, 4A or 4B)

Fuel leakage and/or fuel odour

☐ Damaged or corroded fuel tank, pipes or connections (Chapter 4A or 4B)
☐ Evaporative emissions system fault – petrol models (Chapter 4C)

Excessive noise or fumes from exhaust system

☐ Leaking exhaust system or manifold joints (Chapter 1A, 1B, 4A or 4B)
☐ Leaking, corroded or damaged silencers or pipe (Chapter 1A, 1B, 4A or 4B)
☐ Broken mountings causing body or suspension contact (Chapter 1A or 1B)

Clutch

Pedal travels to floor – no pressure or very little resistance

☐ Air in hydraulic system/faulty master or slave cylinder (Chapter 6)
☐ Faulty hydraulic release system (Chapter 6)
☐ Clutch pedal return spring detached or broken (Chapter 6)
☐ Broken clutch release bearing or fork (Chapter 6)
☐ Broken diaphragm spring in clutch pressure plate (Chapter 6)

Clutch fails to disengage (unable to select gears)

☐ Air in hydraulic system/faulty master or slave cylinder (Chapter 6)
☐ Faulty hydraulic release system (Chapter 6)
☐ Clutch disc sticking on transmission input shaft splines (Chapter 6)
☐ Clutch disc sticking to flywheel or pressure plate (Chapter 6)
☐ Faulty pressure plate assembly (Chapter 6)
☐ Clutch release mechanism worn or incorrectly assembled (Chapter 6)

Clutch slips (engine speed increases, with no increase in vehicle speed)

☐ Faulty hydraulic release system (Chapter 6)
☐ Clutch disc linings excessively worn (Chapter 6)
☐ Clutch disc linings contaminated with oil or grease (Chapter 6)
☐ Faulty pressure plate or weak diaphragm spring (Chapter 6)

Judder as clutch is engaged

☐ Clutch disc linings contaminated with oil or grease (Chapter 6)
☐ Clutch disc linings excessively worn (Chapter 6)
☐ Faulty or distorted pressure plate or diaphragm spring (Chapter 6).
☐ Worn or loose engine or transmission mountings (Chapter 2A or 2B)
☐ Clutch disc hub or transmission input shaft splines worn (Chapter 6)
☐ Faulty dual-mass flywheel, where applicable (Chapter 2A or 2B)

Noise when depressing or releasing clutch pedal

☐ Worn clutch release bearing (Chapter 6)
☐ Worn or dry clutch pedal bushes (Chapter 6)
☐ Worn or dry clutch master cylinder piston (Chapter 6)
☐ Faulty pressure plate assembly (Chapter 6)
☐ Pressure plate diaphragm spring broken (Chapter 6)
☐ Broken clutch disc cushioning springs (Chapter 6)
☐ Faulty dual-mass flywheel, where applicable (Chapter 2A or 2B)

Manual transmission

Noisy in neutral with engine running

☐ Lack of oil (Chapter 1A or 1B)
☐ Input shaft bearings worn (noise apparent with clutch pedal released, but not when depressed) (Chapter 7A)*
☐ Clutch release bearing worn (noise apparent with clutch pedal depressed, possibly less when released) (Chapter 6)

Noisy in one particular gear

☐ Worn, damaged or chipped gear teeth (Chapter 7A)*

Difficulty engaging gears

☐ Clutch fault (Chapter 6)
☐ Worn, damaged, or poorly-adjusted gearchange cables (Chapter 7A)
☐ Lack of lubricant (Chapter 1A or 1B)
☐ Worn synchroniser units (Chapter 7A)*

Jumps out of gear

☐ Worn, damaged, or poorly-adjusted gearchange cables (Chapter 7A)
☐ Worn synchroniser units (Chapter 7A)*
☐ Worn selector forks (Chapter 7A)*

Vibration

☐ Lack of lubricant (Chapter 1A or 1B)
☐ Worn bearings (Chapter 7A)*

Lubricant leaks

☐ Leaking driveshaft or selector shaft oil seal (Chapter 7A)
☐ Leaking housing joint (Chapter 7A)*
☐ Leaking input shaft oil seal (Chapter 7A)*

Although the corrective action necessary to remedy the symptoms described is beyond the scope of the home mechanic, the above information should be helpful in isolating the cause of the condition, so that the owner can communicate clearly with a professional mechanic.

Automatic transmission

Note: *Due to the complexity of the automatic transmission, it is difficult for the home mechanic to properly diagnose and service this unit. For problems other than the following, the car should be taken to a dealer service department or automatic transmission specialist. Do not be too hasty in removing the transmission if a fault is suspected, as most of the testing is carried out with the unit still fitted. Remember that, besides the sensors specific to the transmission, many of the engine management system sensors described in Chapter 4A are essential to the correct operation of the transmission.*

Fluid leakage

☐ Automatic transmission fluid is usually dark red in colour. Fluid leaks should not be confused with engine oil, which can easily be blown onto the transmission by airflow.
☐ To determine the source of a leak, first remove all built-up dirt and grime from the transmission housing and surrounding areas using a degreasing agent, or by steam-cleaning. Drive the car at low speed, so airflow will not blow the leak far from its source. Raise and support the car, and determine where the leak is coming from. The following are common areas of leakage:
a) Fluid pan.
b) Dipstick tube (Chapter 1A).
c) Transmission-to-fluid cooler unions (Chapter 7B).
d) Radiator fluid cooler unions (Chapter 3).
e) Driveshaft seals.

Transmission fluid brown, or has burned smell

☐ Transmission fluid level low (Chapter 1A)

General gear selection problems

☐ Chapter 7B deals with checking the selector cable on automatic transmissions. The following are common problems which may be caused by a faulty selector cable or lever position sensor:
a) Engine starting in gears other than Park or Neutral.
b) Indicator panel indicating a gear other than the one actually being used.
c) Car moves when in Park or Neutral.
d) Poor gear shift quality or erratic gear changes.

Transmission will not downshift (kickdown) with accelerator pedal fully depressed

☐ Low transmission fluid level (Chapter 1A)
☐ Engine management system fault (Chapter 4A)
☐ Faulty transmission sensor or wiring (Chapter 7B)
☐ Incorrect selector cable adjustment (Chapter 7B)

Engine will not start in any gear, or starts in gears other than Park or Neutral

☐ Faulty transmission sensor or wiring (Chapter 7B)
☐ Engine management system fault (Chapter 4A)
☐ Incorrect selector cable adjustment (Chapter 7B)

Transmission slips, shifts roughly, is noisy, or has no drive in forward or reverse gears

☐ Transmission fluid level low (Chapter 1A)
☐ Faulty transmission sensor or wiring (Chapter 7B)
☐ Engine management system fault (Chapter 4A)

Note: *There are many probable causes for the above problems, but diagnosing and correcting them is considered beyond the scope of this manual. Having checked the fluid level and all the wiring as far as possible, a dealer or transmission specialist should be consulted if the problem persists.*

Driveshafts

Vibration when accelerating or decelerating

- ☐ Worn inner constant velocity joint (Chapter 8)
- ☐ Bent or distorted driveshaft (Chapter 8)

Clicking or knocking noise on turns (at slow speed on full-lock)

- ☐ Worn outer constant velocity joint (Chapter 8)
- ☐ Lack of constant velocity joint lubricant, possibly due to damaged gaiter (Chapter 8)

Braking system

Note: *Before assuming that a brake problem exists, make sure that the tyres are in good condition and correctly inflated, that the front wheel alignment is correct, and that the car is not loaded with weight in an unequal manner. Apart from checking the condition of all pipe and hose connections, any faults occurring on the anti-lock braking system should be referred to a Honda dealer for diagnosis.*

Car pulls to one side under braking

- ☐ Worn, defective, damaged or contaminated brake pads/shoes on one side (Chapter 1A, 1B or 9)
- ☐ Seized or partially-seized brake caliper piston or rear wheel cylinder (Chapter 1A, 1B or 9)
- ☐ A mixture of brake pad/shoe materials fitted between sides (Chapter 1A, 1B or 9)
- ☐ Brake caliper mounting bolts loose (Chapter 9)
- ☐ One rear wheel cylinder leaking – drum brake models (Chapter 9)
- ☐ Worn or damaged steering or suspension components (Chapter 1A, 1B or 10)

Noise (grinding or high-pitched squeal) when brakes applied

- ☐ Brake pad/shoe material worn down to metal backing (Chapter 1A, 1B or 9)
- ☐ Excessive corrosion of brake disc/drum (may be apparent after the car has been standing for some time (Chapter 1A, 1B or 9)
- ☐ Foreign object (stone chipping, etc) trapped between brake disc and shield (Chapter 1A, 1B or 9)

Excessive brake pedal travel

- ☐ Faulty master cylinder (Chapter 9)
- ☐ Air in hydraulic system (Chapter 1A, 1B, 6 or 9)
- ☐ Faulty vacuum servo unit (Chapter 9)
- ☐ Rear wheel cylinder leaking – drum brake models (Chapter 9)

Brake pedal feels spongy when depressed

- ☐ Air in hydraulic system (Chapter 1A, 1B, 6 or 9)
- ☐ Rear wheel cylinder leaking – drum brake models (Chapter 9)
- ☐ Deteriorated flexible rubber brake hoses (Chapter 1A, 1B or 9)
- ☐ Master cylinder mounting nuts loose (Chapter 9)
- ☐ Faulty master cylinder (Chapter 9)

Excessive brake pedal effort required to stop car

- ☐ Faulty vacuum servo unit (Chapter 9)
- ☐ Faulty vacuum pump – diesel models (Chapter 9)
- ☐ Disconnected, damaged or insecure brake servo vacuum hose (Chapter 9)
- ☐ Primary or secondary hydraulic circuit failure (Chapter 9)
- ☐ Seized brake caliper piston or rear wheel cylinder (Chapter 9)
- ☐ Brake pads or shoes incorrectly fitted (Chapter 9)
- ☐ Incorrect grade of brake pads/shoes fitted (Chapter 9)
- ☐ Brake pads or shoes contaminated (Chapter 1A, 1B or 9)

Judder felt through brake pedal or steering wheel when braking

Note: *Under heavy braking on models equipped with ABS, vibration may be felt through the brake pedal. This is a normal feature of ABS operation, and does not constitute a fault*

- ☐ Excessive run-out or distortion of front discs (Chapter 1A, 1B or 9)
- ☐ Front brake pads worn (Chapter 1A, 1B or 9)
- ☐ Front brake caliper mounting bolts loose (Chapter 9)
- ☐ Wear in suspension or steering components or mountings (Chapter 1A, 1B or 10)
- ☐ Front wheels out of balance (see *Weekly checks*)

Brakes binding

- ☐ Seized brake caliper piston or rear wheel cylinder (Chapter 9)
- ☐ Incorrectly-adjusted handbrake mechanism (Chapter 9)
- ☐ Faulty master cylinder (Chapter 9)

Rear wheels locking under normal braking

- ☐ Rear brake pads/shoes contaminated or damaged (Chapter 1 or 9)
- ☐ Rear brake discs warped (Chapter 1 or 9)
- ☐ Seized rear brake caliper piston or rear wheel cylinder (Chapter 9)
- ☐ ABS fault (Chapter 9)

ABS warning light stays on

- ☐ Wheel sensor wiring plug corroded, or wiring damaged (Chapter 9)
- ☐ Other wiring fault – check ABS hydraulic unit in engine compartment (Chapter 9)
- ☐ ABS fuse blown (Chapter 12)
- ☐ Low brake fluid level, possibly due to a leak, or system needs bleeding (Chapter 1A, 1B or 9)

Suspension and steering

Note: *Before diagnosing suspension or steering faults, be sure that the trouble is not due to incorrect tyre pressures, mixtures of tyre types, or binding brakes.*

Car pulls to one side

- [ ] Defective tyre (see *Weekly checks*)
- [ ] Excessive wear in suspension or steering components (Chapter 1A, 1B or 10)
- [ ] Incorrect front wheel alignment (Chapter 10)
- [ ] Accident damage to steering or suspension components (Chapter 1A or 1B)

Wheel wobble and vibration

- [ ] Front wheels out of balance (vibration felt mainly through the steering wheel) (see *Weekly checks*)
- [ ] Rear wheels out of balance (vibration felt throughout the car) (see *Weekly checks*)
- [ ] Roadwheels damaged or distorted (see *Weekly checks*)
- [ ] Faulty or damaged tyre (see *Weekly checks*)
- [ ] Worn steering or suspension joints, bushes or components (Chapter 1A, 1B or 10)
- [ ] Wheel nuts loose (Chapter 1A or 1B)

Excessive pitching and/or rolling around corners, or during braking

- [ ] Defective shock absorbers (Chapter 1A, 1B or 10)
- [ ] Broken or weak spring and/or suspension component (Chapter 1A, 1B or 10)
- [ ] Worn or damaged anti-roll bar or mountings (Chapter 1A, 1B or 10)

Wandering or general instability

- [ ] Incorrect front wheel alignment (Chapter 10)
- [ ] Worn steering or suspension joints, bushes or components (Chapter 1A, 1B or 10)
- [ ] Roadwheels out of balance (see *Weekly checks*)
- [ ] Faulty or damaged tyre (see *Weekly checks*)
- [ ] Wheel nuts loose (Chapter 1A or 1B)
- [ ] Defective shock absorbers (Chapter 1A, 1B or 10)

Excessively-stiff steering

- [ ] Seized steering linkage balljoint or suspension balljoint (Chapter 1A, 1B or 10)
- [ ] Incorrect front wheel alignment (Chapter 10)
- [ ] Faulty steering motor or torque sensor (Chapter 10)
- [ ] Faulty steering rack or column (Chapter 10)

Excessive play in steering

- [ ] Worn steering column/intermediate shaft joints (Chapter 10)
- [ ] Worn track rod balljoints (Chapter 1A, 1B or 10)
- [ ] Worn steering rack (Chapter 10)
- [ ] Worn steering or suspension joints, bushes or components (Chapter 1A, 1B or 10)

Lack of power assistance

- [ ] Faulty steering motor or torque sensor (Chapter 10)
- [ ] Faulty steering rack (Chapter 10)

Tyre wear excessive

Tyres worn on inside or outside edges

- [ ] Tyres under-inflated (wear on both edges) (see *Weekly checks*)
- [ ] Incorrect camber or castor angles (wear on one edge only) (Chapter 10)
- [ ] Worn steering or suspension joints, bushes or components (Chapter 1A, 1B or 10)
- [ ] Excessively-hard cornering or braking
- [ ] Accident damage

Tyre treads exhibit feathered edges

- [ ] Incorrect toe setting (tracking) (Chapter 10)

Tyres worn in centre of tread

- [ ] Tyres over-inflated (see *Weekly checks*)

Tyres worn on inside and outside edges

- [ ] Tyres under-inflated (see *Weekly checks*)

Tyres worn unevenly

- [ ] Tyres/wheels out of balance (see *Weekly checks*)
- [ ] Excessive wheel or tyre run-out (buckled wheel rim, faulty tyre)
- [ ] Worn shock absorbers (Chapter 1A, 1B or 10)
- [ ] Faulty tyre (see *Weekly checks*)

Electrical system

Note: *For problems associated with the starting system, refer to the faults listed under Engine earlier in this Section.*

Battery will not hold a charge for more than a few days

- [ ] Battery defective internally – one or more cells failing (Chapter 5A)
- [ ] Battery terminal connections loose or corroded (see *Weekly checks*)
- [ ] Auxiliary drivebelt worn or slipping (Chapter 1A or 1B)
- [ ] Alternator not charging at correct output (Chapter 5A)
- [ ] Alternator or voltage regulator faulty (Chapter 5A)
- [ ] Short-circuit causing continual battery drain (Chapter 5A or 12)

Ignition/no-charge warning light remains illuminated with engine running

- [ ] Auxiliary drivebelt broken, worn, or slipping (Chapter 1A or 1B)
- [ ] Internal fault in alternator or voltage regulator (Chapter 5A)
- [ ] Broken, disconnected, or loose wiring in charging circuit (Chapter 5A or 12)

Ignition/no-charge warning light fails to come on

- [ ] Warning light bulb blown (Chapter 12)
- [ ] Broken, disconnected, or loose wiring in warning light circuit (Chapter 5A or 12)
- [ ] Alternator faulty (Chapter 5A)

Lights inoperative

- [ ] Bulb blown (Chapter 12)
- [ ] Corrosion of bulb or bulbholder contacts (Chapter 12)
- [ ] Blown fuse (Chapter 12)
- [ ] Faulty relay (Chapter 12)
- [ ] Broken, loose, or disconnected wiring (Chapter 12)
- [ ] Faulty switch (Chapter 12)

Instrument readings inaccurate or erratic

Instrument readings increase with engine speed

- [ ] Faulty instrument panel voltage regulator (Chapter 12)

Fuel or temperature gauges give no reading

- [ ] Faulty gauge sender unit (Chapter 3, 4A or 4B)
- [ ] Wiring open-circuit (Chapter 12)
- [ ] Faulty gauge (Chapter 12)

Fuel or temperature gauges give continuous maximum reading

- [ ] Faulty gauge sender unit (Chapter 3, 4A or 4B)
- [ ] Wiring short-circuit (Chapter 12)
- [ ] Faulty gauge (Chapter 12)

Horn inoperative, or unsatisfactory in operation

Horn operates all the time

- [ ] Horn push either earthed or stuck down (Chapter 12)
- [ ] Horn cable-to-horn push earthed (Chapter 12)

Horn fails to operate

- [ ] Blown fuse (Chapter 12)
- [ ] Cable or connections loose, broken or disconnected (Chapter 12)
- [ ] Faulty horn (Chapter 12)

Horn emits intermittent or unsatisfactory sound

- [ ] Cable connections loose (Chapter 12)
- [ ] Horn mountings loose (Chapter 12)
- [ ] Faulty horn (Chapter 12)

Windscreen wipers inoperative, or unsatisfactory in operation

Wipers fail to operate, or operate very slowly

- [ ] Wiper blades stuck to screen, or linkage seized or binding (Chapter 12)
- [ ] Blown fuse (Chapter 12)
- [ ] Battery discharged (Chapter 5A)
- [ ] Wiring/plugs loose, broken or disconnected (Chapter 12)
- [ ] Faulty relay (Chapter 12)
- [ ] Faulty wiper motor (Chapter 12)

Wiper blades sweep over too large or too small an area of the glass

- [ ] Wiper blades incorrectly fitted, or wrong size used (see *Weekly checks*)
- [ ] Wiper arms incorrectly positioned on spindles (Chapter 12)
- [ ] Excessive wear of wiper linkage (Chapter 12)
- [ ] Wiper motor or linkage mountings loose or insecure (Chapter 12)

Wiper blades fail to clean the glass effectively

- [ ] Wiper blade rubbers dirty, worn or perished (see *Weekly checks*)
- [ ] Wiper blades incorrectly fitted, or wrong size used (see *Weekly checks*)
- [ ] Wiper arm tension springs broken, or arm pivots seized (Chapter 12)
- [ ] Insufficient windscreen washer additive to adequately remove road film (see *Weekly checks*)

Windscreen washers inoperative, or unsatisfactory in operation

One or more washer jets inoperative

- [ ] Blocked (or frozen) washer jet
- [ ] Disconnected, kinked or restricted fluid hose (Chapter 12)
- [ ] Insufficient fluid in washer reservoir (see *Weekly checks*)

Washer pump fails to operate

- [ ] Broken or disconnected wiring or connections (Chapter 12)
- [ ] Blown fuse (Chapter 12)
- [ ] Faulty washer switch (Chapter 12)
- [ ] Faulty washer pump (Chapter 12)

Washer pump runs for some time before fluid is emitted from jets

- [ ] Faulty one-way valve in fluid supply hose (Chapter 12)
- [ ] Fluid supply hose leaking (check under or inside car), or partially blocked (Chapter 12)

Electric windows inoperative, or unsatisfactory in operation

Window glass will only move in one direction

- [ ] Faulty switch (Chapter 12)

Window glass slow to move

- [ ] Battery discharged (Chapter 5A)
- [ ] Regulator seized or damaged, or in need of lubrication (Chapter 11)
- [ ] Door internal components or trim fouling regulator (Chapter 11)
- [ ] Faulty motor (Chapter 11)

Window glass fails to move

- [ ] Blown fuse (Chapter 12)
- [ ] Faulty relay (Chapter 12)
- [ ] Broken or disconnected wiring or connections (Chapter 12)
- [ ] Faulty motor (Chapter 11)

One-touch 'auto' feature not working

- [ ] Switch needs resetting after battery disconnection (see *Disconnecting the battery*)

Electrical system (continued)

Central locking system inoperative, or unsatisfactory in operation

Complete system failure

☐ Remote handset battery discharged, where applicable
☐ Blown fuse (Chapter 12)
☐ Faulty relay (Chapter 12)
☐ Broken or disconnected wiring or connections (Chapter 12)
☐ Faulty motor (Chapter 11)

Latch locks but will not unlock, or unlocks but will not lock

☐ Remote handset battery discharged, where applicable
☐ Faulty master switch (Chapter 12)
☐ Broken or disconnected latch operating rods or levers (Chapter 11)
☐ Faulty relay (Chapter 12)
☐ Faulty motor (Chapter 11)

One solenoid/motor fails to operate

☐ Broken or disconnected wiring or connections (Chapter 12)
☐ Faulty door lock (Chapter 11)
☐ Broken, binding or disconnected latch operating rods or levers (Chapter 11)

Notes

Notes

A

ABS (Anti-lock brake system) A system, usually electronically controlled, that senses incipient wheel lockup during braking and relieves hydraulic pressure at wheels that are about to skid.

Air bag An inflatable bag hidden in the steering wheel (driver's side) or the dash or glovebox (passenger side). In a head-on collision, the bags inflate, preventing the driver and front passenger from being thrown forward into the steering wheel or windscreen.

Air cleaner A metal or plastic housing, containing a filter element, which removes dust and dirt from the air being drawn into the engine.

Air filter element The actual filter in an air cleaner system, usually manufactured from pleated paper and requiring renewal at regular intervals.

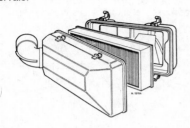

Air filter

Allen key A hexagonal wrench which fits into a recessed hexagonal hole.

Alligator clip A long-nosed spring-loaded metal clip with meshing teeth. Used to make temporary electrical connections.

Alternator A component in the electrical system which converts mechanical energy from a drivebelt into electrical energy to charge the battery and to operate the starting system, ignition system and electrical accessories.

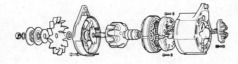

Alternator (exploded view)

Ampere (amp) A unit of measurement for the flow of electric current. One amp is the amount of current produced by one volt acting through a resistance of one ohm.

Anaerobic sealer A substance used to prevent bolts and screws from loosening. Anaerobic means that it does not require oxygen for activation. The Loctite brand is widely used.

Antifreeze A substance (usually ethylene glycol) mixed with water, and added to a vehicle's cooling system, to prevent freezing of the coolant in winter. Antifreeze also contains chemicals to inhibit corrosion and the formation of rust and other deposits that would tend to clog the radiator and coolant passages and reduce cooling efficiency.

Anti-seize compound A coating that reduces the risk of seizing on fasteners that are subjected to high temperatures, such as exhaust manifold bolts and nuts.

Anti-seize compound

Asbestos A natural fibrous mineral with great heat resistance, commonly used in the composition of brake friction materials. Asbestos is a health hazard and the dust created by brake systems should never be inhaled or ingested.

Axle A shaft on which a wheel revolves, or which revolves with a wheel. Also, a solid beam that connects the two wheels at one end of the vehicle. An axle which also transmits power to the wheels is known as a live axle.

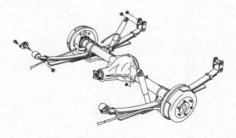

Axle assembly

Axleshaft A single rotating shaft, on either side of the differential, which delivers power from the final drive assembly to the drive wheels. Also called a driveshaft or a halfshaft.

B

Ball bearing An anti-friction bearing consisting of a hardened inner and outer race with hardened steel balls between two races.

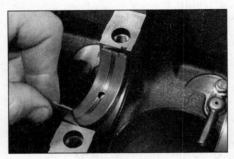

Bearing

Bearing The curved surface on a shaft or in a bore, or the part assembled into either, that permits relative motion between them with minimum wear and friction.

Big-end bearing The bearing in the end of the connecting rod that's attached to the crankshaft.

Bleed nipple A valve on a brake wheel cylinder, caliper or other hydraulic component that is opened to purge the hydraulic system of air. Also called a bleed screw.

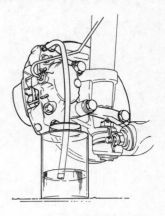

Brake bleeding

Brake bleeding Procedure for removing air from lines of a hydraulic brake system.

Brake disc The component of a disc brake that rotates with the wheels.

Brake drum The component of a drum brake that rotates with the wheels.

Brake linings The friction material which contacts the brake disc or drum to retard the vehicle's speed. The linings are bonded or riveted to the brake pads or shoes.

Brake pads The replaceable friction pads that pinch the brake disc when the brakes are applied. Brake pads consist of a friction material bonded or riveted to a rigid backing plate.

Brake shoe The crescent-shaped carrier to which the brake linings are mounted and which forces the lining against the rotating drum during braking.

Braking systems For more information on braking systems, consult the *Haynes Automotive Brake Manual*.

Breaker bar A long socket wrench handle providing greater leverage.

Bulkhead The insulated partition between the engine and the passenger compartment.

C

Caliper The non-rotating part of a disc-brake assembly that straddles the disc and carries the brake pads. The caliper also contains the hydraulic components that cause the pads to pinch the disc when the brakes are applied. A caliper is also a measuring tool that can be set to measure inside or outside dimensions of an object.

Camshaft A rotating shaft on which a series of cam lobes operate the valve mechanisms. The camshaft may be driven by gears, by sprockets and chain or by sprockets and a belt.

Canister A container in an evaporative emission control system; contains activated charcoal granules to trap vapours from the fuel system.

Canister

Carburettor A device which mixes fuel with air in the proper proportions to provide a desired power output from a spark ignition internal combustion engine.

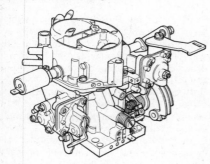

Carburettor

Castellated Resembling the parapets along the top of a castle wall. For example, a castellated balljoint stud nut.

Castellated nut

Castor In wheel alignment, the backward or forward tilt of the steering axis. Castor is positive when the steering axis is inclined rearward at the top.

Catalytic converter A silencer-like device in the exhaust system which converts certain pollutants in the exhaust gases into less harmful substances.

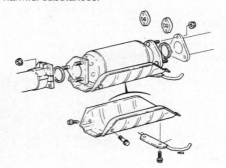

Catalytic converter

Circlip A ring-shaped clip used to prevent endwise movement of cylindrical parts and shafts. An internal circlip is installed in a groove in a housing; an external circlip fits into a groove on the outside of a cylindrical piece such as a shaft.

Clearance The amount of space between two parts. For example, between a piston and a cylinder, between a bearing and a journal, etc.

Coil spring A spiral of elastic steel found in various sizes throughout a vehicle, for example as a springing medium in the suspension and in the valve train.

Compression Reduction in volume, and increase in pressure and temperature, of a gas, caused by squeezing it into a smaller space.

Compression ratio The relationship between cylinder volume when the piston is at top dead centre and cylinder volume when the piston is at bottom dead centre.

Constant velocity (CV) joint A type of universal joint that cancels out vibrations caused by driving power being transmitted through an angle.

Core plug A disc or cup-shaped metal device inserted in a hole in a casting through which core was removed when the casting was formed. Also known as a freeze plug or expansion plug.

Crankcase The lower part of the engine block in which the crankshaft rotates.

Crankshaft The main rotating member, or shaft, running the length of the crankcase, with offset "throws" to which the connecting rods are attached.

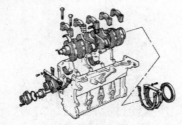

Crankshaft assembly

Crocodile clip See Alligator clip

D

Diagnostic code Code numbers obtained by accessing the diagnostic mode of an engine management computer. This code can be used to determine the area in the system where a malfunction may be located.

Disc brake A brake design incorporating a rotating disc onto which brake pads are squeezed. The resulting friction converts the energy of a moving vehicle into heat.

Double-overhead cam (DOHC) An engine that uses two overhead camshafts, usually one for the intake valves and one for the exhaust valves.

Drivebelt(s) The belt(s) used to drive accessories such as the alternator, water pump, power steering pump, air conditioning compressor, etc. off the crankshaft pulley.

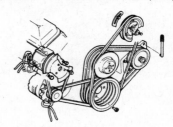

Accessory drivebelts

Driveshaft Any shaft used to transmit motion. Commonly used when referring to the axleshafts on a front wheel drive vehicle.

Driveshaft

Drum brake A type of brake using a drum-shaped metal cylinder attached to the inner surface of the wheel. When the brake pedal is pressed, curved brake shoes with friction linings press against the inside of the drum to slow or stop the vehicle.

Drum brake assembly

E

EGR valve A valve used to introduce exhaust gases into the intake air stream.

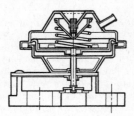

EGR valve

Electronic control unit (ECU) A computer which controls (for instance) ignition and fuel injection systems, or an anti-lock braking system. For more information refer to the *Haynes Automotive Electrical and Electronic Systems Manual*.

Electronic Fuel Injection (EFI) A computer controlled fuel system that distributes fuel through an injector located in each intake port of the engine.

Emergency brake A braking system, independent of the main hydraulic system, that can be used to slow or stop the vehicle if the primary brakes fail, or to hold the vehicle stationary even though the brake pedal isn't depressed. It usually consists of a hand lever that actuates either front or rear brakes mechanically through a series of cables and linkages. Also known as a handbrake or parking brake.

Endfloat The amount of lengthwise movement between two parts. As applied to a crankshaft, the distance that the crankshaft can move forward and back in the cylinder block.

Engine management system (EMS) A computer controlled system which manages the fuel injection and the ignition systems in an integrated fashion.

Exhaust manifold A part with several passages through which exhaust gases leave the engine combustion chambers and enter the exhaust pipe.

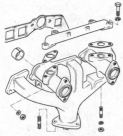

Exhaust manifold

F

Fan clutch A viscous (fluid) drive coupling device which permits variable engine fan speeds in relation to engine speeds.

Feeler blade A thin strip or blade of hardened steel, ground to an exact thickness, used to check or measure clearances between parts.

Feeler blade

Firing order The order in which the engine cylinders fire, or deliver their power strokes, beginning with the number one cylinder.

Flywheel A heavy spinning wheel in which energy is absorbed and stored by means of momentum. On cars, the flywheel is attached to the crankshaft to smooth out firing impulses.

Free play The amount of travel before any action takes place. The "looseness" in a linkage, or an assembly of parts, between the initial application of force and actual movement. For example, the distance the brake pedal moves before the pistons in the master cylinder are actuated.

Fuse An electrical device which protects a circuit against accidental overload. The typical fuse contains a soft piece of metal which is calibrated to melt at a predetermined current flow (expressed as amps) and break the circuit.

Fusible link A circuit protection device consisting of a conductor surrounded by heat-resistant insulation. The conductor is smaller than the wire it protects, so it acts as the weakest link in the circuit. Unlike a blown fuse, a failed fusible link must frequently be cut from the wire for replacement.

G

Gap The distance the spark must travel in jumping from the centre electrode to the side

Adjusting spark plug gap

electrode in a spark plug. Also refers to the spacing between the points in a contact breaker assembly in a conventional points-type ignition, or to the distance between the reluctor or rotor and the pickup coil in an electronic ignition.

Gasket Any thin, soft material - usually cork, cardboard, asbestos or soft metal - installed between two metal surfaces to ensure a good seal. For instance, the cylinder head gasket seals the joint between the block and the cylinder head.

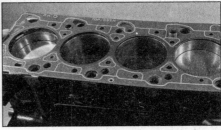

Gasket

Gauge An instrument panel display used to monitor engine conditions. A gauge with a movable pointer on a dial or a fixed scale is an analogue gauge. A gauge with a numerical readout is called a digital gauge.

H

Halfshaft A rotating shaft that transmits power from the final drive unit to a drive wheel, usually when referring to a live rear axle.

Harmonic balancer A device designed to reduce torsion or twisting vibration in the crankshaft. May be incorporated in the crankshaft pulley. Also known as a vibration damper.

Hone An abrasive tool for correcting small irregularities or differences in diameter in an engine cylinder, brake cylinder, etc.

Hydraulic tappet A tappet that utilises hydraulic pressure from the engine's lubrication system to maintain zero clearance (constant contact with both camshaft and valve stem). Automatically adjusts to variation in valve stem length. Hydraulic tappets also reduce valve noise.

I

Ignition timing The moment at which the spark plug fires, usually expressed in the number of crankshaft degrees before the piston reaches the top of its stroke.

Inlet manifold A tube or housing with passages through which flows the air-fuel mixture (carburettor vehicles and vehicles with throttle body injection) or air only (port fuel-injected vehicles) to the port openings in the cylinder head.

J

Jump start Starting the engine of a vehicle with a discharged or weak battery by attaching jump leads from the weak battery to a charged or helper battery.

L

Load Sensing Proportioning Valve (LSPV) A brake hydraulic system control valve that works like a proportioning valve, but also takes into consideration the amount of weight carried by the rear axle.

Locknut A nut used to lock an adjustment nut, or other threaded component, in place. For example, a locknut is employed to keep the adjusting nut on the rocker arm in position.

Lockwasher A form of washer designed to prevent an attaching nut from working loose.

M

MacPherson strut A type of front suspension system devised by Earle MacPherson at Ford of England. In its original form, a simple lateral link with the anti-roll bar creates the lower control arm. A long strut - an integral coil spring and shock absorber - is mounted between the body and the steering knuckle. Many modern so-called MacPherson strut systems use a conventional lower A-arm and don't rely on the anti-roll bar for location.

Multimeter An electrical test instrument with the capability to measure voltage, current and resistance.

N

NOx Oxides of Nitrogen. A common toxic pollutant emitted by petrol and diesel engines at higher temperatures.

O

Ohm The unit of electrical resistance. One volt applied to a resistance of one ohm will produce a current of one amp.

Ohmmeter An instrument for measuring electrical resistance.

O-ring A type of sealing ring made of a special rubber-like material; in use, the O-ring is compressed into a groove to provide the sealing action.

O-ring

Overhead cam (ohc) engine An engine with the camshaft(s) located on top of the cylinder head(s).

Overhead valve (ohv) engine An engine with the valves located in the cylinder head, but with the camshaft located in the engine block.

Oxygen sensor A device installed in the engine exhaust manifold, which senses the oxygen content in the exhaust and converts this information into an electric current. Also called a Lambda sensor.

P

Phillips screw A type of screw head having a cross instead of a slot for a corresponding type of screwdriver.

Plastigage A thin strip of plastic thread, available in different sizes, used for measuring clearances. For example, a strip of Plastigage is laid across a bearing journal. The parts are assembled and dismantled; the width of the crushed strip indicates the clearance between journal and bearing.

Plastigage

Propeller shaft The long hollow tube with universal joints at both ends that carries power from the transmission to the differential on front-engined rear wheel drive vehicles.

Proportioning valve A hydraulic control valve which limits the amount of pressure to the rear brakes during panic stops to prevent wheel lock-up.

R

Rack-and-pinion steering A steering system with a pinion gear on the end of the steering shaft that mates with a rack (think of a geared wheel opened up and laid flat). When the steering wheel is turned, the pinion turns, moving the rack to the left or right. This movement is transmitted through the track rods to the steering arms at the wheels.

Radiator A liquid-to-air heat transfer device designed to reduce the temperature of the coolant in an internal combustion engine cooling system.

Refrigerant Any substance used as a heat transfer agent in an air-conditioning system. R-12 has been the principle refrigerant for many years; recently, however, manufacturers have begun using R-134a, a non-CFC substance that is considered less harmful to the ozone in the upper atmosphere.

Rocker arm A lever arm that rocks on a shaft or pivots on a stud. In an overhead valve engine, the rocker arm converts the upward movement of the pushrod into a downward movement to open a valve.

Rotor In a distributor, the rotating device inside the cap that connects the centre electrode and the outer terminals as it turns, distributing the high voltage from the coil secondary winding to the proper spark plug. Also, that part of an alternator which rotates inside the stator. Also, the rotating assembly of a turbocharger, including the compressor wheel, shaft and turbine wheel.

Runout The amount of wobble (in-and-out movement) of a gear or wheel as it's rotated. The amount a shaft rotates "out-of-true." The out-of-round condition of a rotating part.

S

Sealant A liquid or paste used to prevent leakage at a joint. Sometimes used in conjunction with a gasket.

Sealed beam lamp An older headlight design which integrates the reflector, lens and filaments into a hermetically-sealed one-piece unit. When a filament burns out or the lens cracks, the entire unit is simply replaced.

Serpentine drivebelt A single, long, wide accessory drivebelt that's used on some newer vehicles to drive all the accessories, instead of a series of smaller, shorter belts. Serpentine drivebelts are usually tensioned by an automatic tensioner.

Serpentine drivebelt

Shim Thin spacer, commonly used to adjust the clearance or relative positions between two parts. For example, shims inserted into or under bucket tappets control valve clearances. Clearance is adjusted by changing the thickness of the shim.

Slide hammer A special puller that screws into or hooks onto a component such as a shaft or bearing; a heavy sliding handle on the shaft bottoms against the end of the shaft to knock the component free.

Sprocket A tooth or projection on the periphery of a wheel, shaped to engage with a chain or drivebelt. Commonly used to refer to the sprocket wheel itself.

Starter inhibitor switch On vehicles with an automatic transmission, a switch that prevents starting if the vehicle is not in Neutral or Park.

Strut See MacPherson strut.

T

Tappet A cylindrical component which transmits motion from the cam to the valve stem, either directly or via a pushrod and rocker arm. Also called a cam follower.

Thermostat A heat-controlled valve that regulates the flow of coolant between the cylinder block and the radiator, so maintaining optimum engine operating temperature. A thermostat is also used in some air cleaners in which the temperature is regulated.

Thrust bearing The bearing in the clutch assembly that is moved in to the release levers by clutch pedal action to disengage the clutch. Also referred to as a release bearing.

Timing belt A toothed belt which drives the camshaft. Serious engine damage may result if it breaks in service.

Timing chain A chain which drives the camshaft.

Toe-in The amount the front wheels are closer together at the front than at the rear. On rear wheel drive vehicles, a slight amount of toe-in is usually specified to keep the front wheels running parallel on the road by offsetting other forces that tend to spread the wheels apart.

Toe-out The amount the front wheels are closer together at the rear than at the front. On front wheel drive vehicles, a slight amount of toe-out is usually specified.

Tools For full information on choosing and using tools, refer to the *Haynes Automotive Tools Manual.*

Tracer A stripe of a second colour applied to a wire insulator to distinguish that wire from another one with the same colour insulator.

Tune-up A process of accurate and careful adjustments and parts replacement to obtain the best possible engine performance.

Turbocharger A centrifugal device, driven by exhaust gases, that pressurises the intake air. Normally used to increase the power output from a given engine displacement, but can also be used primarily to reduce exhaust emissions (as on VW's "Umwelt" Diesel engine).

U

Universal joint or U-joint A double-pivoted connection for transmitting power from a driving to a driven shaft through an angle. A U-joint consists of two Y-shaped yokes and a cross-shaped member called the spider.

V

Valve A device through which the flow of liquid, gas, vacuum, or loose material in bulk may be started, stopped, or regulated by a movable part that opens, shuts, or partially obstructs one or more ports or passageways. A valve is also the movable part of such a device.

Valve clearance The clearance between the valve tip (the end of the valve stem) and the rocker arm or tappet. The valve clearance is measured when the valve is closed.

Vernier caliper A precision measuring instrument that measures inside and outside dimensions. Not quite as accurate as a micrometer, but more convenient.

Viscosity The thickness of a liquid or its resistance to flow.

Volt A unit for expressing electrical "pressure" in a circuit. One volt that will produce a current of one ampere through a resistance of one ohm.

W

Welding Various processes used to join metal items by heating the areas to be joined to a molten state and fusing them together. For more information refer to the *Haynes Automotive Welding Manual.*

Wiring diagram A drawing portraying the components and wires in a vehicle's electrical system, using standardised symbols. For more information refer to the *Haynes Automotive Electrical and Electronic Systems Manual.*

Note: *References throughout this index are in the form* "**Chapter number**" • "**Page number**". *So, for example, 2C•15 refers to page 15 of Chapter 2C.*

Note: *References throughout this index are in the form* **"Chapter number"** • **"Page number"**. *So, for example, 2C•15 refers to page 15 of Chapter 2C.*

*Note: References throughout this index are in the form "**Chapter number**" • "**Page number**". So, for example, 2C•15 refers to page 15 of Chapter 2C.*

Note: *References throughout this index are in the form "**Chapter number**" • "**Page number**". So, for example, 2C•15 refers to page 15 of Chapter 2C.*

Haynes Manuals – The Complete **UK Car** List

Title	Book No.
ALFA ROMEO Alfasud/Sprint (74 - 88) up to F *	0292
Alfa Romeo Alfetta (73 - 87) up to E *	0531
AUDI 80, 90 & Coupe Petrol (79 - Nov 88) up to F	0605
Audi 80, 90 & Coupe Petrol (Oct 86 - 90) D to H	1491
Audi 100 & 200 Petrol (Oct 82 - 90) up to H	0907
Audi 100 & A6 Petrol & Diesel (May 91 - May 97) H to P	3504
Audi A3 Petrol & Diesel (96 - May 03) P to 03	4253
Audi A4 Petrol & Diesel (95 - Feb 00) M to V	3575
Audi A4 Petrol & Diesel (Mar 00 - Aug 04) W to 04	4609
AUSTIN A35 & A40 (56 - 67) up to F *	0118
Austin/MG/Rover Maestro 1.3 & 1.6 Petrol (83 - 95) up to M	0922
Austin/MG Metro (80 - May 90) up to G	0718
Austin/Rover Montego 1.3 & 1.6 Petrol (84 - 94) A to L	1066
Austin/MG/Rover Montego 2.0 Petrol (84 - 95) A to M	1067
Mini (59 - 69) up to H *	0527
Mini (69 - 01) up to X	0646
Austin/Rover 2.0 litre Diesel Engine (86 - 93) C to L	1857
Austin Healey 100/6 & 3000 (56 - 68) up to G *	0049
BEDFORD CF Petrol (69 - 87) up to E	0163
Bedford/Vauxhall Rascal & Suzuki Supercarry (86 - Oct 94) C to M	3015
BMW 316, 320 & 320i (4-cyl) (75 - Feb 83) up to Y *	0276
BMW 320, 320i, 323i & 325i (6-cyl) (Oct 77 - Sept 87) up to E	0815
BMW 3- & 5-Series Petrol (81 - 91) up to J	1948
BMW 3-Series Petrol (Apr 91 - 99) H to V	3210
BMW 3-Series Petrol (Sept 98 - 03) S to 53	4067
BMW 520i & 525e (Oct 81 - June 88) up to E	1560
BMW 525, 528 & 528i (73 - Sept 81) up to X *	0632
BMW 5-Series 6-cyl Petrol (April 96 - Aug 03) N to 03	4151
BMW 1500, 1502, 1600, 1602, 2000 & 2002 (59 - 77) up to S *	0240
CHRYSLER PT Cruiser Petrol (00 - 03) W to 53	4058
CITROËN 2CV, Ami & Dyane (67 - 90) up to H	0196
Citroën AX Petrol & Diesel (87 - 97) D to P	3014
Citroën Berlingo & Peugeot Partner Petrol & Diesel (96 - 05) P to 55	4281
Citroën BX Petrol (83 - 94) A to L	0908
Citroën C15 Van Petrol & Diesel (89 - Oct 98) F to S	3509
Citroën C3 Petrol & Diesel (02 - 05) 51 to 05	4197
Citroën CX Petrol (75 - 88) up to F	0528
Citroën Saxo Petrol & Diesel (96 - 04) N to 54	3506
Citroën Visa Petrol (79 - 88) up to F	0620
Citroën Xantia Petrol & Diesel (93 - 01) K to Y	3082
Citroën XM Petrol & Diesel (89 - 00) G to X	3451
Citroën Xsara Petrol & Diesel (97 - Sept 00) R to W	3751
Citroën Xsara Picasso Petrol & Diesel (00 - 02) W to 52	3944
Citroën ZX Diesel (91 - 98) J to S	1922
Citroën ZX Petrol (91 - 98) H to S	1881
Citroën 1.7 & 1.9 litre Diesel Engine (84 - 96) A to N	1379
FIAT 126 (73 - 87) up to E *	0305
Fiat 500 (57 - 73) up to M *	0090
Fiat Bravo & Brava Petrol (95 - 00) N to W	3572
Fiat Cinquecento (93 - 98) K to R	3501
Fiat Panda (81 - 95) up to M	0793
Fiat Punto Petrol & Diesel (94 - Oct 99) L to V	3251
Fiat Punto Petrol (Oct 99 - July 03) V to 03	4066
Fiat Regata Petrol (84 - 88) A to F	1167
Fiat Tipo Petrol (88 - 91) E to J	1625
Fiat Uno Petrol (83 - 95) up to M	0923

Title	Book No.
Fiat X1/9 (74 - 89) up to G *	0273
FORD Anglia (59 - 68) up to G *	0001
Ford Capri II (& III) 1.6 & 2.0 (74 - 87) up to E *	0283
Ford Capri II (& III) 2.8 & 3.0 V6 (74 - 87) up to E	1309
Ford Cortina Mk III 1300 & 1600 (70 - 76) up to P *	0070
Ford Escort Mk I 1100 & 1300 (68 - 74) up to N *	0171
Ford Escort Mk I Mexico, RS 1600 & RS 2000 (70 - 74) up to N *	0139
Ford Escort Mk II Mexico, RS 1800 & RS 2000 (75 - 80) up to W *	0735
Ford Escort (75 - Aug 80) up to V *	0280
Ford Escort Petrol (Sept 80 - Sept 90) up to H	0686
Ford Escort & Orion Petrol (Sept 90 - 00) H to X	1737
Ford Escort & Orion Diesel (Sept 90 - 00) H to X	4081
Ford Fiesta (76 - Aug 83) up to Y	0334
Ford Fiesta Petrol (Aug 83 - Feb 89) A to F	1030
Ford Fiesta Petrol (Feb 89 - Oct 95) F to N	1595
Ford Fiesta Petrol & Diesel (Oct 95 - Mar 02) N to 02	3397
Ford Fiesta Petrol & Diesel (Apr 02 - 05) 02 to 54	4170
Ford Focus Petrol & Diesel (98 - 01) S to Y	3759
Ford Focus Petrol & Diesel (Oct 01 - 04) 51 to 54	4167
Ford Galaxy Petrol & Diesel (95 - Aug 00) M to W	3984
Ford Granada Petrol (Sept 77 - Feb 85) up to B *	0481
Ford Granada & Scorpio Petrol (Mar 85 - 94) B to M	1245
Ford Ka (96 - 02) P to 52	3570
Ford Mondeo Petrol (93 - Sept 00) K to X	1923
Ford Mondeo Petrol & Diesel (Oct 00 - Jul 03) X to 03	3990
Ford Mondeo Petrol & Diesel (July 03 - 07) 03 to 56	4619
Ford Mondeo Diesel (93 - 96) L to N	3465
Ford Orion Petrol (83 - Sept 90) up to H	1009
Ford Sierra 4-cyl Petrol (82 - 93) up to K	0903
Ford Sierra V6 Petrol (82 - 91) up to J	0904
Ford Transit Petrol (Mk 2) (78 - Jan 86) up to C	0719
Ford Transit Petrol (Mk 3) (Feb 86 - 89) C to G	1468
Ford Transit Diesel (Feb 86 - 99) C to T	3019
Ford 1.6 & 1.8 litre Diesel Engine (84 - 96) A to N	1172
Ford 2.1, 2.3 & 2.5 litre Diesel Engine (77 - 90) up to H	1606
FREIGHT ROVER Sherpa Petrol (74 - 87) up to E	0463
HILLMAN Avenger (70 - 82) up to Y	0037
Hillman Imp (63 - 76) up to R *	0022
HONDA Civic (Feb 84 - Oct 87) A to E	1226
Honda Civic (Nov 91 - 96) J to N	3199
Honda Civic Petrol (Mar 95 - 00) M to X	4050
HYUNDAI Pony (85 - 94) C to M	3398
JAGUAR E Type (61 - 72) up to L *	0140
Jaguar MkI & II, 240 & 340 (55 - 69) up to H *	0098
Jaguar XJ6, XJ & Sovereign; Daimler Sovereign (68 - Oct 86) up to D	0242
Jaguar XJ6 & Sovereign (Oct 86 - Sept 94) D to M	3261
Jaguar XJ12, XJS & Sovereign; Daimler Double Six (72 - 88) up to F	0478
Jeep Cherokee Petrol (93 - 96) K to N	1943
LADA 1200, 1300, 1500 & 1600 (74 - 91) up to J	0413
Lada Samara (87 - 91) D to J	1610
LAND ROVER 90, 110 & Defender Diesel (83 - 07) up to 56	3017
Land Rover Discovery Petrol & Diesel (89 - 98) G to S	3016
Land Rover Discovery Diesel (Nov 98 - Jul 04) S to 04	4606
Land Rover Freelander Petrol & Diesel (97 - Sept 03) R to 53	3929
Land Rover Freelander Petrol & Diesel (Oct 03 - 06) 53 to 56	4623
Land Rover Series IIA & III Diesel (58 - 85) up to C	0529

Title	Book No.
Land Rover Series II, IIA & III 4-cyl Petrol (58 - 85) up to C	0314
MAZDA 323 (Mar 81 - Oct 89) up to G	1608
Mazda 323 (Oct 89 - 98) G to R	3455
Mazda 626 (May 83 - Sept 87) up to E	0929
Mazda B1600, B1800 & B2000 Pick-up Petrol (72 - 88) up to F	0267
Mazda RX-7 (79 - 85) up to C *	0460
MERCEDES-BENZ 190, 190E & 190D Petrol & Diesel (83 - 93) A to L	3450
Mercedes-Benz 200D, 240D, 240TD, 300D & 300TD 123 Series Diesel (Oct 76 - 85) up to C	1114
Mercedes-Benz 250 & 280 (68 - 72) up to L *	0346
Mercedes-Benz 250 & 280 123 Series Petrol (Oct 76 - 84) up to B *	0677
Mercedes-Benz 124 Series Petrol & Diesel (85 - Aug 93) C to K	3253
Mercedes-Benz C-Class Petrol & Diesel (93 - Aug 00) L to W	3511
MGA (55 - 62) *	0475
MGB (62 - 80) up to W	0111
MG Midget & Austin-Healey Sprite (58 - 80) up to W *	0265
MINI Petrol (July 01 - 05) Y to 05	4273
MITSUBISHI Shogun & L200 Pick-Ups Petrol (83 - 94) up to M	1944
MORRIS Ital 1.3 (80 - 84) up to B	0705
Morris Minor 1000 (56 - 71) up to K	0024
NISSAN Almera Petrol (95 - Feb 00) N to V	4053
Nissan Bluebird (May 84 - Mar 86) A to C	1223
Nissan Bluebird Petrol (Mar 86 - 90) C to H	1473
Nissan Cherry (Sept 82 - 86) up to D	1031
Nissan Micra (83 - Jan 93) up to K	0931
Nissan Micra (93 - 02) K to 52	3254
Nissan Primera Petrol (90 - Aug 99) H to T	1851
Nissan Stanza (82 - 86) up to D	0824
Nissan Sunny Petrol (May 82 - Oct 86) up to D	0895
Nissan Sunny Petrol (Oct 86 - Mar 91) D to H	1378
Nissan Sunny Petrol (Apr 91 - 95) H to N	3219
OPEL Ascona & Manta (B Series) (Sept 75 - 88) up to F *	0316
Opel Ascona Petrol (81 - 88)	3215
Opel Astra Petrol (Oct 91 - Feb 98)	3156
Opel Corsa Petrol (83 - Mar 93)	3160
Opel Corsa Petrol (Mar 93 - 97)	3159
Opel Kadett Petrol (Nov 79 - Oct 84) up to B	0634
Opel Kadett Petrol (Oct 84 - Oct 91)	3196
Opel Omega & Senator Petrol (Nov 86 - 94)	3157
Opel Rekord Petrol (Feb 78 - Oct 86) up to D	0543
Opel Vectra Petrol (Oct 88 - Oct 95)	3158
PEUGEOT 106 Petrol & Diesel (91 - 04) J to 53	1882
Peugeot 205 Petrol (83 - 97) A to P	0932
Peugeot 206 Petrol & Diesel (98 - 01) S to X	3757
Peugeot 206 Petrol & Diesel (02 - 06) 51 to 06	4613
Peugeot 306 Petrol & Diesel (93 - 02) K to 02	3073
Peugeot 307 Petrol & Diesel (01 - 04) Y to 54	4147
Peugeot 309 Petrol (86 - 93) C to K	1266
Peugeot 405 Petrol (88 - 97) E to P	1559
Peugeot 405 Diesel (88 - 97) E to P	3198
Peugeot 406 Petrol & Diesel (96 - Mar 99) N to T	3394
Peugeot 406 Petrol & Diesel (Mar 99 - 02) T to 52	3982
Peugeot 505 Petrol (79 - 89) up to G	0762
Peugeot 1.7/1.8 & 1.9 litre Diesel Engine (82 - 96) up to N	0950
Peugeot 2.0, 2.1, 2.3 & 2.5 litre Diesel Engines (74 - 90) up to H	1607

* Classic reprint

Title	Book No.
PORSCHE 911 (65 - 85) up to C	0264
Porsche 924 & 924 Turbo (76 - 85) up to C	0397
PROTON (89 - 97) F to P	3255
RANGE ROVER V8 Petrol (70 - Oct 92) up to K	0606
RELIANT Robin & Kitten (73 - 83) up to A *	0436
RENAULT 4 (61 - 86) up to D *	0072
Renault 5 Petrol (Feb 85 - 96) B to N	1219
Renault 9 & 11 Petrol (82 - 89) up to F	0822
Renault 18 Petrol (79 - 86) up to D	0598
Renault 19 Petrol (89 - 96) F to N	1646
Renault 19 Diesel (89 - 96) F to N	1946
Renault 21 Petrol (86 - 94) C to M	1397
Renault 25 Petrol & Diesel (84 - 92) B to K	1228
Renault Clio Petrol (91 - May 98) H to R	1853
Renault Clio Diesel (91 - June 96) H to N	3031
Renault Clio Petrol & Diesel (May 98 - May 01) R to Y	3906
Renault Clio Petrol & Diesel (June 01 - 04) Y to 54	4168
Renault Espace Petrol & Diesel (85 - 96) C to N	3197
Renault Laguna Petrol & Diesel (94 - 00) L to W	3252
Renault Laguna Petrol & Diesel (Feb 01 - Feb 05) X to 54	4283
Renault Mégane & Scénic Petrol & Diesel (96 - 99) N to T	3395
Renault Mégane & Scénic Petrol & Diesel (Apr 99 - 02) T to 52	3916
Renault Megane Petrol & Diesel (Oct 02 - 05) 52 to 55	4284
Renault Scenic Petrol & Diesel (Sept 03 - 06) 53 to 06	4297
ROVER 213 & 216 (84 - 89) A to G	1116
Rover 214 & 414 Petrol (89 - 96) G to N	1689
Rover 216 & 416 Petrol (89 - 96) G to N	1830
Rover 211, 214, 216, 218 & 220 Petrol & Diesel (Dec 95 - 99) N to V	3399
Rover 25 & MG ZR Petrol & Diesel (Oct 99 - 04) V to 54	4145
Rover 414, 416 & 420 Petrol & Diesel (May 95 - 98) M to R	3453
Rover 45/MG ZS Petrol & Diesel (99 - 05) V to 55	4384
Rover 618, 620 & 623 Petrol (93 - 97) K to P	3257
Rover 75/MG ZT Petrol & Diesel (99 - 06) S to 06	4292
Rover 820, 825 & 827 Petrol (86 - 95) D to N	1380
Rover 3500 (76 - 87) up to E *	0365
Rover Metro, 111 & 114 Petrol (May 90 - 98) G to S	1711
SAAB 95 & 96 (66 - 76) up to R *	0198
Saab 90, 99 & 900 (79 - Oct 93) up to L	0765
Saab 900 (Oct 93 - 98) L to R	3512
Saab 9000 (4-cyl) (85 - 98) C to S	1686
Saab 9-3 Petrol & Diesel (98 - Aug 02) R to 02	4614
Saab 9-5 4-cyl Petrol (97 - 04) R to 54	4156
SEAT Ibiza & Cordoba Petrol & Diesel (Oct 93 - Oct 99) L to V	3571
Seat Ibiza & Malaga Petrol (85 - 92) B to K	1609
SKODA Estelle (77 - 89) up to G	0604
Skoda Fabia Petrol & Diesel (00 - 06) W to 06	4376
Skoda Favorit (89 - 96) F to N	1801
Skoda Felicia Petrol & Diesel (95 - 01) M to X	3505
Skoda Octavia Petrol & Diesel (98 - Apr 04) R to 04	4285
SUBARU 1600 & 1800 (Nov 79 - 90) up to H *	0995
SUNBEAM Alpine, Rapier & H120 (67 - 74) up to N *	0051
SUZUKI Supercarry & Bedford/Vauxhall Rascal (86 - Oct 94) C to M	3015
Suzuki SJ Series, Samurai & Vitara (4-cyl) Petrol (82 - 97) up to P	1942
TALBOT Alpine, Solara, Minx & Rapier (75 - 86) up to D	0337

Title	Book No.
Talbot Horizon Petrol (78 - 86) up to D	0473
Talbot Samba (82 - 86) up to D	0823
TOYOTA Avensis Petrol (98 - Jan 03) R to 52	4264
Toyota Carina E Petrol (May 92 - 97) J to P	3256
Toyota Corolla (80 - 85) up to C	0683
Toyota Corolla (Sept 83 - Sept 87) A to E	1024
Toyota Corolla (Sept 87 - Aug 92) E to K	1683
Toyota Corolla Petrol (Aug 92 - 97) K to P	3259
Toyota Corolla Petrol (July 97 - Feb 02) P to 51	4286
Toyota Hi-Ace & Hi-Lux Petrol (69 - Oct 83) up to A	0304
Toyota Yaris Petrol (99 - 05) T to 05	4265
TRIUMPH GT6 & Vitesse (62 - 74) up to N *	0112
Triumph Herald (59 - 71) up to K *	0010
Triumph Spitfire (62 - 81) up to X	0113
Triumph Stag (70 - 78) up to T *	0441
Triumph TR2, TR3, TR3A, TR4 & TR4A (52 - 67) up to F *	0028
Triumph TR5 & 6 (67 - 75) up to P *	0031
Triumph TR7 (75 - 82) up to Y *	0322
VAUXHALL Astra Petrol (80 - Oct 84) up to B	0635
Vauxhall Astra & Belmont Petrol (Oct 84 - Oct 91) B to J	1136
Vauxhall Astra Petrol (Oct 91 - Feb 98) J to R	1832
Vauxhall/Opel Astra & Zafira Petrol (Feb 98 - Apr 04) R to 04	3758
Vauxhall/Opel Astra & Zafira Diesel (Feb 98 - Apr 04) R to 04	3797
Vauxhall/Opel Calibra (90 - 98) G to S	3502
Vauxhall Carlton Petrol (Oct 78 - Oct 86) up to D	0480
Vauxhall Carlton & Senator Petrol (Nov 86 - 94) D to L	1469
Vauxhall Cavalier Petrol (81 - Oct 88) up to F	0812
Vauxhall Cavalier Petrol (Oct 88 - 95) F to N	1570
Vauxhall Chevette (75 - 84) up to B	0285
Vauxhall/Opel Corsa Diesel (Mar 93 - Oct 00) K to X	4087
Vauxhall Corsa Petrol (Mar 93 - 97) K to R	1985
Vauxhall/Opel Corsa Petrol (Apr 97 - Oct 00) P to X	3921
Vauxhall/Opel Corsa Petrol & Diesel (Oct 00 - Sept 03) X to 53	4079
Vauxhall/Opel Corsa Petrol & Diesel (Oct 03 - Aug 06) 53 to 06	4617
Vauxhall/Opel Frontera Petrol & Diesel (91 - Sept 98) J to S	3454
Vauxhall Nova Petrol (83 - 93) up to K	0909
Vauxhall/Opel Omega Petrol (94 - 99) L to T	3510
Vauxhall/Opel Vectra Petrol & Diesel (95 - Feb 99) N to S	3396
Vauxhall/Opel Vectra Petrol & Diesel (Mar 99 - May 02) T to 02	3930
Vauxhall/Opel Vectra Petrol & Diesel (June 02 - 06) 02 to 56	4618
Vauxhall/Opel 1.5, 1.6 & 1.7 litre Diesel Engine (82 - 96) up to N	1222
VW 411 & 412 (68 - 75) up to P *	0091
VW Beetle 1200 (54 - 77) up to S	0036
VW Beetle 1300 & 1500 (65 - 75) up to P	0039
VW 1302 & 1302S (70 - 72) up to L *	0110
VW Beetle 1303, 1303S & GT (72 - 75) up to P	0159
VW Beetle Petrol & Diesel (Apr 99 - 01) T to 51	3798
VW Golf & Jetta Mk 1 Petrol 1.1 & 1.3 (74 - 84) up to A	0716
VW Golf, Jetta & Scirocco Mk 1 Petrol 1.5, 1.6 & 1.8 (74 - 84) up to A	0726
VW Golf & Jetta Mk 1 Diesel (78 - 84) up to A	0451
VW Golf & Jetta Mk 2 Petrol (Mar 84 - Feb 92) A to J	1081
VW Golf & Vento Petrol & Diesel (Feb 92 - Mar 98) J to R	3097

Title	Book No.
VW Golf & Bora Petrol & Diesel (April 98 - 00) R to X	3727
VW Golf & Bora 4-cyl Petrol & Diesel (01 - 03) X to 53	4169
VW Golf & Bora Petrol & Diesel (04 - 07) 53 to 07	4610
VW LT Petrol Vans & Light Trucks (76 - 87) up to E	0637
VW Passat & Santana Petrol (Sept 81 - May 88) up to E	0814
VW Passat 4-cyl Petrol & Diesel (May 88 - 96) E to P	3498
VW Passat 4-cyl Petrol & Diesel (Dec 96 - Nov 00) P to X	3917
VW Passat Petrol & Diesel (Dec 00 - May 05) X to 05	4279
VW Polo & Derby (76 - Jan 82) up to X	0335
VW Polo (82 - Oct 90) up to H	0813
VW Polo Petrol (Nov 90 - Aug 94) H to L	3245
VW Polo Hatchback Petrol & Diesel (94 - 99) M to S	3500
VW Polo Hatchback Petrol (00 - Jan 02) V to 51	4150
VW Polo Petrol & Diesel (02 - May 05) 51 to 05	4608
VW Scirocco (82 - 90) up to H *	1224
VW Transporter 1600 (68 - 79) up to V	0082
VW Transporter 1700, 1800 & 2000 (72 - 79) up to V *	0226
VW Transporter (air-cooled) Petrol (79 - 82) up to Y *	0638
VW Transporter (water-cooled) Petrol (82 - 90) up to H	3452
VW Type 3 (63 - 73) up to M *	0084
VOLVO 120 & 130 Series (& P1800) (61 - 73) up to M *	0203
Volvo 142, 144 & 145 (66 - 74) up to N *	0129
Volvo 240 Series Petrol (74 - 93) up to K	0270
Volvo 262, 264 & 260/265 (75 - 85) up to C *	0400
Volvo 340, 343, 345 & 360 (76 - 91) up to J	0715
Volvo 440, 460 & 480 Petrol (87 - 97) D to P	1691
Volvo 740 & 760 Petrol (82 - 91) up to J	1258
Volvo 850 Petrol (92 - 96) J to P	3260
Volvo 940 Petrol (90 - 96) H to N	3249
Volvo S40 & V40 Petrol (96 - Mar 04) N to 04	3569
Volvo S70, V70 & C70 Petrol (96 - 99) P to V	3573
Volvo V70 / S80 Petrol & Diesel (98 - 05) S to 55	4263

AUTOMOTIVE TECHBOOKS

Title	Book No.
Automotive Electrical and Electronic Systems Manual	3049
Automotive Gearbox Overhaul Manual	3473
Automotive Service Summaries Manual	3475
Automotive Timing Belts Manual – Austin/Rover	3549
Automotive Timing Belts Manual – Ford	3474
Automotive Timing Belts Manual – Peugeot/Citroën	3568
Automotive Timing Belts Manual – Vauxhall/Opel	3577

DIY MANUAL SERIES

Title	Book No.
The Haynes Air Conditioning Manual	4192
The Haynes Manual on Bodywork	4198
The Haynes Manual on Brakes	4178
The Haynes Manual on Carburettors	4177
The Haynes Car Electrical Systems Manual	4251
The Haynes Manual on Diesel Engines	4174
The Haynes Manual on Engine Management	4199
The Haynes Manual on Fault Codes	4175
The Haynes Manual on Practical Electrical Systems	4267
The Haynes Manual on Small Engines	4250
The Haynes Manual on Welding	4176

* Classic reprint

CL22.4/07

Preserving Our Motoring Heritage

< *The Model J Duesenberg Derham Tourster. Only eight of these magnificent cars were ever built – this is the only example to be found outside the United States of America*

Almost every car you've ever loved, loathed or desired is gathered under one roof at the Haynes Motor Museum. Over 300 immaculately presented cars and motorbikes represent every aspect of our motoring heritage, from elegant reminders of bygone days, such as the superb Model J Duesenberg to curiosities like the bug-eyed BMW Isetta. There are also many old friends and flames. Perhaps you remember the 1959 Ford Popular that you did your courting in? The magnificent 'Red Collection' is a spectacle of classic sports cars including AC, Alfa Romeo, Austin Healey, Ferrari, Lamborghini, Maserati, MG, Riley, Porsche and Triumph.

A Perfect Day Out

Each and every vehicle at the Haynes Motor Museum has played its part in the history and culture of Motoring. Today, they make a wonderful spectacle and a great day out for all the family. Bring the kids, bring Mum and Dad, but above all bring your camera to capture those golden memories for ever. You will also find an impressive array of motoring memorabilia, a comfortable 70 seat video cinema and one of the most extensive transport book shops in Britain. The Pit Stop Cafe serves everything from a cup of tea to wholesome, home-made meals or, if you prefer, you can enjoy the large picnic area nestled in the beautiful rural surroundings of Somerset.

> *John Haynes O.B.E., Founder and Chairman of the museum at the wheel of a Haynes Light 12.*

< *Graham Hill's Lola Cosworth Formula 1 car next to a 1934 Riley Sports.*

The Museum is situated on the A359 Yeovil to Frome road at Sparkford, just off the A303 in Somerset. It is about 40 miles south of Bristol, and 25 minutes drive from the M5 intersection at Taunton.

Open 9.30am - 5.30pm (10.00am - 4.00pm Winter) 7 days a week, *except Christmas Day, Boxing Day and New Years Day*

Special rates available for schools, coach parties and outings Charitable Trust No. 292048